The Latin Torah

Fresh Translations of
Genesis, Exodus, Leviticus,
Numbers, Deuteronomy

(A Latin-English,
Verse-by-Verse
Translation)

Translated by John Cunyus
Searchlight Press
Dallas, Texas

The Latin Torah

Fresh Translations of
Genesis, Exodus, Leviticus,
Numbers, Deuteronomy

A Latin-English,
Verse-by-Verse
Translation

ISBN # 978-0-9824802-5-0

1st Printing: January 1, 2010
1st Revision: May 1, 2010
2nd Revision: September 11, 2011
3rd Revision: February 26, 2012

Latin text from *Biblia Sacra Iuxta Vulgatam Versionem*,
Fourth Revised Edition, edited by Roger Gryson,
© 1994 Deutsche Bibelgesellschaft, Stuttgart.
Used by permission.

Searchlight Press
Who are you looking for?
Publishers of thoughtful Christian books since 1994.
5634 Ledgestone Drive
Dallas, Texas 75214
888.896.6081
info@Searchlight-Press.com
www.Searchlight-Press.com
www.JohnCunyus.com

laetatus sum in his quae dicta sunt mihi
in domum Domini ibimus

I was happy among those who said to me,
"Let us go to *the* Lord's house."
(Vulgate Psalm 121:1)

Table of Contents

Genesis

Creation

Genesis 1:1 *in principio creavit Deus caelum et terram*

In beginning
God created sky and land.

1:2 *terra autem erat inanis et vacua et tenebrae super faciem abyssi et spiritus Dei ferebatur super aquas*

But land was
empty and vacant,
and shadows *were*
over abyss's face.
And God's Spirit considered,
above waters.

1:3 *dixitque Deus fiat lux et facta est lux*

And God said,
"Let light be!"
And light came to be.

1:4 *et vidit Deus lucem quod esset bona et divisit lucem ac tenebras*

And God saw light,
that it was good,
and divided light
from shadows.

1:5 *appellavitque lucem diem et tenebras noctem factumque est vespere et mane dies unus*

And He called light "Day,"
and shadows "Night."
And evening came,

and morning,
day one.

1:6 *dixit quoque Deus fiat firmamentum in medio aquarum et dividat aquas ab aquis*

And God also said,
"Let *a* support be
in *the* waters' midst,
and let it divide
waters from waters!"

1:7 *et fecit Deus firmamentum divisitque aquas quae erant sub firmamento ab his quae erant super firmamentum et factum est ita*

And God made *a* support,
and divided waters
which were below *the* support
from those which were
above *the* support.

And *it* became so.

1:8 *vocavitque Deus firmamentum caelum et factum est vespere et mane dies secundus*

And God called *the* support "Sky."
And evening came,
and morning,
second day.

1:9 *dixit vero Deus congregentur aquae quae sub caelo sunt in locum unum et appareat arida factumque est ita*

Indeed, God said,
"Let waters which are
under sky
be gathered in one place,
and let dry appear!"

And *it* became so.

1:10 *et vocavit Deus aridam terram congregationesque aquarum appellavit maria et vidit Deus quod esset bonum*

And God called *the* dry, "Land,"
and waters' gatherings
He called, "Seas."

And God saw that *it* was good,

1:11 *et ait germinet terra herbam virentem et facientem semen et lignum pomiferum faciens fructum iuxta genus suum cuius semen in semet ipso sit super terram et factum est ita*

and said,
"Let land bring forth
green and seed-bearing herbs,
and fruit-bearing wood,
making fruit according
to its kind,
whose seed may be in itself
on land!"

And *it* became so.

1:12 *et protulit terra herbam virentem et adferentem semen iuxta genus suum lignumque faciens*

fructum et habens unumquodque sementem secundum speciem suam et vidit Deus quod esset bonum

And land put forth
green and seed-bearing herb,
according to its kind,
and fruit-bearing wood,
and each one having seed
according to its species.

And God saw
that *all* was good.

1:13 *factumque est vespere et mane dies tertius*

And evening came,
and morning,
third day.

1:14 *dixit autem Deus fiant luminaria in firmamento caeli ut dividant diem ac noctem et sint in signa et tempora et dies et annos*

But God said,
"Let lights be
in sky's support,
that they may divide
day from night,
and be as signs and times,
and days and years –

1:15 *ut luceant in firmamento caeli et inluminent terram et factum est ita*

that they give light
in sky's support
and light up land!"

And *it* became so.

1:16 *fecitque Deus duo magna luminaria luminare maius ut praeesset diei et luminare minus ut praeesset nocti et stellas*

And God made
two great lights:
the great light
that controlled day,
and *the* small light
that controlled night and stars.

1:17 *et posuit eas in firmamento caeli ut lucerent super terram*

And He put them
in sky's support,
that they give light on land.

1:18 *et praeessent diei ac nocti et dividerent lucem ac tenebras et vidit Deus quod esset bonum*

And they controlled
day and night,
and divided light
and darkness.

And God saw
that *all* was good.

1:19 *et factum est vespere et mane dies quartus*

And evening came,
and morning,
fourth day.

1:20 *dixit etiam Deus producant aquae reptile animae viventis et volatile super terram sub firmamento caeli*

God also said,
"Let waters produce
creeping *beings*
with living souls,
and flying *beings* over earth,
under sky's support!"

1:21 *creavitque Deus cete grandia et omnem animam viventem atque motabilem quam produxerant aquae in species suas et omne volatile secundum genus suum et vidit Deus quod esset bonum*

And God made great fish
and every living
and moving soul
which waters produced
in their species,
and all flying *beings*
according to their type.

And God saw that *all* was good.

1:22 *benedixitque eis dicens crescite et multiplicamini et replete aquas maris avesque multiplicentur super terram*

And God blessed them,
saying, "Grow and multiply,
and fill sea's waters!
And let birds
be multiplied over land!"

1:23 *et factum est vespere et mane dies quintus*

And evening came,
and morning,
fifth day.

1:24 *dixit quoque Deus producat terra animam viventem in genere suo iumenta et reptilia et bestias terrae secundum species suas factumque est ita*

And God also said,
"Let earth produce
a living soul in its type,
cattle and crawling *beings*
and land's beasts,
according to their species.

And *it* became so.

1:25 *et fecit Deus bestias terrae iuxta species suas et iumenta et omne reptile terrae in genere suo et vidit Deus quod esset bonum*

And God made land's beasts
according to their species,
and cattle,
and every crawling *being*
of land in its type.

And God saw
that *all* was good,

1:26 *et ait faciamus hominem ad imaginem et similitudinem nostram et praesit piscibus maris et volatilibus caeli et bestiis*

universaeque terrae omnique reptili quod movetur in terra

and said,
"Let us make man
in Our image and likeness,
and let him take precedence
over sea's fish,
and those flying in *the* sky
and all land's beasts,
and every crawling *being*
that moves on land!"

1:27 *et creavit Deus hominem ad imaginem suam ad imaginem Dei creavit illum masculum et feminam creavit eos*

And God created man
in His image.
He created him
in God's image.
He created them
male and female.

1:28 *benedixitque illis Deus et ait crescite et multiplicamini et replete terram et subicite eam et dominamini piscibus maris et volatilibus caeli et universis animantibus quae moventur super terram*

And God blessed them
and said, "Grow and multiply,
and fill land and master it!
And rule sea's fish
and those flying in sky
and all animals which move on land!"

1:29 *dixitque Deus ecce dedi vobis*

omnem herbam adferentem semen
super terram et universa ligna quae
habent in semet ipsis sementem
generis sui ut sint vobis in escam

And God said,
"Look, I have given you
every seed -bearing herb
on land,
and all woods
which have in themselves
seed of their type,
that they may be food
to you,

1:30 *et cunctis animantibus terrae*
omnique volucri caeli et universis
quae moventur in terra et in quibus
est anima vivens ut habeant ad
vescendum et factum est ita

"and to all land's
living *beings*;
and to every winged
being of sky,
and to all *beings*
which move on land,
and in which is *a* living soul,
that they may have them
for food."

And *it* became so.

1:31 *viditque Deus cuncta quae fecit*
et erant valde bona et factum est
vespere et mane dies sextus

And God saw
all that He made,
and *all* was very good.

And evening came,
and morning,
sixth day.

Genesis 2:1 *igitur perfecti sunt caeli et terra et omnis ornatus eorum*

Therefore, sky and land
and all their adornments
were perfected.

2:2 *conplevitque Deus die septimo opus suum quod fecerat et requievit die septimo ab universo opere quod patrarat*

And God completed
on *the* seventh day
His work which He made,
and rested on *the* seventh day
from every work
which He had brought
to completion.

2:3 *et benedixit diei septimo et sanctificavit illum quia in ipso cessaverat ab omni opere suo quod creavit Deus ut faceret*

And He blessed
the seventh day,
and made it holy,
because in it He ceased
from all His work,
which God created,
that it be made.

Man Becomes a Living Soul
2:4 *istae generationes caeli et terrae quando creatae sunt in die quo fecit Dominus Deus caelum et terram*

These *are* sky
and land's generations,

when they were created,
in *the* day when
the Lord God made
sky and land

2:5 *et omne virgultum agri antequam oreretur in terra, omnemque herbam regionis, priusquam germinaret/ non, enim, pluerat Dominus Deus super terram, et homo non erat qui operaretur terram*

and every plant of *the* field,
before it sprung up on land,
and every herb of *the* region
before *it* had germinated,
for *the* Lord God
had not rained on *the* land,
and no man lived
who cultivated *the* land.

2:6 *sed fons ascendebat e terra inrigans universam superficiem terrae*

But *a* spring bubbled up
from *the* land,
watering all *the* land's face.

2:7 *formavit, igitur, Dominus Deus hominem de limo terrae, et inspiravit in faciem eius spiraculum vitae, et factus est homo in animam viventem*

Then *the* Lord God
formed man
from *the* ground's mud,
and blew into life's opening
in his face,

and man was made
into *a* living soul.

Pleasure's Paradise

2:8 *plantaverat autem Dominus Deus paradisum voluptatis a principio in quo posuit hominem quem formaverat*

But *the* Lord God
had planted
pleasure's paradise
at *the* beginning,
in which He placed
man whom He had formed.

2:9 *produxitque Dominus Deus de humo omne lignum pulchrum visu, et ad vescendum suave lignum etiam vitae in medio paradisi lignumque scientiae boni et mali*

And *the* Lord God
produced from soil
every tree beautiful to sight
and sweet for eating –
even *a* tree of life
in paradise's midst,
and *a* tree of knowledge
of good and evil.

2:10 *et fluvius egrediebatur de loco voluptatis ad inrigandum paradisum qui inde dividitur in quattuor capita*

And *a* river rose up
from pleasure's place
to water paradise,
which from there was divided
into four principal divisions.

2:11 *nomen uni Phison ipse est qui circuit omnem terram Evilat ubi nascitur aurum*

The name of one *was* Phison.
This is *the* one that circles
all Evilat's land,
where gold is born.

2:12 *et aurum terrae illius optimum est ibique invenitur bdellium et lapis onychinus*

And that land's gold is choice,
and bdellium and onyx stone
is found there also.

2:13 *et nomen fluvio secundo Geon ipse est qui circuit omnem terram Aethiopiae*

And *the* second river's name
is Geon.
This is *the* one that circles
all Ethiopia's land.

2:14 *nomen vero fluminis tertii Tigris ipse vadit contra Assyrios fluvius autem quartus ipse est Eufrates*

Indeed, *the* third river's name is
Tigris.
This advances
across *the* Assyrians.
But *the* fourth river,
this is Euphrates.

2:15 *tulit ergo Dominus Deus hominem et posuit eum in paradiso* *voluptatis ut operaretur et custodiret illum*

Therefore *the* Lord God
took man
and placed him
in pleasure's paradise,
that he might cultivate
and keep it.

2:16 *praecepitque ei dicens ex omni ligno paradisi comede*

And He commanded him,
saying, "Eat from every tree
of Paradise,

2:17 *de ligno autem scientiae boni et mali ne comedas in quocumque enim die comederis ex eo morte morieris*

"but do not eat
from *the* tree of *the* knowledge
of good and evil.
For in whatever day
you eat from it,
you will die by death."

Man Divided into
Man and Woman

2:18 *dixit quoque Dominus Deus non est bonum esse hominem solum faciamus ei adiutorium similem sui*

And *the* Lord God also said,
"It is not good
to be man alone.
Let us make him
a helper like him."

2:19 *formatis igitur Dominus Deus de humo cunctis animantibus terrae et universis volatilibus caeli adduxit ea ad Adam ut videret quid vocaret ea omne enim quod vocavit Adam animae viventis ipsum est nomen eius*

Therefore *the* Lord God
made from soil
all land's souls
and all sky's birds.
He led them to Adam
so he might see
what he would call them.
For what Adam called
every living soul,
that is its name.

2:20 *appellavitque Adam nominibus suis cuncta animantia et universa volatilia caeli et omnes bestias terrae Adam vero non inveniebatur adiutor similis eius*

And Adam called by name
all living *things,*
and all sky's birds
and all earth's beasts.
Truly, Adam did not find
a helper like him.

2:21 *inmisit ergo Dominus Deus soporem in Adam cumque obdormisset tulit unam de costis eius et replevit carnem pro ea*

Then *the* Lord God sent in
sleep on Adam,
and, when he was sleeping,

He took one of his ribs,
and replaced it with flesh.

2:22 *et aedificavit Dominus Deus
costam quam tulerat de Adam in
mulierem et adduxit eam ad Adam*

And *the* Lord God made
the rib which He had taken
from Adam
into woman,
and He led her to Adam.

2:23 *dixitque Adam hoc nunc os ex
ossibus meis et caro de carne mea
haec vocabitur virago quoniam de
viro sumpta est*

And Adam said,
"This now *is*
bone from my bones
and flesh from my flesh.
She will be called Woman
because she is taken
from Man."

2:24 *quam ob rem relinquet homo
patrem suum et matrem et adherebit
uxori suae et erunt duo in carne una*

From which thing
man will leave
his father and mother,
and will cling to his wife,
and they will be
two in one flesh.

2:25 *erant autem uterque nudi
Adam scilicet et uxor eius et non
erubescebant*

But both of them were naked –
Adam, certainly,
and his wife –
and they were not ashamed.

The Fall

Genesis 3:1 *sed et serpens erat callidior cunctis animantibus terrae quae fecerat Dominus Deus qui dixit ad mulierem cur praecepit vobis Deus ut non comederetis de omni ligno paradisi*

Yet *the* snake also was more clever than all *the* land's animals which *the* Lord God had made. *It* said to *the* woman, "Why did God command you that you not eat from every tree of paradise?"

3:2 *cui respondit mulier de fructu lignorum quae sunt in paradiso vescemur*

The woman answered him, "We will eat from *the* trees' fruit which are in paradise.

3:3 *de fructu vero ligni quod est in medio paradisi praecepit nobis Deus ne comederemus et ne tangeremus illud ne forte moriamur*

"But from *the* tree's fruit which is in *the* middle of paradise, God commanded us *that* we may not eat and we may not touch it, unless perhaps we die."

3:4 *dixit autem serpens ad mulierem nequaquam morte moriemini*

But *the* snake said to *the* woman, "By no means will you die by death!

3:5 *scit enim Deus quod in quocumque die comederitis ex eo aperientur oculi vestri et eritis sicut dii scientes bonum et malum*

"For God knows that in whatever day you will eat from it, your eyes will be opened and you will be like gods, knowing good and harm."

3:6 *vidit igitur mulier quod bonum esset lignum ad vescendum et pulchrum oculis aspectuque delectabile et tulit de fructu illius et comedit deditque viro suo qui comedit*

Therefore, *the* woman saw that *the* tree was good to eat and beautiful to *the* eyes, and delicious looking. And she took its fruit and ate, and gave *it* to her man, who ate.

3:7 *et aperti sunt oculi amborum cumque cognovissent esse se nudos consuerunt folia ficus et fecerunt sibi perizomata*

And both their eyes were open. And when they understood themselves to be naked, they sewed together fig leaves and made themselves coverings.

3:8 *et cum audissent vocem Domini Dei deambulantis in paradiso ad auram post meridiem abscondit se Adam et uxor eius a facie Domini Dei in medio ligni paradisi*

And when they heard *the* Lord God's voice, walking in paradise to *the* afternoon breeze, Adam hid himself and his wife from *the* Lord God's face, among paradise's trees.

3:9 *vocavitque Dominus Deus Adam et dixit ei ubi es*

And *the* Lord God called Adam and said to him, "Where are you?"

3:10 *qui ait vocem tuam audivi in paradiso et timui eo quod nudus essem et abscondi me*

Adam said, "I heard Your voice in paradise and I was afraid, because I was naked. And I hid myself."

3:11 *cui dixit quis enim indicavit tibi quod nudus esses nisi quod ex ligno de quo tibi praeceperam ne comederes comedisti*

To whom He said, "So, who told you that you were naked, unless you ate from *the* tree from which I commanded you that you might not eat?"

3:12 *dixitque Adam mulier quam dedisti sociam mihi dedit mihi de ligno et comedi*

And Adam said, "Woman, whom You gave me as *a* companion, gave to me from *the* tree, and I ate."

3:13 *et dixit Dominus Deus ad mulierem quare hoc fecisti quae respondit serpens decepit me et comedi*

And *the* Lord God said to *the* woman, "Why did you do this?"

She answered, "*The* snake tricked me, and I ate."

3:14 *et ait Dominus Deus ad serpentem quia fecisti hoc maledictus es inter omnia animantia et bestias terrae super pectus tuum gradieris et terram comedes cunctis diebus vitae tuae*

And *the* Lord God said to *the* snake, "Because you did this, you are cursed among all *the* land's animals and beasts. You will go on your breast and eat dirt all your life's days."

3:15 *inimicitias ponam inter te et mulierem et semen tuum et semen illius ipsa conteret caput tuum et tu insidiaberis calcaneo eius*

"I will place hostilities between you and *the* woman, and your seed and her seed. She will crush your head, and you will lie in wait against her heel."

3:16 *mulieri quoque dixit multiplicabo aerumnas tuas et conceptus tuos in dolore paries filios et sub viri potestate eris et ipse dominabitur tui*

To *the* woman likewise He said, "I will multiply your hardships and your conceptions. You will birth children in pain, and will be under man's power. And he will rule you."

3:17 *ad Adam vero dixit quia audisti vocem uxoris tuae et comedisti de ligno ex quo praeceperam tibi ne comederes maledicta terra in opere tuo in laboribus comedes eam cunctis diebus vitae tuae*

Truly, He said to Adam, "Because you listened to your wife's voice, and ate from *the* tree about which I had commanded you that you might not eat, *the* land *is* cursed in your work. You will eat *from it* through hard work all your life's days.

3:18 *spinas et tribulos germinabit tibi et comedes herbas terrae*

"It will bear thorns and spines for you, and you will eat *the* land's herbs.

3:19 *in sudore vultus tui vesceris pane donec revertaris in terram de qua sumptus es quia pulvis es et in pulverem reverteris*

You will eat bread in your face's sweat, until you are turned back into *the* land from which you were taken, because you are dust, and you will return to dust."

3:20 *et vocavit Adam nomen uxoris suae Hava eo quod mater esset cunctorum viventium*

And Adam called his wife's name Eve, because she was mother of all *the* living.

3:21 *fecit quoque Dominus Deus Adam et uxori eius tunicas pellicias et induit eos*

And *the* Lord God likewise made Adam and his wife skin tunics, and clothed them.

3:22 *et ait ecce Adam factus est quasi unus ex nobis sciens bonum et malum nunc ergo ne forte mittat manum suam et sumat etiam de ligno vitae et comedat et vivat in aeternum*

And He said, "Look, Adam has become like one of us, knowing good and harm. Now, therefore, unless perhaps he stretch out his hand and take even from *the* tree of life, and eat, and live in eternity" –

3:23 *emisit eum Dominus Deus de paradiso voluptatis ut operaretur terram de qua sumptus est*

the Lord God sent him out of pleasure's paradise, so he could cultivate *the* land from which he was taken.

3:24 *eiecitque Adam et conlocavit ante paradisum voluptatis cherubin* *et flammeum gladium atque versatilem ad custodiendam viam ligni vitae*

And He threw Adam out and placed Cherubim before pleasure's paradise, and *a* flaming and turning sword, to keeping *the* way to *the* tree of life.

Cain and Abel

Genesis 4:1 *Adam vero cognovit Havam uxorem suam quae concepit et peperit Cain dicens possedi hominem per Dominum*

Truly, Adam knew Eve his wife, who conceived and birthed Cain, saying, "I possessed *a* man through *the* Lord."

4:2 *rursusque peperit fratrem eius Abel fuit autem Abel pastor ovium et Cain agricola*

And again, she birthed his brother, Abel. But Abel was *a* shepherd and Cain *a* farmer.

4:3 *factum est autem post multos dies ut offerret Cain de fructibus terrae munera Domino*

But it happened after many days that Cain offered *the* Lord gifts, from *the* land's fruits.

4:4 *Abel quoque obtulit de primogenitis gregis sui et de adipibus eorum et respexit Dominus ad Abel et ad munera eius*

Abel likewise offered from his flock's firstborn and from their fat. And *the* Lord respected Abel and his offerings,

4:5 *ad Cain vero et ad munera illius non respexit iratusque est Cain vehementer et concidit vultus eius*

but He did not respect Cain and his offerings. And Cain was fiercely angry, and his face fell.

4:6 *dixitque Dominus ad eum quare maestus es et cur concidit facies tua*

And *the* Lord said to him, "Why are you angry, and why has your face fallen?

4:7 *nonne si bene egeris recipies sin autem male statim in foribus peccatum aderit sed sub te erit appetitus eius et tu dominaberis illius*

"If you do well, won't you receive? But if harm, sin immediately will arrive at *the* gates, but its appetite will be under you, and you will master it."

4:8 *dixitque Cain ad Abel fratrem suum egrediamur foras cumque essent in agro consurrexit Cain adversus Abel fratrem suum et interfecit eum*

And Cain said to his brother Abel, "Let's go outside."

And when they were in *the* field, Cain rose up against his brother Abel and killed him.

4:9 *et ait Dominus ad Cain ubi est Abel frater tuus qui respondit nescio num custos fratris mei sum*

And *the* Lord said to Cain, "Where is your brother Abel?"

Cain answered, "I don't know. Surely I'm not my brother's guard!"

4:10 *dixitque ad eum quid fecisti vox sanguinis fratris tui clamat ad me de terra*

And He said to him, "What have you done? Your brother's blood's voice cries out to me from *the* ground.

4:11 *nunc igitur maledictus eris super terram quae aperuit os suum et suscepit sanguinem fratris tui de manu tua*

"Now, therefore, you will be cursed on *the* land which opened its mouth and received your brother's blood from your hand.

4:12 *cum operatus fueris eam non dabit tibi fructus suos vagus et profugus eris super terram*

"When you work it, it will not give you its fruits. You will be *a* wanderer and fugitive on *the* land."

4:13 *dixitque Cain ad Dominum maior est iniquitas mea quam ut veniam merear*

And Cain said to *the* Lord, "My treachery is greater than what I will come to deserve!

4:14 *ecce eicis me hodie a facie terrae et a facie tua abscondar et ero vagus et profugus in terra omnis igitur qui invenerit me occidet me*

"Look, you throw me out today from *the* land's face and I will be hidden from Your face. I will be *a* wanderer and fugitive in *the* land. Therefore all who find me will kill me."

4:15 *dixitque ei Dominus nequaquam ita fiet sed omnis qui occiderit Cain septuplum punietur posuitque Dominus Cain signum ut non eum interficeret omnis qui invenisset eum*

And *the* Lord said to him, "By no means will it be so. But anyone who kills Cain will be punished seven-fold."

And *the* Lord put *a* sign on Cain, so anyone who found him would not kill him.

4:16 *egressusque Cain a facie Domini habitavit in terra profugus ad orientalem plagam Eden*

And, going out from *the* Lord's face, Cain lived in *the* land, *a* fugitive, to *the* east of Eden's region.

Cain and His Descendants

4:17 *cognovit autem Cain uxorem suam quae concepit et peperit Enoch et aedificavit civitatem vocavitque nomen eius ex nomine filii sui Enoch*

But Cain knew his wife, who conceived and birthed Enoch. And *Cain* built *a* city and called its name from his son's name, Enoch.

4:18 *porro Enoch genuit Irad et Irad genuit Maviahel et Maviahel genuit Matusahel et Matusahel genuit Lamech*

Then Enoch fathered Irad, and Irad fathered Maviahel, and Maviahel fathered Matusahel, and Matusahel fathered Lamech,

4:19 *qui accepit uxores duas nomen uni Ada et nomen alteri Sella*

who accepted two wives, one named Ada and *the* other named Sella.

4:20 *genuitque Ada Iabel qui fuit pater habitantium in tentoriis atque pastorum*

And Ada birthed Jabel, who was father of those living in tents and of shepherds.

4:21 *et nomen fratris eius Iubal ipse fuit pater canentium cithara et organo*

And his brother's name was Jubal. He was father of those playing guitar and organ.

4:22 *Sella quoque genuit Thubalcain qui fuit malleator et faber in cuncta opera aeris et ferri* *soror vero Thubalcain Noemma*

Sella likewise birthedThubalcain, who was *a* hammerer and artisan in all works of bronze and iron. And Thubalcain's sister *was* Noemma.

4:23 *dixitque Lamech uxoribus suis Adae et Sellae audite vocem meam uxores Lamech auscultate sermonem meum quoniam occidi virum in vulnus meum et adulescentulum in livorem meum*

And Lamech said to his wives, Ada and Sella, "Hear my voice, Lamech's wives! Listen to my speech, because I killed *a* man in my wound, and *a* youth in my bruising.

4:24 *septuplum ultio dabitur de Cain de Lamech vero septuagies septies*

"Seven-fold revenge will be given for Cain. Truly, seventy times seven for Lamech!"

Adam and Eve's
Further Children

4:25 *cognovit quoque adhuc Adam uxorem suam et peperit filium vocavitque nomen eius Seth dicens posuit mihi Deus semen aliud pro Abel quem occidit Cain*

Adam likewise knew his wife again, and she birthed *a* son. And he called his name Seth, saying, "God appointed me another seed for Abel, whom Cain killed."

4:26 *sed et Seth natus est filius quem vocavit Enos iste coepit invocare nomen Domini*

But *a* son also was born to Seth, whom he called Enos. This man began to invoke *the* Lord's name.

Adam and His Descendants

Genesis 5:1 *hic est liber generationis Adam in die qua creavit Deus hominem ad similitudinem Dei fecit illum*

This is *the* book of Adam's generation. In *the* day which God created man, He made him in God's likeness.

5:2 *masculum et feminam creavit eos et benedixit illis et vocavit nomen eorum Adam in die qua creati sunt*

He created them male and female and blessed them, and called their name Adam, in *the* day which they were created.

5:3 *vixit autem Adam centum triginta annis et genuit ad similitudinem et imaginem suam vocavitque nomen eius Seth*

But Adam lived one hundred thirty years, and fathered *a* son in his likeness and image. And he called his name Seth.

5:4 *et facti sunt dies Adam postquam genuit Seth octingenti anni genuitque filios et filias*

And Adam's days after he fathered Seth became eight hundred years. And he fathered sons and daughters.

5:5 *et factum est omne tempus quod*

vixit Adam anni nongenti triginta et mortuus est

And all *the* time that Adam lived became nine hundred thirty years, and he died.

5:6 *vixit quoque Seth centum quinque annos et genuit Enos*

Seth likewise lived one hundred five years, and fathered Enos.

5:7 *vixitque Seth postquam genuit Enos octingentis septem annis genuitque filios et filias*

And after Seth fathered Enos, he lived eight hundred seven years. And he fathered sons and daughters.

5:8 *et facti sunt omnes dies Seth nongentorum duodecim annorum et mortuus est*

And all Seth's days became nine hundred twelve years, and he died.

5:9 *vixit vero Enos nonaginta annis et genuit Cainan*

Truly, Enos lived ninety years, and fathered Cainan,

5:10 *post cuius ortum vixit octingentis quindecim annis et genuit filios et filias*

after whose birth he lived eight hundred fifteen years. And he fathered sons and daughters.

5:11 *factique sunt omnes dies Enos nongentorum quinque annorum et mortuus est*

And all Enos's days became nine hundred five years, and he died.

5:12 *vixit quoque Cainan septuaginta annis et genuit Malalehel*

Cainan likewise lived seventy years, and fathered Malalehel.

5:13 *et vixit Cainan postquam genuit Malalehel octingentos quadraginta annos genuitque filios et filias*

And after he fathered Malalehel, Cainan lived eight hundred forty years. And he fathered sons and daughters.

5:14 *et facti sunt omnes dies Cainan nongenti decem anni et mortuus est*

And all Cainan's days became nine hundred ten years, and he died.

5:15 *vixit autem Malalehel sexaginta quinque annos et genuit Iared*

But Malalehel lived sixty-five years, and fathered Jared.

5:16 *et vixit Malalehel postquam*

genuit Iared octingentis triginta annis et genuit filios et filias

And after he fathered Jared, Malalehel lived eight hundred thirty years, and fathered sons and daughters.

5:17 *et facti sunt omnes dies Malalehel octingenti nonaginta quinque anni et mortuus est*

And all Malalehel's days became eight hundred ninety-five years, and he died.

5:18 *vixitque Iared centum sexaginta duobus annis et genuit Enoch*

And Jared lived one hundred sixty-two years, and fathered Enoch.

5:19 *et vixit Iared postquam genuit Enoch octingentos annos et genuit filios et filias*

And after he fathered Enoch, Jared lived eight hundred years, and fathered sons and daughters.

5:20 *et facti sunt omnes dies Iared nongenti sexaginta duo anni et mortuus est*

And all Jared's days became nine hundred sixty-two years, and he died.

5:21 *porro Enoch vixit sexaginta quinque annis et genuit Mathusalam*

Further on, Enoch lived sixty-five years, and fathered Methuselah.

5:22 *et ambulavit Enoch cum Deo postquam genuit Mathusalam trecentis annis et genuit filios et filias*

And Enoch walked with God three hundred years after he fathered Methuselah, and fathered sons and daughters.

5:23 *et facti sunt omnes dies Enoch trecenti sexaginta quinque anni*

And all Enoch's days became three hundred sixty-five years.

5:24 *ambulavitque cum Deo et non apparuit quia tulit eum Deus*

And he walked with God and did not appear, because God took him.

5:25 *vixit quoque Mathusalam centum octoginta septem annos et genuit Lamech*

Methuselah likewise lived one hundred eighty-seven years, and fathered Lamech.

5:26 *et vixit Mathusalam postquam genuit Lamech septingentos octoginta duos annos et genuit filios et filias*

And after he fathered Lamech, Methuselah lived seven hundred eighty-two years, and fathered sons and daughters.

5:27 *et facti sunt omnes dies Mathusalae nongenti sexaginta novem anni et mortuus est*

And all Methuselah's days became nine hundred sixty-nine years, and he died.

5:28 *vixit autem Lamech centum octoginta duobus annis et genuit filium*

But Lamech lived one hundred eighty-two years, and fathered *a* son.

5:29 *vocavitque nomen eius Noe dicens iste consolabitur nos ab operibus et laboribus manuum nostrarum in terra cui maledixit Dominus*

And he called his name Noah, saying, "This one will console us from our hands' works and labors, in *the* land which *the* Lord cursed."

5:30 *vixitque Lamech postquam genuit Noe quingentos nonaginta quinque annos et genuit filios et filias*

And after he fathered Noah, Lamech lived five hundred ninety-five years, and fathered sons and daughters.

5:31 *et facti sunt omnes dies Lamech septingenti septuaginta* *septem anni et mortuus est*

And all Lamech's days became seven hundred seventy-seven years, and he died.

5:32 *Noe vero cum quingentorum esset annorum genuit Sem et Ham et Iafeth*

Noah, indeed, when he was five hundred years old, fathered Shem and Ham and Japheth.

Human Wickedness Increases
Genesis 6:1 *cumque coepissent homines multiplicari super terram et filias procreassent*

And when men began to be multiplied on *the* land, and daughters were born,

6:2 *videntes filii Dei filias eorum quod essent pulchrae acceperunt uxores sibi ex omnibus quas elegerant*

God's sons, seeing that their daughters were beautiful, received them *as* wives for themselves from all that they picked out.

6:3 *dixitque Deus non permanebit spiritus meus in homine in aeternum quia caro est eruntque dies illius centum viginti annorum*

And God said, "My Spirit will not stay in man in eternity, because he is flesh. And His days will be one hundred twenty years."

6:4 *gigantes autem erant super terram in diebus illis postquam enim ingressi sunt filii Dei ad filias hominum illaeque genuerunt isti sunt potentes a saeculo viri famosi*

But giants were on *the* land in those days. For after God's sons went in to men's daughters and they birthed them, these were mighty *ones* from *the* age, famous men.

6:5 *videns autem Deus quod multa malitia hominum esset in terra et cuncta cogitatio cordis intenta esset ad malum omni tempore*

But God, seeing that man's great harmfulness was in *the* land, and all *their* heart's thought was directed to harm, all *the* time,

6:6 *paenituit eum quod hominem fecisset in terra et tactus dolore cordis intrinsecus*

it made Him sorry that He had made man in *the* land, and touched *His* heart inside with grief.

6:7 *delebo inquit hominem quem creavi a facie terrae ab homine usque ad animantia a reptili usque ad volucres caeli paenitet enim me fecisse eos*

"I will destroy," He said, "man whom I created from *the* land's face – from man even to animals, from reptiles even to sky's birds, for it saddens Me that I made them."

6:8 *Noe vero invenit gratiam coram Domino*

But Noah found grace before *the* Lord.

6:9 *hae generationes Noe Noe vir iustus atque perfectus fuit in generationibus suis cum Deo ambulavit*

These *are* Noah's generations. Noah was *a* fair and complete man in his generations. He walked with God.

6:10 *et genuit tres filios Sem Ham et Iafeth*

And he fathered three sons: Shem, Ham, and Japheth.

God Judges Humanity, Calls Noah

6:11 *corrupta est autem terra coram Deo et repleta est iniquitate*

But *the* land was corrupt before *the* Lord, and filled with treachery.

6:12 *cumque vidisset Deus terram esse corruptam omnis quippe caro corruperat viam suam super terram*

And when God saw *that the* land was corrupted, all flesh, obviously, had corrupted its way on *the* land,

6:13 *dixit ad Noe finis universae carnis venit coram me repleta est terra iniquitate a facie eorum et ego disperdam eos cum terra*

He said to Noah, "All flesh's end comes before Me. *The* land is filled with treachery from their face, and I will destroy them with *the* land.

6:14 *fac tibi arcam de lignis levigatis mansiunculas in arca facies et bitumine linies intrinsecus et extrinsecus*

"Make yourself *an* ark of wood! You will smooth *it*, and make small rooms in *the* ark. You will line it with pitch inside and outside.

6:15 *et sic facies eam trecentorum cubitorum erit longitudo arcae quinquaginta cubitorum latitudo et triginta cubitorum altitudo illius*

"And you will make it this way. *The* ark's length will be three hundred cubits, *its* width fifty cubits, and its height thirty cubits.

6:16 *fenestram in arca facies et in cubito consummabis summitatem ostium autem arcae pones ex latere deorsum cenacula et tristega facies in ea*

"You will make *a* window in *the* ark, and will finish *its* top in *a* cubit. But you will put *the* ark's doorway on *the* side. And you will make *a* lower, middle, and third floor in it.

6:17 *ecce ego adducam diluvii aquas super terram ut interficiam omnem carnem in qua spiritus vitae est subter caelum universa quae in terra sunt consumentur*

"Look, I will bring in *a* flood of waters over *the* land, so I may kill all flesh in which life's breath exists under *the* sky. All that are in *the* land will be consumed.

6:18 *ponamque foedus meum tecum*

et ingredieris arcam tu et filii tui uxor tua et uxores filiorum tuorum tecum

"And I will place My pact with you, and you will go into *the* ark – you and your sons, your wife and your sons's wives with you.

6:19 *et ex cunctis animantibus universae carnis bina induces in arcam ut vivant tecum masculini sexus et feminini*

"And from all living *beings*, you will bring two of all flesh into *the* ark, so they may live with you – male sex and female:

6:20 *de volucribus iuxta genus suum et de iumentis in genere suo et ex omni reptili terrae secundum genus suum bina de omnibus ingredientur tecum ut possint vivere*

from birds according to their type, and from cattle in their type, and from all *the* land's reptiles according to their type – two from all will go in with you, so they can live.

6:21 *tolles igitur tecum ex omnibus escis quae mandi possunt et conportabis apud te et erunt tam tibi quam illis in cibum*

You will take with you, therefore, some of every food which can be eaten, and you will carry *it* with you. And *it* will be food to you and to them.

6:22 *fecit ergo Noe omnia quae praeceperat illi Deus*

Then Noah did all that God had commanded him.

The Flood

Genesis 7:1 *dixitque Dominus ad eum ingredere tu et omnis domus tua arcam te enim vidi iustum coram me in generatione hac*

And *the* Lord said to him, "Go into *the* ark, you and all your house, for I have seen you *as* fair before me in this generation.

7:2 *ex omnibus animantibus mundis tolle septena septena masculum et feminam de animantibus vero non mundis duo duo masculum et feminam*

"Take seven from all clean animals, seven male and female. But from unclean, *take* two – two male and female.

7:3 *sed et de volatilibus caeli septena septena masculum et feminam ut salvetur semen super faciem universae terrae*

Yet *take* also seven from all sky's birds, seven male and female, so *the* seed will be saved over all land's face.

7:4 *adhuc enim et post dies septem ego pluam super terram quadraginta diebus et quadraginta noctibus et delebo omnem substantiam quam feci de superficie terrae*

"For after seven more days, I will rain over *the* land forty days and forty nights. And I will destroy from *the* land's surface every substance which I made.

7:5 *fecit ergo Noe omnia quae mandaverat ei Dominus*

Therefore, Noah did all that *the* Lord had commanded him.

7:6 *eratque sescentorum annorum quando diluvii aquae inundaverunt super terram*

And he was six hundred years old when *the* waters' floods inundated *the* land.

7:7 *et ingressus est Noe et filii eius uxor eius et uxores filiorum eius cum eo in arcam propter aquas diluvii*

And Noah went into *the* ark – his sons, his wife and his sons wives with him – because of *the* floods' waters.

7:8 *de animantibus quoque mundis et inmundis et de volucribus et ex omni quod movetur super terram*

Likewise, from clean and unclean animals, and from birds, and from all that moves on land,

7:9 *duo et duo ingressa sunt ad Noe in arcam masculus et femina sicut praeceperat Deus Noe*

two by two they went in to Noah in *the* ark – male and female, like God

had commanded Noah.

The Flood Begins

7:10 *cumque transissent septem dies aquae diluvii inundaverunt super terram*

And when seven days had passed, *the* floods' waters inundated *the* land.

7:11 *anno sescentesimo vitae Noe mense secundo septimodecimo die mensis rupti sunt omnes fontes abyssi magnae et cataractae caeli apertae sunt*

The six hundredth year of Noah's life, second month, seventeenth day of the month, all *the* great abyss's fountains were ruptured and *the* sky's waterfalls were opened.

7:12 *et facta est pluvia super terram quadraginta diebus et quadraginta noctibus*

And rain came over *the* land forty days and forty nights.

7:13 *in articulo diei illius ingressus est Noe et Sem et Ham et Iafeth filii eius uxor illius et tres uxores filiorum eius cum eis in arcam*

In that particular day, Noah went in, and Shem and Ham and Japheth his sons, his wife and his sons' three wives with them, to *the* ark.

7:14 *ipsi et omne animal secundum*

genus suum universaque iumenta in genus suum et omne quod movetur super terram in genere suo cunctumque volatile secundum genus suum universae aves omnesque volucres

These, and every animal according to its type, and all cattle in its type, and everything that moves on *the* land in its type, and every flying *creature* according to its type, all birds, and everything that flies

7:15 *ingressae sunt ad Noe in arcam bina et bina ex omni carne in qua erat spiritus vitae*

went into *the* Ark to Noah, two by two, from every flesh in which life's breath existed.

7:16 *et quae ingressa sunt masculus et femina ex omni carne introierunt sicut praeceperat ei Deus et inclusit eum Dominus de foris*

And what went in, came in male and female from every flesh, as God had commanded him. And *the* Lord closed him in from outside.

7:17 *factumque est diluvium quadraginta diebus super terram et multiplicatae sunt aquae et elevaverunt arcam in sublime a terra*

And *the* flood came forty days over *the* land. And waters were multiplied and lifted up *the* ark into *the* highest

parts from *the* land.

7:18 *vehementer inundaverunt et omnia repleverunt in superficie terrae porro arca ferebatur super aquas*

And they flooded fiercely, and all *things* on *the* land's surface were filled. Hereafter, *the* ark floated over *the* waters.

7:19 *et aquae praevaluerunt nimis super terram opertique sunt omnes montes excelsi sub universo caelo*

And waters prevailed greatly over land, and all *the* highest mountains under all *the* sky were covered.

7:20 *quindecim cubitis altior fuit aqua super montes quos operuerat*

The water was fifteen cubits higher than *the* mountains which it covered.

7:21 *consumptaque est omnis caro quae movebatur super terram volucrum animantium bestiarum omniumque reptilium quae reptant super terram universi homines*

And all flesh that moved over *the* land was consumed – birds, animals, and beasts, and all reptiles which crawl on *the* land, all humans

7:22 *et cuncta in quibus spiraculum vitae est in terra mortua sunt*

and all in which life's opening exists died in *the* land.

7:23 *et delevit omnem substantiam quae erat super terram ab homine usque ad pecus tam reptile quam volucres caeli et deleta sunt de terra remansit autem solus Noe et qui cum eo erant in arca*

And it destroyed every substance which was on *the* land – from men even to cattle, reptiles and sky's birds alike. And they were destroyed from *the* land. But only Noah remained, and those who were with him in *the* ark.

7:24 *obtinueruntque aquae terras centum quinquaginta diebus*

And waters held fast *the* lands one hundred fifty days.

The Flood
Begins to Subside

Genesis 8:1 *recordatus autem Deus Noe cunctarumque animantium et omnium iumentorum quae erant cum eo in arca adduxit spiritum super terram et inminutae sunt aquae*

But God remembered Noah and all *the* animals and all *the* cattle that were with him in *the* ark. He brought in *a* wind over *the* land, and waters were diminished.

8:2 *et clausi sunt fontes abyssi et cataractae caeli et prohibitae sunt pluviae de caelo*

And *the* abyss's fountains and *the* sky's waterfalls were closed, and rains from *the* sky were restrained,

8:3 *reversaeque aquae de terra euntes et redeuntes et coeperunt minui post centum quinquaginta dies*

and waters turned back from *the* land, going and returning. And they began to recede after one hundred fifty days.

8:4 *requievitque arca mense septimo vicesima septima die mensis super montes Armeniae*

And *the* ark rested *the* seventh month, seventeenth day of *the* month, over Armenia's mountains.

8:5 *at vero aquae ibant et*

decrescebant usque ad decimum mensem decimo enim mense prima die mensis apparuerunt cacumina montium

But truly waters went and decreased, even to *the* tenth month, for in *the* tenth month, first day of *the* month, *the* mountains' peaks appeared.

Noah Sends Out a Dove

8:6 *cumque transissent quadraginta dies aperiens Noe fenestram arcae quam fecerat dimisit corvum*

And when forty days had passed, Noah, opening *the* ark's window which he made, sent out *a* crow,

8:7 *qui egrediebatur et revertebatur donec siccarentur aquae super terram*

which went out and flew around until *the* waters dried over *the* land.

8:8 *emisit quoque columbam post eum ut videret si iam cessassent aquae super faciem terrae*

He also sent out *a* dove after it, so he could see if *the* waters already had ceased over *the* land's face,

8:9 *quae cum non invenisset ubi requiesceret pes eius reversa est ad eum in arcam aquae enim erant super universam terram extenditque manum et adprehensam intulit in arcam*

which, when it could not find where to rest its foot, came back to him in *the* ark, for waters were over all *the* land. And he stretched out his hand and, taking it, brought it into *the* ark.

8:10 *expectatis autem ultra septem diebus aliis rursum dimisit columbam ex arca*

But, waiting seven days more, he sent *the* dove out again from *the* ark.

8:11 *at illa venit ad eum ad vesperam portans ramum olivae virentibus foliis in ore suo intellexit ergo Noe quod cessassent aquae super terram*

And it came to him at evening, carrying in its mouth *an* olive branch with green leaves. Noah understood, then, that *the* waters had ceased over *the* land.

8:12 *expectavitque nihilominus septem alios dies et emisit columbam quae non est reversa ultra ad eum*

And, nonetheless, he waited seven more days, and sent *the* dove out, which did not come back to him further.

8:13 *igitur sescentesimo primo anno primo mense prima die mensis inminutae sunt aquae super terram et aperiens Noe tectum arcae aspexit viditque quod exsiccata esset superficies terrae*

Therefore, *the* six hundred first year, first month, first day of *the* month, *the* waters were diminished over *the* land. And Noah, opening *the* ark's roof, looked and saw that *the* land's surface was dry.

8:14 *mense secundo septima et vicesima die mensis arefacta est terra*

The second month, twenty-seventh day of *the* month, *the* land was dry.

God Commands Noah
to Go Out

8:15 *locutus est autem Deus ad Noe dicens*

But God spoke to Noah, saying,

8:16 *egredere de arca tu et uxor tua filii tui et uxores filiorum tuorum tecum*

"Go out from *the* ark, you and your wife, your sons and your sons' wives with you!

8:17 *cuncta animantia quae sunt apud te ex omni carne tam in volatilibus quam in bestiis et in universis reptilibus quae reptant super terram educ tecum et ingredimini super terram crescite et multiplicamini super eam*

"Lead out with you all animals which are with you from all flesh, among birds as well as beasts, and all reptiles that crawl on land – and you will go over *the* land. Increase and be multiplied on it!"

8:18 *egressus est ergo Noe et filii eius uxor illius et uxores filiorum eius cum eo*

Therefore, Noah went out and his sons, his wife and his sons' wives with him.

8:19 *sed et omnia animantia iumenta et reptilia quae repunt super terram secundum genus suum arcam egressa sunt*

And also all animals, cattle, and reptiles which crawl over land, according to their type, went out from *the* ark.

Noah Builds an Altar
to the Lord

8:20 *aedificavit autem Noe altare Domino et tollens de cunctis pecoribus et volucribus mundis obtulit holocausta super altare*

But Noah built *an* altar to *the* Lord and, taking from all clean cattle and birds, he offered *a* burnt offering on *the* altar.

8:21 *odoratusque est Dominus odorem suavitatis et ait ad eum nequaquam ultra maledicam terrae propter homines sensus enim et cogitatio humani cordis in malum prona sunt ab adulescentia sua non*

*igitur ultra percutiam omnem
animantem sicut feci*

And *the* Lord smelled *the* odor in
smoothness, and He said to him, "I
will never again curse *the* land
because of men. For man's heart's
sense and thought are prone to harm
from his youth. Therefore, I will not
strike further every animal, like I did.

8:22 *cunctis diebus terrae sementis
et messis frigus et aestus aestas et
hiemps nox et dies non requiescent*

"All *the* land's days   sowing and
harvest, cold and heat, summer and
winter, night and day, will not end.

God Makes
a Covenant with Noah

Genesis 9:1 *benedixitque Deus Noe
et filiis eius et dixit ad eos crescite et
multiplicamini et implete terram*

And God blessed Noah and his sons,
and said to them, "Increase and be
multiplied, and fill *the* land!

9:2 *et terror vester ac tremor sit
super cuncta animalia terrae et
super omnes volucres caeli cum
universis quae moventur in terra
omnes pisces maris manui vestrae
traditi sunt*

"And let terror of you and trembling
be over all land's animals, and all
sky's birds, with all that moves in *the*
land! All sea's fish are given into
your hands.

9:3 *et omne quod movetur et vivit
erit vobis in cibum quasi holera
virentia tradidi vobis omnia*

"And everything that moves and lives
will be to you as food, like I gave
you every green plant –

9:4 *excepto quod carnem cum
sanguine non comedetis*

"except that you will not eat flesh
with blood.

9:5 *sanguinem enim animarum
vestrarum requiram de manu
cunctarum bestiarum et de manu*

hominis de manu viri et fratris eius requiram animam hominis

"For I will require your souls' blood, from all beasts' hand, and from man's hand. From man's hand and his brother's, I will require *a* man's soul.

9:6 *quicumque effuderit humanum sanguinem fundetur sanguis illius ad imaginem quippe Dei factus est homo*

"Whoever pours out human blood let his *own* blood be poured out. Man is made, as you see, in God's image.

9:7 *vos autem crescite et multiplicamini et ingredimini super terram et implete eam*

"But you, increase and be multiplied and go into *the* land and fill it!"

9:8 *haec quoque dixit Deus ad Noe et ad filios eius cum eo*

The Lord said this also to Noah and to his sons with him.

9:9 *ecce ego statuam pactum meum vobiscum et cum semine vestro post vos*

"Look, I will set up My pact with you and with your seed after you –

9:10 *et ad omnem animam viventem quae est vobiscum tam in volucribus quam in iumentis et pecudibus terrae*

cunctis quae egressa sunt de arca et universis bestiis terrae

"and to every living animal which is with you, with birds as well as cattle and *the* land's sheep, with all who have come out from *the* ark, and all *the* land's beasts.

9:11 *statuam pactum meum vobiscum et nequaquam ultra interficietur omnis caro aquis diluvii neque erit deinceps diluvium dissipans terram*

"I will set up My pact with you, and never again will all flesh be killed by *a* flood's waters, nor hereafter will there be *a* flood destroying *the* land completely.

9:12 *dixitque Deus hoc signum foederis quod do inter me et vos et ad omnem animam viventem quae est vobiscum in generationes sempiternas*

And God said, "This *is the* covenant's sign, which I give between Me and you and every living soul which is with you, in everlasting generations.

9:13 *arcum meum ponam in nubibus et erit signum foederis inter me et inter terram*

"I will put My bow in *the* clouds, and it will be *the* covenant's sign between Me and between *the* land.

9:14 *cumque obduxero nubibus caelum apparebit arcus meus in nubibus*

"And when I cover sky with clouds, My bow will appear in *the* clouds.

9:15 *et recordabor foederis mei vobiscum et cum omni anima vivente quae carnem vegetat et non erunt ultra aquae diluvii ad delendam universam carnem*

"And I will remember My covenant with you and with every living soul which imparts energy to flesh. And flood's waters will not be again to *the* destroying of all flesh.

9:16 *eritque arcus in nubibus et videbo illum et recordabor foederis sempiterni quod pactum est inter Deum et inter omnem animam viventem universae carnis quae est super terram*

"And *the* bow will be in *the* clouds, and I will see it and remember *the* everlasting covenant, which is *a* pact between God and between every living soul – all flesh which is on *the* land."

9:17 *dixitque Deus Noe hoc erit signum foederis quod constitui inter me et inter omnem carnem super terram*

And God said to Noah, "This will be the covenant's sign which I have set up between Me and between all flesh on *the* land."

Noah's Sons

9:18 *erant igitur filii Noe qui egressi sunt de arca Sem Ham et Iafeth porro Ham ipse est pater Chanaan*

These, then, were Noah's sons, who went out from *the* ark: Shem, Ham, and Japheth. Afterward, this Ham is Canaan's father.

9:19 *tres isti sunt filii Noe et ab his disseminatum est omne hominum genus super universam terram*

These three are Noah's sons, and from them every human type was spread over all *the* land.

Noah Gets Drunk

9:20 *coepitque Noe vir agricola exercere terram et plantavit vineam*

Noah, *a* farmer, began to work *the* land, and planted *a* vineyard.

9:21 *bibensque vinum inebriatus est et nudatus in tabernaculo suo*

And, drinking wine, he was drunk and naked in his tent.

9:22 *quod cum vidisset Ham pater Chanaan verenda scilicet patris sui esse nuda nuntiavit duobus fratribus suis foras*

Which, when Ham, Canaan's father, saw his father's private parts, *Noah* being naked, he told his two brothers outside.

9:23 *at vero Sem et Iafeth pallium inposuerunt umeris suis et incedentes retrorsum operuerunt verecunda patris sui faciesque eorum aversae erant et patris virilia non viderunt*

And indeed Shem and Japheth put *a* cover on their shoulders and, walking in backwards, covered their father's private parts. And their faces were turned away, and they did not see their father's manhood.

9:24 *evigilans autem Noe ex vino cum didicisset quae fecerat ei filius suus minor*

But Noah, waking up from wine, when he learned what his youngest son had done to him,

9:25 *ait maledictus Chanaan servus servorum erit fratribus suis*

he said, "Canaan be cursed! He will be *the* slaves' slave to his brothers."

9:26 *dixitque benedictus Dominus Deus Sem sit Chanaan servus eius*

And he said, "*The* Lord, Shem's God, be blessed! Let Canaan be his slave!"

9:27 *dilatet Deus Iafeth et habitet in*

tabernaculis Sem sitque Chanaan servus eius

"May God broaden Japheth, and may he live in Shem's tents! And let Canaan be his slave!"

Noah's Death
9:28 *vixit autem Noe post diluvium trecentis quinquaginta annis*

But Noah lived three hundred fifty years after *the* flood.

9:29 *et impleti sunt omnes dies eius nongentorum quinquaginta annorum et mortuus est*

And all his days filled nine hundred fifty years, and he died.

Noah's Descendants

Genesis 10:1 *hae generationes filiorum Noe Sem Ham Iafeth natique sunt eis filii post diluvium*

These are Noah's sons' generations – Shem, Ham, and Japheth.

Children were born to them after *the* flood.

Japheth's Children

10:2 *filii Iafeth Gomer Magog et Madai Iavan et Thubal et Mosoch et Thiras*

Japheth's sons: Gomer, Magog, and Madai. Javan and Thubal and Mosoch and Thiras.

10:3 *porro filii Gomer Aschenez et Rifath et Thogorma*

Afterwards, Gomer's sons were Ashkenaz and Rifath and Thogorma.

10:4 *filii autem Iavan Elisa et Tharsis Cetthim et Dodanim*

But Javan's sons were Elisa and Tharsis, Kittim and Dodanim.

10:5 *ab his divisae sunt insulae gentium in regionibus suis unusquisque secundum linguam et familias in nationibus suis*

The nations' islands were divided from these into their regions, each one according to tongue and families, in their nations.

Ham's Children

10:6 *filii autem Ham Chus et Mesraim et Fut et Chanaan*

But Ham's sons *were* Cush and Mizraim and Fut and Canaan.

10:7 *filii Chus Saba et Hevila et Sabatha et Regma et Sabathaca filii Regma Saba et Dadan*

Cush's sons *were* Saba and Hevila and Sabatha and Regma and Sabathaca. Regma's sons were Sheba and Dadan.

10:8 *porro Chus genuit Nemrod ipse coepit esse potens in terra*

Afterwards, Cush fathered Nimrod. He began to be mighty in *the* land.

10:9 *et erat robustus venator coram Domino ab hoc exivit proverbium quasi Nemrod robustus venator coram Domino*

And he was *a* mighty hunter before *the* Lord. From this *the* proverb came out, "Like Nimrod, mighty hunter before *the* Lord."

10:10 *fuit autem principium regni eius Babylon et Arach et Archad et Chalanne in terra Sennaar*

But his kingdom's beginning was Babylon and Arach and Archad and

Chalanne, in Sennaar's land.

10:11 *de terra illa egressus est Assur et aedificavit Nineven et plateas civitatis et Chale*

Assur went out from that land and built Nineveh and its city's streets, and Chale,

10:12 *Resen quoque inter Nineven et Chale haec est civitas magna*

Resen, likewise, between Nineveh and Chale. This is *a* great city.

10:13 *at vero Mesraim genuit Ludim et Anamim et Laabim Nepthuim*

And indeed, Mizraim fathered Ludim and Anamim and Laabim and Nepthuim

10:14 *et Phetrusim et Cesluim de quibus egressi sunt Philisthim et Capthurim*

and Phetrusim and Cesluim, from whom *the* Philistines went out, and Capthurim.

Canaan's Children
10:15 *Chanaan autem genuit Sidonem primogenitum suum Ettheum*

But Canaan fathered Sidonem, his firstborn, Ettheum,

10:16 *et Iebuseum et Amorreum Gergeseum*

and Jebuseum, and Amorreum, Gergeseum,

10:17 *Eveum et Araceum Sineum*

Eveum and Araceum, Sineum

10:18 *et Aradium Samariten et Amatheum et post haec disseminati sunt populi Chananeorum*

and Aradium, Samariten and Amatheum. And after this, Canaanite peoples were seeded abroad.

10:19 *factique sunt termini Chanaan venientibus a Sidone Geraram usque Gazam donec ingrediaris Sodomam et Gomorram et Adama et Seboim usque Lesa*

And Canaan's borders were made coming from Sidon to Gerara, even to Gaza, until you come to Sodom and Gomorrah and Adamah and Seboim, even to Lesa.

10:20 *hii filii Ham in cognationibus et linguis et generationibus terrisque et gentibus suis*

These are Ham's children in blood-relations and tongues and generations and lands, and his nations.

Shem's Descendants
10:21 *de Sem quoque nati sunt*

patre omnium filiorum Eber fratre Iafeth maiore

From Shem likewise, father of all Eber's children, Japheth's older brother, *children* were born.

10:22 *filii Sem Aelam et Assur et Arfaxad et Lud et Aram*

Shem's sons *were* Elam and Assur and Arfaxad and Lud and Aram.

10:23 *filii Aram Us et Hul et Gether et Mes*

Aram's sons *were* Uz and Hul and Gether and Mes.

10:24 *at vero Arfaxad genuit Sala de quo ortus est Eber*

And indeed Arfaxad fathered Salah, from whom Eber was born.

10:25 *natique sunt Eber filii duo nomen uni Faleg eo quod in diebus eius divisa sit terra et nomen fratris eius Iectan*

And two sons were born to Eber. One's name *was* Peleg, because in his days *the* land is divided. And his brother's name *was* Jectan.

10:26 *qui Iectan genuit Helmodad et Saleph et Asarmoth Iare*

Those whom Jectan fathered *were* Helmodad and Saleph and Asarmoth,

Jare

10:27 *et Aduram et Uzal Decla*

and Aduram and Uzal, Decla

10:28 *et Ebal et Abimahel Saba*

and Ebal and Abimahel, Sheba

10:29 *et Ophir et Evila et Iobab omnes isti filii Iectan*

and Ophir and Evila and Jobab. All these *were* Jectan's sons.

10:30 *et facta est habitatio eorum de Messa pergentibus usque Sephar montem orientalem*

And their home went from Messa, going even to Sephar, *the* eastern mountain.

10:31 *isti filii Sem secundum cognationes et linguas et regiones in gentibus suis*

These *were* Shem's sons, according to blood relations and tongues and regions, among his nations.

10:32 *hae familiae Noe iuxta populos et nationes suas ab his divisae sunt gentes in terra post diluvium*

These were Noah's families, along with his peoples and nations. From these, nations were divided in *the* land after *the* flood.

Ceasing to Listen
and Understand

Genesis 11:1 *erat autem terra labii unius et sermonum eorundem*

But *the* land was of one tongue and *the* same thought.

11:2 *cumque proficiscerentur de oriente invenerunt campum in terra Sennaar et habitaverunt in eo*

And when they set out from *the* east, they found *a* field in Sennaar's land and lived in it.

11:3 *dixitque alter ad proximum suum venite faciamus lateres et coquamus eos igni habueruntque lateres pro saxis et bitumen pro cemento*

And each one said to his neighbor, "Come, let us make bricks, and cook them in fire. And they had bricks for stones and pitch for cement.

11:4 *et dixerunt venite faciamus nobis civitatem et turrem cuius culmen pertingat ad caelum et celebremus nomen nostrum antequam dividamur in universas terras*

And they said, "Come, let us make ourselves *a* city and tower, whose height can touch *the* sky, and we can celebrate our name before we are divided into all *the* lands.

11:5 *descendit autem Dominus ut videret civitatem et turrem quam aedificabant filii Adam*

But *the* Lord came down so He could see *the* city and tower which Adam's children were building.

11:6 *et dixit ecce unus est populus et unum labium omnibus coeperuntque hoc facere nec desistent a cogitationibus suis donec eas opere conpleant*

And He said, "Look, *the* people is one, and *there is* one language to all of them. They have begun to do this, nor will they turn aside from their schemes until they have completed them in work.

11:7 *venite igitur descendamus et confundamus ibi linguam eorum ut non audiat unusquisque vocem proximi sui*

"Come, then, let us go down and confuse their language there, so each one cannot hear his neighbor's voice."

11:8 *atque ita divisit eos Dominus ex illo loco in universas terras et cessaverunt aedificare civitatem*

And so *the* Lord divided them in such manner from that place into all *the* lands. And they ceased to build *the* city.

11:9 *et idcirco vocatum est nomen eius Babel quia ibi confusum est labium universae terrae et inde dispersit eos Dominus super faciem cunctarum regionum*

And therefore its name is called Babel, because *the* tongue of all *the* land was confused there. And from there *the* Lord dispersed them over all *the* region's face.

Shem's Generations
11:10 *hae generationes Sem Sem centum erat annorum quando genuit Arfaxad biennio post diluvium*

These are Shem's generations.

Shem was one hundred years old when he fathered Arfaxad, two years after *the* flood.

11:11 *vixitque Sem postquam genuit Arfaxad quingentos annos et genuit filios et filias*

And Shem lived five hundred years after he fathered Arfaxad, and fathered sons and daughters.

11:12 *porro Arfaxad vixit triginta quinque annos et genuit Sale*

After, Arfaxad lived thiry-five years, and fathered Saleh.

11:13 *vixitque Arfaxad postquam genuit Sale trecentis tribus annis et genuit filios et filias*

And Arfaxad lived three hundred three years after he fathered Saleh, and fathered sons and daughters.

11:14 *Sale quoque vixit triginta annis et genuit Eber*

Saleh likewise lived thirty years and fathered Eber.

11:15 *vixitque Sale postquam genuit Eber quadringentis tribus annis et genuit filios et filias*

And Saleh lived four hundred three years after he fathered Eber, and fathered sons and daughters.

11:16 *vixit autem Eber triginta quattuor annis et genuit Faleg*

But Eber lived thirty-four years and fathered Peleg.

11:17 *et vixit Eber postquam genuit Faleg quadringentis triginta annis et genuit filios et filias*

And Eber lived four hundred thirty years after he fathered Peleg, and fathered sons and daughters.

11:18 *vixit quoque Faleg triginta annis et genuit Reu*

Peleg likewise lived thirty years, and fathered Reu.

11:19 *vixitque Faleg postquam genuit Reu ducentis novem annis et*

genuit filios et filias

And Peleg lived two hundred nine years after he fathered Reu, and fathered sons and daughters.

11:20 *vixit autem Reu triginta duobus annis et genuit Sarug*

But Reu lived thirty-two years, and fathered Sarug.

11:21 *vixitque Reu postquam genuit Sarug ducentis septem annis et genuit filios et filias*

And Reu lived two hundred seven years after he fathered Sarug, and fathered sons and daughters.

11:22 *vixit vero Sarug triginta annis et genuit Nahor*

Truly, Sarug lived thirty years, and fathered Nahor.

11:23 *vixitque Sarug postquam genuit Nahor ducentos annos et genuit filios et filias*

And Sarug lived two hundred years after he fathered Nahor, and fathered sons and daughters.

11:24 *vixit autem Nahor viginti novem annis et genuit Thare*

But Nahor lived twenty-nine years and fathered Thareh.

11:25 *vixitque Nahor postquam genuit Thare centum decem et novem annos et genuit filios et filias*

And Nahor lived one hundred nineteen years after he fathered Thareh, and fathered sons and daughters.

11:26 *vixitque Thare septuaginta annis et genuit Abram et Nahor et Aran*

And Thareh lived seventy years and fathered Abram and Nahor and Haran.

Thareh's Generations

11:27 *hae sunt autem generationes Thare Thare genuit Abram et Nahor et Aran porro Aran genuit Loth*

But these are Thareh's generations.

Thareh fathered Abram and Nahor and Haran. After, Haran fathered Lot.

11:28 *mortuusque est Aran ante Thare patrem suum in terra nativitatis suae in Ur Chaldeorum*

And Haran died before Thareh his father, in *the* land of his birth, in *the* Chaldeans' Ur.

11:29 *duxerunt autem Abram et Nahor uxores nomen autem uxoris Abram Sarai et nomen uxoris Nahor Melcha filia Aran patris Melchae et patris Ieschae*

But Abram and Nahor took wives. And Abram's wife's name *was* Sarai, and Nahor's wife's name *was* Melcha, Haran's daughter – Melcha's father and Jeschah's father.

11:30 *erat autem Sarai sterilis nec habebat liberos*

But Sarai was sterile, nor had children.

11:31 *tulit itaque Thare Abram filium suum et Loth filium Aran filium filii sui et Sarai nurum suam uxorem Abram filii sui et eduxit eos de Ur Chaldeorum ut irent in terram Chanaan veneruntque usque Haran et habitaverunt ibi*

And Thareh took Abram, his son; and Lot, Haran's son, son of his son; and Sarai, his daughter-in-law, wife of his son Abram. And he led them out of *the* Chaldeans' Ur, so he could go to Canaan's land. And he came as far as Haran, and lived there.

11:32 *et facti sunt dies Thare ducentorum quinque annorum et mortuus est in Haran*

And Thareh's days became two hundred five years, and he died in Haran.

God Calls Abram
to Canaan

Genesis 12:1 *dixit autem Dominus ad Abram egredere de terra tua et de cognatione tua et de domo patris tui in terram quam monstrabo tibi*

But *the* Lord said to Abram, "Go out from your land and from your kin and from your father's house, into *a* land which I will show you!

12:2 *faciamque te in gentem magnam et benedicam tibi et magnificabo nomen tuum erisque benedictus*

"And I will make you into *a* great nation, and will bless you, and magnify your name. And you will be blessed.

12:3 *benedicam benedicentibus tibi et maledicam maledicentibus tibi atque in te benedicentur universae cognationes terrae*

"I will bless those blessing you and curse those cursing you. And all *the* land's families will be blessed in you."

12:4 *egressus est itaque Abram sicut praeceperat ei Dominus et ivit cum eo Loth septuaginta quinque annorum erat Abram cum egrederetur de Haran*

So Abram went out, as *the* Lord had commanded him, and Lot went with him. Abram was seventy-five years old when he went out from Haran.

12:5 *tulitque Sarai uxorem suam et Loth filium fratris sui universamque substantiam quam possederant et animas quas fecerant in Haran et egressi sunt ut irent in terram Chanaan cumque venissent in eam*

And he took Sarai, his wife, and Lot, his brother's son, and all *the* substance and souls which they possessed, what they had done in Haran. And they went out so they could go into Canaan's land. And when they had come into it,

12:6 *pertransivit Abram terram usque ad locum Sychem usque ad convallem Inlustrem Chananeus autem tunc erat in terra*

Abram passed through *the* land even to Shechem's place, even to Shining Valley. But *the* Canaanite was in *the* land then.

12:7 *apparuitque Dominus Abram et dixit ei semini tuo dabo terram hanc qui aedificavit ibi altare Domino qui apparuerat ei*

And *the* Lord appeared to Abram and said to him, "I will give this land to your seed."

Abram built an altar there to *the* Lord who appeared to him.

12:8 *et inde transgrediens ad montem qui erat contra orientem Bethel tetendit ibi tabernaculum suum ab occidente habens Bethel et ab oriente Ai aedificavit quoque ibi altare Domino et invocavit nomen eius*

And passing through from there to *a* mountain which was across Bethel to *the* east, he stretched out his tent there, having Bethel on *the* west and Ai on the east. He likewise built *an* altar to *the* Lord there, and invoked His name.

12:9 *perrexitque Abram vadens et ultra progrediens ad meridiem*

And Abram went on, going and making further progress toward *the* south.

Famine Drives Abram to Egypt

12:10 *facta est autem fames in terra descenditque Abram in Aegyptum ut peregrinaretur ibi praevaluerat enim fames in terra*

But famine came into *the* land, and Abram went down into Egypt, so he could stay there, for hunger prevailed in *the* land.

12:11 *cumque prope esset ut ingrederetur Aegyptum dixit Sarai uxori suae novi quod pulchra sis mulier*

And when he was close to going into Egypt, he said to Sarai, his wife, "I knew that you are *a* beautiful woman,

12:12 *et quod cum viderint te Aegyptii dicturi sunt uxor ipsius est et interficient me et te reservabunt*

"and that, when *the* Egyptians see you, they will say 'She is his wife.' And they will kill me and keep you.

12:13 *dic ergo obsecro te quod soror mea sis ut bene sit mihi propter te et vivat anima mea ob gratiam tui*

"Say, then, I pray you, that you are my sister, so *it* may be well with me on your account. And my soul may live, by your grace."

12:14 *cum itaque ingressus esset Abram Aegyptum viderunt Aegyptii mulierem quod esset pulchra nimis*

So when Abram went into Egypt, *the* Egyptians saw *the* woman, that she was exceedingly beautiful.

12:15 *et nuntiaverunt principes Pharaoni et laudaverunt eam apud illum et sublata est mulier in domum Pharaonis*

And Pharaoh's princes told *it*, and they praised her with him. And *the* woman was taken into Pharaoh's house.

12:16 *Abram vero bene usi sunt propter illam fueruntque ei oves et boves et asini et servi et famulae et asinae et cameli*

Abram indeed was well used because of her. And *there* were to him oxen and cattle and donkeys and slaves and female slaves and she-donkeys and camels.

12:17 *flagellavit autem Dominus Pharaonem plagis maximis et domum eius propter Sarai uxorem Abram*

But *the* Lord struck Pharaoh and his house with severe blows because of Sarai, Abram's wife.

12:18 *vocavitque Pharao Abram et dixit ei quidnam est quod fecisti mihi quare non indicasti quod uxor tua esset*

And Pharaoh called Abram and said to him, "What is it that you have done to me? Why didn't you say that she was your wife?"

12:19 *quam ob causam dixisti esse sororem tuam ut tollerem eam mihi in uxorem nunc igitur ecce coniux tua accipe eam et vade*

"For what reason did you say she was your sister, so I took her to me as wife? Now then, look! *There is* your spouse. Take her and go!"

12:20 *praecepitque Pharao super Abram viris et deduxerunt eum et uxorem illius et omnia quae habebat*

And Pharaoh commanded *the* men concerning Abram, and they led him out, and his wife, and all that he had.

Abram Returns to Canaan

Genesis 13:1 *ascendit ergo Abram de Aegypto ipse et uxor eius et omnia quae habebat et Loth cum eo ad australem plagam*

Then Abram went up from Egypt, he and his wife and all that he had, and Lot with him, to *the* south region.

13:2 *erat autem dives valde in possessione argenti et auri*

But he was exceedingly rich, in possession of silver and gold.

13:3 *reversusque est per iter quo venerat a meridie in Bethel usque ad locum ubi prius fixerat tabernaculum inter Bethel et Ai*

And he went back through *the* way which passed from *the* south to Bethel, even to *the* place where he had first pitched *his* tent, between Bethel and Ai,

13:4 *in loco altaris quod fecerat prius et invocavit ibi nomen Domini*

to *the* place where he first built *an* altar. And he invoked *the* Lord's name there.

Abram and Lot Separate

13:5 *sed et Loth qui erat cum Abram fuerunt greges ovium et armenta et tabernacula*

But there were also flocks of sheep and cattle and tents with Lot, who was with Abram.

13:6 *nec poterat eos capere terra ut habitarent simul erat quippe substantia eorum multa et non quibant habitare communiter*

The land wasn't able to hold them, so they could live at *the* same place. Their wealth, as you see, was great, and they couldn't live together.

13:7 *unde et facta est rixa inter pastores gregum Abram et Loth eo autem tempore Chananeus et Ferezeus habitabant in illa terra*

From this also, *a* quarrel developed between Abram's flock's shepherds and Lot's. But at that time, *the* Canaanite and Ferezite lived in that land.

13:8 *dixit ergo Abram ad Loth ne quaeso sit iurgium inter me et te et inter pastores meos et pastores tuos fratres enim sumus*

Therefore, Abram said to Lot, "Let there not be conflict, I ask, between me and you, and between my shepherds and your shepherds, for we are brothers.

13:9 *ecce universa terra coram te est recede a me obsecro si ad sinistram ieris ego ad dexteram tenebo si tu dexteram elegeris ego ad sinistram pergam*

"Look, *the* whole land is before you. Go away from me, I pray! If you go to *the* left, I will hold *the* right. If you choose *the* right, I will go to *the* left."

13:10 *elevatis itaque Loth oculis vidit omnem circa regionem Iordanis quae universa inrigabatur antequam subverteret Dominus Sodomam et Gomorram sicut paradisus Domini et sicut Aegyptus venientibus in Segor*

So Lot lifts up his eye. He saw all *the* region surrounding *the* Jordan coming into Segor, all of which was watered like *the* Lord's paradise and like Egypt, before *the* Lord overthrew Sodom and Gomorrah.

13:11 *elegitque sibi Loth regionem circa Iordanem et recessit ab oriente divisique sunt alterutrum a fratre suo*

And Lot chose for himself *the* region around *the* Jordan, and turned back to *the* east. And they were divided, each one from his brother.

13:12 *Abram habitavit in terra Chanaan Loth moratus est in oppidis quae erant circa Iordanem et habitavit in Sodomis*

Abram lived in Canaan's land. Lot stayed in *the* towns which were near *the* Jordan, and lived in Sodom.

13:13 *homines autem Sodomitae pessimi erant et peccatores coram*

Domino nimis

But Sodom's men were *the* worst, and great sinners before *the* Lord.

The Lord Promises Abram Uncountable Descendants

13:14 *dixitque Dominus ad Abram postquam divisus est Loth ab eo leva oculos tuos et vide a loco in quo nunc es ad aquilonem et ad meridiem ad orientem et ad occidentem*

And *the* Lord said to Abram after Lot separated from him, "Lift up your eyes and look, from *the* place in which you are now to *the* north and south and east and west!"

13:15 *omnem terram quam conspicis tibi dabo et semini tuo usque in sempiternum*

"I will give you and your seed all *the* land which you look on, even to forever.

13:16 *faciamque semen tuum sicut pulverem terrae si quis potest hominum numerare pulverem semen quoque tuum numerare poterit*

"And I will make your seed like *the* land's dust. If someone can count *the* dust, likewise he can count your *seed.*

13:17 *surge et perambula terram in longitudine et in latitudine sua quia* *tibi daturus sum eam*

"Get up and walk through *the* land, in its length and in its breadth, because I will give it to you!"

Abram Lives in Hebron

13:18 *movens igitur Abram tabernaculum suum venit et habitavit iuxta convallem Mambre quod est in Hebron aedificavitque ibi altare Domino*

Abram, therefore, moving his tent, went and lived alongside Mambre Valley, which is in Hebron. And he built *an* altar there to *the* Lord.

War Between Mesopotamia and Canaan

Genesis 14:1 *factum est autem in illo tempore ut Amrafel rex Sennaar et Arioch rex Ponti et Chodorlahomor rex Aelamitarum et Thadal rex Gentium*

But it happened in that time, that Amrafel, Sennaar's king, and Arioch, Pontus's king, and Chodorlahomor, *the* Elamites' king, and Thadal, *the* nations' king

14:2 *inirent bellum contra Bara regem Sodomorum et contra Bersa regem Gomorrae et contra Sennaab regem Adamae et contra Semeber regem Seboim contraque regem Balae ipsa est Segor*

went to war against Bara, *the* Sodomites' king, and against Bersa, Gomorrah's king, and against Sennaab, Adamah's king, and against Semeber, Seboim's king, and against Balah's king (That is, Segor.).

14:3 *omnes hii convenerunt in vallem Silvestrem quae nunc est mare Salis*

All these came together to Silvester valley, which now is *the* Salt Sea.

14:4 *duodecim enim annis servierant Chodorlahomor et tertiodecimo anno recesserunt ab eo*

For twelve years, they had served

Chodorlahomor, and *the* thirteenth year, they turned away from him.

14:5 *igitur anno quartodecimo venit Chodorlahomor et reges qui erant cum eo percusseruntque Rafaim in Astharothcarnaim et Zuzim cum eis et Emim in Savecariathaim*

Therefore, in *the* fourteenth year Chodorlahomor and *the* kings who were with him came and struck *the* Rafaim in Ashtaroth-carnaim and *the* Zuzim with them, and *the* Emim in Saveh-cariathaim,

14:6 *et Chorreos in montibus Seir usque ad campestria Pharan quae est in solitudine*

and *the* Horites on Mount Seir, even to *the* plains of Pharan, which is in *the* desert.

14:7 *reversique sunt et venerunt ad fontem Mesfat ipsa est Cades et percusserunt omnem regionem Amalechitarum et Amorreum qui habitabat in Asasonthamar*

And they turned back and came to Misphat spring, which is Kadesh, and struck all *the* Amalekites' country, and *the* Amorites who lived in Asason-thamar.

Sodom Swept Up
Into the Conflict
14:8 *et egressi sunt rex Sodomorum et rex Gomorrae rexque Adamae et*

rex Seboim necnon et rex Balae quae est Segor et direxerunt contra eos aciem in valle Silvestri

And *the* Sodomites' king and Gomorrah's king and Adamah's king and Seboim's king and even Balah's king, which is Segor, came out, and set *a* line *of battle* against them in Silvester valley –

14:9 *scilicet adversum Chodorlahomor regem Aelamitarum et Thadal regem Gentium et Amrafel regem Sennaar et Arioch regem Ponti quattuor reges adversus quinque*

certainly, against Chodorlahomor, *the* Elamites' king, and Thadal, *the* Nations' king, and Amrafel, Sennaar's king, and Arioch, Pontus's king – four kings against five.

14:10 *vallis autem Silvestris habebat puteos multos bituminis itaque rex Sodomorum et Gomorrae terga verterunt cecideruntque ibi et qui remanserant fugerunt ad montem*

But *there* were many tar pits in Silvester valley, so *the* Sodomites' king and Gomorrah turned back and they fell there. And those who survived fled to *the* mountain.

Lot Taken Captive
14:11 *tulerunt autem omnem substantiam Sodomorum et Gomorrae et universa quae ad cibum*

pertinent et abierunt

But they took all *the* Sodomites' wealth and Gomorrah, and all that concerned food, and they left.

14:12 *necnon et Loth et substantiam eius filium fratris Abram qui habitabat in Sodomis*

And *they* also *took* Lot, Abram's brother's son, who lived in Sodom, and his wealth.

Abram Rescues Lot
14:13 *et ecce unus qui evaserat nuntiavit Abram Hebraeo qui habitabat in convalle Mambre Amorrei fratris Eschol et fratris Aner hii enim pepigerant foedus cum Abram*

And, look, one who escaped told Abram *the* Hebrew, who lived in *the* valley of Mambre *the* Amorite, Eschol's brother, and Aner's brother, for these had made *an* agreement with Abram.

14:14 *quod cum audisset Abram captum videlicet Loth fratrem suum numeravit expeditos vernaculos suos trecentos decem et octo et persecutus est eos usque Dan*

When Abram heard that Lot his brother was captured, as one may see, he numbered his domestic soldiers, three hundred eighteen, and pursued them even to Dan.

14:15 *et divisis sociis inruit super eos nocte percussitque eos et persecutus est usque Hoba quae est ad levam Damasci*

And, dividing his friends, he came in against them by night and struck them. And he pursued *them* even to Hoba, which is to *the* left of Damascus.

14:16 *reduxitque omnem substantiam et Loth fratrem suum cum substantia illius mulieres quoque et populum*

And he brought back all *the* wealth and Lot his brother, with his wealth – women, likewise, and people.

14:17 *egressus est autem rex Sodomorum in occursum eius postquam reversus est a caede Chodorlahomor et regum qui cum eo erant in valle Save quae est vallis Regis*

But *the* Sodomites' king came out to meet him after he returned from slaughtering Chodorlahomor and *the* kings who were with him in Saveh valley, which is *the* King's valley.

Melchisedek Blesses Abram
14:18 *at vero Melchisedech rex Salem proferens panem et vinum erat enim sacerdos Dei altissimi*

And Melchisedech, Salem's king, *came out* also, offering bread and wine, for he was God Most High's priest.

14:19 *benedixit ei et ait benedictus Abram Deo excelso qui creavit caelum et terram*

He blessed him and said, "Abram *be* blessed by God Most High, who created sky and land!

14:20 *et benedictus Deus excelsus quo protegente hostes in manibus tuis sunt et dedit ei decimas ex omnibus*

"And blessed *be* God Most High, by whose protection enemies *are* in your hands!"

And he gave him tenths from all *things.*

Abram Refuses
Sodom's Wealth

14:21 *dixit autem rex Sodomorum ad Abram da mihi animas cetera tolle tibi*

But *the* Sodomites' king said to Abram, "Give me *the* souls, but take *the* rest for yourself."

14:22 *qui respondit ei levo manum meam ad Dominum Deum excelsum possessorem caeli et terrae*

Abram said to him, "I lift up my hand to *the* Lord God Most High, possessor of sky and land,

14:23 *quod a filo subteminis usque ad corrigiam caligae non accipiam ex omnibus quae tua sunt ne dicas ego ditavi Abram*

that I will not accept *anything* – from *a* loom's string even to *a* soldier's shoelace – of all that is yours, so you cannot say, 'I made Abram rich' –

14:24 *exceptis his quae comederunt iuvenes et partibus virorum qui venerunt mecum Aner Eschol et Mambre isti accipient partes suas*

"except what *the* youths have eaten, and *the* portions of *the* men who came with me, Aner, Eschol, and Mambre. These will accept their portions."

The Lord
Appears to Abram

Genesis 15:1 *his itaque transactis factus est sermo Domini ad Abram per visionem dicens noli timere Abram ego protector tuus sum et merces tua magna nimis*

This also happening so, *the* Lord's word came to Abram by *a* vision, saying, "Don't fear, Abram. I am your protector, and your recompense *is* overwhelmingly great."

15:2 *dixitque Abram Domine Deus quid dabis mihi ego vadam absque liberis et filius procuratoris domus meae iste Damascus Eliezer*

And Abram said, "Lord God, what will You give me? I will go without children, and my house manager's son *is* this Eliezer of Damascus."

15:3 *addiditque Abram mihi autem non dedisti semen et ecce vernaculus meus heres meus erit*

And Abram added, "But you have not given me seed. And, look, my native-born servant will be my heir."

15:4 *statimque sermo Domini factus est ad eum dicens non erit hic heres tuus sed qui egredietur de utero tuo ipsum habebis heredem*

And immediately *the* Lord's word came to him, saying, "This *one* will not be your heir, but one who comes out of your womb – you will have him as heir."

15:5 *eduxitque eum foras et ait illi suspice caelum et numera stellas si potes et dixit ei sic erit semen tuum*

And He led him outside and said to him, "Look up at *the* sky and count *the* stars, if you can."

And He said to him, "So your seed will be."

15:6 *credidit Domino et reputatum est ei ad iustitiam*

He believed *the* Lord, and *it* was reputed to him as fairness.

The Lord Recounts
His Story with Abram

15:7 *dixitque ad eum ego Dominus qui eduxi te de Ur Chaldeorum ut darem tibi terram istam et possideres eam*

And He said to him, "I am *the* Lord, who led you from *the* Chaldeans' Ur, so I could give you this land, and you might possess it."

15:8 *at ille ait Domine Deus unde scire possum quod possessurus sim eam*

And he said, "Lord God, from what can I know that I may possess it?"

15:9 *respondens Dominus sume*

inquit mihi vaccam triennem et capram trimam et arietem annorum trium turturem quoque et columbam

Responding, *the* Lord said, "Offer Me *a* three-year-old cow, and *a* three-year-old goat, and *a* ram of three years, *a* dove likewise and *a* pigeon.

15:10 *qui tollens universa haec divisit per medium et utrasque partes contra se altrinsecus posuit aves autem non divisit*

Abram, taking all these, cut each one in half and put each half opposite *the* other. But he did not cut *the* birds in half.

15:11 *descenderuntque volucres super cadavera et abigebat eas Abram*

And birds came down over *the* bodies, and Abram drove them away.

15:12 *cumque sol occumberet sopor inruit super Abram et horror magnus et tenebrosus invasit eum*

And when *the* sun was setting, sleep rushed in over Abram, and great horror and gloom invaded him.

Future Slavery Predicted
15:13 *dictumque est ad eum scito praenoscens quod peregrinum futurum sit semen tuum in terra non sua et subicient eos servituti et*

adfligent quadringentis annis

And it was told him, "Know in advance that your seed may be *a* stranger in *a* land not his. And they will subject them to slavery, and afflict *them* four hundred years.

15:14 *verumtamen gentem cui servituri sunt ego iudicabo et post haec egredientur cum magna substantia*

"Nevertheless, I will judge *the* nation whom they will serve. And after this, they will go out with great wealth.

Abram's End Predicted
15:15 *tu autem ibis ad patres tuos in pace sepultus in senectute bona*

"But you will go to your fathers in peace, buried in *a* good old age.

Return from Slavery Predicted
15:16 *generatione autem quarta revertentur huc necdum enim conpletae sunt iniquitates Amorreorum usque ad praesens tempus*

"But they will come back here in *the* fourth generation, for *the* Amorites' treacheries aren't yet complete, even to *the* present time."

The Lord Makes a Pact with Abram
15:17 *cum ergo occubuisset sol facta est caligo tenebrosa et apparuit*

clibanus fumans et lampas ignis transiens inter divisiones illas

When therefore, *the* sun had set, *a* profound darkness came. And *a* smoking oven and burning torch appeared, passing between *the* severed parts.

15:18 *in die illo pepigit Dominus cum Abram foedus dicens semini tuo dabo terram hanc a fluvio Aegypti usque ad fluvium magnum flumen Eufraten*

On that day, *the* Lord arranged *a* pact with Abram, saying, "I will give this land to your seed, from Egypt's river even to *the* great river, *the* Euphrates river –

15:19 *Cineos et Cenezeos et Cedmoneos*

"Kenites and Kenezites and Cadmonites,

15:20 *et Hettheos et Ferezeos Rafaim quoque*

"and Hittites and Ferezites, Rafaim as well,

15:21 *et Amorreos et Chananeos et Gergeseos et Iebuseos*

"and Amorites and Canaanites and Gergeshites and Jebusites."

Sarai Gives Hagar to Abram as Wife

Genesis 16:1 *igitur Sarai uxor Abram non genuerat liberos sed habens ancillam aegyptiam nomine Agar*

Therefore, Sarai, Abram's wife, had not birthed children, but, having *a* female Egyptian slave named Hagar,

16:2 *dixit marito suo ecce conclusit me Dominus ne parerem ingredere ad ancillam meam si forte saltem ex illa suscipiam filios cumque ille adquiesceret deprecanti*

she said to her husband, "Look, *the* Lord has closed me up, so I cannot give birth. Go into my slave, if perhaps I at least can receive children from her."

And when he had agreed to *her* request,

16:3 *tulit Agar Aegyptiam ancillam suam post annos decem quam habitare coeperant in terra Chanaan et dedit eam viro suo uxorem*

she took Hagar *the* Egyptian, her slave woman, ten years after they had begun to live in Canaan's land. And she gave her to her husband *as* wife.

16:4 *qui ingressus est ad eam at illa concepisse se videns despexit dominam suam*

Abram went in to her, and she, seeing she had conceived, despised her owner.

16:5 *dixitque Sarai ad Abram inique agis contra me ego dedi ancillam meam in sinum tuum quae videns quod conceperit despectui me habet iudicet Dominus inter me et te*

And Sarai said to Abram, "You carry on treachery against me. I gave my slave woman into your embrace, who, seeing that she has conceived, has me in contempt. *The* Lord will judge between me and you."

16:6 *cui respondens Abram ecce ait ancilla tua in manu tua est utere ea ut libet adfligente igitur eam Sarai fugam iniit*

Responding to her, Abram said, "Look, your slave woman is in your hand. Use her as it pleases!"

So *Hagar*, abused by Sarai, started to run away.

God's Angel
Speaks to Hagar
16:7 *cumque invenisset illam angelus Domini iuxta fontem aquae in solitudine qui est in via Sur*

And when *the* Lord's angel had found her beside *a* spring of water in *the* wasteland, which is on *the* road to Sur,

16:8 *dixit ad eam Agar ancilla Sarai unde venis et quo vadis quae respondit a facie Sarai dominae meae ego fugio*

He said to her, "Hagar, Sarai's slave woman, where are you coming from and where are you going?"

She responded, "I'm running away from Sarai, my owner's, face."

16:9 *dixitque ei angelus Domini revertere ad dominam tuam et humiliare sub manibus ipsius*

And *the* Lord's angel said to her, "Go back to your owner and be humble under her hands!"

16:10 *et rursum multiplicans inquit multiplicabo semen tuum et non numerabitur prae multitudine*

And He spoke again, "Multiplying, I will multiply your seed, and it will not be counted for multitude."

16:11 *ac deinceps ecce ait concepisti et paries filium vocabisque nomen eius Ismahel eo quod audierit Dominus adflictionem tuam*

And then He said, "Look, you have conceived and will birth *a* son. And you will call his name Ishmael, because *the* Lord has heard your affliction.

16:12 *hic erit ferus homo manus eius contra omnes et manus omnium contra eum et e regione universorum fratrum suorum figet tabernacula*

"He will be *an* untamed man, his hand against all, and *the* hands of all against him. And he will pitch his tent away from *the* region of all his brothers."

16:13 *vocavit autem nomen Domini qui loquebatur ad eam Tu Deus qui vidisti me dixit enim profecto hic vidi posteriora videntis me*

But she called *the* Lord's name who spoke to her, "You *are* God who has seen me," for she said, "Surely I have seen here *the* back of One who sees me."

16:14 *propterea appellavit puteum illum puteum Viventis et videntis me ipse est inter Cades et Barad*

Because of this, she called that well, "Well of *One* living and watching me."

It is between Kadesh and Barad.

Ishmael Is Born
16:15 *peperitque Abrae filium qui vocavit nomen eius Ismahel*

And she birthed Abram *a* son, who called his name Ishmael.

16:16 *octoginta et sex annorum erat quando peperit ei Agar Ismahelem*

Abram was eighty-six years old when Hagar birthed Ishmael to him.

God Renames
Abram as Abraham

Genesis 17:1 *postquam vero nonaginta et novem annorum esse coeperat apparuit ei Dominus dixitque ad eum ego Deus omnipotens ambula coram me et esto perfectus*

Truly, after he began to be ninety-nine years old, *the* Lord appeared to him and said to him, "I am God omnipotent. Walk before me and be perfect!"

17:2 *ponamque foedus meum inter me et te et multiplicabo te vehementer nimis*

"And I will place My covenant between Me and you, and I will multiply you overwhelmingly much."

17:3 *cecidit Abram pronus in faciem*

Abram fell prone on *his* face.

17:4 *dixitque ei Deus ego sum et pactum meum tecum erisque pater multarum gentium*

And He said to him, "I am God, and My pact *is* with you. And you will be father of many nations."

17:5 *nec ultra vocabitur nomen tuum Abram sed appellaberis Abraham quia patrem multarum gentium constitui te*

"No longer will your name be called Abram. But you will be called Abraham, because I have appointed you father of many nations.

17:6 *faciamque te crescere vehementissime et ponam in gentibus regesque ex te egredientur*

"And I will make you increase overwhelmingly so, and will place you among nations. And kings will come out from you.

17:7 *et statuam pactum meum inter me et te et inter semen tuum post te in generationibus suis foedere sempiterno ut sim Deus tuus et seminis tui post te*

"And I will set up My pact between Me and you, and between your seed after you in their generations, an everlasting agreement, that I may be your God, and to your seed after you.

17:8 *daboque tibi et semini tuo terram peregrinationis tuae omnem terram Chanaan in possessionem aeternam eroque Deus eorum*

"And I will give you and your seed *the* land of your wanderings – all Canaan's land – in *an* eternal possession. And I will be their God.

17:9 *dixit iterum Deus ad Abraham et tu ergo custodies pactum meum et semen tuum post te in generationibus* *suis*

And God again said to Abraham, "And you, therefore, will keep My pact, and your seed after you in their generations.

The Covenant
of Circumcision

17:10 *hoc est pactum quod observabitis inter me et vos et semen tuum post te circumcidetur ex vobis omne masculinum*

"This is *the* pact which you will observe between Me and you and your seed after you. Every male among you will be circumcised.

17:11 *et circumcidetis carnem praeputii vestri ut sit in signum foederis inter me et vos*

"And you will circumcise your foreskin's flesh, so it may be *a* sign of the agreement between Me and you.

17:12 *infans octo dierum circumcidetur in vobis omne masculinum in generationibus vestris tam vernaculus quam empticius circumcidetur et quicumque non fuerit de stirpe vestra*

An eight-day-old infant will be circumcised among you. Every male in your generations, native-born and purchased alike will be circumcised, and whoever is not of your race.

17:13 *eritque pactum meum in carne vestra in foedus aeternum*

"And My pact will be in your flesh, as *an* eternal covenant.

17:14 *masculus cuius praeputii caro circumcisa non fuerit delebitur anima illa de populo suo quia pactum meum irritum fecit*

"*A* male whose foreskin's flesh will not be circumcised, his soul will be removed from his people, because he has made My pact void."

God Renames
Sarai as Sarah

17:15 *dixit quoque Deus ad Abraham Sarai uxorem tuam non vocabis Sarai sed Sarram*

God also said to Abraham, "You will not call Sarai your wife Sarai, but Sarah.

God Promises Abraham
a Son by Sarah

17:16 *et benedicam ei et ex illa dabo tibi filium cui benedicturus sum eritque in nationes et reges populorum orientur ex eo*

"And I will bless her and will give you *a* son from her, whom I will bless. And he will be among nations, and peoples' kings will be born from him."

17:17 *cecidit Abraham in faciem et*

risit dicens in corde suo putasne centenario nascetur filius et Sarra nonagenaria pariet

Abraham fell on his face and laughed, saying in his heart, 'Do you think *a* son will be born to *a* hundred-year-old man, and ninety-year-old Sarah give birth?'

17:18   *dixitque ad Deum utinam Ismahel vivat coram te*

And he said to *the* Lord, "If only Ishmael may live before you!"

17:19   *et ait Deus ad Abraham Sarra uxor tua pariet tibi filium vocabisque nomen eius Isaac et constituam pactum meum illi in foedus sempiternum et semini eius post eum*

And God said to Abraham, "Sarah, your wife, will birth *a* son to you. And you will call his name Isaac, and I will set up My pact with him as *an* everlasting covenant, and with his seed after him.

17:20   *super Ismahel quoque exaudivi te ecce benedicam ei et augebo et multiplicabo eum valde duodecim duces generabit et faciam illum in gentem magnam*

"I have heard you also over Ishmael. Look, I will bless him and increase and multiply him greatly. He will father twelve leaders, and I will make him into *a* great nation.

17:21   *pactum vero meum statuam ad Isaac quem pariet tibi Sarra tempore isto in anno altero*

"But I will set up My pact with Isaac, whom Sarah will birth to you at this time next year."

17:22   *cumque finitus esset sermo loquentis cum eo ascendit Deus ab Abraham*

And when He had finished speaking *the* word with him, God went up from Abraham.

17:23   *tulit autem Abraham Ismahelem filium suum et omnes vernaculos domus suae universosque quos emerat cunctos mares ex omnibus viris domus suae et circumcidit carnem praeputii eorum statim in ipsa die sicut praeceperat ei Deus*

But Abraham took Ishmael his son and all his house's native-born men and all those he had bought, all *the* males from all his house's men, and circumcised their foreskins' flesh at once, on that same day, as God had commanded him.

17:24   *nonaginta novem erat annorum quando circumcidit carnem praeputii sui*

He was ninety-nine years old when his foreskin's flesh was circumcised.

17:25 *et Ismahel filius eius tredecim annos impleverat tempore circumcisionis suae*

And his son Ishmael had completed thirteen years at *the* time of his circumcision.

17:26 *eadem die circumcisus est Abraham et Ismahel filius eius*

That same day, Abraham was circumcised, and his son Ishmael,

17:27 *et omnes viri domus illius tam vernaculi quam empticii et alienigenae pariter circumcisi sunt*

and all his house's men. Native-born and bought and foreign-born alike were circumcised.

Three Men Come to Abraham

Genesis 18:1 *apparuit autem ei Dominus in convalle Mambre sedenti in ostio tabernaculi sui in ipso fervore diei*

But *the* Lord appeared to him in Mambre's valley, while he was sitting in his tent's doorway, in *the* day's own heat.

18:2 *cumque elevasset oculos apparuerunt ei tres viri stantes propter eum quos cum vidisset cucurrit in occursum eorum de ostio tabernaculi et adoravit in terra*

And when he had lifted up his eyes, three men appeared to him, standing near him. He ran from *the* tent's doorway to meet Them, and worshiped on *the* ground.

18:3 *et dixit Domine si inveni gratiam in oculis tuis ne transeas servum tuum*

And he said, "Lord, if I have found grace in Your eyes, do not pass Your slave by.

18:4 *sed adferam pauxillum aquae et lavate pedes vestros et requiescite sub arbore*

"But I will bring *a* little water, and You can wash Your feet and rest under *the* tree.

18:5 *ponam buccellam panis et*

confortate cor vestrum postea transibitis idcirco enim declinastis ad servum vestrum qui dixerunt fac ut locutus es

"I will put out *a* morsel of bread, and You can strengthen your heart. Afterwards You will go on. For therefore You have turned aside to Your slave."

They said, "Do as you have spoken."

18:6 *festinavit Abraham in tabernaculum ad Sarram dixitque ei adcelera tria sata similae commisce et fac subcinericios panes*

Abraham hurried into *the* tent to Sarah and said to her, "Hurry! Mix together three measures of finest flour and make loaves beneath *the* ashes!"

18:7 *ipse vero ad armentum cucurrit et tulit inde vitulum tenerrimum et optimum deditque puero qui festinavit et coxit illum*

He indeed ran to *the* herd and took from it *the* most tender and choice calf. And he gave it to *the* boy, who hurried and cooked it.

18:8 *tulit quoque butyrum et lac et vitulum quem coxerat et posuit coram eis ipse vero stabat iuxta eos sub arbore*

He took likewise butter and milk and

the calf which he had cooked, and he placed *all* before Them. He, indeed, stood beside Them under *the* tree.

18:9 *cumque comedissent dixerunt ad eum ubi est Sarra uxor tua ille respondit ecce in tabernaculo est*

And when They had eaten, They said to him, "Where is Sarah your wife?"

He responded, "Look, she is in *the* tent."

18:10 *cui dixit revertens veniam ad te tempore isto vita comite et habebit filium Sarra uxor tua quo audito Sarra risit post ostium tabernaculi*

He said to him, "I will come to you again at this time, life arranged, and Sarah your wife will have *a* son."

Hearing which, Sarah laughed behind *the* tent's doorway.

18:11 *erant autem ambo senes provectaeque aetatis et desierant Sarrae fieri muliebria*

But both were old and advanced in age, and Sarah's womanhood had ceased to be.

18:12 *quae risit occulte dicens postquam consenui et dominus meus vetulus est voluptati operam dabo*

She laughed secretly, saying, "After I have grown old and my lord is *an* old man will I give *the* desired work?"

18:13 *dixit autem Dominus ad Abraham quare risit Sarra dicens num vere paritura sum anus*

But *the* Lord said to Abraham, "Why did Sarah laugh, saying, 'Will I really give birth, since I am *an* old woman?'

18:14 *numquid Deo est quicquam difficile iuxta condictum revertar ad te hoc eodem tempore vita comite et habebit Sarra filium*

"Is anything too hard for God? I will come back to you according to *the* word at this same time, life arranged, and Sarah will have *a* son."

18:15 *negavit Sarra dicens non risi timore perterrita Dominus autem non est inquit ita sed risisti*

Sarah denied it, terrified by fear, saying, "I did not laugh."

But *the* Lord said, "*It* is not so, but you did laugh."

The Lord Turns
Toward Sodom

18:16 *cum ergo surrexissent inde viri direxerunt oculos suos contra Sodomam et Abraham simul gradiebatur deducens eos*

When, therefore, They had risen from there, *the* Men directed Their eyes toward Sodom. And Abraham went out at once, leading Them.

18:17 *dixitque Dominus num celare potero Abraham quae gesturus sum*

And *the* Lord said, "Can I hide from Abraham what I am going to do,

18:18 *cum futurus sit in gentem magnam ac robustissimam et benedicendae sint in illo omnes nationes terrae*

"when in *the* future he may be *a* great and most mighty nation, and all *the* land's nations may be blessed in him?

18:19 *scio enim quod praecepturus sit filiis suis et domui suae post se ut custodiant viam Domini et faciant iustitiam et iudicium ut adducat Dominus propter Abraham omnia quae locutus est ad eum*

"For I know that he will command his children and his house after him that they keep *the* Lord's way and work fairness and judgment, so *the* Lord may bring for Abraham's sake according to all that He has spoken to him."

18:20 *dixit itaque Dominus clamor Sodomorum et Gomorrae multiplicatus est et peccatum earum adgravatum est nimis*

And *the* Lord spoke this way: "Sodom and Gomorrah's clamor has multiplied, and their sin is overwhelmingly oppressive.

18:21 *descendam et videbo utrum clamorem qui venit ad me opere conpleverint an non est ita ut sciam*

"I will go down and see whether this outcry which has come to Me is so or not, so I can know if they complete *it* by deed."

18:22 *converteruntque se inde et abierunt Sodomam Abraham vero adhuc stabat coram Domino*

And They turned from there and went out toward Sodom. But Abraham still stood before *the* Lord.

18:23 *et adpropinquans ait numquid perdes iustum cum impio*

And, coming close, he said, "You won't destroy *the* fair with *the* lawless, will You?"

18:24 *si fuerint quinquaginta iusti in civitate peribunt simul et non parces loco illi propter quinquaginta iustos si fuerint in eo*

"If there are fifty fair ones in *the* city, will they perish together? And won't You spare that place on account of fifty fair ones, if they are in it?

18:25 *absit a te ut rem hanc facias et occidas iustum cum impio fiatque iustus sicut impius non est hoc tuum qui iudicas omnem terram*

nequaquam facies iudicium

"May it be far from You that You do this thing, and kill *the* fair with *the* lawless, and let *the* fair be like *the* lawless! This is not *fair*! You who judge all *the* land, by no means will you work judgment?"

18:26 *dixitque Dominus ad eum si invenero Sodomis quinquaginta iustos in medio civitatis dimittam omni loco propter eos*

And *the* Lord said to him, "If I find in Sodom fifty fair ones inside *the* city, I will spare *the* whole place because of them."

18:27 *respondens Abraham ait quia semel coepi loquar ad Dominum meum cum sim pulvis et cinis*

Abraham, responding, said, "Because I have begun once, I will speak to my Lord, when I am dust and ashes.

18:28 *quid si minus quinquaginta iustis quinque fuerint delebis propter quinque universam urbem et ait non delebo si invenero ibi quadraginta quinque*

"What if there are five less than fifty fair ones? Will you destroy all *the* city because of five?"

And He said, "I will not destroy if I find forty-five there."

18:29 *rursumque locutus est ad eum sin autem quadraginta inventi fuerint quid facies ait non percutiam propter quadraginta*

And again he said to Him, "But if forty are found, what will You do?"

And He said, "I will not strike on account of forty."

18:30 *ne quaeso inquit indigneris Domine si loquar quid si inventi fuerint ibi triginta respondit non faciam si invenero ibi triginta*

He said, "Do not be indignant, Lord, I pray, if I speak. What if thirty are found there?"

He responded, "I will not act if I find thirty there."

18:31 *quia semel ait coepi loquar ad Dominum meum quid si inventi fuerint ibi viginti dixit non interficiam propter viginti*

He said, "Because I have once begun, I will speak to my Lord. What if twenty are found there?"

He said, "I will not kill on account of twenty."

18:32 *obsecro inquit ne irascaris Domine si loquar adhuc semel quid si inventi fuerint ibi decem dixit non delebo propter decem*

"I pray," he said, "do not get mad, Lord, if I speak one more time. What if ten are found there?"

He said, "I will not destroy on account of ten."

18:33 *abiit Dominus postquam cessavit loqui ad Abraham et ille reversus est in locum suum*

The Lord went out after He finished speaking to Abraham, and *Abraham* went back to his place.

Two Angels Come to Sodom
Genesis 19:1 *veneruntque duo angeli Sodomam vespere sedente Loth in foribus civitatis qui cum vidisset surrexit et ivit obviam eis adoravitque pronus in terra*

And two angels came to Sodom, Lot sitting by evening in *the* city's gate. When he saw them, he got up and went to meet them. And he worshiped, face down on *the* ground.

19:2 *et dixit obsecro domini declinate in domum pueri vestri et manete ibi lavate pedes vestros et mane proficiscimini in viam vestram qui dixerunt minime sed in platea manebimus*

And he said, "I pray, my lords, turn aside into your servant's house and stay there. Wash your feet and set out on your way early."

They said, "No, but we will stay in *the* square."

19:3 *conpulit illos oppido ut deverterent ad eum ingressisque domum illius fecit convivium coxit azyma et comederunt*

He compelled them altogether that they turn aside to him. And going into his house, he made *a* banquet. He cooked unleavened bread and they ate.

19:4 *prius autem quam irent cubitum viri civitatis vallaverunt domum a puero usque ad senem omnis populus simul*

But before they went to bed, *the* city's men surrounded *the* house – from boy even to old man, all *the* people at once.

19:5 *vocaveruntque Loth et dixerunt ei ubi sunt viri qui introierunt ad te nocte educ illos huc ut cognoscamus eos*

And they called Lot and said to him, "Where are *the* men who went into you at night? Bring them here so we can know them!"

19:6 *egressus ad eos Loth post tergum adcludens ostium ait*

Lot, going out to them *and* closing *the* door behind *him*, said,

19:7 *nolite quaeso fratres mei nolite malum hoc facere*

"Do not, I pray, my brothers – do not do this harm!

19:8 *habeo duas filias quae necdum cognoverunt virum educam eas ad vos et abutimini eis sicut placuerit vobis dummodo viris istis nihil faciatis mali quia ingressi sunt sub umbraculum tegminis mei*

"I have two daughters who have not yet known *a* man. I will bring them to you and you can abuse them, if it pleases you, provided that you do no harm to these men who have come under *the* shadow of my roof!"

19:9 *at illi dixerunt recede illuc et rursus ingressus es inquiunt ut advena numquid ut iudices te ergo ipsum magis quam hos adfligemus vimque faciebant Loth vehementissime iam prope erat ut refringeret fores*

And they said, "Go back there!"

And again they said, "You came in as *a* newcomer, so you can judge? Therefore, we will afflict you more than these men!"

And they pushed forcefully against Lot, and *it* was already close, so they could break down the doors.

19:10 *et ecce miserunt manum viri et introduxerunt ad se Loth cluseruntque ostium*

And, look, *the* men put out *their* hands and brought Lot to themselves. And they closed *the* door.

19:11 *et eos qui erant foris percusserunt caecitate a minimo usque ad maximum ita ut ostium invenire non possent*

And they struck those who were outside with blindness, from the least to *the* greatest, so they could not find *the* door.

The Angels Order
Lot to Flee

19:12 *dixerunt autem ad Loth habes hic tuorum quempiam generum aut filios aut filias omnes qui tui sunt educ de urbe hac*

But they said to Lot, "Do you have any family here – sons or daughters? Lead all who are yours out of this city,

19:13 *delebimus enim locum istum eo quod increverit clamor eorum coram Domino qui misit nos ut perdamus illos*

"for we will destroy this place, because their outcry has swollen up before *the* Lord, who sent us so we could destroy them!"

19:14 *egressus itaque Loth locutus est ad generos suos qui accepturi erant filias eius et dixit surgite egredimini de loco isto quia delebit Dominus civitatem hanc et visus est eis quasi ludens loqui*

So Lot, going out, spoke to his sons-in-law, who were to receive his daughters, and said to them, "Get up! Get out of this place, because *the* Lord will destroy this city!"

And to them *it* seemed like *he* was speaking nonsense.

19:15 *cumque esset mane cogebant eum angeli dicentes surge et tolle uxorem tuam et duas filias quas habes ne et tu pariter pereas in scelere civitatis*

And when it was morning, *the* angels urged him, saying, "Get up and take your wife and two daughters whom you have, unless you also perish among this city's crime!

19:16 *dissimulante illo adprehenderunt manum eius et manum uxoris ac duarum filiarum eius eo quod parceret Dominus illi*

He wavering, they took his hand and his wife's and his two daughters', because *the* Lord had spared them.

19:17 *et eduxerunt eum posueruntque extra civitatem ibi locutus est ad eum salva animam tuam noli respicere post tergum nec stes in omni circa regione sed in monte salvum te fac ne et tu simul pereas*

And they led him out and put him outside *the* city there. He said to him, "Save your soul! Don't look behind or stand still in all *the* region around! But make yourself secure in *the* mountain, so you don't perish at once!

19:18 *dixitque Loth ad eos quaeso Domine mi*

And Lot said to them, "My Lord, I pray –

19:19 *quia invenit servus tuus gratiam coram te et magnificasti misericordiam tuam quam fecisti mecum ut salvares animam meam nec possum in monte salvari ne forte adprehendat me malum et moriar*

"because your slave found grace before You and you have magnified Your mercy which You made with me so You could save my soul – I can't be saved on *the* mountain, unless perhaps harm overtake me and I die.

19:20 *est civitas haec iuxta ad quam possum fugere parva et salvabor in ea numquid non modica est et vivet anima mea*

"*There* is this little city close by I can flee to, and I can be saved in it. It's small, isn't it? And my soul will live."

19:21 *dixitque ad eum ecce etiam in hoc suscepi preces tuas ut non subvertam urbem pro qua locutus es*

And He said to him, "Look, even in this I have received your pleas, so I won't overthrow *the* city for which you have spoken.

19:22 *festina et salvare ibi quia non potero facere quicquam donec ingrediaris illuc idcirco vocatum est* *nomen urbis illius Segor*

"Hurry and be saved there, because I can't do anything until you go in there!"

Therefore, that city's name is called Segor.

The Lord Destroys
Sodom and Gomorrah

19:23 *sol egressus est super terram et Loth ingressus est in Segor*

The sun rose over *the* land, and Lot went into Segor.

19:24 *igitur Dominus pluit super Sodomam et Gomorram sulphur et ignem a Domino de caelo*

Therefore *the* Lord rained sulphur and fire from *the* sky over Sodom and Gomorrah, from *the* Lord.

19:25 *et subvertit civitates has et omnem circa regionem universos habitatores urbium et cuncta terrae virentia*

And He overthrew those cities and all *the* surrounding region, all *the* cities' inhabitants and all *the* land's green plants.

19:26 *respiciensque uxor eius post se versa est in statuam salis*

And *Lot's* wife, looking behind her, was turned into *a* salt statue.

Abraham Sees
Sodom's Destruction

19:27 *Abraham autem consurgens mane ubi steterat prius cum Domino*

But Abraham, getting up early where he stood before with *the* Lord,

19:28 *intuitus est Sodomam et Gomorram et universam terram regionis illius viditque ascendentem favillam de terra quasi fornacis fumum*

looked at Sodom and Gomorrah and all that region's land. And he saw glowing ashes rising up from *the* land, like *a* furnace's smoke.

19:29 *cum enim subverteret Deus civitates regionis illius recordatus est Abrahae et liberavit Loth de subversione urbium in quibus habitaverat*

For when God destroyed that region's cities, He remembered Abraham and freed Lot from *the* overthrow of *the* city in which he lived.

Lot Fathers
His Own Grandchildren

19:30 *ascenditque Loth de Segor et mansit in monte duae quoque filiae eius cum eo timuerat enim manere in Segor et mansit in spelunca ipse et duae filiae eius*

And Lot went up from Segor and

stayed on *the* mountain, his two daughters likewise with him, for he was afraid to stay in Segor. And he stayed in *a* cave, he and his two daughters.

19:31 *dixitque maior ad minorem pater noster senex est et nullus virorum remansit in terra qui possit ingredi ad nos iuxta morem universae terrae*

And *the* older said to *the* younger, "Our father is old and none of *the* men are still in *the* land who could come in to us, according to *the* whole land's practice.

19:32 *veni inebriemus eum vino dormiamusque cum eo ut servare possimus ex patre nostro semen*

"Come, let's get him drunk with wine and sleep with him, so we can preserve seed from our father!"

19:33 *dederunt itaque patri suo bibere vinum nocte illa et ingressa est maior dormivitque cum patre at ille non sensit nec quando accubuit filia nec quando surrexit*

So they gave their father wine to drink that night. And *the* older *one* went in and slept with *her* father, and he wasn't aware either when *the* daughter lay down or when she got up.

19:34 *altera quoque die dixit maior*

ad minorem ecce dormivi heri cum patre meo demus ei bibere vinum etiam hac nocte et dormies cum eo ut salvemus semen de patre nostro

Likewise, *the* next day *the* older said to *the* younger, "Look, last night I slept with my father. Let's give him wine to drink tonight too, and you sleep with him, so we can save seed from our father."

19:35 *dederunt et illa nocte patri vinum ingressaque minor filia dormivit cum eo et nec tunc quidem sensit quando concubuerit vel quando illa surrexerit*

So they gave their father wine that night, and *the* younger daughter, going in, slept with him. And then, he was aware neither when she lay down nor when she got up.

19:36 *conceperunt ergo duae filiae Loth de patre suo*

Therefore, Lot's two daughters got pregnant from their father.

19:37 *peperitque maior filium et vocavit nomen eius Moab ipse est pater Moabitarum usque in praesentem diem*

And *the* older birthed *a* son and called his name Moab. He is *the* Moabites' father, even to *the* present day.

19:38 *minor quoque peperit filium*

et vocavit nomen eius Ammon id est filius populi mei ipse est pater Ammanitarum usque hodie

The younger likewise birthed *a* son, and called his name Ammon, that is, "my people's son." He is *the* Ammonites' father, even to today.

Abraham, Sarah, and Abimelech

Genesis 20:1 *profectus inde Abraham in terram australem habitavit inter Cades et Sur et peregrinatus est in Geraris*

Going on from there, Abraham lived in *the* south land, between Kadesh and Sur, and wandered in Gerara.

20:2 *dixitque de Sarra uxore sua soror mea est misit ergo Abimelech rex Gerarae et tulit eam*

And he said about Sarah his wife, "She is my sister."

Therefore Abimelech, Gerara's king, sent and took her.

20:3 *venit autem Deus ad Abimelech per somnium noctis et ait ei en morieris propter mulierem quam tulisti habet enim virum*

But God came to Abimelech through *a* dream at night and said to him, "Look, you will die because of *the* woman whom you took, for she has *a* husband."

20:4 *Abimelech vero non tetigerat eam et ait Domine num gentem ignorantem et iustam interficies*

But Abimelech had not touched her, and he said, "Lord, will you kill *an* unknowing and fair nation?

20:5 *nonne ipse dixit mihi soror mea est et ipsa ait frater meus est in simplicitate cordis mei et munditia manuum mearum feci hoc*

"Didn't he say to me, 'She is my sister?' And she said, 'He is my brother'? I did this in *the* simplicity of my heart and *the* cleanness of my hands."

20:6 *dixitque ad eum Deus et ego scio quod simplici corde feceris et ideo custodivi te ne peccares in me et non dimisi ut tangeres eam*

And God said to him also, "I know that you did it in simplicity of heart and for this reason I kept you, so you did not sin against Me. And I did not allow that you touch her.

20:7 *nunc igitur redde uxorem viro suo quia propheta est et orabit pro te et vives si autem nolueris reddere scito quod morte morieris tu et omnia quae tua sunt*

"Now, then, return *the* wife to her husband, because he is *a* prophet. And he will pray for you and you will live. But if you don't return her, know that you will die *by* death – you and all who are yours!"

20:8 *statimque de nocte consurgens Abimelech vocavit omnes servos suos et locutus est universa verba haec in auribus eorum timueruntque omnes viri valde*

And getting up immediately by night, Abimelech called all his slaves and spoke all those words in their ears. And all *the* men feared greatly.

20:9 *vocavit autem Abimelech etiam Abraham et dixit ei quid fecisti nobis quid peccavimus in te quia induxisti super me et super regnum meum peccatum grande quae non debuisti facere fecisti nobis*

But Abimelech called Abraham also, and said to him, "What have you done to us? What did we sin against you, because you led in over me and over my kingdom *a* great sin? You did to us what you should not have done."

20:10 *rursusque expostulans ait quid vidisti ut hoc faceres*

Again crying out, he said, "What did you see that you did this?"

20:11 *respondit Abraham cogitavi mecum dicens forsitan non est timor Dei in loco isto et interficient me propter uxorem meam*

Abraham answered, "I considered to myself, saying, 'Perhaps there is no fear of God in this place, and they will kill me because of my wife.'

20:12 *alias autem et vere soror mea est filia patris mei et non filia matris meae et duxi eam uxorem*

"But otherwise and also, she is my sister – my father's daughter and not my mother's daughter. And I took her *as* wife.

20:13 *postquam autem eduxit me Deus de domo patris mei dixi ad eam hanc misericordiam facies mecum in omni loco ad quem ingrediemur dices quod frater tuus sim*

"But after God led me out of my father's house, I said to her, "Will you do this mercy to me? In every place to which we go in, will you say that I am your brother?""

20:14 *tulit igitur Abimelech oves et boves et servos et ancillas et dedit Abraham reddiditque illi Sarram uxorem suam*

Therefore Abimelech took sheep and oxen and slaves and slave women and gave them to Abraham. And he returned Sarah his wife to him.

20:15 *et ait terra coram vobis est ubicumque tibi placuerit habita*

And he said, "The land is before you. Live wherever it pleases you."

20:16 *Sarrae autem dixit ecce mille argenteos dedi fratri tuo hoc erit tibi in velamen oculorum ad omnes qui tecum sunt et quocumque perrexeris mementoque te deprehensam*

But he said to Sarah, "Look, I gave your brother *a* thousand silver coins. This will be as *a* covering of *the* eyes to you, to all who are with you, and to whomever you will go. And remember you *were* taken."

20:17 *orante autem Abraham sanavit Deus Abimelech et uxorem ancillasque eius et pepererunt*

But Abraham praying, God healed Abimelech and his wife and female slaves, and they birthed *children*.

20:18 *concluserat enim Deus omnem vulvam domus Abimelech propter Sarram uxorem Abraham*

For God had closed every vulva in Abimelech's house, because of Sarah, Abraham's wife.

Sarah Births Isaac

Genesis 21:1 *visitavit autem Dominus Sarram sicut promiserat et implevit quae locutus est*

But *the* Lord visited Sarah, as He had promised, and fulfilled what He had spoken.

21:2 *concepitque et peperit filium in senectute sua tempore quo praedixerat ei Deus*

And she conceived and birthed *a* son in her old age, *the* time which God had predicted to her.

21:3 *vocavitque Abraham nomen filii sui quem genuit ei Sarra Isaac*

And Abraham called his son's name Isaac, whom Sarah birthed to him.

21:4 *et circumcidit eum octavo die sicut praeceperat ei Deus*

And he circumcised him *the* eighth day, as God had commanded him.

21:5 *cum centum esset annorum hac quippe aetate patris natus est Isaac*

When he was *a* hundred years old – this, of course, *the* father's age – Isaac was born.

21:6 *dixitque Sarra risum fecit mihi Deus quicumque audierit conridebit mihi*

And Sarah said, "God has made laughter for me. And whoever may hear will laugh with me."

21:7 *rursumque ait quis auditurum crederet Abraham quod Sarra lactaret filium quem peperit ei iam seni*

And again she said, "Who would believe Abraham would hear that Sarah would nurse *a* son whom she birthed to him, already old?"

Sarah and Hagar
At Odds Again

21:8 *crevit igitur puer et ablactatus est fecitque Abraham grande convivium in die ablactationis eius*

Therefore, *the* boy grew and was weaned. And Abraham made *a* great feast on *the* day of his weaning.

21:9 *cumque vidisset Sarra filium Agar Aegyptiae ludentem dixit ad Abraham*

And when Sarah saw Hagar *the* Egyptian's son playing, she said to Abraham,

21:10 *eice ancillam hanc et filium eius non enim erit heres filius ancillae cum filio meo Isaac*

"Throw this slave woman and her son out, for *a* slave woman's son will not be *an* heir with my son Isaac!"

21:11 *dure accepit hoc Abraham pro filio suo*

Abraham received this harshly for his son.

21:12 *cui dixit Deus non tibi videatur asperum super puero et super ancilla tua omnia quae dixerit tibi Sarra audi vocem eius quia in Isaac vocabitur tibi semen*

God said to him, "Let it not seem bitter to you concerning *the* boy and concerning your slave woman. All that Sarah says to you, listen to her voice, because seed will be called to you in Isaac.

21:13 *sed et filium ancillae faciam in gentem magnam quia semen tuum est*

"But I will also make *the* slave woman's son into *a* great nation, because he is your seed.

Hagar and Ishmael in the Desert

21:14 *surrexit itaque Abraham mane et tollens panem et utrem aquae inposuit scapulae eius tradiditque puerum et dimisit eam quae cum abisset errabat in solitudine Bersabee*

So Abraham got up early and, taking bread and *a* skin of water, he placed them on her shoulders, and handed *the* boy over. And he sent her away.

When she went out, she wandered in *the* desert of Beersheba.

21:15 *cumque consumpta esset aqua in utre abiecit puerum subter unam arborum quae ibi erant*

And when *the* water in *the* skin was drunk, she put *the* boy down under *a* tree which was there.

21:16 *et abiit seditque e regione procul quantum potest arcus iacere dixit enim non videbo morientem puerum et sedens contra levavit vocem suam et flevit*

And she went away from that place and sat, as far as one can shoot *an* arrow, for she said, "I will not watch *the* boy dying."

And sitting apart, she lifted up her voice and cried.

21:17 *exaudivit autem Deus vocem pueri vocavitque angelus Domini Agar de caelo dicens quid agis Agar noli timere exaudivit enim Deus vocem pueri de loco in quo est*

But God heard *the* boy's voice, and God's angel called Hagar from *the* sky, saying, "What are you doing, Hagar? Don't be afraid, for God has heard *the* boy's voice from *the* place where he is!

21:18 *surge tolle puerum et tene manum illius quia in gentem* *magnam faciam eum*

"Get up! Take *the* boy and hold his hand, because I will make him into *a* great nation!"

21:19 *aperuitque oculos eius Deus quae videns puteum aquae abiit et implevit utrem deditque puero bibere*

And God opened her eyes. *She*, seeing *a* water well, went and filled *the* skin. And she gave *it* to *the* boy to drink.

21:20 *et fuit cum eo qui crevit et moratus est in solitudine et factus est iuvenis sagittarius*

And she was with him, who grew and stayed in *the* desert. And he became *a* young archer.

21:21 *habitavitque in deserto Pharan et accepit illi mater sua uxorem de terra Aegypti*

And he lived in Pharan's desert, and his mother brought him *a* wife from Egypt's land.

Abimelech Fears Abraham

21:22 *eodem tempore dixit Abimelech et Fichol princeps exercitus eius ad Abraham Deus tecum est in universis quae agis*

That same time, Abimelech and Phicol, his army's leader, said to Abraham, "God is with you in all that you do.

21:23 *iura ergo per Dominum ne noceas mihi et posteris meis stirpique meae sed iuxta misericordiam quam feci tibi facies mihi et terrae in qua versatus es advena*

"Swear by *the* Lord, therefore, that you will not harm me and my posterity and my line. But you will do to me according to *the* mercy I did to you, and *the* land in which you wandered as *a* newcomer."

21:24 *dixitque Abraham ego iurabo*

And Abraham said, "I will swear."

21:25 *et increpavit Abimelech propter puteum aquae quem vi abstulerant servi illius*

And he protested to Abimelech about *a* water well, which was taken away by force from his slaves.

21:26 *respondit Abimelech nescivi quis fecerit hanc rem sed et tu non indicasti mihi et ego non audivi praeter hodie*

Abimelech responded, "I don't know who did this thing, but also you haven't told me and I have not heard before today."

21:27 *tulit itaque Abraham oves et boves et dedit Abimelech* *percusseruntque ambo foedus*

So Abraham took sheep and oxen and gave to Abimelech. And *the* two made *an* agreement.

21:28 *et statuit Abraham septem agnas gregis seorsum*

And Abraham stood seven of *the* flock's ewe-lambs apart.

21:29 *cui dixit Abimelech quid sibi volunt septem agnae istae quas stare fecisti seorsum*

Abimelech said to him, "What do these seven ewe-lambs which you made stand apart mean in themselves?"

21:30 *at ille septem inquit agnas accipies de manu mea ut sint in testimonium mihi quoniam ego fodi puteum istum*

And he said, "Accept these seven lambs from my hand, that they may be *a* witness to me that I dug this well."

21:31 *idcirco vocatus est locus ille Bersabee quia ibi uterque iuraverunt*

Therefore, that place is called Beersheba, because both of them swore there.

21:32 *et inierunt foedus pro puteo Iuramenti*

And they entered an agreement for *the* well of Oaths.

21:33 *surrexit autem Abimelech et Fichol princeps militiae eius reversique sunt in terram Palestinorum Abraham vero plantavit nemus in Bersabee et invocavit ibi nomen Domini Dei aeterni*

But Abimelech and Phicol, his military leader, turned back into *the* Palestinians' land. Abraham, indeed, planted *a* forest in Beersheba, and invoked there *the* Lord God's eternal name.

21:34 *et fuit colonus terrae Philisthinorum diebus multis*

And he was *a* settler in *the* Philistines' land many days.

God Tests Abraham

Genesis 22:1 *quae postquam gesta sunt temptavit Deus Abraham et dixit ad eum Abraham ille respondit adsum*

After these things happened, God tested Abraham. And He said to him, "Abraham!"

He answered, "I am here."

22:2 *ait ei tolle filium tuum unigenitum quem diligis Isaac et vade in terram Visionis atque offer eum ibi holocaustum super unum montium quem monstravero tibi*

He said to him, "Take your only begotten son, Isaac whom you love, and go to *the* land of Vision, and offer him there *as a* burnt offering on one of *the* mountains which I will show you."

22:3 *igitur Abraham de nocte consurgens stravit asinum suum ducens secum duos iuvenes et Isaac filium suum cumque concidisset ligna in holocaustum abiit ad locum quem praeceperat ei Deus*

Therefore Abraham, rising up from *the* night, saddled his donkey, leading with him two youths and Isaac, his son. And when he had cut wood for *the* offering, he went out to *the* place to which God had commanded him.

22:4 *die autem tertio elevatis oculis*

vidit locum procul

But *the* third day, lifting up his eyes, he saw *the* place far off.

22:5 *dixitque ad pueros suos expectate hic cum asino ego et puer illuc usque properantes postquam adoraverimus revertemur ad vos*

And he said to *the* servant boys, "Wait here with *the* donkey. The boy and I *are* hurrying even there. After we have worshiped, we will come back to you.

22:6 *tulit quoque ligna holocausti et inposuit super Isaac filium suum ipse vero portabat in manibus ignem et gladium cumque duo pergerent simul*

He took *the* burnt offering's wood also, and put *it* on Isaac, his son. *Abraham*, truly, carried *the* fire and sword in his hands, and *the* two went together.

22:7 *dixit Isaac patri suo pater mi at ille respondit quid vis fili ecce inquit ignis et ligna ubi est victima holocausti*

Isaac said to his father, "My father."

And he answered, "What do you want, son?"

He said, "Look, *here are* fire and wood. Where is *the* burnt offering's victim?"

22:8 *dixit Abraham Deus providebit sibi victimam holocausti fili mi pergebant ergo pariter*

Abraham said, "God Himself will provide *the* burnt offering's victim, my son."

So *the* two went on together.

22:9 *veneruntque ad locum quem ostenderat ei Deus in quo aedificavit altare et desuper ligna conposuit cumque conligasset Isaac filium suum posuit eum in altari super struem lignorum*

And they came to *the* place which God had showed him, in which he built *an* altar. And he placed *the* wood on it. And when he had bound Isaac, his son, he put him on *the* altar, on *the* heap of wood.

22:10 *extenditque manum et arripuit gladium ut immolaret filium*

And he stretched out his hand and picked up *the* sword, so he could offer *his* son.

22:11 *et ecce angelus Domini de caelo clamavit dicens Abraham Abraham qui respondit adsum*

And, look, *the* Lord's angel cried out from *the* sky, saying, "Abraham, Abraham!"

He answered, "Here I am."

22:12 *dixitque ei non extendas manum tuam super puerum neque facias illi quicquam nunc cognovi quod timeas Dominum et non peperceris filio tuo unigenito propter me*

And He said to him, "Don't stretch out your hand over *the* boy, or do anything to him! Now I have known that you fear *the* Lord, and you have not spared your only-begotten son on My account."

22:13 *levavit Abraham oculos viditque post tergum arietem inter vepres herentem cornibus quem adsumens obtulit holocaustum pro filio*

Abraham lifted up his eyes and saw on *the* far side *a* ram among *the* thorn bushes, caught by *its* horns, which, taking up, he offered as *a* burnt offering for *the* son.

22:14 *appellavitque nomen loci illius Dominus videt unde usque hodie dicitur in monte Dominus videbit*

And he called that place's name, "The Lord Will See," from which it is said even today, "On *the* mountain, *the* Lord will see."

The Lord Blesses Abraham
22:15 *vocavit autem angelus Domini Abraham secundo de caelo dicens*

But *the* Lord's angel called Abraham
from *the* sky *a* second time, saying,

22:16 *per memet ipsum iuravi dicit
Dominus quia fecisti rem hanc et
non pepercisti filio tuo unigenito*

"I have sworn by Myself," *the* Lord
said, "because you have done this
thing, and have not spared your only-
begotten son,

22:17 *benedicam tibi et
multiplicabo semen tuum sicut
stellas caeli et velut harenam quae
est in litore maris possidebit semen
tuum portas inimicorum suorum*

"I will bless you and multiply your
seed like *the* sky's stars, and like sand
which is on *the* seashore. Your seed
will possess his enemies' gates.

22:18 *et benedicentur in semine tuo
omnes gentes terrae quia oboedisti
voci meae*

"And all *the* land's nations will be
blessed in your seed, because you
obeyed My voice."

22:19 *reversus est Abraham ad
pueros suos abieruntque Bersabee
simul et habitavit ibi*

But Abraham went back to his
servant boys, and they went to
Beersheba together. And he lived
there.

Nahor's Children

22:20 *his itaque gestis nuntiatum est
Abraham quod Melcha quoque
genuisset filios Nahor fratri suo*

This done so, Abraham also was told
that Melcha likewise had birthed sons
to Nahor, his brother –

22:21 *Hus primogenitum et Buz
fratrem eius Camuhel patrem
Syrorum*

Hus, firstborn, and Buz, his brother;
Camuel, *the* Syrians' father,

22:22 *et Chased et Azau Pheldas
quoque et Iedlaph*

and Hased and Azau, Pheldas
likewise and Jedlaph,

22:23 *ac Bathuel de quo nata est
Rebecca octo istos genuit Melcha
Nahor fratri Abraham*

and Bathuel, from whom Rebecca
was born. These eight Melcha
birthed to Nahor, Abraham's brother.

22:24 *concubina vero illius nomine
Roma peperit Tabee et Gaom et
Thaas et Maacha*

And his concubine, named Roma,
birthed Tabee and Gaom and Thaas
and Maacha.

Sarah Dies

Genesis 23:1 *vixit autem Sarra centum viginti septem annis*

But Sarah lived one hundred twenty-seven years.

23:2 *et mortua est in civitate Arbee quae est Hebron in terra Chanaan venitque Abraham ut plangeret et fleret eam*

And she died in *the* city of Arbee, which is Hebron, in Canaan's land. And Abraham came so he could grieve and weep for her.

Abraham Buys
a Burial Plot

23:3 *cumque surrexisset ab officio funeris locutus est ad filios Heth dicens*

And when he had gotten up from *the* funeral rite, he spoke to Heth's children, saying,

23:4 *advena sum et peregrinus apud vos date mihi ius sepulchri vobiscum ut sepeliam mortuum meum*

"I am *a* newcomer and stranger with you. Give me *a* burial right, so I can bury my dead."

23:5 *responderuntque filii Heth*

And Heth's children answered,

23:6 *audi nos domine princeps Dei es apud nos in electis sepulchris nostris sepeli mortuum tuum nullusque prohibere te poterit quin in monumento eius sepelias mortuum tuum*

"Hear us, Lord. You are God's prince with us. Bury your dead in our best graves! And no one will be able to stop you, so that you may bury your dead in his monument."

23:7 *surrexit Abraham et adoravit populum terrae filios videlicet Heth*

Abraham got up and paid homage to *the* land's people, Heth's children, clearly.

23:8 *dixitque ad eos si placet animae vestrae ut sepeliam mortuum meum audite me et intercedite apud Ephron filium Soor*

And he said to them, "If it pleases your soul that I bury my dead, hear me, and intercede with Ephron, Soor's son,"

23:9 *ut det mihi speluncam duplicem quam habet in extrema parte agri sui pecunia digna tradat mihi eam coram vobis in possessionem sepulchri*

"that he may give me *the* double cave which he has in *the* farthest part of his field. He may give it to me for *the* worthy price before you, as *a* burial possession."

23:10 *habitabat autem Ephron in medio filiorum Heth responditque ad Abraham cunctis audientibus qui ingrediebantur portam civitatis illius dicens*

But Ephron lived among Heth's children, and he responded to Abraham, *in front of* all those listening, who came in through that city's gate, saying,

23:11 *nequaquam ita fiat domine mi sed magis ausculta quod loquor agrum trado tibi et speluncam quae in eo est praesentibus filiis populi mei sepeli mortuum tuum*

"Let it not be done so, my lord, but better – listen to what I say! I give you *the* field and *the* cave that is in it, in my people's children's presence. Bury your dead!"

23:12 *adoravit Abraham coram populo terrae*

Abraham paid homage before *the* land's people,

23:13 *et locutus est ad Ephron circumstante plebe quaeso ut audias me dabo pecuniam pro agro suscipe eam et sic sepeliam mortuum meum in eo*

and said to Ephron, *the* people standing around, "I pray that you hear me. I will give you money for *the* field. Accept it, and thus I will

bury my dead in it."

23:14 *respondit Ephron*

Ephron answered,

23:15 *domine mi audi terram quam postulas quadringentis argenti siclis valet istud est pretium inter me et te sed quantum est hoc sepeli mortuum tuum*

"Listen, my lord. *The* land which you ask for is worth four hundred silver shekels. That is *the* price. But what is that between me and you? Bury your dead!"

23:16 *quod cum audisset Abraham adpendit pecuniam quam Ephron postulaverat audientibus filiis Heth quadringentos siclos argenti et probati monetae publicae*

When Abraham heard that, he took *the* money which Ephron had asked in *the* hearing of Heth's children, four hundred silver shekels, and *the* official public coinage.

23:17 *confirmatusque est ager quondam Ephronis in quo erat spelunca duplex respiciens Mambre tam ipse quam spelunca et omnes arbores eius in cunctis terminis per circuitum*

And *the* field was confirmed at once by Ephron, in which was *the* double cave, looking on Mambre, *the* cave likewise and all its trees, in all its boundaries around,

23:18 *Abrahae in possessionem videntibus filiis Heth et cunctis qui intrabant portam civitatis illius*

to Abraham as *a* possession, in *the* sight of Heth's children and those who entered that city's gates.

23:19 *atque ita sepelivit Abraham Sarram uxorem suam in spelunca agri duplici qui respiciebat Mambre haec est Hebron in terra Chanaan*

And so Abraham buried Sarah his wife, in *the* field's double cave which looked on Mambre. This is Hebron, in Canaan's land.

23:20 *et confirmatus est ager et antrum quod erat in eo Abrahae in possessionem monumenti a filiis Heth*

And *the* field was confirmed to Abraham, and *the* cavern that was in it, as *a* memorial possession from Heth's children.

Abraham Seeks
a Wife for Isaac

Genesis 24:1 *erat autem Abraham senex dierumque multorum et Dominus in cunctis benedixerat ei*

But Abraham was *an* old man of many days, and *the* Lord had blessed him in all *ways*.

24:2 *dixitque ad servum seniorem domus suae qui praeerat omnibus quae habebat pone manum tuam subter femur meum*

And he said to his house's senior slave, who had charge of all that he had, "Put your hand under my thigh,

24:3 *ut adiurem te per Dominum Deum caeli et terrae ut non accipias uxorem filio meo de filiabus Chananeorum inter quos habito*

"so I can make you swear by *the* Lord God of sky and land that you will not accept *a* wife for my son from *the* Canaanites' daughters, among whom I live.

24:4 *sed ad terram et ad cognationem meam proficiscaris et inde accipias uxorem filio meo Isaac*

"But you may set out to my land and kin, and will accept from there *a* wife for my son Isaac.

24:5 *respondit servus si noluerit mulier venire mecum in terram hanc* *num reducere debeo filium tuum ad locum de quo egressus es*

The slave answered, "If *the* woman doesn't want to come with me to this land, must I return your son to *the* place from which you came out?"

24:6 *dixit Abraham cave nequando reducas illuc filium meum*

Abraham said, "Take care! By no means will you bring my son back there.

24:7 *Dominus Deus caeli qui tulit me de domo patris mei et de terra nativitatis meae qui locutus est mihi et iuravit dicens semini tuo dabo terram hanc ipse mittet angelum suum coram te et accipies inde uxorem filio meo*

"*The* Lord, sky's God, who took me from my father's house and *the* land of my birth, who spoke to me and swore, saying, 'I will give this land to your seed,' He will send His angel before you. And you will accept *a* wife from there for my son.

24:8 *sin autem noluerit mulier sequi te non teneberis iuramento filium tantum meum ne reducas illuc*

"But if *the* woman doesn't want to follow you, you won't be bound by *the* oath. Regardless, don't return my son there!"

24:9 *posuit ergo servus manum sub femore Abraham domini sui et iuravit illi super sermone hoc*

So he put his hand under Abraham his lord's thigh, and swore to him concerning this word.

24:10 *tulitque decem camelos de grege domini sui et abiit ex omnibus bonis eius portans secum profectusque perrexit Mesopotamiam ad urbem Nahor*

And he took ten camels from his lord's flock and went out, carrying some of all his goods with him. And setting out, he went on to Mesopotamia, to Nahor's city.

Abraham's Servant
Meets Rebecca

24:11 *cumque camelos fecisset accumbere extra oppidum iuxta puteum aquae vespere eo tempore quo solent mulieres egredi ad hauriendam aquam dixit*

And when he had made *the* camels sit outside *a* town, alongside *a* water well at evening, at *the* time when women are accustomed to go out to draw up water, he said,

24:12 *Domine Deus domini mei Abraham occurre obsecro hodie mihi et fac misericordiam cum domino meo Abraham*

"Lord, God of my lord Abraham,

meet me today, I pray, and work mercy with my lord Abraham!

24:13 *ecce ego sto propter fontem aquae et filiae habitatorum huius civitatis egredientur ad hauriendam aquam*

"Look, I am standing before *a* water spring, and this city's inhabitants' daughters will come out to draw up water.

24:14 *igitur puella cui ego dixero inclina hydriam tuam ut bibam et illa responderit bibe quin et camelis tuis dabo potum ipsa est quam praeparasti servo tuo Isaac et per hoc intellegam quod feceris misericordiam cum domino meo*

"Therefore, *the* girl to whom I say, 'Turn your pitcher down so I can drink,' and she answers, 'Drink, then, and I will give your camels *a* drink,' – she is the one whom You have prepared for Your slave Isaac. And by this I will know that You have worked mercy with my lord."

24:15 *necdum intra se verba conpleverat et ecce Rebecca egrediebatur filia Bathuel filii Melchae uxoris Nahor fratris Abraham habens hydriam in scapula*

The word was not yet completed inside him, and, look, Rebecca, daughter of Bathuel, son of Melcha, wife of Nahor, Abraham's brother, came out, having *a* pitcher on *her* shoulder –

24:16 *puella decora nimis virgoque pulcherrima et incognita viro descenderat autem ad fontem et impleverat hydriam ac revertebatur*

an overwhelmingly beautiful girl and most lovely young woman, and *she had* not known *a* man. But she came down to *the* spring and filled *the* pitcher and went back.

24:17 *occurritque ei servus et ait pauxillum mihi ad sorbendum praebe aquae de hydria tua*

And *the* slave met her and said, "Give me *a* little water to drink from your pitcher."

24:18 *quae respondit bibe domine mi celeriterque deposuit hydriam super ulnam suam et dedit ei potum*

She said, "Drink, my lord," and she quickly put *the* pitcher on her forearm and gave him *a* drink.

24:19 *cumque ille bibisset adiecit quin et camelis tuis hauriam aquam donec cuncti bibant*

And when he had drunk, she said also, "And I will haul up water for your camels until all have drunk."

24:20 *effundensque hydriam in canalibus recurrit ad puteum ut* *hauriret aquam et haustam omnibus camelis dedit*

And, pouring out *the* pitcher into *the* channels, she went back to *the* well so she could haul up water. And she gave *a* drink to all *the* camels.

24:21 *ille autem contemplabatur eam tacitus scire volens utrum prosperum fecisset iter suum Dominus an non*

But he watched her quietly, wanting to know whether *the* Lord had made his journey prosper or not.

24:22 *postquam ergo biberunt cameli protulit vir inaures aureas adpendentes siclos duos et armillas totidem pondo siclorum decem*

Therefore, after *the* camels had drunk, *the* man took out gold earrings weighing two shekels, and as many armlets, ten shekels' weight.

24:23 *dixitque ad eam cuius es filia indica mihi est in domo patris tui locus ad manendum*

And he said to her, "Whose daughter are you? Tell me. Is there room to stay in your father's place?

24:24 *quae respondit filia Bathuelis sum filii Melchae quem peperit Nahor*

She answered, "I am *the* daughter of Bathuel, Melcha's son, whom she birthed to Nahor."

24:25 *et addidit dicens palearum quoque et faeni plurimum est apud nos et locus spatiosus ad manendum*

And she added, saying, "*There* is straw and much hay alike with us, and *the* place is spacious to stay *in*."

24:26 *inclinavit se homo et adoravit Dominum*

The man bowed down and paid homage to *the* Lord,

24:27 *dicens benedictus Dominus Deus domini mei Abraham qui non abstulit misericordiam et veritatem suam a domino meo et recto me itinere perduxit in domum fratris domini mei*

saying, "*The* Lord, God of my lord Abraham, *be* blessed, who has not taken His mercy and truth away from my lord, and has led me by *the* right path to my lord's brother's house."

The Servant Meets Rebecca's Family

24:28 *cucurrit itaque puella et nuntiavit in domum matris suae omnia quae audierat*

So *the* girl ran and told in her mother's house all that she had heard.

24:29 *habebat autem Rebecca fratrem nomine Laban qui festinus egressus est ad hominem ubi erat fons*

But Rebecca had *a* brother named Laban, who quickly went out to *the* man where *the* spring was.

24:30 *cumque vidisset inaures et armillas in manibus sororis suae et audisset cuncta verba referentis haec locutus est mihi homo venit ad virum qui stabat iuxta camelos et propter fontem aquae*

And when he saw *the* earrings and armbands in his sister's hands, and heard all *the* words recounting, '*The* man said this to me,' he went to *the* man, who was standing beside *the* camels and close to *the* water spring.

24:31 *dixitque ad eum ingredere benedicte Domini cur foris stas praeparavi domum et locum camelis*

And he said to him, "Come in, *the* Lord's blessed *one*! Why are you standing outside? I have prepared *the* house and *the* camels' place."

24:32 *et introduxit eum hospitium ac destravit camelos deditque paleas et faenum et aquam ad lavandos pedes camelorum et virorum qui venerant cum eo*

And he brought him into *the* lodging and unsaddled *the* camels. And he gave straw and hay and water, to wash *the* feet of *the* camels and men who came with him.

24:33 *et adpositus est in conspectu eius panis qui ait non comedam donec loquar sermones meos respondit ei loquere*

And bread was placed in his sight, who said, "I will not eat until I speak my words."

He responded to him, "Speak!"

24:34 *at ille servus inquit Abraham sum*

And he said, "I am Abraham's slave,

24:35 *et Dominus benedixit domino meo valde magnificatusque est et dedit ei oves et boves argentum et aurum servos et ancillas camelos et asinos*

"and *the* Lord has blessed my lord greatly, and he is magnified. And He gave him sheep and oxen, silver and gold, slaves and slave women, camels and donkeys.

24:36 *et peperit Sarra uxor domini mei filium domino meo in senectute sua deditque illi omnia quae habuerat*

"And Sarah, my lord's wife, birthed my lord *a* son in her old age. And he has given him all that he has.

24:37 *et adiuravit me dominus meus dicens non accipies uxorem filio meo de filiabus Chananeorum in quorum terra habito*

"And my lord swore to me, saying, 'You will not accept *a* wife for my son from *the* Canaanites' daughters, in whose land I live.

24:38 *sed ad domum patris mei perges et de cognatione mea accipies uxorem filio meo*

"'But you will go to my father's house, and will accept *a* wife for my son from my kin.'

24:39 *ego vero respondi domino meo quid si noluerit venire mecum mulier*

"But I answered my lord, 'What if *the* woman doesn't want to come with me?'

24:40 *Dominus ait in cuius conspectu ambulo mittet angelum suum tecum et diriget viam tuam accipiesque uxorem filio meo de cognatione mea et de domo patris mei*

"He said, '*The* Lord, in whose sight I walk, will send His angel with you and guide your way. And you will accept *a* wife for my son from my kin, and from my father's house.'

24:41 *innocens eris a maledictione mea cum veneris ad propinquos meos et non dederint tibi*

"'You will be innocent from my curse when you come to my next-of-kin and they will not give *her* to you.'

24:42 *veni ergo hodie ad fontem et dixi Domine Deus domini mei Abraham si direxisti viam meam in qua nunc ambulo*

"I came to *the* spring today, therefore, and said, 'Lord God of my lord Abraham, if You have guided my way in which I am now walking,

24:43 *ecce sto iuxta fontem aquae et virgo quae egredietur ad hauriendam aquam audierit a me da mihi pauxillum aquae ad bibendum ex hydria tua*

"look! I'm standing beside *a* water well. And *a* young woman who comes out to haul up water will hear from me, 'Give me *a* little water to drink from your pitcher,'

24:44 *et dixerit mihi et tu bibe et camelis tuis hauriam ipsa est mulier quam praeparavit Dominus filio domini mei*

"'and she will say to me, 'You drink, and I will haul up *water* for your camels' – she is *the* woman whom *the* Lord has prepared for my lord's son.'

24:45 *dum haec mecum tacitus volverem apparuit Rebecca veniens cum hydria quam portabat in scapula descenditque ad fontem et hausit aquam et aio ad eam da mihi paululum bibere*

"When I was considering this quietly in myself, Rebecca appeared, coming with *a* pitcher which she carried on her shoulder. And she went down to *the* spring and hauled up water. And I said to her, 'Give me *a* little to drink.'

24:46 *quae festina deposuit hydriam de umero et dixit mihi et tu bibe et camelis tuis potum tribuam bibi et adaquavit camelos*

"*She* quickly put *the* pitcher on her forearm and said to me, 'You drink, and I will give your camels *a* drink.' I drank and she watered *the* camels.

24:47 *interrogavique eam et dixi cuius es filia quae respondit filia Bathuelis sum filii Nahor quem peperit illi Melcha suspendi itaque inaures ad ornandam faciem eius et armillas posui in manibus*

"And I questioned her and said, 'Whose daughter are you?'

"She answered, 'I am *the* daughter of Bathuel, Nahor's son, whom Melcha birthed to him.'

"So I hung *the* earrings to adorn her

face, and put *the* armlets in *her* hands.

24:48 *pronusque adoravi Dominum benedicens Domino Deo domini mei Abraham qui perduxisset me recto itinere ut sumerem filiam fratris domini mei filio eius*

"And I paid homage to *the* Lord face down, blessing *the* Lord, God of my lord Abraham, who had led me by *the* right path, so I could find *a* daughter from my lord's brother for his son.

24:49 *quam ob rem si facitis misericordiam et veritatem cum domino meo indicate mihi sin autem aliud placet et hoc dicite ut vadam ad dextram sive ad sinistram*

"From which thing, if you work mercy and truth with my lord, tell me! But if something else is pleasing, tell me this too, so I can go to *the* right or to *the* left."

24:50 *responderunt Laban et Bathuel a Domino egressus est sermo non possumus extra placitum eius quicquam aliud tecum loqui*

Laban and Bathuel answered, "This word came out from *the* Lord. We cannot say anything else to you beyond His pleasure.

24:51 *en Rebecca coram te est tolle eam et proficiscere et sit uxor filii domini tui sicut locutus est Dominus*

"Look, Rebecca *is* before you. Take her and set out, and may she be wife to your lord's son, as *the* Lord has spoken!"

24:52 *quod cum audisset puer Abraham adoravit in terra Dominum*

When Abraham's servant had heard that, he paid homage to *the* Lord on *the* ground.

24:53 *prolatisque vasis argenteis et aureis ac vestibus dedit ea Rebeccae pro munere fratribus quoque eius et matri dona obtulit*

And taking out silver and gold vessels and garments, he gave them as gifts to Rebecca. He likewise brought out presents for her brothers and mother.

24:54 *initoque convivio vescentes pariter et bibentes manserunt ibi surgens autem mane locutus est puer dimittite me ut vadam ad dominum meum*

And, entering *the* feast, eating and drinking together, they stayed there. But, getting up early, *the* servant said, "Let me go, so I can go to my lord."

24:55 *responderunt fratres eius et mater maneat puella saltem decem dies apud nos et postea proficiscetur*

Her brothers and mother answered,

"Let *the* girl stay at least ten days with us, and afterwards she will go."

24:56 *nolite ait me retinere quia Dominus direxit viam meam dimittite me ut pergam ad dominum meum*

He said, "Don't keep me, because *the* Lord guided my way. Let me go, so I can go to my lord."

24:57 *dixerunt vocemus puellam et quaeramus ipsius voluntatem*

They said, "We will call *the* girl and find out her desire."

24:58 *cumque vocata venisset sciscitati sunt vis ire cum homine isto quae ait vadam*

And called, when she had come they asked, "Do you want to go with this man?"

She said, "I will go."

24:59 *dimiserunt ergo eam et nutricem illius servumque Abraham et comites eius*

So they let her and her nurse go, and Abraham's slave and his companions

24:60 *inprecantes prospera sorori suae atque dicentes soror nostra es crescas in mille milia et possideat semen tuum portas inimicorum suorum*

praying prosperity to their sister, and saying, "You are our sister. May you grow into *a* thousand thousands, and may your seed possess his enemies' gates!"

24:61 *igitur Rebecca et puellae illius ascensis camelis secutae sunt virum qui festinus revertebatur ad dominum suum*

So Rebecca and her girls, being mounted on *the* camels, followed *the* man, who quickly went back to his lord.

Isaac and Rebecca Meet

24:62 *eo tempore Isaac deambulabat per viam quae ducit ad puteum cuius nomen est Viventis et videntis habitabat enim in terra australi*

At that time, Isaac was walking down *the* road that led to *the* well whose name is "Of *the* Living and Seeing," for he was living in *the* south land.

24:63 *et egressus fuerat ad meditandum in agro inclinata iam die cumque levasset oculos vidit camelos venientes procul*

And he had gone out to meditate in *the* field, *the* day already ending. And when he lifted up *his* eyes, he saw camels coming far off.

24:64 *Rebecca quoque conspecto Isaac descendit de camelo*

Rebecca too, seeing Isaac, came down from *the* camel,

24:65 *et ait ad puerum quis est ille homo qui venit per agrum in occursum nobis dixit ei ipse est dominus meus at illa tollens cito pallium operuit se*

and said to *the* servant, "Who is that man who is coming through *the* field to meet us?"

He said to her, "He is my lord."

And she, quickly taking *the* veil, covered herself.

24:66 *servus autem cuncta quae gesserat narravit Isaac*

But *the* slave told Isaac all that had happened.

24:67 *qui introduxit eam in tabernaculum Sarrae matris suae et accepit uxorem et in tantum dilexit ut dolorem qui ex morte matris acciderat temperaret*

He brought her into Sarah his mother's tent and received her *as* wife. And he delighted in her so much that *the* grief which followed his mother's death was eased.

Abraham Marries Kethurah

Genesis 25:1 *Abraham vero aliam duxit uxorem nomine Cetthuram*

Abraham then married another wife named Kethurah,

25:2 *quae peperit ei Zamram et Iexan et Madan et Madian et Iesboch et Sue*

who birthed him Zamram and Jexan and Madan and Midian and Jesboch and Sue.

25:3 *Iexan quoque genuit Saba et Dadan filii Dadan fuerunt Assurim et Lathusim et Loommim*

Jexan likewise fathered Sabah and Dadan. Dadan's sons were Assurim and Lathusim and Lo-omim.

25:4 *at vero ex Madian ortus est Epha et Opher et Enoch et Abida et Eldaa omnes hii filii Cetthurae*

And then from Midian, Epha and Opher and Enoch and Abidah and Eldaah were born. All these were Kethurah's children.

25:5 *deditque Abraham cuncta quae possederat Isaac*

And Abraham gave all he possessed to Isaac.

25:6 *filiis autem concubinarum largitus est munera et separavit eos*

ab Isaac filio suo dum adhuc ipse viveret ad plagam orientalem

But he gave generous gifts to his concubines' children, and separated them from his son Isaac while he was still living, toward *the* eastern plain.

Abraham Dies

25:7 *fuerunt autem dies vitae eius centum septuaginta quinque anni*

But his life's days were one hundred seventy-five years,

25:8 *et deficiens mortuus est in senectute bona provectaeque aetatis et plenus dierum congregatusque est ad populum suum*

and, faltering, he died in *a* good old age, and life's advance, and full of days. And he was gathered to his people.

25:9 *et sepelierunt eum Isaac et Ismahel filii sui in spelunca duplici quae sita est in agro Ephron filii Soor Hetthei e regione Mambre*

And Isaac and Ishmael, his sons, buried him in *the* double cave which was located in *the* field of Ephron *the* Hittite, Soor's son, in Mambre's region,

25:10 *quem emerat a filiis Heth ibi sepultus est ipse et Sarra uxor eius*

which he bought from Heth's

children. He was buried there, and Sarah his wife.

25:11 *et post obitum illius benedixit Deus Isaac filio eius qui habitabat iuxta puteum nomine Viventis et videntis*

And after his death, God blessed Isaac his son, who lived beside *the* well called "Of *the* Living and Seeing."

Ishmael's Children

25:12 *hae sunt generationes Ismahel filii Abraham quem peperit ei Agar Aegyptia famula Sarrae*

These are *the* generations of Ishmael, Abraham's son, whom Hagar *the* Egyptian, Sarah's household slave, birthed to him.

25:13 *et haec nomina filiorum eius in vocabulis et generationibus suis primogenitus Ismahelis Nabaioth dein Cedar et Abdeel et Mabsam*

And these are his children's names, in his designations and generations. Ishmael's firstborn was Nabaioth, then Kedar and Abdeel and Mabsam;

25:14 *Masma quoque et Duma et Massa*

Masmah too, and Dumah and Massah;

25:15 *Adad et Thema Itur et Naphis*

et Cedma

Hadad and Themah, Itur and Naphis and Cedma.

25:16 *isti sunt filii Ismahel et haec nomina per castella et oppida eorum duodecim principes tribuum suarum*

These are Ishmael's sons, and these *the* names, by their strongholds and towns – twelve princes of his tribes.

25:17 *anni vitae Ismahel centum triginta septem deficiens mortuus est et adpositus ad populum suum*

The years of Ishmael's life were one hundred thirty-seven. Faltering, he died and *was* placed with his people.

25:18 *habitavit autem ab Evila usque Sur quae respicit Aegyptum introeuntibus Assyrios coram cunctis fratribus suis obiit*

But he lived from Evila even to Sur, which looks on Egypt, going into *the* Assyrians. He died before all his brothers.

Isaac's Generations

25:19 *hae quoque sunt generationes Isaac filii Abraham Abraham genuit Isaac*

These likewise are the generations of Isaac, Abraham's son. Abraham fathered Isaac,

25:20 *qui cum quadraginta esset annorum duxit uxorem Rebeccam filiam Bathuel Syri de Mesopotamiam sororem Laban*

who, when he was forty years old, married Rebecca, Laban's sister, daughter of *the* Syrian Bathuel, from Mesopotamia.

25:21 *deprecatusque est Dominum pro uxore sua eo quod esset sterilis qui exaudivit eum et dedit conceptum Rebeccae*

And he pleaded with *the* Lord for his wife, because she was sterile. *He* heard him and gave Rebecca conception.

Rebecca Births
Esau and Jacob

25:22 *sed conlidebantur in utero eius parvuli quae ait si sic mihi futurum erat quid necesse fuit concipere perrexitque ut consuleret Dominum*

But *the* little ones in her womb fought each other. *She* said, "If *the* future was so to me, why did I have to conceive?"

And she went so she could consult *the* Lord,

25:23 *qui respondens ait duae gentes in utero tuo sunt et duo populi ex ventre tuo dividentur populusque populum superabit et maior minori serviet*

who, answering, said, "Two nations are in your uterus, and two peoples will be divided from your womb. And people will overcome people, and *the* older will serve *the* younger."

25:24 *iam tempus pariendi venerat et ecce gemini in utero repperti sunt*

The time of giving birth had already come, and, look, twins in *her* uterus were discovered.

25:25 *qui primus egressus est rufus erat et totus in morem pellis hispidus vocatumque est nomen eius Esau protinus alter egrediens plantam fratris tenebat manu et idcirco appellavit eum Iacob*

The first one who came out was red, and all in *the* manner of hairy skin. And his name was called Esau. *The* other, immediately coming out, had his brother's heel in hand, and therefore, she called him Jacob.

25:26 *sexagenarius erat Isaac quando nati sunt parvuli*

Isaac was sixty when *the* little ones were born.

25:27 *quibus adultis factus est Esau vir gnarus venandi et homo agricola Iacob autem vir simplex habitabat in tabernaculis*

When Esau became *an* adult, he was *a* skilled hunter and *a* man of *the* field. But Jacob, *a* simple man, lived in tents.

Esau Sells His Birthright

25:28 *Isaac amabat Esau eo quod de venationibus illius vesceretur et Rebecca diligebat Iacob*

Isaac loved Esau because he would eat from his game, and Rebecca delighted in Jacob.

25:29 *coxit autem Iacob pulmentum ad quem cum venisset Esau de agro lassus*

But Jacob cooked *a* stew, to whom, when Esau had come from *the* field exhausted,

25:30 *ait da mihi de coctione hac rufa quia oppido lassus sum quam ob causam vocatum est nomen eius Edom*

he said, "Give me some of this red stuff, because I am so worn out!"

(From which cause, his name was called Edom.)

25:31 *cui dixit Iacob vende mihi primogenita tua*

Jacob said to him, "Sell me your birthright!"

25:32 *ille respondit en morior quid*

mihi proderunt primogenita

He answered, "Look, I'm dying! What good will *a* birthright be to me?"

25:33 *ait Iacob iura ergo mihi iuravit Esau et vendidit primogenita*

Jacob said, "Swear to me, then!"

Esau swore, and sold *the* birthright.

25:34 *et sic accepto pane et lentis edulio comedit et bibit et abiit parvipendens quod primogenita vendidisset*

And so, accepting bread and edible lentils, he ate and drank and went out, little considering that he had sold *the* birthright.

The Lord Appears to Isaac

Genesis 26:1 *orta autem fame super terram post eam sterilitatem quae acciderat in diebus Abraham abiit Isaac ad Abimelech regem Palestinorum in Gerara*

But hunger sprung up over *the* land, after that sterility which happened in Abraham's days. Isaac went to Abimelech, *the* Palestinians' king, in Gerara.

26:2 *apparuitque ei Dominus et ait ne descendas in Aegyptum sed quiesce in terra quam dixero tibi*

And *the* Lord appeared to him and said, "Don't go down to Egypt, but keep calm in *the* land which I will tell you,

26:3 *et peregrinare in ea eroque tecum et benedicam tibi tibi enim et semini tuo dabo universas regiones has conplens iuramentum quod spopondi Abraham patri tuo*

and be *an* alien in it. I will be with you and bless you, for I will give you and your seed all these regions, fulfilling *the* oath which I swore to Abraham your father.

26:4 *et multiplicabo semen tuum sicut stellas caeli daboque posteris tuis universas regiones has et benedicentur in semine tuo omnes gentes terrae*

"And I will multiply your seed like *the* sky's stars. And I will give your descendants all these regions. And all *the* land's nations will be blessed in your seed,

26:5 *eo quod oboedierit Abraham voci meae et custodierit praecepta et mandata mea et caerimonias legesque servaverit*

because Abraham obeyed My voice and kept My precepts and commandments and ceremonies, and he might serve laws.

26:6 *mansit itaque Isaac in Geraris*

So Isaac stayed in Gerara.

Isaac Fears the Palestinians

26:7 *qui cum interrogaretur a viris loci illius super uxore sua respondit soror mea est timuerat enim confiteri quod sibi esset sociata coniugio reputans ne forte interficerent eum propter illius pulchritudinem*

Isaac, when questioned by that place's men about his wife, answered, "She is my sister" – for he was afraid to confess that she was joined to him in marriage, thinking, 'Unless, perhaps, they kill me because of her beauty.'

26:8 *cumque pertransissent dies plurimi et ibi demoraretur prospiciens Abimelech Palestinorum rex per fenestram vidit eum iocantem* *cum Rebecca uxore sua*

And when many days had passed and he stayed there, Abimelech, *the* Palestinians' king, looking through *the* window, saw him playing with Rebecca his wife.

26:9 *et accersito ait perspicuum est quod uxor tua sit cur mentitus es sororem tuam esse respondit timui ne morerer propter eam*

And, summoning him, he said, "It is clear that she is your wife. Why have you lied *that* she is your sister?"

He answered, "I was afraid I would be killed because of her."

26:10 *dixitque Abimelech quare inposuisti nobis potuit coire quispiam de populo cum uxore tua et induxeras super nos grande peccatum praecepitque omni populo dicens*

And Abimelech said, "Why have you put this on us? Someone from *the* people could have had sex with your wife, and you would have covered us with *a* great sin."

And he commanded all *the* people, saying,

26:11 *qui tetigerit hominis huius uxorem morte morietur*

"Who touches this man's wife will

die by death."

Isaac Prospers
26:12 *seruit autem Isaac in terra illa et invenit in ipso anno centuplum benedixitque ei Dominus*

But Isaac sowed in that land and found in that same year *a* hundredfold *return*. And *the* Lord blessed him.

26:13 *et locupletatus est homo et ibat proficiens atque succrescens donec magnus vehementer effectus est*

And *the* man was enriched, and was accomplishing and growing until he had become very great.

26:14 *habuit quoque possessionem ovium et armentorum et familiae plurimum ob haec invidentes ei Palestini*

He had possession also of sheep and cattle and *a* great family, from which *the* Palestinians, envying him,

Palestinian Hostility
26:15 *omnes puteos quos foderant servi patris illius Abraham illo tempore obstruxerunt implentes humo*

blocked at that time all *the* wells which his father Abraham's slaves had dug, filling *them* with dirt –

26:16 *in tantum ut ipse Abimelech diceret ad Isaac recede a nobis quoniam potentior nostri factus es valde*

so much so that Abimelech himself said to Isaac, "Go away from us, because you have become much stronger than us!"

26:17 *et ille discedens veniret ad torrentem Gerarae habitaretque ibi*

And he, leaving, went to Gerara creek and lived there.

26:18 *rursum fodit alios puteos quos foderant servi patris sui Abraham et quos illo mortuo olim obstruxerant Philisthim appellavitque eos hisdem nominibus quibus ante pater vocaverat*

He dug again other wells which his father Abraham's slaves had dug and which, he being dead, *the* Philistines had formerly blocked. And he called them by *the* same names which his father had called *them* before.

26:19 *foderunt in torrente et reppererunt aquam vivam*

They dug into *the* flow and found living water.

26:20 *sed et ibi iurgium fuit pastorum Gerarae adversum pastores Isaac dicentium nostra est aqua quam ob rem nomen putei ex eo quod acciderat vocavit Calumniam*

But in that place also there was *a* conflict of Gerara's shepherds against Isaac's shepherds, saying, "*The* water is ours."

From which thing, he called *the* well's name "Accusation," because of what happened.

26:21 *foderunt et alium et pro illo quoque rixati sunt appellavitque eum Inimicitias*

They also dug another, and they brawled likewise for this one. And he called it "Hostility."

26:22 *profectus inde fodit alium puteum pro quo non contenderunt itaque vocavit nomen illius Latitudo dicens nunc dilatavit nos Dominus et fecit crescere super terram*

Going from there he dug another well, for which they did not contend. So he called its name "Broadness," saying, "Now *the* Lord has broadened us and made us grow on *the* land."

The Lord Appears to Isaac in Beersheba

26:23 *ascendit autem ex illo loco in Bersabee*

But he climbed up from that place to Beersheba,

26:24 *ubi apparuit ei Dominus in ipsa nocte dicens ego sum Deus Abraham patris tui noli metuere quia tecum sum benedicam tibi et multiplicabo semen tuum propter servum meum Abraham*

where *the* Lord appeared to him in that same night, saying, "I am God of Abraham your father. Do not be afraid, because I am with you! I will bless you and multiply your seed, on account of My slave Abraham."

26:25 *itaque aedificavit ibi altare et invocato nomine Domini extendit tabernaculum praecepitque servis suis ut foderent puteum*

So he built *an* altar there and, invoking *the* Lord's name, he pitched *a* tent and commanded his slaves that they dig *a* well.

Abimelech Tries to Make Peace with Isaac

26:26 *ad quem locum cum venissent de Geraris Abimelech et Ochozath amicus illius et Fichol dux militum*

To which place, when Abimelech, and Ochozath his friend, and Phicol *the* army commander had come from Gerara,

26:27 *locutus est eis Isaac quid venistis ad me hominem quem odistis et expulistis a vobis*

Isaac said to them, "Why have you come to me, *a* man whom you hated and expelled from among you?"

26:28 *qui responderunt vidimus tecum esse Dominum et idcirco nunc diximus sit iuramentum inter nos et ineamus foedus*

They responded, "We have seen that *the* Lord is with you. And therefore now we say, let there be *an* oath between us, and let us enter *an* agreement,

26:29 *ut non facias nobis quicquam mali sicut et nos nihil tuorum adtigimus nec fecimus quod te laederet sed cum pace dimisimus auctum benedictione Domini*

"that you will not do us any harm, as we also have touched nothing of yours, nor have we done that which has wounded you. But we let you go with peace, enlarged by *the* Lord's blessing."

26:30 *fecit ergo eis convivium et post cibum et potum*

He made, therefore, *a* feast for them, and after food and drink,

26:31 *surgentes mane iuraverunt sibi mutuo dimisitque eos Isaac pacifice in locum suum*

getting up early, they swore among themselves mutually. And Isaac let them go peacefully to their place.

26:32 *ecce autem venerunt in ipso die servi Isaac adnuntiantes ei de puteo quem foderant atque dicentes invenimus aquam*

But look, Isaac's slaves came that same day, telling him about *the* well which they had dug and saying, "We found water."

26:33 *unde appellavit eum Abundantiam et nomen urbi inpositum est Bersabee usque in praesentem diem*

From which he called it "Abundance." And Beersheba became *the* city's name, even to *the* present day.

Esau's Wives

26:34 *Esau vero quadragenarius duxit uxores Iudith filiam Beeri Hetthei et Basemath filiam Helon eiusdem loci*

Esau, forty years old, took wives – Judith, Beeri *the* Hittite's daughter; and Basemath, daughter of Helon, of *the* same place –

26:35 *quae ambae offenderant animum Isaac et Rebeccae*

who both offended Isaac and Rebecca's soul.

Isaac Prepares for Death

Genesis 27:1 *senuit autem Isaac et caligaverunt oculi eius et videre non poterat vocavitque Esau filium suum maiorem et dixit ei fili mi qui respondit adsum*

But Isaac had grown old and his eyes were shadowed, and he could not see. And he called Esau his older son and said to him, "My son."

He answered, "I am here."

27:2 *cui pater vides inquit quod senuerim et ignorem diem mortis meae*

The father said to him, "You see that I have gotten old, and I do not know *the* day of my death."

27:3 *sume arma tua faretram et arcum et egredere foras cumque venatu aliquid adprehenderis*

"Take your arms, quiver and bow, and go outside, and when you have taken some by hunting,

27:4 *fac mihi inde pulmentum sicut velle me nosti et adfer ut comedam et benedicat tibi anima mea antequam moriar*

"make me from it food like you know I like, and bring it, so I can eat! And my soul may bless you before I die."

Rebecca Plots for Jacob

27:5 *quod cum audisset Rebecca et ille abisset in agrum ut iussionem patris expleret*

When Rebecca heard that, and he had gone into *the* field so he could fulfill *his* father's order,

27:6 *dixit filio suo Iacob audivi patrem tuum loquentem cum Esau fratre tuo et dicentem ei*

she said to her son Jacob, "I heard your father talking to Esau your brother and saying to him,

27:7 *adfer mihi venationem tuam et fac cibos ut comedam et benedicam tibi coram Domino antequam moriar*

"'Bring me your game and make food so I can eat! And I will bless you before *the* Lord, before I die.'

27:8 *nunc ergo fili mi adquiesce consiliis meis*

"Now, then, my son, agree to my counsels

27:9 *et pergens ad gregem adfer mihi duos hedos optimos ut faciam ex eis escas patri tuo quibus libenter vescitur*

and, going to *the* flock, bring me two choice young goats, so I can make from them *the* food that your father eats gladly.

27:10 *quas cum intuleris et comederit benedicat tibi priusquam moriatur*

"When you have taken it in and he has eaten, he may bless you before he dies."

27:11 *cui ille respondit nosti quod Esau frater meus homo pilosus sit et ego lenis*

He answered her, "You know that Esau my brother is *a* hairy man and I *am* smooth.

27:12 *si adtractaverit me pater meus et senserit timeo ne putet sibi voluisse inludere et inducat super me maledictionem pro benedictione*

"If my father touches me and feels, I'm afraid he'll think to himself that *I* want to mock him, and it will bring over me cursing for blessing."

27:13 *ad quem mater in me sit ait ista maledictio fili mi tantum audi vocem meam et perge adferque quae dixi*

His mother said to him, "Let that curse be on me, my son. Just hear my voice, and go and bring what I said."

27:14 *abiit et adtulit deditque matri paravit illa cibos sicut noverat velle patrem illius*

He went out and brought *it* in and gave *it* to *his* mother. She prepared food like she knew his father liked.

27:15 *et vestibus Esau valde bonis quas apud se habebat domi induit eum*

And she dressed him well in Esau's good clothes, which she had with her in *the* house.

27:16 *pelliculasque hedorum circumdedit manibus et colli nuda protexit*

She wrapped his hands in *the* goats' skin and covered *his* bare neck.

Isaac Blesses Jacob
27:17 *dedit pulmentum et panes quos coxerat tradidit*

She gave *him the* meat and handed him *the* bread which she had cooked.

27:18 *quibus inlatis dixit pater mi et ille respondit audio quis tu es fili mi*

He, going in, said, "My father."

And he answered, "I am listening. Who are you, my son?"

27:19 *dixitque Iacob ego sum Esau primogenitus tuus feci sicut praecepisti mihi surge sede et comede de venatione mea ut benedicat mihi anima tua*

And Jacob said, "I am Esau, your firstborn. I did as you commanded me. Get up, sit, and eat some of my game, so your soul may bless me."

27:20 *rursum Isaac ad filium suum quomodo inquit tam cito invenire potuisti fili mi qui respondit voluntatis Dei fuit ut cito mihi occurreret quod volebam*

Isaac again said to his son, "How could you find it so quickly, my son?"

He answered, "It was of God's will that what I wanted quickly met with me."

27:21 *dixitque Isaac accede huc ut tangam te fili mi et probem utrum tu sis filius meus Esau an non*

And Isaac said, "Come here so I can touch you, my son, and see whether you are my son Esau or not."

27:22 *accessit ille ad patrem et palpato eo dixit Isaac vox quidem vox Iacob est sed manus manus sunt Esau*

He went to *his* father and Isaac, touching him, said, "*The* voice is Jacob's voice, but *the* hands are Esau's hands."

27:23 *et non cognovit eum quia pilosae manus similitudinem maioris expresserant benedicens ergo illi*

And he did not know him, because his hands imitated hairiness like *his* older *brother's*. Therefore, blessing him,

27:24 *ait tu es filius meus Esau respondit ego sum*

he said, "Are you my son Esau?"

He answered, "I am."

27:25 *at ille offer inquit mihi cibos de venatione tua fili mi ut benedicat tibi anima mea quos cum oblatos comedisset obtulit ei etiam vinum quo hausto*

And he said, "Give me meat from your game, my son, so my soul may bless you" – which, when he had eaten *the* offerings, he brought him wine also, which *he* drained.

27:26 *dixit ad eum accede ad me et da mihi osculum fili mi*

He said to him, "Come to me and give me *a* kiss, my son."

27:27 *accessit et osculatus est eum statimque ut sensit vestimentorum illius flagrantiam benedicens ait ecce odor filii mei sicut odor agri cui benedixit Dominus*

He came and kissed him, and, immediately, as he sensed *the* smell of his clothes, he said, blessing, "Look, my son's scent is like *the*

scent of *a* field *the* Lord has blessed!

27:28 *det tibi Deus de rore caeli et de pinguedine terrae abundantiam frumenti et vini*

"May God give you grain and wine's abundance, from *the* sky's dew and from *the* land's fatness!

27:29 *et serviant tibi populi et adorent te tribus esto dominus fratrum tuorum et incurventur ante te filii matris tuae qui maledixerit tibi sit maledictus et qui benedixerit benedictionibus repleatur*

"And may peoples serve you and tribes pay homage to you! Be your brothers' lord, and may your mother's sons bow down before you! Let those who curse you be cursed, and those who bless you be filled with blessings!"

Esau and Isaac Discover the Fraud

27:30 *vix Isaac sermonem impleverat et egresso Iacob foras venit Esau*

Isaac had hardly finished speaking and Jacob gone outside when Esau came.

28:31 *coctosque de venatione cibos intulit patri dicens surge pater mi et comede de venatione filii tui ut benedicat mihi anima tua*

And he brought in roasted meat from hunting to *his* father, saying, "Get up, my father, and eat from your son's hunting, so your soul may bless me!"

27:32 *dixitque illi Isaac quis enim es tu qui respondit ego sum primogenitus filius tuus Esau*

And Isaac said to him, "Who are you?"

He answered, "I am your firstborn son, Esau."

27:33 *expavit Isaac stupore vehementi et ultra quam credi potest admirans ait quis igitur ille est qui dudum captam venationem adtulit mihi et comedi ex omnibus priusquam tu venires benedixique ei et erit benedictus*

Isaac became frightened by *a* great numbness, and, wondering more than he could believe, he said, "Then who is he who *a* little while ago brought taken game to me, and I ate from all of it before you came? And I blessed him and he will be blessed."

27:34 *auditis Esau sermonibus patris inrugiit clamore magno et consternatus ait benedic etiam mihi pater mi*

Esau, hearing his father's words, shouted with *a* great cry and, stricken, said, "Bless even me, my father!"

27:35 *qui ait venit germanus tuus fraudulenter et accepit benedictionem tuam*

Isaac said, "Your twin came deceptively and received your blessing."

27:36 *at ille subiunxit iuste vocatum est nomen eius Iacob subplantavit enim me en altera vice primogenita mea ante tulit et nunc secundo subripuit benedictionem meam rursumque ad patrem numquid non reservasti ait et mihi benedictionem*

And *Esau* added, "His name is called Jacob fairly, for he undermined me *a* second *time*. He took my birthright before, and now *a* second time, he stole my blessing."

And again he said to *the* father, "Didn't you reserve *a* blessing even for me?"

27:37 *respondit Isaac dominum tuum illum constitui et omnes fratres eius servituti illius subiugavi frumento et vino stabilivi eum tibi post haec fili mi ultra quid faciam*

Isaac responded, "I made him your lord, and subjected all his brothers to his service. I made firm for him grain and wine. After all this, my son, what more can I do for you?"

27:38 *cui Esau num unam inquit tantum benedictionem habes pater*

mihi quoque obsecro ut benedicas
cumque heiulatu magno fleret

Esau said to him, "Do you have only one blessing, my father? I pray you bless *me* also!"

And with *a* great wail, he wept.

27:39 *motus Isaac dixit ad eum in pinguedine terrae et in rore caeli desuper*

Moved, Isaac said to him, "In *the* land's fatness and in *the* sky's dew from above

27:40 *erit benedictio tua vives gladio et fratri tuo servies tempusque veniet cum excutias et solvas iugum eius de cervicibus tuis*

will your blessing be. You will live by *the* sword and serve your brother. And *the* time will come when you may shake off and loosen his yoke from your necks."

27:41 *oderat ergo semper Esau Iacob pro benedictione qua benedixerat ei pater dixitque in corde suo veniant dies luctus patris mei ut occidam Iacob fratrem meum*

Therefore Esau always hated Jacob, for *the* blessing with which *the* father blessed him. And he said in his heart, "Days of grieving will come for my father, so I can kill Jacob my brother."

Rebecca Plots to Save Jacob

27:42 *nuntiata sunt haec Rebeccae quae mittens et vocans Iacob filium suum dixit ad eum ecce Esau frater tuus minatur ut occidat te*

This was told to Rebecca, who, sending and calling Jacob her son, said to him, "Look, Esau your brother is threatening that he will kill you.

27:43 *nunc ergo fili audi vocem meam et consurgens fuge ad Laban fratrem meum in Haran*

"Now, then, son, listen to my voice! And, getting up, go to Laban my brother in Haran!

27:44 *habitabisque cum eo dies paucos donec requiescat furor fratris tui*

"And you will live with him *a* few days, until your brother's fury calms down,

27:45 *et cesset indignatio eius obliviscaturque eorum quae fecisti in eum postea mittam et adducam te inde huc cur utroque orbabor filio in una die*

"and his indignation may cease and what you have done to him may be forgotten. Afterward I will send and bring you from there. Why will I be bereaved of each son in one day?"

27:46 *dixit quoque Rebecca ad Isaac taedet me vitae meae propter filias Heth si acceperit Iacob uxorem de stirpe huius terrae nolo vivere*

Rebecca likewise said to Isaac, "It wearies me of my life because of *the* Hittites' daughters. If Jacob marries *a* wife of this land's type, I don't want to live."

Isaac Sends Jacob Away with Another Blessing

Genesis 28:1 *vocavit itaque Isaac Iacob et benedixit praecepitque ei dicens noli accipere coniugem de genere Chanaan*

So Isaac called Jacob. And he blessed and commanded him, saying, "Don't take *a* spouse from Canaan's race,

28:2 *sed vade et proficiscere in Mesopotamiam Syriae ad domum Bathuel patrem matris tuae et accipe tibi inde uxorem de filiabus Laban avunculi tui*

"but go and set out for Syrian Mesopotamia, to Bathuel, your mother's father's house. And accept for yourself *a* wife from there, from Laban your uncle's daughters.

28:3 *Deus autem omnipotens benedicat tibi et crescere te faciat atque multiplicet ut sis in turbas populorum*

"But God omnipotent bless you, and make you increase and multiply, so you may become multitudes of peoples!

28:4 *et det tibi benedictiones Abraham et semini tuo post te ut possideas terram peregrinationis tuae quam pollicitus est avo tuo*

"And may He give you and your seed

after you Abraham's blessings, so you may possess *the* land of your sojournings, which was promised to your grandfather."

28:5 *cumque dimisisset eum Isaac profectus venit in Mesopotamiam Syriae ad Laban filium Bathuel Syri fratrem Rebeccae matris suae*

And when Isaac had let him go, setting out, he came into Syrian Mesopotamia, to Laban, son of *the* Syrian Bathuel, brother of his mother Rebecca.

Esau Marries
Among the Ishmaelites

28:6 *videns autem Esau quod benedixisset pater suus Iacob et misisset eum in Mesopotamiam Syriae ut inde uxorem duceret et quod post benedictionem praecepisset ei dicens non accipies coniugem de filiabus Chanaan*

But Esau, seeing that his father had blessed Jacob and sent him to Syrian Mesopotamia, that he could marry *a* wife from there, and that after blessing, he had commanded him saying, "Don't receive *a* spouse from Canaan's daughters,"

28:7 *quodque oboediens Iacob parentibus isset in Syriam*

and that Jacob, obeying his parents, had gone to Syria,

28:8 *probans quoque quod non libenter aspiceret filias Chanaan pater suus*

understanding also that his father did not look gladly on Canaan's daughters,

28:9 *ivit ad Ismahelem et duxit uxorem absque his quas prius habebat Maeleth filiam Ismahel filii Abraham sororem Nabaioth*

he went to Ishmael and married *a* wife, apart from those he had before: Maheleth, daughter of Ishmael, Abraham's son, Nabaioth's sister.

Jacob's Journey

28:10 *igitur egressus Iacob de Bersabee pergebat Haran*

Then Jacob, going out from Beersheba, went to Haran.

28:11 *cumque venisset ad quendam locum et vellet in eo requiescere post solis occubitum tulit de lapidibus qui iacebant et subponens capiti suo dormivit in eodem loco*

And when he had come to *a* certain place and wanted to rest in it after sunset, he took one of *the* stones which had fallen, and, putting *it* under his head, he slept in that place.

28:12 *viditque in somnis scalam stantem super terram et cacumen illius tangens caelum angelos* *quoque Dei ascendentes et descendentes per eam*

And he saw in sleep *a* ladder standing on *the* ground, and its top touching *the* sky, God's angels likewise climbing up and down by it.

28:13 *et Dominum innixum scalae dicentem sibi ego sum Dominus Deus Abraham patris tui et Deus Isaac terram in qua dormis tibi dabo et semini tuo*

And *the* Lord *was* leaning on *the* ladder, saying, "I am *the* Lord, Abraham your father's God, and Isaac's God. I will give you and your seed *the* land in which you sleep.

28:14 *eritque germen tuum quasi pulvis terrae dilataberis ad occidentem et orientem septentrionem et meridiem et benedicentur in te et in semine tuo cunctae tribus terrae*

"And your offspring will be like *the* land's dust. I will broaden you to east and west, north and south. And all *the* land's tribes will be blessed in you and in your seed.

28:15 *et ero custos tuus quocumque perrexeris et reducam te in terram hanc nec dimittam nisi conplevero universa quae dixi*

"And I will be your keeper wherever you will go. And I will bring you

back to this land. I will not let you go until I have completed all that I said."

28:16 *cumque evigilasset Iacob de somno ait vere Dominus est in loco isto et ego nesciebam*

And when Jacob woke up from sleep, he said, "Truly *the* Lord is in this place, and I didn't know."

28:17 *pavensque quam terribilis inquit est locus iste non est hic aliud nisi domus Dei et porta caeli*

And fearing, he said, "How terrible is this place! This is none other than God's house and sky's gate!"

28:18 *surgens ergo mane tulit lapidem quem subposuerat capiti suo et erexit in titulum fundens oleum desuper*

Getting up early, then, he took *the* stone which he'd put under his head, and stood it up as *a* memorial, pouring oil over *it*.

28:19 *appellavitque nomen urbis Bethel quae prius Luza vocabatur*

And he called that city's name Bethel, which was called Luza before.

28:20 *vovit etiam votum dicens si fuerit Deus mecum et custodierit me in via per quam ambulo et dederit* *mihi panem ad vescendum et vestem ad induendum*

So he swore *a* vow, saying, "If God will be with me and guard me in *the* way by which I walk, and will give me bread to eat and clothing to wear,

28:21 *reversusque fuero prospere ad domum patris mei erit mihi Dominus in Deum*

"and returning, I come back prosperously to my father's house, *the* Lord will be as God to me,

28:22 *et lapis iste quem erexi in titulum vocabitur Domus Dei cunctorumque quae dederis mihi decimas offeram tibi*

"and this stone which I set up as *a* memorial will be called God's House. And I will offer You tithes of all which You give me.

Jacob Comes to Haran

Genesis 29:1 *profectus ergo Iacob venit ad terram orientalem*

Setting out, then, Jacob came to *the* eastern land.

29:2 *et vidit puteum in agro tresque greges ovium accubantes iuxta eum nam ex illo adaquabantur pecora et os eius grandi lapide claudebatur*

And he saw *a* well in *a* field, and three flocks of sheep lying beside it, for *the* animals drank from it, and its mouth was closed by *a* large stone.

29:3 *morisque erat ut cunctis ovibus congregatis devolverent lapidem et refectis gregibus rursum super os putei ponerent*

And *the* custom was that, with all *the* sheep gathered, they would move *the* stone away and, *the* flocks refreshed, they would put *the* stone over *the* well's mouth again.

29:4 *dixitque ad pastores fratres unde estis qui responderunt de Haran*

And he said to *the* shepherds, "Brothers, where are you from?"

They answered, "From Haran."

29:5 *quos interrogans numquid ait nostis Laban filium Nahor dixerunt novimus*

Questioning them again, he said, "Do you know Laban, Nahor's son?"

They said, "We know *him.*"

29:6 *sanusne est inquit valet inquiunt et ecce Rahel filia eius venit cum grege suo*

"Is he well?" he asked.

"He is well," they said. "And, look, Rachel his daughter is coming with her flock."

29:7 *dixitque Iacob adhuc multum diei superest nec est tempus ut reducantur ad caulas greges date ante potum ovibus et sic ad pastum eas reducite*

And Jacob said, "*There* is still *a* lot of daylight left, and it isn't time that they bring *the* flocks to *the* folds. First give *the* sheep *a* drink, and so take them back to pasture."

29:8 *qui responderunt non possumus donec omnia pecora congregentur et amoveamus lapidem de ore putei ut adaquemus greges*

They answered, "We can't until all *the* animals are gathered, and we move *the* stone away from *the* well's mouth so we can water the flocks.

29:9 *adhuc loquebantur et ecce Rahel veniebat cum ovibus patris sui nam gregem ipsa pascebat*

They were still talking and, look, Rachel came with her father's sheep, for she shepherded *the* flock.

29:10 *quam cum vidisset Iacob et sciret consobrinam suam ovesque Laban avunculi sui amovit lapidem quo puteus claudebatur*

When Jacob saw her and knew his cousin and Laban his uncle's sheep, he moved away *the* stone that closed *the* well.

29:11 *et adaquato grege osculatus est eam elevataque voce flevit*

And, watering *the* flock, he kissed her and, lifting up *his* voice, wept.

29:12 *et indicavit ei quod frater esset patris eius et filius Rebeccae at illa festinans nuntiavit patri suo*

And he told her that he was brother of her father and Rebecca's son. And she, hurrying, told her father,

29:13 *qui cum audisset venisse Iacob filium sororis suae cucurrit obviam conplexusque eum et in oscula ruens duxit in domum suam auditis autem causis itineris*

who, when he had heard that Jacob, his sister's son, had come, ran on *the* way. And hugging him and falling on him in kisses, led him into his house. But hearing *the* journey's reason,

29:14 *respondit os meum es et caro mea et postquam expleti sunt dies mensis unius*

he answered, "You are my mouth and my flesh."

Jacob Agrees to Serve
Laban for Rachel

And after one month's days were completed,

29:15 *dixit ei num quia frater meus es gratis servies mihi dic quid mercedis accipias*

he said to him, "Because you are my brother, will you serve me for free? Tell what pay you will accept!"

29:16 *habebat vero filias duas nomen maioris Lia minor appellabatur Rahel*

Truly, he had two daughters. *The* older's name was Lia. *The* younger was called Rachel.

29:17 *sed Lia lippis erat oculis Rahel decora facie et venusto aspectu*

But Lia was bleary-eyed. Rachel's face *was* beautiful and of lovely appearance.

29:18 *quam diligens Iacob ait serviam tibi pro Rahel filia tua minore septem annis*

Jacob, loving her, said, "I will serve you seven years for Rachel, your younger daughter."

29:19 *respondit Laban melius est ut tibi eam dem quam viro alteri mane apud me*

Laban answered, "It is better that I give her to you than to some other man. Stay with me."

29:20 *servivit igitur Iacob pro Rahel septem annis et videbantur illi pauci dies prae amoris magnitudine*

So Jacob served seven years for Rachel, and they seemed like *a* few days to him because of great love.

29:21 *dixitque ad Laban da mihi uxorem meam quia iam tempus expletum est ut ingrediar ad eam*

And he said to Laban, "Give me my wife because *the* time is already completed, so I can go in to her."

Laban Deceives Jacob

29:22 *qui vocatis multis amicorum turbis ad convivium fecit nuptias*

Laban, calling *a* great crowd of friends to *the* feast, made *a* wedding.

29:23 *et vespere filiam suam Liam introduxit ad eum*

And by night he brought his daughter Lia to him,

29:24 *dans ancillam filiae Zelpham nomine ad quam cum ex more Iacob fuisset ingressus facto mane vidit Liam*

giving her his daughter's female slave named Zelpha. When Jacob had gone into her after *the* custom, morning coming, he saw Lia.

29:25 *et dixit ad socerum quid est quod facere voluisti nonne pro Rahel servivi tibi quare inposuisti mihi*

And he said to his father-in-law, "What is it that you wanted to do? Haven't I served you for Rachel? Why have you imposed on me?"

29:26 *respondit Laban non est in loco nostro consuetudinis ut minores ante tradamus ad nuptias*

Laban answered, "It isn't our custom in this place that we give *the* younger to marriage first.

29:27 *imple ebdomadem dierum huius copulae et hanc quoque dabo tibi pro opere quo serviturus es mihi septem annis aliis*

"Complete *a* week of days for this marriage, and I will give you her likewise, for *the* work that you will serve me seven more years.

29:28 *adquievit placito et ebdomade transacta Rahel duxit uxorem*

He agreed peacefully and, *the* week passed, he took Rachel *as* wife,

29:29 *cui pater servam Balam dederat*

to whom *her* father gave her slave Balah.

29:30 *tandemque potitus optatis nuptiis amorem sequentis priori praetulit serviens apud eum septem annis aliis*

And, at length acquiring *the* marriage, he preferred *the* latter love to *the* former, serving with him another seven years.

Lia Births Children
29:31 *videns autem Dominus quod despiceret Liam aperuit vulvam eius sorore sterili permanente*

But *the* Lord, seeing that he despised Lia, opened her vulva, her sister remaining sterile.

29:32 *quae conceptum genuit filium vocavitque nomen eius Ruben dicens vidit Dominus humilitatem meam nunc amabit me vir meus*

She, conceiving, birthed *a* son and called his name Reuben, saying, "*The* Lord saw my humiliation. Now my husband will love me."

29:33 *rursumque concepit et peperit filium et ait quoniam audivit*

Dominus haberi me contemptui dedit etiam istum mihi vocavitque nomen illius Symeon

And she conceived again and birthed *a* son. And she said, "Because *the* Lord heard that he had me in contempt, He gave me even this *one*."

And she called his name Simeon.

29:34 *concepit tertio et genuit alium dixitque nunc quoque copulabitur mihi maritus meus eo quod pepererim illi tres filios et idcirco appellavit nomen eius Levi*

She conceived *a* third time and birthed another *son*. And she said, "Now my husband will have sex with me, because I have born him three sons."

And therefore she called his name Levi.

29:35 *quarto concepit et peperit filium et ait modo confitebor Domino et ob hoc vocavit eum Iudam cessavitque parere*

She conceived *a* fourth time and birthed *a* son. And she said, "I will confess to *the* Lord in this manner."

And from this, she called him Judah. And she ceased to bear *children*.

Rachel Gives Jacob
Her Slave Balah

Genesis 30:1 *cernens autem Rahel quod infecunda esset invidit sorori et ait marito suo da mihi liberos alioquin moriar*

But Rachel, perceiving that she was infertile, envied her sister and said to her husband, "Give me children or else I will die!"

30:2 *cui iratus respondit Iacob num pro Deo ego sum qui privavit te fructu ventris tui*

Jacob, angry, answered her, "Am I in God's place, who has deprived you of your womb's fruit?"

30:3 *at illa habeo inquit famulam Balam ingredere ad eam ut pariat super genua mea et habeam ex ea filios*

And she said, "I have *a* slave named Balah. Go into her, so she can give birth on my knee! And I will have sons from her."

30:4 *deditque illi Balam in coniugium quae*

And she gave him Balah in marriage, who

30:5 *ingresso ad se viro concepit et peperit filium*

the man going into her, conceived

and birthed *a* son.

30:6 *dixitque Rahel iudicavit mihi Dominus et exaudivit vocem meam dans mihi filium et idcirco appellavit nomen illius Dan*

And Rachel said, "*The* Lord has judged me and heard my voice, giving me *a* son."

And therefore, she called his name Dan.

30:7 *rursumque Bala concipiens peperit alterum*

And Balah, again conceiving, birthed another,

30:8 *pro quo ait Rahel conparavit me Deus cum sorore mea et invalui vocavitque eum Nepthalim*

for whom Rachel said, "God compared me with my sister, and I was stronger."

And she called his name Napthali.

Lia Gives Jacob
Her Slave Zelpha
30:9 *sentiens Lia quod parere desisset Zelpham ancillam suam marito tradidit*

Lia, sensing that she had stopped bearing children, handed her female slave Zelpha over to *the* husband,

30:10 *qua post conceptum edente filium*

who, after conceiving *a* son, *while* eating,

30:11 *dixit feliciter et idcirco vocavit nomen eius Gad*

said, "Happily!"

And therefore, she called his name Gad.

30:12 *peperit quoque Zelpha alterum*

Zelpha likewise birthed another.

30:13 *dixitque Lia hoc pro beatitudine mea beatam quippe me dicent mulieres propterea appellavit eum Aser*

And Lia said, "This *one is* for my blessing. Women of course will call me blessed."

Because of this, she called his name Asher.

30:14 *egressus autem Ruben tempore messis triticeae in agro repperit mandragoras quos matri Liae detulit dixitque Rahel da mihi partem de mandragoris filii tui*

But Reuben, going out into *the* field at wheat harvest time, found mandrakes which he took to his mother Lia. And Rachel said, "Give me part of your son's mandrakes!"

30:15 *illa respondit parumne tibi videtur quod praeripueris maritum mihi nisi etiam mandragoras filii mei tuleris ait Rahel dormiat tecum hac nocte pro mandragoris filii tui*

She answered, "Does it seem small to you that you snatched my husband away from me? Do you even have to take away my son's mandrakes?"

Rachel said, "He can sleep with you tonight for your son's mandrakes."

30:16 *redeuntique ad vesperam de agro Iacob egressa est in occursum Lia et ad me inquit intrabis quia mercede conduxi te pro mandragoris filii mei dormivit cum ea nocte illa*

And Lia went out to meet Jacob, returning from *the* field at evening. And she said, "You will come in to me because I hired you at price, for my son's mandrakes."

And he slept with her that night.

30:17 *et exaudivit Deus preces eius concepitque et peperit filium quintum*

And God heard her prayers, and she conceived and birthed *a* fifth son.

30:18 *et ait dedit Deus mercedem mihi quia dedi ancillam meam viro*

meo appellavitque nomen illius Isachar

And she said, "God gave me pay, because I gave my slave woman to my husband."

And she called his name Issachar.

30:19 *rursum Lia concipiens peperit sextum filium*

Lia, conceiving again, birthed *a* sixth son.

30:20 *et ait ditavit me Deus dote bona etiam hac vice mecum erit maritus meus eo quod genuerim ei sex filios et idcirco appellavit nomen eius Zabulon*

And she said, "God enriched me with *a* good dowry. By this exchange, my husband will be with me also, because I have birthed him six sons."

And therefore she called his name Zebulon.

30:21 *post quem peperit filiam nomine Dinam*

After him, she birthed *a* daughter named Dinah.

30:22 *recordatus quoque Dominus Rahelis exaudivit eam et aperuit vulvam illius*

The Lord, likewise remembering

Rachel, heard her and opened her vulva.

30:23 *quae concepit et peperit filium dicens abstulit Deus obprobrium meum*

She conceived and birthed *a* son, saying, "God has taken away my reproach."

30:24 *et vocavit nomen illius Ioseph dicens addat mihi Dominus filium alterum*

And she called his name Joseph, saying, "May *the* Lord add to me another son!"

Jacob Wants to Go Home
30:25 *nato autem Ioseph dixit Iacob socero suo dimitte me ut revertar in patriam et ad terram meam*

But Joseph being born, Jacob said to his father-in-law, "Let me go, so I can go back to my country and to my land."

30:26 *da mihi uxores et liberos meos pro quibus servivi tibi ut abeam tu nosti servitutem qua servivi tibi*

"Give me my wives and children, for whom I have served you, so I can go. You know *the* service which I have served you."

30:27 *ait ei Laban inveniam gratiam in conspectu tuo experimento didici quod benedixerit mihi Deus propter te*

Laban said to him, "May I find grace in your sight! I know by experience that God has blessed me because of you.

30:28 *constitue mercedem tuam quam dem tibi*

"Name your price which I may give you!"

30:29 *at ille respondit tu nosti quomodo servierim tibi et quanta in manibus meis fuerit possessio tua*

And he answered, "You know how I have served you, and how great your possession has been in my hands.

30:30 *modicum habuisti antequam venirem et nunc dives effectus es benedixitque tibi Dominus ad introitum meum iustum est igitur ut aliquando provideam etiam domui meae*

"You had little before I came, and now you have become rich. And *the* Lord blessed you at my coming. *It* is fair, therefore, that I provide something even for my house."

30:31 *dixitque Laban quid dabo tibi at ille ait nihil volo sed si feceris quod postulo iterum pascam et custodiam pecora tua*

And Laban said, "What will I give you?"

And he said, "I want nothing. But if you will do what I ask, I will shepherd and keep your animals again.

30:32 *gyra omnes greges tuos et separa cunctas oves varias et sparso vellere et quodcumque furvum et maculosum variumque fuerit tam in ovibus quam in capris erit merces mea*

"Go through all your flocks and separate all *the* sheep with varied and spotted fleece. And whatever is dark and spotted and varied, whether in sheep or in goats, will be my pay."

30:33 *respondebitque mihi cras iustitia mea quando placiti tempus advenerit coram te et omnia quae non fuerint varia et maculosa et furva tam in ovibus quam in capris furti me arguent*

"And my fairness will answer me tomorrow, when *the* pleasing time will come before you. And all that are not varied and spotted and dark, whether in sheep or in goats, will prove me *a* thief.

30:34 *dixit Laban gratum habeo quod petis*

Laban said, "I have pleasure *at* what you ask."

30:35 *et separavit in die illo capras et oves hircos et arietes varios atque maculosos cunctum autem gregem unicolorem id est albi et nigri velleris tradidit in manu filiorum suorum*

And he separated on that day nanny goats and sheep, he-goats and rams, varied and spotted. But all *the* same-colored flock, that is white and black fleeced, he gave into his sons' hands.

30:36 *et posuit spatium itineris inter se et generum dierum trium qui pascebat reliquos greges eius*

And he put *a* three day's journey's space between him and *his* son-in-law, who shepherded *the* rest of his flocks.

Jacob Practices Selective Breeding

30:37 *tollens ergo Iacob virgas populeas virides et amigdalinas et ex platanis ex parte decorticavit eas detractisque corticibus in his quae spoliata fuerant candor apparuit illa vero quae integra erant viridia permanserunt atque in hunc modum color effectus est varius*

Jacob therefore, taking green branches from poplars and almond trees and plane-trees, he cut them apart and *was* stripping off *the* barks. In those which where stripped, whiteness appeared. Those indeed which were whole, *the* green remained. And in this way, *the* color became varied.

30:38 *posuitque eas in canalibus ubi effundebatur aqua ut cum venissent greges ad bibendum ante oculos haberent virgas et in aspectu earum conciperent*

And he put them in *the* channels where *the* water was poured out, so when *the* flocks came to drink *the* staffs were before their eyes, and they conceived in their sight.

30:39 *factumque est ut in ipso calore coitus oves intuerentur virgas et parerent maculosa et varia et diverso colore respersa*

And it happened that *the* sheep mating in that heat saw *the* staffs and birthed spotted and varied and sprinkled, in diverse color.

30:40 *divisitque gregem Iacob et posuit virgas ante oculos arietum erant autem alba quaeque et nigra Laban cetera vero Iacob separatis inter se gregibus*

And Jacob divided *the* flock, and placed *the* staffs before *the* rams' eyes. But *the* white and black alike were Laban's. *The* others, truly, *were* Jacob's, *when the* flocks were separated between them.

30:41 *igitur quando primo tempore ascendebantur oves ponebat Iacob*

virgas in canalibus aquarum ante oculos arietum et ovium ut in earum contemplatione conciperent

Therefore, when at *the* first season *the* sheep went up, Jacob put staffs in *the* water channels before *the* rams' and ewes' eyes, so they could mate in their sight.

30:42 *quando vero serotina admissura erat et conceptus extremus non ponebat eas factaque sunt ea quae erant serotina Laban et quae primi temporis Iacob*

And when *the* later season came and *the* last heat, he did not place them. And it happened that those conceived later were Laban's, and those at *the* first time Jacob's.

30:43 *ditatusque est homo ultra modum et habuit greges multos ancillas et servos camelos et asinos*

And *the* man became rich beyond measure, and had many flocks, and female and male slaves, camels, and donkeys.

Jacob Is Alarmed
by Laban's Hostility

Genesis 31:1 *postquam autem audivit verba filiorum Laban dicentium tulit Iacob omnia quae fuerunt patris nostri et de illius facultate ditatus factus est inclitus*

But after he heard Laban's sons' words, saying, "Jacob took all that was our father's, and from this skill *his* wealth has become glorious,"

31:2 *animadvertit quoque faciem Laban quod non esset erga se sicut heri et nudius tertius*

he noticed also that Laban's face was not agreeable to him like yesterday and *the* day before.

31:3 *maxime dicente sibi Domino revertere in terram patrum tuorum et ad generationem tuam eroque tecum*

The Lord saying strongly to him, "Go back to your fathers' land, and to your generation, and I will be with you,"

31:4 *misit et vocavit Rahel et Liam in agrum ubi pascebat greges*

he sent, and called Rachel and Lia into *the* field where he was pastoring flocks.

31:5 *dixitque eis video faciem patris vestri quod non sit erga me sicut heri et nudius tertius Deus autem patris*

mei fuit mecum

And he said to them, "I see your father's face, that it is not agreeable toward me like yesterday and *the* day before. But my father's God was with me,

31:6 *et ipsae nostis quod totis viribus meis servierim patri vestro*

"and you know that I have served your father with all my strength.

31:7 *sed pater vester circumvenit me et mutavit mercedem meam decem vicibus et tamen non dimisit eum Deus ut noceret mihi*

"But your father went around me and changed my pay ten times. And yet God did not let him go so he could harm me.

31:8 *si quando dixit variae erunt mercedes tuae pariebant omnes oves varios fetus quando vero e contrario ait alba quaeque accipies pro mercede omnes greges alba pepererunt*

"If when he said *the* various colored *ones* will be your pay, all *the* sheep birthed varied-colored lambs indeed. But when on *the* contrary he said, "Likewise you will receive *the* white ones for pay," all *the* flocks birthed white.

31:9 *tulitque Deus substantiam*

patris vestri et dedit mihi

"And God took your father's wealth and gave it to me.

31:10 *postquam enim conceptus ovium tempus advenerat levavi oculos meos et vidi in somnis ascendentes mares super feminas varios et maculosos et diversorum colorum*

"For after *the* time came for *the* sheep to mate, I lifted up my eyes and saw in dreams varied and spotted and different-colored males mounting on females.

31:11 *dixitque angelus Dei ad me in somnis Iacob et ego respondi adsum*

And God's angel said to me in dreams, "Jacob."

And I answered, "I am here."

31:12 *qui ait leva oculos tuos et vide universos masculos ascendentes super feminas varios respersos atque maculosos vidi enim omnia quae fecit tibi Laban*

He said, "Lift up your eyes and see all *the* males mounting on *the* females *are* various-colored and spotted. For I have seen all that Laban did to you.

31:13 *ego sum Deus Bethel ubi unxisti lapidem et votum vovisti mihi nunc ergo surge et egredere de terra*

hac revertens in terram nativitatis tuae

"I am Bethel's God, where you anointed *the* stone and promised Me *a* vow. Now, then, get up and go out from this land, returning to your native land!"

31:14 *responderunt Rahel et Lia numquid habemus residui quicquam in facultatibus et hereditate domus patris nostri*

Rachel and Lia answered, "We don't have anything left in *the* skills and inheritance of our father's house, do we?

31:15 *nonne quasi alienas reputavit nos et vendidit comeditque pretium nostrum*

"Hasn't he considered us like strangers, and sold and eaten our price?

31:16 *sed Deus tulit opes patris nostri et nobis eas tradidit ac filiis nostris unde omnia quae praecepit fac*

"But God took our father's riches and handed them to us and our children. From which, all that He has commanded, do!"

**Jacob and Family
Leave Mesopotamia**
31:17 *surrexit itaque Iacob et*

inpositis liberis et coniugibus suis super camelos abiit

So Jacob got up and, putting his children and wives on camels, went away.

31:18 *tulitque omnem substantiam et greges et quicquid in Mesopotamiam quaesierat pergens ad Isaac patrem suum in terram Chanaan*

And he took all *the* wealth and flocks and whatever he had sought in Mesopotamia, going to Isaac his father in Canaan's land.

31:19 *eo tempore Laban ierat ad tondendas oves et Rahel furata est idola patris sui*

At that time Laban had gone to shear sheep, and Rachel stole her father's idols.

31:20 *noluitque Iacob confiteri socero quod fugeret*

And Jacob didn't want to tell *the* father-in-law that he was fleeing.

Laban Pursues Jacob

31:21 *cumque abisset tam ipse quam omnia quae iuris eius erant et amne transmisso pergeret contra montem Galaad*

And when he had gone, he and all that was his right, and, *the* river crossed, was going beside Mount Galaad,

31:22 *nuntiatum est Laban die tertio quod fugeret Iacob*

Laban was told *the* third day that Jacob had fled.

31:23 *qui adsumptis fratribus suis persecutus est eum diebus septem et conprehendit in monte Galaad*

Laban, taking his brothers, followed him seven days and caught up *to him* on Mount Galaad.

31:24 *viditque in somnis dicentem sibi Dominum cave ne quicquam aspere loquaris contra Iacob*

And he saw in dreams *the* Lord saying to him, "Take care that you not say anything harshly against Jacob!"

31:25 *iamque Iacob extenderat in monte tabernaculum cum ille consecutus eum cum fratribus suis in eodem monte Galaad fixit tentorium*

And Jacob already had pitched tent on *the* mountain when he, following him with his brothers, fixed tents on *the* same Mount Galaad.

Laban and Jacob Confront One Another

31:26 *et dixit ad Iacob quare ita egisti ut clam me abigeres filias*

meas quasi captivas gladio

And he said to Jacob, "Why have you done so, that unknown to me, you've stolen my daughters like *the* sword's captives?

31:27 *cur ignorante me fugere voluisti nec indicare mihi ut prosequerer te cum gaudio et canticis et tympanis et cithara*

"Why did you want to flee, me not knowing, nor tell me, so I might have sent you off with joy and songs and tympanies and guitars?

31:28 *non es passus ut oscularer filios meos ac filias stulte operatus es et nunc*

"You haven't allowed that I kiss my sons and daughters. You've worked foolishly, and now

31:29 *valet quidem manus mea reddere tibi malum sed Deus patris vestri heri dixit mihi cave ne loquaris cum Iacob quicquam durius*

"my hand is strong enough at least to repay harm to you. But your father's God said to me yesterday, 'Take care that you not say anything stern with Jacob!'"

31:30 *esto ad tuos ire cupiebas et desiderio tibi erat domus patris tui cur furatus es deos meos*

"You wanted to go, to be with yours, and your father's house was desire to you. Why have you stolen my gods?"

31:31 *respondit Iacob quod inscio te profectus sum timui ne violenter auferres filias tuas*

Jacob responded, "That I set out without you knowing *was* because I was afraid you would take your daughters away violently.

31:32 *quod autem furti arguis apud quemcumque inveneris deos tuos necetur coram fratribus nostris scrutare quicquid tuorum apud me inveneris et aufer haec dicens ignorabat quod Rahel furata esset idola*

"But that you charge theft, let anyone with whom you find your gods be killed before our brothers. Look for anything of yours! If you find it with me, take it!"

Saying this, he did not know that Rachel had stolen *the* idols.

31:33 *ingressus itaque Laban tabernaculum Iacob et Liae et utriusque famulae non invenit cumque intrasset tentorium Rahelis*

So Laban, going into *the* tents of Jacob and Lia and both handmaids, did not find *them*. And when he came into Rachel's tent,

31:34 *illa festinans abscondit idola subter stramen cameli et sedit desuper scrutantique omne tentorium et nihil invenienti*

she quickly hid *the* idols under *the* camel's saddle and sat on *them*, and *her father* searching *the* whole tent and finding nothing.

31:35 *ait ne irascatur dominus meus quod coram te adsurgere nequeo quia iuxta consuetudinem feminarum nunc accidit mihi sic delusa sollicitudo quaerentis est*

She said, "Don't let my lord be mad that I cannot get up before you, because now it falls on me according to *the* manner of women."

So deceived, he searched anxiously.

Jacob Rebukes Laban
31:36 *tumensque Iacob cum iurgio ait quam ob culpam meam et ob quod peccatum sic exarsisti post me*

And Jacob, swelling with anger, said, "For what fault of mine and for what sin have you have you blazed up after me so,

31:37 *et scrutatus es omnem supellectilem meam quid invenisti de cuncta substantia domus tuae pone hic coram fratribus meis et fratribus tuis et iudicent inter me et te*

"and searched all my house

furnishings? What did you find from all your house's wealth? Put it here before my brothers and your brothers, and let them judge between me and you!

31:38 *idcirco viginti annis fui tecum oves tuae et caprae steriles non fuerunt arietes gregis tui non comedi*

"So twenty years I was with you! Your sheep and goats weren't sterile. I didn't eat your flock's rams.

31:39 *nec captum a bestia ostendi tibi ego damnum omne reddebam quicquid furto perierat a me exigebas*

"Nor did I show you ones torn by animals. I repaid every loss. Whatever was taken by theft, you required from me.

31:40 *die noctuque aestu urebar et gelu fugiebat somnus ab oculis meis*

"Day and night I burned with heat and cold. Sleep fled from my eyes.

31:41 *sic per viginti annos in domo tua servivi tibi quattuordecim pro filiabus et sex pro gregibus tuis inmutasti quoque mercedem meam decem vicibus*

"So I slaved for you for twenty years in your house – fourteen for daughters and six for your flocks! You likewise changed my pay ten times!

31:42 *nisi Deus patris mei Abraham et Timor Isaac adfuisset mihi forsitan modo nudum me dimisisses adflictionem meam et laborem manuum mearum respexit Deus et arguit te heri*

"If Abraham my father's God and Isaac's Fear had not been with me, perhaps recently you would have sent me away naked! God has seen my affliction and my hand's labors, and accused you yesterday!"

Laban and Jacob
Make an Uneasy Peace

31:43 *respondit ei Laban filiae et filii et greges tui et omnia quae cernis mea sunt quid possum facere filiis et nepotibus meis*

Laban answered him, "Your daughters and sons and flocks and all that you see are mine! What can I do to my children and grandchildren?

31:44 *veni ergo et ineamus foedus ut sit testimonium inter me et te*

"Come therefore, and let's make an agreement, so it can be testimony between me and you!

31:45 *tulit itaque Iacob lapidem et erexit illum in titulum*

So Jacob took *a* stone and set it up as *a* memorial.

31:46 *dixitque fratribus suis adferte lapides qui congregantes fecerunt tumulum comederuntque super eum*

And he said to his brothers, "Bring stones," who, gathering *them*, made *a* heap. And they ate on it,

31:47 *quem vocavit Laban tumulus Testis et Iacob acervum Testimonii uterque iuxta proprietatem linguae suae*

which Laban called *the* mound of Witness, and Jacob *the* heap of Testimony, each according to his tongue's character.

31:48 *dixitque Laban tumulus iste testis erit inter me et te hodie et idcirco appellatum est nomen eius Galaad id est tumulus Testis*

And Laban said, "This mound will be witness between me and you today."

And therefore its name is called Galaad, that is, "Mound of Witness."

31:49 *intueatur Dominus et iudicet inter nos quando recesserimus a nobis*

"May *the* Lord consider and judge between us when we have gone away from each other!

31:50 *si adflixeris filias meas et si introduxeris uxores alias super eas nullus sermonis nostri testis est* *absque Deo qui praesens respicit*

"If you afflict my daughters and if you bring in other wives above them, no one is witness to our words apart from God, who present, looks on."

31:51 *dixitque rursus ad Iacob en tumulus hic et lapis quem erexi inter me et te*

And he said to Jacob again, "Look, this mound and stone which I erected between me and you –

31:52 *testis erit tumulus inquam iste et lapis sint in testimonio si aut ego transiero illum pergens ad te aut tu praeterieris malum mihi cogitans*

"this mound will be witness, I say, and this stone may be as testimony, if either I pass it going to you or you pass it, plotting harm to me.

31:53 *Deus Abraham et Deus Nahor iudicet inter nos Deus patris eorum iuravit Iacob per Timorem patris sui Isaac*

"Abraham's God and Nahor's God judge between us, their father's God!"

Jacob swore by his father Isaac's Fear.

31:54 *immolatisque victimis in monte vocavit fratres suos ut ederent panem qui cum comedissent*

manserunt ibi

And burning offerings on *the* mountain, he called his brothers so they could eat bread, who, when they had eaten, stayed there.

31:55 *Laban vero de nocte consurgens osculatus est filios et filias suas et benedixit illis reversus in locum suum*

But Laban, getting up by night, kissed his sons and daughters. And he blessed them, going back to his place.

Jacob Sends
Messengers to Esau

Genesis 32:1 *Iacob quoque abiit itinere quo coeperat fueruntque ei obviam angeli Dei*

Jacob likewise went on by *the* way which he had begun. And God's angels came to meet him,

32:2 *quos cum vidisset ait castra Dei sunt haec et appellavit nomen loci illius Manaim id est Castra*

who, when he saw them, said, "These are God's camps."

And he called that place's name Manaim (that is, Camps).

32:3 *misit autem et nuntios ante se ad Esau fratrem suum in terram Seir regionis Edom*

But he sent messengers before him to his brother Esau in Seir's land, Edom's region.

32:4 *praecepitque eis dicens sic loquimini domino meo Esau haec dicit frater tuus Iacob apud Laban peregrinatus sum et fui usque in praesentem diem*

And he commanded them, saying, "Speak so to my lord Esau. 'Your brother Jacob says this: I stayed with Laban and was *there* even to *the* present day.

32:5 *habeo boves et asinos oves et servos atque ancillas mittoque nunc legationem ad dominum meum ut inveniam gratiam in conspectu tuo*

"'I have oxen and donkeys, sheep and slaves and slave women. Now I am sending *a* mission to my lord, so I can find grace in your sight.'"

32:6 *reversi sunt nuntii ad Iacob dicentes venimus ad Esau fratrem tuum et ecce properat in occursum tibi cum quadringentis viris*

The messengers came back to Jacob, saying, "We came to your brother Esau, and, look! He is hurrying to meet you with four hundred men."

32:7 *timuit Iacob valde et perterritus divisit populum qui secum erat greges quoque et oves et boves et camelos in duas turmas*

Jacob feared greatly and, terrified, divided *the* people with him into two companies, (there were flocks as well, and sheep and oxen and camels)

32:8 *dicens si venerit Esau ad unam turmam et percusserit eam alia turma quae reliqua est salvabitur*

saying, "If Esau comes to one company and strikes it, *the* other company which is left will be safe."

32:9 *dixitque Iacob Deus patris mei Abraham et Deus patris mei Isaac*

Domine qui dixisti mihi revertere in terram tuam et in locum nativitatis tuae et benefaciam tibi

And Jacob said, "Lord, God of my father Abraham and God of my father Isaac, who said to me, 'Go back into your land and to your birthplace and I will do well for you,'

32:10 *minor sum cunctis miserationibus et veritate quam explesti servo tuo in baculo meo transivi Iordanem istum et nunc cum duabus turmis regredior*

"I am not worthy of all *the* mercies and truth which you filled out to your slave. I crossed this Jordan with my staff, and now I come back with two companies.

32:11 *erue me de manu fratris mei de manu Esau quia valde eum timeo ne forte veniens percutiat matrem cum filiis*

"Rescue me from my brother's hand, from Esau's hand, because I fear him greatly, unless coming, he strike down mother with children!

32:12 *tu locutus es quod bene mihi faceres et dilatares semen meum sicut harenam maris quae prae multitudine numerari non potest*

"You said that You would do well with me and broaden my seed like the sea's sand, which can't be counted for multitude."

32:13 *cumque dormisset ibi nocte illa separavit de his quae habebat munera Esau fratri suo*

And when he had slept there that night, he separated from what he had *a* gift for his brother Esau:

32:14 *capras ducentas hircos viginti oves ducentas arietes viginti*

two hundred nanny goats, twenty male goats, two hundred sheep, twenty rams,

32:15 *camelos fetas cum pullis suis triginta vaccas quadraginta et tauros viginti asinas viginti et pullos earum decem*

thirty breeding camels with their foals, forty cows and twenty bulls, twenty donkeys and ten of their colts.

32:16 *et misit per manus servorum suorum singulos seorsum greges dixitque pueris suis antecedite me et sit spatium inter gregem et gregem*

And he sent them by his slaves' hands, each flock separately. And he said to his servants, "Go before me, and let there be space between flock and flock."

32:17 *et praecepit priori dicens si obvium habueris Esau fratrem meum et interrogaverit te cuius es et quo* *vadis et cuius sunt ista quae sequeris*

And he commanded them before, saying, "If you meet Esau my brother on *the* road, and he questions you, 'Whose are you, and where are you going, and whose are these that you are following?'

32:18 *respondebis servi tui Iacob munera misit domino meo Esau ipse quoque post nos venit*

"You will answer, '*They are* your slave Jacob's. He sent gifts to my lord Esau. He likewise is coming after us.'"

32:19 *similiter mandata dedit secundo ac tertio et cunctis qui sequebantur greges dicens hisdem verbis loquimini ad Esau cum inveneritis eum*

He gave *the* same command to *the* second and third and to all who followed *the* flocks, saying, "Speak these same words to Esau when you find him!"

32:20 *et addetis ipse quoque servus tuus Iacob iter nostrum insequitur dixit enim placabo illum muneribus quae praecedunt et postea videbo forsitan propitiabitur mihi*

"And you will add, 'Your slave Jacob himself is following our way, for he said, I will please him with *the* gifts which go before, and afterwards I

will see if perhaps he will be favorable to me.'"

Jacob Wrestles
with the Angel

32:21 *praecesserunt itaque munera ante eum ipse vero mansit nocte illa in Castris*

So *the* gifts went before him. He, indeed, stayed that night in Camps.

32:22 *cumque mature surrexisset tulit duas uxores suas et totidem famulas cum undecim filiis et transivit vadum Iaboc*

And when he had gotten up early, he took his two wives and both handmaids with *the* eleven sons, and crossed *the* Jabbok ford.

32:23 *transductisque omnibus quae ad se pertinebant*

And taking all that pertained to him across,

32:24 *remansit solus et ecce vir luctabatur cum eo usque mane*

he stayed behind alone. And look, *a* Man wrestled with him until morning,

32:25 *qui cum videret quod eum superare non posset tetigit nervum femoris eius et statim emarcuit*

who, when He saw that He couldn't overcome him, touched his thigh's nerve and it immediately withered.

32:26 *dixitque ad eum dimitte me iam enim ascendit aurora respondit non dimittam te nisi benedixeris mihi*

And He said to him, "Let Me go, for dawn is already rising!"

He answered, "I will not let You go unless You bless me!"

32:27 *ait ergo quod nomen est tibi respondit Iacob*

He said therefore, "What is your name?

And he answered, "Jacob."

32:28 *at ille nequaquam inquit Iacob appellabitur nomen tuum sed Israhel quoniam si contra Deum fortis fuisti quanto magis contra homines praevalebis*

And He said, "Your name won't be called Jacob any longer, but Israel, because if you were mighty against God, how much more will you prevail against men!"

32:29 *interrogavit eum Iacob dic mihi quo appellaris nomine respondit cur quaeris nomen meum et benedixit ei in eodem loco*

And Jacob demanded of him, "Tell me by what name You are called?"

He answered, "Why do you ask My name?"

And He blessed him in that same place.

32:30 *vocavitque Iacob nomen loci illius Phanuhel dicens vidi Deum facie ad faciem et salva facta est anima mea*

And Jacob called that place's name Phanuel, saying, "I saw God face-to-face, and my soul was made secure."

32:31 *ortusque est ei statim sol postquam transgressus est Phanuhel ipse vero claudicabat pede*

And *the* sun rose immediately on him after he crossed over from Phanuel. He, truly, was lame in foot.

32:32 *quam ob causam non comedunt filii Israhel nervum qui emarcuit in femore Iacob usque in praesentem diem eo quod tetigerit nervum femoris eius et obstipuerit*

For this reason, Jacob's children will not eat *the* nerve which withered in Jacob's thigh even to *the* present day, because He touched his thigh nerve and stunned *it*.

Esau Meets Jacob

Genesis 33:1 *levans autem Iacob oculos suos vidit venientem Esau et cum eo quadringentos viros divisitque filios Liae et Rahel ambarumque famularum*

But Jacob, lifting up his eyes, saw Esau coming and with him four hundred men. And he divided *the* children of Lia and of Rachel and of both handmaids.

33:2 *et posuit utramque ancillam et liberos earum in principio Liam vero et filios eius in secundo loco Rahel autem et Ioseph novissimos*

And he put both female slaves and their children at *the* first, Lia indeed and her children in second place, but Rachel and Joseph at *the* end.

33:3 *et ipse praegrediens adoravit pronus in terram septies donec adpropinquaret frater eius*

And he, going before, paid homage face-down on *the* ground seven times until his brother came near.

33:4 *currens itaque Esau obviam fratri suo amplexatus est eum stringensque collum et osculans flevit*

So Esau, running to meet his brother, embraced him and, holding *his* neck close and kissing, wept.

33:5 *levatisque oculis vidit mulieres et parvulos earum et ait quid sibi volunt isti et si ad te pertinent respondit parvuli sunt quos donavit mihi Deus servo tuo*

And lifting his eyes, he saw *the* women and their little ones and said, "What do these want in themselves, and do they belong to you?"

And he answered, "*The* little ones are *the* ones God has given me, to your slave."

33:6 *et adpropinquantes ancillae et filii earum incurvati sunt*

And, *the* slave women and their sons coming near, they bowed down.

33:7 *accessitque Lia cum liberis suis et cum similiter adorassent extremi Ioseph et Rahel adoraverunt*

And Lia came close with her children, and when she likewise had paid homage, at *the* end Joseph and Rachel paid homage.

33:8 *quaenam sunt inquit istae turmae quas obvias habui respondit ut invenirem gratiam coram domino meo*

"What are," he said, "these companies which I had on *the* way?"

He answered, "So I might find grace before my lord."

33:9 *et ille habeo ait plurima frater mi sint tua tibi*

And he said, "I have many, my brother. Let yours be to you."

33:10 *dixit Iacob noli ita obsecro sed si inveni gratiam in oculis tuis accipe munusculum de manibus meis sic enim vidi faciem tuam quasi viderim vultum Dei esto mihi propitius*

And Jacob said, "Not so, I pray. But if I have found grace in your eyes, accept *a* small gift from my hands. For so I have seen your face, as if I had seen God's face. Be well-disposed to me,

33:11 *et suscipe benedictionem quam adtuli tibi et quam donavit mihi Deus tribuens omnia vix fratre conpellente suscipiens*

"and accept *the* blessing which I have brought to you, and that God has given me, *who is* giving all things!"

Receiving it reluctantly, compelled by his brother,

33:12 *ait gradiamur simul eroque socius itineris tui*

Esau said, "Let us go together, and I will be *a* companion on your way."

33:13 *dixit Iacob nosti domine mi quod parvulos habeam teneros et*

oves ac boves fetas mecum quas si plus in ambulando fecero laborare morientur una die cuncti greges

Jacob said, "You know, my lord, that I have young little ones and sheep and oxen with calves with me, which, if I make them work more in walking, all *the* flocks will die in one day.

33:14 *praecedat dominus meus ante servum suum et ego sequar paulatim vestigia eius sicut videro posse parvulos meos donec veniam ad dominum meum in Seir*

"Let my lord go before his slave, and I will follow your footsteps slowly, as I see my little ones are able, until I come to my lord in Seir."

33:15 *respondit Esau oro te ut de populo qui mecum est saltem socii remaneant viae tuae non est inquit necesse hoc uno indigeo ut inveniam gratiam in conspectu domini mei*

Esau answered, "I pray you that at least companions from *the* people with me may stay behind on your way."

He said, "It isn't necessary. This one thing I lack: that I may find grace in my lord's sight."

33:16 *reversus est itaque illo die Esau itinere quo venerat in Seir*

So Esau went back that day to Seir on *the* road by which he had come.

Jacob Goes to Soccoth

33:17 *et Iacob venit in Soccoth ubi aedificata domo et fixis tentoriis appellavit nomen loci illius Soccoth id est Tabernacula*

And Jacob came to Soccoth, where, building *a* house and pitching tents, he called that place's name Soccoth (that is, Tents).

33:18 *transivitque in Salem urbem Sycimorum quae est in terra Chanaan postquam regressus est de Mesopotamiam Syriae et habitavit iuxta oppidum*

And he crossed into Salem, *a* city of *the* Shechemites, which is in Canaan's land, after he came back from Syrian Mesopotamia. And he lived alongside *the* town.

33:19 *emitque partem agri in qua fixerat tabernaculum a filiis Emor patris Sychem centum agnis*

And he bought part of *the* field in which he fixed his tent from Emor's sons, Shechem's father, for one hundred lambs.

33:20 *et erecto ibi altari invocavit super illud Fortissimum Deum Israhel*

And building *an* altar there, he invoked over it Israel's Most Mighty God.

Shechem Rapes Dinah

Genesis 34:1 *egressa est autem Dina filia Liae ut videret mulieres regionis illius*

But Dinah, Lia's daughter, went out so she could see that region's women.

34:2 *quam cum vidisset Sychem filius Emor Evei princeps terrae illius adamavit et rapuit et dormivit cum illa vi opprimens virginem*

When Shechem, son of Emor *the* Hevite, that land's prince, saw her, he lusted and took *her* and slept with her, overcoming *the* young woman by force.

34:3 *et conglutinata est anima eius cum ea tristemque blanditiis delinivit*

And his soul stuck to her, and, since she *was* sad, he soothed *her* with smooth words.

34:4 *et pergens ad Emor patrem suum accipe mihi inquit puellam hanc coniugem*

And going to Emor his father, he said, "Get this girl *as* wife for me!"

34:5 *quod cum audisset Iacob absentibus filiis et in pastu occupatis pecorum siluit donec redirent*

When Jacob had heard this, his sons absent and occupied with *the* animals in pasture, he was silent until they came back.

34:6 *egresso autem Emor patre Sychem ut loqueretur ad Iacob*

But *when* Emor, Shechem's father, *had* come out so he could speak to Jacob,

34:7 *ecce filii eius veniebant de agro auditoque quod acciderat irati sunt valde eo quod foedam rem esset operatus in Israhel et violata filia Iacob rem inlicitam perpetrasset*

look, his sons came from *the* field. And hearing what had happened, they were furious because he had done *a* loathsome thing in Israel, and Jacob's daughter raped, had perpetrated *an* unlawful act.

34:8 *locutus est itaque Emor ad eos Sychem filii mei adhesit anima filiae vestrae date eam illi uxorem*

So Emor said to them, "My son Shechem's soul sticks fast to your daughter. Give her to him as wife,

34:9 *et iungamus vicissim conubia filias vestras tradite nobis et filias nostras accipite*

"and we will join in marriage in turn! Give us your daughters and marry our daughters,

34:10 *et habitate nobiscum terra in*

potestate vestra est exercete negotiamini et possidete eam

and live with us! *The* land is in your power. Cultivate *it*, do business, and possess it!"

34:11 *sed et Sychem ad patrem et ad fratres eius ait inveniam gratiam coram vobis et quaecumque statueritis dabo*

Yet Shechem also said to *her* father and to her brothers, "I will find grace before you, and whatever you decide, I will give.

34:12 *augete dotem munera postulate libens tribuam quod petieritis tantum date mihi puellam hanc uxorem*

"Raise *the* dowry! Ask for gifts! I will give what you ask freely, only give that girl to me as wife."

Jacob's Sons Plot Revenge
34:13 *responderunt filii Iacob Sychem et patri eius in dolo saevientes ob stuprum sororis*

Jacob's sons answered Shechem and his father deceitfully, raging at their sister's rape.

34:14 *non possumus facere quod petitis nec dare sororem nostram homini incircumciso quod inlicitum et nefarium est apud nos*

"We can't do what you ask or give our sister to *an* uncircumcised man, because it is illegal and detestable with us.

34:15 *sed in hoc valebimus foederari si esse volueritis nostri similes et circumcidatur in vobis omne masculini sexus*

"But we will be able to make *an* agreement in this – if you want to be like us, and everyone of the male sex among you be circumcised.

34:16 *tunc dabimus et accipiemus mutuo filias nostras ac vestras et habitabimus vobiscum erimusque unus populus*

"Then we will give and receive mutually our daughters and yours, and will live with you. And we will be one people.

34:17 *sin autem circumcidi nolueritis tollemus filiam nostram et recedemus*

"But if you don't want to be circumcised, we will take our daughter and go away."

Emor and Shechem Agree to Terms
34:18 *placuit oblatio eorum Emor et Sychem filio eius*

Their offering pleased Emor and Shechem his son,

34:19 *nec distulit adulescens quin statim quod petebatur expleret amabat enim puellam valde et ipse erat inclitus in omni domo patris sui*

nor did *the* young man delay, so that immediately he fulfilled what had been asked. For he loved *the* girl greatly, and he was renowned in all his father's house.

34:20 *ingressique portam urbis locuti sunt populo*

And going in *the* city's gate, they said to *the* people,

34:21 *viri isti pacifici sunt et volunt habitare nobiscum negotientur in terra et exerceant eam quae spatiosa et lata cultoribus indiget filias eorum accipiemus uxores et nostras illis dabimus*

"These men are peaceful and want to live with us. Let them do business in the land and work it, because it is spacious and wide and lacks farmers! We will accept their daughters as wives and give ours to them.

34:22 *unum est quod differtur tantum bonum si circumcidamus masculos nostros ritum gentis imitantes*

"*There* is one thing that separates from so great *a* good. Let us circumcise our males, imitating *this* nation's rite,

34:23 *et substantia eorum et pecora et cuncta quae possident nostra erunt tantum in hoc adquiescamus et habitantes simul unum efficiemus populum*

"and their wealth and cattle and all that they possess will be ours. Only in this must we agree and, living together, we will make one people."

Simeon and Levi
Avenge Their Sister

34:24 *adsensi sunt omnes circumcisis cunctis maribus*

They agreed, circumcising all *the* males.

34:25 *et ecce die tertio quando gravissimus vulnerum dolor est arreptis duo Iacob filii Symeon et Levi fratres Dinae gladiis ingressi sunt urbem confidenter interfectisque omnibus masculis*

And, look, *the* third day, when *the* wound's pain was worst, two of Jacob's sons – Simeon and Levi, Dinah's brothers, taking swords, came into *the* city confidently and killed all *the* males.

34:26 *Emor et Sychem pariter necaverunt tollentes Dinam de domo Sychem sororem suam*

They killed Emor and Shechem together, taking Dinah their sister from Shechem's house.

34:27 *quibus egressis inruerunt super occisos ceteri filii Iacob et depopulati sunt urbem in ultionem stupri*

They going out, Jacob's other sons rushed in over *the* killed and plundered *the* city in revenge of *the* dishonor,

34:28 *oves eorum et armenta et asinos cunctaque vastantes quae in domibus et in agris erant*

taking away their sheep and cattle and donkeys and all things that were in *the* houses and fields,

34:29 *parvulos quoque et uxores eorum duxere captivas*

likewise leading their little ones and wives captive.

Jacob Rebukes
Simeon and Levi

34:30 *quibus patratis audacter Iacob dixit ad Symeon et Levi turbastis me et odiosum fecistis Chananeis et Ferezeis habitatoribus terrae huius nos pauci sumus illi congregati percutient me et delebor ego et domus mea*

These *things* boldly completed, Jacob said to Simeon and Levi, "You have troubled me and made me hated to *the* Canaanites and Ferezites, this land's inhabitants. We are few. They, gathering together, will strike me and I will be destroyed, and my house.

34:31 *responderunt numquid ut scorto abuti debuere sorore nostra*

They answered, "They shouldn't have abused our sister like *a* whore, should they?"

God Calls Jacob
Back to Bethel

Genesis 35:1 *interea locutus est Deus ad Iacob surge et ascende Bethel et habita ibi facque altare Deo qui apparuit tibi quando fugiebas Esau fratrem tuum*

Meanwhile, God said to Jacob, "Get up and go up to Bethel and live there. Build *an* altar to God, who appeared to you when you fled from Esau your brother!"

35:2 *Iacob vero convocata omni domo sua ait abicite deos alienos qui in medio vestri sunt et mundamini ac mutate vestimenta vestra*

Jacob indeed, gathering all his house, said, "Throw out *the* alien gods who are in your midst, and be clean, and change your clothes!

35:3 *surgite et ascendamus in Bethel ut faciamus ibi altare Deo qui exaudivit me in die tribulationis meae et fuit socius itineris mei*

"Get up, and we will go up to Bethel, so we can build *an* altar there to God, who heard me in my trouble's day and was *a* Companion on my journey.

35:4 *dederunt ergo ei omnes deos alienos quos habebant et inaures quae erant in auribus eorum at ille infodit ea subter terebinthum quae est post urbem Sychem*

They gave him, therefore, all *the* strange gods which they had, and *the* earrings which were in their ears. And he buried them under *the* terebinth tree which is behind *the* city of Shechem.

35:5 *cumque profecti essent terror Dei invasit omnes per circuitum civitates et non sunt ausi persequi recedentes*

And when they had set out, God's terror invaded all peoples from *the* surrounding cities, and they did not dare to pursue them, pulling back.

35:6 *venit igitur Iacob Luzam quae est in terra Chanaan cognomento Bethel ipse et omnis populus cum eo*

Therefore Jacob came to Luz, which is in Canaan's land, called Bethel – he and all *the* people with him.

35:7 *aedificavitque ibi altare et appellavit nomen loci Domus Dei ibi enim apparuit ei Deus cum fugeret fratrem suum*

And he built *an* altar there, and called *the* place's name God's House, for God appeared to him there when he fled from his brother.

35:8 *eodem tempore mortua est Debbora nutrix Rebeccae et sepulta ad radices Bethel subter quercum vocatumque est nomen loci quercus Fletus*

At that time, Deborah, Rebecca's nurse, died and was buried at Bethel's roots, under *an* oak tree. And that place's name was called Oak of Weeping.

Another Account of God's Appearance at Bethel

35:9 *apparuit autem iterum Deus Iacob postquam reversus est de Mesopotamiam Syriae benedixitque ei*

But God appeared to Jacob again after he came back from Syrian Mesopotamia, and He blessed him,

35:10 *dicens non vocaberis ultra Iacob sed Israhel erit nomen tuum et appellavit eum Israhel*

saying, "You will not be called Jacob any more, but Israel will be your name." And He called him Israel.

35:11 *dixitque ei ego Deus omnipotens cresce et multiplicare gentes et populi nationum erunt ex te reges de lumbis tuis egredientur*

And He said to him, "I am God omnipotent. Grow and be multiplied! Nations and nations' peoples will be from you. Kings will come out from your loins.

35:12 *terramque quam dedi Abraham et Isaac dabo tibi et semini tuo post te*

"And *the* land which I gave to Abraham and Isaac, I will give to you and to your seed after you."

35:13 *et recessit ab eo*

And He went away from him.

35:14 *ille vero erexit titulum lapideum in loco quo locutus ei fuerat Deus libans super eum libamina et effundens oleum*

He indeed put up *a* memorial stone in *the* place where God had spoken to him, pouring *a* drink offering over it and pouring out oil,

35:15 *vocansque nomen loci Bethel*

and calling *the* place's name Bethel.

Rachel's Death

35:16 *egressus inde venit verno tempore ad terram quae ducit Efratham in qua cum parturiret Rahel*

Going out from there, he came in springtime to *the* land that led to Ephratha, in which when Rachel had given birth,

35:17 *ob difficultatem partus periclitari coepit dixitque ei obsetrix noli timere quia et hunc habebis filium*

she began to struggle from *the* difficulty of *the* birth. And *the* nurse said to her, "Don't be afraid, because you will have this son too."

35:18 *egrediente autem anima prae dolore et inminente iam morte vocavit nomen filii sui Benoni id est filius doloris mei pater vero appellavit eum Beniamin id est filius dexterae*

But life going out before *the* pain and death already imminent, she called her son's name Benoni (that is, My suffering's son). But *his* father called him Benjamin (that is, *"The* right *hand's* son).

35:19 *mortua est ergo Rahel et sepulta in via quae ducit Efratham haec est Bethleem*

So Rachel died and was buried on *the* road which led to Ephratha (that is Bethlehem).

35:20 *erexitque Iacob titulum super sepulchrum eius hic est titulus monumenti Rahel usque in praesentem diem*

And Jacob set up *a* title over her grave. This is Rachel's monument's title, even to *the* present day.

Jacob Lives
in the Flocks' Tower
35:21 *egressus inde fixit tabernaculum trans turrem Gregis*

Going out from there, he pitched his tent across from *the* Flocks' tower.

35:22 *cumque habitaret in illa regione abiit Ruben et dormivit cum Bala concubina patris sui quod illum minime latuit erant autem filii Iacob duodecim*

And when he lived in that region, Reuben went out and slept with Balah, his father's concubine, which he had not hidden from him.

List of Jacob's Sons
But twelve sons were to Jacob:

35:23 *filii Liae primogenitus Ruben et Symeon et Levi et Iudas et Isachar et Zabulon*

Lia's sons: firstborn Reuben, and Simeon, and Levi, and Judah, and Issachar, and Zebulon;

35:24 *filii Rahel Ioseph et Beniamin*

Rachel's sons: Joseph and Benjamin;

35:25 *filii Balae ancillae Rahelis Dan et Nepthalim*

Balah, Rachel's slave-woman's sons: Dan and Napthali;

35:26 *filii Zelphae ancillae Liae Gad et Aser hii filii Iacob qui nati sunt ei in Mesopotamiam Syriae*

Zelpha, Lia's slave-woman's sons: Gad and Asher.

These were Jacob's sons, who were born to him in Syrian Mesopotamia.

Isaac's Death

35:27 *venit etiam ad Isaac patrem suum in Mambre civitatem Arbee haec est Hebron in qua peregrinatus est Abraham et Isaac*

He also came to Isaac his father in Mambre, *the* city of Arbee. This is Hebron, in which Abraham was *a* sojourner and Isaac.

35:28 *et conpleti sunt dies Isaac centum octoginta annorum*

And Isaac's days completed one hundred eighty years.

35:29 *consumptusque aetate mortuus est et adpositus populo suo senex et plenus dierum et sepelierunt eum Esau et Iacob filii sui*

And consumed by age, he died and was placed with his people, old and full of days. And Esau and Jacob, his sons, buried him.

Esau's Generations

Genesis 36:1 *hae sunt autem generationes Esau ipse est Edom*

But these are Esau's generations. He is Edom.

36:2 *Esau accepit uxores de filiabus Chanaan Ada filiam Elom Hetthei et Oolibama filiam Anae filiae Sebeon Evei*

Esau married wives from Canaan's daughters: Ada, daughter of Elom *the* Hittite, and Oholibamah, daughter of Ana, daughter of Sebeon *the* Hivite;

36:3 *Basemath quoque filiam Ismahel sororem Nabaioth*

Basemath likewise, Ishmael's daughter, Nabaioth's sister.

36:4 *peperit autem Ada Eliphaz Basemath genuit Rauhel*

But Ada birthed Eliphaz. Basemath birthed Rauhel.

36:5 *Oolibama edidit Hieus et Hielom et Core hii filii Esau qui nati sunt ei in terra Chanaan*

Oholibamah produced Hieus and Hielom and Coreh. These were Esau's sons who were born to him in Canaan's land.

36:6 *tulit autem Esau uxores suas et*

filios et filias et omnem animam domus suae et substantiam et pecora et cuncta quae habere poterat in terra Chanaan et abiit in alteram regionem recessitque a fratre suo Iacob

But Esau took his wives and sons and daughters and every soul in his house and wealth and cattle and all that he had been able to gather in Canaan's land, and went into another region. And he went away from his brother Jacob,

36:7 *divites enim erant valde et simul habitare non poterant nec sustinebat eos terra peregrinationis eorum prae multitudine gregum*

for they were very rich and couldn't live together, nor could their sojourning's land sustain them because of *the* multitude of *the* flocks.

36:8 *habitavitque Esau in monte Seir ipse est Edom*

And Esau lived on Mount Seir. He is Edom.

36:9 *hae sunt generationes Esau patris Edom in monte Seir*

These are Esau's generations, Edom's father on Mount Seir,

36:10 *et haec nomina filiorum eius Eliphaz filius Ada uxoris Esau*

Rauhel quoque filius Basemath uxoris eius

and these are his sons' names: Eliphaz, son of Esau's wife Ada; Rauhel also, son of Basemath his wife.

36:11 *fueruntque filii Eliphaz Theman Omar Sephu et Gatham et Cenez*

And Eliphaz's sons were Theman, Omar, Sephu, and Gatham and Cenez.

36:12 *erat autem Thamna concubina Eliphaz filii Esau quae peperit ei Amalech hii sunt filii Adae uxoris Esau*

But Thamna was concubine of Eliphaz, Esau's son, who birthed him Amalek. These are *the* sons of Ada, Esau's wife.

36:13 *filii autem Rauhel Naath et Zara Semma et Meza hii filii Basemath uxoris Esau*

But Rauhel's sons were Naath and Zara, Semma and Mesa. These *were* sons of Basemath, Esau's wife.

36:14 *isti quoque erant filii Oolibama filiae Ana filiae Sebeon uxoris Esau quos genuit ei Hieus et Hielom et Core*

These likewise were *the* sons of

Oholibama, Ana's daughter, Sebeon's daughter, Esau's wife, who birthed him Hieus and Hielom and Coreh.

36:15 *hii duces filiorum Esau filii Eliphaz primogeniti Esau dux Theman dux Omar dux Sephu dux Cenez*

These were *the* leaders of Esau's children: sons of Eliphaz, Esau's firstborn: Duke Theman; Duke Omar; Duke Sephu; Duke Cenez;

36:16 *dux Core dux Gatham dux Amalech hii filii Eliphaz in terra Edom et hii filii Adae*

Duke Coreh; Duke Gatham; Duke Amalek. These *are* Eliphaz's sons in Edom's land, and these *are* Ada's sons.

36:17 *hii quoque filii Rauhel filii Esau dux Naath dux Zara dux Semma dux Meza hii duces Rauhel in terra Edom isti filii Basemath uxoris Esau*

These likewise *are* sons of Rauhel, Esau's son: Duke Naath, Duke Zara; Duke Semma; Duke Meza. These *are* Rauhel's dukes in Edom's land. These *are* sons of Basemoth, Esau's wife.

36:18 *hii autem filii Oolibama uxoris Esau dux Hieus dux Hielom dux Core hii duces Oolibama filiae*

Ana uxoris Esau

But these *are* sons of Oholibamah, Esau's wife: Duke Hieus, Duke Hielom, Duke Coreh. These *are* dukes of Oholibamah, Ana's daughter, Esau's wife.

36:19 *isti filii Esau et hii duces eorum ipse est Edom*

These are Esau's sons, and these are their leaders. He is Edom.

36:20 *isti filii Seir Horrei habitatores terrae Lotham et Sobal et Sebeon et Anan*

These are *the* sons of Seir *the* Horite, *the* land's inhabitants: Lotham and Sobal and Sebeon and Ana,

36:21 *Dison et Eser et Disan hii duces Horrei filii Seir in terra Edom*

Dison and Eser and Disan. These are *the* Horites' leaders, Seir's sons in Edom's land.

36:22 *facti sunt autem filii Lotham Horrei et Heman erat autem soror Lotham Thamna*

But these became Lotham's sons: Horrei and Heman. But Thamna was Lotham's sister.

36:23 *et isti filii Sobal Alvam et Maneeth et Hebal Sephi et Onam*

And these *are* Sobal's sons: Alvan and Maneeth and Hebal, Sephi and Onam.

36:24 *et hii filii Sebeon Ahaia et Anam iste est Ana qui invenit aquas calidas in solitudine cum pasceret asinos Sebeon patris sui*

And these *are* Sebeon's sons: Ahaiah and Ana. This is *the* Ana who found hot waters in *the* wilderness, when he shepherded *the* donkeys of Sebeon his father.

36:25 *habuitque filium Disan et filiam Oolibama*

And he had *a* son Disan and *a* daughter Oholibamah.

36:26 *et isti filii Disan Amdan et Esban et Iethran et Charan*

And these *are* Disan's sons: Amdah and Esbah and Jethrah and Charah.

36:27 *hii quoque filii Eser Balaan et Zevan et Acham*

These also *are* Eser's sons: Balaah and Zevah and Achah.

36:28 *habuit autem filios Disan Hus et Aran*

But Disan had sons: Hus and Arah.

36:29 *isti duces Horreorum dux Lothan dux Sobal dux Sebeon dux Ana*

These *are the* Horrites' leaders: Duke Lothan, Duke Sobal, Duke Sebeon, Duke Ana,

36:30 *dux Dison dux Eser dux Disan isti duces Horreorum qui imperaverunt in terra Seir*

Duke Dison, Duke Eser, Duke Disan. These are *the* Horites' leaders who ruled in Seir's land.

Kings in Edom's Land

36:31 *reges autem qui regnaverunt in terra Edom antequam haberent regem filii Israhel fuerunt hii*

But *the* kings who reigned in Edom's land before Israel's children had kings were these:

36:32 *Bale filius Beor nomenque urbis eius Denaba*

Baleh, Beor's son; and his city's name was Denaba.

36:33 *mortuus est autem Bale et regnavit pro eo Iobab filius Zare de Bosra*

But Baleh died and Jobab, Zareh's son, reigned for him from Bosra.

36:34 *cumque mortuus esset Iobab regnavit pro eo Husan de terra Themanorum*

And when Jobab was dead, Husan from *the* Themanites' land reigned in his place.

36:35 *hoc quoque mortuo regnavit pro eo Adad filius Badadi qui percussit Madian in regione Moab et nomen urbis eius Ahuith*

This likewise dead, Adad, son of Badadi, reigned for him, who struck Midian in Moab's region. And his city's name *was* Ahuith.

36:36 *cumque mortuus esset Adad regnavit pro eo Semla de Maserecha*

And when Adad was dead, Semla from Maserecha reigned in his place.

36:37 *hoc quoque mortuo regnavit pro eo Saul de fluvio Rooboth*

This also dead, Saul from Rohoboth River reigned for him.

36:38 *cumque et hic obisset successit in regnum Baalanam filius Achobor*

And when this also had died, Baalanam, Achobor's son, succeeded to *the* kingdom

36:39 *isto quoque mortuo regnavit pro eo Adad nomenque urbis eius Phau et appellabatur uxor illius Meezabel filia Matred filiae Mizaab*

He likewise dead, Adad reigned for

him. And his city's name *was* Phau, and his wife was called Meezabel, Matred's daughter, Mizaab's daughter.

36:40 *haec ergo nomina Esau in cognationibus et locis et vocabulis suis dux Thamna dux Alva dux Ietheth*

These, therefore, are Esau's names, in his clans and places and languages: Duke Thamna, Duke Alva, Duke Jetheth,

36:41 *dux Oolibama dux Ela dux Phinon*

Duke Oholibamah, Duke Ela, Duke Phinon,

36:42 *dux Cenez dux Theman dux Mabsar*

Duke Cenez, Duke Thema, Duke Mabsar,

36:43 *dux Mabdiel dux Iram hii duces Edom habitantes in terra imperii sui ipse est Esau pater Idumeorum*

Duke Mabdiel, Duke Iram. These are Edom's leaders, living in *the* land of his rule. He is Esau, *the* Edomites' father.

Joseph and His Brothers

Genesis 37:1 *habitavit autem Iacob in terra Chanaan in qua peregrinatus est pater suus*

But Jacob lived in Canaan's land, in which his father had sojourned.

37:2 *et hae sunt generationes eius Ioseph cum sedecim esset annorum pascebat gregem cum fratribus suis adhuc puer et erat cum filiis Balae et Zelphae uxorum patris sui accusavitque fratres suos apud patrem crimine pessimo*

And these *are* his generations.

Joseph, when he was sixteen years old, shepherded *a* flock with his brothers, still *a* boy. And he was with *the* sons of Balah and Zelpha, his father's wives, and accused his brothers before *their* father of *a* dismal crime.

37:3 *Israhel autem diligebat Ioseph super omnes filios suos eo quod in senectute genuisset eum fecitque ei tunicam polymitam*

But Israel loved Joseph more than all his brothers, because he had been born to him in old age. And he made him *a* tunic of many-colored threads.

37:4 *videntes autem fratres eius quod a patre plus cunctis filiis amaretur oderant eum nec poterant ei quicquam pacificum loqui*

But his brothers, seeing that he was loved more by *their* father than all his brothers, hated him, nor could they say anything peaceful to him.

Joseph's Dreams

37:5 *accidit quoque ut visum somnium referret fratribus quae causa maioris odii seminarium fuit*

It happened likewise that, seeing *a* dream, he brought *it* to his brothers, from which cause greater hatred was seeded.

37:6 *dixitque ad eos audite somnium meum quod vidi*

And he said to them, "Listen to *the* dream which I saw!

37:7 *putabam ligare nos manipulos in agro et quasi consurgere manipulum meum et stare vestrosque manipulos circumstantes adorare manipulum meum*

"I thought to bind bundles with you in *the* field, and *it was* like my bundle stood up and stood. And your bundles stood around to pay homage to my bundle."

37:8 *responderunt fratres eius numquid rex noster eris aut subiciemur dicioni tuae haec ergo causa somniorum atque sermonum invidiae et odii fomitem ministravit*

His brothers answered, "Will you be

our king, or will we be subject to your authority?"

So these dreams and words added kindling to envy and hatred.

37:9 *aliud quoque vidit somnium quod narrans fratribus ait vidi per somnium quasi solem et lunam et stellas undecim adorare me*

He saw another dream as well which, telling his brothers, he said, "I saw in *a* dream *and it was* like sun and moon and eleven stars paying homage to me."

37:10 *quod cum patri suo et fratribus rettulisset increpavit eum pater et dixit quid sibi vult hoc somnium quod vidisti num ego et mater tua et fratres adorabimus te super terram*

When he had told it to his father and brothers, *his* father rebuked him and said, "What does this dream which you saw want in itself? Will I and your mother and brothers adore you on *the* ground?"

37:11 *invidebant igitur ei fratres sui pater vero rem tacitus considerabat*

Therefore his brothers envied him, but *the* father considered *the* affair quietly.

Israel Sends Joseph
to His Brothers

37:12 *cumque fratres illius in pascendis gregibus patris morarentur in Sychem*

And when his brothers stayed in Shechem to shepherd *their* father's flocks,

37:13 *dixit ad eum Israhel fratres tui pascunt oves in Sycimis veni mittam te ad eos quo respondente*

Israel said to him, "Your brothers are feeding sheep in Shechem. Go! I will send you to them."

He, responding,

37:14 *praesto sum ait vade et vide si cuncta prospera sint erga fratres tuos et pecora et renuntia mihi quid agatur missus de valle Hebron venit in Sychem*

said, "I'm ready."

Israel said, "Go and see if all is well with your brothers and *the* animals. And come tell me what is going on."

Sent from Hebron valley, he came to Shechem.

37:15 *invenitque eum vir errantem in agro et interrogavit quid quaereret*

And *a* man found him wandering in *a*

field and asked him what he was looking for.

37:16 *at ille respondit fratres meos quaero indica mihi ubi pascant greges*

And he answered, "I'm looking for my brothers. Tell me where they are feeding *the* flocks."

37:17 *dixitque ei vir recesserunt de loco isto audivi autem eos dicentes eamus in Dothain perrexit ergo Ioseph post fratres suos et invenit eos in Dothain*

And *the* man said to him, "They went away from this place. But I heard them saying, 'Let's go to Dothain.'"

So Joseph went on after his brothers and found them in Dothain.

Joseph's Brothers
Plot Against Him

37:18 *qui cum vidissent eum procul antequam accederet ad eos cogitaverunt illum occidere*

They, when they saw him far off, before he came to them, plotted to kill him.

37:19 *et mutuo loquebantur ecce somniator venit*

And they said to each other, "Look, *the* dreamer is coming.

37:20 *venite occidamus eum et mittamus in cisternam veterem dicemusque fera pessima devoravit eum et tunc apparebit quid illi prosint somnia sua*

"Come! Let's kill him and throw him in *an* old cistern. And we can say, '*A* wild animal ate him.' And then what will come of his dreams will be clear."

37:21 *audiens hoc Ruben nitebatur liberare eum de manibus eorum et dicebat*

Hearing this, Reuben pressed to free him from their hands. And he said,

37:22 *non interficiamus animam eius nec effundatis sanguinem sed proicite eum in cisternam hanc quae est in solitudine manusque vestras servate innoxias hoc autem dicebat volens eripere eum de manibus eorum et reddere patri suo*

"Let's not kill his soul or pour out his blood. But throw him into this cistern which is in *the* desert, and preserve your hands' innocence!"

He said this, wanting to rescue him from their hands and return him to his father.

37:23 *confestim igitur ut pervenit ad fratres nudaverunt eum tunica talari et polymita*

As soon, then, as he came to *the* brothers, they stripped him of his long tunic of many colors.

37:24 *miseruntque in cisternam quae non habebat aquam*

And they threw him into *a* cistern which didn't have water.

Joseph Sold into Slavery

37:25 *et sedentes ut comederent panem viderunt viatores Ismahelitas venire de Galaad et camelos eorum portare aromata et resinam et stacten in Aegyptum*

And sitting down so they could eat bread, they saw Ishmaelite travelers and their camels coming from Galaad, carrying spices and resin and medicinal gum to Egypt.

37:26 *dixit ergo Iudas fratribus suis quid nobis prodest si occiderimus fratrem nostrum et celaverimus sanguinem ipsius*

So Judah said to his brothers, "What good is it to us if we kill our brother and hide his blood?

37:27 *melius est ut vendatur Ismahelitis et manus nostrae non polluantur frater enim et caro nostra est adquieverunt fratres sermonibus eius*

"It's better that he be sold to *the* Ishmaelites and our hands not be polluted. For he is our brother and flesh."

The brothers agreed with his words.

37:28 *et praetereuntibus Madianitis negotiatoribus extrahentes eum de cisterna vendiderunt Ismahelitis viginti argenteis qui duxerunt eum in Aegyptum*

And, negotiating with *the* passing Midianites, taking him from *the* cistern, they sold him to *the* Ishmaelites for twenty silver coins. *They* led him to Egypt.

37:29 *reversusque Ruben ad cisternam non invenit puerum*

And Reuben, coming back to *the* cistern, did not find *the* boy.

37:30 *et scissis vestibus pergens ad fratres ait puer non conparet et ego quo ibo*

And tearing his clothes, going to *the* brothers, he said, "*The* boy isn't in sight, and I – where will I go?"

Joseph's Brothers
Deceive Israel

37:31 *tulerunt autem tunicam eius et in sanguinem hedi quem occiderant tinxerunt*

So they took his tunic and dipped it in *the* blood of *a* young goat they had killed,

37:32 *mittentes qui ferrent ad patrem et dicerent hanc invenimus vide utrum tunica filii tui sit an non*

sending *some* who carried it to *his* father and said, "We found this. See if it's your son's tunic or not."

Jacob's Inconsolable Grief

37:33 *quam cum agnovisset pater ait tunica filii mei est fera pessima comedit eum bestia devoravit Ioseph*

When *his* father had looked at it, he said, "This is my son's tunic. *A* wild animal has eaten him. *A* beast has devoured Joseph."

37:34 *scissisque vestibus indutus est cilicio lugens filium multo tempore*

Tearing his clothes, he dressed in sackcloth, grieving his son *a* long time.

37:35 *congregatis autem cunctis liberis eius ut lenirent dolorem patris noluit consolationem recipere et ait descendam ad filium meum lugens in infernum et illo perseverante in fletu*

But even though all his children *were* gathering so they could ease *their* father's pain, he did not want to receive comfort. And he said, "I will go down grieving to my son in *the* inferno."

And while he continued to weep,

37:36 *Madianei vendiderunt Ioseph in Aegypto Putiphar eunucho Pharaonis magistro militiae*

the Midianites sold Joseph in Egypt to Potiphar, Pharaoh's eunuch, *a* military instructor.

Judah's Children

Genesis 38:1 *eo tempore descendens Iudas a fratribus suis divertit ad virum odollamitem nomine Hiram*

Going down at that time from his brothers, Judah turned aside to *an* Adullamite man named Hiras.

38:2 *viditque ibi filiam hominis chananei vocabulo Suae et uxore accepta ingressus est ad eam*

And he saw there *the* daughter of *a* Canaanite man named Suah, and, taking her as wife, went in to her.

38:3 *quae concepit et peperit filium vocavitque nomen eius Her*

She conceived and birthed *a* son, and called his name Er.

38:4 *rursum concepto fetu natum filium nominavit Onam*

Conceiving again, birthing *a* baby son, she called him Onan.

38:5 *tertium quoque peperit quem appellavit Sela quo nato parere ultra cessavit*

Likewise she birthed *a* third whom she named Sela, who, being born, she ceased to bear further.

Thamar and Judah's Sons

38:6 *dedit autem Iudas uxorem primogenito suo Her nomine Thamar*

But Judah gave *a* wife named Thamar to his firstborn Er.

38:7 *fuitque Her primogenitus Iudae nequam in conspectu Domini et ab eo occisus est*

And Er, Judah's firstborn, was worthless in *the* Lord's sight, and he was killed from Him.

38:8 *dixit ergo Iudas ad Onam filium suum ingredere ad uxorem fratris tui et sociare illi ut suscites semen fratri tuo*

So Judah said to his son Onan, "Go into your brother's wife and join to her, so you can raise up seed to your brother."

38:9 *ille sciens non sibi nasci filios introiens ad uxorem fratris sui semen fundebat in terram ne liberi fratris nomine nascerentur*

He, knowing that sons would not be born to him, going into his brother's wife poured *his* seed on *the* ground, so children would not be born in his brother's name.

38:10 *et idcirco percussit eum Dominus quod rem detestabilem faceret*

And therefore *the* Lord struck him, because he had done *a* detestable thing.

38:11 *quam ob rem dixit Iudas Thamar nurui suae esto vidua in domo patris tui donec crescat Sela filius meus timebat enim ne et ipse moreretur sicut fratres eius quae abiit et habitavit in domo patris sui*

From which thing, Judah said to Thamar his daughter-in-law, "Be *a* widow in your father's house until my son Sela grows," for he feared that even he might die like his brothers. *She* went out and lived in her father's house.

38:12 *evolutis autem multis diebus mortua est filia Suae uxor Iudae qui post luctum consolatione suscepta ascendebat ad tonsores ovium suarum ipse et Hiras opilio gregis Odollamita in Thamnas*

But many days passing, Suah's daughter, Judah's wife died. He accepting consolation after grief, went up to his sheep's shearers, he and *the* Adullamite Hiras, shepherd of *his* flock in Thamnas.

38:13 *nuntiatumque est Thamar quod socer illius ascenderet in Thamnas ad tondendas oves*

And Thamar was told that her father-in-law had gone up to Thamnas to shear sheep.

38:14 *quae depositis viduitatis vestibus adsumpsit theristrum et mutato habitu sedit in bivio itineris quod ducit Thamnam eo quod crevisset Sela et non eum accepisset maritum*

She, setting aside widow's clothing, took up summer clothes and, *her* dress changed, sat in *the* crossroad of *the* way that leads to Thamnas, because Sela had grown and she had not received him as spouse.

38:15 *quam cum vidisset Iudas suspicatus est esse meretricem operuerat enim vultum suum ne cognosceretur*

When Judah saw her, he took her to be *a* prostitute, for she had covered her face that she not be recognized.

38:16 *ingrediensque ad eam ait dimitte me ut coeam tecum nesciebat enim quod nurus sua esset qua respondente quid mihi dabis ut fruaris concubitu meo*

And going in to her, he said, "Allow me, so I can make love with you," for he did not know that she was his daughter-in-law.

She, answering, said, "What will you give me so you can enjoy having sex with me?"

38:17 *dixit mittam tibi hedum de gregibus rursum illa dicente patiar quod vis si dederis mihi arrabonem* *donec mittas quod polliceris*

He said, "I will send you *a* young goat from *the* flock."

She, answering again, *said*, "I'll endure what you want if you'll give me *a* deposit, until you send what you promised."

38:18 *ait Iudas quid vis tibi pro arrabone dari respondit anulum tuum et armillam et baculum quem manu tenes ad unum igitur coitum concepit mulier*

Judah said, "What do you want for yourself as *a* deposit?"

She answered, "Give me your ring and armband and *the* staff which you have in your hand."

So *the* woman at one intercourse conceived.

38:19 *et surgens abiit depositoque habitu quem adsumpserat induta est viduitatis vestibus*

And getting up, she went out. And leaving *the* clothes she had put on, she dressed *again* in widow's clothing.

38:20 *misit autem Iudas hedum per pastorem suum Odollamitem ut reciperet pignus quod dederat mulieri qui cum non invenisset eam*

But Judah sent *a* goat by his Adullamite shepherd, so he could recover *the* pledge which he had given *the* woman. *The shepherd*, when he couldn't find her,

38:21 *interrogavit homines loci illius ubi est mulier quae sedebat in bivio respondentibus cunctis non fuit in loco isto meretrix*

asked that place's men, "Where is *the* woman who was sitting in *the* crossroad?"

All of them answering *said* there was no prostitute in that place.

38:22 *reversus est ad Iudam et dixit ei non inveni eam sed et homines loci illius dixerunt mihi numquam ibi sedisse scortum*

He came back to Judah and said to him, "I did not find her. But that place's men even told me no whore had sat there."

38:23 *ait Iudas habeat sibi certe mendacii nos arguere non poterit ego misi hedum quem promiseram et tu non invenisti eam*

Judah said, "Let her have *it* herself. Surely she can't accuse us of *a* lie. I sent *the* goat which I promised, and you did not find her."

Thamar Shames Judah
38:24 *ecce autem post tres menses*

nuntiaverunt Iudae dicentes fornicata est Thamar nurus tua et videtur uterus illius intumescere dixit Iudas producite eam ut conburatur

But look, after three months, they told Judah saying, "Thamar your daughter-in-law has fornicated, and her womb seems to be growing."

Judah said, "Bring her so she can be burned."

38:25 *quae cum educeretur ad poenam misit ad socerum suum dicens de viro cuius haec sunt concepi cognosce cuius sit anulus et armilla et baculus*

She, when she was brought to punishment, sent to her father-in-law saying, "I conceived from *the* man whose things these are. Do you recognize whose are *the* ring and armband and staff?"

38:26 *qui agnitis muneribus ait iustior me est quia non tradidi eam Sela filio meo attamen ultra non cognovit illam*

He, acknowledging *the* gifts, said, "She is fairer than me, because I did not give her to Sela my son."

But still, he did not know her further.

Thamar Gives Birth
38:27 *instante autem partu apparuerunt gemini in utero atque in*

ipsa effusione infantum unus protulit manum in qua obsetrix ligavit coccinum dicens

But in *the* moment of birth, twins appeared in her womb. And in *the* infants' coming forth, one *baby* put out *its* hand, on which *the* midwife tied *a* red string, saying,

38:28 *iste egreditur prior*

"This one is coming out first."

38:29 *illo vero retrahente manum egressus est alter dixitque mulier quare divisa est propter te maceria et ob hanc causam vocavit nomen eius Phares*

But he taking back *his* hand, *the* other *baby* came out.

And *the* woman said, "Why is *the* wall broken through for you?"

And for this reason she called his name Phares.

38:30 *postea egressus est frater in cuius manu erat coccinum quem appellavit Zara*

Afterwards, *the* brother came out on whose hand was *the* red thread, whom she called Zara.

Joseph in Egypt

Genesis 39:1 *igitur Ioseph ductus est in Aegyptum emitque eum Putiphar eunuchus Pharaonis princeps exercitus vir aegyptius de manu Ismahelitarum a quibus perductus erat*

So Joseph was led into Egypt. Potiphar, Pharaoh's eunuch, *an* army leader, *an* Egyptian man, bought him from *the* Ishmaelites' hand, by whom he had been brought in.

39:2 *fuitque Dominus cum eo et erat vir in cunctis prospere agens habitabatque in domo domini sui*

Yet *the* Lord was with him, and he was *a* man working prosperously in all things. And he lived in his lord's house,

39:3 *qui optime noverat esse Dominum cum eo et omnia quae gereret ab eo dirigi in manu illius*

who knew well *the* Lord to be with him, and all that he did to be guided by Him in his hand.

39:4 *invenitque Ioseph gratiam coram domino suo et ministrabat ei a quo praepositus omnibus gubernabat creditam sibi domum et universa quae tradita fuerant*

And Joseph found grace before his lord and ministered to him, from whom, *made* overseer of all, he governed *the* house entrusted to him and all things that were handed over *to him.*

39:5 *benedixitque Dominus domui Aegyptii propter Ioseph et multiplicavit tam in aedibus quam in agris cunctam eius substantiam*

And *the* Lord blessed *the* Egyptian's house for Joseph's sake, and multiplied all his wealth, both in houses and in fields,

39:6 *nec quicquam aliud noverat nisi panem quo vescebatur erat autem Ioseph pulchra facie et decorus aspectu*

nor did he worry over anything else, except *the* bread which he ate.

Potiphar's Wife
Lusts for Joseph

But Joseph was beautiful in face and handsome in appearance.

39:7 *post multos itaque dies iecit domina oculos suos in Ioseph et ait dormi mecum*

So after many days, his lord's wife cast her eyes on Joseph and said, "Sleep with me!"

39:8 *qui nequaquam adquiescens operi nefario dixit ad eam ecce dominus meus omnibus mihi traditis ignorat quid habeat in domo sua*

He, by no means acquiescing to *the* wicked act, said to her, "Look, my lord having handed all things to me, ignores what he has in his house,

39:9 *nec quicquam est quod non in mea sit potestate vel non tradiderit mihi praeter te quae uxor eius es quomodo ergo possum malum hoc facere et peccare in Deum meum*

"nor is *there* anything that isn't in my power or that he hasn't handed over to me, except for you, who are his wife. How, then, can I do this harm and sin against my God?"

39:10 *huiuscemodi verbis per singulos dies et mulier molesta erat adulescenti et ille recusabat stuprum*

Through such words day by day *the* woman also was molesting *the* youth, yet he refused sexual intercourse.

39:11 *accidit autem ut quadam die intraret Ioseph domum et operis quippiam absque arbitris faceret*

But it happened that *a* certain day Joseph had entered *the* house and was doing something, without bringing *a* witness.

39:12 *et illa adprehensa lacinia vestimenti eius diceret dormi mecum qui relicto in manu illius pallio fugit et egressus est foras*

And she, grabbing his clothing's fringe, said, "Sleep with me!"

He, leaving his covering in her hand, fled and went outside.

Potiphar's Wife Denounces Joseph

39:13 *cumque vidisset mulier vestem in manibus suis et se esse contemptam*

And when *the* woman saw *the* garment in her hands and felt herself rejected,

39:14 *vocavit homines domus suae et ait ad eos en introduxit virum hebraeum ut inluderet nobis ingressus est ad me ut coiret mecum cumque ego succlamassem*

she called her house's men and said to them, "Look, he brought this Hebrew man in so he could ridicule us! He came into me so he could have sex with me, and when I cried out,

39:15 *et audisset vocem meam reliquit pallium quod tenebam et fugit foras*

"and he heard my voice, he left *his* covering which I held and fled outside."

39:16 *in argumentum ergo fidei retentum pallium ostendit marito revertenti domum*

As proof therefore of faith, holding *the* garment, she showed it to her husband *when he* came back to *the* house.

39:17 *et ait ingressus est ad me servus hebraeus quem adduxisti ut inluderet mihi*

And she said, "*The* Hebrew slave whom you brought in came in to me so he could ridicule me.

39:18 *cumque vidisset me clamare reliquit pallium et fugit foras*

"And when he saw me cry out, he left *his* covering and fled outside."

Joseph Jailed

39:19 *his auditis dominus et nimium credulus verbis coniugis iratus est valde*

The lord, hearing this and too trusting of his wife's words, was very angry.

39:20 *tradiditque Ioseph in carcerem ubi vincti regis custodiebantur et erat ibi clausus*

And he handed Joseph over into *the* jail where *the* king's captives were kept, and he was closed up there.

39:21 *fuit autem Dominus cum Ioseph et misertus illius dedit ei gratiam in conspectu principis carceris*

But *the* Lord was with Joseph and *had* compassion for him. He gave him grace in *the* chief jailor's sight,

39:22 *qui tradidit in manu ipsius universos vinctos qui in custodia tenebantur et quicquid fiebat sub ipso erat*

who handed all *the* captives who were kept in custody over into his hand. And anything that happened was under him,

39:23 *nec noverat aliquid cunctis ei creditis Dominus enim erat cum illo et omnia eius opera dirigebat*

nor was *the jailor* concerned with anything of all *that was* entrusted to him, for *the* Lord was with *Joseph* and guided all his hands' works.

Two High Officials Imprisoned

Genesis 40:1 *his ita gestis accidit ut peccarent duo eunuchi pincerna regis Aegypti et pistor domino suo*

These carrying so, it happened that two of Egypt's king's eunuchs sinned against their lord: *his* wine steward and baker.

40:2 *iratusque Pharao contra eos nam alter pincernis praeerat alter pistoribus*

And Pharaoh, angry with them (for one was first wine steward, and *the* other first baker)

40:3 *misit eos in carcerem principis militum in quo erat vinctus et Ioseph*

threw them in *the* chief of soldiers' jail, in which Joseph also was captive.

40:4 *at custos carceris tradidit eos Ioseph qui et ministrabat eis aliquantum temporis fluxerat et illi in custodia tenebantur*

And *the* jail's keeper handed them over to Joseph, who ministered to them. *A* period of time passed and they were held in custody.

40:5 *videruntque ambo somnium nocte una iuxta interpretationem congruam sibi*

And both saw *a* dream one night, according to interpretation appropriate to themselves.

40:6 *ad quos cum introisset Ioseph mane et vidisset eos tristes*

When Joseph had gone in to them early and saw them sad,

40:7 *sciscitatus est dicens cur tristior est hodie solito facies vestra*

he asked saying, "Why is your face sadder today than usual?"

40:8 *qui responderunt somnium vidimus et non est qui interpretetur nobis dixitque ad eos Ioseph numquid non Dei est interpretatio referte mihi quid videritis*

They answered, "We saw *a* dream, and *there* is no one who can interpret it to us."

And Joseph said to them, "Interpretation is God's, isn't it? Tell me what you saw!"

The Wine Steward's Dream

40:9 *narravit prior praepositus pincernarum somnium videbam coram me vitem*

The wine stewards' commander told his dream first, "I saw *a* vine before me

40:10 *in qua erant tres propagines crescere paulatim gemmas et post flores uvas maturescere*

"in which three branches were growing buds little by little, and after flowers, grapes were maturing.

40:11 *calicemque Pharaonis in manu mea tuli ergo uvas et expressi in calicem quem tenebam et tradidi poculum Pharaoni*

"And, Pharaoh's cup in my hand, I took therefore grapes and squeezed them into *the* chalice which I had and gave Pharaoh *a* drink."

40:12 *respondit Ioseph haec est interpretatio somnii tres propagines tres adhuc dies sunt*

Joseph answered, "This is *the* dream's interpretation. Three branches are three remaining days,

40:13 *post quos recordabitur Pharao magisterii tui et restituet te in gradum pristinum dabisque ei calicem iuxta officium tuum sicut facere ante consueveras*

"after which, Pharaoh will remember your office and restore you to *the* prior rank. And you will give him *the* cup according to your office, as you were accustomed to do before."

40:14 *tantum memento mei cum tibi bene fuerit et facies mecum misericordiam ut suggeras Pharaoni et educat me de isto carcere*

"Only remember me when it goes well with you, and do mercy with me, so you suggest to Pharaoh and he lead me out of this jail,

40:15 *quia furto sublatus sum de terra Hebraeorum et hic innocens in lacum missus sum*

because I was taken away by theft from *the* Hebrews' land, and thrown into *the* pit here innocent!"

The Baker's Dream
40:16 *videns pistorum magister quod prudenter somnium dissolvisset ait et ego vidi somnium quod haberem tria canistra farinae super caput meum*

The chief baker, seeing that he had explained *the* dream prudently, said, "I saw *a* dream too, that I had three baskets of flour on my head.

40:17 *et in uno canistro quod erat excelsius portare me omnes cibos qui fiunt arte pistoria avesque comedere ex eo*

"And in one of *the* baskets I carried, which was highest, were all *the* foods which are made by *the* baker's art, and *the* birds eating from it."

40:18 *respondit Ioseph haec est interpretatio somnii tria canistra tres adhuc dies sunt*

Joseph answered, "This *is* the dream's interpretation. Three baskets are three remaining days,

40:19 *post quos auferet Pharao caput tuum ac suspendet te in cruce et lacerabunt volucres carnes tuas*

after which Pharaoh will take away your head and hang you on *a* cross. And birds will mangle your flesh."

Joseph's Interpretations Come True

40:20 *exin dies tertius natalicius Pharaonis erat qui faciens grande convivium pueris suis recordatus est inter epulas magistri pincernarum et pistorum principis*

Three days after was Pharaoh's birthday, who, making *a* great feast for his servants, remembered between courses *the* chief wine steward and head baker.

40:21 *restituitque alterum in locum suum ut porrigeret regi poculum*

And he restored one to his place, so he could pour *the* king's drink.

40:22 *alterum suspendit in patibulo ut coniectoris veritas probaretur*

The other he hanged on *a* gallows, so *the* dream interpreter's truth could be proved.

40:23 *et tamen succedentibus prosperis praepositus pincernarum oblitus est interpretis sui*

And nevertheless, returning to prosperity, *the* chief wine steward forgot his interpreter.

Pharaoh Dreams

Genesis 41:1 *post duos annos vidit Pharao somnium putabat se stare super fluvium*

After two years, Pharaoh saw *a* dream. He seemed to himself to stand over *the* river,

41:2 *de quo ascendebant septem boves pulchrae et crassae nimis et pascebantur in locis palustribus*

from which seven beautiful and very fat cows climbed up. And they ate in *the* marshy places.

41:3 *aliae quoque septem emergebant de flumine foedae confectaeque macie et pascebantur in ipsa amnis ripa in locis virentibus*

Likewise seven others emerged from *the* river, foul and poorly-built, and they ate on *the* same river bank, in *a* place of green plants.

41:4 *devoraveruntque eas quarum mira species et habitudo corporum erat expergefactus Pharao*

And they ate up those whose appearance and bodily form was beautiful. Pharaoh, waking up,

41:5 *rursum dormivit et vidit alterum somnium septem spicae pullulabant in culmo uno plenae atque formonsae*

slept again and saw another dream. Seven heads *of grain* sprouted in one stalk, full and finely formed.

41:6 *aliae quoque totidem spicae tenues et percussae uredine oriebantur*

A similar number of heads of grain likewise grew, thin and struck by blight,

41:7 *devorantes omnem priorum pulchritudinem evigilans post quietem*

eating up all *the* prior beautiful ones.

Pharaoh Demands
an Interpretation

Waking up after quiet,

41:8 *et facto mane pavore perterritus misit ad coniectores Aegypti cunctosque sapientes et accersitis narravit somnium nec erat qui interpretaretur*

and terrified by fear, *it* already *being* morning, he sent to Egypt's dream interpreters and all *the* wise men. And, *they* coming near, he told *the* dream, but *there* was no one who could interpret *it*.

41:9 *tunc demum reminiscens pincernarum magister ait confiteor peccatum meum*

Then *the* wine stewards' chief, finally

remembering, said, "I confess my sin.

41:10 *iratus rex servis suis me et magistrum pistorum retrudi iussit in carcerem principis militum*

"The king, angry with his slaves, commanded me and *the* bakers' chief to be thrown into *the* soldiers' chief's jail,

41:11 *ubi una nocte uterque vidimus somnium praesagum futurorum*

where one night both of us saw dreams foretelling *the* future.

41:12 *erat ibi puer hebraeus eiusdem ducis militum famulus cui narrantes somnia*

A Hebrew boy was there, *a* servant of *the* same soldiers' commander, to whom *we were* telling *the* dreams.

41:13 *audivimus quicquid postea rei probavit eventus ego enim redditus sum officio meo et ille suspensus est in cruce*

Everything we heard was borne out afterwards by events, for I was returned to my office and he was hanged on *a* cross.

Joseph Brought to Pharaoh
41:14 *protinus ad regis imperium eductum de carcere Ioseph totonderunt ac veste mutata*

obtulerunt ei

Immediately leading Joseph from *the* jail at *the* king's command, they shaved him and, changing his clothes, presented him.

41:15 *cui ille ait vidi somnia nec est qui edisserat quae audivi te prudentissime conicere*

Pharaoh said to him, "I saw dreams, nor is there anyone who can unlock what *I saw.* I have heard that you can interpret most prudently."

41:16 *respondit Ioseph absque me Deus respondebit prospera Pharaoni*

Joseph answered, "Apart from me God will respond with favor to Pharaoh."

41:17 *narravit ergo ille quod viderat putabam me stare super ripam fluminis*

So he told what he saw. "I seemed to be standing on *the* riverbank,

41:18 *et septem boves de amne conscendere pulchras nimis et obesis carnibus quae in pastu paludis virecta carpebant*

"and seven cows came up together from *the* water, very beautiful and with fat flesh, who grazed in *the* swampy greenery of *the* pasture.

41:19 *et ecce has sequebantur aliae septem boves in tantum deformes et macilentae ut numquam tales in terra Aegypti viderim*

"And look! Seven other cows followed these, so deformed and thin that I've never seen such in Egypt's land –

41:20 *quae devoratis et consumptis prioribus*

who, eating up and consuming *the* prior ones,

41:21 *nullum saturitatis dedere vestigium sed simili macie et squalore torpebant evigilans rursum sopore depressus*

"it gave no fullness to their appearance, but they were lethargic, just as thin and filthy. Waking up, again pushed down by sleep,

41:22 *vidi somnium septem spicae pullulabant in culmo uno plenae atque pulcherrimae*

"I saw *a* dream – seven heads *of grain* sprouting in one stalk, full and most beautiful.

41:23 *aliae quoque septem tenues et percussae uredine oriebantur stipula*

"Likewise another seven, thin and struck by blight, grew from *the* stalk,

41:24 *quae priorum pulchritudinem devorarunt narravi coniectoribus somnium et nemo est qui edisserat*

"which ate up *the* earlier ones' beauty. I told *the* interpreters *the* dream, and there is no one who could unlock *it*.

Joseph Interprets Pharaoh's Dream

41:25 *respondit Ioseph somnium regis unum est quae facturus est Deus ostendit Pharaoni*

Joseph answered, "*The* king's dream is one. God has shown Pharaoh what will come.

41:26 *septem boves pulchrae et septem spicae plenae septem ubertatis anni sunt eandemque vim somnii conprehendunt*

"Seven beautiful cows and seven full heads *of grain* are seven nourishing years. And both dreams include *the* same force.

41:27 *septem quoque boves tenues atque macilentae quae ascenderunt post eas et septem spicae tenues et vento urente percussae septem anni sunt venturae famis*

"Likewise *the* seven thin and meager cows which came up after them and *the* seven thin heads of grain, struck by *a* burning wind, are seven coming years of famine,

41:28 *qui hoc ordine conplebuntur*

"which will be completed in this order.

41:29 *ecce septem anni venient fertilitatis magnae in universa terra Aegypti*

"Look, seven years of great fertility will come in all Egypt's land,

41:30 *quos sequentur septem anni alii tantae sterilitatis ut oblivioni tradatur cuncta retro abundantia consumptura est enim fames omnem terram*

"which will be followed by seven other years of such sterility that all earlier abundance will be handed over to oblivion. For famine will eat up all *the* land,

41:31 *et ubertatis magnitudinem perditura inopiae magnitudo*

"and great nourishing lost in great poverty.

41:32 *quod autem vidisti secundo ad eandem rem pertinens somnium firmitatis indicium est eo quod fiat sermo Dei et velocius impleatur*

"But because you saw *the* second dream pertaining to *the* same thing, *the* judgment is firm, because God's word is done and will be fulfilled quickly.

41:33 *nunc ergo provideat rex virum sapientem et industrium et praeficiat eum terrae Aegypti*

"Now then, let *the* king provide *a* wise and industrious man, and make him first in Egypt's land,

41:34 *qui constituat praepositos per singulas regiones et quintam partem fructuum per septem annos fertilitatis*

who will appoint overseers in each of *the* regions. And let *a* fifth part of *the* fruit of *the* seven fertile years,

41:35 *qui iam nunc futuri sunt congreget in horrea et omne frumentum sub Pharaonis potestate condatur serveturque in urbibus*

which already now are coming, be gathered into storehouses. And let all *the* grain be stored under Pharaoh's power, and guarded in cities.

41:36 *et paretur futurae septem annorum fami quae pressura est Aegyptum et non consumetur terra inopia*

"And let it be prepared for *the* seven future years of famine which will pressure Egypt. And let *the* land not be consumed by poverty."

Pharaoh Approves
Joseph's Counsel

41:37 *placuit Pharaoni consilium et cunctis ministris eius*

The counsel pleased Pharaoh and all his ministers.

41:38 *locutusque est ad eos num invenire poterimus talem virum qui spiritu Dei plenus sit*

And he said to them, "Could we find such *a* man who would be full of God's spirit?"

41:39 *dixit ergo ad Ioseph quia ostendit Deus tibi omnia quae locutus es numquid sapientiorem et similem tui invenire potero*

Therefore he said to Joseph, "Because God showed you all that you have said, could I find someone wiser and like you?

41:40 *tu eris super domum meam et ad tui oris imperium cunctus populus oboediet uno tantum regni solio te praecedam*

"You will be over my house, and all *the* people will obey *the* command at your word, so that only in *the* royal throne will I go before you."

41:41 *dicens quoque rursum Pharao ad Ioseph ecce constitui te super universam terram Aegypti*

Pharaoh, again speaking to Joseph, said, "Look, I have placed you over all Egypt's land."

41:42 *tulit anulum de manu sua et dedit in manu eius vestivitque eum stola byssina et collo torquem auream circumposuit*

He took *the* ring from his hand and gave *it* into his hand, and dressed him in *a* linen stole, and put *a* gold chain around *his* neck.

41:43 *fecitque ascendere super currum suum secundum clamante praecone ut omnes coram eo genuflecterent et praepositum esse scirent universae terrae Aegypti*

And he made him climb up into his second chariot, *a* herald proclaiming that all must kneel before him, and they should know him to be governor of all Egypt's land.

41:44 *dixit quoque rex ad Ioseph ego sum Pharao absque tuo imperio non movebit quisquam manum aut pedem in omni terra Aegypti*

And *the* king said to Joseph also, "I am Pharaoh. Without your command, no one will move hand or foot in all Egypt's land."

Pharaoh Changes
Joseph's Name

41:45 *vertitque nomen illius et vocavit eum lingua aegyptiaca*

Salvatorem mundi dedit quoque illi uxorem Aseneth filiam Putiphare sacerdotis Heliopoleos egressus itaque Ioseph ad terram Aegypti

And he changed his name and called him "World Savior" in *the* Egyptian tongue. And he also gave him Aseneth, daughter of Potiphar priest of Heliopolis, as wife. So Joseph, going out to Egypt's land,

41:46 *triginta autem erat annorum quando stetit in conspectu regis Pharaonis circuivit omnes regiones Aegypti*

was thirty years old when he stood in King Pharaoh's sight. He traveled around all Egypt's regions.

41:47 *venitque fertilitas septem annorum et in manipulos redactae segetes congregatae sunt in horrea Aegypti*

And *the* seven fertile years came, and grain reduced to bundles was gathered in Egypt's storehouses.

41:48 *omnis etiam frugum abundantia in singulis urbibus condita est*

All *the* grain's abundance also was gathered into each of *the* cities.

41:49 *tantaque fuit multitudo tritici ut harenae maris coaequaretur et copia mensuram excederet*

And *the* wheat's multitude was such that it equaled *the* sea's sand, and *the* abundance exceeded measure.

Joseph Fathers Two Sons

41:50 *nati sunt autem Ioseph filii duo antequam veniret fames quos ei peperit Aseneth filia Putiphare sacerdotis Heliopoleos*

But two sons were born to Joseph before *the* famine came, whom Aseneth, daughter of Potiphar priest of Heliopolis, birthed to him.

41:51 *vocavitque nomen primogeniti Manasse dicens oblivisci me fecit Deus omnium laborum meorum et domum patris mei*

And he called *the* firstborn's name Manasseh, saying, "*The* Lord made me forget all my labors and my father's house."

41:52 *nomen quoque secundi appellavit Ephraim dicens crescere me fecit Deus in terra paupertatis meae*

Likewise, he called *the* second one's name Ephraim, saying, "God made me increase in *the* land of my poverty."

41:53 *igitur transactis septem annis ubertatis qui fuerant in Aegypto*

Therefore, *the* seven nourishing years which were in Egypt *having* passed,

The Famine Begins

41:54 *coeperunt venire septem anni inopiae quos praedixerat Ioseph et in universo orbe fames praevaluit in cuncta autem terra Aegypti erat panis*

seven poor years began which Joseph had predicted, and famine prevailed in all *the* world. But *there* was bread in all Egypt's land.

41:55 *qua esuriente clamavit populus ad Pharaonem alimenta petens quibus ille respondit ite ad Ioseph et quicquid vobis dixerit facite*

The people, who *were* hungry, cried out to Pharaoh begging food, to whom he responded, "Go to Joseph, and do whatever he says to you!"

41:56 *crescebat autem cotidie fames in omni terra aperuitque Ioseph universa horrea et vendebat Aegyptiis nam et illos oppresserat fames*

But *the* famine increased daily in all *the* land, and Joseph opened all *the* storehouses and sold *food* to *the* Egyptians, for they also were oppressed by hunger.

41:57 *omnesque provinciae veniebant in Aegyptum ut emerent escas et malum inopiae temperarent*

And all *the* provinces came to Egypt so they could buy food and temper poverty's harm.

Jacob Sends His Sons
to Egypt

Genesis 42:1 *audiens autem Iacob quod alimenta venderentur in Aegypto dixit filiis suis quare neglegitis*

But Jacob, hearing that food was being sold in Egypt, said to his sons, "Why will you do nothing?

42:2 *audivi quod triticum venundetur in Aegypto descendite et emite nobis necessaria ut possimus vivere et non consumamur inopia*

"I heard that wheat is for sale in Egypt. Go down and buy us necessities, so we can live and not be eaten up by poverty!"

42:3 *descendentes igitur fratres Ioseph decem ut emerent frumenta in Aegypto*

Therefore, ten of Joseph's brothers going down so they could buy food in Egypt,

42:4 *Beniamin domi retento ab Iacob qui dixerat fratribus eius ne forte in itinere quicquam patiatur mali*

(Benjamin *was* kept home by Jacob, who said to his brothers, "No, unless perhaps he suffer some harm on *the* journey.")

42:5 *ingressi sunt terram Aegypti*

cum aliis qui pergebant ad emendum erat autem fames in terra Chanaan

they went into Egypt's land with others who went down to buy *food*, for famine was in Canaan's land.

Joseph's Brothers
Come Before Him

42:6 *et Ioseph princeps Aegypti atque ad illius nutum frumenta populis vendebantur cumque adorassent eum fratres sui*

And Joseph *was* Egypt's prince, and *the* one at whose nod food was sold to *the* peoples. And when his brothers had paid homage to him,

42:7 *et agnovisset eos quasi ad alienos durius loquebatur interrogans eos unde venistis qui responderunt de terra Chanaan ut emamus victui necessaria*

and he had recognized them, he spoke harshly, as if to strangers, interrogating them, "Where did you come from?"

They answered, "From Canaan's land, so we can buy necessary food."

42:8 *et tamen fratres ipse cognoscens non est agnitus ab eis*

And though he recognized them, *he* was not recognized by them.

42:9 *recordatusque somniorum*

quae aliquando viderat ait exploratores estis ut videatis infirmiora terrae venistis

And remembering *the* dreams which he had seen once, he said, "You are spies. You came so you could see *the* land's weaknesses."

42:10 *qui dixerunt non est ita domine sed servi tui venerunt ut emerent cibos*

They said, "It isn't so, lord, but your slaves came so they could buy food!

42:11 *omnes filii unius viri sumus pacifici venimus nec quicquam famuli tui machinantur mali*

"We are all sons of one man. We come peacefully, nor are your servants planning any harm,"

42:12 *quibus ille respondit aliter est inmunita terrae huius considerare venistis*

to whom he answered, "It is otherwise! You came to consider this land's unfortified *places*."

42:13 *et illi duodecim inquiunt servi tui fratres sumus filii viri unius in terra Chanaan minimus cum patre nostro est alius non est super*

And they said, "Your slaves are twelve brothers. We are sons of one man in Canaan's land. *The* youngest

is with our father. Another is not above."

42:14 *hoc est ait quod locutus sum exploratores estis*

He said, "This is what I said. You are spies.

42:15 *iam nunc experimentum vestri capiam per salutem Pharaonis non egrediemini hinc donec veniat frater vester minimus*

"Soon now I will try your experience. By Pharaoh's health, you will not leave here until your youngest brother comes.

42:16 *mittite e vobis unum et adducat eum vos autem eritis in vinculis donec probentur quae dixistis utrum falsa an vera sint alioquin per salutem Pharaonis exploratores estis*

"Send one of you and bring him in! But you will be in chains until what you have said can be proved, whether they are true or false. Otherwise, by Pharaoh's health you are spies!"

42:17 *tradidit ergo eos custodiae tribus diebus*

So he handed them into custody for three days.

42:18 *die autem tertio eductis de carcere ait facite quod dixi et vivetis*

Deum enim timeo

But bringing them from jail *the* third day, he said, "Do what I said and you will live, for I fear God.

42:19 *si pacifici estis frater vester unus ligetur in carcere vos autem abite et ferte frumenta quae emistis in domos vestras*

"If you are peaceful, let one of your brothers be bound in jail. But you go out and bring *the* food which you bought to your houses.

42:20 *et fratrem vestrum minimum ad me adducite ut possim vestros probare sermones et non moriamini fecerunt ut dixerat*

"And bring me your youngest brother so I can prove your words, and you may not die."

They did as he said.

42:21 *et locuti sunt invicem merito haec patimur quia peccavimus in fratrem nostrum videntes angustiam animae illius cum deprecaretur nos et non audivimus idcirco venit super nos ista tribulatio*

And they said in turn, "We suffer this rightly because we sinned against our brother, seeing his soul's anguish when he pleaded with us and we did not listen. Therefore this trouble comes over us."

42:22 *e quibus unus Ruben ait numquid non dixi vobis nolite peccare in puerum et non audistis me en sanguis eius exquiritur*

And one of them, Reuben, said, "Didn't I say to you, 'Don't sin against *the* boy,' and you didn't listen to me? Look, his blood is required!"

42:23 *nesciebant autem quod intellegeret Ioseph eo quod per interpretem loquebatur ad eos*

But they didn't know that Joseph understood, because he spoke to them by *an* interpreter.

42:24 *avertitque se parumper et flevit et reversus locutus est ad eos*

And he turned himself away for *a* moment and wept. And turning back he spoke to them,

Joseph Dismisses
His Brothers
42:25 *tollens Symeon et ligans illis praesentibus iussitque ministris ut implerent saccos eorum tritico et reponerent pecunias singulorum in sacculis suis datis supra cibariis in via qui fecerunt ita*

taking Simeon and binding him before those present. And he commanded his ministers that they fill their bags with wheat and replace each one's money in his bag, putting on top food for *the* journey. *They* did so.

42:26 *at illi portantes frumenta in asinis profecti sunt*

And they, carrying grain on donkeys, set out.

42:27 *apertoque unus sacco ut daret iumento pabulum in diversorio contemplatus pecuniam in ore sacculi*

And one, opening *a* bag so he could give fodder as food in *a* lodging place, seeing *the* money in *the* sack's mouth,

42:28 *dixit fratribus suis reddita est mihi pecunia en habetur in sacco et obstupefacti turbatique dixerunt mutuo quidnam est hoc quod fecit nobis Deus*

said to his brothers, "*The* money is returned to me. Look, it's in *the* sack!"

And amazed and disturbed, they said to each other, "What is this that God has done to us?"

The Brothers
Report to Jacob

42:29 *veneruntque ad Iacob patrem suum in terra Chanaan et narraverunt ei omnia quae accidissent sibi dicentes*

And they came to Jacob their father

in Canaan's land and told him all that had happened to them, saying,

42:30 *locutus est nobis dominus terrae dure et putavit nos exploratores provinciae*

"*The* land's ruler spoke harshly to us and thought us spies of *the* province,

42:31 *cui respondimus pacifici sumus nec ullas molimur insidias*

"to whom we said, 'We are peaceful, nor are we planning any traps.

42:32 *duodecim fratres uno patre geniti sumus unus non est super minimus cum patre versatur in terra Chanaan*

"'We are twelve brothers born to one father. One is not above. *The* youngest lives with *the* father in Canaan's land.'

42:33 *qui ait nobis sic probabo quod pacifici sitis fratrem vestrum unum dimittite apud me et cibaria domibus vestris necessaria sumite et abite*

"*He* said to us, 'So I will prove whether you are peaceful! Leave one of your brothers with me and take up your houses' necessary food and go.

42:34 *fratremque vestrum minimum adducite ad me ut sciam quod non sitis exploratores et istum qui tenetur* *in vinculis recipere possitis ac deinceps emendi quae vultis habeatis licentiam*

"'Bring your youngest brother to me, so I can know whether you are spies, and you can receive this *one* who is held in chains. And thereafter you can have freedom to buy what you want.'"

The Brothers Discover Their Money Returned

42:35 *his dictis cum frumenta effunderent singuli reppererunt in ore saccorum ligatas pecunias exterritisque simul omnibus*

This said, when they poured out *the* grain, each one found *the* money bound in *the* bags' mouth. And all *of them were* terrified together.

42:36 *dixit pater Iacob absque liberis me esse fecistis Ioseph non est super Symeon tenetur in vinculis Beniamin auferetis in me haec mala omnia reciderunt*

Father Jacob said, "You have made me be without children. Joseph isn't above. Simeon is held in chains. You will take Benjamin away. All these harms have happened to me!"

42:37 *cui respondit Ruben duos filios meos interfice si non reduxero illum tibi trade in manu mea et ego eum restituam*

Reuben answered him, "Kill my two sons if I don't bring him back to you! Put *him* in my hand and I will restore him!"

42:38 *at ille non descendet inquit filius meus vobiscum frater eius mortuus est ipse solus remansit si quid ei adversi acciderit in terra ad quam pergitis deducetis canos meos cum dolore ad inferos*

And he said, "My son will not go down with you. His brother is dead and he only is left. If something bad happens to him in *the* land to which you bring him, you will lead my gray hairs down to *the* dead with grief."

Food Again Runs Short
In Jacob's House

Genesis 43:1 *interim fames omnem terram vehementer premebat*

Meanwhile, famine pressed all *the* land fiercely.

43:2 *consumptisque cibis quos ex Aegypto detulerant dixit Iacob ad filios suos revertimini et emite pauxillum escarum*

And *when the* food which they had brought from Egypt *was* consumed, Jacob said to his sons, "Go back and buy *a* little food."

43:3 *respondit Iudas denuntiavit nobis vir ille sub testificatione iurandi dicens non videbitis faciem meam nisi fratrem vestrum minimum adduxeritis vobiscum*

Judah answered, "That man told us under sworn oath saying, 'You will not see my face unless you bring your youngest brother with you.'

43:4 *si ergo vis mittere eum nobiscum pergemus pariter et ememus tibi necessaria*

"If therefore you want to send him with us, we will go together and buy you *the* necessities.

43:5 *si autem non vis non ibimus vir enim ut saepe diximus denuntiavit nobis dicens non videbitis faciem meam absque fratre vestro minimo*

"But if you don't want, we won't go – for *the* man, as we've often said, told us saying, 'You won't see my face without your youngest brother.'"

43:6 *dixit eis Israhel in meam hoc fecistis miseriam ut indicaretis ei et alium habere vos fratrem*

Israel said to them, "You made this misery in me, that you told him you also had another brother."

43:7 *at illi responderunt interrogavit nos homo per ordinem nostram progeniem si pater viveret si haberemus fratrem et nos respondimus ei consequenter iuxta id quod fuerat sciscitatus numquid scire poteramus quod dicturus esset adducite vobiscum fratrem vestrum*

And they answered, "*The* man questioned us in order about our birth, if our father was alive, if we had *a* brother. And we answered him in order, according to what he had questioned. How could we have known that he would say, 'Bring your brother with you'?"

43:8 *Iudas quoque dixit patri suo mitte puerum mecum ut proficiscamur et possimus vivere ne moriamur nos et parvuli nostri*

Judah also said to his father, "Send

the boy with me so we can set out and we can live, so we and our little ones won't die.

43:9 *ego suscipio puerum de manu mea require illum nisi reduxero et tradidero eum tibi ero peccati in te reus omni tempore*

"I receive *the* boy. Require him from my hand. If I don't bring him back and give him to you, I will be guilty of sin against you for all time.

43:10 *si non intercessisset dilatio iam vice altera venissemus*

"If delay had not interrupted, we could already have come again."

Israel Sends the Brothers Back with Benjamin

43:11 *igitur Israhel pater eorum dixit ad eos si sic necesse est facite quod vultis sumite de optimis terrae fructibus in vasis vestris et deferte viro munera modicum resinae et mellis et styracis et stactes et terebinthi et amigdalarum*

So Israel their father said to them, "If it has to be so, do what you want. Take from *the* land's best fruits in your vessels and give *the* man gifts: *a* little resin and honey and fragrant gum and myrrh and terebinth and almonds.

43:12 *pecuniamque duplicem ferte vobiscum et illam quam invenistis in*

sacculis reportate ne forte errore factum sit

"And take double money with you, and tell what you found in your sacks, unless perhaps it was done in error.

43:13 *sed et fratrem vestrum tollite et ite ad virum*

"But take your brother also and go to *the* man.

43:14 *Deus autem meus omnipotens faciat vobis eum placabilem et remittat vobiscum fratrem vestrum quem tenet et hunc Beniamin ego autem quasi orbatus absque liberis ero*

"But may my omnipotent God make him favorable to you, and may he send back with you your brother whom he has and this Benjamin. But I will be like one bereaved without children."

The Brothers Again Before Joseph

43:15 *tulerunt ergo viri munera et pecuniam duplicem et Beniamin descenderuntque in Aegyptum et steterunt coram Ioseph*

So *the* men took gifts and double money and Benjamin. And they went down into Egypt and stood before Joseph.

43:16 *quos cum ille vidisset et Beniamin simul praecepit dispensatori domus suae dicens introduc viros domum et occide victimas et instrue convivium quoniam mecum sunt comesuri meridie*

When he had seen them with Benjamin, he at once commanded his house steward saying, "Bring the men to the house and kill victims and set up *a* feast, because they will eat with me at midday."

43:17 *fecit ille sicut fuerat imperatum et introduxit viros domum*

He did as he was ordered and brought *the* men into *the* house.

43:18 *ibique exterriti dixerunt mutuo propter pecuniam quam rettulimus prius in saccis nostris introducti sumus ut devolvat in nos calumniam et violenter subiciat servituti et nos et asinos nostros*

And terrified there, they said to each other, "We are brought in here because of *the* money that we brought before in our sacks, so he can fall on us in false accusation and subject us and our donkeys violently to slavery."

Joseph's Brothers Try to Explain Themselves

43:19 *quam ob rem in ipsis foribus accedentes ad dispensatore*

From which thing, coming near *the* steward at *the* doors themselves,

43:20 *locuti sunt oramus domine ut audias iam ante descendimus ut emeremus escas*

they said, "We pray, lord, that you listen. We already came down before so we could buy food,

43:21 *quibus emptis cum venissemus ad diversorium aperuimus sacculos nostros et invenimus pecuniam in ore saccorum quam nunc eodem pondere reportamus*

which bought, when we had come to *the* lodging place we opened our bags and found *the* money in our bags' mouth, which now we are bringing back of *the* same weight.

43:22 *sed et aliud adtulimus argentum ut emamus quae necessaria sunt non est in nostra conscientia quis eam posuerit in marsuppiis nostris*

"But we also brought other silver so we could buy *the* things that are needed. Who put it in our bags is not in our conscience."

43:23 *at ille respondit pax vobiscum nolite timere Deus vester et Deus patris vestri dedit vobis thesauros in sacculis vestris nam pecuniam quam dedistis mihi probatam ego habeo* *eduxitque ad eos Symeon*

And he answered, "Peace *be* with you. Don't be afraid. Your God and your father's God gave you treasure in your bags, for I have proof of *the* money which you gave me."

And he led Simeon out to them.

43:24 *et introductis domum adtulit aquam et laverunt pedes suos deditque pabula asinis eorum*

And, bringing *them* into *the* house, he brought water and they washed their feet. And he gave fodder to their donkeys.

43:25 *illi vero parabant munera donec ingrederetur Ioseph meridie audierant enim quod ibi comesuri essent panem*

They indeed prepared gifts until Joseph came in at midday, for they heard that they would eat bread there.

Joseph Comes
to His Brothers

43:26 *igitur ingressus est Ioseph domum suam obtuleruntque ei munera tenentes in manibus et adoraverunt proni in terram*

Therefore Joseph came into his house. And they gave him *the* gifts *they* had in *their* hands and paid homage face-down on *the* ground.

43:27 *at ille clementer resalutatis eis interrogavit dicens salvusne est pater vester senex de quo dixeratis mihi adhuc vivit*

And he, greeting them again peacefully, asked them saying, "Is your old father well, of whom you told me? Is he still alive?"

43:28 *qui responderunt sospes est servus tuus pater noster adhuc vivit et incurvati adoraverunt eum*

They answered, "Your slave our father is well and still lives."

And, bending down, they paid homage to him.

43:29 *adtollens autem oculos Ioseph vidit Beniamin fratrem suum uterinum et ait iste est frater vester parvulus de quo dixeratis mihi et rursum Deus inquit misereatur tui fili mi*

But lifting up his eyes, Joseph saw Benjamin his full brother and said, "Is this your little brother about whom you spoke to me?"

And again he said, "God have mercy on you, my son."

43:30 *festinavitque quia commota fuerant viscera eius super fratre suo et erumpebant lacrimae et introiens cubiculum flevit*

And he hurried because his insides were moved over his brother, and tears burst forth. And going into *his* room, he wept.

43:31 *rursusque lota facie egressus continuit se et ait ponite panes*

And his face washed, coming out again, he contained himself and said, "Put out *the* bread."

43:32 *quibus adpositis seorsum Ioseph et seorsum fratribus Aegyptiis quoque qui vescebantur simul seorsum inlicitum est enim Aegyptiis comedere cum Hebraeis et profanum putant huiuscemodi convivium*

which *was* placed separately to Joseph and separately to *the* brothers, *the* Egyptians likewise who ate at *the* same time separate (for it is unlawful for Egyptians to eat with Hebrews, and they consider this kind of feast profane).

43:33 *sederunt coram eo primogenitus iuxta primogenita sua et minimus iuxta aetatem suam et mirabantur nimis*

They sat before him, *the* firstborn according to his birth order and *the* youngest according to his age, and they marveled greatly.

43:34 *sumptis partibus quas ab eo acceperant maiorque pars venit Beniamin ita ut quinque partibus excederet biberuntque et inebriati sunt cum eo*

Taking up *the* portions which they received from him, *the* larger portion came to Benjamin, so that it exceeded five portions. And they drank and were drunk with him.

Joseph Calls
His Brothers Back

Genesis 44:1 *praecepit autem Ioseph dispensatori domus suae dicens imple saccos eorum frumento quantum possunt capere et pone pecuniam singulorum in summitate sacci*

But Joseph commanded his house steward saying, "Fill their sacks with as much grain as they can hold, and put each one's money at *the* top of *the* sack.

44:2 *scyphum autem meum argenteum et pretium quod dedit tritici pone in ore sacci iunioris factumque est ita*

But put my silver goblet and *the* price which he gave for *the* wheat in *the* mouth of *the* youngest one's bag.

And it was done so.

44:3 *et orto mane dimissi sunt cum asinis suis*

And morning risen, they were dismissed with their donkeys.

44:4 *iamque urbem exierant et processerant paululum tum Ioseph arcessito dispensatore domus surge inquit persequere viros et adprehensis dicito quare reddidistis malum pro bono*

And after they had already left *the* city and set out *a* little, then Joseph, summoning *the* house steward, said, "Get up, follow *the* men and, catching them, say, 'Why did you repay harm for good?'

44:5 *scyphum quem furati estis ipse est in quo bibit dominus meus et in quo augurari solet pessimam rem fecistis*

"*The* goblet which you stole, it is *the* one in which my lord drinks and in which he is accustomed to practice divination. You've done *a* terrible thing!"

44:6 *fecit ille ut iusserat et adprehensis per ordinem locutus est*

He did as *Joseph* had commanded and, catching *them*, he spoke according to *the* order.

44:7 *qui responderunt quare sic loquitur dominus noster ut servi tui tantum flagitii commiserint*

They answered, "Why does our lord speak so, as if your slaves had committed such *an* outrage?

44:8 *pecuniam quam invenimus in summitate saccorum reportavimus ad te de terra Chanaan et quomodo consequens est ut furati simus de domo domini tui aurum vel argentum*

"We brought back to you from Canaan's land *the* money which we found in *the* top of *the* bags. And how does it follow that we would steal gold or silver from your lord's house?

44:9 *apud quemcumque fuerit inventum servorum tuorum quod quaeris moriatur et nos servi erimus domini nostri*

"Let whoever is found among your slaves with what you seek die, and we will be our lord's slaves!"

44:10 *qui dixit fiat iuxta vestram sententiam apud quem fuerit inventum ipse sit servus meus vos autem eritis innoxii*

He said, "Let it be done according to your sentence. Let him with whom it is found be my slave, but you will be innocent."

44:11 *itaque festinato deponentes in terram saccos aperuerunt singuli*

And so, quickly putting *the* bags on *the* ground, each one opened them,

44:12 *quos scrutatus incipiens a maiore usque ad minimum invenit scyphum in sacco Beniamin*

which *were* searched, beginning with *the* oldest even to *the* youngest. He found *the* goblet in Benjamin's sack.

Joseph's Brothers Return to Him

44:13 *at illi scissis vestibus oneratisque rursum asinis reversi sunt in oppidum*

And they, tearing their clothes and loading *the* donkeys again, turned back to *the* town.

44:14 *primusque Iudas cum fratribus ingressus est ad Ioseph necdum enim de loco abierat omnesque ante eum in terra pariter corruerunt*

And Judah first, with his brothers, went in to Joseph, for he had not gone out from that place. And they fell before him together on *the* ground.

44:15 *quibus ille ait cur sic agere voluistis an ignoratis quod non sit similis mei in augurandi scientia*

He said to them, "Why did you want to act so? Can it be you didn't know that there is no one like me in *the* knowledge of divination?"

Judah Pleads for Benjamin

44:16 *cui Iudas quid respondebimus inquit domino meo vel quid loquemur aut iusti poterimus obtendere Deus invenit iniquitatem servorum tuorum en omnes servi sumus domini mei et nos et apud quem inventus est scyphus*

To whom Judah said, "What can we answer my lord, or what can we say? Or how can we obtain justice? God found your slaves' treachery. Look, we are all my lord's slaves – we also, and the one with whom *the* cup was found."

44:17 *respondit Ioseph absit a me ut sic agam qui furatus est scyphum ipse sit servus meus vos autem abite liberi ad patrem vestrum*

Joseph answered, "May it be far from me that I do so! *The* one who stole *the* cup – let him be my slave! But *the rest of* you, go free to your father!"

44:18 *accedens propius Iudas confidenter ait oro domine mi loquatur servus tuus verbum in auribus tuis et ne irascaris famulo tuo tu es enim post Pharaonem*

Judah, coming close, spoke boldly, "I pray, my lord, let your slave speak *a* word in your ears and do not be angry with your servant, for you are after Pharaoh.

44:19 *dominus meus interrogasti prius servos tuos habetis patrem aut fratrem*

"My lord questioned your slaves before, 'Do you have *a* father or brother?'

44:20 *et nos respondimus tibi*

domino meo est nobis pater senex et puer parvulus qui in senecta illius natus est cuius uterinus frater est mortuus et ipsum solum habet mater sua pater vero tenere diligit eum

"And we answered you to my lord, 'We have *an* old father and *a* little boy, who was born in his old age, whose full brother is dead.' And *the* father has him only from his mother. Truly he loves him tenderly.

44:21 *dixistique servis tuis adducite eum ad me et ponam oculos meos super illum*

"And you said to your slaves, 'Bring him to me and I will place my eyes on him!'

44:22 *suggessimus domino meo non potest puer relinquere patrem suum si enim illum dimiserit morietur*

"We suggested to my lord, '*The* boy can't leave his father. For if he lets him go, he will die.'

44:23 *et dixisti servis tuis nisi venerit frater vester minimus vobiscum non videbitis amplius faciem meam*

"And you said to your slaves, 'Unless your youngest brother comes with you, you will not see my face again.'

44:24 *cum ergo ascendissemus ad famulum tuum patrem nostrum* *narravimus ei omnia quae locutus est dominus meus*

"When therefore we had gone up to your servant our father, we told him all that my lord had spoken.

44:25 *et dixit pater noster revertimini et emite nobis parum tritici*

"And our father said, 'Go back and buy us *a* little wheat,'

44:26 *cui diximus ire non possumus si frater noster minimus descendet nobiscum proficiscemur simul alioquin illo absente non audemus videre faciem viri*

to whom we said, 'We can't go if our little brother doesn't come down with us. If we set out together again, him absent, we dare not see *the* man's face.'

44:27 *atque ille respondit vos scitis quod duos genuerit mihi uxor mea*

"And he answered, 'You know that my wife birthed two to me.

44:28 *egressus est unus et dixistis bestia devoravit eum et hucusque non conparet*

"'One has gone out and you said *a* beast ate him, and so far he does not appear.

44:29 *si tuleritis et istum et aliquid ei in via contigerit deducetis canos meos cum maerore ad inferos*

"'If you take him too and something happens to him on *the* way, you will lead my gray hairs to *the* dead with grief.'

44:30 *igitur si intravero ad servum tuum patrem nostrum et puer defuerit cum anima illius ex huius anima pendeat*

"Therefore, if I go into your slave our father and *the* boy is missing, when his soul depends on his life,

44:31 *videritque eum non esse nobiscum morietur et deducent famuli tui canos eius cum dolore ad inferos*

"and he sees that he is not with us, he will die, and your servants will lead his gray hairs with sorrow to *the* dead.

44:32 *ego proprie servus tuus qui in meam hunc recepi fidem et spopondi dicens nisi reduxero eum peccati reus ero in patrem meum omni tempore*

"I, especially, *will be* your slave, who received this one into my trust and promised saying, 'If I don't bring him back, I will be guilty of sin against my father through all time.'

44:33 *manebo itaque servus tuus pro puero in ministerium domini mei et puer ascendat cum fratribus suis*

"So I will stay as your slave in *the* boy's place, in serving my lord. And may *the* boy go up with his brothers.

44:34 *non enim possum redire ad patrem absente puero ne calamitatis quae oppressura est patrem meum testis adsistam*

"For I can't go back to *the* father again without *the* boy, unless I be witness to *the* calamity that will oppress my father!"

Joseph Reveals Himself

Genesis 45:1 *non se poterat ultra cohibere Ioseph multis coram adstantibus unde praecepit ut egrederentur cuncti foras et nullus interesset alienus agnitioni mutuae*

Joseph couldn't hold himself back further before *the* many standing around. From this, he commanded that all should go outside, and no stranger be present at *the* mutual recognition.

45:2 *elevavitque vocem cum fletu quam audierunt Aegyptii omnisque domus Pharaonis*

And he lifted up his voice with weeping, which *the* Egyptians and all of Pharaoh's house heard.

45:3 *et dixit fratribus suis ego sum Ioseph adhuc pater meus vivit nec poterant respondere fratres nimio timore perterriti*

And he said to his brothers, "I am Joseph. Is my father still living?"

The brothers couldn't answer, greatly terrified by fear,

45:4 *ad quos ille clementer accedite inquit ad me et cum accessissent prope ego sum ait Ioseph frater vester quem vendidistis in Aegypto*

to whom he spoke peacefully, "Come near to me."

And when they had come near, he said, "I am Joseph your brother, whom you sold into Egypt.

45:5 *nolite pavere nec vobis durum esse videatur quod vendidistis me in his regionibus pro salute enim vestra misit me Deus ante vos in Aegyptum*

"Don't be afraid or let it seem harsh to you that you sold me into these lands. For God sent me before you into Egypt for your health.

45:6 *biennium est quod fames esse coepit in terra et adhuc quinque anni restant quibus nec arari poterit nec meti*

"This is *the* second year since *the* famine began to be in *the* land, and five years still remain in which it won't be possible to plow or reap.

45:7 *praemisitque me Deus ut reservemini super terram et escas ad vivendum habere possitis*

"And God sent me before so you could be preserved on *the* land and you could have food to live.

45:8 *non vestro consilio sed Dei huc voluntate missus sum qui fecit me quasi patrem Pharaonis et dominum universae domus eius ac principem in omni terra Aegypti*

"I have been sent here not by your counsel but by God's will, who made me like *a* father to Pharaoh and lord of all his house and prince in all Egypt's land.

45:9 *festinate et ascendite ad patrem meum et dicetis ei haec mandat filius tuus Ioseph Deus me fecit dominum universae terrae Aegypti descende ad me ne moreris*

"Hurry and go up to my father and say to him, 'Your son Joseph commands this: God made me lord of all Egypt's land. Come down to me! Don't delay!

45:10 *et habita in terra Gessen erisque iuxta me tu et filii tui et filii filiorum tuorum oves tuae et armenta tua et universa quae possides*

"'And live in Gessen's land! You will be beside me, and your children and your children's children, your sheep and your cattle and all that you have.

45:11 *ibique te pascam adhuc enim quinque anni residui sunt famis ne et tu pereas et domus tua et omnia quae possides*

"'And I will feed you there – for five years of famine are still left – so you also won't perish and your house and all that you have.'

45:12 *en oculi vestri et oculi fratris mei Beniamin vident quod os meum loquatur ad vos*

"Look, your eyes and Benjamin my brother's eyes see that my mouth speaks to you.

45:13 *nuntiate patri meo universam gloriam meam et cuncta quae vidistis in Aegypto festinate et adducite eum ad me*

"Tell my father all my glory and all that you have seen in Egypt! Hurry and bring him to me!

Joseph Embraces
His Brothers

45:14 *cumque amplexatus recidisset in collum Beniamin fratris sui flevit illo quoque flente similiter super collum eius*

And when he had fallen on Benjamin's neck embracing *him*, he wept, *Benjamin* likewise weeping together on his neck.

45:15 *osculatusque est Ioseph omnes fratres suos et ploravit super singulos post quae ausi sunt loqui ad eum*

And Joseph kissed all his brothers and wept over each one individually, after which they dared to speak to him.

Pharaoh Summons
Jacob to Egypt

45:16 *auditumque est et celebri sermone vulgatum in aula regis venerunt fratres Ioseph et gavisus est*

Pharao atque omnis familia eius

And it was heard and *the* crowd's rumor repeated in *the* king's court: "Joseph's brothers have come."

And Pharaoh was glad and all his family.

45:17 *dixitque ad Ioseph ut imperaret fratribus suis dicens onerantes iumenta ite in terram Chanaan*

And he said to Joseph that he should command his brothers, saying, "Packing grain, go into Canaan's land

45:18 *et tollite inde patrem vestrum et cognationem et venite ad me et ego dabo vobis omnia bona Aegypti ut comedatis medullam terrae*

"and bring your father and clan from there. And come to me and I will give you all Egypt's good *things*, so you can eat *the* land's marrow.

45:19 *praecipe etiam ut tollant plaustra de terra Aegypti ad subvectionem parvulorum suorum et coniugum ac dicito tollite patrem vestrum et properate quantocius venientes*

"Command also that they bring wagons from Egypt's land for transporting their little ones and wives, and tell them, 'Bring your father and hurry, *the* sooner coming *the* better.

45:20 *ne dimittatis quicquam de supellectili vestra quia omnes opes Aegypti vestrae erunt*

"'Do not let go of any of your furnishings, because all Egypt's riches will be yours.'"

Israel's Sons Set Out to Bring Him to Egypt

45:21 *fecerunt filii Israhel ut eis mandatum fuerat quibus dedit Ioseph plaustra secundum Pharaonis imperium et cibaria in itinere*

Israel's sons did as it had been commanded them, to whom Joseph gave wagons and provisions for *the* journey, according to Pharaoh's order.

45:22 *singulisque proferri iussit binas stolas Beniamin vero dedit trecentos argenteos cum quinque stolis optimis*

And he ordered each one to be given two garments. To Benjamin, though, he give three hundred silver coins with five premium garments,

45:23 *tantundem pecuniae et vestium mittens patri suo addens eis asinos decem qui subveherent ex omnibus divitiis Aegypti et totidem asinas triticum in itinere panesque portantes*

sending *the* same amount of money and clothing to his father, adding to them ten male donkeys who carried some of all Egypt's riches, and *the* same number of female donkeys carrying wheat and bread on *the* journey.

45:24 *dimisit ergo fratres suos et proficiscentibus ait ne irascamini in via*

Therefore he dismissed his brothers and, *they* setting out, he said, "Don't argue on *the* way."

45:25 *qui ascendentes ex Aegypto venerunt in terram Chanaan ad patrem suum Iacob*

They, going up from Egypt, came into Canaan's land, to their father Jacob.

45:26 *et nuntiaverunt ei dicentes Ioseph vivit et ipse dominatur in omni terra Aegypti quo audito quasi de gravi somno evigilans tamen non credebat eis*

And they told him saying, "Joseph lives and he rules in all Egypt's land."

He, hearing like one waking up from *a* deep sleep, nevertheless did not believe them.

45:27 *illi contra referebant omnem ordinem rei cumque vidisset plaustra et universa quae miserat revixit* *spiritus eius*

They brought all *the* things ordered, and when he had seen *the* wagons and all that he had sent, his spirit revived.

45:28 *et ait sufficit mihi si adhuc Ioseph filius meus vivit vadam et videbo illum antequam moriar*

And he said, "It is enough to me if Joseph my son still lives. I will go and see him before I die."

God Appears to Israel in Beersheba

Genesis 46:1 *profectusque Israhel cum omnibus quae habebat venit ad puteum Iuramenti et mactatis ibi victimis Deo patris sui Isaac*

Israel, setting out with all that he had, came to *the* well of Oath, and, sacrificing victims there to his father Isaac's God,

46:2 *audivit eum per visionem nocte vocantem se et dicentem sibi Iacob Iacob cui respondit ecce adsum*

he heard Him in *a* vision by night calling him and saying to him, "Jacob, Jacob."

Jacob responded to Him, "Look, I am here!"

46:3 *ait illi Deus ego sum Fortissimus Deus patris tui noli timere et descende in Aegyptum quia in gentem magnam faciam te ibi*

God said to him, "I am *the* Mightiest God of your father. Do not be afraid! And go down into Egypt, because I will make you into *a* great nation there.

46:4 *ego descendam tecum illuc et ego inde adducam te revertentem Ioseph quoque ponet manum suam super oculos tuos*

"I will go down there with you, and I

will lead you up from there. Joseph likewise, turning back, will place his hand over your eyes."

Jacob Goes to Egypt

46:5 *surrexit Iacob a puteo Iuramenti tuleruntque eum filii cum parvulis et uxoribus suis in plaustris quae miserat Pharao ad portandum senem*

Jacob went up from *the* well of Oath, and *his* sons brought him with little ones and their wives in *the* wagons which Pharaoh had sent to carry *the* old man

46:6 *et omnia quae possederat in terra Chanaan venitque in Aegyptum cum omni semine suo*

and all that he possessed in Canaan's land. And he came into Egypt with all his seed:

46:7 *filii eius et nepotes filiae et cuncta simul progenies*

his sons and grandsons, daughters and all offspring together.

Jacob's Children

46:8 *haec sunt autem nomina filiorum Israhel qui ingressi sunt in Aegyptum ipse cum liberis suis primogenitus Ruben*

But these are Israel's sons' names, who went into Egypt: he with his children:

Firstborn Reuben;

Lia's Children

46:9 *filii Ruben Enoch et Phallu et Esrom et Charmi*

Reuben's sons *were* Enoch and Phallu and Esrom and Charmi.

46:10 *filii Symeon Iemuhel et Iamin et Ahod et Iachin et Saher et Saul filius Chananitidis*

Simeon's sons *were* Jemuhel and Jamin and Ahod and Jachin and Saher, and Saul, *a* Canaanite's son.

46:11 *filii Levi Gerson Caath et Merari*

Levi's sons *were* Gerson, Caath, and Merari.

46:12 *filii Iuda Her et Onan et Sela et Phares et Zara mortui sunt autem Her et Onan in terra Chanaan natique sunt filii Phares Esrom et Amul*

Judah's sons *were* Er and Onan and Selah and Phares and Zara (but Er and Onan died in Canaan's land, and sons were born to Phares: Esrom and Amul);

46:13 *filii Isachar Thola et Phua et Iob et Semron*

Issachar's sons *were* Thola and Phua and Job and Semron.

46:14 *filii Zabulon Sared et Helon et Iahelel*

Zebulon's sons *were* Sared and Helon and Jahelel.

46:15 *hii filii Liae quos genuit in Mesopotamiam Syriae cum Dina filia sua omnes animae filiorum eius et filiarum triginta tres*

These were *the* sons which Lia birthed in Syrian Mesopotamia, with her daughter Dinah. All her sons and daughters' souls *were* thirty-three.

Zelpha's Children
46:16 *filii Gad Sephion et Haggi Suni et Esebon Heri et Arodi et Areli*

Gad's children *were* Sephion and Haggi, Suni and Hesebon, Heri and Arodi and Areli.

46:17 *filii Aser Iamne et Iesua et Iesui et Beria Sara quoque soror eorum filii Beria Heber et Melchihel*

Asher's sons *were* Jamne and Jesua and Jesui and Beriah; Sarah as well, their sister. Beriah's sons *were* Heber and Melchihel.

46:18 *hii filii Zelphae quam dedit Laban Liae filiae suae et hos genuit Iacob sedecim animas*

These *were* Zelpha's sons, whom Laban gave to Lia his daughter. And Jacob fathered sixteen souls from them.

Rachel's Children
46:19 *filii Rahel uxoris Iacob Ioseph et Beniamin*

The sons of Rachel, Jacob's wife, *were* Joseph and Benjamin.

46:20 *natique sunt Ioseph filii in terra Aegypti quos genuit ei Aseneth filia Putiphare sacerdotis Heliopoleos Manasses et Ephraim*

And sons were born to Joseph in Egypt's land, whom Aseneth, daughter of Potiphar priest of Heliopolis, birthed to him: Manasseh and Ephraim.

46:21 *filii Beniamin Bela et Bechor et Asbel Gera et Naaman et Ehi et Ros Mophim et Opphim et Ared*

Benjamin's sons *were* Belah and Bechor and Asbel; Gerah and Naaman and Ehi and Ros; Mophim and Opphim and Ared.

46:22 *hii filii Rahel quos genuit Iacob omnes animae quattuordecim*

These *were* Rachel's sons, whom Jacob fathered. All *the* souls *numbered* fourteen.

Balah's Children
46:23 *filii Dan Usim*

Dan's son *was* Usim.

46:24 *filii Nepthalim Iasihel et Guni et Hieser et Sallem*

Napthali's sons *were* Jasihel and Guni and Hieser and Sallem.

46:25 *hii filii Balae quam dedit Laban Raheli filiae suae et hos genuit Iacob omnes animae septem*

These *were* Balah's sons, whom Laban gave to Rachel his daughter. And Jacob fathered them, all seven souls.

46:26 *cunctae animae quae ingressae sunt cum Iacob in Aegyptum et egressae de femore illius absque uxoribus filiorum sexaginta sex*

All *the* souls who went in to Egypt with Jacob and came out from his thigh, apart from his sons' wives, *were* sixty-six.

46:27 *filii autem Ioseph qui nati sunt ei in terra Aegypti animae duae omnis anima domus Iacob quae ingressa est Aegyptum fuere septuaginta*

But Joseph's two sons who were born to him in Egypt's land *were* two souls. All Jacob's house's souls who went in to Egypt were seventy.

Jacob and Joseph Reunited

46:28 *misit autem Iudam ante se ad Ioseph ut nuntiaret ei et ille occurreret in Gessen*

But he sent Judah before him to Joseph so he could tell him, and he came to meet *him* in Gessen,

46:29 *quo cum pervenisset iuncto Ioseph curru suo ascendit obviam patri ad eundem locum vidensque eum inruit super collum eius et inter amplexus flevit*

who, when he had come, Joseph went up by his chariot to meet his father in *the* same place. And seeing him, he fell on his neck and between embraces wept.

46:30 *dixitque pater ad Ioseph iam laetus moriar quia vidi faciem tuam et superstitem te relinquo*

And *the* father said to Joseph, "Now I can die happy, because I have seen your face, and I leave you behind living."

46:31 *et ille locutus est ad fratres et ad omnem domum patris sui ascendam et nuntiabo Pharaoni dicamque ei fratres mei et domus patris mei qui erant in terra Chanaan venerunt ad me*

And he spoke to *the* brothers and to all his father's house, "I will go up and tell Pharaoh, and say to him, 'My brothers and my father's house, who were in Canaan's land, have come to me.

46:32 *et sunt viri pastores ovium curamque habent alendorum gregum pecora sua et armenta et omnia quae habere potuerunt adduxerunt secum*

"'And *the* men are shepherds. They have *the* work of tending sheep, feeding their flocks and herds. And they brought with them all that they were able to have.

46:33 *cumque vocaverit vos et dixerit quod est opus vestrum*

"And when he has called you and said, 'What is your work?'

46:34 *respondebitis viri pastores sumus servi tui ab infantia nostra usque in praesens et nos et patres nostri haec autem dicetis ut habitare possitis in terra Gessen quia detestantur Aegyptii omnes pastores ovium*

"you will answer, 'Your slaves are shepherds from our infancy even to *the* present, both we and our fathers.' But you will say this so you can live in Gessen's land, because *the* Egyptians detest all shepherds of sheep."

Jacob and His Sons
Before Pharaoh

Genesis 47:1 *ingressus ergo Ioseph nuntiavit Pharaoni dicens pater meus et fratres oves eorum et armenta et cuncta quae possident venerunt de terra Chanaan et ecce consistunt in terra Gessen*

Therefore Joseph, going in, told Pharaoh saying, "My father and brothers have come from Canaan's land with their sheep and cattle and all that they have. And look, they are stopping in Gessen's land."

47:2 *extremos quoque fratrum suorum quinque viros statuit coram rege*

Likewise, he stood five men, *the* last of his brothers, before *the* king.

47:3 *quos ille interrogavit quid habetis operis responderunt pastores ovium sumus servi tui et nos et patres nostri*

He asked them, "What do you have for work?"

They answered, "Your slaves are shepherds of sheep, both we and our fathers.

47:4 *ad peregrinandum in terra tua venimus quoniam non est herba gregibus servorum tuorum ingravescente fame in regione Chanaan petimusque ut esse nos* *iubeas servos tuos in terra Gessen*

"We have come to sojourn in your land because there is no grass for your slaves' flocks, *the* famine growing heavy in Canaan's region. And we ask that you command us your slaves to be in Gessen's land."

47:5 *dixit itaque rex ad Ioseph pater tuus et fratres tui venerunt ad te*

So *the* king said to Joseph, "Your father and your brothers have come to you.

47:6 *terra Aegypti in conspectu tuo est in optimo loco fac habitare eos et trade eis terram Gessen quod si nosti esse in eis viros industrios constitue illos magistros pecorum meorum*

"Egypt's land is in your sight. Make them live in *the* best place and hand them Gessen's land. If you know that there are industrious men among them, make them keepers of my herds."

47:7 *post haec introduxit Ioseph patrem suum ad regem et statuit eum coram eo qui benedicens illi*

After this, Joseph introduced his father to *the* king and stood him before him, who, blessing him,

47:8 *et interrogatus ab eo quot sunt dies annorum vitae tuae*

was questioned by him also, "How many are *the* days of your life's years?"

47:9 *respondit dies peregrinationis vitae meae centum triginta annorum sunt parvi et mali et non pervenerunt usque ad dies patrum meorum quibus peregrinati sunt*

He answered, "*The* days of my life's pilgrimage are one hundred thirty years, few and *full of* harm, and have not come even to those which my fathers have passed through."

47:10 *et benedicto rege egressus est foras*

And, blessing *the* king, he went out.

The Famine Worsens
47:11 *Ioseph vero patri et fratribus suis dedit possessionem in Aegypto in optimo loco terrae solo Ramesses ut praeceperat Pharao*

Joseph indeed gave *a* possession in Egypt to his father and brothers in *the* land's best place, Ramesses alone, as Pharaoh had ordered.

47:12 *et alebat eos omnemque domum patris sui praebens cibaria singulis*

And he fed them and all his father's house, providing each one food,

47:13 *in toto enim orbe panis deerat*

et oppresserat fames terram maxime Aegypti et Chanaan

for bread was lacking in all *the* world, and hunger pressed *the* land down greatly, Egypt and Canaan.

47:14 *e quibus omnem pecuniam congregavit pro venditione frumenti et intulit eam in aerarium regis*

And by this he gathered all *the* money for buying grain and took it into *the* king's treasury.

Joseph Reduces the Egyptians to Slavery

47:15 *cumque defecisset emptoris pretium venit cuncta Aegyptus ad Ioseph dicens da nobis panes quare morimur coram te deficiente pecunia*

And when *the* buyers' money had given out, all Egypt came to Joseph saying, "Give us bread! Why are we dying before you, *the* money being gone?"

47:16 *quibus ille respondit adducite pecora vestra et dabo vobis pro eis cibos si pretium non habetis*

He answered them, "Bring your cattle and I will give you food for them, if you don't have money."

47:17 *quae cum adduxissent dedit eis alimenta pro equis et ovibus et bubus et asinis sustentavitque eos illo anno pro commutatione pecorum*

When they had brought them, he gave them food in exchange for horses and sheep and oxen and donkeys. And he sustained them that year in exchange for animals.

47:18 *veneruntque anno secundo et dixerunt ei non celamus dominum nostrum quod deficiente pecunia pecora simul defecerint nec clam te est quod absque corporibus et terra nihil habeamus*

And they came the second year and said to him, "We don't hide from our lord that, lacking money, *the* animals together are gone. Nor is it hidden from you that, aside from bodies and land, we have nothing.

47:19 *cur ergo morimur te vidente et nos et terra nostra tui erimus eme nos in servitutem regiam et praebe semina ne pereunte cultore redigatur terra in solitudinem*

"Why then are we dying, you watching? Both we and our land will be yours. Buy us into *the* royal service and give seed, unless farming ending, *the* land turn back to desert."

47:20 *emit igitur Ioseph omnem terram Aegypti vendentibus singulis possessiones suas prae magnitudine famis subiecitque eam Pharaoni*

Therefore Joseph bought all Egypt's land, each one selling his possessions before *the* famine's magnitude. And he subjected them to Pharaoh,

47:21 *et cunctos populos eius a novissimis terminis Aegypti usque ad extremos fines eius*

and all its peoples, from Egypt's last borders even to its boundaries' limits,

47:22 *praeter terram sacerdotum quae a rege tradita fuerat eis quibus et statuta cibaria ex horreis publicis praebebantur et idcirco non sunt conpulsi vendere possessiones suas*

except *the* priests' land, which was given them by *the* king, to whom also food was provided, appointed from public storehouses. And therefore, they weren't forced to sell their possessions.

47:23 *dixit ergo Ioseph ad populos en ut cernitis et vos et terram vestram Pharao possidet accipite semina et serite agros*

Joseph said therefore to *the* peoples, "Look, as you know, Pharaoh possesses both you and your land. Receive seed and sow fields,

47:24 *ut fruges habere possitis quintam partem regi dabitis quattuor reliquas permitto vobis in sementem et in cibos famulis et liberis vestris*

"so you can have crops. You will give *a* fifth part to *the* king. I permit you *the* four remaining *parts* as seed

and as food for your servants and children."

47:25 *qui responderunt salus nostra in manu tua est respiciat nos tantum dominus noster et laeti serviemus regi*

They answered, "Our health is in your hand. Only may our lord consider *us*, and we will serve *the* king happily."

47:26 *ex eo tempore usque in praesentem diem in universa terra Aegypti regibus quinta pars solvitur et factum est quasi in legem absque terra sacerdotali quae libera ab hac condicione fuit*

From that time even to *the* present day, *a* fifth part is paid to *the* kings in all Egypt's land. And it became like *a* law, apart from *the* priestly land which was free from this condition.

Jacob's Life in Egypt
47:27 *habitavit ergo Israhel in Aegypto id est in terra Gessen et possedit eam auctusque est et multiplicatus nimis*

So Israel lived in Egypt (that is, in Gessen's land), and possessed it. And he was enlarged and multiplied greatly.

47:28 *et vixit in ea decem et septem annis factique sunt omnes dies vitae illius centum quadraginta septem* *annorum*

And he lived seventeen years in it, and all his life's days came to one hundred forty-seven years.

47:29 *cumque adpropinquare cerneret mortis diem vocavit filium suum Ioseph et dixit ad eum si inveni gratiam in conspectu tuo pone manum sub femore meo et facies mihi misericordiam et veritatem ut non sepelias me in Aegypto*

And when he knew that *the* day of death was coming near, he called his son Joseph and said to him, "If I have found grace in your sight, put your hand under my thigh and work mercy and truth to me, that you not bury me in Egypt.

47:30 *sed dormiam cum patribus meis et auferas me de hac terra condasque in sepulchro maiorum cui respondit Ioseph ego faciam quod iussisti*

"But I will sleep with my fathers. And you will take me from this land and put me in *the* elders' tomb."

Joseph answered him, "I will do what you have commanded."

47:31 *et ille iura ergo inquit mihi quo iurante adoravit Israhel Deum conversus ad lectuli caput*

And he said, "Swear to me!"

He swearing, Israel worshiped God, turning to *the* head of *the* bed.

Jacob Prepares for Death
Genesis 48:1 *his ita transactis nuntiatum est Ioseph quod aegrotaret pater eius qui adsumptis duobus filiis Manasse et Ephraim ire perrexit*

This happening so, Joseph was told that *his* father was sick. *He* taking his two sons, Manasseh and Ephraim, got up to go.

48:2 *dictumque est seni ecce filius tuus Ioseph venit ad te qui confortatus sedit in lectulo*

And *it* was told *the* old man, "Look, your son Joseph is coming to you."

He, strengthened, sat in *the* bed.

48:3 *et ingresso ad se ait Deus omnipotens apparuit mihi in Luza quae est in terra Chanaan benedixitque mihi*

And *Joseph* coming in to him, *Israel* said, "God omnipotent appeared to me in Luza, which is in Canaan's land, and He blessed me.

48:4 *et ait ego te augebo et multiplicabo et faciam in turbas populorum daboque tibi terram hanc et semini tuo post te in possessionem sempiternam*

"And He said, 'I will increase and multiply and make you into *a* crowd of peoples. And I will give you and

your seed after you this land as *an* everlasting possession.'

48:5 *duo igitur filii tui qui nati sunt tibi in terra Aegypti antequam huc venirem ad te mei erunt Ephraim et Manasses sicut Ruben et Symeon reputabuntur mihi*

"Therefore your two sons who were born to you in Egypt's land before I came to you there will be mine. Ephraim and Manasseh will be considered like Reuben and Simeon to me.

48:6 *reliquos autem quos genueris post eos tui erunt et nomine fratrum suorum vocabuntur in possessionibus suis*

"But *the* rest whom you father after them will be yours, and they will be called by their brothers' name in their possessions.

48:7 *mihi enim quando veniebam de Mesopotamiam mortua est Rahel in terra Chanaan in ipso itinere eratque vernum tempus et ingrediebar Ephratam et sepelivi eam iuxta viam Ephratae quae alio nomine appellatur Bethleem*

"For Rachel died to me in Canaan's land when I came from Mesopotamia, on *the* same journey. And it was springtime, and I was going to Ephratha. And I buried her beside *the* road to Ephratha (whose other name is called Bethlehem)."

Jacob Blesses
Ephraim and Manasseh

48:8 *videns autem filios eius dixit ad eum qui sunt isti*

But seeing his sons, he said to him, "Who are these?"

48:9 *respondit filii mei sunt quos dedit mihi Deus in hoc loco adduc inquit eos ad me ut benedicam illis*

He answered, "*They* are my sons, whom God gave me in this place."

"Bring them to me," he said, "so I can bless them,"

48:10 *oculi enim Israhel caligabant prae nimia senectute et clare videre non poterat adplicitosque ad se deosculatus et circumplexus*

for Israel's eyes were clouded by great age, and he could not see clearly. And *the children* brought near to him, *he* kissed and embraced *them*.

48:11 *dixit ad filium non sum fraudatus aspectu tuo insuper ostendit mihi Deus semen tuum*

He said to *the* son, "I am not defrauded of your sight. Even more, God has shown me your seed."

48:12 *cumque tulisset eos Ioseph de*

gremio patris adoravit pronus in terram

And when Joseph had taken them from his father's lap, he paid homage, face-down on *the* ground.

48:13 *et posuit Ephraim ad dexteram suam id est ad sinistram Israhel Manassen vero in sinistra sua ad dexteram scilicet patris adplicuitque ambos ad eum*

And he put Ephraim at his right (that is at Israel's left), Manasseh indeed at his left, at *the* father's right of course. And he brought both to him.

48:14 *qui extendens manum dextram posuit super caput Ephraim iunioris fratris sinistram autem super caput Manasse qui maior natu erat commutans manus*

Israel, extending his right hand, put *it* on Ephraim, *the* younger brother's, head. But *the* left he put on Manasseh's head, who was older born, crossing hands.

48:15 *benedixitque Ioseph filio suo et ait Deus in cuius conspectu ambulaverunt patres mei Abraham et Isaac Deus qui pascit me ab adulescentia mea usque in praesentem diem*

And he blessed Joseph his son and said, "God, in whose sight my fathers Abraham and Isaac walked – God, who feeds me from my youth even to *the* present day –

48:16 *angelus qui eruit me de cunctis malis benedicat pueris et invocetur super eos nomen meum nomina quoque patrum meorum Abraham et Isaac et crescant in multitudinem super terram*

"*the* Angel who rescued me from all harms – bless *the* boys! And may my name be invoked over them, and likewise *the* names of my fathers Abraham and Isaac, and may they grow into *a* multitude on *the* land!"

48:17 *videns autem Ioseph quod posuisset pater suus dexteram manum super caput Ephraim graviter accepit et adprehensam patris manum levare conatus est de capite Ephraim et transferre super caput Manasse*

But Joseph, seeing that his father had put his right hand over Ephraim's head, received *it* gravely. And, catching *the* father's hand, he tried to lift *it* from Ephraim's head and put *it* on Manasseh's head.

48:19 *dixitque ad patrem non ita convenit pater quia hic est primogenitus pone dexteram tuam super caput eius*

And he said to *the* father, "It isn't appropriate so, father, because this is *the* firstborn. Put your right hand on his head."

48:19 *qui rennuens ait scio fili mi scio et iste quidem erit in populos et multiplicabitur sed frater eius iunior maior illo erit et semen illius crescet in gentes*

Israel, refusing, said, "I know, my son, I know. And this one too will be as peoples and be multiplied. But his younger brother will be greater than him, and his seed will grow into nations."

48:20 *benedixitque eis in ipso tempore dicens in te benedicetur Israhel atque dicetur faciat tibi Deus sicut Ephraim et sicut Manasse constituitque Ephraim ante Manassen*

And he blessed them at that time saying, "May Israel be blessed in you, and may it be said, "God make you like Ephraim and like Manasseh.'"

And he set Ephraim before Manasseh.

48:21 *et ait ad Ioseph filium suum en ego morior et erit Deus vobiscum reducetque vos ad terram patrum vestrorum*

And he said to Joseph his son, "Look, I am dying and God will be with you. And He will bring you back to your fathers' land.

48:22 *do tibi partem unam extra fratres tuos quam tuli de manu Amorrei in gladio et arcu meo*

"I give you one portion beyond your brothers, which I took from *the* Amorites' hand by my sword and bow."

Jacob's Dying Prophecy
Genesis 49:1 *vocavit autem Iacob filios suos et ait eis congregamini ut adnuntiem quae ventura sunt vobis diebus novissimis*

But Jacob called his sons and said to them, "Come together so I can tell what will come to you in *the* last days!

49:2 *congregamini et audite filii Iacob audite Israhel patrem vestrum*

"Gather together and hear, Jacob's sons! Listen to Israel your father!

For Reuben
49:3 *Ruben primogenitus meus tu fortitudo mea et principium doloris mei prior in donis maior imperio*

"Reuben my firstborn, you are my strength and my pain's beginning, first in authority.

49:4 *effusus es sicut aqua non crescas quia ascendisti cubile patris tui et maculasti stratum eius*

"You were poured out like water. May you not grow, because you went up to your father's bed and stained his couch!

For Simeon and Levi
49:5 *Symeon et Levi fratres vasa iniquitatis bellantia*

"Simeon and Levi *are* brothers,

treachery's vessels making war.

49:6 *in consilio eorum ne veniat anima mea et in coetu illorum non sit gloria mea quia in furore suo occiderunt virum et in voluntate sua suffoderunt murum*

"May my soul not go in their counsel nor my glory in their activity, because in their fury they killed *a* man and in their will they undermined *a* wall.

49:7 *maledictus furor eorum quia pertinax et indignatio illorum quia dura dividam eos in Iacob et dispergam illos in Israhel*

"Their fury *is* cursed because *it is* stubborn, and their indignation because *it is* harsh. I will divide them in Jacob and scatter them in Israel.

For Judah

49:8 *Iuda te laudabunt fratres tui manus tua in cervicibus inimicorum tuorum adorabunt te filii patris tui*

"Judah, your brothers will praise you. Your hands *will be* on your enemies' necks. Your father's sons will pay homage to you.

49:9 *catulus leonis Iuda a praeda fili mi ascendisti requiescens accubuisti ut leo et quasi leaena quis suscitabit eum*

"Judah is *a* young lion. You went up from *the* prey, my son! Resting, you lay down like *a* lion. And like *a* lioness, who will rouse him?

49:10 *non auferetur sceptrum de Iuda et dux de femoribus eius donec veniat qui mittendus est et ipse erit expectatio gentium*

"*The* scepter will not be taken away from Judah and *the* leader from his thighs, until he who will be sent may come. And he will be *the* nations' expectation,

49:11 *ligans ad vineam pullum suum et ad vitem o fili mi asinam suam lavabit vino stolam suam et sanguine uvae pallium suum*

"binding his colt to *the* vineyard and his donkey to *the* vine, O my son. He will wash his garment in wine and his covering in *the* grape's blood.

49:12 *pulchriores oculi eius vino et dentes lacte candidiores*

"His eyes *are* more beautiful than wine, and *his* teeth whiter than milk.

For Zebulon

49:13 *Zabulon in litore maris habitabit et in statione navium pertingens usque ad Sidonem*

"Zebulon will live on *the* seashore and on *the* ships' station, stretching even to Sidon.

For Issachar
49:14 *Isachar asinus fortis accubans inter terminos*

"Issachar *will be a* strong donkey, lying down between borders.

49:15 *vidit requiem quod esset bona et terram quod optima et subposuit umerum suum ad portandum factusque est tributis serviens*

"He saw rest, that it was good; and *the* land, that it was choice; and put his shoulder to serving. And he became *the one* serving under tribute.

For Dan
49:16 *Dan iudicabit populum suum sicut et alia tribus Israhel*

"Dan will judge his people, as also Israel's other tribes.

49:17 *fiat Dan coluber in via cerastes in semita mordens ungulas equi ut cadat ascensor eius retro*

"May Dan be *a* cobra on *the* road, *a* horned viper on *the* path, biting *a* horse's hooves so its rider falls backwards!

49:18 *salutare tuum expectabo Domine*

"I will expect your security, Lord.

For Gad
49:19 *Gad accinctus proeliabitur*

ante eum et ipse accingetur retrorsum

"Gad, girded, will battle before him, and he will be bound backwards.

For Asher
49:20 *Aser pinguis panis eius et praebebit delicias regibus*

"Asher, his bread *will be* fat, and he will provide kings with delicacies.

For Napthali
49:21 *Nepthalim cervus emissus et dans eloquia pulchritudinis*

"Napthali is *a* deer sent out and giving beautiful eloquence.

For Joseph
49:22 *filius adcrescens Ioseph filius adcrescens et decorus aspectu filiae discurrerunt super murum*

"Joseph is *a* growing son, *a* growing son and handsome in appearance. Daughters have run around over *the* wall,

49:23 *sed exasperaverunt eum et iurgati sunt invideruntque illi habentes iacula*

"yet they irritated him and they quarreled. And those having javelins envied *him.*

49:24 *sedit in forti arcus eius et dissoluta sunt vincula brachiorum et* *manuum illius per manus potentis Iacob inde pastor egressus est lapis Israhel*

"His bow sat among *the* mighty, and his arms' and his hands' chains were loosened by Jacob's mighty *One*. From there he went out as *a* pastor, Israel's jewel.

49:25 *Deus patris tui erit adiutor tuus et Omnipotens benedicet tibi benedictionibus caeli desuper benedictionibus abyssi iacentis deorsum benedictionibus uberum et vulvae*

"God your father will be your helper, and *the* Omnipotent will bless you by *the* sky's blessings above, *the* abyss's blessings throwing below, *the* blessings of breasts and vulva.

49:26 *benedictiones patris tui confortatae sunt benedictionibus patrum eius donec veniret desiderium collium aeternorum fiant in capite Ioseph et in vertice nazarei inter fratres suos*

"Your father's blessings are strengthened by his father's blessings, until *the* desire of eternal hills may come. Let them be on Joseph's head, and on *the* crown of *the* Nazarite among his brothers.

For Benjamin
49:27 *Beniamin lupus rapax mane comedet praedam et vespere dividet spolia*

"Benjamin is *a* hungry wolf. He will eat prey at morning and divide plunder at evening.

Jacob's Final Instructions
49:28 *omnes hii in tribubus Israhel duodecim haec locutus est eis pater suus benedixitque singulis benedictionibus propriis*

All these *are* among Israel's twelve tribes. Their father has spoken these to them, and blessed each one with appropriate blessings.

49:29 *et praecepit eis dicens ego congregor ad populum meum sepelite me cum patribus meis in spelunca duplici quae est in agro Ephron Hetthei*

And he commanded them saying, "I will be gathered to my people. Bury me with my fathers in *the* double cave which is in Ephron *the* Hittite's field,

49:30 *contra Mambre in terra Chanaan quam emit Abraham cum agro ab Ephron Hettheo in possessionem sepulchri*

across from Mambre in Canaan's land, which Abraham bought with *the* field from Ephron *the* Hittite, as *a* burial possession.

49:31 *ibi sepelierunt eum et Sarram*

uxorem eius ibi sepultus est Isaac cum Rebecca coniuge ibi et Lia condita iacet

"They buried him there, and Sarah his wife. Isaac is buried there with Rebecca his wife. There also Lia's mummy was stored."

49:32 *finitisque mandatis quibus filios instruebat collegit pedes suos super lectulum et obiit adpositusque est ad populum suum*

And finishing *the* commandments which he taught his sons, he drew his feet up on *the* bed and died. And he was placed with his people.

Egypt Mourns Jacob

Genesis 50:1 *quod cernens Ioseph ruit super faciem patris flens et deosculans eum*

Joseph, realizing that *Israel had died*, fell on his father's face, weeping and kissing him.

50:2 *praecepitque servis suis medicis ut aromatibus condirent patrem*

And he commanded his slaves *the* doctors to embalm *the* father with spices,

50:3 *quibus iussa explentibus transierunt quadraginta dies iste quippe mos erat cadaverum conditorum flevitque eum Aegyptus septuaginta diebus*

fulfilling which commandment, forty days passed. This, of course, was *the* custom of embalming corpses. And Egypt wept for him seventy days.

Joseph Buries His Father

50:4 *et expleto planctus tempore locutus est Ioseph ad familiam Pharaonis si inveni gratiam in conspectu vestro loquimini in auribus Pharaonis*

And *the* time of mourning completed, Joseph spoke to Pharaoh's family, "If I have found grace in your sight, speak in Pharaoh's ears,

50:5 *eo quod pater meus adiuraverit me dicens en morior in sepulchro meo quod fodi mihi in terra Chanaan sepelies me ascendam igitur et sepeliam patrem meum ac revertar*

"because my father made me swear saying, 'Look, I am dying. You will bury me in *the* grave which I dug myself in Canaan's land.' I am going up myself, therefore, and I will bury my father and come back."

50:6 *dixitque ei Pharao ascende et sepeli patrem tuum sicut adiuratus es*

And Pharaoh said to him, "Go up and bury your father, as you have sworn."

50:7 *quo ascendente ierunt cum eo omnes senes domus Pharaonis cunctique maiores natu terrae Aegypti*

Joseph going up, all *the* old men of Pharaoh's house and all *the* older born of Egypt's land went with him,

50:8 *domus Ioseph cum fratribus suis absque parvulis et gregibus atque armentis quae dereliquerant in terra Gessen*

and Joseph's house with his brothers, apart from little ones and flocks and herds which they left in Gessen's land.

50:9 *habuit quoque in comitatu*

currus et equites et facta est turba non modica

He had chariots and cavalry in attendance as well, and *the* crowd became not insignificant.

50:10 *veneruntque ad aream Atad quae sita est trans Iordanem ubi celebrantes exequias planctu magno atque vehementi impleverunt septem dies*

And they came to Atad's threshing floor, which was located across *the* Jordan, where they filled seven days celebrating funeral rights with great and severe grief.

50:11 *quod cum vidissent habitatores terrae Chanaan dixerunt planctus magnus est iste Aegyptiis et idcirco appellaverunt nomen loci illius Planctus Aegypti*

When *the* inhabitants of Canaan's land had seen that, they said, "This great grief is to *the* Egyptians."

And therefore they call that place's name "Egypt's Grief."

50:12 *fecerunt ergo filii Iacob sicut praeceperat eis*

So Jacob's sons did as he had commanded them.

50:13 *et portantes eum in terram Chanaan sepelierunt in spelunca* *duplici quam emerat Abraham cum agro in possessionem sepulchri ab Ephron Hettheo contra faciem Mambre*

And, carrying him into Canaan's land, they buried him in *the* double cave which Abraham had bought with *the* field as *a* burial possession from Ephron *the* Hittite, across *from* Mambre's face.

50:14 *reversusque est Ioseph in Aegyptum cum fratribus suis et omni comitatu sepulto patre*

And Joseph went back to Egypt with his brothers and all *the* company *that had* buried *his* father.

Joseph's Brother
Ask His Forgiveness

50:15 *quo mortuo timentes fratres eius et mutuo conloquentes ne forte memor sit iniuriae quam passus est et reddat nobis malum omne quod fecimus*

Israel being dead, *Joseph's* brothers, fearing and speaking among themselves, *said* "Unless perhaps he remembers *the* injury which he suffered, and pays us back *the* harm which we did!"

50:16 *mandaverunt ei pater tuus praecepit nobis antequam moreretur*

And they commanded him, "Our father ordered us before he died

50:17 *ut haec tibi verbis illius diceremus obsecro ut obliviscaris sceleris fratrum tuorum et peccati atque malitiae quam exercuerunt in te nos quoque oramus ut servis Dei patris tui dimittas iniquitatem hanc quibus auditis flevit Ioseph*

"that we speak these words to you. 'I pray that you will forget your brothers' crimes and sins and malice which they worked against you.' We likewise pray that you may forgive *the* treachery of *the* slaves of your father's God."

Hearing this, Joseph wept.

50:18 *veneruntque ad eum fratres sui et proni in terram dixerunt servi tui sumus*

And his brothers came to him and, face-down on *the* ground, they said, "We are your slaves."

50:19 *quibus ille respondit nolite timere num Dei possumus rennuere voluntatem*

He answered them, "Don't be afraid. Can we disapprove God's will?

50:20 *vos cogitastis de me malum et Deus vertit illud in bonum ut exaltaret me sicut inpraesentiarum cernitis et salvos faceret multos populos*

"You plotted harm for me and God

turned it into good, so He could lift me up like you presently see, and make many peoples secure.

50:21 *nolite metuere ego pascam vos et parvulos vestros consolatusque est eos et blande ac leniter est locutus*

"Don't fear. I will feed you and your little ones."

And he consoled them and spoke gently and leniently.

Joseph after Jacob's Death
50:22 *et habitavit in Aegypto cum omni domo patris sui vixitque centum decem annis et vidit Ephraim filios usque ad tertiam generationem filii quoque Machir filii Manasse nati sunt in genibus Ioseph*

And he lived in Egypt with all his father's house. And he lived one hundred ten years, and saw Ephraim's children even to *the* third generation. Machir's sons too, Manasseh's sons, were born on Joseph's knees.

50:23 *quibus transactis locutus est fratribus suis post mortem meam Deus visitabit vos et ascendere faciet de terra ista ad terram quam iuravit Abraham Isaac et Iacob*

Which done, he spoke to his brothers, "After my death, God will visit you and make you go up from this land to *the* land which He swore to Abraham, Isaac, and Jacob."

50:24 *cumque adiurasset eos atque dixisset Deus visitabit vos asportate vobiscum ossa mea de loco isto*

And when he had made them swear and said, "God will visit you. Take my bones away from this place" –

50:25 *mortuus est expletis centum decem vitae suae annis et conditus aromatibus repositus est in loculo in Aegypto*

he died, his life's days filling one hundred ten years. And, embalmed with spices, he was placed in *a* coffin in Egypt.

Exodus

Israel's Family in Egypt

Exodus 1:1 *haec sunt nomina filiorum Israhel qui ingressi sunt Aegyptum cum Iacob singuli cum domibus suis introierunt*

These are *the* names of Israel's sons who went into Egypt with Jacob. Each entered with their houses:

1:2 *Ruben Symeon Levi Iuda*

Reuben; Simeon; Levi; Judah;

1:3 *Isachar Zabulon et Beniamin*

Issachar; Zebulon; and Benjamin;

1:4 *Dan et Nepthalim Gad et Aser*

Dan; and Napthali; Gad; and Asher.

1:5 *erant igitur omnes animae eorum qui egressi sunt de femore Iacob septuaginta Ioseph autem in Aegypto erat*

They, therefore, were all *the* souls who came out from Jacob's thigh, seventy.

Israel's Descendants
After Joseph's Death

But Joseph was in Egypt,

1:6 *quo mortuo et universis fratribus eius omnique cognatione illa*

who *once* dead, and all his brothers,

and all that family,

1:7 *filii Israhel creverunt et quasi germinantes multiplicati sunt ac roborati nimis impleverunt terram*

Israel's children increased and were multiplied like *seeds* springing up, and, overwhelmingly strong, filled *the* land.

Pharaoh Faces
an Immigration Issue

1:8 *surrexit interea rex novus super Aegyptum qui ignorabat Ioseph*

Meanwhile, *a* new king rose up over Egypt who did not know Joseph.

1:9 *et ait ad populum suum ecce populus filiorum Israhel multus et fortior nobis*

And he said to his people, "Look, *the* people, Israel's children, is large and stronger than us.

1:10 *venite sapienter opprimamus eum ne forte multiplicetur et si ingruerit contra nos bellum addatur inimicis nostris expugnatisque nobis egrediatur e terra*

"Come, let's push it down by cleverness, unless perhaps it multiply, and if war threatens us, it will be added to our enemies, and go out from *the* land by fighting against us!

1:11 *praeposuit itaque eis magistros*

operum ut adfligerent eos oneribus aedificaveruntque urbes tabernaculorum Pharaoni Phiton et Ramesses

So he appointed them officials over their work, so they could afflict them with heavy loads. And they built Pharaoh's shrine cities, Phiton and Ramesses.

1:12 *quantoque opprimebant eos tanto magis multiplicabantur et crescebant*

And *the* more they pushed them down, *the* more they were multiplied and grew.

1:13 *oderantque filios Israhel Aegyptii et adfligebant inludentes eis*

And *the* Egyptians hated and afflicted Israel's children, mocking them.

1:14 *atque ad amaritudinem perducebant vitam eorum operibus duris luti et lateris omnique famulatu quo in terrae operibus premebantur*

And they brought their life to bitterness by hard work in clay and bricks and every service, by which they were oppressed in *the* land's works.

Pharaoh Conspires
to Kill Hebrew Babies
1:15 *dixit autem rex Aegypti obsetricibus Hebraeorum quarum*

una vocabatur Sephra altera Phua

But Egypt's king spoke to *the* Hebrew midwives, one of whom was called Sephra and *the* other Phua,

1:16 *praecipiens eis quando obsetricabitis Hebraeas et partus tempus advenerit si masculus fuerit interficite illum si femina reservate*

commanding them, "When you midwife *the* Hebrew women and *the* time for birth comes, if it's male, kill it! If it's female, keep *it*!"

Women Resist Pharaoh's Order
1:17 *timuerunt autem obsetrices Deum et non fecerunt iuxta praeceptum regis Aegypti sed conservabant mares*

But *the* midwives feared God and did not work according to *the* Egyptian king's commandment. But they preserved *the* males.

1:18 *quibus ad se accersitis rex ait quidnam est hoc quod facere voluistis ut pueros servaretis*

The king, summoning them, said, "What is this that you want to do, so you save *the* boys?"

1:19 *quae responderunt non sunt hebraeae sicut aegyptiae mulieres ipsae enim obsetricandi habent scientiam et priusquam veniamus ad eas pariunt*

They answered, "Hebrew women aren't like Egyptian woman, for they already have *an* understanding of midwifery, and they give birth before we come to them."

1:20 *bene ergo fecit Deus obsetricibus et crevit populus confortatusque est nimis*

So God did well by *the* midwives, and *the* people increased and was strengthened overwhelmingly.

1:21 *et quia timuerant obsetrices Deum aedificavit illis domos*

And because *the* midwives feared God, He built them houses.

Pharaoh Again Commands Infanticide

1:22 *praecepit autem Pharao omni populo suo dicens quicquid masculini sexus natum fuerit in flumen proicite quicquid feminei reservate*

But Pharaoh commanded all his people, saying, "Throw whatever is born of male sex in *the* river! Whatever is female, keep!"

Moses Is Born

Exodus 2:1 *egressus est post haec vir de domo Levi accepta uxore stirpis suae*

After this, *a* man from Levi's house went out, receiving *a* wife of his lineage.

2:2 *quae concepit et peperit filium et videns eum elegantem abscondit tribus mensibus*

She conceived and birthed *a* son and, seeing him finely formed, hid him three months.

Moses Abandoned in the Basket

2:3 *cumque iam celare non posset sumpsit fiscellam scirpeam et linivit eam bitumine ac pice posuitque intus infantulum et exposuit eum in carecto ripae fluminis*

And when she could no longer hide him, she took *a* large woven basket of bulrushes and lined it with pitch and tar. And she put *the* baby inside and exposed him in *the* rushes on *the* river bank.

2:4 *stante procul sorore eius et considerante eventum rei*

His sister *was* standing at *a* distance and watching *the* thing's outcome.

Pharaoh's Daughter
Saves the Baby

2:5 *ecce autem descendebat filia Pharaonis ut lavaretur in flumine et puellae eius gradiebantur per crepidinem alvei quae cum vidisset fiscellam in papyrione misit unam e famulis suis et adlatam*

But, look, Pharaoh's daughter came down so she could wash in *the* river. And her servant girls walked along *the* bath's retaining wall. *She*, when she saw *the* basket in *the* papyrus bushes, sent one of her servants. And *the basket* brought,

2:6 *aperiens cernensque in ea parvulum vagientem miserta eius ait de infantibus Hebraeorum est*

opening and seeing *the* little one in it crying, she said, pitying him, "He is one of *the* Hebrews' babies."

2:7 *cui soror pueri vis inquit ut vadam et vocem tibi hebraeam mulierem quae nutrire possit infantulum*

The boy's sister said to her, "Do you want that I go and call you *a* Hebrew woman who can nurse *the* baby?"

2:8 *respondit vade perrexit puella et vocavit matrem eius*

She answered, "Go!"

The girl went out and called her

mother,

2:9 *ad quam locuta filia Pharaonis accipe ait puerum istum et nutri mihi ego tibi dabo mercedem tuam suscepit mulier et nutrivit puerum adultumque tradidit filiae Pharaonis*

speaking to whom Pharaoh's daughter said, "Take this boy and nurse him for me. I will give you your pay."

The woman took and nursed *the* boy, and gave him grown up to Pharaoh's daughter,

2:10 *quem illa adoptavit in locum filii vocavitque nomen eius Mosi dicens quia de aqua tuli eum*

whom she adopted in place of *a* son. And she called his name Moses, saying, "Because I took him from water."

Moses Sees
the Hebrews' Suffering

2:11 *in diebus illis postquam creverat Moses egressus ad fratres suos vidit adflictionem eorum et virum aegyptium percutientem quendam de Hebraeis fratribus suis*

In those days, after he had grown, Moses, going out to his brothers, saw their affliction, and *an* Egyptian man beating one of his Hebrew brothers.

2:12 *cumque circumspexisset huc*

atque illuc et nullum adesse vidisset percussum Aegyptium abscondit sabulo

And when he had looked around here and there and saw no one present, he struck *the* Egyptian down and hid *his body* in *the* sand.

2:13 *et egressus die altero conspexit duos Hebraeos rixantes dixitque ei qui faciebat iniuriam quare percutis proximum tuum*

And going out *the* next day, he saw two Hebrews brawling. And he said to *the* one who caused *the* injury, "Why are you hitting your neighbor?"

2:14 *qui respondit quis constituit te principem et iudicem super nos num occidere me tu dicis sicut occidisti Aegyptium timuit Moses et ait quomodo palam factum est verbum istud*

He responded, "Who made you prince and judge over us? Are you ordering me killed, like you killed *the* Egyptian?"

Moses was afraid and said, "How has this word become known?"

2:15 *audivitque Pharao sermonem hunc et quaerebat occidere Mosen qui fugiens de conspectu eius moratus est in terra Madian et sedit iuxta puteum*

And Pharaoh heard this word and sought to kill Moses, who, fleeing from his sight, stayed in Midian's land. And he sat beside *a* well.

Moses Defends
Jethro's Daughters

2:16 *erant sacerdoti Madian septem filiae quae venerunt ad hauriendas aquas et impletis canalibus adaquare cupiebant greges patris sui*

There were seven daughters of *a* Midianite priest who came to haul up water and, filling *the water* channels, they wanted to water their father's flocks.

2:17 *supervenere pastores et eiecerunt eas surrexitque Moses et defensis puellis adaquavit oves earum*

Shepherds came up and threw them out. And Moses got up and, defending *the* girls, watered their sheep.

2:18 *quae cum revertissent ad Raguhel patrem suum dixit ad eas cur velocius venistis solito*

When they had come back to Raguel their father, he said to them, "Why have you come back faster than usual?"

2:19 *responderunt vir aegyptius liberavit nos de manu pastorum insuper et hausit aquam nobiscum* *potumque dedit ovibus*

They answered, "*An* Egyptian man freed us from *the* shepherds' hands above and hauled up water for us. And he gave *the* sheep *a* drink."

2:20 *at ille ubi est inquit quare dimisistis hominem vocate eum ut comedat panem*

And he said, "Where is he? Why did you let *the* man go? Call him, so he can eat bread!"

Moses Marries Sephora
2:21 *iuravit ergo Moses quod habitaret cum eo accepitque Sefforam filiam eius*

Therefore Moses swore that he would live with him. And he received Sephora, his daughter,

2:22 *quae peperit filium quem vocavit Gersam dicens advena fui in terra aliena*

who birthed *a* son whom he called Gersam, saying, "I was *a* newcomer in *a* strange land."

Israel Cries Out to God
2:23 *post multum temporis mortuus est rex Aegypti et ingemescentes filii Israhel propter opera vociferati sunt ascenditque clamor eorum ad Deum ab operibus*

After *a* long time, Egypt's king died,

and Israel's children, groaning in anguish because of *their* labor, cried out loudly. And their cry concerning *their* labors went up to God.

2:24 *et audivit gemitum eorum ac recordatus foederis quod pepigerat cum Abraham et Isaac et Iacob*

And He heard their moan and, remembering *the* covenant that He had made with Abraham and Isaac and Jacob,

2:25 *respexit filios Israhel et cognovit eos*

He looked on Israel's children and knew them.

The Lord Appears in Sinai

Exodus 3:1 *Moses autem pascebat oves Iethro cognati sui sacerdotis Madian cumque minasset gregem ad interiora deserti venit ad montem Dei Horeb*

But Moses fed *the* sheep of Jethro, his kinsman, Midian's priest. And when he had driven *the* flock to *the* desert's interior, he came to God's mountain, Horeb.

3:2 *apparuitque ei Dominus in flamma ignis de medio rubi et videbat quod rubus arderet et non conbureretur*

And *the* Lord appeared to him in *a* flame of fire, from *the* middle of *a* bramble bush. And he saw that *the* bush was burning, yet it wasn't consumed.

3:3 *dixit ergo Moses vadam et videbo visionem hanc magnam quare non conburatur rubus*

So Moses said, "I will go and see this great vision. Why isn't *the* bush burned up?

The Lord Speaks
to Moses

3:4 *cernens autem Dominus quod pergeret ad videndum vocavit eum de medio rubi et ait Moses Moses qui respondit adsum*

But *the* Lord, discerning that he had

gone on to see, called him from *the* middle of *the* bush and said, "Moses, Moses!"

He answered, "I am here."

3:5 *at ille ne adpropies inquit huc solve calciamentum de pedibus tuis locus enim in quo stas terra sancta est*

And He said, "Don't come near here! Untie *the* sandals from your feet, for *the* place in which you stand is holy!

3:6 *et ait ego sum Deus patris tui Deus Abraham Deus Isaac Deus Iacob abscondit Moses faciem suam non enim audebat aspicere contra Deum*

And He said, "I am your father's God, Abraham's God, Isaac's God, Jacob's God."

Moses hid his face, for he didn't dare to look toward God.

3:7 *cui ait Dominus vidi adflictionem populi mei in Aegypto et clamorem eius audivi propter duritiam eorum qui praesunt operibus*

The Lord said to him, "I have seen my people's affliction in Egypt, and I have heard his cry because of *the* harshness of those who control *their* works.

3:8 *et sciens dolorem eius descendi ut liberarem eum de manibus Aegyptiorum et educerem de terra illa in terram bonam et spatiosam in terram quae fluit lacte et melle ad loca Chananei et Hetthei et Amorrei Ferezei et Evei et Iebusei*

"And, knowing his pain, I have come down so I can free *him* from *the* Egyptians' hands, and lead *him* from that land into *a* good and spacious land, into *a* land that flows with milk and honey, to *the* place of Canaanites and Hittites and Amorites, Ferezites and Hivites and Jebusites.

3:9 *clamor ergo filiorum Israhel venit ad me vidique adflictionem eorum qua ab Aegyptiis opprimuntur*

Therefore Israel's children's cry came to me, and I saw *the* affliction with which they are pressed down by *the* Egyptians.

3:10 *sed veni mittam te ad Pharaonem ut educas populum meum filios Israhel de Aegypto*

"But come! I will send you to Pharaoh, so you can lead my people, Israel's children, out of Egypt."

Moses Hesitates

3:11 *dixit Moses ad Deum quis ego sum ut vadam ad Pharaonem et educam filios Israhel de Aegypto*

Moses said to God, "Who am I that I should go to Pharaoh and lead Israel's children from Egypt?"

3:12 *qui dixit ei ero tecum et hoc habebis signum quod miserim te cum eduxeris populum de Aegypto immolabis Deo super montem istum*

The Lord said to him, "I will be with you, and you will have this sign that I have sent you. When you lead *the* people from Egypt, you will burn offerings to God on this mountain.

3:13 *ait Moses ad Deum ecce ego vadam ad filios Israhel et dicam eis Deus patrum vestrorum misit me ad vos si dixerint mihi quod est nomen eius quid dicam eis*

Moses said to God, "Look, I will go to Israel's children and say to them, 'Your fathers' God sent me to you.' If they say to me, 'What is His name?' what will I tell them?"

3:14 *dixit Deus ad Mosen ego sum qui sum ait sic dices filiis Israhel qui est misit me ad vos*

God said to Moses, "I am who I am."

He said, "So you will say to Israel's children, 'Who is' sent me to you.'"

3:15 *dixitque iterum Deus ad Mosen haec dices filiis Israhel Dominus Deus patrum vestrorum Deus Abraham Deus Isaac et Deus Iacob misit me ad vos hoc nomen mihi est*

*in aeternum et hoc memoriale meum
in generationem et generatione*

And God spoke to Moses again,
"You will say this to Israel's children.
'The Lord God of your fathers,
Abraham's God, Isaac's God, and
Jacob's God, sent me to you. This is
My name in eternity, and this my
memorial in generation after
generation.'

3:16 *vade congrega seniores Israhel
et dices ad eos Dominus Deus
patrum vestrorum apparuit mihi
Deus Abraham et Deus Isaac et Deus
Iacob dicens visitans visitavi vos et
omnia quae acciderunt vobis in
Aegypto*

"Go! Gather Israel's elders, and say
to them, *'The* Lord God of your
fathers appeared to me – Abraham's
God and Isaac's God and Jacob's
God – saying, 'Visiting, I have
visited you, and all that has happened
to you in Egypt.'

3:17 *et dixi ut educam vos de
adflictione Aegypti in terram
Chananei et Hetthei et Amorrei
Ferezei et Evei et Iebusei ad terram
fluentem lacte et melle*

"'And I said that I will lead you out
from Egypt's affliction, into *the* land
of *the* Canaanites and Hittites and
Amorites, Ferezites and Hivites and
Jebusites, to *a* land flowing with milk
and honey.

3:18 *et audient vocem tuam
ingredierisque tu et seniores Israhel
ad regem Aegypti et dices ad eum
Dominus Deus Hebraeorum vocavit
nos ibimus viam trium dierum per
solitudinem ut immolemus Domino
Deo nostro*

"And they will listen to your voice.
And you and Israel's elders will go in
to Egypt's king, and you will say to
him, *'The* Lord, *the* Hebrews' God,
called us. We will go three days'
journey into *the* desert, so we can
burn sacrifices to *the* Lord our God.'

3:19 *sed ego scio quod non dimittet
vos rex Aegypti ut eatis nisi per
manum validam*

"But I know that Egypt's king will
not release you so you can go, except
by *a* strong hand.

3:20 *extendam enim manum meam
et percutiam Aegyptum in cunctis
mirabilibus meis quae facturus sum
in medio eorum post haec dimittet
vos*

"For I will stretch out My hand and
strike Egypt in all My miracles,
which I will do in their midst. After
this, he will release you.

3:22 *daboque gratiam populo huic
coram Aegyptiis et cum egrediemini
non exibitis vacui*

"And I will give this people grace

before *the* Egyptians. And when you go out, you will not leave empty-handed.

3:23 *sed postulabit mulier a vicina sua et ab hospita vasa argentea et aurea ac vestes ponetisque eas super filios et filias vestras et spoliabitis Aegyptum*

"But *a* woman will demand from neighbor and landlord vessels of silver and gold, and clothing. And you will put them on your sons and your daughters, and you will plunder Egypt.

Moses Continues
to Resist God's Call

Exodus 4:1 *respondens Moses ait non credent mihi neque audient vocem meam sed dicent non apparuit tibi Dominus*

Moses, answering, said, "They won't believe me or listen to my voice. But they'll say, '*The* Lord didn't appear to you'."

4:2 *dixit ergo ad eum quid est hoc quod tenes in manu tua respondit virga*

He said to him, therefore, "What is this that you have in your hand?"

He answered, "*A* staff."

4:3 *ait proice eam in terram proiecit et versa est in colubrum ita ut fugeret Moses*

He said, "Throw it on the ground!"

He threw it and it turned into *a* snake, so Moses fled.

4:4 *dixitque Dominus extende manum tuam et adprehende caudam eius extendit et tenuit versaque est in virgam*

And *the* Lord said, "Stretch out your hand and take its tail!"

He stretched *it* out and took *it*, and it turned into *a* staff.

4:5 *ut credant inquit quod apparuerit tibi Dominus Deus patrum tuorum Deus Abraham Deus Isaac Deus Iacob*

"So they will believe," He said, "that *the* Lord God of your fathers appeared to you, Abraham's God, Isaac's God, Jacob's God.

4:6 *dixitque Dominus rursum mitte manum in sinum tuum quam cum misisset in sinum protulit leprosam instar nivis*

And *the* Lord spoke again, "Put your hand in your chest!"

When he had put it in his chest, he took it out leprous, like snow.

4:7 *retrahe ait manum in sinum tuum retraxit et protulit iterum et erat similis carni reliquae*

"Draw it back," He said, "to your chest."

He drew *it* back and took *it* out again, and it was like *the* rest of *his* flesh.

4:8 *si non crediderint inquit tibi neque audierint sermonem signi prioris credent verbo signi sequentis*

"If they won't believe," He said, "or listen to *the* first sign's message, they will believe *the* following sign's message.

4:9 *quod si nec duobus quidem his signis crediderint neque audierint vocem tuam sume aquam fluminis et effunde eam super aridam et quicquid hauseris de fluvio vertetur in sanguinem*

"Which, if they won't believe these two signs or listen to your voice, take *the* river's water and pour it over dry land, and whatever you draw up from *the* river will be turned to blood."

Moses Claims
He Cannot Speak Well

4:10 *ait Moses obsecro Domine non sum eloquens ab heri et nudius tertius et ex quo locutus es ad servum tuum inpeditioris et tardioris linguae sum*

Moses said, "I pray, Lord. I am not eloquent from yesterday and *the* third day. And since You spoke to Your slave, my tongue is more hindered and slower."

4:11 *dixit Dominus ad eum quis fecit os hominis aut quis fabricatus est mutum et surdum videntem et caecum nonne ego*

The Lord said to him, "Who made man's mouth or who formed *the* mute and deaf, *the* seeing and blind? Isn't *it* I?

4:12 *perge igitur et ego ero in ore tuo doceboque te quid loquaris*

"Go, therefore, and I will be in your mouth! And I will teach you what you will say."

4:13 *at ille obsecro inquit Domine mitte quem missurus es*

And he said, "I pray, Lord, send whom You will send!"

Aaron's Coming Predicted
4:14 *iratus Dominus in Mosen ait Aaron frater tuus Levites scio quod eloquens sit ecce ipse egreditur in occursum tuum vidensque te laetabitur corde*

The Lord, angry at Moses, said, "Aaron *the* Levite *is* your brother. I know that he is eloquent. Look, he is coming out to meet you, and seeing you, he will be happy in heart.

4:15 *loquere ad eum et pone verba mea in ore eius ego ero in ore tuo et in ore illius et ostendam vobis quid agere debeatis*

"Speak to Him and put My word in his mouth. I will be in your mouth and in his mouth, and I will show you *both* what you must do.

4:16 *ipse loquetur pro te ad populum et erit os tuum tu autem eris ei in his quae ad Deum pertinent*

"He will speak for you to *the* people and will be your mouth. But you will be to him as these which pertain to God.

4:17 *virgam quoque hanc sume in manu tua in qua facturus es signa*

"Take up this staff in your hand as well, in which you will work signs."

Moses Returns to Egypt
4:18 *abiit Moses et reversus est ad Iethro cognatum suum dixitque ei vadam et revertar ad fratres meos in Aegyptum ut videam si adhuc vivunt cui ait Iethro vade in pace*

Moses went out and came back to Jethro, his kinsman. And he said to him, "I will go and return to my brothers in Egypt, so I can see if they are still alive."

Jethro said to him, "Go in peace."

4:19 *dixit ergo Dominus ad Mosen in Madian vade revertere in Aegyptum mortui sunt omnes qui quaerebant animam tuam*

So *the* Lord said to Moses in Midian, "Go, return to Egypt! All who sought your life are dead."

4:20 *tulit Moses uxorem et filios suos et inposuit eos super asinum reversusque est in Aegyptum portans virgam Dei in manu sua*

Moses took his wife and sons and put them on *a* donkey, and he went back to Egypt, carrying God's staff in his hand.

The Lord Predicts
Pharaoh's Hard Heart

4:21 *dixitque ei Dominus revertenti in Aegyptum vide ut omnia ostenta quae posui in manu tua facias coram Pharaone ego indurabo cor eius et non dimittet populum*

And *the* Lord said to him *as he was* going back to Egypt, "See that you work before Pharaoh all *the* wonders that I have put in your hand! I will harden his heart, and he won't release *the* people.

4:22 *dicesque ad eum haec dicit Dominus filius meus primogenitus meus Israhel*

"And you will say to him, "*The* Lord says this: 'Israel *is* My firstborn son.'

4:23 *dixi tibi dimitte filium meum ut serviat mihi et noluisti dimittere eum ecce ego interficiam filium tuum primogenitum*

"I have said to you, 'Release My son so he can serve Me', and you didn't want to release him. Look, I will kill your firstborn son."

The Lord Wants
to Kill Moses

4:24 *cumque esset in itinere in diversorio occurrit ei Dominus et volebat occidere eum*

And when he was on *the* way, in *a* lodging place, *the* Lord met him and wanted to kill him.

4:25 *tulit ilico Seffora acutissimam petram et circumcidit praeputium filii sui tetigitque pedes eius et ait sponsus sanguinum tu mihi es*

Sephora immediately took *a* sharpened rock and circumcised her son's foreskin. And she touched his feet and said, "You are *a* bridegroom of blood to me."

4:26 *et dimisit eum postquam dixerat sponsus sanguinum ob circumcisionem*

And He released him, after she said, "*A* bridegroom of blood," for *the* circumcision's sake.

Moses and Aaron Meet

4:27 *dixit autem Dominus ad Aaron vade in occursum Mosi in deserto qui perrexit ei obviam in montem Dei et osculatus est eum*

But *the* Lord said to Aaron, "Go to meet Moses in *the* desert!"

He went out to him on *the* way to God's mountain, and he kissed him.

4:28 *narravitque Moses Aaron omnia verba Domini quibus miserat eum et signa quae mandaverat*

And Moses told Aaron all *the* words

of *the* Lord who had sent him, and all *the* signs which He had commanded.

Moses and Aaron
Gather Israel's Elders

4:29 *veneruntque simul et congregaverunt cunctos seniores filiorum Israhel*

And they came together and gathered all Israel's children's elders.

4:30 *locutusque est Aaron omnia verba quae dixerat Dominus ad Mosen et fecit signa coram populo*

And Aaron spoke all *the* words which *the* Lord had spoken to Moses, and he did *the* signs before *the* people.

4:31 *et credidit populus audieruntque quod visitasset Dominus filios Israhel et quod respexisset adflictionem eorum et proni adoraverunt*

And *the* people believed and listened, because *the* Lord had visited Israel's children, and because He had looked on their affliction. And they worshiped face-down.

Moses and Aaron
Demand Israel's Release

Exodus 5:1 *post haec ingressi sunt Moses et Aaron et dixerunt Pharaoni haec dicit Dominus Deus Israhel dimitte populum meum ut sacrificet mihi in deserto*

After this, Moses and Aaron went in and said to Pharaoh, "*The* Lord, Israel's God, says this: Release My people so it can sacrifice to Me in *the* desert!"

5:2 *at ille respondit quis est Dominus ut audiam vocem eius et dimittam Israhel nescio Dominum et Israhel non dimittam*

And he answered, "Who is *the* Lord that I should listen to his voice and release Israel? I don't know *the* Lord and I won't release Israel."

5:3 *dixerunt Deus Hebraeorum vocavit nos ut eamus viam trium dierum in solitudinem et sacrificemus Domino Deo nostro ne forte accidat nobis pestis aut gladius*

They said, "*The* Hebrews' God called us so we could go three days' journey into *the* wasteland and sacrifice to *the* Lord our God, unless perhaps plague or sword fall on us."

5:4 *ait ad eos rex Aegypti quare Moses et Aaron sollicitatis populum ab operibus suis ite ad onera vestra*

And Egypt's king said to them, "Moses and Aaron, why have you disturbed *the* people from its work? Go to your burdens!"

5:5 *dixitque Pharao multus est populus terrae videtis quod turba succreverit quanto magis si dederitis eis requiem ab operibus*

And Pharaoh said, "*The* land's people is large. You see that *the* turmoil has increased. How much more if you give them rest from their labors!

Pharaoh Increases
the People's Burdens
5:6 *praecepit ergo in die illo praefectis operum et exactoribus populi dicens*

So he commanded on that day *the* work's overseers and *the* people's taskmasters, saying,

5:7 *nequaquam ultra dabitis paleas populo ad conficiendos lateres sicut prius sed ipsi vadant et colligant stipulam*

"You will no longer give *the* people husks for making bricks as before, but they will go and collect stubble.

5:8 *et mensuram laterum quos prius faciebant inponetis super eos nec minuetis quicquam vacant enim et idcirco vociferantur dicentes eamus et sacrificemus Deo nostro*

"And you will impose on them *the* measure of bricks which they made before, nor will you diminish it any. For they are idle and for this reason they cry out saying, 'Let us go and sacrifice to our God.'

5:9 *opprimantur operibus et expleant ea ut non adquiescant verbis mendacibus*

"Let them be pressed down by works and complete them, so they won't give in to lying words."

5:10 *igitur egressi praefecti operum et exactores ad populum dixerunt sic dicit Pharao non do vobis paleas*

Going out, therefore, *the* work's overseers and taskmasters said to *the* people, "Pharaoh says this: 'I will not give you husks.'

5:11 *ite et colligite sicubi invenire potueritis nec minuetur quicquam de opere vestro*

"Go and collect *it*, if you can find it anywhere! Nor will anything be lessened from your work.'"

5:12 *dispersusque est populus per omnem terram Aegypti ad colligendas paleas*

And *the* people was scattered over all Egypt's land, collecting husks.

5:13 *praefecti quoque operum*

instabant dicentes conplete opus vestrum cotidie ut prius facere solebatis quando dabantur vobis paleae

The work's overseers likewise threatened them, saying, "Complete your daily work like you used to do before, when husks were given to you!"

5:14 *flagellatique sunt qui praeerant operibus filiorum Israhel ab exactoribus Pharaonis dicentibus quare non impletis mensuram laterum sicut prius nec heri nec hodie*

And those who were over Israel's children's work were beaten by Pharaoh's taskmasters, saying, "Why haven't you completed *the* quota of bricks like before – neither yesterday nor today!"

Israel Complains to Pharaoh

5:15 *veneruntque praepositi filiorum Israhel et vociferati sunt ad Pharaonem dicentes cur ita agis contra servos tuos*

And Israel's children's commanders came and complained to Pharaoh, saying, "Why are you acting so against your slaves?

5:16 *paleae non dantur nobis et lateres similiter imperantur en famuli tui flagellis caedimur et*

iniuste agitur contra populum tuum

"Husks aren't given to us, but bricks are commanded *the* same! Look, your servants are struck by whips, and it happens unfairly against your people!"

5:17 *qui ait vacatis otio et idcirco dicitis eamus et sacrificemus Domino*

Pharaoh said, "You are idle in leisure and for this reason you say, 'Let us go and sacrifice to *the* Lord.'

5:18 *ite ergo et operamini paleae non dabuntur vobis et reddetis consuetum numerum laterum*

"Go, therefore, and work! Husks won't be given you, yet you will return *the* usual number of bricks."

5:19 *videbantque se praepositi filiorum Israhel in malo eo quod diceretur eis non minuetur quicquam de lateribus per singulos dies*

And Israel's overseers saw themselves in harm, because he had said to them, "It will not be reduced at all from *the* bricks required each day."

5:20 *occurreruntque Mosi et Aaron qui stabant ex adverso egredientes a Pharaone*

And they met Moses and Aaron, who

stood opposite them going out from Pharaoh.

5:21 *et dixerunt ad eos videat Dominus et iudicet quoniam fetere fecistis odorem nostrum coram Pharao et servis eius et praebuistis ei gladium ut occideret nos*

And they said to them, "May *the* Lord see and judge, because you have made us *a* rotting odor before Pharaoh and his slaves! And you have provided him *a* sword, so he could kill us!"

5:22 *reversusque Moses ad Dominum ait Domine cur adflixisti populum istum quare misisti me*

And Moses, turning back to *the* Lord, said, "Lord, why have You afflicted this people? Why have you sent me?

5:23 *ex eo enim quo ingressus sum ad Pharaonem ut loquerer nomine tuo adflixit populum tuum et non liberasti eos*

"For since the *time* that I went in to Pharaoh so I could speak in Your name, he has afflicted Your people and You have not freed them!"

God Reaffirms
His Covenant with Israel

Exodus 6:1 *dixit Dominus ad Mosen nunc videbis quae facturus sum Pharaoni per manum enim fortem dimittet eos et in manu robusta eiciet illos de terra sua*

The Lord said to Moses, "Now you will see what I will do to Pharaoh, for he will release them by *a* strong hand and throw them out of his land with *a* robust hand."

6:2 *locutusque est Dominus ad Mosen dicens ego Dominus*

And *the* Lord spoke to Moses, saying, "I *am the* Lord

6:3 *qui apparui Abraham Isaac et Iacob in Deo omnipotente et nomen meum Adonai non indicavi eis*

"who appeared to Abraham, Isaac, and Jacob as God omnipotent. Yet I did not tell them My name, Adonai.

6:4 *pepigique cum eis foedus ut darem illis terram Chanaan terram peregrinationis eorum in qua fuerunt advenae*

"And I made *a* covenant with them, that I would give them Canaan's land, their sojournings' land, in which they were newcomers.

6:5 *ego audivi gemitum filiorum Israhel quo Aegyptii oppresserunt* *eos et recordatus sum pacti mei*

"I have heard Israel's children's groaning because *the* Egyptians have pressed them down, and I have remembered My pact.

6:6 *ideo dic filiis Israhel ego Dominus qui educam vos de ergastulo Aegyptiorum et eruam de servitute ac redimam in brachio excelso et iudiciis magnis*

"Therefore, say to Israel's children, 'I am *the* Lord, who will lead you from *the* Egyptians' prison and rescue you from slavery. And I will redeem by *a* raised arm and mighty judgments.

6:7 *et adsumam vos mihi in populum et ero vester Deus scietisque quod ego sim Dominus Deus vester qui eduxerim vos de ergastulo Aegyptiorum*

"And I will take you up to Myself as *a* people, and I will be your God. And you will know that I am *the* Lord your God, who has led you from *the* Egyptians' prison,

6:8 *et induxerim in terram super quam levavi manum meam ut darem eam Abraham Isaac et Iacob daboque illam vobis possidendam ego Dominus*

"and I have led you into *the* land over which I lifted up My hand, so I could give it to Abraham, Isaac, and Jacob.

And I will give it to you as *a* possession. I am *the* Lord."

Moses Tells the People

6:9 *narravit ergo Moses omnia filiis Israhel qui non adquieverunt ei propter angustiam spiritus et opus durissimum*

So Moses told all *these things* to Israel's children, who did not assent to him because of spirit's anguish and most difficult work.

God Sends Moses
to Pharaoh Again

6:10 *locutusque est Dominus ad Mosen dicens*

And *the* Lord spoke to Moses, saying,

6:11 *ingredere et loquere ad Pharao regem Aegypti ut dimittat filios Israhel de terra sua*

"Go in and speak to Pharaoh, Egypt's king, that he release Israel's children from his land."

6:12 *respondit Moses coram Domino ecce filii Israhel non me audiunt et quomodo audiet me Pharao praesertim cum sim incircumcisus labiis*

Moses answered before *the* Lord, "Look, Israel's children don't listen to me, and how will Pharaoh hear me, especially when I am of uncircumcised lips?"

6:13 *locutus est Dominus ad Mosen et Aaron et dedit mandatum ad filios Israhel et ad Pharao regem Aegypti ut educerent filios Israhel de terra Aegypti*

The Lord spoke to Moses and Aaron, and gave *a* commandment to Israel's children and to Pharaoh, Egypt's king, that they lead Israel's children from Egypt's land.

Israel's Leaders

6:14 *isti sunt principes domorum per familias suas filii Ruben primogeniti Israhelis Enoch et Phallu Aesrom et Charmi*

These are *the* houses' princes by their families:
the sons of Reuben, Israel's firstborn: Enoch and Phallu, Aesrom and Charmi –

6:15 *hae cognationes Ruben filii Symeon Iamuhel et Iamin et Aod Iachin et Soer et Saul filius Chananitidis hae progenies Symeon*

these are Reuben's clans.

Simeon's sons *were* Jamuel and Jamin and Aod; Jachin and Soer and Saul, *a* Canaanite woman's son – these *are* Simeon's descendants.

Levi's Descendants

6:16 *et haec nomina filiorum Levi per cognationes suas Gerson et Caath et Merari anni autem vitae Levi fuerunt centum triginta septem*

And these *are the* names of Levi's children by their clans: Gerson and Caath and Merari (but *the* years of Levi's life were one hundred thirty-seven).

6:17 *filii Gerson Lobeni et Semei per cognationes suas*

Gershon's sons *were* Lobeni and Shemei, by their clans.

6:18 *filii Caath Amram et Isuar et Hebron et Ozihel annique vitae Caath centum triginta tres*

Caath's sons *were* Amram and Isuar and Hebron and Ozihel (*the* years of Caath's life were one hundred thirty-three).

6:19 *filii Merari Mooli et Musi hae cognationes Levi per familias suas*

Merari's sons *were* Mooli and Musi. These are Levi's clans, by their families.

6:20 *accepit autem Amram uxorem Iocabed patruelem suam quae peperit ei Aaron et Mosen fueruntque anni vitae Amram centum triginta septem*

But Amram accepted *as* wife Jocabed, his cousin, who birthed him

Aaron and Moses. And *the* years of Amram's life were one hundred thirty-seven.

6:21 *filii quoque Isuar Core et Napheg et Zechri*

Likewise, Isuar's sons *were* Core and Napheg and Zechri.

6:22 *filii quoque Ozihel Misahel et Elsaphan et Sethri*

Likewise, Ozihel's sons *were* Misael and Elsaphan and Sethri.

6:23 *accepit autem Aaron uxorem Elisabe filiam Aminadab sororem Naasson quae peperit ei Nadab et Abiu et Eleazar et Ithamar*

But Aaron received *as* wife Elisabe, daughter of Aminadab, Naasson's sister, who birthed him Nadab and Abiu and Eleazar and Ithamar.

6:24 *filii quoque Core Asir et Helcana et Abiasab hae sunt cognationes Coritarum*

Core's sons likewise *were* Asir and Helcana and Abiasab. These are *the* Coreite clans.

6:25 *at vero Eleazar filius Aaron accepit uxorem de filiabus Phutihel quae peperit ei Finees hii sunt principes familiarum leviticarum per cognationes suas*

And indeed Eleazar, Aaron's son, received *a* wife from Phutiel's daughters, who birthed him Phineas. These are *the* princes of *the* Levitical families, by their clans.

6:26 *iste est Aaron et Moses quibus praecepit Dominus ut educerent filios Israhel de terra Aegypti per turmas suas*

This is Aaron and Moses, whom *the* Lord commanded that they lead Israel's children from Egypt's land by their companies.

6:27 *hii sunt qui loquuntur ad Pharao regem Aegypti ut educant filios Israhel de Aegypto iste Moses et Aaron*

These are *the ones* who spoke to Pharaoh, Egypt's king, so they could lead Israel's children out of Egypt – this Moses and Aaron,

6:28 *in die qua locutus est Dominus ad Mosen in terra Aegypti*

on *the* day when *the* Lord spoke to Moses in Egypt's land.

6:29 *et locutus est Dominus ad Mosen dicens ego Dominus loquere ad Pharao regem Aegypti omnia quae ego loquor tibi*

And *the* Lord spoke to Moses, saying, "I *am the* Lord. Say to Pharaoh, Egypt's king, all that I say to you.

6:30 *et ait Moses coram Domino en incircumcisus labiis sum quomodo audiet me Pharao*

And Moses said before *the* Lord, "Look, I am of uncircumcised lips. How will Pharaoh listen to me?"

The Lord Explains
His Purposes to Moses

Exodus 7:1 *dixitque Dominus ad Mosen ecce constitui te Deum Pharaonis Aaron frater tuus erit propheta tuus*

And *the* Lord said to Moses, "Look, I have appointed you God to Pharaoh. Aaron your brother will be your prophet.

7:2 *tu loqueris omnia quae mando tibi ille loquetur ad Pharaonem ut dimittat filios Israhel de terra sua*

"You will speak all that I command you. He will speak to Pharaoh, that he release Israel's children from his land.

7:3 *sed ego indurabo cor eius et multiplicabo signa et ostenta mea in terra Aegypti*

"But I will harden his heart and multiply My signs and wonders in Egypt's land.

7:4 *et non audiet vos inmittamque manum meam super Aegyptum et educam exercitum et populum meum filios Israhel de terra Aegypti per iudicia maxima*

"And he will not hear you. And I will send My hand in over Egypt, and lead out My army and people, Israel's children, from Egypt's land by *the* greatest judgments.

7:5 *et scient Aegyptii quod ego sim Dominus qui extenderim manum meam super Aegyptum et eduxerim filios Israhel de medio eorum*

"And *the* Egyptians will know that I am *the* Lord, who stretched out My hand over Egypt and led Israel's children out from their midst."

Moses and Aaron Obey

7:6 *fecit itaque Moses et Aaron sicut praeceperat Dominus ita egerunt*

So Moses and Aaron did. As *the* Lord had commanded, so they did.

Moses and Aaron's Ages

7:7 *erat autem Moses octoginta annorum et Aaron octoginta trium quando locuti sunt ad Pharaonem*

But Moses was eighty years old and Aaron eighty-three when they spoke to Pharaoh.

The Second Encounter with Pharaoh

7:8 *dixitque Dominus ad Mosen et Aaron*

And *the* Lord said to Moses and Aaron,

7:9 *cum dixerit vobis Pharao ostendite signa dices ad Aaron tolle virgam tuam et proice eam coram Pharao ac vertatur in colubrum*

"When Pharaoh has said to you, 'Show signs!' you will say to Aaron, 'Take your staff and throw it down before Pharaoh!' And it will turn into *a* snake."

7:10 *ingressi itaque Moses et Aaron ad Pharaonem fecerunt sicut praeceperat Dominus tulitque Aaron virgam coram Pharao et servis eius quae versa est in colubrum*

So Moses and Aaron, going in to Pharaoh, did as *the* Lord had commanded. And Aaron took *the* staff which turned into *a* snake before Pharaoh and his slaves.

7:11 *vocavit autem Pharao sapientes et maleficos et fecerunt etiam ipsi per incantationes aegyptias et arcana quaedam similiter*

But Pharaoh called wise men and magicians and they also did something similar through Egyptian incantations and mysteries.

7:12 *proieceruntque singuli virgas suas quae versae sunt in dracones sed devoravit virga Aaron virgas eorum*

And each one threw down their staffs which turned into dragons, but Aaron's staff devoured their staffs.

7:13 *induratumque est cor Pharaonis et non audivit eos sicut* *praeceperat Dominus*

And Pharaoh's heart was hardened and he did not listen to them, as *the* Lord had commanded.

The River Turned to Blood

7:14 *dixit autem Dominus ad Mosen ingravatum est cor Pharaonis non vult dimittere populum*

But *the* Lord said to Moses, "Pharaoh's heart is weighed down. He doesn't want to release *the* people.

7:15 *vade ad eum mane ecce egredietur ad aquas et stabis in occursum eius super ripam fluminis et virgam quae conversa est in draconem tolles in manu tua*

"Go to him! Look, he goes out early to *the* waters, and you will stand to meet him on *the* river bank. And you will take *the* staff which turned into *a* dragon in your hand.

7:16 *dicesque ad eum Dominus Deus Hebraeorum misit me ad te dicens dimitte populum meum ut mihi sacrificet in deserto et usque ad praesens audire noluisti*

"And you will say to him, '*The* Lord, *the* Hebrews' God, sent me to you, saying, 'Release My people so it can sacrifice to Me in *the* desert, and even to *the* present you haven't wanted to listen!'

7:17 *haec igitur dicit Dominus in hoc scies quod Dominus sim ecce percutiam virga quae in manu mea est aquam fluminis et vertetur in sanguinem*

"Therefore, *the* Lord says this: 'You will know that I am *the* Lord in this: Look, I will strike *the* river's waters by *the* staff which is in my hand, and it will be turned into blood!'

7:18 *pisces quoque qui sunt in fluvio morientur et conputrescent aquae et adfligentur Aegyptii bibentes aquam fluminis*

"*The* fish that are in *the* river will die as well, and *the* waters will putrefy, and *the* Egyptians will be afflicted, drinking *the* river's water."

7:19 *dixit quoque Dominus ad Mosen dic ad Aaron tolle virgam tuam et extende manum tuam super aquas Aegypti et super fluvios eorum et rivos ac paludes et omnes lacus aquarum ut vertantur in sanguinem et sit cruor in omni terra Aegypti tam in ligneis vasis quam in saxeis*

The Lord also said to Moses, "Say to Aaron, 'Take your staff and stretch out your hand over Egypt's waters and over their rivers and streams and marshes and all their reservoirs of waters, so they be turned to blood and let gore be in all Egypt's land, whether in wooden vessels or in stone.'"

7:20 *feceruntque ita Moses et Aaron sicut praeceperat Dominus et elevans virgam percussit aquam fluminis coram Pharao et servis eius quae versa est in sanguinem*

And Moses and Aaron did so as *the* Lord had commanded. And, lifting up *the* staff, he struck *the* river's water, which was turned to blood before Pharaoh and his slaves.

7:21 *et pisces qui erant in flumine mortui sunt conputruitque fluvius et non poterant Aegyptii bibere aquam fluminis et fuit sanguis in tota terra Aegypti*

And *the* fish which were in *the* river died, and *the* river putrefied, and *the* Egyptians couldn't drink *the* river water. And it was blood in all Egypt's land.

7:22 *feceruntque similiter malefici Aegyptiorum incantationibus suis et induratum est cor Pharaonis nec audivit eos sicut praeceperat Dominus*

But *the* Egyptians' magicians did *a* similar *thing* by their incantations and Pharaoh's heart was hardened, nor did he listen to them, as *the* Lord had commanded.

7:23 *avertitque se et ingressus est domum suam nec adposuit cor etiam hac vice*

And he turned himself away and went into his house, nor did he set *his* heart this time also.

7:24 *foderunt autem omnes Aegyptii per circuitum fluminis aquam ut biberent non enim poterant bibere de aqua fluminis*

But all *the* Egyptians dug around *the* river so they could drink water, for they couldn't drink from *the* river's water.

7:25 *impletique sunt septem dies postquam percussit Dominus fluvium*

And seven days were completed after *the* Lord struck *the* river.

Frogs Cover
Egypt's Land

Exodus 8:1 *dixitque Dominus ad Mosen ingredere ad Pharao et dices ad eum haec dicit Dominus dimitte populum meum ut sacrificet mihi*

And *the* Lord said to Moses, "Go in to Pharaoh! And you will say to him, '*The* Lord says this: release My people so it can sacrifice to Me!'

8:2 *sin autem nolueris dimittere ecce ego percutiam omnes terminos tuos ranis*

"'But if you do not want to release *them*, look! I will strike all your borders with frogs.

8:3 *et ebulliet fluvius ranas quae ascendent et ingredientur domum tuam et cubiculum lectuli tui et super stratum tuum et in domos servorum tuorum et in populum tuum et in furnos tuos et in reliquias ciborum tuorum*

"'And *the* river will boil over with frogs, who will climb up and go into your house and your bedroom and on your bed, and in your slaves' houses, and among your people, and in your ovens, and in *the* rest of your food.

8:4 *et ad te et ad populum tuum et ad omnes servos tuos intrabunt ranae*

"And frogs will come in to you and to your people and to all your slaves.'"

8:5 *dixitque Dominus ad Mosen dic Aaron extende manum tuam super fluvios et super rivos ac paludes et educ ranas super terram Aegypti*

And *the* Lord said to Moses, "Tell Aaron, 'Stretch out your hand over rivers and over streams and over marshes, and bring frogs over Egypt's land!'"

8:6 *extendit Aaron manum super aquas Aegypti et ascenderunt ranae operueruntque terram Aegypti*

Aaron stretched out his hand over Egypt's waters, and frogs came up and covered Egypt's land.

8:7 *fecerunt autem et malefici per incantationes suas similiter eduxeruntque ranas super terram Aegypti*

But *the* magicians also did *something* similar by their incantations, and they brought frogs over Egypt's land.

Pharaoh Asks That
the Frogs Be Removed

8:8 *vocavit autem Pharao Mosen et Aaron et dixit orate Dominum ut auferat ranas a me et a populo meo et dimittam populum ut sacrificet Domino*

But Pharaoh called Moses and Aaron

and said, "Pray to *the* Lord that He take *the* frogs away from me and my people, and I will release *the* people so they can sacrifice to *the* Lord."

8:9 *dixitque Moses Pharaoni constitue mihi quando deprecer pro te et pro servis tuis et pro populo tuo ut abigantur ranae a te et a domo tua et tantum in flumine remaneant*

And Moses said to Pharaoh, "Set for me when I should pray for you and for your slaves and for your people that *the* frogs be removed from you and from your house, and remain only in the river."

8:10 *qui respondit cras at ille iuxta verbum inquit tuum ut scias quoniam non est sicut Dominus Deus noster*

He answered, "Tomorrow."

And *Moses* said, "According to your word, so you may know that no one is like *the* Lord our God.

8:11 *et recedent ranae a te et a domo tua et a servis tuis et a populo tuo tantum in flumine remanebunt*

"And *the* frogs will recede from you and from your house and from your slaves and from your people, and will remain only in *the* river."

**Moses Prays
About the Frogs**
8:12 *egressique sunt Moses et*

Aaron a Pharaone et clamavit Moses ad Dominum pro sponsione ranarum quam condixerat Pharaoni

And Moses and Aaron went out from Pharaoh. And Moses cried to *the* Lord for *the* promise *concerning the* frogs which he had agreed on with Pharaoh.

8:13 *fecitque Dominus iuxta verbum Mosi et mortuae sunt ranae de domibus et de villis et de agris*

And *the* Lord did according to Moses' word, and *the* frogs died out from *the* houses and villages and fields.

8:14 *congregaveruntque eas in inmensos aggeres et conputruit terra*

And they gathered them in great heaps and *the* land rotted.

Pharaoh Changes His Mind
8:15 *videns autem Pharao quod data esset requies ingravavit cor suum et non audivit eos sicut praeceperat Dominus*

But Pharaoh, seeing that respite was given, hardened his heart and did not listen to them, as *the* Lord had commanded.

8:16 *dixitque Dominus ad Mosen loquere ad Aaron extende virgam tuam et percute pulverem terrae et sint scinifes in universa terra Aegypti*

And *the* Lord said to Moses, "Say to Aaron, 'Stretch out your staff and strike *the* land's dust, so *there* may be biting flies in all Egypt's land.

8:17 *feceruntque ita et extendit Aaron manu virgam tenens percussitque pulverem terrae et facti sunt scinifes in hominibus et in iumentis omnis pulvis terrae versus est in scinifes per totam terram Aegypti*

And they did so. And Aaron stretched out *the* staff he had in hand and struck *the* land's dust, and it became biting flies on men and on cattle. All *the* land's dust was turned into biting flies through all Egypt's land.

Pharaoh's Magicians
Can't Duplicate the Sign

8:18 *feceruntque similiter malefici incantationibus suis ut educerent scinifes et non potuerunt erantque scinifes tam in hominibus quam in iumentis*

And *the* magicians did something similar by their incantations so they could lead in biting flies, but they couldn't. And *the* biting flies were on men and on cattle alike.

8:19 *et dixerunt malefici ad Pharao digitus Dei est induratumque est cor Pharaonis et non audivit eos sicut praeceperat Dominus*

And *the* magicians said to Pharaoh, "This is God's finger."

Yet Pharaoh's heart was hardened and he did not listen to them, as *the* Lord had commanded.

8:20 *dixit quoque Dominus ad Mosen consurge diluculo et sta coram Pharaone egreditur enim ad aquas et dices ad eum haec dicit Dominus dimitte populum meum ut sacrificet mihi*

The Lord said to Moses as well, "Get up early and stand before Pharaoh, for he goes out to the waters. And you will say to him, '*The* Lord says this: Release My people so they can sacrifice to Me!

8:21 *quod si non dimiseris eum ecce ego inmittam in te et in servos tuos et in populum tuum et in domos tuas omne genus muscarum et implebuntur domus Aegyptiorum muscis diversi generis et in universa terra in qua fuerint*

"'Which, if you will not release him, look! I will send in on you and on your slaves and on your people and on your houses every species of flies, and *the* Egyptians' houses will be filled with different types of flies, and in all the land in which they are.

8:22 *faciamque mirabilem in die illa terram Gessen in qua populus meus est ut non sint ibi muscae et* *scias quoniam ego Dominus in medio terrae*

"'And I will make Gessen's land *a* miracle in that day, in which My people lives, that *the* flies may not be there. And you will know that I am *the* Lord in the land's midst.

8:23 *ponamque divisionem inter populum meum et populum tuum cras erit signum istud*

"'And I will place *a* division between My people and your people. This sign will be tomorrow.'"

8:24 *fecitque Dominus ita et venit musca gravissima in domos Pharaonis et servorum eius et in omnem terram Aegypti corruptaque est terra ab huiuscemodi muscis*

And *the* Lord did so, and *the* heaviest fly came into *the* houses of Pharaoh and his slaves, and in all Egypt's land. And *the* land was corrupted by such flies.

Pharaoh Relents
In Part

8:25 *vocavit Pharao Mosen et Aaron et ait eis ite sacrificate Deo vestro in terra*

Pharaoh called Moses and Aaron and said to them, "Go, sacrifice to your God in *the* land!"

8:26 *et ait Moses non potest ita fieri*

abominationes enim Aegyptiorum immolabimus Domino Deo nostro quod si mactaverimus ea quae colunt Aegyptii coram eis lapidibus nos obruent

And Moses said, "It can't be done so, for we will offer *the* Egyptians' abominations to *the* Lord our God, that if we sacrifice that which *the* Egyptians serve before them, they will crush us with stones.

8:27 *via trium dierum pergemus in solitudine et sacrificabimus Domino Deo nostro sicut praeceperit nobis*

"We will go three days' journey into *the* wasteland and sacrifice to *the* Lord our God, as He commanded us."

8:28 *dixitque Pharao ego dimittam vos ut sacrificetis Domino Deo vestro in deserto verumtamen longius ne abeatis rogate pro me*

And Pharaoh said, "I release you so you can sacrifice to *the* Lord your God in *the* desert. Nevertheless, you may not go farther. Pray for me!"

8:29 *et ait Moses egressus a te orabo Dominum et recedet musca a Pharaone et a servis et a populo eius cras verumtamen noli ultra fallere ut non dimittas populum sacrificare Domino*

And Moses, going out, said, "I will

pray to *the* Lord for you, and *the* fly will recede from Pharaoh and his slaves and his people tomorrow. Nevertheless, don't deceive us further, that you not release *the* people to sacrifice to *the* Lord!"

8:30 *egressusque Moses a Pharao oravit Dominum*

And Moses, going out from Pharaoh, prayed to *the* Lord,

8:31 *qui fecit iuxta verbum illius et abstulit muscas a Pharao et a servis et a populo eius non superfuit ne una quidem*

who did according to his word and took away *the* flies from Pharaoh and his slaves and his people. And not *a* single one remained.

Pharaoh Changes His Mind Again

8:32 *et ingravatum est cor Pharaonis ita ut ne hac quidem vice dimitteret populum*

And so Pharaoh's heart was hardened, that he would not release *the* people this time either.

The Lord Again Commands Pharaoh

Exodus 9:1 *dixit autem Dominus ad Mosen ingredere ad Pharaonem et loquere ad eum haec dicit Dominus Deus Hebraeorum dimitte populum meum ut sacrificet mihi*

But *the* Lord said to Moses, "Go in to Pharaoh and say to him, '*The* Lord, *the* Hebrews' God, says this: Release My people so it can sacrifice to Me!

9:2 *quod si adhuc rennuis et retines eos*

"'Because, if you still refuse and retain them,

9:3 *ecce manus mea erit super agros tuos et super equos et asinos et camelos et boves et oves pestis valde gravis*

"'look, My hand will be over your fields and over horses and donkeys and camels and oxen and sheep, *an* overwhelmingly serious plague.

9:4 *et faciet Dominus mirabile inter possessiones Israhel et possessiones Aegyptiorum ut nihil omnino intereat ex his quae pertinent ad filios Israhel*

"'And *the* Lord will work miraculously between Israel's possessions and *the* Egyptians' possessions, that nothing at all of those which belong to Israel's children will die.

9:5 *constituitque Dominus tempus dicens cras faciet Dominus verbum istud in terra*

"And *the* Lord has appointed *a* time, saying, 'Tomorrow *the* Lord will do this word in *the* land.'"

9:6 *fecit ergo Dominus verbum hoc altero die mortuaque sunt omnia animantia Aegyptiorum de animalibus vero filiorum Israhel nihil omnino periit*

Therefore, *the* Lord did this word, and *the* following day all *the* Egyptians' animals died. But nothing at all among Israel's children's animals perished.

Pharaoh Investigates the Sign

9:7 *et misit Pharao ad videndum nec erat quicquam mortuum de his quae possidebat Israhel ingravatumque est cor Pharaonis et non dimisit populum*

And Pharaoh sent to see, yet nothing was dead among what Israel possessed. Yet Pharaoh's heart was hardened and he did not release *the* people.

Swelling Sores in Egypt

9:8 *et dixit Dominus ad Mosen et Aaron tollite plenas manus cineris de camino et spargat illud Moses in*

caelum coram Pharao

And *the* Lord said to Moses and Aaron, "Take handfuls of ashes from *a* furnace, and let Moses scatter them in *the* sky before Pharaoh.

9:9 *sitque pulvis super omnem terram Aegypti erunt enim in hominibus et in iumentis vulnera et vesicae turgentes in universa terra Aegypti*

"And let *the* dust be over all Egypt's land, for wounds will be in men and in cattle, and swelling sores in all Egypt's land."

9:10 *tuleruntque cinerem de camino et steterunt contra Pharao et sparsit illud Moses in caelum factaque sunt vulnera vesicarum turgentium in hominibus et in iumentis*

And they took ashes from *the* furnace and stood before Pharaoh. And Moses scattered it in *the* sky. And they became wounds of swelling sores in men and in cattle.

9:11 *nec poterant malefici stare coram Mosen propter vulnera quae in illis erant et in omni terra Aegypti*

Nor could *the* magicians stand before Moses, because of *the* wounds which were in them and in all Egypt's land.

9:12 *induravitque Dominus cor Pharaonis et non audivit eos sicut* *locutus est Dominus ad Mosen*

Yet *the* Lord hardened Pharaoh's heart, and he did not listen to what *the* Lord said to Moses.

9:13 *dixit quoque Dominus ad Mosen mane consurge et sta coram Pharao et dices ad eum haec dicit Dominus Deus Hebraeorum dimitte populum meum ut sacrificet mihi*

The Lord also said to Moses, "Get up early and stand before Pharaoh! And you will say to him, '*The* Lord says this: Release My people so it can sacrifice to Me,

9:14 *quia in hac vice mittam omnes plagas meas super cor tuum super servos tuos et super populum tuum ut scias quod non sit similis mei in omni terra*

"for in this turn I will send all My blows over your heart, over your slaves, and over your people, so you may know that no one is like Me in all *the* land!

9:15 *nunc enim extendens manum percutiam te et populum tuum peste peribisque de terra*

"'For now, stretching out My hand, I will strike you and your people by plague, and you will perish from *the* land."

9:16 *idcirco autem posui te ut*

ostendam in te fortitudinem meam et narretur nomen meum in omni terra

"'But I have appointed you for this reason, so I may show My strength in you, and My name may be told in all *the* land.

9:17 *adhuc retines populum meum et non vis eum dimittere*

"'You still retain My people and do not want to release him.

9:18 *en pluam hac ipsa hora cras grandinem multam nimis qualis non fuit in Aegypto a die qua fundata est usque in praesens tempus*

"Look! I will rain at this hour tomorrow *a* great, overwhelming hail, such as has not been in Egypt from *the* day which it was founded even to *the* present time.

9:19 *mitte ergo iam nunc et congrega iumenta tua et omnia quae habes in agro homines enim et iumenta et universa quae inventa fuerint foris nec congregata de agris cecideritque super ea grando morientur*

"'Send, therefore, already now, and gather your cattle and all that you have in the field, for men and cattle and all that will be found outside, nor gathered from the fields and *the* hail will fall on them, will die.'"

Distinction Between Those Who Believe and Those Who Don't

9:20 *qui timuit verbum Domini de servis Pharao fecit confugere servos suos et iumenta in domos*

One who feared *the* Lord's word among Pharaoh's slaves made his slaves and cattle flee together into houses.

9:21 *qui autem neglexit sermonem Domini dimisit servos suos et iumenta in agris*

But *one* who neglected *the* Lord's word left his slaves and cattle in *the* fields.

9:22 *et dixit Dominus ad Mosen extende manum tuam in caelum ut fiat grando in universa terra Aegypti super homines et super iumenta et super omnem herbam agri in terra Aegypti*

And *the* Lord said to Moses, "Stretch out your hand to *the* sky so hail may be in all Egypt's land, over men and over cattle and over *the* plant of every field in Egypt's land."

9:23 *extenditque Moses virgam in caelum et Dominus dedit tonitrua et grandinem ac discurrentia fulgura super terram pluitque Dominus grandinem super terram Aegypti*

And Moses stretched out *the* staff to *the* sky, and *the* Lord gave thunder and hail and scattering lightning over *the* land. And *the* Lord rained hail over Egypt's land.

9:24 *et grando et ignis inmixta pariter ferebantur tantaeque fuit magnitudinis quanta ante numquam apparuit in universa terra Aegypti ex quo gens illa condita est*

And hail and fire mixed together were brought. And *the* magnitude was so great that never before had such appeared in all Egypt's land, since *the* time that nation was founded.

9:25 *et percussit grando in omni terra Aegypti cuncta quae fuerunt in agris ab homine usque ad iumentum cunctam herbam agri percussit grando et omne lignum regionis confregit*

And *the* hail struck in all Egypt's land. And it struck all who were in *the* field, from men even to cattle. And *the* hail struck all *the* field's plants and broke each of *the* region's trees.

Israel's Children Spared

9:26 *tantum in terra Gessen ubi erant filii Israhel grando non cecidit*

Only in Gessen's land, where Israel's children were, did hail not fall.

Pharaoh Begs for Mercy

9:27 *misitque Pharao et vocavit Mosen et Aaron dicens ad eos peccavi etiam nunc Dominus iustus ego et populus meus impii*

And Pharaoh sent and called Moses and Aaron, saying to them, "I have sinned. Even now *the* Lord *is* fair. I and my people *are* lawless.

9:28 *orate Dominum et desinant tonitrua Dei et grando ut dimittam vos et nequaquam hic ultra maneatis*

"Pray to *the* Lord and let God's thunder and hail end, so I can release you, and you by no means will remain here further!"

9:29 *ait Moses cum egressus fuero de urbe extendam palmas meas ad Dominum et cessabunt tonitrua et grando non erit ut scias quia Domini est terra*

Moses said, "When I go out of *the* city, I will stretch out my palms to *the* Lord. And *the* thunders will cease and *the* hail will not be, so you may know that *the* land is *the* Lord's.

9:30 *novi autem quod et tu et servi tui necdum timeatis Dominum Deum*

"But I have known that neither you nor your slaves yet fear *the* Lord God.

9:31 *linum ergo et hordeum laesum est eo quod hordeum esset virens et linum iam folliculos germinaret*

The flax and *the* barley, therefore, was struck, because *the* barley was green and *the* flax had already germinated pods.

9:32 *triticum autem et far non sunt laesa quia serotina erant*

But *the* wheat and spelt were not struck, because they were late in coming.

9:33 *egressusque Moses a Pharaone et ex urbe tetendit manus ad Dominum et cessaverunt tonitrua et grando nec ultra stillavit pluvia super terram*

And Moses, going out from Pharaoh and from *the* city, stretched *his* hand to *the* Lord and *the* thunder and hail ceased, nor did another raindrop fall on *the* ground.

9:34 *videns autem Pharao quod cessasset pluvia et grando et tonitrua auxit peccatum.*

But Pharaoh, seeing that *the* rain had ceased and *the* hail and thunder, increased sin.

9:35 *et ingravatum est cor eius et servorum illius et induratum nimis nec dimisit filios Israhel sicut praeceperat Dominus per manum Mosi*

And his heart was hardened and his servants' *hearts* also, hardened overwhelmingly, nor did he release Israel's children, as *the* Lord had commanded through Moses' hand.

The Lord Again
Commands Pharaoh

Exodus 10:1 *et dixit Dominus ad Mosen ingredere ad Pharao ego enim induravi cor eius et servorum illius ut faciam signa mea haec in eo*

And *the* Lord said to Moses, "Go in to Pharaoh, for I have hardened his heart and his slaves' *hearts*, so I can work these My signs in him.

10:2 *et narres in auribus filii tui et nepotum tuorum quotiens contriverim Aegyptios et signa mea fecerim in eis et sciatis quia ego Dominus*

"And you may tell in your children and your grandchildren's ears how often I crushed *the* Egyptians and worked My signs among them. And they may know that I *am the* Lord."

10:3 *introierunt ergo Moses et Aaron ad Pharaonem et dixerunt ad eum haec dicit Dominus Deus Hebraeorum usquequo non vis subici mihi dimitte populum meum ut sacrificet mihi*

So Moses and Aaron went in to Pharaoh and said to him, "*The* Lord, *the* Hebrews' God, says this: 'How long do you not want to be subject to Me? Release My people so it can sacrifice to Me!

10:4 *sin autem resistis et non vis dimittere eum ecce ego inducam cras* *lucustam in fines tuos*

"'But if you resist and don't want to release him, look! I will bring *the* locust into your borders tomorrow,

10:5 *quae operiat superficiem terrae nec quicquam eius appareat sed comedatur quod residuum fuit grandini conrodet enim omnia ligna quae germinant in agris*

"'which may cover *the* land's surface, nor may any of it appear. But it will eat what was left by *the* hail, for it will chew up all *the* trees which grow in *the* fields.

10:6 *et implebunt domos tuas et servorum tuorum et omnium Aegyptiorum quantam non viderunt patres tui et avi ex quo orti sunt super terram usque in praesentem diem avertitque se et egressus est a Pharaone*

"'And they will fill your houses and your slaves' *houses* and all *the* Egyptians' *houses*, to an extent that neither your fathers nor ancestors have seen, from the time in which they were brought forth on *the* land even to *the* present day.'"

And he turned himself away and went out from Pharaoh.

Pharaoh's Own Slaves Plead With Him

10:7 *dixerunt autem servi Pharaonis*

ad eum usquequo patiemur hoc scandalum dimitte homines ut sacrificent Domino Deo suo nonne vides quod perierit Aegyptus

But Pharaoh's slaves said to him, "How long will we put up with this scandal? Release *the* men so they can sacrifice to *the* Lord their God! Don't you see that Egypt is dying?"

10:8 *revocaveruntque Mosen et Aaron ad Pharaonem qui dixit eis ite sacrificate Domino Deo vestro quinam sunt qui ituri sunt*

And they called Moses and Aaron back to Pharaoh, who said to them, "Go! Sacrifice to *the* Lord your God! Who then are those who will go?"

10:9 *ait Moses cum parvulis nostris et senibus pergemus cum filiis et filiabus cum ovibus et armentis est enim sollemnitas Domini nostri*

Moses said, "We will go with our little ones and elders, with sons and daughters, with sheep and cattle, for it is *a* solemn rite to our Lord."

10:10 *et respondit sic Dominus sit vobiscum quomodo ego dimittam vos et parvulos vestros cui dubium est quod pessime cogitetis*

And Pharaoh answered, "*The* Lord be with you so! How will I release you and your little ones? To whom is it doubtful that you plot destructively?

10:11 *non fiet ita sed ite tantum viri et sacrificate Domino hoc enim et ipsi petistis statimque eiecti sunt de conspectu Pharaonis*

"It will not be so, but you go – only *the* men – and sacrifice to *the* Lord, for this also you yourself have demanded!"

And immediately they were thrown out of Pharaoh's presence.

The Lord Brings the Locusts

10:12 *dixit autem Dominus ad Mosen extende manum tuam super terram Aegypti ad lucustam ut ascendat super eam et devoret omnem herbam quae residua fuit grandini*

But *the* Lord said to Moses, "Stretch out your hand to *the* locust over Egypt's land, that it come up over it and devour every plant that was left by *the* hail!"

10:13 *extendit Moses virgam super terram Aegypti et Dominus induxit ventum urentem tota illa die ac nocte et mane facto ventus urens levavit lucustas*

Moses stretched out *the* staff over Egypt's land, and *the* Lord brought in *a* burning wind all that day and night. And morning come, *the* burning wind lifted up *the* locusts,

10:14 *quae ascenderunt super universam terram Aegypti et sederunt in cunctis finibus Aegyptiorum innumerabiles quales ante illud tempus non fuerant nec postea futurae sunt*

which came up over all Egypt's land and sat in all Egypt's borders, innumerable, *the* likes of which before that time had not been, nor afterwards will be.

10:15 *operueruntque universam superficiem terrae vastantes omnia devorata est igitur herba terrae et quicquid pomorum in arboribus fuit quae grando dimiserat nihilque omnino virens relictum est in lignis et in herbis terrae in cuncta Aegypto*

And they covered all *the* land's surface, devastating all. Therefore *the* land's grass was devoured and whatever fruit was in *the* trees which *the* hail had left. And nothing of any greenery was left on trees and in *the* land's plants in all Egypt.

Pharaoh Hurriedly Calls
Moses and Aaron Back

10:16 *quam ob rem festinus Pharao vocavit Mosen et Aaron et dixit eis peccavi in Dominum Deum vestrum et in vos*

From which thing, Pharaoh hurriedly called Moses and Aaron and said to them, "I have sinned against *the* Lord your God and against you.

10:17 *sed nunc dimittite peccatum mihi etiam hac vice et rogate Dominum Deum vestrum ut auferat a me mortem istam*

"But now, forgive my sin even this time, and pray to *the* Lord your God that He take this death away from me!"

10:18 *egressusque est de conspectu Pharaonis et oravit Dominum*

And *Moses* went out from Pharaoh's sight and prayed to *the* Lord,

10:19 *qui flare fecit ventum ab occidente vehementissimum et arreptam lucustam proiecit in mare Rubrum non remansit ne una quidem in cunctis finibus Aegypti*

who caused *a* wind to blow most fiercely from *the* west. And seizing *the* locust, it threw them into *the* Red Sea. Not even one of them remained in all Egypt's borders.

Pharaoh Again
Changes His Mind

10:20 *et induravit Dominus cor Pharaonis nec dimisit filios Israhel*

Yet *the* Lord hardened Pharaoh's heart, nor did he release Israel's children.

10:21 *dixit autem Dominus ad Mosen extende manum tuam in caelum et sint tenebrae super terram Aegypti tam densae ut palpari queant*

But *the* Lord said to Moses, "Stretch out your hand to *the* sky and let shadows be over Egypt's land, so dense that they be able to touch *them*.

10:22 *extendit Moses manum in caelum et factae sunt tenebrae horribiles in universa terra Aegypti tribus diebus*

Moses stretched out his hand to *the* sky, and terrible shadows came into all Egypt's land for three days.

10:23 *nemo vidit fratrem suum nec movit se de loco in quo erat ubicumque autem habitabant filii Israhel lux erat*

No one saw his brother or moved himself from *the* place in which he was. But wherever Israel's children lived *there* was light.

Pharaoh Again Offers
a Partial Release

10:24 *vocavitque Pharao Mosen et Aaron et dixit eis ite sacrificate Domino oves tantum vestrae et armenta remaneant parvuli vestri eant vobiscum*

And Pharaoh called Moses and Aaron and said to them, "Go! Sacrifice to *the* Lord! Let only your sheep and cattle remain. Your little ones may go with you."

10:25 *ait Moses hostias quoque et holocausta dabis nobis quae offeramus Domino Deo nostro*

Moses said, "Will you also give us victims and burnt offerings that we can offer *the* Lord our God?

10:26 *cuncti greges pergent nobiscum non remanebit ex eis ungula quae necessaria sunt in cultum Domini Dei nostri praesertim cum ignoremus quid debeat immolari donec ad ipsum locum perveniamus*

"All *the* flocks will go with us. Not one hoof will remain from them, which are necessary in *the* Lord our God's worship – especially when we do not know what we must offer until we come to that place."

Pharaoh Bans
Moses and Aaron
From His Presence

10:27 *induravit autem Dominus cor Pharaonis et noluit dimittere eos*

But *the* Lord hardened Pharaoh's heart, and he did not want to release them.

10:28 *dixitque Pharao ad eum recede a me cave ne ultra videas faciem meam quocumque die apparueris mihi morieris*

And Pharaoh said to him, "Go away from me! Take care that you never see my face again! In whatever day you appear before me, you will die!"

10:28 *respondit Moses ita fiat ut locutus es non videbo ultra faciem tuam*

Moses answered, "Let it be so, as you said. I will not see your face again."

The Decisive Blow Predicted

Exodus 11:1 *et dixit Dominus ad Mosen adhuc una plaga tangam Pharaonem et Aegyptum et post haec dimittet vos et exire conpellet*

And *the* Lord said to Moses, "I will touch Pharaoh and Egypt with yet one more blow, and after this he will release you and compel *you* to leave.

11:2 *dices ergo omni plebi ut postulet vir ab amico suo et mulier a vicina sua vasa argentea et aurea*

"Therefore, you will say to all *the* people, that *a* man ask from his friend and *a* woman from her neighbor vessels of silver and gold.

11:3 *dabit autem Dominus gratiam populo coram Aegyptiis fuitque Moses vir magnus valde in terra Aegypti coram servis Pharao et omni populo*

"But *the* Lord will give *the* people grace before *the* Egyptians."

And Moses was *an* overwhelmingly great man in all Egypt's land, before Pharaoh's slaves and all *the* people.

11:4 *et ait haec dicit Dominus media nocte egrediar in Aegyptum*

And he said, "*The* Lord says this: 'I will go out at midnight into Egypt.

11:5 *et morietur omne*

primogenitum in terra Aegyptiorum a primogenito Pharaonis qui sedet in solio eius usque ad primogenitum ancillae quae est ad molam et omnia primogenita iumentorum

"'And every firstborn in Egypt's land will die, from Pharaoh's firstborn who sits on his throne even to *the* slave-woman's firstborn who is at *the* millstone, and all *the* cattle's firstborn.

11:6 *eritque clamor magnus in universa terra Aegypti qualis nec ante fuit nec postea futurus est*

"'And *a* great outcry will be in all Egypt's land, *the* likes of which never was before nor will be after.

11:7 *apud omnes autem filios Israhel non muttiet canis ab homine usque ad pecus ut sciatis quanto miraculo dividat Dominus Aegyptios et Israhel*

"'But with all Israel's children not *a* dog will bark, from men even to animals, so you may know how miraculously *the* Lord divides *the* Egyptians and Israel.'

11:8 *descendentque omnes servi tui isti ad me et adorabunt me dicentes egredere tu et omnis populus qui subiectus est tibi post haec egrediemur*

"And all these your slaves will go

down to me and pay homage to me, saying, 'Go out – you and all *the* people who are subject to you!' After this, we will go out."

11:9 *et exivit a Pharaone iratus nimis dixit autem Dominus ad Mosen non audiet vos Pharao ut multa signa fiant in terra Aegypti*

And he left Pharaoh, very angry. But *the* Lord said to Moses, "Pharaoh will not listen to you, so many signs may be done in Egypt's land."

11:10 *Moses autem et Aaron fecerunt omnia ostenta quae scripta sunt coram Pharaone et induravit Dominus cor Pharaonis nec dimisit filios Israhel de terra sua*

But Moses and Aaron did before Pharaoh all *the* wonders which were written. And *the* Lord hardened Pharaoh's heart, nor did he release Israel's children from his land.

Passover Ritual Commanded
Exodus 12:1 *dixit quoque Dominus ad Mosen et Aaron in terra Aegypti*

The Lord likewise said to Moses and Aaron in Egypt's land,

12:2 *mensis iste vobis principium mensuum primus erit in mensibus anni*

"This month will be *the* beginning of months for you. It will be first among *the* year's months.

12:3 *loquimini ad universum coetum filiorum Israhel et dicite eis decima die mensis huius tollat unusquisque agnum per familias et domos suas*

"Speak to all *the* gathering of Israel's children and say to them, '*The* tenth day of this month, let each one take *a* lamb for his families and houses.'

12:4 *sin autem minor est numerus ut sufficere possit ad vescendum agnum adsumet vicinum suum qui iunctus est domui eius iuxta numerum animarum quae sufficere possunt ad esum agni*

"'But if *the* number is too small, so it can be possible to eat *the* lamb, he will take up his neighbor who is alongside his house, according to *the* number of souls who can suffice to eat *the* lamb.

12:5 *erit autem agnus absque macula masculus anniculus iuxta quem ritum tolletis et hedum*

"'But *the* lamb will be without defect, *a* yearling male, according to which rite you will take also *a* young goat.

12:6 *et servabitis eum usque ad quartamdecimam diem mensis huius immolabitque eum universa multitudo filiorum Israhel ad vesperam*

"'And you will keep it even to *the* fourteenth day of this month. And all Israel's children's multitude will offer it at sunset.

12:7 *et sument de sanguine ac ponent super utrumque postem et in superliminaribus domorum in quibus comedent illum*

And they will take from *the* blood and put it on each doorpost and on *the* houses' lintels in which they will eat it.

12:8 *et edent carnes nocte illa assas igni et azymos panes cum lactucis agrestibus*

"'And they will eat *the* flesh that night, roasted in fire, and unleavened bread with wild leaves.

12:9 *non comedetis ex eo crudum quid nec coctum aqua sed assum tantum igni caput cum pedibus eius*

et intestinis vorabitis

"'You will not eat from it that *which is* uncooked, nor cooked in water, but roasted only in fire. You will eat its head with its feet and intestines.

12:10 *nec remanebit ex eo quicquam usque mane si quid residui fuerit igne conburetis*

"'Nor will anything remain from it even to morning. If *there* is some left over, you will burn it with fire.

12:11 *sic autem comedetis illum renes vestros accingetis calciamenta habebitis in pedibus tenentes baculos in manibus et comedetis festinantes est enim phase id est transitus Domini*

"'But you will eat it like this. You will dress yourselves. You will have shoes on feet, having staffs in hands. And you will eat hurrying. For it is Passover (that is, *the* Lord's passing through).

God Tells Israel
What He Will Do

12:12 *et transibo per terram Aegypti nocte illa percutiamque omne primogenitum in terra Aegypti ab homine usque ad pecus et in cunctis diis Aegypti faciam iudicia ego Dominus*

"'And I will pass through Egypt's land that night, and I will strike every firstborn in Egypt's land – from men even to cattle. And I will work judgment among all Egypt's gods. I *am the* Lord.

12:13 *erit autem sanguis vobis in signum in aedibus in quibus eritis et videbo sanguinem ac transibo vos nec erit in vobis plaga disperdens quando percussero terram Aegypti*

"'But *the* blood will be to you as *a* sign in houses, in wherever you are. And I will see *the* blood and pass over you, nor will *the* destroying blow be among you when I strike Egypt's land.

An Everlasting Observance

12:14 *habebitis autem hanc diem in monumentum et celebrabitis eam sollemnem Domino in generationibus vestris cultu sempiterno*

"'But you will have this day as *a* memorial, and you will celebrate it solemnly to *the* Lord in your generations, *an* everlasting observance.

12:15 *septem diebus azyma comedetis in die primo non erit fermentum in domibus vestris quicumque comederit fermentatum peribit anima illa de Israhel a primo die usque ad diem septimum*

"'You will eat unleavened *bread* seven days. From *the* first day, no

yeast will be in your houses. Whoever will eat yeast from *the* first day even to *the* seventh, that soul will perish from Israel.

12:16 *dies prima erit sancta atque sollemnis et dies septima eadem festivitate venerabilis nihil operis facietis in eis exceptis his quae ad vescendum pertinent*

"'*The* first day will be holy and solemn, and *the* seventh day *the* same, *a* dignified festivity. You will do no work in them, except those that pertain to eating.

12:17 *et observabitis azyma in eadem enim ipsa die educam exercitum vestrum de terra Aegypti et custodietis diem istum in generationes vestras ritu perpetuo*

And you will observe unleavened *bread*, for in that same day I will lead your army from Egypt's land. And you will keep that day in your generations as *an* everlasting rite.

12:18 *primo mense quartadecima die mensis ad vesperam comedetis azyma usque ad diem vicesimam primam eiusdem mensis ad vesperam*

"'From *the* first month, fourteenth day of *the* month at evening, you will eat unleavened *bread* even to *the* twenty-first day of *the* same month at evening.

12:19 *septem diebus fermentum non invenietur in domibus vestris qui comederit fermentatum peribit anima eius de coetu Israhel tam de advenis quam de indigenis terrae*

"'For seven days, yeast will not be found in your houses. One who eats yeast, his soul will perish from Israel's gathering, as with newcomers so also with *the* land's native born.

12:20 *omne fermentatum non comedetis in cunctis habitaculis vestris edetis azyma*

"'You will not eat any yeast in all your dwellings. You will eat unleavened *bread.*'"

Moses Instructs
Israel's Elders

12:21 *vocavit autem Moses omnes seniores filiorum Israhel et dixit ad eos ite tollentes animal per familias vestras immolate phase*

But Moses called all Israel's children's elders, and said to them, "Go, taking *an* animal for your families! Offer *the* Passover!

12:22 *fasciculumque hysopi tinguite sanguine qui est in limine et aspergite ex eo superliminare et utrumque postem nullus vestrum egrediatur ostium domus suae usque mane*

"Dip *a* bundle of hyssop in *the* blood which is in *the* threshold and sprinkle some of it on *the* lintel and both doorposts! None of you will go out your house's door until morning!

12:23 *transibit enim Dominus percutiens Aegyptios cumque viderit sanguinem in superliminari et in utroque poste transcendet ostium et non sinet percussorem ingredi domos vestras et laedere*

"For *the* Lord will pass through, striking *the* Egyptians. And when He will see *the* blood on your lintel and in both doorposts, He will pass beyond *the* door. And he will not allow *the* one who strikes down to go into your houses and wound.

12:24 *custodi verbum istud legitimum tibi et filiis tuis usque in aeternum*

"Keep this word as lawful to yourself and your children, even to eternity!

12:25 *cumque introieritis terram quam Dominus daturus est vobis ut pollicitus est observabitis caerimonias istas*

"And when you have entered *the* land which *the* Lord will give you as He promised, you will observe these ceremonies.

12:26 *et cum dixerint vobis filii vestri quae est ista religio*

"And when your children say to you, 'What is this binding rite?'

12:27 *dicetis eis victima transitus Domini est quando transivit super domos filiorum Israhel in Aegypto percutiens Aegyptios et domos nostras liberans incurvatusque populus adoravit*

"you will say to them, '*It* is *the* offering of *the* Lord's passing through, when He passed over Israel's children's houses in Egypt, striking down *the* Egyptians and freeing our houses."

And, bending down, *the* people paid homage,

12:28 *et egressi filii Israhel fecerunt sicut praeceperat Dominus Mosi et Aaron*

And Israel's children, going out, did as *the* Lord had commanded Moses and Aaron.

The Lord Strikes Down Egypt's Firstborn

12:29 *factum est autem in noctis medio percussit Dominus omne primogenitum in terra Aegypti a primogenito Pharaonis qui sedebat in solio eius usque ad primogenitum captivae quae erat in carcere et omne primogenitum iumentorum*

But it happened at midnight. *The* Lord struck down every firstborn in Egypt's land, from Pharaoh's firstborn who sat on his throne, even to *the* captive's firstborn who was in prison, and every firstborn among cattle.

12:30 *surrexitque Pharao nocte et omnes servi eius cunctaque Aegyptus et ortus est clamor magnus in Aegypto neque enim erat domus in qua non iaceret mortuus*

And Pharaoh got up by night and all his slaves and all Egypt. And *a* great cry rose up in Egypt, for *there* was no house in which one had not fallen dead.

Pharaoh Releases Israel

12:31 *vocatisque Mosen et Aaron nocte ait surgite egredimini a populo meo et vos et filii Israhel ite immolate Domino sicut dicitis*

And calling Moses and Aaron by night, he said, "Get up! Go out from my people! And you and Israel's children, go! Burn offerings to *the* Lord, as you say!

12:32 *oves vestras et armenta adsumite ut petieratis et abeuntes benedicite mihi*

"Take up your sheep and cattle as you demanded and, going out, bless me!"

12:33 *urguebantque Aegyptii populum de terra exire velociter* *dicentes omnes moriemur*

And *the* Egyptians urged *the* people to go out from *the* land quickly, saying, "We all will die!"

12:34 *tulit igitur populus conspersam farinam antequam fermentaretur et ligans in palliis posuit super umeros suos*

So *the* people took strewn flour before it could ferment and, binding *it* in cloaks, put *it* on their shoulders.

12:35 *feceruntque filii Israhel sicut praeceperat Moses et petierunt ab Aegyptiis vasa argentea et aurea vestemque plurimam*

And Israel's children did as Moses had commanded, and they demanded from *the* Egyptians vessels of silver and gold and many garments.

12:36 *dedit autem Dominus gratiam populo coram Aegyptiis ut commodarent eis et spoliaverunt Aegyptios*

But *the* Lord gave *the* people favor before *the* Egyptians, that they accommodated them. And they plundered *the* Egyptians.

Israel Sets Out From Egypt

12:37 *profectique sunt filii Israhel de Ramesse in Soccoth sescenta ferme milia peditum virorum absque parvulis*

And Israel's children set out from Ramesses in Soccoth, nearly six hundred thousand men on foot, apart from little ones.

12:38 *sed et vulgus promiscuum innumerabile ascendit cum eis oves et armenta et animantia diversi generis multa nimis*

Yet *an* indiscriminate rabble, innumerable, also went up with them. Sheep and cattle and diverse species of animals *were* overwhelmingly many.

12:39 *coxeruntque farinam quam dudum conspersam de Aegypto tulerant et fecerunt subcinericios panes azymos neque enim poterant fermentari cogentibus exire Aegyptiis et nullam facere sinentibus moram nec pulmenti quicquam occurrerant praeparare*

And they baked flour which recently was strewn from Egypt. They took and made unleavened bread under ashes, for they couldn't be leavened. *They were* compelled to leave by *the* Egyptians, and no one allowed to make delay, nor had they happened to prepare any food.

12:40 *habitatio autem filiorum Israhel qua manserant in Aegypto fuit quadringentorum triginta annorum*

But Israel's children's residence in

which they had stayed in Egypt was four hundred thirty years,

12:41 *quibus expletis eadem die egressus est omnis exercitus Domini de terra Aegypti*

which, completed, all *the* Lord's army went out that same day from Egypt's land.

12:42 *nox est ista observabilis Domini quando eduxit eos de terra Aegypti hanc observare debent omnes filii Israhel in generationibus suis*

That is *the* night of *the* Lord's observation, when He led them from Egypt's land. All Israel's children must observe this in their generations.

Who May Eat the Passover
12:43 *dixitque Dominus ad Mosen et Aaron haec est religio phase omnis alienigena non comedet ex eo*

And *the* Lord said to Moses and Aaron, "This is *the* Passover obligation. No foreigner may eat from it.

12:44 *omnis autem servus empticius circumcidetur et sic comedet*

"But every bought slave will be circumcised, and so he will eat.

12:45 *advena et mercennarius non edent ex eo*

"Newcomer and hired soldier will not eat from it.

12:46 *in una domo comedetur nec efferetis de carnibus eius foras nec os illius confringetis*

"It will be eaten in one house, nor will you take any of its meat outside, nor will you break its bones.

Conditions for Passover Participation
12:47 *omnis coetus filiorum Israhel faciet illud*

"All Israel's children's assembly will work it,

12:48 *quod si quis peregrinorum in vestram voluerit transire coloniam et facere phase Domini circumcidetur prius omne masculinum eius et tunc rite celebrabit eritque sicut indigena terrae si quis autem circumcisus non fuerit non vescetur ex eo*

"which, if some sojourner among you wants to cross over to settle and work *the* Lord's Passover, let each of his males be circumcised first. And then he will celebrate *the* rite, and he will be like *the* land's native born. But if someone won't be circumcised, he will not eat from it.

12:49 *eadem lex erit indigenae et colono qui peregrinatur apud vos*

"*The* same law will be for *the* native born and *the* settler who sojourns with you."

12:50 *fecerunt omnes filii Israhel sicut praeceperat Dominus Mosi et Aaron*

All Israel's children did as *the* Lord had commanded Moses and Aaron.

12:51 *et in eadem die eduxit Dominus filios Israhel de terra Aegypti per turmas suas*

And on that same day, *the* Lord led Israel's children out of Egypt's land by their columns.

More Instructions
Concerning Passover

Exodus 13:1 *locutusque est Dominus ad Mosen dicens*

And *the* Lord spoke to Moses, saying,

13:2 *sanctifica mihi omne primogenitum quod aperit vulvam in filiis Israhel tam de hominibus quam de iumentis mea sunt enim omnia*

"Make holy to Me every firstborn who opens *the* vulva among Israel's children, whether from men or from cattle, for all are Mine."

13:3 *et ait Moses ad populum mementote diei huius in qua egressi estis de Aegypto et de domo servitutis quoniam in manu forti eduxit vos Dominus de loco isto ut non comedatis fermentatum panem*

And Moses said to *the* people, "Remember this day in which you came out of Egypt and out of slavery's house, that you will not eat leavened bread, for *the* Lord led you out by *a* mighty hand from that place.

13:4 *hodie egredimini mense novarum frugum*

Today you go out, in *the* month of first fruits.

13:5 *cumque te introduxerit Dominus in terram Chananei et*

Hetthei et Amorrei et Evei et Iebusei quam iuravit patribus tuis ut daret tibi terram fluentem lacte et melle celebrabis hunc morem sacrorum mense isto

"And when *the* Lord has brought you into *the* land of Canaanites and Hittites and Amorites and Hivites and Jebusites, which He swore to your fathers that He would give you – *a* land flowing with milk and honey – you will celebrate this holy rite in that month.

13:6 *septem diebus vesceris azymis et in die septimo erit sollemnitas Domini*

"You will feed on unleavened *bread* seven days, and *the* Lord's solemnity will be on *the* seventh day.

13:7 *azyma comedetis septem diebus non apparebit apud te aliquid fermentatum nec in cunctis finibus tuis*

"You will eat unleavened *bread* seven days. Nothing leavened will appear with you, or in all your borders

13:8 *narrabisque filio tuo in die illo dicens hoc est quod fecit Dominus mihi quando egressus sum de Aegypto*

"And you will tell your child in that day, saying, 'This is what *the* Lord

did for me when I came out of Egypt.'

13:9 *et erit quasi signum in manu tua et quasi monumentum ante oculos tuos et ut lex Domini semper in ore tuo in manu enim forti eduxit te Dominus de Aegypto*

"And it will be like *a* sign in your hand and like *a* memorial before you eyes, so *the* Lord's law *may be* always in your mouth. For *the* Lord led you out of Egypt by *a* mighty hand.

13:10 *custodies huiuscemodi cultum statuto tempore a diebus in dies*

"You will observe *the* ritual this way at *the* appointed time, from days to days.

Every Firstborn
Is the Lord's

13:11 *cumque introduxerit te in terram Chananei sicut iuravit tibi et patribus tuis et dederit eam tibi*

"And when He has brought you into Canaan's land as He swore to you and your fathers, and has given it to you,

13:12 *separabis omne quod aperit vulvam Domino et quod primitivum est in pecoribus tuis quicquid habueris masculini sexus consecrabis Domino*

"you will separate to *the* Lord everything that opens *the* vulva, and whatever is first among your cattle. Whatever you have of male sex, you will consecrate to *the* Lord.

13:13 *primogenitum asini mutabis ove quod si non redemeris interficies omne autem primogenitum hominis de filiis tuis pretio redimes*

"You will exchange *a* donkey's firstborn for sheep, which, if you will not buy *it* back, you will kill. But every firstborn male among your children you will buy back at price.

13:14 *cumque interrogaverit te filius tuus cras dicens quid est hoc respondebis ei in manu forti eduxit nos Dominus de Aegypto de domo servitutis*

"And when your child questions you tomorrow, saying, 'What is this?' you will answer him, '*The* Lord led us out of Egypt, out of slavery's house, by *a* mighty hand.

13:15 *nam cum induratus esset Pharao et nollet nos dimittere occidit Dominus omne primogenitum in terra Aegypti a primogenito hominis usque ad primogenitum iumentorum idcirco immolo Domino omne quod aperit vulvam masculini sexus et omnia primogenita filiorum meorum redimo*

"'For when Pharaoh's heart was hardened and he didn't want to release *us*, *the* Lord killed every firstborn in Egypt's land, from *the* firstborn of men even to *the* firstborn of cattle. Therefore, I offer *the* Lord everything of male sex that opens *the* vulva, and I buy back all *the* firstborn of my children.'

13:16 *erit igitur quasi signum in manu tua et quasi adpensum quid ob recordationem inter oculos tuos eo quod in manu forti eduxerit nos Dominus de Aegypto*

"Therefore, it will be like *a* sign in your hand and like *a* suspended weight of remembrance between your eyes, because *the* Lord led us out of Egypt by *a* mighty hand.

The Route of the Exodus

13:17 *igitur cum emisisset Pharao populum non eos duxit Dominus per viam terrae Philisthim quae vicina est reputans ne forte paeniteret eum si vidisset adversum se bella consurgere et reverteretur in Aegyptum*

Therefore, when Pharaoh sent *the* people out, *the* Lord did not lead them by *the* road to *the* Philistines' land, which is near, thinking 'Unless perhaps it make him sorry if he sees war rise up against him, and he turn back to Egypt.'

13:18 *sed circumduxit per viam deserti quae est iuxta mare Rubrum* *et armati ascenderunt filii Israhel de terra Aegypti*

But He led them around through *the* desert road which is beside *the* Red Sea. And armed, Israel's children went up from Egypt's land.

13:19 *tulit quoque Moses ossa Ioseph secum eo quod adiurasset filios Israhel dicens visitabit vos Deus efferte ossa mea hinc vobiscum*

Moses likewise took Joseph's bones with him, because he had made Israel's children swear, saying, "God will visit you. Take my bones with you from here!"

13:20 *profectique de Soccoth castrametati sunt in Etham in extremis finibus solitudinis*

And, setting out from Soccoth, they camped in Etham, in *the* last limits of *the* wasteland.

The Lord Leads

13:21 *Dominus autem praecedebat eos ad ostendendam viam per diem in columna nubis et per noctem in columna ignis ut dux esset itineris utroque tempore*

But *the* Lord went before them to show *the* way, in *a* column of cloud by day and in *a* column of fire by night, so He could be Leader on *the* journey at both times.

13:22 *numquam defuit columna nubis per diem nec columna ignis per noctem coram populo*

Neither *the* column of cloud by day nor *the* column of fire by night ever faltered before *the* people.

The Lord Hardens
Pharaoh's Heart Again

Exodus 14:1 *locutus est autem Dominus ad Mosen dicens*

But *the* Lord spoke to Moses, saying,

14:2 *loquere filiis Israhel reversi castrametentur e regione Phiahiroth quae est inter Magdolum et mare contra Beelsephon in conspectu eius castra ponetis super mare*

"Say to Israel's children, 'Let them camp, turning from Phiahiroth's region, which is between Magdolum and *the* sea, across from Beelsephon, in its sight. You will place *the* camps beside *the* sea.'

14:3 *dicturusque est Pharao super filiis Israhel coartati sunt in terra conclusit eos desertum*

"And Pharaoh will say about Israel's children, 'They are hemmed in within *the* land. *The* desert has closed them in.'

14:4 *et indurabo cor eius ac persequetur vos et glorificabor in Pharao et in omni exercitu eius scientque Aegyptii quia ego sum Dominus feceruntque ita*

"And I will harden his heart and he will pursue you. And I will be glorified in Pharaoh and in all his army, and *the* Egyptians may know that I am *the* Lord."

And they did so.

Pharaoh Pursues Israel

14:5 *et nuntiatum est regi Aegyptiorum quod fugisset populus inmutatumque est cor Pharaonis et servorum eius super populo et dixerunt quid voluimus facere ut dimitteremus Israhel ne serviret nobis*

And it was told to *the* Egyptians' king that *the* people had fled. And Pharaoh's heart was changed and that of his slaves concerning *the* people. And they said, "What did we want to do that we released Israel, so he not serve us?"

14:6 *iunxit ergo currum et omnem populum suum adsumpsit secum*

So he yoked *the* chariot and took all his people with him.

14:7 *tulitque sescentos currus electos quicquid in Aegypto curruum fuit et duces totius exercitus*

And he took six hundred chosen chariots, whatever was among Egypt's chariots, and *the* leaders of *the* whole army.

14:8 *induravitque Dominus cor Pharaonis regis Aegypti et persecutus est filios Israhel at illi egressi erant in manu excelsa*

And *the* Lord hardened *the* heart of

Pharaoh, Egypt's king, and he pursued Israel's children. And they had gone out beneath *a* most exalted hand.

14:9 *cumque persequerentur Aegyptii vestigia praecedentium reppererunt eos in castris super mare omnis equitatus et currus Pharaonis et universus exercitus erant in Ahiroth contra Beelsephon*

And when *the* Egyptians pursued, following *their* footsteps, they found them in camps beside *the* sea. All Pharaoh's cavalry and chariots and *the* whole army was in Ahiroth, across from Beelsephon.

Israel Reproaches Moses
14:10 *cumque adpropinquasset Pharao levantes filii Israhel oculos viderunt Aegyptios post se et timuerunt valde clamaveruntque ad Dominum*

And when Pharaoh had come close, Israel's children, lifting up *their* eyes, saw *the* Egyptians behind them and feared greatly. And they cried out to *the* Lord.

14:11 *et dixerunt ad Mosen forsitan non erant sepulchra in Aegypto ideo tulisti nos ut moreremur in solitudine quid hoc facere voluisti ut educeres nos ex Aegypto*

And they said to Moses, "Were there perhaps no graves in Egypt? Did you take us out for this reason, so we could die in *the* wasteland? What did you want to do *in* this, that you led us out of Egypt?"

14:12 *nonne iste est sermo quem loquebamur ad te in Aegypto dicentes recede a nobis ut serviamus Aegyptiis multo enim melius est servire eis quam mori in solitudine*

"Isn't this *the* word which we spoke to you in Egypt, saying, 'Go away from us so we can serve *the* Egyptians!' For it is much better to serve them than to die in *the* wasteland!"

Moses Answers
14:13 *et ait Moses ad populum nolite timere state et videte magnalia Domini quae facturus est hodie Aegyptios enim quos nunc videtis nequaquam ultra videbitis usque in sempiternum*

And Moses said to *the* people, "Don't be afraid! Stand and see *the* Lord's great signs, which will happen today! For *the* Egyptians whom you now see, you will never see again, even in everlasting *time*.

14:14 *Dominus pugnabit pro vobis et vos tacebitis*

"*The* Lord will fight for you, and you will be quiet."

The Lord Commands Moses

14:15 *dixitque Dominus ad Mosen quid clamas ad me loquere filiis Israhel ut proficiscantur*

And *the* Lord said to Moses, "What are you shouting to me? Say to Israel's children that they set out.

14:16 *tu autem eleva virgam tuam et extende manum super mare et divide illud ut gradiantur filii Israhel in medio mari per siccum*

"But you, lift up your staff and stretch out *the* hand over *the* sea and divide it, so Israel's children can go into *the* middle of *the* sea through dry ground!

14:17 *ego autem indurabo cor Aegyptiorum ut persequantur vos et glorificabor in Pharaone et in omni exercitu eius in curribus et in equitibus illius*

"But I will harden *the* Egyptians' hearts, so they follow you. And I will be glorified in Pharaoh and in all his army, in his chariots and in his cavalry.

14:18 *et scient Aegyptii quia ego sum Dominus cum glorificatus fuero in Pharaone et in curribus atque in equitibus eius*

"And *the* Egyptians will know that I am *the* Lord, when I am glorified in Pharaoh and in his chariots and in his cavalry.

God Fights for Israel

14:19 *tollensque se angelus Dei qui praecedebat castra Israhel abiit post eos et cum eo pariter columna nubis priora dimittens post tergum*

And God's Angel who went before Israel's camp, taking Himself, went behind them, and with Him at once *the* column of cloud. Leaving *the* front, *He went* behind.

14:20 *stetit inter castra Aegyptiorum et castra Israhel et erat nubes tenebrosa et inluminans noctem ut ad se invicem toto noctis tempore accedere non valerent*

He stood between *the* Egyptians' camp and Israel's camp and was shadowy clouds. And *He continued* illuminating *the* night, so that they were not strong enough to come close to Him in turn, through all *the* nighttime.

14:21 *cumque extendisset Moses manum super mare abstulit illud Dominus flante vento vehementi et urente tota nocte et vertit in siccum divisaque est aqua*

And when Moses had stretched out his hand over *the* sea, *the* Lord took it away, blowing *a* fierce, burning wind all night. And it turned into dry *ground* and *the* water was divided.

14:22 *et ingressi sunt filii Israhel per medium maris sicci erat enim aqua quasi murus a dextra eorum et leva*

And Israel's children went in through *the* middle of *the* dry sea, for *the* water *was* like *a* wall to their right, and lifted up.

The Egyptians
Again Pursue

14:23 *persequentesque Aegyptii ingressi sunt post eos omnis equitatus Pharaonis currus eius et equites per medium maris*

And pursuing, *the* Egyptians went in after them – all Pharaoh's cavalry, his chariots and riders – through *the* middle of *the* sea.

14:24 *iamque advenerat vigilia matutina et ecce respiciens Dominus super castra Aegyptiorum per columnam ignis et nubis interfecit exercitum eorum*

And *the* morning vigil had already come and, look! *The* Lord, looking down on *the* Egyptians' camp through *the* column of fire and cloud, destroyed their army.

14:25 *et subvertit rotas curruum ferebanturque in profundum dixerunt ergo Aegyptii fugiamus Israhelem Dominus enim pugnat pro eis contra nos*

And He overturned *the* chariots' wheels, and they were carried off in *the* depth. So *the* Egyptians said, "Let us flee Israel, for *the* Lord fights for them against us!"

The Lord Calls
the Waters Back Together

14:26 *et ait Dominus ad Mosen extende manum tuam super mare ut revertantur aquae ad Aegyptios super currus et equites eorum*

And *the* Lord said to Moses, "Stretch out your hand over *the* sea, that *the* waters may turn back to *the* Egyptians, over their chariots and riders!"

14:27 *cumque extendisset Moses manum contra mare reversum est primo diluculo ad priorem locum fugientibusque Aegyptiis occurrerunt aquae et involvit eos Dominus in mediis fluctibus*

And when Moses had stretched out his hand against *the* sea, it went back at first light to its prior place. And, *the* Egyptians fleeing, *the* waters met and *the* Lord covered them in *the* middle of *the* floods.

Pharaoh's Army
Utterly Destroyed

14:28 *reversaeque sunt aquae et operuerunt currus et equites cuncti exercitus Pharaonis qui sequentes ingressi fuerant mare ne unus quidem superfuit ex eis*

And *the* waters turned back and covered chariots and riders, all Pharaoh's army which, pursuing, had gone into *the* sea. Not one of them came out of it.

Israel Escapes

14:29 *filii autem Israhel perrexerunt per medium sicci maris et aquae eis erant quasi pro muro a dextris et a sinistris*

But Israel's children went on through *the* middle of *the* dry sea, and *the* waters were to them like *a* wall to *the* right and to *the* left.

14:30 *liberavitque Dominus in die illo Israhel de manu Aegyptiorum*

And *the* Lord freed Israel in that day from *the* Egyptians' hands.

14:31 *et viderunt Aegyptios mortuos super litus maris et manum magnam quam exercuerat Dominus contra eos timuitque populus Dominum et crediderunt Domino et Mosi servo eius*

And they saw *the* Egyptians dead on *the* seashore, and *the* great hand which *the* Lord had used against them, and *the* people feared *the* Lord. And they believed *the* Lord and Moses, His slave.

Israel Sings
the Lord's Victory

Exodus 15:1 *tunc cecinit Moses et filii Israhel carmen hoc Domino et dixerunt cantemus Domino gloriose enim magnificatus est equum et ascensorem deiecit in mare*

Then Moses and Israel's children sang this song to *the* Lord, and said, "Let us sing to *the* Lord, for He is gloriously lifted up! He threw horse and rider into *the* sea.

15:2 *fortitudo mea et laus mea Dominus et factus est mihi in salutem iste Deus meus et glorificabo eum Deus patris mei et exaltabo eum*

"*The* Lord is my strength and my praise and has become to me as security. This is my God and I will glorify Him – my father's God, and I will exalt Him.

15:3 *Dominus quasi vir pugnator Omnipotens nomen eius*

The Lord, like *a* fighting man – Omnipotent *is* His name.

15:4 *currus Pharaonis et exercitum eius proiecit in mare electi principes eius submersi sunt in mari Rubro*

"He threw
Pharaoh's chariots
and his army into *the* sea.
His chosen princes
were plunged
into *the* Red Sea.

15:5 *abyssi operuerunt eos descenderunt in profundum quasi lapis*

"*The* abysses
covered them.
They went down
into *the* depth like rocks.

15:6 *dextera tua Domine magnifice in fortitudine dextera tua Domine percussit inimicum*

"Your right hand, Lord,
magnificently in might –
Your right hand, Lord,
struck *the* enemy.

15:7 *et in multitudine gloriae tuae deposuisti adversarios meos misisti iram tuam quae devoravit eos ut stipulam*

"And in
Your glory's multitude,
You put down
my adversaries.
You sent Your anger
which devoured them
like stubble.

15:8 *et in spiritu furoris tui congregatae sunt aquae stetit unda*

fluens congregatae sunt abyssi in medio mari

"And in Your spirit's fury,
waters were gathered.
The flowing wave stood.
Abysses were gathered
in *the* sea's midst.

15:9 *dixit inimicus persequar et conprehendam dividam spolia implebitur anima mea evaginabo gladium meum interficiet eos manus mea*

"*The* enemy said,
'I will pursue and capture.
I will divide spoil.
My soul will be filled.
I will unsheathe
my sword.
My hand will kill them.'

15:10 *flavit spiritus tuus et operuit eos mare submersi sunt quasi plumbum in aquis vehementibus*

"Your wind blew
and *the* sea covered them.
They were submerged
like lead in raging waters.

15:11 *quis similis tui in fortibus Domine quis similis tui magnificus in sanctitate terribilis atque laudabilis et faciens mirabilia*

"Who is like you
in strengths, Lord?
Who is like you –

lifted up in holiness,
terrifying and worthy
of praise –
and working wonders?

15:12 *extendisti manum tuam et devoravit eos terra*

"You stretched out
Your hand
and *the* land
devoured them.

15:13 *dux fuisti in misericordia tua populo quem redemisti et portasti eum in fortitudine tua ad habitaculum sanctum tuum*

"You were leader
in Your mercy
to *the* people
whom You bought back.
You carried him
in Your strength
to Your holy dwelling.

15:14 *adtenderunt populi et irati sunt dolores obtinuerunt habitatores Philisthim*

"Peoples paid attention
and were angry.
Pains took hold
of Philistia's inhabitants.

15:15 *tunc conturbati sunt principes Edom robustos Moab obtinuit tremor obriguerunt omnes habitatores Chanaan*

"Then Edom's princes
were troubled.
Trembling took
Moab's mighty ones.
All Canaan's inhabitants
stiffened *in fear*.

15:16 *inruat super eos formido et pavor in magnitudine brachii tui fiant inmobiles quasi lapis donec pertranseat populus tuus Domine donec pertranseat populus tuus iste quem possedisti*

"May terror
rush in over them,
and fear
at Your arm's greatness!
Make them immobile,
like stones,
until Your people
passes through, Lord –
until Your people
passes through,
this *people*, which You
have possessed!

15:17 *introduces eos et plantabis in monte hereditatis tuae firmissimo habitaculo tuo quod operatus es Domine sanctuarium Domine quod firmaverunt manus tuae*

"You will bring them in
and plant them
in Your inheritance's mountain,
Your most firm dwelling –
which You have made, Lord –
a sanctuary, Lord,
which Your hands

have formed.

15:18 *Dominus regnabit in aeternum et ultra*

"*The* Lord will reign
in eternity and beyond,

15:19 *ingressus est enim equus Pharao cum curribus et equitibus eius in mare et reduxit super eos Dominus aquas maris filii autem Israhel ambulaverunt per siccum in medio eius*

"for Pharaoh's horse
went into *the* sea
with his chariots
and riders,
and *the* Lord brought
the sea's waters
back over them.
But Israel's children
walked by dry *ground*
in its midst."

Mary and the Woman
Sing and Celebrate
15:20 *sumpsit ergo Maria prophetis soror Aaron tympanum in manu egressaeque sunt omnes mulieres post eam cum tympanis et choris*

Therefore, Mary *the* prophet, Aaron's sister, took *a* tympani in her hand. All *the* women went out after her with tympanies and dancers,

15:21 *quibus praecinebat dicens cantemus Domino gloriose enim*

magnificatus est equum et ascensorem eius deiecit in mare

to whom she prophesied, saying,

"Let us sing
to *the* Lord,
for He is
gloriously lifted up!
He threw horse
and its rider
down into *the* sea."

The People Set Out
into Sinai
15:22 *tulit autem Moses Israhel de mari Rubro et egressi sunt in desertum Sur ambulaveruntque tribus diebus per solitudinem et non inveniebant aquam*

But Moses took Israel from *the* Red Sea, and they went out into Sur's desert. And they walked three days through *the* wasteland and did not find water.

Mara, Bitterness
15:23 *et venerunt in Marath nec poterant bibere aquas de Mara eo quod essent amarae unde et congruum loco nomen inposuit vocans illud Mara id est amaritudinem*

And they came to Marath, but weren't able to drink *the* waters from Mara, because they were bitter. From this, he imposed *a* suitable name on that place, calling it Mara

(that is, bitterness.)

15:24 *et murmuravit populus contra Mosen dicens quid bibemus*

And *the* people griped against Moses, saying, "What will we drink?"

15:25 *at ille clamavit ad Dominum qui ostendit ei lignum quod cum misisset in aquas in dulcedinem versae sunt ibi constituit ei praecepta atque iudicia et ibi temptavit eum*

And he cried out to *the* Lord, who showed him wood, which, when he had thrown it into *the* waters, they were turned into sweetness. There He appointed him precepts and judgments. And there He tested him,

15:26 *dicens si audieris vocem Domini Dei tui et quod rectum est coram eo feceris et oboedieris mandatis eius custodierisque omnia praecepta illius cunctum languorem quem posui in Aegypto non inducam super te ego enim Dominus sanator tuus*

saying, "If you will hear *the* Lord your God's voice, and do what is right before Him, and obey His commandments, and keep all His precepts, I will not lead in over you all *the* sickness which I placed in Egypt, for I am *the* Lord your healer."

Israel Camps at Elim
15:27 *venerunt autem in Helim ubi erant duodecim fontes aquarum et septuaginta palmae et castrametati sunt iuxta aquas*

But Israel came to Helim, where *there* were twelve water springs and seventy palm trees. And they camped alongside *the* waters.

Israel Complains
of Hunger

Exodus 16:1 *profectique sunt de Helim et venit omnis multitudo filiorum Israhel in desertum Sin quod est inter Helim et Sinai quintodecimo die mensis secundi postquam egressi sunt de terra Aegypti*

And they set out from Helim, and *the* whole multitude of Israel's children came into Sin's desert, which is between Helim and Sinai, *the* fifteenth day, second month, after they came out of Egypt's land.

16:2 *et murmuravit omnis congregatio filiorum Israhel contra Mosen et contra Aaron in solitudine*

And all Israel's children's assembly griped against Moses and against Aaron in *the* wasteland.

16:3 *dixeruntque ad eos filii Israhel utinam mortui essemus per manum Domini in terra Aegypti quando sedebamus super ollas carnium et comedebamus panes in saturitate cur eduxistis nos in desertum istud ut occideretis omnem multitudinem fame*

And Israel's children said to them, "If only we had died by *the* Lord's hand in Egypt's land, when we sat beside pots of meat and ate bread to *the* full! Why did you lead us into this desert, so you could kill *the* whole multitude with hunger?"

16:4 *dixit autem Dominus ad Mosen ecce ego pluam vobis panes de caelo egrediatur populus et colligat quae sufficiunt per singulos dies ut temptem eum utrum ambulet in lege mea an non*

But *the* Lord said to Moses, "Look, I will rain bread from *the* sky over you. Let *the* people go out and collect what suffices for each day, so I can test him, whether he will walk in My law or not.

16:5 *die autem sexta parent quod inferant et sit duplum quam colligere solebant per singulos dies*

"But *the* sixth day, let them prepare what can be brought, and let it be twice what they are used to collecting for each day."

16:6 *dixeruntque Moses et Aaron ad omnes filios Israhel vespere scietis quod Dominus eduxerit vos de terra Aegypti*

And Moses and Aaron said to all Israel's children, "At evening you will know that *the* Lord led you out of Egypt's land.

16:7 *et mane videbitis gloriam Domini audivit enim murmur vestrum contra Dominum nos vero quid sumus quia mussitatis contra nos*

"And at morning you will see *the* Lord's glory, for He has heard your complaint against *the* Lord. We, truly – what are we that you complain about us?"

16:8 *et ait Moses dabit Dominus vobis vespere carnes edere et mane panes in saturitate eo quod audierit murmurationes vestras quibus murmurati estis contra eum nos enim quid sumus nec contra nos est murmur vestrum sed contra Dominum*

And Moses said, "*The* Lord will give you meat to eat at evening and bread to *the* full at morning, because He has heard your griping which you griped against Him. For we – what are we? Your gripe isn't against us but against *the* Lord!"

16:9 *dixitque Moses ad Aaron dic universae congregationi filiorum Israhel accedite coram Domino audivit enim murmur vestrum*

And Moses said to Aaron, "Say to *the* whole congregation of Israel's children, 'Come near before *the* Lord, for He has heard your complaint!'"

16:10 *cumque loqueretur Aaron ad omnem coetum filiorum Israhel respexerunt ad solitudinem et ecce gloria Domini apparuit in nube*

And when Aaron had spoken to *the* whole gathering of Israel's children, they looked toward *the* wasteland and, look! *The* Lord's glory appeared in *a* cloud.

God Rains Down
Quail and Manna

16:11 *locutus est autem Dominus ad Mosen dicens*

But *the* Lord spoke to Moses, saying,

16:12 *audivi murmurationes filiorum Israhel loquere ad eos vespere comedetis carnes et mane saturabimini panibus scietisque quod sim Dominus Deus vester*

"I have heard Israel's children's complaints. Say to them, 'At evening you will eat meat, and at morning you will be filled with bread. And you will know that I am *the* Lord your God.'"

16:13 *factum est ergo vespere et ascendens coturnix operuit castra mane quoque ros iacuit per circuitum castrorum*

It happened, therefore, at evening. And quail, coming up, covered *the* camps. At morning, as well, dew fell around *the* camps.

16:14 *cumque operuisset superficiem terrae apparuit in solitudine minutum et quasi pilo tunsum in similitudinem pruinae super terram*

And after it had covered *the* ground's surface, *a* small thing appeared in *the* wasteland, and like *something* pulped by *a* pestle, in *the* likeness of frost over *the* ground.

16:15 *quod cum vidissent filii Israhel dixerunt ad invicem man hu quod significat quid est hoc ignorabant enim quid esset quibus ait Moses iste est panis quem dedit Dominus vobis ad vescendum*

When Israel's children had seen it, they said to each other, "*Man hu,*" which means, "What is this?"

For they did not know what it was. Moses said to them, "This is *the* bread which *the* Lord has given you to eat.

16:16 *hic est sermo quem praecepit Dominus colligat ex eo unusquisque quantum sufficiat ad vescendum gomor per singula capita iuxta numerum animarum vestrarum quae habitant in tabernaculo sic tolletis*

"This is *the* word which *the* Lord commanded: 'Let each one collect from it as much as is needed to eat, *a* gomor for each head. According to *the* number of your souls who live in *your* tent, so you will take.'"

16:17 *feceruntque ita filii Israhel et collegerunt alius plus alius minus*

And Israel's children did so. And they collected, one more *and* one less.

16:18 *et mensi sunt ad mensuram gomor nec qui plus collegerat habuit amplius nec qui minus paraverat repperit minus sed singuli iuxta id quod edere poterant congregarunt*

And they measured by *the* gomor's measure. Yet one who collected more did not have too much, nor one find too little who prepared less. But all gathered, according to what they could eat.

16:19 *dixitque Moses ad eos nullus relinquat ex eo in mane*

And Moses said to them, "Let no one keep any of it till morning."

16:20 *qui non audierunt eum sed dimiserunt quidam ex eis usque mane et scatere coepit vermibus atque conputruit et iratus est contra eos Moses*

They did not listen to him, but kept some of it to morning. And it began to swarm with maggots and rot. And Moses was angry with them.

16:21 *colligebant autem mane singuli quantum sufficere poterat ad vescendum cumque incaluisset sol liquefiebat*

But each collected at morning as much as would be needed to eat.

And when *the* sun had heated up, it melted.

Twice the Collection
Before the Sabbath

16:22 *in die vero sexta collegerunt cibos duplices id est duo gomor per singulos homines venerunt autem omnes principes multitudinis et narraverunt Mosi*

Indeed, on *the* sixth day they collected twice *the* food – that is, two gomors for each of *the* men. But all *the* multitude's princes came and told Moses,

16:23 *qui ait eis hoc est quod locutus est Dominus requies sabbati sanctificata erit Domino cras quodcumque operandum est facite et quae coquenda sunt coquite quicquid autem reliquum fuerit reponite usque in mane*

who said to them, "This is what *the* Lord has said. Tomorrow will be *a* holy Sabbath rest to *the* Lord. Do whatever must be done, and cook whatever must be cooked! But whatever is left, put back until morning."

16:24 *feceruntque ita ut praeceperat Moses et non conputruit neque vermis inventus est in eo*

And they did so, as Moses had commanded. And it did not rot, nor were worms found in it.

16:24 *dixitque Moses comedite illud hodie quia sabbatum est Domino non invenietur hodie in agro*

And Moses said, "Eat it today, because it is *the* Sabbath to *the* Lord. It will not be found in *the* field today.

16:26 *sex diebus colligite in die autem septimo sabbatum est Domino idcirco non invenietur*

"Gather it six days, but *the* seventh day is *a* Sabbath to *the* Lord. Therefore, it will not be found."

Some Disobey
the Sabbath Commandment

16:27 *venit septima dies et egressi de populo ut colligerent non invenerunt*

The seventh day came and some of *the* people, going out so they could gather, did not find any.

16:28 *dixit autem Dominus ad Mosen usquequo non vultis custodire mandata mea et legem meam*

But *the* Lord said to Moses, "How long will you not want to keep My mandates and My law?

16:29 *videte quod Dominus dederit vobis sabbatum et propter hoc tribuerit vobis die sexto cibos duplices maneat unusquisque apud semet ipsum nullus egrediatur de loco suo die septimo*

"See that *the* Lord has given you *the* Sabbath and, because of this, has granted you double food on *the* sixth day! Let each one stay with his own! No one may go out of his place *the* seventh day!"

16:30 *et sabbatizavit populus die septimo*

And *the* people kept *the* Sabbath *the* seventh day.

About the Manna

16:31 *appellavitque domus Israhel nomen eius man quod erat quasi semen coriandri album gustusque eius quasi similae cum melle*

And Israel's house called its name manna, which was like coriander seed, white. And its taste *was* like wheat flour with honey.

16:32 *dixit autem Moses iste est sermo quem praecepit Dominus imple gomor ex eo et custodiatur in futuras retro generationes ut noverint panem quo alui vos in solitudine quando educti estis de terra Aegypti*

But Moses said, "This is *the* word which *the* Lord has commanded: 'Fill *a* gomor from it, and let it be kept to future generations afterward, so they may know *the* bread which I fed you in *the* wasteland, when you were led out of Egypt's land.'

16:33 *dixitque Moses ad Aaron sume vas unum et mitte ibi man quantum potest capere gomor et repone coram Domino ad servandum in generationes vestras*

And Moses said to Aaron, "Take one vessel and put manna there, as much as *a* gomor can hold! And put it before *the* Lord, to save for your generations!

16:34 *sicut praecepit Dominus Mosi posuitque illud Aaron in tabernaculo reservandum*

Aaron put it in *the* tabernacle to keep, as *the* Lord had commanded Moses.

16:35 *filii autem Israhel comederunt man quadraginta annis donec venirent in terram habitabilem hoc cibo aliti sunt usquequo tangerent fines terrae Chanaan*

But Israel's children ate manna forty years, until they came into *an* inhabitable land. They were fed with this food until they touched *the* borders of Canaan's land.

16:36 *gomor autem decima pars est oephi*

But *a* gomor is *a* tenth part of *an* ephah.

The People Thirst

Exodus 17:1 *igitur profecta omnis multitudo filiorum Israhel de deserto Sin per mansiones suas iuxta sermonem Domini castrametata est in Raphidim ubi non erat aqua ad bibendum populo*

Therefore, all Israel's children's multitude, setting out from Sin's desert through their stages according to *the* Lord's word, camped in Raphidim, where *there* was no water for *the* people to drink.

17:2 *qui iurgatus contra Mosen ait da nobis aquam ut bibamus quibus respondit Moses quid iurgamini contra me cur temptatis Dominum*

They, quarreling with Moses, said, "Give us water so we can drink!"

He answered them, "Why are you quarreling against me? Why are you testing *the* Lord?"

17:3 *sitivit ergo populus ibi pro aquae penuria et murmuravit contra Mosen dicens cur nos exire fecisti de Aegypto ut occideres et nos et liberos nostros ac iumenta siti*

So *the* people thirsted there for lack of water. And they griped against Moses, saying, "Why did you make us come out of Egypt, so you could kill both us and our children and cattle with thirst?"

17:4 *clamavit autem Moses ad Dominum dicens quid faciam populo huic adhuc pauxillum et lapidabunt me*

But Moses cried out to *the* Lord, saying, "What will I do for this people? Yet *a* little and they will stone me!"

17:5 *ait Dominus ad Mosen antecede populum et sume tecum de senibus Israhel et virgam qua percussisti fluvium tolle in manu tua et vade*

The Lord said to Moses, "Go in front of *the* people and take with you some of Israel's elders. Take in your hand *the* staff with which you struck *the* river and go!

17:6 *en ego stabo coram te ibi super petram Horeb percutiesque petram et exibit ex ea aqua ut bibat populus fecit Moses ita coram senibus Israhel*

"Look, I will stand before you there on *the* rock of Horeb. And you will strike *the* rock, and water will come out of it so *the* people can drink."

Moses did so before Israel's elders.

17:7 *et vocavit nomen loci illius Temptatio propter iurgium filiorum Israhel et quia temptaverunt Dominum dicentes estne Dominus in nobis an non*

And he called that place's name Testing, because of Israel's children's quarrel and because they tested *the* Lord, saying, "Is *the* Lord among us or not?"

Amalek Fights Against Israel

17:8 *venit autem Amalech et pugnabat contra Israhel in Raphidim*

But Amalek came and fought against Israel in Raphidim.

17:9 *dixitque Moses ad Iosue elige viros et egressus pugna contra Amalech cras ego stabo in vertice collis habens virgam Dei in manu mea*

And Moses said to Joshua, "Choose men and, going out, fight against Amalek! Tomorrow I will stand on *the* hilltop, having God's staff in my hand."

17:10 *fecit Iosue ut locutus ei erat Moses et pugnavit contra Amalech Moses autem et Aaron et Hur ascenderunt super verticem collis*

Joshua did as Moses had told him, and he fought against Amalek. But Moses and Aaron and Hur climbed up on *the* hilltop.

Aaron and Hur Sustain Moses' Hands

17:11 *cumque levaret Moses manus vincebat Israhel sin autem paululum*

remisisset superabat Amalech

And when Moses lifted up his hand, Israel won. But if he relaxed *a* little, Amalek won.

17:12 *manus autem Mosi erant graves sumentes igitur lapidem posuerunt subter eum in quo sedit Aaron autem et Hur sustentabant manus eius ex utraque parte et factum est ut manus ipsius non lassarentur usque ad occasum solis*

But Moses' hands were heavy. Taking, therefore, *a* stone, they put it under him, on which he sat. But Aaron and Hur held up his hands from both sides, and it happened that his hands did not weaken until *the* sun set.

17:13 *fugavitque Iosue Amalech et populum eius in ore gladii*

And Joshua chased Amalek and its people away with *the* sword's mouth.

The Lord Promises to Destroy Amalek

17:14 *dixit autem Dominus ad Mosen scribe hoc ob monumentum in libro et trade auribus Iosue delebo enim memoriam Amalech sub caelo*

But the Lord said to Moses, "Write this as *a* memorial in *a* book, and hand it over into Joshua's ears, for I will destroy Amalek's memory under *the* sky."

Moses Builds an Altar

17:15 *aedificavitque Moses altare et vocavit nomen eius Dominus exaltatio mea dicens*

And Moses built *an* altar and called its name, "*The* Lord *is* my exaltation," saying,

17:16 *quia manus solii Domini et bellum Dei erit contra Amalech a generatione in generationem*

"Because *the* hand of *the* Lord's throne and God's war will be against Amalek from generation to generation."

Moses Reunited with His Family

Exodus 18:1 *cumque audisset Iethro sacerdos Madian cognatus Mosi omnia quae fecerat Deus Mosi et Israhel populo suo eo quod eduxisset Dominus Israhel de Aegypto*

And when Jethro, Midian's priest, Moses' kinsman, had heard all that God had done for Moses and Israel, His people, because *the* Lord had led Israel out of Egypt,

18:2 *tulit Sefforam uxorem Mosi quam remiserat*

he took Sephora, Moses' wife, whom he had sent back,

18:3 *et duos filios eius quorum unus vocabatur Gersan dicente patre advena fui in terra aliena*

and his two sons, one of whom was called Gersan, his father saying "I was *a* newcomer in *a* strange land."

18:4 *alter vero Eliezer Deus enim ait patris mei adiutor meus et eruit me de gladio Pharaonis*

The other, indeed, *he called* Eliezer, for he said, "My father's God is my helper, and he rescued me from Pharaoh's sword."

18:5 *venit ergo Iethro cognatus Mosi et filii eius et uxor ad Mosen in* *desertum ubi erat castrametatus iuxta montem Dei*

So Jethro, Moses' kinsman, and his sons and wife came to Moses in *the* desert, where he was camped alongside God's mountain.

18:6 *et mandavit Mosi dicens ego cognatus tuus Iethro venio ad te et uxor tua et duo filii tui cum ea*

And he sent to Moses, saying, "I am your kinsman, Jethro. I am coming to you *with* your wife, and your two sons with her."

Moses Tells Jethro
All That Has Happened
18:7 *qui egressus in occursum cognati sui adoravit et osculatus est eum salutaveruntque se mutuo verbis pacificis cumque intrasset tabernaculum*

He, going out to meet his kinsman, paid homage and kissed him. And they greeted each other with peaceful words. And when he had entered *the* tabernacle,

18:8 *narravit Moses cognato suo cuncta quae fecerat Deus Pharaoni et Aegyptiis propter Israhel universum laborem qui accidisset eis in itinere quo liberarat eos Dominus*

Moses told his kinsman all that God had done to Pharaoh and *the* Egyptians on Israel's behalf – *the* whole labor that had fallen on them on *the* way, that *the* Lord had freed them.

18:9 *laetatusque est Iethro super omnibus bonis quae fecerat Dominus Israheli eo quod eruisset eum de manu Aegyptiorum*

And Jethro was happy over all *the* good that *the* Lord had done for Israel, because He had rescued him from *the* Egyptians' hands.

Jethro Blesses the Lord
18:10 *et ait benedictus Dominus qui liberavit vos de manu Aegyptiorum et de manu Pharaonis qui eruit populum suum de manu Aegypti*

He said, "*The* Lord *is* blessed, who freed you from *the* Egyptians' hands and from Pharaoh's hands, who rescued His people from Egypt's hand!

18:11 *nunc cognovi quia magnus Dominus super omnes deos eo quod superbe egerint contra illos*

"Now I have known that *the* Lord is great over all gods, because they acted proudly against them."

18:12 *obtulit ergo Iethro cognatus Mosi holocausta et hostias Deo veneruntque Aaron et omnes senes Israhel ut comederent panem cum eo coram Domino*

So Jethro, Moses' kinsman, took burnt offerings and victims to God. And Aaron and all Israel's elders came, so they could eat bread with him before *the* Lord.

Jethro Mentors Moses

18:13 *altero autem die sedit Moses ut iudicaret populum qui adsistebat Mosi de mane usque ad vesperam*

But *the* next day, Moses sat down, so he could judge *the* people, who appeared before Moses from morning even to evening.

18:14 *quod cum vidisset cognatus eius omnia scilicet quae agebat in populo ait quid est hoc quod facis in plebe cur solus sedes et omnis populus praestolatur de mane usque ad vesperam*

When his kinsman had seen that – all *the* things, certainly, that he did among *the* people – he said, "What is this that you are doing among *the* people? Why do you sit alone and all *the* people stand around from morning even to evening?"

18:15 *cui respondit Moses venit ad me populus quaerens sententiam Dei*

Moses answered him, "*The* people comes to me, wanting God's sentence."

18:16 *cumque acciderit eis aliqua disceptatio veniunt ad me ut iudicem*

inter eos et ostendam praecepta Dei et leges eius

"And when any dispute falls on them, they come to me so I can judge between them. And I will show God's precepts and His laws."

18:17 *at ille non bonam inquit rem facis*

And he said, "You aren't doing *a* good thing.

18:18 *stulto labore consumeris et tu et populus iste qui tecum est ultra vires tuas est negotium solus illud non poteris sustinere*

"You are eaten up by foolish work, both you and this people who is with you. *The* business is beyond your strength. You can't bear it alone.

18:19 *sed audi verba mea atque consilia et erit Deus tecum esto tu populo in his quae ad Deum pertinent ut referas quae dicuntur ad eum*

"But listen to my words and advice, and God will be with you. You be for *the* people in those *matters* which pertain to God, so you can bring what they will say to Him.

18:20 *ostendasque populo caerimonias et ritum colendi viamque per quam ingredi debeant et opus quod facere*

And You can show *the* people *the* ceremonies and ritual to practice, and *the* way by which they ought to go, and *the* work which *is* to do.

18:21 *provide autem de omni plebe viros potentes et timentes Deum in quibus sit veritas et qui oderint avaritiam et constitue ex eis tribunos et centuriones et quinquagenarios et decanos*

"But provide them from all *the* people strong men, and *ones* fearing God, in whom truth may be, and who hate greed. And appoint from them tribunes and centurions and commanders of fifties and tens.

18:22 *qui iudicent populum omni tempore quicquid autem maius fuerit referant ad te et ipsi minora tantummodo iudicent leviusque tibi sit partito in alios onere*

These will judge *the* people all *the* time. But if anything big happens, they will bring it to you. And these will judge *the* merely small. And let *it* be easier on you, *with* part of *the* work on others!

18:23 *si hoc feceris implebis imperium Dei et praecepta eius poteris sustentare et omnis hic populus revertetur cum pace ad loca sua*

"If you do this, you will satisfy God's command, and you can bear His

precepts. And all this people may return to its places with peace.

Moses Listens
to Jethro's Suggestions
18:24 *quibus auditis Moses fecit omnia quae ille suggesserat*

Moses, listening to him, did all that he had suggested.

18:25 *et electis viris strenuis de cuncto Israhel constituit eos principes populi tribunos et centuriones et quinquagenarios et decanos*

And, *when* strong men *were* chosen from all Israel, he appointed them *the* people's princes: tribunes, and centurions, and commanders of fifties and tens,

18:26 *qui iudicabant plebem omni tempore quicquid autem gravius erat referebant ad eum faciliora tantummodo iudicantes*

who judged the people all *the* time. But anything that was weighty , they referred to him, judging only *the* lighter cases *themselves*.

18:27 *dimisitque cognatum qui reversus abiit in terram suam*

And he released his kinsman who, turning around, went back into his land.

Israel Camps Before
the Lord's Mountain

Exodus 19:1 *mense tertio egressionis Israhel de terra Aegypti in die hac venerunt in solitudinem Sinai*

In *the* third month of Israel's going out of Egypt's land, on that day, they came into Sinai's wasteland.

19:2 *nam profecti de Raphidim et pervenientes usque in desertum Sinai castrametati sunt in eodem loco ibique Israhel fixit tentoria e regione montis*

For, setting out from Raphidim and coming into Sinai's desert, they camped in *the* same place. And Israel fixed tents out of *the* mountain region.

Who Israel Can Be
To the Lord

19:3 *Moses autem ascendit ad Deum vocavitque eum Dominus de monte et ait haec dices domui Iacob et adnuntiabis filiis Israhel*

But Moses climbed up to God. And *the* Lord called him from *the* mountain and said, "You will say this to Jacob's house, and announce *it* to Israel's children:

19:4 *vos ipsi vidistis quae fecerim Aegyptiis quomodo portaverim vos super alas aquilarum et adsumpserim mihi*

"'You yourselves have seen what I did to *the* Egyptians – how I carried you on eagles' wings and took you up to Myself.

19:5 *si ergo audieritis vocem meam et custodieritis pactum meum eritis mihi in peculium de cunctis populis mea est enim omnis terra*

"'If, therefore, you will listen to My voice and keep My pact, you will be to Me as *a* private possession among all *the* peoples, for all *the* land is Mine.

19:6 *et vos eritis mihi regnum sacerdotale et gens sancta haec sunt verba quae loqueris ad filios Israhel*

"'And you will be to Me *a* priestly kingdom and *a* holy nation.' These are *the* words which you will say to Israel's children."

The People Agree
to God's Terms

19:7 *venit Moses et convocatis maioribus natu populi exposuit omnes sermones quos mandaverat Dominus*

Moses came and, calling *the* people's elder born together, laid out all *the* words which *the* Lord had commanded.

19:8 *responditque universus populus simul cuncta quae locutus est Dominus faciemus cumque* *rettulisset Moses verba populi ad Dominum*

And *the* whole people answered together, "We will do all that *the* Lord has spoken."

And when Moses had carried back *the* people's words to *the* Lord,

19:9 *ait ei Dominus iam nunc veniam ad te in caligine nubis ut audiat me populus loquentem ad te et credat tibi in perpetuum nuntiavit ergo Moses verba populi ad Dominum*

the Lord said to him, "Now already I will come to you in gloomy clouds, so *the* people may hear Me speaking to you and believe in you forever."

So Moses told *the* people's words to *the* Lord.

The Lord Commands the People to Be Ready

19:10 *qui dixit ei vade ad populum et sanctifica illos hodie et cras laventque vestimenta sua*

The Lord said to him, "Go to *the* people and make them holy today and tomorrow, and let them wash their clothes.

19:11 *et sint parati in diem tertium die enim tertio descendet Dominus coram omni plebe super montem Sinai*

"And let them be ready on *the* third day, for on *the* third day *the* Lord will come down before *the* whole people on Mount Sinai.

19:12 *constituesque terminos populo per circuitum et dices cavete ne ascendatis in montem nec tangatis fines illius omnis qui tetigerit montem morte morietur*

"And you will appoint boundaries for *the* people around, and you will say, 'Take care that you not climb up on *the* mountain or touch its boundaries! Everyone who touches *the* mountain will die by death!'

19:13 *manus non tanget eum sed lapidibus opprimetur aut confodietur iaculis sive iumentum fuerit sive homo non vivet cum coeperit clangere bucina tunc ascendant in montem*

"'Do not let *a* hand touch him, but let *him* be crushed with stones or shot through with arrows. Whether it be cattle or man, it will not live! When *the* trumpet begins to sound, then they will climb up onto *the* mountain.'"

Moses Prepares the People

19:14 *descenditque Moses de monte ad populum et sanctificavit eum cumque lavissent vestimenta sua*

And Moses came down to *the* people from *the* mountain, and he sanctified him. And when they had washed their clothes,

19:15 *ait ad eos estote parati in diem tertium ne adpropinquetis uxoribus vestris*

he said to them, "Be ready *the* third day! Let none of you approach your wives!"

The Lord Appears on Sinai

19:16 *iam advenerat tertius dies et mane inclaruerat et ecce coeperunt audiri tonitrua ac micare fulgura et nubes densissima operire montem clangorque bucinae vehementius perstrepebat timuit populus qui erat in castris*

The third day already had come and morning had become bright. And look, thunders began to be heard and lightnings to shake and densest clouds to cover *the* mountain, and *the* sound of mightiest trumpets rang out. And *the* people who was in *the* camps was afraid.

19:17 *cumque eduxisset eos Moses in occursum Dei de loco castrorum steterunt ad radices montis*

And when Moses had led them out from *the* encampments' place to meet God, they stood at *the* mountain's roots.

19:18 *totus autem mons Sinai fumabat eo quod descendisset*

Dominus super eum in igne et ascenderet fumus ex eo quasi de fornace eratque mons omnis terribilis

But all Mount Sinai smoked, because *the* Lord had come down on it in fire. And smoke came up from it like from *a* furnace, and all *the* mountain was terrifying.

19:19 *et sonitus bucinae paulatim crescebat in maius et prolixius tendebatur Moses loquebatur et Dominus respondebat ei*

And *the* trumpet sound increased greatly by degrees and extended tremendously. Moses spoke and *the* Lord answered him.

The Lord Calls Moses
Up the Mountain

19:20 *descenditque Dominus super montem Sinai in ipso montis vertice et vocavit Mosen in cacumen eius quo cum ascendisset*

And *the* Lord came down on Mount Sinai, in *the* mountain's very summit, and called Moses to its peak, where, when he had climbed up,

19:21 *dixit ad eum descende et contestare populum ne forte velint transcendere terminos ad videndum Dominum et pereat ex eis plurima multitudo*

He said to him, "Go down and bear

solemn witness to *the* people, unless perhaps they want to cross *the* boundaries to *the* living Lord, and *a* great multitude perish from among them!

19:22 *sacerdotes quoque qui accedunt ad Dominum sanctificentur ne percutiat eos*

"Let *the* priests, likewise, who will come close to *the* Lord, be made holy, so He not strike them down!

19:23 *dixitque Moses ad Dominum non poterit vulgus ascendere in montem Sinai tu enim testificatus es et iussisti dicens pone terminos circa montem et sanctifica illum*

And Moses said to *the* Lord, "*The* crowd can't come up onto Mount Sinai, for You have testified and commanded, saying, 'Put boundaries around *the* mountain and make it holy.'"

19:24 *cui ait Dominus vade descende ascendesque tu et Aaron tecum sacerdotes autem et populus ne transeant terminos nec ascendant ad Dominum ne forte interficiat illos*

The Lord said to him, "Go! Climb down! And you will climb up and Aaron with you. But let *the* priests and people not pass beyond *the* boundaries or climb up to *the* Lord, unless perhaps He kill them!

19:25 *descendit Moses ad populum et omnia narravit eis*

Moses went down to *the* people and told them all these *things*.

The Ten Commandments
Exodus 20:1 *locutus quoque est Dominus cunctos sermones hos*

The Lord also spoke all these words:

God Our Liberator
20:2 *ego sum Dominus Deus tuus qui eduxi te de terra Aegypti de domo servitutis*

"I am *the* Lord your God, who led you out of Egypt's land, out of slavery's house.

I
20:3 *non habebis deos alienos coram me*

"You will not have alien gods before Me.

II
20:4 *non facies tibi sculptile neque omnem similitudinem quae est in caelo desuper et quae in terra deorsum nec eorum quae sunt in aquis sub terra*

"You will not make yourselves sculpted images, neither in *the* likeness of all that is in sky above or that *is* in land below or those that are in waters under land.

20:5 *non adorabis ea neque coles ego sum Dominus Deus tuus fortis zelotes visitans iniquitatem patrum in filiis in tertiam et quartam generationem eorum qui oderunt me*

"You will not adore or serve them. I am *the* Lord your God, mighty, jealous, visiting *a* father's treachery in children to *the* third and fourth generation of those who have hated Me,

20:6 *et faciens misericordiam in milia his qui diligunt me et custodiunt praecepta mea*

"and working mercy in thousands of those who love Me and keep My precepts.

III
20:7 *non adsumes nomen Domini Dei tui in vanum nec enim habebit insontem Dominus eum qui adsumpserit nomen Domini Dei sui frustra*

"You will not take up *the* Lord your God's name in vain, for *the* Lord will not have him innocent who takes up *the* Lord his God's name for nothing.

IV
20:8 *memento ut diem sabbati sanctifices*

"Remember, so you may keep *the* Sabbath day holy!

20:9 *sex diebus operaberis et facies omnia opera tua*

"You will work six days and do all your tasks.

20:10 *septimo autem die sabbati Domini Dei tui non facies omne opus tu et filius tuus et filia tua servus tuus et ancilla tua iumentum tuum et advena qui est intra portas tuas*

"But *the* seventh day is *the* Lord your God's Sabbath. You will not do any work – you and your son and your daughter, your slave and your slave woman, your cattle and *the* newcomer who is in your gates.

20:11 *sex enim diebus fecit Dominus caelum et terram et mare et omnia quae in eis sunt et requievit in die septimo idcirco benedixit Dominus diei sabbati et sanctificavit eum*

"For *the* Lord made sky and land and sea and all those that are in them in six days, and He rested on *the* seventh day. For this reason, *the* Lord blessed *the* Sabbath day and made it holy.

V

20:12 *honora patrem tuum et matrem tuam ut sis longevus super terram quam Dominus Deus tuus dabit tibi*

"Honor your father and your mother, so you may be long-lived on *the* land which *the* Lord your God will give you.

VI

20:13 *non occides*

"You will not murder.

VII

20:14 *non moechaberis*

"You will not commit adultery.

VIII

20:15 *non furtum facies*

"You will not work theft.

IX

20:16 *non loqueris contra proximum tuum falsum testimonium*

"You will not speak false testimony against your neighbor.

X

20:17 *non concupisces domum proximi tui nec desiderabis uxorem eius non servum non ancillam non bovem non asinum nec omnia quae illius sunt*

"You will not lust after your neighbor's house, or desire his wife, or slave, or slave woman, or ox, or donkey, or all *things* that are his."

The People Fear

20:18 *cunctus autem populus videbat voces et lampadas et sonitum bucinae montemque fumantem et perterriti ac pavore concussi steterunt procul*

But all *the* people saw voices and lightnings and *the* trumpet's sound and *the* mountain smoking, and, terrified and struck by fear, they stood far off,

20:19 *dicentes Mosi loquere tu nobis et audiemus non loquatur nobis Dominus ne forte moriamur*

saying to Moses, "You speak to us and we will listen! Let *the* Lord not speak to us, unless perhaps we die!"

20:20 *et ait Moses ad populum nolite timere ut enim probaret vos venit Deus et ut terror illius esset in vobis et non peccaretis*

And Moses said to *the* people, "Don't be afraid, for God comes so He can prove you, and so His terror can be in you, and you might not sin!"

20:21 *stetitque populus de longe Moses autem accessit ad caliginem in qua erat Deus*

And *the* people stood far away. But Moses came near to *the* gloom in which God was.

Instructions for Worship

20:22 *dixit praeterea Dominus ad Mosen haec dices filiis Israhel vos vidistis quod de caelo locutus sum vobis*

The Lord said to Moses thereafter, "You will say this to Israel's children: 'You have seen that I have spoken to you from *the* sky.

20:23 *non facietis mecum deos argenteos nec deos aureos facietis vobis*

"'You will not make silver gods with Me, nor will you make yourselves golden gods.

20:24 *altare de terra facietis mihi et offeretis super eo holocausta et pacifica vestra oves vestras et boves in omni loco in quo memoria fuerit nominis mei veniam ad te et benedicam tibi*

"'You will make Me an altar of earth, and offer on it your sheep and cattle *as* burnt offerings and peace offerings. I will come to you and bless you in every place where My name's memory will be.

20:25 *quod si altare lapideum feceris mihi non aedificabis illud de sectis lapidibus si enim levaveris cultrum tuum super eo polluetur*

"'Yet if you make Me *a* stone altar, you will not build it from cut stones. For if you lift up your knife over it, it will be polluted.

20:26 *non ascendes per gradus ad altare meum ne reveletur turpitudo tua*

"'You will not climb up to My altar by steps, unless your nakedness be uncovered.'"

Exodus 21:1 *haec sunt iudicia quae propones eis*

"These are *the* judgments that you will put before them.

Rules Concerning Hebrew Slavery

21:2 *si emeris servum hebraeum sex annis serviet tibi in septimo egredietur liber gratis*

"If you buy *a* Hebrew slave, he will serve you six years. In *the* seventh, he will go out free without price.

21:3 *cum quali veste intraverit cum tali exeat si habens uxorem et uxor egredietur simul*

"With whatever kind of clothing he comes in, he will go out with *the* like. If having *a* wife, *the* wife also will go out together.

21:4 *sin autem dominus dederit illi uxorem et peperit filios et filias mulier et liberi eius erunt domini sui ipse vero exibit cum vestitu suo*

"But if *the* master will give him *a* wife and *the* woman births sons and daughters, his children will be his master's. But he will go out with his clothing.

21:5 *quod si dixerit servus diligo dominum meum et uxorem ac liberos non egrediar liber*

"*But* if *the* slave will say, 'I love my master and wife and children. I will not go free' –

21:6 *offeret eum dominus diis et adplicabitur ad ostium et postes perforabitque aurem eius subula et erit ei servus in saeculum*

"*the* master will bring him to *the* gods and place him near door and doorposts. And he will pierce his ear with *an* awl, and he will be *a* slave to him in *the* age.

A Daughter Sold as Slave
21:7 *si quis vendiderit filiam suam in famulam non egredietur sicut ancillae exire consuerunt*

"If someone should sell his daughter as *a* handmaid, she will not go out as female slaves are accustomed to go out.

21:8 *si displicuerit oculis domini sui cui tradita fuerit dimittet eam populo autem alieno vendendi non habet potestatem si spreverit eam*

"If she displeases her master's eyes, to whom she was handed over, let him release her. But he does not have authority to sell her to foreign people if he has scorned her.

21:9 *sin autem filio suo desponderit eam iuxta morem filiarum faciet illi*

"But if he has promised her to his son, he will do for her according to *the* custom of daughters.

21:10 *quod si alteram ei acceperit providebit puellae nuptias et vestimenta et pretium pudicitiae non negabit*

"But if he marries another to him, he will provide *the* girl wedding and clothing and will not deny her chastity's price.

21:11 *si tria ista non fecerit egredietur gratis absque pecunia*

"If he will not do these three, she will go out free, without price.

Murder and Manslaughter
21:12 *qui percusserit hominem volens occidere morte moriatur*

Let one who strikes down *a* man, wanting to kill, die by death.

21:13 *qui autem non est insidiatus sed Deus illum tradidit in manu eius constituam tibi locum quo fugere debeat*

"But one who has not plotted, but God handed him over into his hand, I will appoint *a* place to him where he must flee.

21:14 *si quis de industria occiderit proximum suum et per insidias ab altari meo evelles eum ut moriatur*

"But if someone should kill his neighbor from planning and by plots, you will tear him from My altar so He can die.

21:15 *qui percusserit patrem suum et matrem morte moriatur*

"Let one who strikes his father and mother die by death.

Kidnaping into Slavery
21:16 *qui furatus fuerit hominem et vendiderit eum convictus noxae morte moriatur*

"Let one who will steal *a* man and sell him, proved guilty of *the* crime, die by death.

Cursing Parents
21:17 *qui maledixerit patri suo et matri morte moriatur*

"Let one who will curse his father and mother die by death.

Injuries in a Brawl
21:18 *si rixati fuerint viri et percusserit alter proximum suum lapide vel pugno et ille mortuus non fuerit sed iacuerit in lectulo*

"If men are brawling and one should strike his neighbor by stone or fist, and he does not die but is laid prostrate in bed,

21:19 *si surrexerit et ambulaverit foris super baculum suum innocens erit qui percussit ita tamen ut operas eius et inpensas in medicos restituat*

"if he gets up again and walks outside on his staff, *the* one who struck him so will be innocent, except that he will repay his works and expenses in doctors.

Injuring a Slave
21:20 *qui percusserit servum suum vel ancillam virga et mortui fuerint in manibus eius criminis reus erit*

"One who strikes his slave or slave woman with *a* staff, and they will die at his hands, will be guilty of *a* crime.

21:21 *sin autem uno die supervixerit vel duobus non subiacebit poenae quia pecunia illius est*

"But if he should survive one or two days, he will not be subject to punishment, because he is his property.

Causing a Miscarriage
21:22 *si rixati fuerint viri et percusserit quis mulierem praegnantem et abortivum quidem fecerit sed ipsa vixerit subiacebit damno quantum expetierit maritus mulieris et arbitri iudicarint*

"If men are brawling and someone strikes *a* pregnant woman and indeed she will miscarry, but she will live, he will be subject to as much loss as *the* woman's husband will demand and arbitrators will judge.

Eye for Eye

21:23 *sin autem mors eius fuerit subsecuta reddet animam pro anima*

"But if her death will follow, he will pay back soul for soul,

21:24 *oculum pro oculo dentem pro dente manum pro manu pedem pro pede*

"eye for eye, tooth for tooth, hand for hand, foot for foot,

21:25 *adustionem pro adustione vulnus pro vulnere livorem pro livore*

"burn for burn, wound for wound, bruising for bruising

Harming a Slave

21:26 *si percusserit quispiam oculum servi sui aut ancillae et luscos eos fecerit dimittet liberos pro oculo quem eruit*

"If someone should strike his slave or slave woman's eye and will make him blind in one eye, he will set *the* children free for *the* eye which he took away.

21:27 *dentem quoque si excusserit servo vel ancillae suae similiter dimittet eos liberos*

"Likewise, if he should knock out his slave or slave woman's tooth, he will

set *the* children free as well.

A Dangerous Animal

21:28 *si bos cornu petierit virum aut mulierem et mortui fuerint lapidibus obruetur et non comedentur carnes eius dominusque bovis innocens erit*

"If *an* ox should gore *a* man or woman and they die, it will be crushed with stones, and its flesh will not be eaten. And *the* ox's master will be innocent.

21:29 *quod si bos cornipeta fuerit ab heri et nudius tertius et contestati sunt dominum eius nec reclusit eum occideritque virum aut mulierem et bos lapidibus obruetur et dominum illius occident*

"But if *the* ox was inclined to gore from yesterday and *the* day before, and its master was told, but did not pen it up, and it kills *a* man or woman, *the* ox will be crushed with stones and they will kill *the* man.

21:30 *quod si pretium ei fuerit inpositum dabit pro anima sua quicquid fuerit postulatus*

"But if *a* price will be imposed on him, he will give whatever will be demanded for his soul.

21:31 *filium quoque et filiam si cornu percusserit simili sententiae subiacebit*

"If also it should strike son or daughter with *the* horn, he will be subject to *the* same sentence.

21:32 *si servum ancillamque invaserit triginta siclos argenti dabit domino bos vero lapidibus opprimetur*

"If it should gore *a* slave or slave woman, he will give *their* master thirty silver coins, but *the* ox will be put down with stones.

Careless Property Damage

21:33 *si quis aperuerit cisternam et foderit et non operuerit eam cecideritque bos vel asinus in eam*

"If someone should open *a* cistern and dig it out, and not cover it, and *an* ox or donkey fall in it,

21:34 *dominus cisternae reddet pretium iumentorum quod autem mortuum est ipsius erit*

the cistern's owner will pay *the* animals' price. But what is dead will be his.

21:35 *si bos alienus bovem alterius vulnerarit et ille mortuus fuerit vendent bovem vivum et divident pretium cadaver autem mortui inter se dispertient*

"If one person's ox will wound another's ox and it die, they will sell *the* living ox and divide *the* price. But *the* dead body they will distribute among themselves.

21:36 *sin autem sciebat quod bos cornipeta esset ab heri et nudius tertius et non custodivit eum dominus suus reddet bovem pro bove et cadaver integrum accipiet*

"But if he knew that *the* ox was inclined to gore from yesterday and *the* day before, and its master did not watch him, he will pay back ox for ox, and will accept *the* whole dead body.

Restitution for Theft

Exodus 22:1 *si quis furatus fuerit bovem aut ovem et occiderit vel vendiderit quinque boves pro uno bove restituet et quattuor oves pro una ove*

"If someone should steal *an* ox or sheep and kill or sell it, he will pay back five oxen for one ox, and four sheep for one sheep.

Concerning Theft

22:2 *si effringens fur domum sive suffodiens fuerit inventus et accepto vulnere mortuus fuerit percussor non erit reus sanguinis*

"If *a* thief is found, breaking into or digging under *a* house and, receiving *a* wound, will die, *the* one striking will not be guilty of blood.

22:3 *quod si orto sole hoc fecerit homicidium perpetravit et ipse morietur si non habuerit quod pro furto reddat venundabitur*

"But if, *the* sun risen, he will do this, he has perpetrated homicide and will die.   If *the thief* does not have something to pay back for *the* theft, he will be sold.

22:4 *si inventum fuerit apud eum quod furatus est vivens sive bos sive asinus sive ovis duplum restituet*

"If what was stolen is found alive with him, whether ox or donkey or sheep, he will pay back double.

Inadvertent Property Damage

22:5 *si laeserit quispiam agrum vel vineam et dimiserit iumentum suum ut depascatur aliena quicquid optimum habuerit in agro suo vel in vinea pro damni aestimatione restituet*

"If someone will strike *a* field or vineyard and let his animal go so it eats anything choice another may have in his field or vineyard, he will pay back *the* estimated damages.

22:6 *si egressus ignis invenerit spinas et conprehenderit acervos frugum sive stantes segetes in agris reddet damnum qui ignem succenderit*

"If fire, going in, should find thorns and take heaps of grain or standing grain in fields, *one* who kindled *the* fire will repay *the* damage.

22:7 *si quis commendaverit amico pecuniam aut vas in custodiam et ab eo qui susceperat furto ablata fuerint si invenitur fur duplum reddet*

"If someone should entrust property or *a* vessel in care to *a* friend, and it be taken by theft from *the* one who received it, if *the* thief is found, he will repay double.

22:8 *si latet dominus domus adplicabitur ad deos et iurabit quod* *non extenderit manum in rem proximi sui*

"If he remains hidden, *the* house's owner will be taken to *the* gods, and he will swear that he did not stretch out *his* hand against his neighbor in *the* matter

22:9 *ad perpetrandam fraudem tam in bove quam in asino et ove ac vestimento et quicquid damnum inferre potest ad deos utriusque causa perveniet et si illi iudicaverint duplum restituet proximo suo*

"to working *a* fraud, either in ox or in donkey, in sheep or clothing or anything that can bring damage. Each one's cause will come to *the* gods and, if they judge, he will pay his neighbor back double.

22:10 *si quis commendaverit proximo suo asinum bovem ovem et omne iumentum ad custodiam et mortuum fuerit aut debilitatum vel captum ab hostibus nullusque hoc viderit*

"If someone should entrust his neighbor with *a* donkey, ox, sheep, or any animal to keep, and it dies or gets sick or is captured by enemies, and no one sees this,

22:11 *iusiurandum erit in medio quod non extenderit manum ad rem proximi sui suscipietque dominus iuramentum et ille reddere non*

cogetur

"*an* oath will be between them that he did not stretch out his hand against his neighbor in *the* affair. And *the* owner will accept *the* oath and he will not be compelled to repay.

22:12 *quod si furto ablatum fuerit restituet damnum domino*

"But if it was taken by theft, he will pay *the* owner damages.

22:13 *si comestum a bestia deferet ad eum quod occisum est et non restituet*

"If it *was* eaten by *a* wild animal, he will bring him back him what was killed, and he will not pay *it* back.

22:14 *qui a proximo suo quicquam horum mutuo postularit et debilitatum aut mortuum fuerit domino non praesente reddere conpelletur*

"One who will borrow from his neighbor any of these things, and it gets sick or dies, *the* owner not present, he will be compelled to repay.

22:15 *quod si inpraesentiarum fuit dominus non restituet maxime si conductum venerat pro mercede operis sui*

"But if *the* owner was present, he will not repay, especially if it came hired at *a* price for its work.

Sex with a Young Woman

22:16 *si seduxerit quis virginem necdum desponsatam et dormierit cum ea dotabit eam et habebit uxorem*

"If someone seduces *a* young woman not yet engaged, and sleeps with her, he will pay her *a* dowry and have *her* as wife.

22:17 *si pater virginis dare noluerit reddet pecuniam iuxta modum dotis quam virgines accipere consuerunt*

"If *the* young woman's father doesn't want to give her, he will pay money according to *the* manner of dowries which young women are accustomed to receive.

Miscellaneous Laws

22:18 *maleficos non patieris vivere*

"You will not allow sorcerers to live.

22:19 *qui coierit cum iumento morte moriatur*

"Let one who has sex with *an* animal die by death.

22:20 *qui immolat diis occidetur praeter Domino soli*

"One who sacrifices to gods, except to *the* Lord alone, will be killed.

22:21 *advenam non contristabis neque adfliges eum advenae enim et ipsi fuistis in terra Aegypti*

"You will not discourage *a* newcomer or afflict him, for you also were newcomers in Egypt's land.

Widow and Orphan

22:22 *viduae et pupillo non nocebitis*

"You will not harm widow or orphan.

22:23 *si laeseritis eos vociferabuntur ad me et ego audiam clamorem eorum*

"If you harm them, they will cry out to Me and I will hear their cry.

22:24 *et indignabitur furor meus percutiamque vos gladio et erunt uxores vestrae viduae et filii vestri pupilli*

"And My fury will be enraged and I will strike you by *the* sword. And your wives will be widows and your children orphans.

Lending to the Poor

22:25 *si pecuniam mutuam dederis populo meo pauperi qui habitat tecum non urgues eum quasi exactor nec usuris opprimes*

"If you give *a* loan of money to *the* poor of My people who lives with you, you will not threaten him like *an* extortioner or push him down with usuries.

22:26 *si pignus a proximo tuo acceperis vestimentum ante solis occasum redde ei*

"If you accept *a* garment *as a* pledge from your neighbor, give *it* back to him before sunset,

22:27 *ipsum enim est solum quo operitur indumentum carnis eius nec habet aliud in quo dormiat si clamaverit ad me exaudiam eum quia misericors sum*

"for it is his only *garment*, with which clothing he covers his flesh, nor does he have another in which he can sleep. If he cries out to Me, I will hear him, because I am merciful.

Respecting Those in Authority

22:28 *diis non detrahes et principi populi tui non maledices*

"You will not slander gods, and you will not curse your people's leaders.

Tithes and Offerings

22:29 *decimas tuas et primitias non tardabis offerre primogenitum filiorum tuorum dabis mihi*

"You will not delay in offering your tithes and first fruits. You will give *the* firstborn of your sons to Me.

22:30 *de bubus quoque et ovibus similiter facies septem diebus sit cum matre sua die octavo reddes illum mihi*

"You will do *the* same from bulls and sheep as well. Let it be with its mother seven days. *The* eighth day, you will offer it to Me.

22:31 *viri sancti eritis mihi carnem quae a bestiis fuerit praegustata non comedetis sed proicietis canibus*

"You will be holy men to Me. You will not eat meat which was tasted in advance by wild animals, but will throw it to dogs.

Liars
Exodus 23:1 *non suscipies vocem mendacii nec iunges manum tuam ut pro impio dicas falsum testimonium*

"You will not support *a* lie's voice, or join your hand so you give false testimony for *the* lawless.

Don't Follow the Crowd
23:2 *non sequeris turbam ad faciendum malum nec in iudicio plurimorum adquiesces sententiae ut a vero devies*

"You will not follow *a* crowd to do harm, or acquiesce in judgment to *the* majority's opinions, so you turn away from truth.

23:3 *pauperis quoque non misereberis in negotio*

"Likewise, you will not prefer *the* poor in business.

Your Enemy's Property
23:4 *si occurreris bovi inimici tui aut asino erranti reduc ad eum*

"If you find your enemy's ox or donkey wandering, bring it to him!

23:5 *si videris asinum odientis te iacere sub onere non pertransibis sed sublevabis cum eo*

"If you see *the* donkey of one who hates you fallen under *a* load, you will not walk by, but will lift *it* up with him.

Fairness in Judgment
23:6 *non declinabis in iudicio pauperis*

"You will not turn away from *the* poor *person's* judgment.

23:7 *mendacium fugies insontem et iustum non occides quia aversor impium*

"You will flee lying. You will not kill *the* innocent and fair, because I turn away in disgust from *the* lawless,

23:8 *nec accipias munera quae excaecant etiam prudentes et subvertunt verba iustorum*

"nor will you receive bribes that blind even *the* prudent, and undermine *the* fair *ones'* words.

How to Treat Strangers
23:9 *peregrino molestus non eris scitis enim advenarum animas quia et ipsi peregrini fuistis in terra Aegypti*

"You will not harass *a* stranger, for you understand newcomers' souls, because you also were sojourners in Egypt's land.

Laws of Seven
23:10 *sex annis seminabis terram tuam et congregabis fruges eius*

"You will sow your land for six years and gather its fruits.

23:11 *anno autem septimo dimittes eam et requiescere facies ut comedant pauperes populi tui et quicquid reliqui fuerit edant bestiae agri ita facies in vinea et in oliveto tuo*

"But you will leave it alone *the* seventh year and cause it to rest, so your people's poor may eat. And whatever is left *the* field's beasts will eat. You will do so in your vineyard and olive orchard.

23:12 *sex diebus operaberis septima die cessabis ut requiescat bos et asinus tuus et refrigeretur filius ancillae tuae et advena*

"You will work six days. *The* seventh day you will cease, so your ox and donkey can rest and your slave woman's son and newcomer may cool off.

Keep the Lord's Words
23:13 *omnia quae dixi vobis custodite et per nomen externorum deorum non iurabitis neque audietur ex ore vestro*

"Keep all that I have said to you! And you will not swear by *the* name of alien gods, nor let *them* be heard from your mouth.

The Lord's Feasts
23:14 *tribus vicibus per singulos annos mihi festa celebrabitis*

"You will celebrate feasts to Me three times each year.

Unleavened Bread
23:15 *sollemnitatem azymorum custodies septem diebus comedes azyma sicut praecepi tibi tempore mensis novorum quando egressus es de Aegypto non apparebis in conspectu meo vacuus*

"You will keep *the* solemnity of unleavened *bread*. You will eat unleavened *bread* seven days as I commanded you, at *the* time of new months, when you came out of Egypt. You will not appear empty-handed in My sight.

First Fruits and Harvest
23:16 *et sollemnitatem messis primitivorum operis tui quaecumque serueris in agro sollemnitatem quoque in exitu anni quando congregaveris omnesfruges tuas de agro*

"And *you will keep the* solemnity of *the* harvest of your efforts' first fruits, whatever you sow in your field; likewise *the* solemnity of *the* year's end, when you have gathered all your crops from *the* field.

23:17 *ter in anno apparebit omne masculinum tuum coram Domino*

Deo

"Each of your males will appear three times each year before *the* Lord God.

23:18 *non immolabis super fermento sanguinem victimae meae nec remanebit adeps sollemnitatis meae usque mane*

"You will not offer My victim's blood over yeast, nor will My solemnity's fat remain until morning.

23:19 *primitias frugum terrae tuae deferes in domum Domini Dei tui nec coques hedum in lacte matris suae*

"You will bring your land's first fruits into *the* Lord your God's house, nor will you cook *a* goat in its mother's milk.

My Angel
Will Go Before You
23:20 *ecce ego mittam angelum meum qui praecedat te et custodiat in via et introducat ad locum quem paravi*

"Look, I will send My angel, who will go before you and guard *you* in *the* way, and bring *you* into *the* place that I have prepared.

23:21 *observa eum et audi vocem eius nec contemnendum putes quia non dimittet cum peccaveritis et est nomen meum in illo*

"Watch him and listen to his voice, and do not think him one to despise, because he will not forgive when you sin, and My name is in him.

23:22 *quod si audieris vocem eius et feceris omnia quae loquor inimicus ero inimicis tuis et adfligam adfligentes te*

"But if you will listen to his voice and do all that I speak, I will be enemy to your enemies and will afflict those afflicting you.

23:23 *praecedetque te angelus meus et introducet te ad Amorreum et Hettheum et Ferezeum Chananeumque et Eveum et Iebuseum quos ego contribo*

"And My angel will go before you and bring you to *the* Amorites and Hittites and Ferezites and Canaanites and Hevites and Jebusites, whom I will wear down.

Don't Worship Their Gods
23:24 *non adorabis deos eorum nec coles eos non facies opera eorum sed destrues eos et confringes statuas eorum*

"You will not worship their gods or serve them. You will not do their works, but you will destroy them and smash their statues.

23:25 *servietisque Domino Deo vestro ut benedicam panibus tuis et* *aquis et auferam infirmitatem de medio tui*

"And you will serve *the* Lord your God, so I will bless your bread and waters and take away sickness from among you.

23:26 *non erit infecunda nec sterilis in terra tua numerum dierum tuorum implebo*

"*An* infertile or sterile *one* will not be in your land. I will fill up *the* number of your days.

God Will Drive
the Nations Out

23:27 *terrorem meum mittam in praecursum tuum et occidam omnem populum ad quem ingredieris cunctorumque inimicorum tuorum coram te terga vertam*

"I will send My terror in before you and will kill all *the* people to whom you will go in. And I will turn *the* backs of all your enemies before you,

23:28 *emittens crabrones prius qui fugabunt Eveum et Chananeum et Hettheum antequam introeas*

"sending hornets before who will make *the* Hevites and Canaanites and Hittites flee before you enter.

23:29 *non eiciam eos a facie tua anno uno ne terra in solitudinem redigatur et crescant contra te*

bestiae

"I will not throw them out before your face in one year, so *the* land may not return to wasteland and wild animals increase against you.

23:30 *paulatim expellam eos de conspectu tuo donec augearis et possideas terram*

"I will expel them little by little before your sight, until you are increased and can possess *the* land.

23:31 *ponam autem terminos tuos a mari Rubro usque ad mare Palestinorum et a deserto usque ad Fluvium tradam manibus vestris habitatores terrae et eiciam eos de conspectu vestro*

"But I will place your borders from *the* Red Sea even to *the* Palestinians' sea, and from *the* desert even to *the* River. I will hand *the* land's inhabitants over into your hands, and I will throw them out of your sight.

23:32 *non inibis cum eis foedus nec cum diis eorum*

"You will not enter into *a* pact with them, or with their gods.

23:33 *non habitent in terra tua ne forte peccare te faciant in me si servieris diis eorum quod tibi certo erit in scandalum*

"They may not live in your land, unless perhaps they make you sin against me if your serve their gods, which certainly will be to you as *a* stumbling block."

God Commands Moses and the Elders to Come Up Onto the Mountain

Exodus 24:1 *Mosi quoque dixit ascende ad Dominum tu et Aaron Nadab et Abiu et septuaginta senes ex Israhel et adorabitis procul*

To Moses also He said, "Climb up to *the* Lord, you and Aaron, Nadab and Abiu and seventy elders from Israel! And you will worship far off.

24:2 *solusque Moses ascendet ad Dominum et illi non adpropinquabunt nec populus ascendet cum eo*

"And Moses only will climb up to *the* Lord. And they will not come close, nor will *the* people climb up with him.

The Covenant Sacrifice

24:3 *venit ergo Moses et narravit plebi omnia verba Domini atque iudicia responditque cunctus populus una voce omnia verba Domini quae locutus est faciemus*

So Moses came and told the people all *the* Lord's words and judgments. And *the* whole people answered with one voice, "We will do all *the* Lord's words, which He has spoken."

24:4 *scripsit autem Moses universos sermones Domini et mane consurgens aedificavit altare ad* *radices montis et duodecim titulos per duodecim tribus Israhel*

But Moses wrote all *the* Lord's sayings and, getting up early, built *an* altar at *the* mountain's roots, and twelve titles for Israel's twelve tribes.

24:5 *misitque iuvenes de filiis Israhel et obtulerunt holocausta immolaveruntque victimas pacificas Domino vitulos*

And he sent youths from Israel's children. And they took burnt offerings and sacrificed calves *as* peace offerings to *the* Lord.

24:6 *tulit itaque Moses dimidiam partem sanguinis et misit in crateras partem autem residuam fudit super altare*

So Moses took *a* half portion of the blood and put it in basins, but part of *the* rest he poured on *the* altar.

Moses Reads
the Book of the Covenant
24:7 *adsumensque volumen foederis legit audiente populo qui dixerunt omnia quae locutus est Dominus faciemus et erimus oboedientes*

And taking up *the* Book of *the* Covenant, he read it, *the* people hearing, who said, "All that *the* Lord has spoken we will do. And we will be obedient."

24:8 *ille vero sumptum sanguinem respersit in populum et ait hic est sanguis foederis quod pepigit Dominus vobiscum super cunctis sermonibus his*

He, indeed, taking blood, sprinkled it among *the* people and said, "This is *the* covenant's blood, which *the* Lord has struck with you concerning all of these words."

Moses and the Elders
See God
24:9 *ascenderuntque Moses et Aaron Nadab et Abiu et septuaginta de senioribus Israhel*

And Moses and Aaron, Nadab and Abiu and seventy of Israel's elders climbed up,

24:10 *et viderunt Deum Israhel sub pedibus eius quasi opus lapidis sapphirini et quasi caelum cum serenum est*

and they saw Israel's God. Under His feet *was something* like *a* work of sapphire stones, and like *the* sky when it is clear.

24:11 *nec super eos qui procul recesserant de filiis Israhel misit manum suam videruntque Deum et comederunt ac biberunt*

Nor did He send His hand against those who had withdrawn far away among Israel's children. And they saw God and ate and drank.

God Commands Moses
to Come Up

24:12 *dixit autem Dominus ad Mosen ascende ad me in montem et esto ibi daboque tibi tabulas lapideas et legem ac mandata quae scripsi ut doceas eos*

But *the* Lord said to Moses, "Climb up to me on *the* mountain and be there. And I will give you stone tables and *the* law and commandments which I have written, so you may teach them."

24:13 *surrexerunt Moses et Iosue minister eius ascendensque Moses in montem Dei*

Moses rose up and Joshua, his minister. And Moses, climbing onto God's mountain,

24:14 *senioribus ait expectate hic donec revertamur ad vos habetis Aaron et Hur vobiscum si quid natum fuerit quaestionis referetis ad eos*

said to *the* elders, "Wait here until we come back to you. You will have Aaron and Hur with you. If some controversies begin, you will refer to them."

The Lord's Glory
on the Mountain

24:15 *cumque ascendisset Moses*

operuit nubes montem

And when Moses had gone up, *a* cloud covered *the* mountain.

24:16 *et habitavit gloria Domini super Sinai tegens illum nube sex diebus septimo autem die vocavit eum de medio caliginis*

And *the* Lord's glory stayed over Sinai, covering it with cloud for six days. But *the* seventh day, He called him from *the* middle of darkness.

24:17 *erat autem species gloriae Domini quasi ignis ardens super verticem montis in conspectu filiorum Israhel*

But *the* appearance of *the* Lord's glory *was* like fire burning on *the* mountain heights in *the* sight of Israel's children.

24:18 *ingressusque Moses medium nebulae ascendit in montem et fuit ibi quadraginta diebus et quadraginta noctibus*

And Moses, going into *the* middle of *the* cloud, climbed onto *the* mountain and was there forty days and forty nights.

**The Lord
Appoints an Offering**
Exodus 25:1 *locutusque est Dominus ad Mosen dicens*

And *the* Lord spoke to Moses, saying,

25:2 *loquere filiis Israhel ut tollant mihi primitias ab omni homine qui offert ultroneus accipietis eas*

"Speak to Israel's children, so they bring Me first fruits. You will accept them from all *the* people who bring voluntary *offerings.*

25:3 *haec sunt autem quae accipere debetis aurum et argentum et aes*

"But these are *the* things which you must receive: gold and silver and bronze;

25:4 *hyacinthum et purpuram coccumque bis tinctum et byssum pilos caprarum*

"blue dye and purple dye, scarlet twice dyed and stained, fine flax and goat hair;

25:5 *et pelles arietum rubricatas pelles ianthinas et ligna setthim*

"and red ram skins, and violet-colored skins, and acacia wood;

25:6 *oleum ad luminaria concinnanda aromata in unguentum*

et thymiama boni odoris

"oil for making candles; scented oils in ointment, and incense of good odor;

25:7 *lapides onychinos et gemmas ad ornandum ephod ac rationale*

"onyx stones and gems for adorning ephod and breastplate.

**The Reason
for the Offering**
25:8 *facientque mihi sanctuarium et habitabo in medio eorum*

"And they will make Me *a* sanctuary and dwelling among them,

25:9 *iuxta omnem similitudinem tabernaculi quod ostendam tibi et omnium vasorum in cultum eius sicque facietis illud*

"according to every likeness of *the* tabernacle which I will show you, and all *the* vessels in its worship. And you will make it so.

The Covenant Box
25:10 *arcam de lignis setthim conpingite cuius longitudo habeat duos semis cubitos latitudo cubitum et dimidium altitudo cubitum similiter ac semissem*

"Put together *a* box of acacia wood, whose length will be two and half cubits; width *a* cubit and *a* half;

height *a* cubit and *a* half as well.

25:11 *et deaurabis eam auro mundissimo intus et foris faciesque supra coronam auream per circuitum*

"And you will cover it with purest gold inside and out. And over it you will make *a* golden crown around;

25:12 *et quattuor circulos aureos quos pones per quattuor arcae angulos duo circuli sint in latere uno et duo in altero*

"and four golden circles, which you will put on *the* box's four corners: two circles may be in one side, and two on *the* other.

25:13 *facies quoque vectes de lignis setthim et operies eos auro*

"And you will also make poles of acacia wood and cover them with gold.

25:14 *inducesque per circulos qui sunt in arcae lateribus ut portetur in eis*

"And you will put them through *the* circles which are on *the* box's sides, so it can be carried by them,

25:15 *qui semper erunt in circulis nec umquam extrahentur ab eis*

"which always will be in *the* circles,

nor ever taken out of them.

25:16 *ponesque in arcam testificationem quam dabo tibi*

"And you will put into *the* box *the* testimony which I will give you.

The Place of Atonement

25:17 *facies et propitiatorium de auro mundissimo duos cubitos et dimidium tenebit longitudo eius cubitum ac semissem latitudo*

"You will also make *an* atonement seat from purest gold. Its length will be two and *a* half cubits, and width *a* cubit and *a* half.

25:18 *duos quoque cherubin aureos et productiles facies ex utraque parte oraculi*

"Likewise, you will make two cherubim of hammered gold, on each of *the* oracle's sides.

25:19 *cherub unus sit in latere uno et alter in altero*

"Let one cherub be on one side and *the* other on *the* other.

25:20 *utrumque latus propitiatorii tegant expandentes alas et operientes oraculum respiciantque se mutuo versis vultibus in propitiatorium quo operienda est arca*

"Let them cover both sides of *the*

atonement seat, spreading *their* wings, and covering *the* oracle. Let them look at each other, turning faces to *the* atonement seat with which *the* box is covered –

25:21 *in qua pones testimonium quod dabo tibi*

"in which you will put *the* testimony which I will give you."

Where God Will Speak
25:22 *inde praecipiam et loquar ad te supra propitiatorio scilicet ac medio duorum cherubin qui erunt super arcam testimonii cuncta quae mandabo per te filiis Israhel*

"I will teach and speak to you from there, over *the* atonement seat, of course, and between *the* two cherubim which will be over *the* box of testimony, all that I will command Israel's children through you.

The Table
25:23 *facies et mensam de lignis setthim habentem duos cubitos longitudinis et in latitudine cubitum et in altitudine cubitum ac semissem*

"You will also make *a* table of acacia wood, having two cubits length, and one cubit in width, and *a* cubit and *a* half in height.

25:24 *et inaurabis eam auro purissimo faciesque illi labium aureum per circuitum*

"And you will cover it with purest gold, and make it *a* golden lip around.

25:25 *et ipsi labio coronam interrasilem altam quattuor digitis et super illam alteram coronam aureolam*

"and to this lip *a* carved crown four fingers high, and over it another golden crown.

25:26 *quattuor quoque circulos aureos praeparabis et pones eos in quattuor angulis eiusdem mensae per singulos pedes*

"You will prepare likewise four gold circles and put them on *the* four corners of this table, for each foot.

25:27 *subter coronam erunt circuli aurei ut mittantur vectes per eos et possit mensa portari*

"*The* golden circles will be under *the* crown, so poles can be put through them and *the* table can be carried.

25:28 *ipsosque vectes facies de lignis setthim et circumdabis auro ad subvehendam mensam*

"You will make *the* poles of acacia wood and surround them with gold, for carrying *the* table.

25:29 *parabis et acetabula ac fialas turibula et cyatos in quibus* *offerenda sunt libamina ex auro purissimo*

"You will prepare also from purest gold small cups and drinking plates, censers and wine ladles, in which drink offerings will be offered

25:30 *et pones super mensam panes propositionis in conspectu meo semper*

"And you will place on *the* table *the* bread of propositions, in My sight always.

The Candelabra

25:31 *facies et candelabrum ductile de auro mundissimo hastile eius et calamos scyphos et spherulas ac lilia ex ipso procedentia*

"You will also make *a* candelabra, formed from purest gold, its shaft and branches, bowls and small balls and lilies coming out from *the* same.

25:32 *sex calami egredientur de lateribus tres ex uno latere et tres ex altero*

"Six branches will go out from *the* sides: three from one side, and three from the other.

25:33 *tres scyphi quasi in nucis modum per calamos singulos spherulaque simul et lilium et tres similiter scyphi instar nucis in calamo altero spherulaque et lilium*

hoc erit opus sex calamorum qui producendi sunt de hastili

"Three bowls like in *the* manner of nuts for each branch, and *a* small bowl and lily together; and three bowls resembling nuts in *the* other branch, and *a* small bowl and lily. This will be *the* work of *the* six branches which will come out from *the* shaft.

25:34 *in ipso autem candelabro erunt quattuor scyphi in nucis modum spherulaeque per singulos et lilia*

"But in *the* candelabra itself will be four bowls in *the* manner of nuts, and small bowls for each, and lilies;

25:35 *spherula sub duobus calamis per tria loca qui simul sex fiunt procedentes de hastili uno*

"small bowls under two branches, for three places, which together make six, proceeding from one shaft.

25:36 *et spherae igitur et calami ex ipso erunt universa ductilia de auro purissimo*

And *the* small bowls, therefore, and *the* branches will all be formed *the* same, from purest gold.

The Lamps

25:37 *facies et lucernas septem et pones eas super candelabrum ut* *luceant ex adverso*

"You will make also seven lamps and put them on *the* candelabra, so they may shine from outside;

25:38 *emunctoria quoque et ubi quae emuncta sunt extinguantur fient de auro purissimo*

"snuffers also, and where what is snuffed may be extinguished. They will be made of purest gold.

25:39 *omne pondus candelabri cum universis vasis suis habebit talentum auri mundissimi*

"All *the* candelabra's weight, with all its vessels, will be *a* talent of purest gold.

25:40 *inspice et fac secundum exemplar quod tibi in monte monstratum est*

"Inspect and make *it* according to *the* model which was shown to you on *the* mountain!"

The Tabernacle

Exodus 26:1 *tabernaculum vero ita fiet decem cortinas de bysso retorta et hyacintho ac purpura coccoque bis tincto variatas opere plumario facies*

"And *the* tabernacle will be made this way. You will make ten curtains of twisted flax and blue and purple and scarlet twice dyed, embroidered by work of various colors.

26:2 *longitudo cortinae unius habebit viginti octo cubitos latitudo quattuor cubitorum erit unius mensurae fient universa tentoria*

"One curtain's length will be twenty-eight cubits, its width four cubits. All the partitions will be made from one measure.

26:3 *quinque cortinae sibi iungentur mutuo et aliae quinque nexu simili coherebunt*

"Five curtains will be joined to each other, and *the* other five will be connected by similar ties.

26:4 *ansulas hyacinthinas in lateribus ac summitatibus facies cortinarum ut possint invicem copulari*

"You will make blue dyed ties on *the* curtains' sides and tops, so they can be joined together in turn.

26:5 *quinquagenas ansulas cortina habebit in utraque parte ita insertas ut ansa contra ansam veniat et altera alteri possit aptari*

"*The* curtain will have fifty ties in each part. You will insert them this way: so tie may come against tie, and one may be fitted to *the* other.

26:6 *facies et quinquaginta circulos aureos quibus cortinarum vela iungenda sunt ut unum tabernaculum fiat*

"You will make also fifty golden circles, by which *the* curtains' veils may be joined, so one tabernacle may be made.

The Tabernacle's Roof

26:7 *facies et saga cilicina undecim ad operiendum tectum tabernaculi*

"You will also make eleven goat hair cloaks for covering *the* tabernacle's top.

26:8 *longitudo sagi unius habebit triginta cubitos et latitudo quattuor aequa erit mensura sagorum omnium*

"One cloak will have thirty cubits' length and four *cubits'* width. *The* measure of all *the* cloaks will be equal.

26:9 *e quibus quinque iunges seorsum et sex sibi mutuo copulabis ita ut sextum sagum in fronte tecti duplices*

"And from them you will fasten five above and six to *the* others. You will join them this way, so *the* sixth cloak doubles in *the* roof's front.

26:10 *facies et quinquaginta ansas in ora sagi unius ut coniungi cum altero queat et quinquaginta ansas in ora sagi alterius ut cum altero copuletur*

"You will also make fifty ties in *the* mouths of one cloak, so it can be joined with *the* other, and fifty ties in *the* other cloak's mouth, so it can be fastened with *the* other;

26:11 *quinquaginta fibulas aeneas quibus iungantur ansae et unum ex omnibus operimentum fiat*

"fifty copper joins, which will be connected to handles, and let all of them be made one covering.

26:12 *quod autem superfuerit in sagis quae parantur tecto id est unum sagum quod amplius est ex medietate eius operies posteriora tabernaculi*

"But *from* what is left over from *the* cloaks which are joined in *the* roof – that is, one cloak which is more – you will cover *the* tabernacle's back with half of it.

26:13 *et cubitus ex una parte pendebit et alter ex altera qui plus est in sagorum longitudine utrumque latus tabernaculi protegens*

"And *a* cubit from one part will hang down, and *the* other from *the* other which is extra in *the* cloaks' length, protecting both sides of *the* tabernacle.

26:14 *facies et operimentum aliud tecto de pellibus arietum rubricatis et super hoc rursum aliud operimentum de ianthinis pellibus*

"You will also make another covering, *a* roof of red ram skins, and over this again another covering of violet-colored skins.

The Tabernacle's Framing

26:15 *facies et tabulas stantes tabernaculi de lignis setthim*

"You will also make *the* tabernacle's standing frames from acacia wood,

26:16 *quae singulae denos cubitos in longitudine habeant et in latitudine singulos ac semissem*

each one of which will have ten cubits' length and one and *a* half in width.

26:17 *in lateribus tabulae duae incastraturae fient quibus tabula alteri tabulae conectatur atque in hunc modum cunctae tabulae parabuntur*

"In *the* wall frames' two sides let notches be made, by which *a* frame may be connected to another frame, and in this way all *the* frames will be prepared;

26:18 *quarum viginti erunt in latere meridiano quod vergit ad austrum*

"twenty of which will be on *the* southern side, which inclines toward *the* south.

26:19 *quibus quadraginta bases argenteas fundes ut binae bases singulis tabulis per duos angulos subiciantur*

"You will cast for them forty silver bases, so two bases may be placed under each of *the* frames, for two corners.

26:20 *in latere quoque secundo tabernaculi quod vergit ad aquilonem viginti tabulae erunt*

"Likewise, twenty frames will be in *the* tabernacle's second side, which inclines to *the* north;

26:21 *quadraginta habentes bases argenteas binae bases singulis tabulis subponentur*

"having forty silver bases. Let twin bases be placed beneath each of the frames.

26:22 *ad occidentalem vero plagam tabernaculi facies sex tabulas*

"You will make six frames for *the* tabernacle's west quarter,

26:23 *et rursum alias duas quae in angulis erigantur post tergum tabernaculi*

"and again two others, which may be erected in *the* corners, at *the* tabernacle's back.

26:24 *eruntque coniunctae a deorsum usque sursum et una omnes conpago retinebit duabus quoque tabulis quae in angulis ponendae sunt similis iunctura servabitur*

"And *the* junctions will be from below to above. And one structure will retain all. *The* joint likewise will serve *the* two frames which are hung together in *the* corners.

26:25 *et erunt simul tabulae octo bases earum argenteae sedecim duabus basibus per unam tabulam supputatis*

"And *the* eight frames will be together on their sixteen silver bases. You will count up two bases for each frame.

26:26 *facies et vectes de lignis setthim quinque ad continendas tabulas in uno latere tabernaculi*

"You will also make five poles from acacia wood, to hang *the* frames in one side of *the* tabernacle,

26:27 *et quinque alios in altero et eiusdem numeri ad occidentalem plagam*

"and five others in *the* other side, and *the* same number toward *the* western quarter,

26:28 *qui mittentur per medias tabulas a summo usque ad summum*

"which can be placed through *the* middle of *the* frames, from *the* top to *the* top.

26:29 *ipsasque tabulas deaurabis et fundes eis anulos aureos per quos vectes tabulata contineant quos operies lamminis aureis*

"You will cover these frames with gold and cast for them golden rings, through which *the* poles may hold *the* frames, which *poles* you will cover with gold laminate.

26:30 *et eriges tabernaculum iuxta exemplum quod tibi in monte monstratum est*

"And you will set up *the* tabernacle according to *the* model which was shown you on *the* mountain.

The Veil
Inside the Tabernacle

26:31 *facies et velum de hyacintho et purpura coccoque bis tincto et bysso retorta opere plumario et pulchra varietate contextum*

"You will also make *a* veil of blue, and purple, and scarlet twice dyed, and twisted flax covered with embroideries, and *a* beautiful many-colored texture;

26:32 *quod adpendes ante quattuor columnas de lignis setthim quae ipsae quidem deauratae erunt et habebunt capita aurea sed bases argenteas*

"which you will hang before four columns of acacia wood, which themselves will be covered with gold and will have golden head pieces, but silver bases.

The Tabernacle's
Inner Arrangement

26:33 *inseretur autem velum per circulos intra quod pones arcam testimonii et quo sanctuarium et sanctuarii sanctuaria dividentur*

"But you will hang *the* veil inside by rings, inside of which you will put *the* ark of testimony, and by which *the* sanctuary and *the* sanctuary's sanctuary will be divided.

26:34 *pones et propitiatorium super arcam testimonii in sancta*

sanctorum

"You will also put *the* atonement seat over *the* ark of testimony, in *the* holy of holies,

26:35 *mensamque extra velum et contra mensam candelabrum in latere tabernaculi meridiano mensa enim stabit in parte aquilonis*

"and *the* table outside *the* veil, and *the* candelabra on *the* tabernacle's south side, for *the* table will stand in *the* northern part.

26:36 *facies et tentorium in introitu tabernaculi de hyacintho et purpura coccoque bis tincto et bysso retorta opere plumarii*

"You will also make *a* partition at *the* tabernacle's entrance of blue, and purple, and scarlet twice-dyed, and twisted flax, covered with embroideries.

26:37 *et quinque columnas deaurabis lignorum setthim ante quas ducetur tentorium quarum erunt capita aurea et bases aeneae*

"And you will cover five acacia wood columns in gold, before which *the* partition will be led, whose head pieces will be gold and bases silver.

The Altar

Exodus 27:1 *facies et altare de lignis setthim quod habebit quinque cubitos in longitudine et totidem in latitudine id est quadrum et tres cubitos in altitudine*

"You will also make *an* altar from acacia wood, which will have five cubits in length and *the* same in width – that is, square – and three cubits in height.

27:2 *cornua autem per quattuor angulos ex ipso erunt et operies illud aere*

"But horns will be in it, from *the* four corners, and you will cover it with brass.

27:3 *faciesque in usus eius lebetas ad suscipiendos cineres et forcipes atque fuscinulas et ignium receptacula omnia vasa ex aere fabricabis*

"And you will make in its use copper cauldrons for receiving ashes, and tongs, and forks, and *a* receptacle for fire. You will make all *the* vessels from brass,

27:4 *craticulamque in modum retis aeneam per cuius quattuor angulos erunt quattuor anuli aenei*

"and *a* copper grate in *the* manner of *a* net. Four copper rings will be for each of *the* four corners,

27:5 *quos pones subter arulam altaris eritque craticula usque ad altaris medium*

which you will place under *the* altar's base. And *the* grate will be even to *the* middle of *the* altar.

27:6 *facies et vectes altaris de lignis setthim duos quos operies lamminis aeneis*

"And you will make *the* altar's two poles of acacia wood, which you will cover with brass laminate.

27:7 *et induces per circulos eruntque ex utroque latere altaris ad portandum*

"And you will put them through *the* rings, and they will be on each of *the* altar's sides to carry *it*.

27:8 *non solidum sed inane et cavum intrinsecus facies illud sicut tibi in monte monstratum est*

"You will not make it solid, but empty, and *a* cavity inside, as was shown you on *the* mountain.

The Tabernacle's Courtyard

27:9 *facies et atrium tabernaculi in cuius plaga australi contra meridiem erunt tentoria de bysso retorta centum cubitos unum latus tenebit in longitudine*

"You will also make *the* tabernacle's

courtyard. In its southern quarter, pointing south, *the* partitions will be of twisted flax. It will have one hundred cubits for one side in length,

27:10 *et columnas viginti cum basibus totidem aeneis quae capita cum celaturis suis habebunt argentea*

"and twenty columns, with *the* same number of bases of copper, whose head pieces with their canopies will have silver.

27:11 *similiter in latere aquilonis per longum erunt tentoria centum cubitorum columnae viginti et bases aeneae eiusdem numeri et capita earum cum celaturis suis argentea*

Similarly, on *the* north side, for *its* length, *the* partitions will be one hundred cubits, twenty columns and bronze bases of *the* same number, and their head pieces with their canopies *of* silver.

27:12 *in latitudine vero atrii quod respicit ad occidentem erunt tentoria per quinquaginta cubitos et columnae decem basesque totidem*

"And *the* courtyard's width, which looks to the west, *the* partitions will be for fifty cubits, and ten columns, and as many bases.

27:13 *in ea quoque atrii latitudine quae respicit ad orientem quinquaginta cubiti erunt*

"Likewise, in *the* courtyard's side that faces to *the* east, *there* will be fifty cubits,

27:14 *in quibus quindecim cubitorum tentoria lateri uno deputabuntur columnaeque tres et bases totidem*

"in *the* partitions of which on one side fifteen cubits will be assigned, and three columns, and *the* same number of bases.

27:15 *et in latere altero erunt tentoria cubitos obtinentia quindecim columnas tres et bases totidem*

"And *the* partitions in *the* other side will be occupying fifteen cubits, three columns, and *the* same number of bases.

The Courtyard's Entrance
27:16 *in introitu vero atrii fiet tentorium cubitorum viginti ex hyacintho et purpura coccoque bis tincto et bysso retorta opere plumarii columnas habebit quattuor cum basibus totidem*

"And in *the* courtyard's entrance will be made partitions of twenty cubits from blue, and purple, and red twice dyed, and twisted flax, worked with embroideries. It will have four columns with *the* same number of bases.

27:17 *omnes columnae atrii per circuitum vestitae erunt argenti lamminis capitibus argenteis et basibus aeneis*

"All *the* courtyard's columns will be clothed around with silver plate, *its* head pieces of silver and bases of brass.

27:18 *in longitudine occupabit atrium cubitos centum in latitudine quinquaginta altitudo quinque cubitorum erit fietque de bysso retorta et habebit bases aeneas*

"*The* courtyard will occupy one hundred cubits in length, fifty in width. It will be five cubits tall. And it will be made of twisted flax and will have bronze bases.

27:19 *cuncta vasa tabernaculi in omnes usus et caerimonias tam paxillos eius quam atrii ex aere facies*

"You will make from bronze all *the* tabernacle's vessels for all uses and ceremonies, from its tent stakes to its courtyard.

An Ever-burning Lamp
Before the Lord

27:20 *praecipe filiis Israhel ut adferant tibi oleum de arboribus olivarum purissimum piloque contusum ut ardeat lucerna semper*

"Command Israel's children, so they bring you purest oil from olive trees, and ground by *a* pestle, so *a* lamp may always burn

27:21 *in tabernaculo testimonii extra velum quod oppansum est testimonio et conlocabunt eam Aaron et filii eius ut usque mane luceat coram Domino perpetuus erit cultus per successiones eorum a filiis Israhel*

"in *the* tabernacle of testimony, outside *the* veil which is spread out before *the* testimony. And Aaron and his sons will arrange it so it may shine even to morning before *the* Lord. *It* will be *a* continuous rite for their successors from Israel's children."

Priesthood Formally Established

Exodus 28:1 *adplica quoque ad te Aaron fratrem tuum cum filiis suis de medio filiorum Israhel ut sacerdotio fungantur mihi Aaron Nadab et Abiu Eleazar et Ithamar*

"Likewise, join to yourself from Israel's children's midst Aaron your brother with his sons, so they may perform priestly duties to Me: Aaron, Nadab and Abiu, Eleazar and Ithamar.

Priestly Garments

28:2 *faciesque vestem sanctam fratri tuo in gloriam et decorem*

"And you will make *a* holy garment for your brother, in glory and beauty.

28:3 *et loqueris cunctis sapientibus corde quos replevi spiritu prudentiae ut faciant vestes Aaron in quibus sanctificatus ministret mihi*

"And you will speak to all *the* wise in heart, whom I have filled by *a* prudent spirit, so they may make Aaron's robes, in which, made holy, he will minister to Me.

28:4 *haec autem erunt vestimenta quae facient rationale et superumerale tunicam et lineam strictam cidarim et balteum facient vestimenta sancta Aaron fratri tuo et filiis eius ut sacerdotio fungantur mihi*

"But these will be *the* garments which they will make: *a* breastplate, and *an* overlay, *a* tunic and *a* closely-woven linen *garment*, and *a* head-dress, and *a* shoulder band. They will make these holy garments for Aaron your brother and his sons, so they may carry out priestly duties to Me.

28:5 *accipientque aurum et hyacinthum et purpuram coccumque bis tinctum et byssum*

"And they will take gold, and blue, and purple, and scarlet twice-dyed, and twisted flax.

28:6 *facient autem superumerale de auro et hyacintho ac purpura coccoque bis tincto et bysso retorta opere polymito*

"But they will make *the* overlay of gold, and blue, and purple, and scarlet twice-dyed, and twisted flax, woven of different colored threads.

28:7 *duas oras iunctas habebit in utroque latere summitatum ut in unum redeant*

"It will have two borders joined on top on either side, so they may buckle in one.

28:8 *ipsaque textura et cuncta operis varietas erit ex auro et hyacintho et purpura coccoque bis tincto et bysso retorta*

"It will be of *the* same texture and all covered with embroideries, from gold, and blue, and purple, and scarlet twice-dyed, and twisted flax.

The Tribes' Names
Near the Priest's Heart

28:9 *sumesque duos lapides onychinos et sculpes in eis nomina filiorum Israhel*

"And you will take two onyx stones, and carve in them *the* names of Israel's children:

28:10 *sex nomina in lapide uno et sex reliqua in altero iuxta ordinem nativitatis eorum*

"six names in one stone, and *the* remaining six in *the* other, according to their birth order.

28:11 *opere sculptoris et celatura gemmarii sculpes eos nominibus filiorum Israhel inclusos auro atque circumdatos*

"You will sculpt them by *a* sculptor's work and *a* jeweler's engraving, *the* names of Israel's children set in gold and carved around.

28:12 *et pones in utroque latere superumeralis memoriale filiis Israhel portabitque Aaron nomina eorum coram Domino super utrumque umerum ob recordationem*

"And you will place *them as a*

memorial of Israel's children on either side of *the* overlay, and Aaron will carry their names before *the* Lord over both shoulders as *a* recollection.

28:13 *facies et uncinos ex auro*

"You will also make hooks of gold,

28:14 *et duas catenulas auri purissimi sibi invicem coherentes quas inseres uncinis*

"and two small chains of purest gold, attaching to themselves in turn, in which you will insert *the* hooks.

The Breastplate

28:15 *rationale quoque iudicii facies opere polymito iuxta texturam superumeralis ex auro hyacintho et purpura coccoque bis tincto et bysso retorta*

"Judgment's breastplate likewise you will make of embroidered work, like *the* overlay's texture, from gold, blue, and purple, and scarlet twice-dyed, and twisted flax.

28:16 *quadrangulum erit et duplex mensuram palmi habebit tam in longitudine quam in latitudine*

"It will be four-sided and doubled, and will have *a* palm's measure in length as well as in width.

28:17 *ponesque in eo quattuor*

ordines lapidum in primo versu erit lapis sardius et topazius et zmaragdus

"And you will put in it four rows of stones. In the first row will be stones of carnelian and topaz and emerald;

28:18 *in secundo carbunculus sapphyrus et iaspis*

"in *the* second, garnet and sapphire and jasper;

28:19 *in tertio ligyrius achates et amethistus*

"in *the* third, ligure, agate, and amethyst;

28:20 *in quarto chrysolitus onychinus et berillus inclusi auro erunt per ordines suos*

"in *the* fourth, chrysolite, onyx, and beryl. All will be set with gold, in their rows.

28:21 *habebuntque nomina filiorum Israhel duodecim nominibus celabuntur singuli lapides nominibus singulorum per duodecim tribus*

"And they will have Israel's children's names. They will be engraved with twelve names, on each stone *the* name of *an* individual tribe, for twelve tribes.

28:22 *facies in rationali catenas*

sibi invicem coherentes ex auro purissimo

"You will make chains in *the* breastplate from purest gold, joining to themselves in turn,

28:23 *et duos anulos aureos quos pones in utraque rationalis summitate*

"and two gold rings, which you will put on either side of *the* top of *the* breastplate.

28:24 *catenasque aureas iunges anulis qui sunt in marginibus eius*

"And you will join *the* golden chains to *the* rings which are on its edges.

28:25 *et ipsarum catenarum extrema duobus copulabis uncinis in utroque latere superumeralis quod rationale respicit*

"And you will join *the* same chains' two ends to *the* hooks on either side of *the* overlay, which looks on *the* breastplate.

28:26 *facies et duos anulos aureos quos pones in summitatibus rationalis et in oris quae e regione sunt superumeralis et posteriora eius aspiciunt*

"You will also make two gold rings, which you will put on *the* breastplate's top, and in *the* borders that are on that part of *the* overlay, and will face behind it;

28:27 *nec non et alios duos anulos aureos qui ponendi sunt in utroque latere superumeralis deorsum quod respicit contra faciem iuncturae inferioris ut aptari possit cum superumerali*

"in addition, two other gold rings which will be hung on either side beneath *the* breastplate, which looks against *the* lower junction's face, so it can be joined with *the* overlay.

28:28 *et stringatur rationale anulis suis cum anulis superumeralis vitta hyacinthina ut maneat iunctura fabrefacta et a se invicem rationale et superumerale nequeant separari*

"And *the* breastplate will be tied by its rings to *the* overlay by *a* blue-colored cord, so *the* junction may remain in place and, in turn, *the* breastplate and overlay may not be separated from each other.

28:29 *portabitque Aaron nomina filiorum Israhel in rationali iudicii super pectus suum quando ingreditur sanctuarium memoriale coram Domino in aeternum*

"And Aaron will carry *the* names of Israel's children in judgment's breastplate over his chest when he goes into *the* sanctuary, as *a* memorial before *the* Lord in eternity.

28:30 *pones autem in rationali iudicii doctrinam et veritatem quae erunt in pectore Aaron quando ingreditur coram Domino et gestabit iudicium filiorum Israhel in pectore suo in conspectu Domini semper*

"But you will place teaching and truth into judgment's breastplate, which will be on Aaron's chest when he goes before *the* Lord. And he will carry Israel's children's judgment on his chest, in *the* Lord's sight always.

The Tunic
28:31 *facies et tunicam superumeralis totam hyacinthinam*

"You will also make *the* overlay's tunic completely of blue-colored thread.

28:32 *in cuius medio supra erit capitium et ora per gyrum eius textilis sicut fieri solet in extremis vestium partibus ne facile rumpatur*

"in *the* middle of which above will be *a* hole for *the* head and *a* woven border around it, as is customarily made in *the* outermost parts of clothing, so it may not be easily broken.

28:33 *deorsum vero ad pedes eiusdem tunicae per circuitum quasi mala punica facies ex hyacintho et purpura et cocco bis tincto mixtis in medio tintinabulis*

"And below at *the* same tunic's feet, you will make around it like pomegranates, from violet and purple and scarlet twice-dyed with little bells mixed between,

28:34 *ita ut tintinabulum sit aureum et malum rursumque tintinabulum aliud aureum et malum punicum*

"so that *there* may be *a* golden bell and *a* pomegranate, and another golden bell in turn and *a* pomegranate.

Why Aaron
Wears the Garment

28:35 *et vestietur ea Aaron in officio ministerii ut audiatur sonitus quando ingreditur et egreditur sanctuarium in conspectu Domini et non moriatur*

"And Aaron will put it on in his ministerial office, so *the* sound can be heard when he goes into and comes out of *the* sanctuary in *the* Lord's sight, and he may not die.

Holy to the Lord

28:36 *facies et lamminam de auro purissimo in qua sculpes opere celatoris Sanctum Domino*

"You will also make *a* plate of purest gold, in which you will carve by *the* jeweler's work, 'Holy to *the* Lord.'

28:37 *ligabisque eam vitta hyacinthina et erit super tiaram*

"And you will tie it by *a* blue ribbon, and it will be over *the* crown,

28:38 *inminens fronti pontificis portabitque Aaron iniquitates eorum quae obtulerint et sanctificaverint filii Israhel in cunctis muneribus et donariis suis erit autem lammina semper in fronte eius ut placatus eis sit Dominus*

"hanging over *the* high priest's forehead. Aaron will carry *the* lawlessness of those *things* which Israel's children have offered and sacrificed, in all their gifts and offerings. But *the* plate will always be on his forehead, so *the* Lord may be placated.

28:39 *stringesque tunicam bysso et tiaram byssinam facies et balteum opere plumarii*

"And you will draw tight *a* tunic of twisted flax, and make *a* flax headpiece, and *a* shoulder band covered with embroideries.

28:40 *porro filiis Aaron tunicas lineas parabis et balteos ac tiaras in gloriam et decorem*

"Further, you will prepare linen tunics and shoulder bands and head pieces, in glory and beauty, for Aaron's sons.

28:41 *vestiesque his omnibus Aaron fratrem tuum et filios eius cum eo et* *cunctorum consecrabis manus sanctificabisque illos ut sacerdotio fungantur mihi*

"And you will dress Aaron your brother and his sons with him in all these. And you will consecrate all their hands, and sanctify them, so they may carry out priestly duties to Me.

Linen Thigh Coverings

28:42 *facies et feminalia linea ut operiant carnem turpitudinis suae a renibus usque ad femina*

"You will also make linen thigh coverings, so you may cover their shame's flesh, from kidneys even to thighs.

28:43 *et utentur eis Aaron et filii eius quando ingredientur tabernaculum testimonii vel quando adpropinquant ad altare ut ministrent in sanctuario ne iniquitatis rei moriantur legitimum sempiternum erit Aaron et semini eius post eum*

"And Aaron and his sons will use them when they go into testimony's tabernacle, or when they approach *the* altar so they can minister in *the* sanctuary, so they not die by guilt of lawlessness. *This* will be an everlasting rule to Aaron and his seed after him.

Offerings to Consecrate Priests

Exodus 29:1 *sed et hoc facies ut mihi in sacerdotio consecrentur tolle vitulum de armento et arietes duos inmaculatos*

"Yet you will also do this so they may be consecrated to me in priestly service. Take *a* calf from *the* herd and two spotless rams,

29:2 *panesque azymos et crustula absque fermento quae conspersa sint oleo lagana quoque azyma oleo lita de simila triticea cuncta facies*

"unleavened bread and *a* small cake without yeast, which are sprinkled with oil, unleavened wafers with oil as well. You will make *them* all from wheat flour.

29:3 *et posita in canistro offeres vitulum autem et duos arietes*

"And you will offer them, placed in baskets. But you will bring *the* calf and *the* two rams,

29:4 *et Aaron ac filios eius adplicabis ad ostium tabernaculi testimonii cumque laveris patrem cum filiis aqua*

"and Aaron and his sons to *the* tabernacle of testimony's entry.

Rite of Consecrating Priests
And when you have washed by water

the father with the sons,

29:5 *indues Aaron vestimentis suis id est linea et tunica et superumerali et rationali quod constringes balteo*

"you will dress Aaron in his vestments – that is the undergarment and tunic and overlay and breastplate, which you will tie to the shoulder strap.

29:6 *et pones tiaram in capite eius et lamminam sanctam super tiaram*

"And you will place the headpiece on his head and the holy plate over the headpiece.

29:7 *et oleum unctionis fundes super caput eius atque hoc ritu consecrabitur*

"And you will pour anointing oil over his head, and he will be made holy by this rite.

29:8 *filios quoque illius adplicabis et indues tunicis lineis cingesque balteo*

"Likewise, you will take his sons and dress them in tunics *and* undergarments, and tie on shoulder straps –

29:9 *Aaron scilicet et liberos eius et inpones eis mitras eruntque sacerdotes mei in religione perpetua postquam initiaveris manus eorum*

"Aaron, of course, and his children – and you will put head pieces on them. And they will be priests to Me in *an* everlasting rite, after you have initiated their hands.

Offering the Calf

29:10 *adplicabis et vitulum coram tabernaculo testimonii inponentque Aaron et filii eius manus super caput illius*

"And you will take the calf before testimony's tabernacle, and Aaron and his sons will lay hands on its head.

29:11 *et mactabis eum in conspectu Domini iuxta ostium tabernaculi testimonii*

"And you will slaughter it in the Lord's sight, beside the opening to testimony's tabernacle.

29:12 *sumptumque de sanguine vituli pones super cornua altaris digito tuo reliquum autem sanguinem fundes iuxta basim eius*

"And taking some of the calf's blood, you will put it on the altar's horns with your finger. But you will pour the rest of the blood alongside its base.

29:13 *sumes et adipem totum qui operit intestina et reticulum iecoris ac duos renes et adipem qui super eos est et offeres incensum super* *altare*

"You will also take all *the* fat that covers *the* intestines, and *the* liver's covering, and *the* two kidneys, and *the* fat that is over them, and you will offer *as* incense over *the* altar.

29:14 *carnes vero vituli et corium et fimum conbures foris extra castra eo quod pro peccato sit*

"But *the* calf's flesh and hide and dung you will burn outside, beyond *the* camp, so that it may be for sin.

The First Ram
29:15 *unum quoque arietum sumes super cuius caput ponent Aaron et filii eius manus*

"Likewise, you will take one ram, over whose head Aaron and his sons will lay hands.

29:16 *quem cum mactaveris tolles de sanguine eius et fundes circa altare*

"When you have slaughtered it, you will take some of its blood and pour it around *the* altar.

29:17 *ipsum autem arietem secabis in frusta lotaque intestina eius ac pedes pones super concisas carnes et super caput illius*

"But you will cut *the* same ram into pieces and wash its intestines and

feet. And you will place *them* on *the* cut up flesh and on its head.

29:18 *et offeres totum arietem in incensum super altare oblatio est Domini odor suavissimus victimae Dei*

"And you will offer *the* whole ram as incense on *the* altar. It is *the* Lord's offering, *the* smoothest odor of God's victim.

The Second Ram
29:19 *tolles quoque arietem alterum super cuius caput Aaron et filii eius ponent manus*

"Likewise, you will take *the* other ram, over whose head Aaron and his sons will lay hands.

29:20 *quem cum immolaveris sumes de sanguine ipsius et pones super extremum dextrae auriculae Aaron et filiorum eius et super pollices manus eorum et pedis dextri fundesque sanguinem super altare per circuitum*

"When you have offered it, you will take some of its blood and put it on *the* tip of Aaron and his sons' right ear, and over *the* thumbs of their right hands and *big toes of* their right feet. And you will pour *the* blood over *the* altar, around *it*.

29:21 *cumque tuleris de sanguine qui est super altare et de oleo* *unctionis asperges Aaron et vestes eius filios et vestimenta eorum consecratisque et ipsis et vestibus*

"And when you have taken some of *the* blood which is on *the* altar and some of *the* anointing oil, you will sprinkle Aaron and his sons and their vestments. And they will be made holy, both them and *the* vestments.

29:22 *tolles adipem de ariete et caudam et arvinam quae operit vitalia ac reticulum iecoris et duos renes atque adipem qui super eos est armumque dextrum eo quod sit aries consecrationum*

"You will take *the* ram's fat and tail, and *the* lard which covers *the* vital organs, and *the* liver's covering, and *the* two kidneys and *the* fat which is over them, and *the* right shoulder, so that it may be *the* ram of consecration;

The Grain Offerings

29:23 *tortam panis unius crustulum conspersum oleo laganum de canistro azymorum quod positum est in conspectu Domini*

"*a* cake of bread, one small cake sprinkled with oil, *an* unleavened wafer from *the* basket which was placed in *the* Lord's sight;

29:24 *ponesque omnia super manus Aaron et filiorum eius et sanctificabis eos elevans coram Domino*

"and you will place all *these* in Aaron and his sons' hands. And they will sanctify them, raising them before *the* Lord.

29:25 *suscipiesque universa de manibus eorum et incendes super altare in holocaustum odorem suavissimum in conspectu Domini quia oblatio eius est*

"And you will receive all these from their hands and burn them on *the* altar as *a* burnt offering, *a* smoothest odor in *the* Lord's sight, because *it* is His offering.

The Priests' Portion

29:26 *sumes quoque pectusculum de ariete quo initiatus est Aaron sanctificabisque illud elatum coram Domino et cedet in partem tuam*

"Likewise, you will take *the* breast from the ram by which Aaron was initiated, and you will make it holy, lifted before *the* Lord. And it is granted as your portion.

29:27 *sanctificabis et pectusculum consecratum et armum quem de ariete separasti*

"You will sanctify also *the* consecrated breast and forequarter which you separated from *the* ram,

29:28 *quo initiatus est Aaron et filii*

eius cedentque in partem Aaron et filiorum eius iure perpetuo a filiis Israhel quia primitiva sunt et initia de victimis eorum pacificis quae offerunt Domino

"by which Aaron was initiated and his sons. And they will grant them to Aaron and his sons, *a* perpetual law for Israel's children, because they are first fruits and *the* beginnings of their peace offerings, which they will offer to *the* Lord.

Ongoing Use
of Holy Vestments
29:29 *vestem autem sanctam qua utitur Aaron habebunt filii eius post eum ut unguantur in ea et consecrentur manus eorum*

"But *the* holy vestment which Aaron uses, his sons will have after him, so they may be anointed in it and their hands be consecrated.

29:30 *septem diebus utetur illa qui pontifex pro eo fuerit constitutus de filiis eius et qui ingredietur tabernaculum testimonii ut ministret in sanctuario*

"*The* one from his sons who will be appointed high priest in his place, and *the* one who goes into testimony's tabernacle so he can minister in *the* sanctuary, will use it for seven days.

Who May Eat
the Offering?
29:31 *arietem autem consecrationum tolles et coques carnes eius in loco sancto*

"But you will take *the* consecration ram and cook its meat in *the* holy place.

29:32 *quibus vescetur Aaron et filii eius panes quoque qui sunt in canistro in vestibulo tabernaculi testimonii comedent*

"which Aaron will eat, and his sons. They will likewise eat *the* bread that is in *the* basket in *the* court of testimony's tabernacle,

29:33 *ut sit placabile sacrificium et sanctificentur offerentium manus alienigena non vescetur ex eis quia sancti sunt*

"so it may be *a* pleasing sacrifice, and *the* hands offering *it* may be made holy. *A* stranger will not eat from them, because they are holy.

No Leftovers
29:34 *quod si remanserit de carnibus consecratis sive de panibus usque mane conbures reliquias igni non comedentur quia sanctificata sunt*

"But if something from *the* consecrated meat should remain to morning, even of *the* bread, you will burn *the* leftovers with fire. They will not be eaten, because they are holy.

Carrying Out
the Commands

29:35 *omnia quae praecepi tibi facies super Aaron et filiis eius septem diebus consecrabis manus eorum*

"All things that I have commanded you, you will do for Aaron and his sons. You will consecrate their hands for seven days.

29:36 *et vitulum pro peccato offeres per singulos dies ad expiandum mundabisque altare cum immolaris expiationis hostiam et ungues illud in sanctificationem*

"And you will offer *a* calf for sin each day, for atonement. And you will cleanse *the* altar when you burn *the* atonement offerings, and anoint it in holiness.

29:37 *septem diebus expiabis altare et sanctificabis et erit sanctum sanctorum omnis qui tetigerit illud sanctificabitur*

"Seven days you will make atonement for *the* altar and sanctify *it*, and it will be *the* holy of holies. Everyone who touches it will become holy.

The Continuing Sacrifice

29:38 *hoc est quod facies in altari agnos anniculos duos per singulos dies iugiter*

"This is what you will offer on *the* altar: two yearling lambs each day, continuously –

29:39 *unum agnum mane et alterum vespere*

"one lamb at morning and *the* other at evening;

29:40 *decimam partem similae conspersae oleo tunso quod habeat mensuram quartam partem hin et vinum ad libandum eiusdem mensurae in agno uno*

"*a* tenth portion of flour sprinkled with pulped oil, which will have *a* fourth portion of *a* hin's measure; and wine to drink of *the* same measure, with one lamb.

29:41 *alterum vero agnum offeres ad vesperam iuxta ritum matutinae oblationis et iuxta ea quae diximus in odorem suavitatis*

"You will offer *the* other lamb at evening, according to *the* rite of *the* morning offering, and according to what we have said, as *an* odor of smoothness,

29:42 *sacrificium Domino oblatione perpetua in generationes vestras ad*

ostium tabernaculi testimonii coram Domino ubi constituam ut loquar ad te

"*a* sacrifice to *the* Lord, *a* perpetual offering in your generations, at *the* entrance to testimony's tabernacle before *the* Lord, where I will appoint, so I may speak to you.

29:43 *ibique praecipiam filiis Israhel et sanctificabitur altare in gloria mea*

"And I will command Israel's children there, and he will be sanctified by *the* altar to My glory.

29:44 *sanctificabo et tabernaculum testimonii cum altari et Aaron cum filiis eius ut sacerdotio fungantur mihi*

"And I will sanctify also testimony's tabernacle with *the* altar, and Aaron with his sons, so they may perform priestly duties to Me.

29:45 *et habitabo in medio filiorum Israhel eroque eis Deus*

"And I will live among Israel's children, and I will be God to them.

29:46 *et scient quia ego Dominus Deus eorum qui eduxi eos de terra Aegypti ut manerem inter illos ego Dominus Deus ipsorum*

"And they will know that I am *the* Lord their God, who led them from Egypt's land so I could dwell among them. I am *the* Lord their God.

The Incense Altar

Exodus 30:1 *facies quoque altare in adolendum thymiama de lignis setthim*

"You will also make *an* altar for burning incense from acacia wood,

30:2 *habens cubitum longitudinis et alterum latitudinis id est quadrangulum et duos cubitos in altitudine cornua ex ipso procedent*

"having *a* cubit's length and another in width – that is, square – and two cubits in height. Horns will come out from it.

30:3 *vestiesque illud auro purissimo tam craticulam eius quam parietes per circuitum et cornua faciesque ei coronam auream per gyrum*

"And you will dress it in purest gold, its grate as well as its walls around and horns. And you will make *a* golden crown around *it*,

30:4 *et duos anulos aureos sub corona per singula latera ut mittantur in eos vectes et altare portetur*

"and two gold rings under *the* crown on each side, so poles can be placed in them and *the* altar be carried.

30:5 *ipsos quoque vectes facies de lignis setthim et inaurabis*

"You will also make *these* poles of acacia wood, and cover them with gold.

30:6 *ponesque altare contra velum quod ante arcam pendet testimonii coram propitiatorio quo tegitur testimonium ubi loquar tibi*

"And you will put *the* altar beside *the* veil which hangs before *the* ark of testimony, before *the* atonement seat which covers *the* testimony, where I speak to you.

30:7 *et adolebit incensum super eo Aaron suave fraglans mane quando conponet lucernas incendet illud*

"And Aaron will burn pleasant-burning incense on it early. When he arranges *the* lamps, he will light it.

30:8 *et quando conlocat eas ad vesperum uret thymiama sempiternum coram Domino in generationes vestras*

"And when he sets them at evening, he will burn everlasting incense before *the* Lord, in your generations.

30:9 *non offeretis super eo thymiama conpositionis alterius nec oblationem et victimam nec liba libabitis*

"You will not offer on it incense of another composition, or *an* offering or victim, nor will you pour *a* drink offering.

30:10 *et deprecabitur Aaron super cornua eius semel per annum in sanguine quod oblatum est pro peccato et placabit super eo in generationibus vestris sanctum sanctorum erit Domino*

"And Aaron will pray on its horns once *a* year, with *the* blood which is offered for sin. And he will make peace over it in your generations. It will holy of holies to *the* Lord."

Funding the Tabernacle

30:11 *locutusque est Dominus ad Mosen dicens*

And *the* Lord spoke to Moses, saying,

30:12 *quando tuleris summam filiorum Israhel iuxta numerum dabunt singuli pretium pro animabus suis Domino et non erit plaga in eis cum fuerint recensiti*

"When you take the count of Israel's children, according to number, each one will give to *the* Lord *the* price of their lives. And plague will not be among them when they are counted.

30:13 *hoc autem dabit omnis qui transit ad nomen dimidium sicli iuxta mensuram templi siclus viginti obolos habet media pars sicli offeretur Domino*

"But each one who passes through to *being* named will give this: half *a* shekel, according to *the* temple measure. *A* shekel has twenty coins. *A* half part of *a* shekel will be offered to *the* Lord.

30:14 *qui habetur in numero a viginti annis et supra dabit pretium*

"One who has twenty years or more in *the* numbering will give *the* price.

30:15 *dives non addet ad medium sicli et pauper nihil minuet*

"*The* rich will not add to half *a* shekel, and *the* poor will reduce nothing.

30:16 *susceptamque pecuniam quae conlata est a filiis Israhel trades in usus tabernaculi testimonii ut sit monumentum eorum coram Domino et propitietur animabus illorum*

"You will give *the* received money which is collected from Israel's children into *the* use of testimony's tabernacle, so it may be their monument before *the* Lord, and it will make peace to their souls."

The Brass Wash Basin

30:17 *locutusque est Dominus ad Mosen dicens*

And *the* Lord spoke to Moses, saying,

30:18 *facies et labium aeneum cum basi sua ad lavandum ponesque illud inter tabernaculum testimonii et altare et missa aqua*

"You will also make *a* brass basin with its base for washing. And you will place it between testimony's tabernacle and *the* altar. And putting in water,

30:19 *lavabunt in eo Aaron et filii eius manus suas ac pedes*

"Aaron and his sons will wash their hands and feet in it

30:20 *quando ingressuri sunt tabernaculum testimonii et quando accessuri ad altare ut offerant in eo thymiama Domino*

"when they go into testimony's tabernacle, and when they come to *the* altar so they can offer *the* Lord incense in it,

30:21 *ne forte moriantur legitimum sempiternum erit ipsi et semini eius per successiones*

"unless perhaps they die. It will be *an* everlasting law to him and his seed by successions."

The Anointing Oil
30:22 *locutusque est Dominus ad Mosen*

And *the* Lord spoke to Moses,

30:23 *dicens sume tibi aromata prima et zmyrnae electae quingentos siclos et cinnamomi medium id est ducentos quinquaginta calami similiter ducentos quinquaginta*

saying, "Take yourself prime spices and choice myrrh, five hundred shekels' weight; and half *that* of cinnamon – that is, two hundred fifty shekels; sweet cane also, two hundred fifty *shekels;*

30:24 *cassiae autem quingentos siclos in pondere sanctuarii olei de olivetis mensuram hin*

"but five hundred shekels of cassia, in *the* sanctuary's measure; oil from olives, *a* hin's measure.

30:25 *faciesque unctionis oleum sanctum unguentum conpositum opere unguentarii*

"And you will make holy anointing oil, composite ointment, made by *the* ointment-maker.

Ritual Anointing
30:26 *et ungues ex eo tabernaculum testimonii et arcam testamenti*

"And you will anoint from it testimony's tabernacle and *the* covenant box,

30:27 *mensamque cum vasis suis candelabrum et utensilia eius altaria thymiamatis*

"and *the* table with its vessels, *the* candelabra and its utensils, *the* altars of incense

30:28 *et holocausti et universam supellectilem quae ad cultum eorum pertinent*

"and burnt offerings, and all *the* items that pertain to their ritual.

30:29 *sanctificabisque omnia et erunt sancta sanctorum qui tetigerit ea sanctificabitur*

"And you will sanctify all of them, and they will be holy of holies. Who touches them will be made holy.

30:30 *Aaron et filios eius ungues sanctificabisque eos ut sacerdotio fungantur mihi*

"You will anoint Aaron and his sons and make them holy, so they may carry out priestly duties to Me.

30:31 *filiis quoque Israhel dices hoc oleum unctionis sanctum erit mihi in generationes vestras*

"Likewise, you will say to Israel's children, 'This holy anointing oil will be for Me in your generations.

30:32 *caro hominis non unguetur ex eo et iuxta conpositionem eius non facietis aliud quia sanctificatum est et sanctum erit vobis*

"'Human flesh will not be anointed from it, and you will not make another according to its composition, because it is sanctified. And it will be holy to you.

30:33 *homo quicumque tale conposuerit et dederit ex eo alieno exterminabitur de populo suo*

"'Whatever man who makes it and gives some of it to *a* stranger will be exterminated from his people.'"

Instructions for Incense

30:34 *dixitque Dominus ad Mosen sume tibi aromata stacten et onycha galbanen boni odoris et tus lucidissimum aequalis ponderis erunt omnia*

And *the* Lord said to Moses, "Take for yourself spices of medicinal gum and onych, resin of good odor and clearest frankincense. And all will be of equal measure.

30:35 *faciesque thymiama conpositum opere unguentarii mixtum diligenter et purum et sanctificatione dignissimum*

"And you will make incense, compounded by *the* ointment-maker's work, mixed carefully and pure and most worthy of holy usage.

30:36 *cumque in tenuissimum pulverem universa contuderis pones ex eo coram testimonio tabernaculi* *in quo loco apparebo tibi sanctum sanctorum erit vobis thymiama*

"And when you have crushed it all into finest powder, you will put some of it before testimony's tabernacle, in which place I will appear to you. And *the* incense will be holy of holies to you.

30:37 *talem conpositionem non facietis in usus vestros quia sanctum est Domino*

"You will not make such *a* composition for your uses, because *it* is holy to *the* Lord.

30:38 *homo quicumque fecerit simile ut odore illius perfruatur peribit de populis suis*

"And whatever man makes something similar so he can enjoy its odor, will perish from his people."

God Appoints Those
Who Will Make the Tabernacle

Exodus 31:1 *locutusque est Dominus ad Mosen dicens*

And *the* Lord spoke to Moses, saying,

31:2 *ecce vocavi ex nomine Beselehel filium Uri filii Hur de tribu Iuda*

"Look, I have called by name Beselel, Uri's son, Hur's son, from Judah's tribe.

31:3 *et implevi eum spiritu Dei sapientia intellegentia et scientia in omni opere*

"And I have filled him by God's spirit with wisdom, intelligence, and knowledge in every work

31:4 *ad excogitandum fabre quicquid fieri potest ex auro et argento et aere*

"to thinking out skillfully whatever can be made from gold and silver and brass

31:5 *marmore et gemmis et diversitate lignorum*

"marble and gems and various woods."

31:6 *dedique ei socium Hooliab filium Achisamech de tribu Dan et in*

corde omnis eruditi posui sapientiam
ut faciant cuncta quae praecepi tibi

"And I have given him Hooliab, Achisamech's son, from Dan's tribe, as friend. And I have placed wisdom in every learned heart, so they can make all that I have commanded you:

31:7 *tabernaculum foederis et arcam testimonii et propitiatorium quod super eam est et cuncta vasa tabernaculi*

"*the* covenant tabernacle and testimony's ark and *the* atonement seat which is over it, and all *the* tabernacle's vessels;

31:8 *mensamque et vasa eius candelabrum purissimum cum vasis suis et altaria thymiamatis*

"*the* table and its vessels; *the* most pure candelabra with its vessels; and *the* altars of incense

31:9 *et holocausti et omnia vasa eorum labium cum basi sua*

"and burnt offerings and all their vessels; *the* basin with its base;

31:10 *vestes sanctas in ministerio Aaron sacerdoti et filiis eius ut fungantur officio suo in sacris*

"holy vestments in ministry for Aaron *the* priest and his sons, so they can carry out their office in holiness;

31:11 *oleum unctionis et thymiama aromatum in sanctuario omnia quae praecepi tibi facient*

"*the* anointing oil and aromatic incense in *the* sanctuary. All that I have commanded you, they will make."

Sabbath Keeping
31:12 *et locutus est Dominus ad Mosen dicens*

And *the* Lord spoke to Moses, saying,

31:13 *loquere filiis Israhel et dices ad eos videte ut sabbatum meum custodiatis quia signum est inter me et vos in generationibus vestris ut sciatis quia ego Dominus qui sanctifico vos*

"Speak to Israel's children and say to them, 'See that you keep My Sabbath, because it is *a* sign between Me and you in your generations, so you may know that I *am the* Lord who sanctifies you.

31:14 *custodite sabbatum sanctum est enim vobis qui polluerit illud morte morietur qui fecerit in eo opus peribit anima illius de medio populi sui*

"'Keep *the* Sabbath holy, for it is for you. One who pollutes it will die by death. Who does work in it, his soul will perish from among his people.

31:15 *sex diebus facietis opus in die septimo sabbatum est requies sancta Domino omnis qui fecerit opus in hac die morietur*

"'Six days you will do work. In *the* seventh day is Sabbath, *a* holy rest to *the* Lord. Everyone who does work in that day will die.

31:16 *custodiant filii Israhel sabbatum et celebrent illud in generationibus suis pactum est sempiternum*

"'Let Israel's children keep *the* Sabbath and celebrate it in their generations. It is *an* everlasting pact

31:17 *inter me et filios Israhel signumque perpetuum sex enim diebus fecit Dominus caelum et terram et in septimo ab opere cessavit*

"'between Me and Israel's children, and *a* perpetual sign, for in six days *the* Lord made sky and land, and on *the* seventh He ceased from work.'"

The Completed Words

31:18 *dedit quoque Mosi conpletis huiuscemodi sermonibus in monte Sinai duas tabulas testimonii lapideas scriptas digito Dei*

Likewise, *when* these words *were* completed, He gave Moses on Mount Sinai two stone tables of testimony, written by God's finger.

The People Grow Restless

Exodus 32:1 *videns autem populus quod moram faceret descendendi de monte Moses congregatus adversus Aaron ait surge fac nobis deos qui nos praecedant Mosi enim huic viro qui nos eduxit de terra Aegypti ignoramus quid acciderit*

But *the* people, seeing that Moses made *a* delay coming down from *the* mountain, gathered against Aaron. It said, "Get up! Make us gods who can go before us! For we don't know what happened to this man Moses who led us out of Egypt's land."

32:2 *dixitque ad eos Aaron tollite inaures aureas de uxorum filiorumque et filiarum vestrarum auribus et adferte ad me*

And Aaron said to them, "Take *the* gold earrings from your wives, sons, and daughters' ears, and bring them to me!"

32:3 *fecit populus quae iusserat deferens inaures ad Aaron*

The people did what he commanded, bringing *the* earrings to Aaron.

32:4 *quas cum ille accepisset formavit opere fusorio et fecit ex eis vitulum conflatilem dixeruntque hii sunt dii tui Israhel qui te eduxerunt de terra Aegypti*

When he had received them, he formed *them* by *the* metal worker's craft, and made from them *a* molded calf. And they said, "These are your gods, Israel, who led you out of Egypt's land"

32:5 *quod cum vidisset Aaron aedificavit altare coram eo et praeconis voce clamavit dicens cras sollemnitas Domini est*

When he saw it, Aaron built *an* altar before it and proclaimed by *a* herald's voice, saying, "Tomorrow is *the* Lord's solemnity."

32:6 *surgentesque mane obtulerunt holocausta et hostias pacificas et sedit populus comedere ac bibere et surrexerunt ludere*

And, rising up early, they brought burnt offerings and peace victims. And *the* people sat down to eat and drink, and got up to play.

The Lord Sends Moses Down the Mountain

32:7 *locutus est autem Dominus ad Mosen vade descende peccavit populus tuus quem eduxisti de terra Aegypti*

But *the* Lord said to Moses, "Go! Climb down! Your people, whom you led out of Egypt's land, has sinned.

32:8 *recesserunt cito de via quam*

ostendisti eis feceruntque sibi vitulum conflatilem et adoraverunt atque immolantes ei hostias dixerunt isti sunt dii tui Israhel qui te eduxerunt de terra Aegypti

"They turned away quickly from *the* way that you showed them, and made themselves *a* molded calf. And they worshiped and, burning offerings to it, they said, 'These are your gods, Israel, who led you out of Egypt's land.'"

The Lord Tests Moses

32:9 *rursumque ait Dominus ad Mosen cerno quod populus iste durae cervicis sit*

And again *the* Lord said to Moses, "I see that this people is hard-necked.

32:10 *dimitte me ut irascatur furor meus contra eos et deleam eos faciamque te in gentem magnam*

"Let Me go so My fury may be enraged against them. And I will destroy them and make you into *a* great nation."

32:11 *Moses autem orabat Dominum Deum suum dicens cur Domine irascitur furor tuus contra populum tuum quem eduxisti de terra Aegypti in fortitudine magna et in manu robusta*

But Moses prayed to *the* Lord his God, saying, "Why, Lord, is Your fury enraged against Your people, whom You led out of Egypt's land in great strength and in *a* mighty hand?

32:12 *ne quaeso dicant Aegyptii callide eduxit eos ut interficeret in montibus et deleret e terra quiescat ira tua et esto placabilis super nequitia populi tui*

"Let *the* Egyptians not say, I beg, 'He led them out skillfully so He could kill them in *the* desert and destroy them from *the* land.' Let Your anger rest, and be pacified over Your people's worthlessness!

32:13 *recordare Abraham Isaac et Israhel servorum tuorum quibus iurasti per temet ipsum dicens multiplicabo semen vestrum sicut stellas caeli et universam terram hanc de qua locutus sum dabo semini vestro et possidebitis eam semper*

"Remember Abraham, Isaac, and Israel, Your slaves, to whom You swore by Yourself, saying, 'I will multiply your seed like *the* sky's stars, and I will give your seed all this land of which I have spoken. And you will possess it always.'"

32:14 *placatusque est Dominus ne faceret malum quod locutus fuerat adversus populum suum*

And *the* Lord was placated, so He did not do *the* harm that He had spoken against His people.

Moses Turns Back
from the Mountain

32:15 *et reversus est Moses de monte portans duas tabulas testimonii manu scriptas ex utraque parte*

And Moses turned back from *the* mountain, carrying *the* two tables of testimony, written on either side,

32:16 *et factas opere Dei scriptura quoque Dei erat sculpta in tabulis*

and made by God's work. God's writing was also in *the* tables.

32:17 *audiens autem Iosue tumultum populi vociferantis dixit ad Mosen ululatus pugnae auditur in castris*

But Joshua, hearing *the* people's tumult shouting, said to Moses, "*A* battle cry is heard in *the* camps."

32:18 *qui respondit non est clamor adhortantium ad pugnam neque vociferatio conpellentium ad fugam sed vocem cantantium ego audio*

Moses answered, "It isn't *a* cry urging to battle or *a* shout compelling to flee. But I hear *the* voice of singing."

32:19 *cumque adpropinquasset ad castra vidit vitulum et choros iratusque valde proiecit de manu tabulas et confregit eas ad radices montis*

And when he came close to *the* camps, he saw *the* calf and *the* dancing and, very angry, threw down *the* tables from his hand and broke them at *the* mountain's roots.

32:20 *arripiensque vitulum quem fecerant conbusit et contrivit usque ad pulverem quem sparsit in aqua et dedit ex eo potum filiis Israhel*

And taking *the* calf which they had made, he burned and crushed it even to dust, which he scattered in water and gave to Israel's children *to* drink from it.

Moses Questions Aaron

32:21 *dixitque ad Aaron quid tibi fecit hic populus ut induceres super eum peccatum maximum*

And he said to Aaron, "What did *the* people do to you here that you led *the* greatest sin over him?"

32:22 *cui ille respondit ne indignetur dominus meus tu enim nosti populum istum quod pronus sit ad malum*

He answered him, "Don't be mad, my lord, for you know this people – that it is prone to evil.

32:23 *dixerunt mihi fac nobis deos*

qui praecedant nos huic enim Mosi qui nos eduxit de terra Aegypti nescimus quid acciderit

"They said to me, 'Make us gods who can go before us, because we don't know what happened to this Moses who led us out of Egypt's land.'

32:24 *quibus ego dixi quis vestrum habet aurum tulerunt et dederunt mihi et proieci illud in ignem egressusque est hic vitulus*

"I said to them, 'Who of you has gold?'

"They took *it* and gave *it* to me, and I threw it into fire, and this calf came out."

Moses and the Levites
Wreak Vengeance

32:25 *videns ergo Moses populum quod esset nudatus spoliaverat enim eum Aaron propter ignominiam sordis et inter hostes nudum constituerat*

So Moses, seeing that *the* people was naked – for Aaron had stripped him because of his squalor's shame, and had set him nude between enemies –

32:26 *et stans in porta castrorum ait si quis est Domini iungatur mihi congregatique sunt ad eum omnes filii Levi*

and standing in *the* camps' gate, said, "Who*ever* is *the* Lord's, let him join me!"

And all Levi's children gathered to him.

32:27 *quibus ait haec dicit Dominus Deus Israhel ponat vir gladium super femur suum ite et redite de porta usque ad portam per medium castrorum et occidat unusquisque fratrem et amicum et proximum suum*

He said to them, "*The* Lord, Israel's God, says this: Let each man put his sword on his thigh. Go and return from gate even to gate, through *the* middle of *the* camps, and let each one kill his brother and friend and neighbor!"

32:28 *fecerunt filii Levi iuxta sermonem Mosi cecideruntque in die illo quasi tria milia hominum*

Levi's children did according to Moses' word, and nearly three thousand men fell in that day.

32:29 *et ait Moses consecrastis manus vestras hodie Domino unusquisque in filio et fratre suo ut detur vobis benedictio*

And Moses said, "You have set aside your hands to *the* Lord today, each one in his son and brother, so blessing may be given to you."

32:30 *facto autem die altero locutus est Moses ad populum peccastis peccatum maximum ascendam ad Dominum si quo modo eum quivero deprecari pro scelere vestro*

But *the* next day coming, Moses said to *the* people, "You have sinned *a* great sin! I will climb up to *the* Lord, if somehow I can pray to him over your crime."

Moses Pleads with God
for the People

32:31 *reversusque ad Dominum ait obsecro peccavit populus iste peccatum magnum feceruntque sibi deos aureos aut dimitte eis hanc noxam*

And turning back to *the* Lord, he said, "I pray, this people sinned *a* great sin and made themselves golden gods. Either forgive them this injury

32:32 *aut si non facis dele me de libro tuo quem scripsisti*

or, if you won't do it, erase me from Your book which You have written!"

32:33 *cui respondit Dominus qui peccaverit mihi delebo eum de libro meo*

The Lord answered him, "I will erase *the* one who sinned against Me from My book.

32:34 *tu autem vade et duc populum*

istum quo locutus sum tibi angelus meus praecedet te ego autem in die ultionis visitabo et hoc peccatum eorum

"But you, go and lead this people where I have told you. My angel will go before you, but I will visit also this their sin in revenge's day.

32:35 *percussit ergo Dominus populum pro reatu vituli quem fecit Aaron*

So *the* Lord struck *the* people for *the* guilt of *the* calf which Aaron made.

The Lord Commands
Israel to Go to Canaan

Exodus 33:1 *locutusque est Dominus ad Mosen vade ascende de loco isto tu et populus tuus quem eduxisti de terra Aegypti in terram quam iuravi Abraham Isaac et Iacob dicens semini tuo dabo eam*

And *the* Lord said to Moses, "Go! Climb up from this place, you and *the* people whom you led from Egypt's land, into *the* land which I swore to Abraham, Isaac, and Jacob, saying, 'I will give it to your seed.'

33:2 *et mittam praecursorem tui angelum ut eiciam Chananeum et Amorreum et Hettheum et Ferezeum et Eveum et Iebuseum*

"And I will send *an* angel before you, so I can throw out *the* Canaanite and Amorite and Hittite and Ferezite and Hivite and Jebusite,

33:3 *et intres in terram fluentem lacte et melle non enim ascendam tecum quia populus durae cervicis est ne forte disperdam te in via*

"and you may enter into *a* land flowing with milk and honey. For I will not go up with you, because *the* people is hard-necked, unless perhaps I destroy you on *the* way.

33:4 *audiens populus sermonem hunc pessimum luxit et nullus ex more indutus est cultu suo*

The people, hearing this saddest word, mourned, and no one was dressed in *the* manner of his worship.

Israel's Adornment

33:5 *dixitque Dominus ad Mosen loquere filiis Israhel populus durae cervicis es semel ascendam in medio tui et delebo te iam nunc depone ornatum tuum ut sciam quid faciam tibi*

And *the* Lord said to Moses, "Speak to Israel's children: 'You are hard-necked people. I will go up once among you and destroy you. Now already, put off your adornment, so I may know what I will do with you.'"

33:6 *deposuerunt ergo filii Israhel ornatum suum a monte Horeb*

So Israel's children put off its adornment at Mount Horeb.

Moses Sets Up
the Covenant Tabernacle

33:7 *Moses quoque tollens tabernaculum tetendit extra castra procul vocavitque nomen eius tabernaculum foederis et omnis populus qui habebat aliquam quaestionem egrediebatur ad tabernaculum foederis extra castra*

Moses, likewise, taking *the* tabernacle, pitched it outside the camps far off. And he called its name *the* Covenant Tabernacle. And each of *the* people who had any dispute went out to *the* Covenant Tabernacle, outside *the* camps.

33:8 *cumque egrederetur Moses ad tabernaculum surgebat universa plebs et stabat unusquisque in ostio papilionis sui aspiciebantque tergum Mosi donec ingrederetur tentorium*

And when Moses went out to *the* tabernacle, *the* whole people got up and stood, each one at *the* mouth of his tent. And they watched Moses' back until he went into *the* tent.

33:9 *ingresso autem illo tabernaculum foederis descendebat columna nubis et stabat ad ostium loquebaturque cum Mosi*

But he going into to *the* Covenant Tabernacle, *the* column of cloud came down and stood at *the* opening and spoke with Moses.

33:10 *cernentibus universis quod columna nubis staret ad ostium tabernaculi stabantque ipsi et adorabant per fores tabernaculorum suorum*

All discerning that *the* column of cloud stood at *the* tabernacle's entry, they stood and worshiped from outside their tents.

Moses Speaks Face-to-Face
with the Lord
33:11 *loquebatur autem Dominus ad Mosen facie ad faciem sicut loqui*

solet homo ad amicum suum cumque ille reverteretur in castra minister eius Iosue filius Nun puer non recedebat de tabernaculo

But *the* Lord spoke to Moses face-to-face, as *a* man is used to talking to his friend. And when he came back into *the* camps, his minister Joshua, Nun's son, *a* youth, did not come back from *the* tabernacle.

Moses Asks the Lord
To Go Before Them
33:12 *dixit autem Moses ad Dominum praecipis ut educam populum istum et non indicas mihi quem missurus es mecum praesertim cum dixeris novi te ex nomine et invenisti gratiam coram me*

But Moses said to *the* Lord, "You command that I lead this people out, and You don't show me whom You will send with me, especially since You said, 'I have known you by name, and you have found grace before Me.'

33:13 *si ergo inveni gratiam in conspectu tuo ostende mihi viam tuam ut sciam te et inveniam gratiam ante oculos tuos respice populum tuum gentem hanc*

"If, therefore, I have found grace in Your sight, show me Your way, so I may know You and find grace before Your eyes. Look on this people!"

33:14 *dixitque Dominus facies mea praecedet te et requiem dabo tibi*

And *the* Lord said, "My face will go before you, and I will give you rest."

33:15 *et ait Moses si non tu ipse praecedes ne educas nos de loco isto*

And Moses said, "If You Yourself won't go before, don't lead us out from this place.

33:16 *in quo enim scire poterimus ego et populus tuus invenisse nos gratiam in conspectu tuo nisi ambulaveris nobiscum ut glorificemur ab omnibus populis qui habitant super terram*

"For in what can we know – I and Your people – that we have found grace in Your sight, unless You walk with us, so we can be glorified from all *the* peoples who live in *the* land?"

33:17 *dixit autem Dominus ad Mosen et verbum istud quod locutus es faciam invenisti enim gratiam coram me et te ipsum novi ex nomine*

But *the* Lord said to Moses, "I will do this word also that you have spoken, for you have found grace before Me and I have known you personally by name."

Moses Asks to See
the Lord's Glory
33:18 *qui ait ostende mihi gloriam tuam*

Moses said, "Show me Your glory!"

33:19 *respondit ego ostendam omne bonum tibi et vocabo in nomine Domini coram te et miserebor cui voluero et clemens ero in quem mihi placuerit*

He answered, "I will show every good to you, and will call in *the* Lord's name before you. And I will have mercy on whom I desire, and will be gentle in one who pleases Me."

33:20 *rursumque ait non poteris videre faciem meam non enim videbit me homo et vivet*

And again He said, "You cannot see My face, for man will not see Me and live."

33:21 *et iterum ecce inquit est locus apud me stabis super petram*

And again He said, "Look, *there* is *a* place with me. You will stand on *the* rock,

33:22 *cumque transibit gloria mea ponam te in foramine petrae et protegam dextera mea donec transeam*

"and when My glory passes by, I will put you in *the* rock's opening and protect you by My right hand until I pass by.

33:23 *tollamque manum meam et videbis posteriora mea faciem autem meam videre non poteris*

"And I will lift My hand and you will see My back, but you cannot see My face."

God Calls Moses
Back Up the Mountain

Exodus 34:1 *ac deinceps praecide ait tibi duas tabulas lapideas instar priorum et scribam super eas verba quae habuerunt tabulae quas fregisti*

And then He said, "Cut out two stone tables, like *the* prior ones, and I will write on them *the* words which *the* tables you broke had.

34:2 *esto paratus mane ut ascendas statim in montem Sinai stabisque mecum super verticem montis*

"Be ready early, so you can climb immediately onto Mount Sinai. And you will stand with Me on *the* mountaintop.

34:3 *nullus ascendat tecum nec videatur quispiam per totum montem boves quoque et oves non pascantur e contra*

"No one may climb up with you, nor may anyone be seen in all *the* mountain. Oxen and sheep likewise may not eat on it."

34:4 *excidit ergo duas tabulas lapideas quales ante fuerant et de nocte consurgens ascendit in montem Sinai sicut ei praeceperat Dominus portans secum tabulas*

So he cut out *the* two stone tables, like those before. And getting up by night, he climbed onto Mount Sinai like *the* Lord had commanded, carrying *the* tables with him.

The Lord and Moses
on the Mountain

34:5 *cumque descendisset Dominus per nubem stetit Moses cum eo invocans nomen Domini*

And when *the* Lord had come down in *the* cloud, Moses stood with Him, invoking *the* Lord's name,

34:6 *quo transeunte coram eo ait Dominator Domine Deus misericors et clemens patiens et multae miserationis ac verus*

where, passing before him, he said, "Master, Lord God, merciful and kind, patient and of many compassions and true –

34:7 *qui custodis misericordiam in milia qui aufers iniquitatem et scelera atque peccata nullusque apud te per se innocens est qui reddis iniquitatem patrum in filiis ac nepotibus in tertiam et quartam progeniem*

"who keep mercy among thousands, who take away treachery and crime and sin – and no one is innocent in himself with You – who repay *a* father's treachery in children and grandchildren to *the* third and fourth generation."

34:8 *festinusque Moses curvatus est*

pronus in terram et adorans

And Moses quickly kneeled down prone on *the* ground and, worshiping,

34:9 *ait si inveni gratiam in conspectu tuo Domine obsecro ut gradiaris nobiscum populus enim durae cervicis est et auferas iniquitates nostras atque peccata nosque possideas*

said, "If I have found grace in your sight, Lord, I pray that You go with us – for *the* people is hard-necked – and *pray* that You take away our treacheries and sins, and possess us."

34:10 *respondit Dominus ego inibo pactum videntibus cunctis signa faciam quae numquam sunt visa super terram nec in ullis gentibus ut cernat populus in cuius es medio opus Domini terribile quod facturus sum*

The Lord answered, "I will enter a pact before all who see. I will do signs which were never seen on *the* land or in other nations, so *the* people in whose midst you are may discern *the* Lord's terrifying works, which I will do.

34:11 *observa cuncta quae hodie mando tibi ego ipse eiciam ante faciem tuam Amorreum et Chananeum et Hettheum Ferezeum quoque et Eveum et Iebuseum*

"Keep all that I command you today! I myself will throw out *the* Amorite and Canaanite and Hittite and Ferezite before your face, and *the* Hivite and Jebusite as well.

34:12 *cave ne umquam cum habitatoribus terrae illius iungas amicitias quae tibi sint in ruinam*

"Take care that you never join in friendship with any of that land's inhabitants, who may be to you as ruin!

34:13 *sed aras eorum destrue confringe statuas lucosque succide*

"But destroy their altars, shatter *their* statues, and cut down *their* sacred groves!

Keep Away
From Their Gods
34:14 *noli adorare deum alienum Dominus Zelotes nomen eius Deus est aemulator*

"You will not bow down before *an* alien god. *The* Zealous Lord *is* His name. *He* is *a* jealous God.

34:15 *ne ineas pactum cum hominibus illarum regionum ne cum fornicati fuerint cum diis suis et adoraverint simulacra eorum vocet te quispiam ut comedas de immolatis*

"You may not enter *a* pact with that region's men, unless, when they have

fornicated with their gods and worshiped their images, somebody call you and you eat from *the* offerings.

34:16 *nec uxorem de filiabus eorum accipies filiis tuis ne postquam ipsae fuerint fornicatae fornicari faciant et filios tuos in deos suos*

"You will not accept *a* wife for your sons from their daughters, unless, after they have fornicated, they make your sons fornicate to their gods also.

34:17 *deos conflatiles non facies tibi*

"You will not make gods of cast metal.

Passover
34:18 *sollemnitatem azymorum custodies septem diebus vesceris azymis sicut praecepi tibi in tempore mensis novorum mense enim verni temporis egressus es de Aegypto*

"You will keep *the* solemnity of unleavened *bread*. Seven days you will eat unleavened *bread*, as I commanded you, in *the* time of *the* month of new grain. For in *the* month of springtime you came out of Egypt.

Firstborn
34:19 *omne quod aperit vulvam generis masculini meum erit de*

cunctis animantibus tam de bubus quam de ovibus meum erit

"Everything of male gender that opens *a* vulva will be Mine from all animals. They will be Mine alike from bulls and from sheep.

34:20 *primogenitum asini redimes ove sin autem nec pretium pro eo dederis occidetur primogenitum filiorum tuorum redimes nec apparebis in conspectu meo vacuus*

"You will buy back *a* donkey's firstborn with *a* sheep. But if you won't give *the* price for it, let it be killed. You will buy back *the* firstborn of your sons, nor will you appear empty-handed in My sight.

Sabbath
34:21 *sex diebus operaberis die septimo cessabis arare et metere*

"You will work six days. *The* seventh day you will cease to plow and reap.

Festivals
34:22 *sollemnitatem ebdomadarum facies tibi in primitiis frugum messis tuae triticeae et sollemnitatem quando redeunte anni tempore cuncta conduntur*

"You will do *the* solemnity of weeks for yourself with *the* first fruits of your wheat harvest; and *the* solemnity when, *the* time of year

returning, all is put away.

Three Times Each Year
34:23 *tribus temporibus anni apparebit omne masculinum tuum in conspectu omnipotentis Domini Dei Israhel*

"Three times *a* year each of your males will appear in *the* omnipotent Lord's sight, Israel's God,

34:24 *cum enim tulero gentes a facie tua et dilatavero terminos tuos nullus insidiabitur terrae tuae ascendente te et apparente in conspectu Domini Dei tui ter in anno*

"for when I have taken away *the* nations from your face and broadened your borders, no one will plot against your land, you going and appearing in *the* Lord your God's sight three times each year.

34:25 *non immolabis super fermento sanguinem hostiae meae neque residebit mane de victima sollemnitatis phase*

"You will not offer My victim's blood over yeast, nor will *the* leftovers of *the* Passover observance's offering remain until morning.

Offer to God
34:26 *primitias frugum terrae tuae offeres in domum Domini Dei tui non coques hedum in lacte matris*

suae

"You will offer *the* first fruits of your land's crops in *the* Lord your God's house. You will not cook *a* lamb in its mother's milk.

Moses Writes
the Lord's Words

34:27 *dixitque Dominus ad Mosen scribe tibi verba haec quibus et tecum et cum Israhel pepigi foedus*

And the Lord said to Moses, "Write these words for yourself, by which I have struck an agreement with you and with Israel!"

34:28 *fecit ergo ibi cum Domino quadraginta dies et quadraginta noctes panem non comedit et aquam non bibit et scripsit in tabulis verba foederis decem*

So he did *it* there with *the* Lord, forty days and forty nights. He did not eat bread and did not drink water. And he wrote on tables *the* ten words of *the* covenant.

Moses' Face Horned

34:29 *cumque descenderet Moses de monte Sinai tenebat duas tabulas testimonii et ignorabat quod cornuta esset facies sua ex consortio sermonis Dei*

And when Moses had come down from Mount Sinai, he had two tables of testimony. And he did not know that his face was horned from sharing God's words.

34:30 *videntes autem Aaron et filii Israhel cornutam Mosi faciem timuerunt prope accedere*

But Aaron and Israel's children, seeing Moses' face horned, were afraid to come near.

34:31 *vocatique ab eo reversi sunt tam Aaron quam principes synagogae et postquam locutus est*

And, called by him, both Aaron and *the* gathering's princes returned *to him*. And afterward he spoke.

34:32 *venerunt ad eum etiam omnes filii Israhel quibus praecepit cuncta quae audierat a Domino in monte Sinai*

All Israel's children came to him also, to whom he commanded all that he had heard from *the* Lord on Mount Sinai.

34:33 *impletisque sermonibus posuit velamen super faciem suam*

And, finishing *the* words, he put *a* veil over his face

34:34 *quod ingressus ad Dominum et loquens cum eo auferebat donec exiret et tunc loquebatur ad filios Israhel omnia quae sibi fuerant imperata*

that he took off, going into *the* Lord and speaking with Him, until he had gone out. And then he spoke to Israel's children all that had been commanded him.

34:35 *qui videbant faciem egredientis Mosi esse cornutam sed operiebat rursus ille faciem suam si quando loquebatur ad eos*

They saw his face to be horned when Moses came out, but he covered his face again whenever he talked to them.

Moses Tells Israel the Law
Exodus 35:1 *igitur congregata omni turba filiorum Israhel dixit ad eos haec sunt quae iussit Dominus fieri*

Therefore, all *the* crowd of Israel's children gathered, he said to them, "These are *the* things that *the* Lord commanded to be done."

Sabbath
35:2 *sex diebus facietis opus septimus dies erit vobis sanctus sabbatum et requies Domini qui fecerit opus in eo occidetur*

"You will do work six days. *The* seventh day will be holy to you, *the* Sabbath and *the* Lord's rest. Who does work in it will die.

35:3 *non succendetis ignem in omnibus habitaculis vestris per diem sabbati*

"You will not kindle fire in all your dwellings on *the* Sabbath day."

Moses Calls for an Offering
35:4 *et ait Moses ad omnem catervam filiorum Israhel iste est sermo quem praecepit Dominus dicens*

And Moses said to every company of Israel's children, "This is *the* word which the Lord commanded, saying,

35:5 *separate apud vos primitias*

Domino omnis voluntarius et proni animi offerat eas Domino aurum et argentum et aes

"Separate with you first fruits to *the* Lord. Let each freely and with *a* humbled soul offer them to *the* Lord – gold and silver and bronze;

35:6 *hyacinthum purpuram coccumque bis tinctum et byssum pilos caprarum*

"blue, purple, and scarlet twice-dyed, and twisted flax; goat hair

35:7 *et pelles arietum rubricatas et ianthinas*

"and ram skins dyed red and violet;

35:8 *ligna setthim*

"acacia wood

35:9 *et oleum ad luminaria concinnanda et ut conficiatur unguentum et thymiama suavissimum*

"and oil prepared for lamps and so anointing oil and smoothest incense may be made;

35:10 *lapides onychinos et gemmas ad ornatum superumeralis et rationalis*

"onyx stones and gems to decorate *the* overlay and breastplate.

35:11 *quisquis vestrum est sapiens veniat et faciat quod Dominus imperavit*

"Let whoever is wise among you come and make what *the* Lord commanded:

35:12 *tabernaculum scilicet et tectum eius atque operimentum anulos et tabulata cum vectibus paxillos et bases*

"*the* tabernacle, of course, and its roof and covering; rings and boards with poles, pegs, and bases;

35:13 *arcam et vectes propitiatorium et velum quod ante illud oppanditur*

"*the* ark and poles, *the* atonement seat, and *the* veil which is spread before it;

35:14 *mensam cum vectibus et vasis et propositionis panibus*

"*the* table with its poles and vessels and *the* bread of propositions;

35:15 *candelabrum ad luminaria sustentanda vasa illius et lucernas et oleum ad nutrimenta ignium*

"*the* candelabra to hold up *the* lamps, its vessels and lanterns, and oil to feed *the* fire;

35:16 *altare thymiamatis et vectes*

oleum unctionis et thymiama ex aromatibus tentorium ad ostium tabernaculi

"*the* incense altar and poles, anointing oil and incense from spices; *the* partitions at *the* tabernacle's opening;

35:17 *altare holocausti et craticulam eius aeneam cum vectibus et vasis suis labrum et basim eius*

"*the* altar of burnt offerings and its bronze grate, with its poles and vessels, its basin and base;

35:18 *cortinas atrii cum columnis et basibus tentorium in foribus vestibuli*

"*the* courtyard's curtains with columns and bases; *the* partitions outside *the* vestibule;

35:19 *paxillos tabernaculi et atrii cum funiculis suis*

"*the* tabernacle and courtyard's pegs, with their ties;

35:20 *vestimenta quorum usus est in ministerio sanctuarii vestes Aaron pontificis ac filiorum eius ut sacerdotio fungantur mihi*

"*the* vestments whose use is in *the* sanctuary's ministry, Aaron's high priestly garments and his sons, so they may carry out priestly duties to Me."

Israel Obeys

35:21 *egressaque omnis multitudo filiorum Israhel de conspectu Mosi*

And all *the* multitude of Israel's children, going out from Moses' sight,

35:22 *obtulit mente promptissima atque devota primitias Domino ad faciendum opus tabernaculi testimonii quicquid in cultum et ad vestes sanctas necessarium erat*

brought first fruits to *the* Lord by *a* most prompt and devoted mind, to doing *the* work of testimony's tabernacle, whatever was necessary in its worship, and for *the* holy vestments

35:23 *viri cum mulieribus praebuerunt armillas et inaures anulos et dextralia omne vas aureum in donaria Domini separatum est*

Men with women presented armbands and gold earrings and bracelets. Each gold vessel in *the* offering was set aside to *the* Lord.

35:24 *si quis habuit hyacinthum purpuram coccumque bis tinctum byssum et pilos caprarum pelles arietum rubricatas et ianthinas*

If someone had blue, purple, and scarlet twice-dyed, twisted flax and goat hair, red and violet-dyed ram skins,

35:25 *argenti et aeris metalla obtulerunt Domino lignaque setthim in varios usus*

silver and copper metal, and acacia wood, they offered *them* to *the* Lord for various uses.

The Learned Women
35:26 *sed et mulieres doctae dederunt quae neverant hyacinthum purpuram et vermiculum ac byssum*

And learned women even gave what they had woven: blue, purple, and violet, and twisted flax,

35:27 *et pilos caprarum sponte propria cuncta tribuentes*

and goat hair, all giving of their own will.

The Princes
35:28 *principes vero obtulerunt lapides onychinos et gemmas ad superumerale et rationale*

"*The* princes, indeed, offered onyx stones and gems for *the* overlay and breastplate,

35:29 *aromataque et oleum ad luminaria concinnanda et ad praeparandum unguentum ac thymiama odoris suavissimi conponendum*

"and spices and oil for preparing *the* lamps, and for preparing anointing oil, and *for* making incense of *the* smoothest odor.

All the People
35:30 *omnes viri et mulieres mente devota obtulerunt donaria ut fierent opera quae iusserat Dominus per manum Mosi cuncti filii Israhel voluntaria Domino dedicaverunt*

All *the* men and women with *a* devoted mind offered gifts so *the* work that *the* Lord had commanded by Moses' hand could be made. All Israel's children dedicated *the* free-will gifts to *the* Lord.

Beselel Called
35:31 *dixitque Moses ad filios Israhel ecce vocavit Dominus ex nomine Beselehel filium Uri filii Hur de tribu Iuda*

And Moses said to Israel's children, "Look, the Lord has called by name Beselel, Uri's son, Hur's son, from Judah's tribe.

35:32 *implevitque eum spiritu Dei sapientiae et intellegentiae et scientiae omni doctrina*

"And He has filled him with God's spirit, wisdom and intelligence and knowledge of all learning,

35:33 *ad excogitandum et faciendum opus in auro et argento et aere sculpendisque lapidibus et opere carpentario quicquid fabre*

adinveniri potest

for devising and making works in gold and silver and copper, and sculpting stone and carpentry work – whatever can be skillfully devised.

35:34 *dedit in corde eius Hooliab quoque filium Achisamech de tribu Dan*

"And he gave in his heart Hooliab, likewise, Achisamech's son, from Dan's tribe.

35:35 *ambos erudivit sapientia ut faciant opera abietarii polymitarii ac plumarii de hyacintho et purpura coccoque bis tincto et bysso et texant omnia ac nova quaeque repperiant*

"He taught both wisdom so they may do works in wood, woven cloth, and embroideries, from blue, and purple, and scarlet twice-dyed, and twisted flax. And they may weave all and invent new things.

The Offerings Overflow

Exodus 36:1 *fecit ergo Beselehel et Hooliab et omnis vir sapiens quibus dedit Dominus sapientiam et intellectum ut scirent fabre operari quae in usus sanctuarii necessaria sunt et quae praecepit Dominus*

So Beselel and Hooliab and every wise man to whom *the* Lord gave wisdom and understanding so they knew how to work skillfully, made *the* things that were necessary in *the* sanctuary's use, and that *the* Lord had commanded.

36:2 *cumque vocasset eos Moses et omnem eruditum virum cui dederat Deus sapientiam et qui sponte sua obtulerant se ad faciendum opus*

And when Moses had called them and every learned man to whom God had given wisdom, and *those* who of their free will offered themselves to doing *the* work,

36:3 *tradidit eis universa donaria filiorum Israhel qui cum instarent operi cotidie mane vota populus offerebat*

he gave them all Israel's children's donations. When they approached to work, *the* people offered gifts each morning.

36:4 *unde artifices venire conpulsi*

From this *the* artisans, compelled to

come,

36:5 *dixerunt Mosi plus offert populus quam necessarium est*

said to Moses, "*The* people offer more than is needed."

36:6 *iussit ergo Moses praeconis voce cantari nec vir nec mulier quicquam ultra offerat in opere sanctuarii sicque cessatum est a muneribus offerendis*

Therefore, Moses commanded to be sung by *the* herald's voice, "Neither man nor woman may offer anything more in *the* sanctuary's work."

And so *the people* ceased from offering gifts,

36:7 *eo quod oblata sufficerent et superabundarent*

because *the* offerings sufficed and overflowed.

The Materials Made

36:8 *feceruntque omnes corde sapientes ad explendum opus tabernaculi cortinas decem de bysso retorta et hyacintho et purpura coccoque bis tincto opere vario et arte polymita*

And they made all by *a* wise heart, toward completing *the* tabernacle's work: ten curtains of twisted flax and blue and purple, scarlet twice-dyed,

various embroidered work and multicolored weaving –

36:9 *quarum una habebat in longitudine viginti octo cubitos et in latitudine quattuor una mensura erat omnium cortinarum*

one of which had twenty-eight cubits in length and four in width. One measure was for all *the* curtains.

36:10 *coniunxitque cortinas quinque alteram alteri et alias quinque sibi invicem copulavit*

And he joined five curtains one to another, and *the* other five he coupled in turn to *the* others.

36:11 *fecit et ansas hyacinthinas in ora cortinae unius ex utroque latere et in ora cortinae alterius similiter*

He also made blue loops in *the* curtain's border, on each side, and in *the* other curtain's edge similarly,

36:12 *ut contra se invicem venirent ansae et mutuo iungerentur*

so *the* loops could come against each other in turn and be joined together.

36:13 *unde et quinquaginta fudit circulos aureos qui morderent cortinarum ansas et fieret unum tabernaculum*

From this also he cast fifty golden

circles which bit at *the* curtains' loops, and it might be made one tabernacle.

Cloaks

36:14 *fecit et saga undecim de pilis caprarum ad operiendum tectum tabernaculi*

He also made eleven goat hair cloaks for covering *the* tabernacle's roof.

36:15 *unum sagum habebat in longitudine cubitos triginta et in latitudine cubitos quattuor unius mensurae erant omnia saga*

One cloak had thirty cubits in length and four cubits in width. All *the* cloaks were from one measure.

36:16 *quorum quinque iunxit seorsum et sex alia separatim*

Five of them he joined apart, and six others separately.

36:17 *fecitque ansas quinquaginta in ora sagi unius et quinquaginta in ora sagi alterius ut sibi invicem iungerentur*

And he made fifty loops in *the* border of one cloak and fifty in *the* border of *the* other cloak, so they could be joined in turn to each other,

36:18 *et fibulas aeneas quinquaginta quibus necteretur tectum et unum pallium ex omnibus*

sagis fieret

and fifty brass joins by which *the* roof could be tied. And one covering was made from all *the* cloaks.

The Tabernacle's Cover

36:19 *fecit et opertorium tabernaculi de pellibus arietum rubricatis aliudque desuper velamentum de pellibus ianthinis*

He also made *the* tabernacle's covering from red ram skins, and another cover above from blue skins.

36:20 *fecit et tabulas tabernaculi de lignis setthim stantes*

He also made *the* tabernacle's boards from standing acacia wood.

36:21 *decem cubitorum erat longitudo tabulae unius et unum ac semis cubitum latitudo retinebat*

The length of one board was ten cubits, and it retained one and *a* half cubits' width.

36:22 *binae incastraturae erant per singulas tabulas ut altera alteri iungeretur sic fecit in omnibus tabulis tabernaculi*

Two openings were in each board, so it could be joined one to another. He made it so in all *the* tabernacle's boards,

36:23 *e quibus viginti ad plagam meridianam erant contra austrum*

out of which twenty were toward *the* southern quarter, leaning south,

36:24 *cum quadraginta basibus argenteis duae bases sub una tabula ponebantur ex utraque angulorum parte ubi incastraturae laterum in angulis terminantur*

with forty silver bases. Two bases were placed under one board and from each side of *the* corners, where *the* side openings ended in *the* corners.

36:25 *ad plagam quoque tabernaculi quae respicit ad aquilonem fecit viginti tabulas*

Likewise, he made twenty boards for *the* tabernacle's quarter that faced to *the* north,

36:26 *cum quadraginta argenteis basibus duas bases per singulas tabulas*

with forty silver bases, two bases for each board.

36:27 *contra occidentem vero id est ad eam partem tabernaculi quae mare respicit fecit sex tabulas*

And facing west – that is, to that part of *the* tabernacle that looked toward *the* sea – he made six boards,

36:28 *et duas alias per singulos angulos tabernaculi retro*

and two others for each of *the* tabernacle's corners behind,

36:29 *quae iunctae erant deorsum usque sursum et in unam conpagem pariter ferebantur ita fecit ex utraque parte per angulos*

which were joined from beneath to above and were brought together in one action. So he did from each side, for *the* corners,

36:30 *ut octo essent simul tabulae et haberent bases argenteas sedecim binas scilicet bases sub singulis tabulis*

so eight boards were together, and they had sixteen silver bases, two bases, of course, under each board.

Poles
36:31 *fecit et vectes de lignis setthim quinque ad continendas tabulas unius lateris tabernaculi*

He also made five poles of acacia wood, to hold together *the* boards on one of *the* tabernacle's sides,

36:32 *et quinque alios ad alterius lateris tabulas coaptandas et extra hos quinque alios vectes ad occidentalem plagam tabernaculi contra mare*

and five others on *the* other side, fitted to *the* boards, and beyond these five other poles for *the* tabernacle's western quarter, facing *the* sea.

36:33 *fecit quoque vectem alium qui per medias tabulas ab angulo usque ad angulum perveniret*

He likewise made another pole that went through *the* middle of *the* boards from corner to corner.

36:34 *ipsa autem tabulata deauravit et circulos eorum fecit aureos per quos vectes induci possint quos et ipsos aureis lamminis operuit*

But these boards he covered with gold. And he made their rings of gold, through which *the* poles could be threaded, and which also he covered with gold plate.

36:35 *fecit et velum de hyacintho purpura vermiculo ac bysso retorta opere polymitario varium atque distinctum*

He also made *a* veil of blue, purple, violet, and twisted flax, made with varied and distinctive embroidery,

36:36 *et quattuor columnas de lignis setthim quas cum capitibus deauravit fusis basibus earum argenteis*

and four columns of acacia wood which, with *the* head pieces he plated with gold, their bases cast from silver.

36:37 *fecit et tentorium in introitu tabernaculi ex hyacintho purpura vermiculo byssoque retorta opere plumarii*

He also made partitions for *the* tabernacle's entrance, from blue, purple, violet, and twisted flax, with embroidered work,

36:38 *et columnas quinque cum capitibus suis quas operuit auro basesque earum fudit aeneas*

and five columns with their head pieces, which he covered in gold. And he cast their bases with bronze.

Beselel Makes the Ark

Exodus 37:1 *fecit autem Beselehel et arcam de lignis setthim habentem duos semis cubitos in longitudinem et cubitum ac semissem in latitudinem altitudo quoque uno cubito fuit et dimidio vestivitque eam auro purissimo intus ac foris*

But Beselel also made *a* box of acacia wood, having two and *a* half cubits in length and *a* cubit and *a* half in width. Its height was also one and *a* half cubits. And he dressed it with purest gold, inside and out.

37:2 *et fecit illi coronam auream per gyrum*

And he made *a* golden crown around it,

37:3 *conflans quattuor anulos aureos per quattuor angulos eius duos anulos in latere uno et duos in altero*

casting four golden rings for each of its four corners: two rings on one side and two on *the* other.

37:4 *vectes quoque fecit de lignis setthim quos vestivit auro*

He likewise made poles of acacia wood, which he dressed with gold,

37:5 *et quos misit in anulos qui erant in lateribus arcae ad portandum eam*

and which he put through *the* rings which were on *the* box's sides, for carrying it.

37:6 *fecit et propitiatorium id est oraculum de auro mundissimo duorum cubitorum et dimidio in longitudine et cubito ac semisse in latitudine*

He also made *the* atonement seat – that is *the* oracle – of purest gold, two and a half cubits in length and *a* cubit and *a* half in width;

37:7 *duos etiam cherubin ex auro ductili quos posuit ex utraque parte propitiatorii*

two cherubim as well from formed gold, which he placed on either side of *the* atonement seat.

37:8 *cherub unum in summitate huius partis et cherub alterum in summitate partis alterius duos cherubin in singulis summitatibus propitiatorii*

One cherub *was* on *the* top of its side, and *the* other cherub on *the* other side's top – two cherubim, *one* on each side of *the* atonement seat,

37:9 *extendentes alas et tegentes propitiatorium seque mutuo et illud respectantes*

stretching wings and covering *the* atonement seat, and looking on it and each other.

The Table

37:10 *fecit et mensam de lignis setthim in longitudine duorum cubitorum et in latitudine unius cubiti quae habebat in altitudine cubitum ac semissem*

He also made *the* table of acacia wood, two cubits in length and one cubit in width, which had *a* cubit and *a* half in height.

37:11 *circumdeditque eam auro mundissimo et fecit illi labium aureum per gyrum*

And he covered it with purest gold, and made *a* golden lip around it,

37:12 *ipsique labio coronam interrasilem quattuor digitorum et super eandem alteram coronam auream*

and in this lip *a* carved crown four fingers *breadth*, and over it another golden crown.

37:13 *fudit et quattuor circulos aureos quos posuit in quattuor angulis per singulos pedes mensae*

He also cast four golden circles, which he placed on *the* four corners for each of *the* table's feet,

37:14 *contra coronam misitque in eos vectes ut possit mensa portari*

against *the* crown. And he placed poles through them so *the* table could be carried.

37:15 *ipsos quoque vectes fecit de lignis setthim et circumdedit eos auro*

He made these poles likewise of acacia wood and covered them with gold.

37:16 *et vasa ad diversos usus mensae acetabula fialas cyatos et turibula ex auro puro in quibus offerenda sunt liba*

And *he made* vessels for *the* table's various uses: small cups, drinking plates, wine ladles, and censers from pure gold, in which libations were offered.

The Candelabra

37:17 *fecit et candelabrum ductile de auro mundissimo de cuius vecte calami scyphi spherulae ac lilia procedebant*

And he made *the* candelabra, formed from purest gold, from which branches bearing spherical bowls and lilies proceeded,

37:18 *sex in utroque latere tres calami ex parte una et tres ex altera*

six on *the* two sides: three branches from one part and three from *the* other.

37:19 *tres scyphi in nucis modum per calamos singulos spherulaeque simul et lilia et tres scyphi instar nucis in calamo altero spherulaeque simul et lilia aequum erat opus sex calamorum qui procedebant de stipite candelabri*

Three bowls *were* in *the* form of nuts for each branch, and spherical bowls and lilies together; and three bowls like nuts in another branch, and spherical bowls and lilies. *The* work was *the* same in *the* six branches which came out from *the* candelabra's shaft.

37:20 *in ipso autem vecte erant quattuor scyphi in nucis modum spherulaeque per singulos et lilia*

But four bowls like nuts were in *the* shaft, and spherical bowls and lilies on each one,

37:21 *et spherae sub duobus calamis per loca tria qui simul sex fiunt calami procedentes de vecte uno*

and spheres under two branches, through three places, which together become six branches coming out from one shaft.

37:22 *et spherae igitur et calami ex ipso erant universa ductilia de auro purissimo*

And *the* spheres therefore and *the*

branches from them were all formed from purest gold.

37:23 *fecit et lucernas septem cum emunctoriis suis et vasa ubi quae emuncta sunt extinguuntur de auro mundissimo*

He also made seven lamps with their snuffers from purest gold, and vessels where what was snuffed could be put out.

37:24 *talentum auri adpendebat candelabrum cum omnibus vasis suis*

He weighed out *a* talent of gold for *the* candelabra, with all its vessels.

The Incense Altar
37:25 *fecit et altare thymiamatis de lignis setthim habens per quadrum singulos cubitos et in altitudine duos e cuius angulis procedebant cornua*

He also made *the* incense altar from acacia wood, having one cubit per side, square, and two *cubits* in height, and from whose corners horns proceeded.

37:26 *vestivitque illud auro purissimo cum craticula ac parietibus et cornibus*

And he dressed it with purest gold, with *the* grate and walls and horns.

37:27 *fecitque ei coronam aureolam per gyrum et duos anulos aureos sub* *corona per singula latera ut mittantur in eos vectes et possit altare portari*

And he made *a* golden crown around it, and two golden rings under *the* crown for each side, so poles could be put in them and *the* altar could be carried.

37:28 *ipsos autem vectes fecit de lignis setthim et operuit lamminis aureis*

But he made these poles of acacia wood and covered *them* with gold plate.

37:29 *conposuit et oleum ad sanctificationis unguentum et thymiama de aromatibus mundissimis opere pigmentarii*

He also mixed oil for *the* ointment of sanctification, and incense of purest spices, by *the* perfume-maker's work.

The Altar
of Burnt Offerings

Exodus 38:1 *fecit et altare holocausti de lignis setthim quinque cubitorum per quadrum et trium in altitudine*

He also made *the* altar of burnt offerings from acacia wood, five cubits per side, square, and three in height,

38:2 *cuius cornua de angulis procedebant operuitque illud aeneis lamminis*

whose horns came out from *the* corners, and he covered it with bronze plate.

38:3 *et in usus eius paravit ex aere vasa diversa lebetas forcipes fuscinulas uncinos et ignium receptacula*

And he prepared for its uses various vessels from brass: cauldrons, tongs, forks, hooks, and fire receptacles.

38:4 *craticulamque eius in modum retis fecit aeneam et subter eam in altaris medio arulam*

And he made its grate of brass in *the* likeness of *a* net, and under it *a* hearth in *the* middle of *the* altar,

38:5 *fusis quattuor anulis per totidem retiaculi summitates ad inmittendos vectes ad portandum*

casting four rings for all *the* grate's tops, for putting *the* poles through to carry *it*.

38:6 *quos et ipsos fecit de lignis setthim et operuit lamminis aeneis*

He also made those of acacia wood and covered them with brass plate.

38:7 *induxitque in circulos qui in altaris lateribus eminebant ipsum autem altare non erat solidum sed cavum ex tabulis et intus vacuum*

And he led them through *the* circles that stuck out from *the* altar's sides. And *the* altar was not solid, but hollow, *built* from boards and empty inside.

The Brass Basin
38:8 *fecit et labrum aeneum cum base sua de speculis mulierum quae excubabant in ostio tabernaculi*

He also made *a* brass basin with its base from the mirrors of *the* women who stood at *the* tabernacle's entrance.

The Partitions and Columns
38:9 *et atrium in cuius australi plaga erant tentoria de bysso retorta cubitorum centum*

And *he made the* courtyard, in whose south quarter were partitions of twisted flax of one hundred cubits;

38:10 *columnae aeneae viginti cum basibus suis capita columnarum et tota operis celatura argentea*

twenty brass columns with their bases, *the* columns' head pieces, and all *the* coverings of worked silver.

38:11 *aeque ad septentrionalis plagam tentoria columnae basesque et capita columnarum eiusdem et mensurae et operis ac metalli erant*

Equally, to *the* northern quarter, *the* partitions, columns and bases and *the* columns' head pieces were *the* same in measure and work and metal.

38:12 *in ea vero plaga quae occidentem respicit fuere tentoria cubitorum quinquaginta columnae decem cum basibus suis aeneae et capita columnarum celata argentea*

And in *the* quarter that looks west were fifty cubits of partitions, ten columns with their bronze bases, and *the* columns' head pieces covered with silver.

38:13 *porro contra orientem quinquaginta cubitorum paravit tentoria*

Furthermore, he prepared fifty cubits of partitions facing east,

38:14 *e quibus quindecim cubitos columnarum trium cum basibus suis unum tenebat latus*

and from them one had *a* side of fifteen cubits, with three columns and its bases,

38:15 *et in parte altera quia utraque introitum tabernaculi facit quindecim aeque cubitorum erant tentoria columnae tres et bases totidem*

and in *the* other side (for it makes *the* two sides of *the* tabernacle's entrance) *the* partitions were fifteen cubits as well, three columns, and as many bases.

38:16 *cuncta atrii tentoria byssus torta texuerat*

All *the* courtyard's partitions were woven of twisted flax.

38:17 *bases columnarum fuere aeneae capita autem earum cum celaturis suis argentea sed et ipsas columnas atrii vestivit argento*

The columns' bases were bronze, but their head pieces with their coverings were silver, and *the* same columns of *the* courtyard he dressed in silver.

38:18 *et in introitu eius opere plumario fecit tentorium ex hyacintho purpura vermiculo ac bysso retorta quod habebat viginti cubitos in longitudine altitudo vero quinque cubitorum erat iuxta mensuram quam cuncta atrii habebant tentoria*

And in its entrance, he made *the* partitions with embroidered work from blue, purple, violet, and twisted flax, which had twenty cubits in length and five cubits' height. It was according to *the* measure that all *the* courtyard's partitions had.

38:19 *columnae autem ingressus fuere quattuor cum basibus aeneis capitaque earum et celaturae argenteae*

But *there* were four columns coming in, with bronze bases and their head pieces and coverings of silver.

38:20 *paxillos quoque tabernaculi et atrii per gyrum fecit aeneos*

He made *the* tabernacle and courtyard's tent pegs all around of brass.

The Weight
of the Furnishing
38:21 *haec sunt instrumenta tabernaculi testimonii quae numerata sunt iuxta praeceptum Mosi in caerimonias Levitarum per manum Ithamar filii Aaron sacerdotis*

These are *the* instruments of *the* tabernacle of testimony, which were numbered according to Moses' command in *the* Levites' ceremonies, by *the* hand of Ithamar, son of Aaron *the* priest,

38:22 *quas Beselehel filius Uri filii Hur de tribu Iuda Domino per Mosen iubente conpleverat*

which Beselel, Uri's son, Hur's son, from Judah's tribe, had completed, *the* Lord commanding through Moses.

38:23 *iuncto sibi socio Hooliab filio Achisamech de tribu Dan qui et ipse artifex lignorum egregius fuit et polymitarius atque plumarius ex hyacintho purpura vermiculo et bysso*

His friend Hooliab, Achisamech's son, from Dan's tribe, who himself also was *an* exceptional craftsman of woods and multi-colored weavings and embroideries from blue, purple, *and* violet, and fine linen, *worked* together with him.

The Weight of Gold
38:24 *omne aurum quod expensum est in opere sanctuarii et quod oblatum in donariis viginti novem talentorum fuit et septingentorum triginta siclorum ad mensuram sanctuarii*

All *the* gold that was spent in *the* sanctuary's work and which was given in donations was twenty-nine talents and seven hundred thirty shekels, by *the* sanctuary's measure.

38:25 *oblatum est autem ab his qui transierant ad numerum a viginti*

annis et supra de sescentis tribus milibus et quingentis quinquaginta armatorum

But it was given by those who had passed through *the* age of twenty and above, from six hundred three thousand, five hundred fifty men fit for arms.

The Weight of Silver
38:26 *fuerunt praeterea centum talenta argenti e quibus conflatae sunt bases sanctuarii et introitus ubi velum pendet*

There were as well *a* hundred talents of silver, from which *the* sanctuary's bases were cast, and *the* entrance where *the* veil hung.

38:27 *centum bases factae sunt de talentis centum singulis talentis per bases singulas supputatis*

One hundred bases were made from *the* hundred talents, *a* talent calculated for each base.

38:28 *de mille autem septingentis et septuaginta quinque fecit capita columnarum quas et ipsas vestivit argento*

But from one thousand, seven hundred, and seventy-five *shekels* he made *the* columns' head pieces, which also he dressed in silver.

The Weight of Bronze

38:29 *aeris quoque oblata sunt talenta septuaginta duo milia et quadringenti supra sicli*

Likewise, seventy-two thousand talents of bronze were given, and four hundred shekels above,

38:30 *ex quibus fusae sunt bases in introitu tabernaculi testimonii et altare aeneum cum craticula sua omniaque vasa quae ad usum eius pertinent*

from which *the* bases at *the* tabernacle of testimony's entrance were cast, and *the* bronze altar with its grate, and all *the* vessels which pertained to its use,

38:31 *et bases atrii tam in circuitu quam in ingressu eius et paxilli tabernaculi atque atrii per gyrum*

and *the* courtyard's bases, those around it and in its entrance, and *the* tent pegs from *the* tabernacle and *the* courtyard around.

The Priestly Vestments

Exodus 39:1 *de hyacintho vero et purpura vermiculo ac bysso fecit vestes quibus indueretur Aaron quando ministrabat in sanctis sicut praecepit Dominus Mosi*

And he made *the* vestments which Aaron wore when he ministered in *the* holy places, from blue and purple and violet and fine flax, as *the* Lord commanded Moses.

The Overlay

39:2 *fecit igitur superumerale de auro hyacintho et purpura coccoque bis tincto et bysso retorta*

Therefore, he made *the* overlay from gold, blue, and purple, and scarlet twice-dyed, and twisted flax,

39:3 *opere polymitario inciditque bratteas aureas et extenuavit in fila ut possint torqueri cum priorum colorum subtemine*

by *the* embroider's work. And he threaded gold leaf and made *it* thin into thread, so it could be woven in with *the* prior colors in *the* loom;

39:4 *duasque oras sibi invicem copulatas in utroque latere summitatum*

and *the* two borders joined to each other in turn on either side at *the* top;

39:5 *et balteum ex hisdem coloribus*

sicut praeceperat Dominus Mosi

and *the* shoulder piece from *the* same colors, as *the* Lord had commanded Moses.

39:6 *paravit et duos lapides onychinos adstrictos et inclusos auro et sculptos arte gemmaria nominibus filiorum Israhel*

He also prepared two onyx stones, tightly-sewn and set in gold and carved by *the* jeweler's art with Israel's sons' names.

39:7 *posuitque eos in lateribus superumeralis in monumentum filiorum Israhel sicut praeceperat Dominus Mosi*

And he put them on *the* overlay's sides as *a* memorial of Israel's sons, as *the* Lord had commanded Moses.

The Breastplate

39:8 *fecit et rationale opere polymito iuxta opus superumeralis ex auro hyacintho purpura coccoque bis tincto et bysso retorta*

He also made *the* breastplate by embroidered work like *the* overlay's work, from gold, blue, purple, scarlet twice-dyed, and twisted flax,

39:9 *quadrangulum duplex mensurae palmi*

quadrangular, two palms' measure.

39:10 *et posuit in eo gemmarum ordines quattuor in primo versu erat sardius topazius zmaragdus*

And he placed in it four rows of gems. In *the* first row was carnelian, topaz, emerald;

39:11 *in secundo carbunculus sapphyrus iaspis*

in *the* second garnet, sapphire, jasper;

39:12 *in tertio ligyrius achates amethistus*

in *the* third ligure, agate, and amethyst;

39:13 *in quarto chrysolitus onychinus berillus circumdati et inclusi auro per ordines suos*

in *the* fourth, chrysolite, onyx, beryl. *All were* set and enclosed with gold through their rows.

39:14 *ipsique lapides duodecim sculpti erant nominibus duodecim tribuum Israhel singuli per nomina singulorum*

And *the* same twelve stones were carved with *the* names of Israel's twelve tribes, one *stone* for each name.

39:15 *fecerunt in rationali et catenulas sibi invicem coherentes de auro purissimo*

And they also made in *the* breastplate little chains joining to themselves, from purest gold,

39:16 *et duos uncinos totidemque anulos aureos porro anulos posuerunt in utroque latere rationalis*

and two hooks, and *the* same number of golden rings. Afterwards, they put *the* rings on either side of *the* breastplate,

39:17 *e quibus penderent duae catenae aureae quas inseruerunt uncinis qui in superumeralis angulis eminebant*

from which they hung two golden chains, which they joined to *the* hooks that came out from *the* breastplate's corners.

39:18 *haec et ante et retro ita conveniebant sibi ut superumerale et rationale mutuo necterentur*

These came together so before and behind, so *the* overlay and breastplate could be tied together,

39:19 *stricta ad balteum et anulis fortius copulata quos iungebat vitta hyacinthina ne laxe fluerent et a se invicem moverentur sicut praecepit Dominus Mosi*

secured to *the* shoulder piece and joined by strong rings, which *a* blue ribbon tied, so they wouldn't hang loosely and be moved from each other in turn, as *the* Lord had commanded Moses.

The Tunic

39:20 *fecerunt quoque tunicam superumeralis totam hyacinthinam*

They likewise made *the* overlay's tunic completely of blue *thread*;

39:21 *et capitium in superiori parte contra medium oramque per gyrum capitii textilem*

and *the* head opening in *the* top part at *the* middle, and *the* border of *the* head opening woven around;

39:22 *deorsum autem ad pedes mala punica ex hyacintho purpura vermiculo ac bysso retorta*

but below at *the* feet, pomegranates from blue, purple, violet, and twisted flax,

39:23 *et tintinabula de auro mundissimo quae posuerunt inter mala granata in extrema parte tunicae per gyrum*

and little bells of purest gold, which they put between *the* pomegranates around *the* bottom of *the* tunic –

39:24 *tintinabulum aureum et malum punicum quibus ornatus incedebat pontifex quando ministerio* *fungebatur sicut praecepit Dominus Mosi*

small golden bells and pomegranates, adorned with which *the* high priest approached when he performed ministry, as *the* Lord had commanded Moses.

Various Items
39:25 *fecerunt et tunicas byssinas opere textili Aaron et filiis eius*

They also made linen tunics by *the* weaver's art for Aaron and his sons;

39:26 *et mitras cum coronulis suis ex bysso*

and head pieces with their little crowns from flax;

39:27 *feminalia quoque linea byssina*

thigh coverings also of fine flax;

39:28 *cingulum vero de bysso retorta hyacintho purpura ac vermiculo distinctum arte plumaria sicut praecepit Dominus Mosi*

and *a* sash of twisted flax, blue, purple, and violet, distinguished by *the* embroider's art, as *the* Lord had commanded Moses.

39:29 *fecerunt et lamminam sacrae venerationis de auro purissimo scripseruntque in ea opere gemmario*

Sanctum Domini

They also made *the* plate of holy worship of purest gold, and they wrote on it by *the* jeweler's work, "*The* Lord's Holy *One*."

39:30 *et strinxerunt eam cum mitra vitta hyacinthina sicut praecepit Dominus Mosi*

and they tied it to *the* head piece by *a* blue ribbon, as *the* Lord had commanded Moses.

The Work Completed
39:31 *perfectum est igitur omne opus tabernaculi et tecti testimonii feceruntque filii Israhel cuncta quae praeceperat Dominus Mosi*

Therefore, all *the* work of *the* tabernacle and *the* testimony's covering was completed. And Israel's children made all that *the* Lord had commanded Moses.

39:32 *et obtulerunt tabernaculum et tectum et universam supellectilem anulos tabulas vectes columnas ac bases*

And they offered *the* tabernacle and *the* covering and all *the* furnishings: rings, boards, poles, columns, and bases;

39:33 *opertorium de pellibus arietum rubricatis et aliud operimentum de ianthinis pellibus* *a* covering of red ram skins and another covering of blue skins;

39:34 *velum arcam vectes propitiatorium*

the veil, ark, poles, atonement seat;

39:35 *mensam cum vasis et propositionis panibus*

the table with vessels and *the* bread of propositions;

39:36 *candelabrum lucernas et utensilia eorum cum oleo*

the candelabra, lamps, and their utensils, with oil;

39:37 *altare aureum et unguentum thymiama ex aromatibus*

the golden altar and anointing oil, *the* incense from spices,

39:38 *et tentorium in introitu tabernaculi*

and *the* partitions at *the* tabernacle's entrance;

39:39 *altare aeneum retiaculum vectes et vasa eius omnia labrum cum basi sua tentoria atrii et columnas cum basibus suis*

the brass altar, grate, poles, and all its vessels; *the* basin with its base; *the* courtyard's partitions and columns,

with their bases;

39:40 *tentorium in introitu atrii funiculosque illius et paxillos nihil ex vasis defuit quae in ministerium tabernaculi et in tectum foederis iussa sunt fieri*

the partitions at *the* courtyard's entrance, their ties and tent pegs. Nothing was neglected from *the* vessels that were commanded to be made for *the* tabernacle's ministry and for *the* covenant covering.

39:41 *vestes quoque quibus sacerdotes utuntur in sanctuario Aaron scilicet et filii eius*

Likewise, *the* vestments which *the* priests used in *the* sanctuary – Aaron, of course, and his sons –

39:42 *obtulerunt filii Israhel sicut praeceperat Dominus*

Israel's children offered as *the* Lord had commanded.

39:43 *quae postquam Moses cuncta vidit expleta benedixit eis*

After Moses saw it all completed, he blessed them.

The Lord Commands . . .

Exodus 40:1 *locutusque est Dominus ad Mosen dicens*

And *the* Lord spoke to Moses, saying,

40:2 *mense primo die prima mensis eriges tabernaculum testimonii*

"You will set up testimony's tabernacle *the* first month, *the* first day of *the* month.

40:3 *et pones in eo arcam dimittesque ante illam velum*

"And you will put *the* ark in it, and unfold *the* veil before it.

40:4 *et inlata mensa pones super eam quae rite praecepta sunt candelabrum stabit cum lucernis suis*

"And, bringing in *the* table, you will place on it what things are commanded for ritual. You will stand up *the* candelabra with its lamps,

40:5 *et altare aureum in quo adoletur incensum coram arca testimonii tentorium in introitu tabernaculi pones*

"and *the* golden altar, in which incense is burned before *the* covenant box. You will place partitions in *the* tabernacle's entrance,

40:6 *et ante illud altare holocausti*

"and before it *the* altar of burnt offerings;

40:7 *labrum inter altare et tabernaculum quod implebis aqua*

"*the* basin, which you will fill with water, between *the* altar and *the* tabernacle.

40:8 *circumdabisque atrium tentoriis et ingressum eius*

"And you will surround *the* courtyard and its entrance with partitions.

Anoint Its Vessels

40:9 *et adsumpto unctionis oleo ungues tabernaculum cum vasis suis ut sanctificentur*

"And, taking up *the* anointing oil, you will anoint *the* tabernacle with its vessels, so they may be made holy:

40:10 *altare holocausti et omnia vasa eius*

"*the* altar of burnt offerings and all its vessels;

40:11 *labrum cum basi sua omnia unctionis oleo consecrabis ut sint sancta sanctorum*

"*the* basin with its base. You will consecrate all with *the* anointing oil, so they may be holy of holies.

Preparing Aaron
and His Sons

40:12 *adplicabisque Aaron et filios eius ad fores tabernaculi testimonii et lotos aqua*

"And you will take Aaron and his sons to *the* door of testimony's tabernacle and, washing with water,

40:13 *indues sanctis vestibus ut ministrent mihi et unctio eorum in sacerdotium proficiat sempiternum*

"you will dress them in *the* holy vestments so they can minister to me, and their anointing may make *them* into *an* everlasting priesthood."

Moses Obeys the Lord

40:14 *fecitque Moses omnia quae praeceperat Dominus*

And Moses did all that *the* Lord had commanded.

40:15 *igitur mense primo anni secundi in prima die mensis conlocatum est tabernaculum*

So the tabernacle was put together *the* first month of *the* second year, *the* first day of *the* month.

40:16 *erexitque illud Moses et posuit tabulas ac bases et vectes statuitque columnas*

And Moses set it up and placed *the* boards and bases and poles. And he stood up *the* columns

40:17 *et expandit tectum super tabernaculum inposito desuper operimento sicut Dominus imperarat*

and spread *the* roof over *the* tabernacle, placing *a* covering above *it* as *the* Lord had ordered.

40:18 *posuit et testimonium in arca subditis infra vectibus et oraculum desuper*

And he also put *the* testimony in *the* ark, putting *the* poles under *it* and *the* oracle above.

40:19 *cumque intulisset arcam in tabernaculum adpendit ante eam velum ut expleret Domini iussionem*

And when he had brought *the* ark into *the* tabernacle, he hung *the* veil before it, so he could complete *the* Lord's command.

40:20 *posuit et mensam in tabernaculo testimonii ad plagam septentrionalem extra velum*

He also put *the* table in testimony's tabernacle, facing *the* northern quarter, outside *the* veil,

40:21 *ordinatis coram propositionis panibus sicut praeceperat Dominus Mosi*

ordering *the* bread of propositions

before, as *the* Lord had commanded Moses.

40:22 *posuit et candelabrum in tabernaculum testimonii e regione mensae in parte australi*

And he also put *the* candelabra in testimony's tabernacle, in *the* south part, away from *the* table's area,

40:23 *locatis per ordinem lucernis iuxta praeceptum Domini*

the lamps located by order, according to *the* Lord's command.

40:24 *posuit et altare aureum sub tecto testimonii contra velum*

He also set *the* golden altar under testimony's roof, against *the* veil.

40:25 *et adolevit super eo incensum aromatum sicut iusserat Dominus*

And he burned aromatic incense on it, as *the* Lord had commanded.

40:26 *posuit et tentorium in introitu tabernaculi*

And he placed partitions in *the* tabernacle's entrance,

40:27 *et altare holocausti in vestibulo testimonii offerens in eo holocaustum et sacrificia ut Dominus imperarat*

and *the* altar of burnt offerings in testimony's entry, offering *a* burnt offering and sacrifices on it as *the* Lord had ordered.

40:28 *labrum quoque statuit inter tabernaculum testimonii et altare implens illud aqua*

He likewise stood *the* basin between testimony's tabernacle and *the* altar, filling it with water.

40:29 *laveruntque Moses et Aaron ac filii eius manus suas et pedes*

And Moses and Aaron and his sons washed their hands and feet

40:30 *cum ingrederentur tectum foederis et accederent ad altare sicut praeceperat Dominus*

when they went under *the* covenant roof and came to *the* altar, as *the* Lord had commanded.

40:31 *erexit et atrium per gyrum tabernaculi et altaris ducto in introitu eius tentorio postquam cuncta perfecta sunt*

He also set up *the* courtyard around *the* tabernacle and altars, guiding *the* partition to its entrance.

**The Lord's Glory
Fills the Tabernacle**

After all was completed,

40:32 *operuit nubes tabernaculum testimonii et gloria Domini implevit illud*

a cloud covered testimony's tabernacle and *the* Lord's glory filled it,

40:33 *nec poterat Moses ingredi tectum foederis nube operiente omnia et maiestate Domini coruscante quia cuncta nubes operuerat*

nor could Moses go in under *the* covenant's roof, *the* cloud covering everything and *the* Lord's majesty flashing, for *the* cloud had covered all.

40:34 *si quando nubes tabernaculum deserebat proficiscebantur filii Israhel per turmas suas*

Whenever *the* cloud left *the* tabernacle, Israel's children set out by their columns.

40:35 *si pendebat desuper manebant in eodem loco*

If it hung above, they stayed in *the* same place.

40:36 *nubes quippe Domini incubabat per diem tabernaculo et ignis in nocte videntibus populis Israhel per cunctas mansiones suas*

The Lord's cloud, of course, covered *the* tabernacle by day, and *His* fire by night, Israel's people watching from all their lodgings

Leviticus

Leviticus 1:1 *vocavit autem Mosen et locutus est ei Dominus de tabernaculo testimonii dicens*

But *the* Lord called Moses and spoke to him from testimony's tabernacle, saying,

A Burnt Offering
From Cattle
1:2 *loquere filiis Israhel et dices ad eos homo qui obtulerit ex vobis hostiam Domino de pecoribus id est de bubus et ovibus offerens victimas*

"Speak to Israel's children and you will say to them, '*A* man from you who will offer *a* sacrfice to *the* Lord from animals – that is, offering victims from bulls and sheep –

1:3 *si holocaustum fuerit eius oblatio ac de armento masculum inmaculatum offeret ad ostium tabernaculi testimonii ad placandum sibi Dominum*

"if his offering will be *a* burnt offering and from *the* herd, he will offer *a* spotless male at *the* entrance to testimony's tabernacle, to placating *the* Lord with himself.

1:4 *ponetque manus super caput hostiae et acceptabilis erit atque in expiationem eius proficiens*

"'And he will lay hands on *the* offering's head, and it will be acceptable in accomplishing his

forgiveness.

1:5 *immolabitque vitulum coram Domino et offerent filii Aaron sacerdotes sanguinem eius fundentes super altaris circuitum quod est ante ostium tabernaculi*

"'And he will kill *the* calf before *the* Lord, and Aaron's sons, *the* priests, will offer its blood, pouring it around over *the* altar which is before *the* tabernacle's entry.

1:6 *detractaque pelle hostiae artus in frusta concident*

"'And taking off *the* victim's hide, they will chop *the* joints in pieces,

1:7 *et subicient in altari ignem strue lignorum ante conposita*

"'and throw fire on *the* altar, *which is* piled with wood placed before.

1:8 *et membra quae caesa sunt desuper ordinantes caput videlicet et cuncta quae adherent iecori*

"'And, arranging on top of *the altar the* members which are cut up – *the* head, of course, and all that adheres to *the* liver,

1:9 *intestinis et pedibus lotis aqua adolebitque ea sacerdos super altare in holocaustum et suavem odorem Domino*

"'*the* intestines and feet washed with water – *the* priest will burn them on *the* altar as *a* burnt offering and *a* smooth odor to *the* Lord.

From Sheep or Goats

1:10 *quod si de pecoribus oblatio est de ovibus sive de capris holocaustum anniculum et absque macula offeret*

"'And if *the* offering from *the* animals is *a* burnt offering from sheep or from goats, he will offer *a* yearling male without defect.

1:11 *immolabitque ad latus altaris quod respicit ad aquilonem coram Domino sanguinem vero illius fundent super altare filii Aaron per circuitum*

"'And he will kill it at *the* altar's side that looks to *the* north, before *the* Lord. And Aaron's sons will pour its blood around over *the* altar.

1:12 *dividentque membra caput et omnia quae adherent iecori et inponent super ligna quibus subiciendus est ignis*

"'And they will divide *the* members – *the* head and all that adheres to *the* liver – and place them on *the* wood from which *the* fire is lit.

1:13 *intestina vero et pedes lavabunt aqua et oblata omnia adolebit sacerdos super altare in*

holocaustum et odorem suavissimum Domino

"'And they will wash *the* intestines and feet with water, and *the* priest will burn all *the* offering on *the* altar as *a* burnt offering and smoothest odor to *the* Lord.

Doves and Pigeons

1:14 *sin autem de avibus holocausti oblatio fuerit Domino de turturibus et pullis columbae*

"'But if *the* holocaust's offering to *the* Lord is from birds – from doves or young pigeons –

1:15 *offeret eam sacerdos ad altare et retorto ad collum capite ac rupto vulneris loco decurrere faciet sanguinem super crepidinem altaris*

"'*the* priest will offer it at *the* altar. And, twisting *the* head at *the* neck and breaking it at *the* place's wound, he will make *the* blood run over *the* altar's rim.

1:16 *vesiculam vero gutturis et plumas proiciet propter altare ad orientalem plagam in loco in quo cineres effundi solent*

"'But *the* throat's crop and feathers he will throw out near *the* altar at *the* east side, in *the* place in which ashes are customarily poured out.

1:17 *confringetque ascellas eius et*

non secabit nec ferro dividet eam et adolebit super altare lignis igne subposito holocaustum est et oblatio suavissimi odoris Domino

"'And he will break its wings and not cut *them*, nor divide it with *a* knife. And he will burn it in fire on *the* altar, *the* wood placed beneath. It is *a* holocaust and offering, *the* smoothest odor to *the* Lord.'"

Rules for Grain Offerings

Leviticus 2:1 *anima cum obtulerit oblationem sacrificii Domino simila erit eius oblatio fundetque super eam oleum et ponet tus*

"'When *a* soul will offer *a* sacrifice's oblation to *the* Lord, his offering will be wheat flour. And he will pour oil over it and place incense.

2:2 *ac deferet ad filios Aaron sacerdotes quorum unus tollet pugillum plenum similae et olei ac totum tus et ponet memoriale super altare in odorem suavissimum Domino*

"'And he will bring it to Aaron's sons, *the* priests, one of whom will take *a* fistful of flour and oil and all *the* incense, and place *them as a* memorial on *the* altar, as *a* smoothest odor to *the* Lord.

2:3 *quod autem reliquum fuerit de sacrificio erit Aaron et filiorum eius sanctum sanctorum de oblationibus Domini*

"'But what will remain from *the* sacrifice will be for Aaron and his sons, holy of holies from *the* Lord's offerings.

2:4 *cum autem obtuleris sacrificium coctum in clibano de simila panes scilicet absque fermento conspersos oleo et lagana azyma oleo lita*

"'But when you offer *a* sacrifice of flour baked in *an* oven – bread, of course, without yeast, sprinkled with oil, and unleavened cakes smeared with oil –

2:5 *si oblatio tua fuerit de sartagine similae conspersae oleo et absque fermento*

"'if your offering will be of flour from *the* frying pan, sprinkled with oil and without yeast,

2:6 *divides eam minutatim et fundes supra oleum*

"'you will divide it in pieces and pour oil over *it.*

2:7 *sin autem de craticula sacrificium aeque simila oleo conspergetur*

"'But if *the* sacrifice *is* from the griddle, *the* flour equally will be sprinkled with oil,

2:8 *quam offeres Domino tradens manibus sacerdotis*

"'which you will offer to *the* Lord, giving it into *the* priests' hands.

2:9 *qui cum obtulerit eam tollet memoriale de sacrificio et adolebit super altare in odorem suavitatis Domino*

"'*The priest,* when you have offered it, will take *a* memorial from *the* sacrifice and burn it on *the* altar, as *an* odor of smoothness to *the* Lord.

2:10 *quicquid autem reliquum est erit Aaron et filiorum eius sanctum sanctorum de oblationibus Domini*

"'But whatever is left will be for Aaron and his sons, holy of holies from *the* Lord's offerings.

2:11 *omnis oblatio quae offertur Domino absque fermento fiet nec quicquam fermenti ac mellis adolebitur in sacrificio Domini*

"'Every gift which is offered to *the* Lord will be made without yeast, nor will anything of yeast or honey be burned in sacrifice to *the* Lord.

2:12 *primitias tantum eorum offeretis et munera super altare vero non ponentur in odorem suavitatis*

"'You will offer only their first fruits and gifts. And they will not be placed on *the* altar as *an* odor of smoothness.

2:13 *quicquid obtuleris sacrificii sale condies nec auferes sal foederis Dei tui de sacrificio tuo in omni oblatione offeres sal*

"'Whatever you offer in sacrifice you will season with salt, nor will you take away *the* salt of God's covenant from your sacrifice. You will offer salt in every offering.

2:14 *sin autem obtuleris munus primarum frugum tuarum Domino de spicis adhuc virentibus torres eas igni et confringes in morem farris et sic offeres primitias tuas Domino*

"'But if you offer *the* gift of your crops' first fruits to *the* Lord, from grain still green, roast them in fire and break them up in *the* manner of coarse meal. And so you will offer your first fruits to *the* Lord,

2:15 *fundens supra oleum et tus inponens quia oblatio Domini est*

"'pouring oil over *them* and placing incense, because *it* is *the* Lord's offering –

2:16 *de qua adolebit sacerdos in memoriam muneris partem farris fracti et olei ac totum tus*

"'from which *the* priest will burn as *a* memorial of *the* gift part of *the* coarse meal and oil and all *the* incense.'"

Peace Offerings
Leviticus 3:1 *quod si hostia pacificorum fuerit eius oblatio et de bubus voluerit offerre marem sive feminam inmaculata offeret coram Domino*

"'But if his offering will be *a* peace victim, and he wants to offer male or female from cattle, he will offer *one* without defect before *the* Lord.

3:2 *ponetque manum super caput victimae suae quae immolabitur in introitu tabernaculi fundentque filii Aaron sacerdotes sanguinem per circuitum altaris*

"'And he will put his hand on his victim's head, which will be killed in *the* tabernacle's entrance. And Aaron's sons, *the* priests, will pour *the* blood around *the* altar.

3:2 *et offerent de hostia pacificorum in oblationem Domini adipem qui operit vitalia et quicquid pinguedinis intrinsecus est*

"'And they will offer from *the* peace sacrifice, as *the* Lord's offering, *the* fat which covers *the* vital organs and whatever fatness is inside,

3:4 *duos renes cum adipe quo teguntur ilia et reticulum iecoris cum renunculis*

the two kidneys with *the* fat that covers them, *the* loins and *the* liver's covering, with *the* smaller organs.

3:5 *adolebuntque ea super altare in holocaustum lignis igne subposito in oblationem suavissimi odoris Domino*

"'And they will burn them on *the* altar as *a* holocaust, *the* wood's fire placed beneath, as *an* offering of *the* smoothest odor to *the* Lord.

Offering Sheep
3:6 *si vero de ovibus fuerit eius oblatio et pacificorum hostia sive masculum sive feminam obtulerit inmaculata erunt*

"'But if his offering and peace sacrifice will be from sheep, whether he offer male or female, they will be without defect.

Offering a Lamb
3:7 *si agnum obtulerit coram Domino*

"'If he will offer *a* lamb before *the* Lord,

3:8 *ponet manum super caput victimae suae quae immolabitur in vestibulo tabernaculi testimonii fundentque filii Aaron sanguinem eius per altaris circuitum*

"'he will place hands on his victim's head, which will be killed in *the* entrance to testimony's tabernacle.

And Aaron's sons will pour its blood around *the* altar.

3:9 *et offerent de pacificorum hostia sacrificium Domino adipem et caudam totam*

"'And they will offer *the* Lord from *the* peace victim *a* sacrifice of *the* fat and all *the* tail,

3:10 *cum renibus et pinguedinem quae operit ventrem atque universa vitalia et utrumque renunculum cum adipe qui est iuxta ilia reticulumque iecoris cum renunculis*

"'with *the* kidneys and *the* fat that covers *the* gut, and all *the* vital organs, and *the* small kidney with *the* fat which is beside *the* loins, and *the* liver's covering with *the* small organs.

3:11 *et adolebit ea sacerdos super altare in pabulum ignis et oblationis Domini*

"'And *the* priest will burn it on *the* altar, as *the* fire's fuel and *the* Lord's offering.

Offering a Goat
3:12 *si capra fuerit eius oblatio et obtulerit eam Domino*

"'If his offering is *a* goat, and he will offer it to *the* Lord,

3:13 *ponet manum suam super*

caput eius immolabitque eam in introitu tabernaculi testimonii et fundent filii Aaron sanguinem eius per altaris circuitum

"'he will place his hand on its head and it will be killed in *the* entrance to testimony's tabernacle. And Aaron's sons will pour out its blood around *the* altar.

3:14 *tollentque ex ea in pastum ignis dominici adipem qui operit ventrem et qui tegit universa vitalia*

"'And they will take from it as food for *the* Lord's fire *the* fat that covers *the* gut and that touches all *the* vital organs,

3:15 *duos renunculos cum reticulo qui est super eos iuxta ilia et arvinam iecoris cum renunculis*

the two kidneys with *the* covering that is over them, alongside *the* loins, and *the* liver's suet with *the* smaller organs.

3:16 *adolebitque ea sacerdos super altare in alimoniam ignis et suavissimi odoris omnis adeps Domini erit*

And *the* priest will burn them on *the* altar as *the* fire's nourishment and smoothest odor. All *the* fat will be *the* Lord's,

3:17 *iure perpetuo in*

generationibus et cunctis habitaculis vestris nec adipes nec sanguinem omnino comedetis

by *a* perpetual law in all your generations and dwellings. You will eat no fat or blood at all.'"

A Priest's Sin Offering

Leviticus 4:1 *locutusque est Dominus ad Mosen dicens*

And *the* Lord spoke to Moses, saying,

4:2 *loquere filiis Israhel anima cum peccaverit per ignorantiam et de universis mandatis Domini quae praecepit ut non fierent quippiam fecerit*

"Speak to Israel's children, 'When *a* soul sins through ignorance, and from all *the* Lord's precepts which He commanded, so he does anything that may not be done –

4:3 *si sacerdos qui est unctus peccaverit delinquere faciens populum offeret pro peccato suo vitulum inmaculatum Domino*

"'if *a* priest who is anointed sins, making *the* people offend, he will offer *the* Lord for his sin *a* calf without defect.

4:4 *et adducet illum ad ostium tabernaculi testimonii coram Domino ponetque manum super caput eius et immolabit eum Domino*

"'And he will lead it to *the* entrance of testimony's tabernacle before *the* Lord, and lay hands on its head, and kill it to *the* Lord.

4:5 *hauriet quoque de sanguine vituli inferens illud in tabernaculum testimonii*

"'Likewise, he will carry some of *the* calf's blood, bringing it into testimony's tabernacle.

4:6 *cumque intinxerit digitum in sanguinem asperget eo septies coram Domino contra velum sanctuarii*

"'And when he has dipped *a* finger in *the* blood, he will sprinkle it seven times before *the* Lord, before *the* sanctuary's veil.

4:7 *ponetque de eodem sanguine super cornua altaris thymiamatis gratissimi Domino quod est in tabernaculo testimonii omnem autem reliquum sanguinem fundet in basim altaris holocausti in introitu tabernaculi*

"'And he will place some of *the* same blood on *the* horns of *the* altar of most graceful incense to *the* Lord, which is in testimony's tabernacle. But he will pour out all *the* blood that remains in *the* base of *the* altar of burnt offerings at *the* tabernacle's entrance.

4:8 *et adipem vituli auferet pro peccato tam eum qui operit vitalia quam omnia quae intrinsecus sunt*

"'And he will take away for sin *the* calf's fat – that which covers the vital organs and all that are inside,

4:9 *duos renunculos et reticulum quod est super eos iuxta ilia et adipem iecoris cum renunculis*

"'*the* two kidneys and *the* covering that is over them beside *the* loins, and *the* liver's fat with *the* little organs –

4:10 *sicut aufertur de vitulo hostiae pacificorum et adolebit ea super altare holocausti*

as is taken away from *the* calf of *the* peace victim, and he will burn them over *the* altar of burnt offerings.

4:11 *pellem vero et omnes carnes cum capite et pedibus et intestinis et fimo*

"'And *the* hide and all *the* meat, with *the* head and feet and intestines and dung

4:12 *et reliquo corpore efferet extra castra in locum mundum ubi cineres effundi solent incendetque ea super lignorum struem quae in loco effusorum cinerum cremabuntur*

and *the* rest of the body, he will take outside *the* camp into *a* clean place, where they are accustomed to pour out ashes. And he will burn them over piled wood, that they may be cremated in *the* place of poured out ashes.

Sin Offering
for the Whole People

4:13 *quod si omnis turba Israhel ignoraverit et per inperitiam fecerit quod contra mandatum Domini est*

"'And if Israel's whole crowd doesn't know and through ignorance does what is against *the* Lord's commandment,

4:14 *et postea intellexerit peccatum suum offeret vitulum pro peccato adducetque eum ad ostium tabernaculi*

"'and afterwards understands its sin, it will offer *a* calf for sin. And *the* people* will lead it to *the* tabernacle's entrance,

4:15 *et ponent seniores populi manus super caput eius coram Domino immolatoque vitulo in conspectu Domini*

"'and *the* people's elders will lay hands on its head before *the* Lord. And, *the* calf being killed in *the* Lord's sight,

4:16 *inferet sacerdos qui unctus est de sanguine eius in tabernaculum testimonii*

the priest who is anointed will take some of its blood into testimony's tabernacle.

4:17 *tincto digito aspergens septies*

contra velum

"'*His* finger dipped *in the blood*, sprinkling seven times before *the* veil,

4:18 *ponetque de eodem sanguine in cornibus altaris quod est coram Domino in tabernaculo testimonii reliquum autem sanguinem fundet iuxta basim altaris holocaustorum quod est in ostio tabernaculi testimonii*

"'he will also put some of *the* same blood on *the* horns of *the* altar which is before *the* Lord in testimony's tabernacle. But he will pour out *the* rest of *the* blood beside *the* base of *the* altar of burnt offerings, which is in *the* entrance of testimony's tabernacle.

4:19 *omnemque eius adipem tollet et adolebit super altare*

"'And he will take all its fat and burn *it* on *the* altar,

4:20 *sic faciens et de hoc vitulo quomodo fecit et prius et rogante pro eis sacerdote propitius erit Dominus*

"'doing so also from this calf as he did before. And, *the* priest praying for them, *the* Lord will be satisfied.

4:21 *ipsum autem vitulum efferet extra castra atque conburet sicut et priorem vitulum quia pro peccato est multitudinis*

"'But he will take *the* calf itself outside *the* camp and burn it as *the* prior calf, because *it* is for *the* multitude's sin.

Sin Offering for a Prince

4:22 *si peccaverit princeps et fecerit unum e pluribus per ignorantiam quod Domini lege prohibetur*

"'But if *a* prince sins and does through ignorance one of *the* many *things* that is prohibited by *the* Lord's law,

4:23 *et postea intellexerit peccatum suum offeret hostiam Domino hircum de capris inmaculatum*

"'and afterwards understands his sins, he will offer *the* Lord *as a* victim *a* he-goat without defect, from *the* flock.

4:24 *ponetque manum suam super caput eius cumque immolaverit eum in loco ubi solet mactari holocaustum coram Domino quia pro peccato est*

"'And he will lay his hand on its head. And when he has killed it in *the* place where *it* is customary to kill *the* burnt offering before *the* Lord, because *it* is for sin,

4:25 *tinguet sacerdos digitum in sanguine hostiae pro peccato tangens cornua altaris holocausti et reliquum fundens ad basim eius*

"'*the* priest will dip *a* finger in *the* victim's blood for sin, touching *the* altar of burnt offerings' horns and pouring out *the* rest at its base.

4:26 *adipem vero adolebit supra sicut in victimis pacificorum fieri solet rogabitque pro eo et pro peccato eius ac dimittetur ei*

"'And he will burn *the* fat on it, as is customarily done with peace offerings. And he will pray for him and for his sin, and *it* will be forgiven him.

Sin Offering
for an Ordinary Person

4:27 *quod si peccaverit anima per ignorantiam de populo terrae ut faciat quicquam ex his quae Domini lege prohibentur atque delinquat*

"'And if *a* soul from *the* land's people sins through ignorance and does something from those which are prohibited by *the* Lord's law, and falls short,

4:28 *et cognoverit peccatum suum offeret capram inmaculatam*

"'and recognizes his sin, he will offer *a* she-goat without defect.

4:29 *ponetque manum super caput hostiae quae pro peccato est et immolabit eam in loco holocausti*

"'And he will lay hands on *the*

victim's head, which is for sin, and will kill it in *the* place of burnt offerings.

4:30 *tolletque sacerdos de sanguine in digito suo et tangens cornua altaris holocausti reliquum fundet ad basim eius*

"'And *the* priest will take some of *the* blood on his finger and, touching *the* horns of *the* altar of burnt offerings, will pour out *the* rest at its base.

4:31 *omnem autem auferens adipem sicut auferri solet de victimis pacificorum adolebit super altare in odorem suavitatis Domino rogabitque pro eo et dimittetur ei*

"'But taking away all *the* fat as is customary to take away from peace offerings, he will burn *it* to *the* Lord on *the* altar as *an* odor of smoothness. And he will pray for him, and *it* will be forgiven him.

4:32 *sin autem de pecoribus obtulerit victimam pro peccato ovem scilicet inmaculatam*

"'But if he offers for sin *a* victim from *the* flock – *a* sheep, of course, without defect –

4:33 *ponet manum super caput eius et immolabit eam in loco ubi solent holocaustorum caedi hostiae*

"'he will lay hands on its head and

kill it in *the* place where burnt offerings' victims are customarily slaughtered.

4:34 *sumetque sacerdos de sanguine eius digito suo et tangens cornua altaris holocausti reliquum fundet ad basim eius*

"'And *the* priest will take up some of its blood on his finger and, touching *the* horns of *the* altar of burnt offerings, he will pour out *the* rest at its base.

4:35 *omnem quoque auferens adipem sicut auferri solet adeps arietis qui immolatur pro pacificis et cremabit super altare in incensum Domini rogabitque pro eo et pro peccato eius et dimittetur illi*

"'Likewise taking away all *the* fat, as is customary to take *the* ram's fat which is offered for peace, he will burn *it* also on *the* altar as *the* Lord's incense. And he will pray for him and for his sin, and *it* will be forgiven him.

Don't Hide
What Others Swore

Leviticus 5:1 *si peccaverit anima et audierit vocem iurantis testisque fuerit quod aut ipse vidit aut conscius est nisi indicaverit portabit iniquitatem suam*

"'If *a* soul sins, and hears *the* voice of one swearing. and is witness either that he saw or was aware, unless he tells, he will carry his treachery.

Touching Unclean Things

5:2 *anima quae tetigerit aliquid inmundum sive quod occisum a bestia est aut per se mortuum vel quodlibet aliud reptile et oblita fuerit inmunditiae suae rea est et deliquit*

"'*A* soul that touches something unclean, whether that be *a* killed animal, or *one* that died of itself, or any sort of crawling thing, and forgets his uncleanness, is guilty and falls short.

5:3 *et si tetigerit quicquam de inmunditia hominis iuxta omnem inpuritatem qua pollui solet oblitaque cognoverit postea subiacebit delicto*

"'And if he should touch something from human uncleanness, according to every impurity by which it is customary to be polluted, and forgetting, afterwards recognizes *it*, he will be subject to penalty.

Swearing and Forgetting

5:4 *anima quae iuraverit et protulerit labiis suis ut vel male quid faceret vel bene et id ipsum iuramento et sermone firmaverit oblitaque postea intellexerit delictum suum*

"'*A* soul that swears and puts forward by his lips – whether he does harm or good, and he himself swearing and affirming by word, and afterward forgetting, will understand his offense –

5:5 *agat paenitentiam pro peccato*

"'let him act out penance for sin.

5:6 *et offerat agnam de gregibus sive capram orabitque pro eo sacerdos et pro peccato eius*

"'And let him offer *a* female lamb from flocks or herds. And *the* priest will pray for him and for his sin.

5:7 *sin autem non potuerit offerre pecus offerat duos turtures vel duos pullos columbarum Domino unum pro peccato et alterum in holocaustum*

"'But if he can't offer *a* large animal, let him offer *the* Lord two doves or two young pigeons, one for sin and *the* other as *a* burnt offering.

5:8 *dabitque eos sacerdoti qui primum offerens pro peccato*

retorquebit caput eius ad pinnulas ita ut collo hereat et non penitus abrumpatur

"'And he will give them to *the* priest, who, offering first for sin, will twist its head back to *the* wings, so that *the* neck is wounded, and is not broken deeply.

5:9 *et asperget de sanguine eius parietem altaris quicquid autem reliquum fuerit faciet destillare ad fundamentum eius quia pro peccato est*

"'And he will sprinkle from its blood on *the* altar's walls. But whatever is left he will make drip down at its base, because it is for sin.

5:10 *alterum vero adolebit holocaustum ut fieri solet rogabitque pro eo sacerdos et pro peccato eius et dimittetur ei*

"'*The* other, indeed, he will burn as *a* holocaust, as is customarily done. And *the* priest will pray for him and for his sin, and *it* will be forgiven him.

5:11 *quod si non quiverit manus eius offerre duos turtures vel duos pullos columbae offeret pro peccato similam partem oephi decimam non mittet in eam oleum nec turis aliquid inponet quia pro peccato est*

"'But if his hand isn't able to offer

two doves or two young pigeons, he will offer for sin wheat flour, *a* tenth part of *an* ephah. He will not put oil in it or place any incense on it, because it is for sin.

5:12 *tradetque eam sacerdoti qui plenum ex toto pugillum hauriens cremabit super altare in monumentum eius qui obtulit*

"'And he will hand it to *the* priest who, grabbing *a* handful for all with his fist, will burn it on *the* altar as his memorial who offered *it*,

5:13 *rogans pro illo et expians reliquam vero partem ipse habebit in munere*

"'praying for him and making atonement. But *the* remaining portion he will have as *a* gift.'"

5:14 *locutus est Dominus ad Mosen dicens*

The Lord spoke to Moses, saying,

5:15 *anima si praevaricans caerimonias per errorem in his quae Domino sunt sanctificata peccaverit offeret pro delicto suo arietem inmaculatum de gregibus qui emi potest duobus siclis iuxta pondus sanctuarii*

"'If *a* soul, transgressing by error *the* ceremonies in which things are sanctified to *the* Lord, should sin, he

will offer for his sin *a* ram without defect from *the* flock, which can be bought for two shekels, according to *the* sanctuary measure.

5:16 *ipsumque quod intulit damni restituet et quintam partem ponet supra tradens sacerdoti qui rogabit pro eo offerens arietem et dimittetur ei*

"'And he will pay back *the* damage that he himself brought in, and will add *a* fifth part above *it*, handing it to *the* priest, who will pray for him, offering *the* ram, and *it* will be forgiven him.

5:17 *anima si peccaverit per ignorantiam feceritque unum ex his quae Domini lege prohibentur et peccati rea intellexerit iniquitatem suam*

"'If *a* soul sins through ignorance and does one of those things prohibited by *the* Lord's law and, guilty of sin, should understand his treachery,

5:18 *offeret arietem inmaculatum de gregibus sacerdoti iuxta mensuram aestimationemque peccati qui orabit pro eo quod nesciens fecerit et dimittetur ei*

"'he will offer *the* priest *a* ram without defect from *the* flock, according to *the* measure and estimation of sin. *The priest* will pray for him because he did it unknowing, and *it* will be forgiven him,

5:19 *quia per errorem deliquit in Dominum*

because through error he fell short in *the* Lord.'"

Sinning By Fraud

Leviticus 6:1 *locutus est Dominus ad Mosen dicens*

And *the* Lord spoke to Moses, saying,

6:2 *anima quae peccaverit et contempto Domino negaverit depositum proximo suo quod fidei eius creditum fuerat vel vi aliquid extorserit aut calumniam fecerit*

"'*A* soul that sins and, in contempt of *the* Lord, denies *a* deposit to his neighbor that was credited as his pledge, or by force extorts something or works oppression,

6:3 *sive rem perditam invenerit et infitians insuper peierarit et quodlibet aliud ex pluribus fecerit in quibus peccare solent homines*

"'or finds *a* lost thing and, denying *it,* also swears falsely, and does whatever else of *the* many things in which men are accustomed to sin,

6:4 *convicta delicti reddet*

"'convicted of *the* offense, he will repay

6:5 *omnia quae per fraudem voluit obtinere integra et quintam insuper partem domino cui damnum intulerat*

all that he wanted to obtain by fraud entirely, and *a* fifth part above, to *the* owner to whom he did damage.

6:6 *pro peccato autem suo offeret arietem inmaculatum de grege et dabit eum sacerdoti iuxta aestimationem mensuramque delicti*

"'But he will offer for his sin *a* ram without defect from *the* flock. And he will give it to *the* priest, according to *the* estimation and measure of *the* offense,

6:7 *qui rogabit pro eo coram Domino et dimittetur illi pro singulis quae faciendo peccaverit*

who will pray for him before *the* Lord. And *it* will be forgiven him for each of *the* things, which doing, he sinned.'"

The Law
of Burnt Offerings

6:8 *locutus est Dominus ad Mosen dicens*

The Lord spoke to Moses, saying,

6:9 *praecipe Aaron et filiis eius haec est lex holocausti cremabitur in altari tota nocte usque mane ignis ex eodem altari erit*

"Command Aaron and his sons, 'This is *the* law of burnt offering. It will be burned on *the* altar all night, until morning. *The* fire will be from *the* same altar.

6:10 *vestietur sacerdos tunica et feminalibus lineis tolletque cineres quos vorans ignis exusit et ponens iuxta altare*

"'*The* priest will be dressed in *the* tunic and linen thigh coverings. And he will take *the* ashes which *the* devouring fire burned up and, placing *them* beside *the* altar,

6:11 *spoliabitur prioribus vestimentis indutusque aliis efferet eos extra castra et in loco mundissimo usque ad favillam consumi faciet*

"'he will take off *the* prior garments and, dressing in others, will take them outside *the* camp into *a* most clean place. And he will cause them to be consumed to ashes.

6:12 *ignis autem in altari semper ardebit quem nutriet sacerdos subiciens ligna mane per singulos dies et inposito holocausto desuper adolebit adipes pacificorum*

"'But *the* fire on *the* altar will always burn, which *the* priest will feed, placing wood beneath it early every day, and putting *the* burnt offering above. He will burn *the* fat of *the* peace offerings.

6:13 *ignis est iste perpetuus qui numquam deficiet in altari*

"'This is *the* perpetual fire which will

never go out on *the* altar.

The Law of
Sacrifice and Libation

6:14 *haec est lex sacrificii et libamentorum quae offerent filii Aaron coram Domino et coram altari*

"'This is *the* law of *the* sacrifice and libations which Aaron's sons will offer before *the* Lord and before *the* altar.

6:15 *tollet sacerdos pugillum similae quae conspersa est oleo et totum tus quod super similam positum est adolebitque illud in altari in monumentum odoris suavissimi Domino*

"'*The* priest will take *a* fistful of wheat flour which is sprinkled with oil, and all *the* incense which is placed on *the* wheat. And he will burn it on *the* altar as *a* monument of *the* smoothest odor to *the* Lord.

6:16 *reliquam autem partem similae comedet Aaron cum filiis suis absque fermento et comedet in loco sancto atrii tabernaculi*

"'But Aaron with his sons will eat *the* remaining part of *the* wheat, without yeast. And he will eat in *the* holy place, *the* tabernacle's courtyard.

6:17 *ideo autem non fermentabitur quia pars eius in Domini offertur*

incensum sanctum sanctorum erit sicut pro peccato atque delicto

"'And for this reason it will not be fermented, because it is his portion in *the* Lord. Let *the* incense be offered as *the* holy of holies. It will be like *those* for sin and offense.

6:18 *mares tantum stirpis Aaron comedent illud legitimum ac sempiternum est in generationibus vestris de sacrificiis Domini omnis qui tetigerit illa sanctificabitur*

"'Only males of Aaron's line will eat it. It is an everlasting law in your generations from *the* Lord's sacrifice. Everyone who touches them will be made holy.'"

6:19 *et locutus est Dominus ad Mosen dicens*

And *the* Lord spoke to Moses, saying,

6:20 *haec est oblatio Aaron et filiorum eius quam offerre debent Domino in die unctionis suae decimam partem oephi offerent similae in sacrificio sempiterno medium eius mane et medium vespere*

"'This is *the* offering of Aaron and his sons, which they must offer *the* Lord on *the* day of their anointing. They will offer wheat flour, *a* tenth part of *an* ephah, as *an* enduring sacrifice – half of it at morning and half at evening,

6:21 *quae in sartagine oleo conspersa frigetur offeret autem eam calidam in odorem suavissimum Domino*

"'which will be roasted on *a* grill, sprinkled with oil. But he will offer it hot, as *a* smoothest odor to *the* Lord –

6:22 *sacerdos qui patri iure successerit et tota cremabitur in altari*

"'*the* priest, who legally succeeds *his* father – and he will burn all on *the* altar.

6:23 *omne enim sacrificium sacerdotum igne consumetur nec quisquam comedet ex eo*

"'For every priest's sacrifice will be consumed by fire, nor will anyone eat from it.'"

The Law for Sin Offerings

6:24 *locutus est Dominus ad Mosen dicens*

The Lord spoke to Moses, saying,

6:25 *loquere Aaron et filiis eius ista est lex hostiae pro peccato in loco ubi offertur holocaustum immolabitur coram Domino sanctum sanctorum est*

"Say to Aaron and his sons, 'This is *the* law of *the* offering for sin. In *the* place where *the* holocaust is offered, it will be killed before *the* Lord. *It* is holy of holies.

6:26 *sacerdos qui offert comedet eam in loco sancto in atrio tabernaculi*

"'*The* priest who offers *it* will eat it in *the* holy place, in *the* tabernacle's courtyard.

6:27 *quicquid tetigerit carnes eius sanctificabitur si de sanguine illius vestis fuerit aspersa lavabitur in loco sancto*

"'Whatever touches its flesh will be made holy. If *a* garment is sprinkled with its blood, it will be washed in *the* holy place.

6:28 *vas autem fictile in quo cocta est confringetur quod si vas aeneum fuerit defricabitur et lavabitur aqua*

"'But *an* earthenware vessel in which it is cooked will be broken. But if it is bronze, it will be scoured and washed with water.

6:29 *omnis masculus de genere sacerdotali vescetur carnibus eius quia sanctum sanctorum est*

"'Every male from *the* priestly line will eat its flesh, because it is holy of holies.

6:30 *hostia enim quae caeditur pro peccato cuius sanguis infertur in tabernaculum testimonii ad expiandum in sanctuario non comedetur sed conburetur igni*

"'Yet *the* victim which is slaughtered for sin, whose blood is brought into testimony's tabernacle as atonement in *the* sanctuary, will not be eaten, but burned with fire.'"

Offerings for an Offense

Leviticus 7:1 *haec quoque est lex hostiae pro delicto sancta sanctorum est*

"'This likewise is *the* law of victims for *an* offense. *It* is holy of holies.

7:2 *idcirco ubi immolatur holocaustum mactabitur et victima pro delicto sanguis eius per gyrum fundetur altaris*

"'Therefore, where *the* burnt offering is killed, *the* victim for *an* offense also will be slaughtered. Its blood will be poured out around *the* altar.

7:3 *offerent ex ea caudam et adipem qui operit vitalia*

"'They will offer from it *the* tail and *the* fat that covers *the* vitals,

7:4 *duos renunculos et pinguedinem quae iuxta ilia est reticulumque iecoris cum renunculis*

"'*the* two kidneys and *the* fat that is beside *the* loins, *the* liver's covering with *the* small organs.

7:5 *et adolebit ea sacerdos super altare incensum est Domini pro delicto*

"'And *the* priest will burn it on *the* altar. It is *the* Lord's incense for *an* offense.

7:6 *omnis masculus de sacerdotali genere in loco sancto vescetur his carnibus quia sanctum sanctorum est*

"'Every male from *the* priestly line will eat this meat in *the* holy place, because it is holy of holies.

7:7 *sicut pro peccato offertur hostia ita et pro delicto utriusque hostiae lex una erit ad sacerdotem qui eam obtulerit pertinebit*

"'As *a* victim is offered for sin, so also for *an* offense. *It* will be one law for both victims. *The offering* will belong to *the* priest who offers it.

7:8 *sacerdos qui offert holocausti victimam habebit pellem eius*

"'*The* priest who offers *the* holocaust's victim will have its hide.

7:9 *et omne sacrificium similae quod coquitur in clibano et quicquid in craticula vel in sartagine praeparatur eius erit sacerdotis a quo offertur*

"'And every sacrifice of wheat flour cooked in *an* oven, and whatever is prepared on *a* grill or in *a* frying pan, will be *the* priest's by whom it is offered.

7:10 *sive oleo conspersa sive arida fuerit cunctis filiis Aaron aequa mensura per singulos dividetur*

"'Whether sprinkled with oil or dry, *it* will be to all Aaron's sons in equal measure. It will be divided among each.

The Law
for Peace Offerings

7:11 *haec est lex hostiae pacificorum quae offertur Domino*

"'This is *the* law of *the* peace offering, which is offered to *the* Lord.

7:12 *si pro gratiarum actione fuerit oblatio offerent panes absque fermento conspersos oleo et lagana azyma uncta oleo coctamque similam et collyridas olei admixtione conspersas*

"'If *the* gift is given for *an* act of favor, they will offer bread without yeast sprinkled with oil, and unleavened cakes smeared with oil, and cooked wheat, and rolls mixed with sprinkled oil.

7:13 *panes quoque fermentatos cum hostia gratiarum quae immolatur pro pacificis*

"'leavened bread also with *the* offering of favor, which is killed for peace.

7:14 *ex quibus unus pro primitiis offeretur Domino et erit sacerdotis qui fundet hostiae sanguinem*

"'One of them will be offered to *the* Lord for first fruits, and will be *the* priest's who pours out *the* victim's blood.

7:15 *cuius carnes eadem comedentur die nec remanebit ex eis quicquam usque mane*

"'*The offering's* meat will be eaten *the* same day, nor will anything from them remain until morning.

7:16 *si voto vel sponte quisquam obtulerit hostiam eadem similiter edetur die sed et si quid in crastinum remanserit vesci licitum est*

"'If *a* vow or any sort of promise is offered, *the* victim likewise will be eaten *the* same day. But if something should remain to *the* next day, *it* is lawful to eat.

7:17 *quicquid autem tertius invenerit dies ignis absumet*

"'But whatever is found *the* third day will be consumed by fire.

Respect What Is Offered!

7:18 *si quis de carnibus victimae pacificorum die tertio comederit irrita fiet oblatio nec proderit offerenti quin potius quaecumque anima tali se edulio contaminarit praevaricationis rea erit*

"'If one should eat from *the* peace offering's flesh *the* third day, *the* gift will be made void, nor will it benefit *the* one offering. But rather whatever soul should eat so will contaminate himself. He will be guilty of transgressing.

7:19 *caro quae aliquid tetigerit inmundum non comedetur sed conburetur igni qui fuerit mundus vescetur ea*

"'Flesh that anything unclean touches will not be eaten, but burned in fire. One who will be clean will eat it.

7:20 *anima polluta quae ederit de carnibus hostiae pacificorum quae oblata est Domino peribit de populis suis*

"'*A* polluted soul that eats from *the* peace offering's flesh, which is offered to *the* Lord, will perish from his people.

7:21 *et quae tetigerit inmunditiam hominis vel iumenti sive omnis rei quae polluere potest et comederit de huiuscemodi carnibus interibit de populis suis*

"'And who will touch uncleanness, whether of men or cattle or anything that can be polluted, and will eat from such meat, will die from his people.'"

Don't Eat Fat

7:22 *locutusque est Dominus ad Mosen dicens*

And *the* Lord spoke to Moses, saying,

7:23 *loquere filiis Israhel adipem bovis et ovis et caprae non comedetis*

"Say to Israel's children, 'You will not eat *the* fat of cattle or sheep or goat.

7:24 *adipem cadaveris morticini et eius animalis quod a bestia captum est habebitis in usus varios*

"'You will have for various uses *the* fat of *a* body that died of itself, and *of an* animal that *a* wild beast has taken.

7:25 *si quis adipem qui offerri debet in incensum Domini comederit peribit de populo suo*

"'If one who ought to offer fat as *the* Lord's incense should eat it, he will perish from his people.

Don't Eat Blood
7:26 *sanguinem quoque omnis animalis non sumetis in cibo tam de avibus quam de pecoribus*

"'Likewise, you will not take up *the* blood of any animal as food, whether of birds or of beasts.

7:27 *omnis anima quae ederit sanguinem peribit de populis suis*

"'Every soul that eats blood will perish from his people.'"

The Libations
with the Peace Offering
7:28 *locutus est Dominus ad Mosen dicens*

The Lord spoke to Moses, saying,

7:29 *loquere filiis Israhel qui offert victimam pacificorum Domino offerat simul et sacrificium id est libamenta eius*

"Speak to Israel's children, 'Who offers *the* Lord *a* peace offering will offer at *the* same time also *a* sacrifice – that is, his libations.

7:30 *tenebit manibus adipem hostiae et pectusculum cumque ambo oblata Domino consecrarit tradet sacerdoti*

"'He will have in hands *the* victim's fat and breast. And when each offering is consecrated to *the* Lord, he will hand them to *the* priest,

7:31 *qui adolebit adipem super altare pectusculum autem erit Aaron et filiorum eius*

who will burn *the* fat on *the* altar. But *the* breast will be for Aaron and his sons.

7:32 *armus quoque dexter de pacificorum hostiis cedet in primitias sacerdotis*

"'Likewise, *the* right forequarter of *the* peace offerings will fall as first fruits to *the* priest

7:33 *qui obtulerit sanguinem et adipem filiorum Aaron ipse habebit et armum dextrum in portione sua*

"'who offers *the* blood and fat, from Aaron's sons. He will have also *the* right forequarter as his portion.

7:34 *pectusculum enim elationis et armum separationis tuli a filiis Israhel de hostiis eorum pacificis et dedi Aaron sacerdoti ac filiis eius lege perpetua ab omni populo Israhel*

"'For I have taken *the* breast of exaltation and *the* forequarter of separation from Israel's children, from their peace offerings, and given *them* to Aaron *the* priest and his sons, *an* enduring law, from all Israel's people.'"

7:35 *haec est unctio Aaron et filiorum eius in caerimoniis Domini die qua obtulit eos Moses ut sacerdotio fungerentur*

This is Aaron and his sons' anointing in *the* Lord's ceremonies on *the* day which Moses offered them, so they could carry out priestly duties,

7:36 *et quae praecepit dari eis Dominus a filiis Israhel religione perpetua in generationibus suis*

and which *the* Lord commanded be given them from Israel's children, *a* perpetual rite in their generations.

7:37 *ista est lex holocausti et sacrificii pro peccato atque delicto et pro consecratione et pacificorum victimis*

This is *the* law of burnt offering and of *the* sacrifice for sin and *an* offense, and for consecration and for peace offerings,

7:38 *quas constituit Dominus Mosi in monte Sinai quando mandavit filiis Israhel ut offerrent oblationes suas Domino in deserto Sinai*

which *the* Lord appointed for Moses on Mount Sinai, when He commanded Israel's children that they offer *the* Lord sacrifices in *the* Sinai desert.

Aaron's Ordination

Leviticus 8:1 *locutusque est Dominus ad Mosen dicens*

And *the* Lord spoke to Moses, saying,

8:2 *tolle Aaron cum filiis suis vestes eorum et unctionis oleum vitulum pro peccato duos arietes canistrum cum azymis*

"Take Aaron with his sons, their vestments and anointing oil, *a* calf for sin, two rams, *a* basket with unleavened *bread,*

8:3 *et congregabis omnem coetum ad ostium tabernaculi*

"and you will gather *the* whole assembly at *the* tabernacle's opening."

8:4 *fecit Moses ut Dominus imperarat congregataque omni turba ante fores*

Moses did as *the* Lord had commanded. And, all *the* crowd gathered before *the* entrance,

8:5 *ait iste est sermo quem iussit Dominus fieri*

he said, "This is *the* word that *the* Lord commanded to be done."

Dressing Them for Ordination

8:6 *statimque obtulit Aaron et filios eius cumque lavisset eos*

And he immediately offered Aaron and his sons. And when he had washed them,

8:7 *vestivit pontificem subucula linea accingens eum balteo et induens tunica hyacinthina et desuper umerale inposuit*

he dressed *the* high priest in *the* linen underclothes, girding *the* shoulder piece on him, and dressed him with *the* violet tunic. And he placed *the* overlay above,

8:8 *quod adstringens cingulo aptavit rationali in quo erat doctrina et veritas*

stringing it by *a* belt. He fit *the* breastplate, in which was teaching and truth.

8:9 *cidarim quoque texit caput et super eam contra frontem posuit lamminam auream consecratam in sanctificationem sicut praeceperat ei Dominus*

He covered *the* head as well with *the* head-dress, and over it against *the* forehead he placed *the* consecrated gold plate for sanctification, as *the* Lord had commanded him.

8:10 *tulit et unctionis oleum quo levit tabernaculum cum omni supellectili sua*

He also took *the* anointing oil, with which he sealed *the* tabernacle with all its furnishings.

8:11 *cumque sanctificans aspersisset altare septem vicibus unxit illud et omnia vasa eius labrumque cum basi sua sanctificavit oleo*

And when, sanctifying, he had sprinkled *the* altar seven times, he anointed it and all its vessels. He sanctified with oil *the* basin with its base,

8:12 *quod fundens super caput Aaron unxit eum et consecravit*

pouring which over Aaron's head, he anointed him and made him holy.

8:13 *filios quoque eius oblatos vestivit tunicis lineis et cinxit balteo inposuitque mitras ut iusserat Dominus*

His sons likewise offered, he dressed *them* in linen tunics and tied *the* shoulder piece. And he placed head pieces *on them*, as *the* Lord had commanded.

The Sacrificial Calf
8:14 *obtulit et vitulum pro peccato cumque super caput eius posuissent*

Aaron et filii eius manus suas

He also offered *the* calf for sin and, when Aaron and his sons had placed their hands on its head,

8:15 *immolavit eum hauriens sanguinem et tincto digito tetigit cornua altaris per gyrum quo expiato et sanctificato fudit reliquum sanguinem ad fundamenta eius*

he killed it, drawing *the* blood. And, dipping *a* finger, he touched *the* altar's horns around, which, atoned for and sanctified, he poured out *the* rest of *the* blood at its base.

8:16 *adipem autem qui erat super vitalia et reticulum iecoris duosque renunculos cum arvinulis suis adolevit super altare*

But he burned on *the* altar *the* fat which was over *the* vitals, and *the* liver's covering, and *the* smaller organs with their suet –

8:17 *vitulum cum pelle carnibus et fimo cremans extra castra sicut praeceperat Dominus*

burning *the* calf with its hide, meat, and excrement outside *the* camps, as *the* Lord had commanded.

The Sacrificial Rams
8:18 *obtulit et arietem in holocaustum super cuius caput cum inposuissent Aaron et filii eius*

manus suas

He also offered *the* ram as *a* burnt offering, over whose head, when Aaron and his sons had laid on their hands,

8:19 *immolavit eum et fudit sanguinem eius per altaris circuitum*

he killed it and poured its blood around *the* altar.

8:20 *ipsumque arietem in frusta concidens caput eius et artus et adipem adolevit igni*

And, cutting *the* same ram into pieces, he burned its head and limbs and fat in fire,

8:21 *lotis prius intestinis et pedibus totumque simul arietem incendit super altare eo quod esset holocaustum suavissimi odoris Domino sicut praeceperat ei*

first washing *the* intestines and feet. And he burned *the* whole ram together on *the* altar, because it was *a* holocaust of smoothest odor to *the* Lord, as He had commanded him.

8:22 *obtulit et arietem secundum in consecrationem sacerdotum posueruntque super caput illius Aaron et filii eius manus suas*

He also offered *the* second ram in *the* consecration of *the* priests. And

Aaron and his sons laid their hands on its head,

8:23 *quem cum immolasset Moses sumens de sanguine tetigit extremum auriculae dextrae Aaron et pollicem manus eius dextrae similiter et pedis*

which, when Moses had killed it, taking some of *the* blood, he touched *the* tip of Aaron's right ear and *the* thumb of his right hand, and *the* same also of his foot.

8:24 *obtulit et filios Aaron cumque de sanguine arietis immolati tetigisset extremum auriculae singulorum dextrae et pollices manus ac pedis dextri reliquum fudit super altare per circuitum*

He also offered Aaron's sons, and when, from *the* blood of *the* offered ram, he had touched *the* tip of each one's right ear and *the* thumb of his right hand and foot, he poured *the* rest around over *the* altar.

8:25 *adipem vero et caudam omnemque pinguedinem quae operit intestina reticulumque iecoris et duos renes cum adipibus suis et armo dextro separavit*

Indeed, he separated *the* fat and *the* tail and all *the* fatness that covers *the* intestines, *the* liver's covering and *the* kidneys with their fat, and *the* right forequarter.

8:26 *tollens autem de canistro azymorum quod erat coram Domino panem absque fermento et collyridam conspersam oleo laganumque posuit super adipes et armum dextrum*

But taking from *the* basket of unleavened bread that was before *the* Lord, bread without yeast, and rolls sprinkled with oil, and cakes, he placed *them* on *the* fat and *the* right forequarter,

8:27 *tradens simul omnia Aaron et filiis eius qui postquam levaverunt ea coram Domino*

handing all together to Aaron and his sons, who afterwards lifted them before *the* Lord.

8:28 *rursum suscepta de manibus eorum adolevit super altare holocausti eo quod consecrationis esset oblatio in odorem suavitatis sacrificii Domini*

Receiving them again from their hands, he burned them on *the* altar of burnt offerings, because it was *the* offering of consecration, as *the* smoothest odor of *the* Lord's sacrifice.

8:29 *tulit et pectusculum elevans illud coram Domino de ariete consecrationis in partem suam sicut praeceperat ei Dominus*

He took also *the* breast from *the* ram of consecration as his portion, lifting it before *the* Lord, as *the* Lord had commanded him.

8:30 *adsumensque unguentum et sanguinem qui erat in altari aspersit super Aaron et vestimenta eius et super filios illius ac vestes eorum*

And, taking *the* anointing oil and *the* blood which was on *the* altar, he sprinkled it over Aaron and his vestments and over his sons and their vestments.

Seven Days of Consecration

8:31 *cumque sanctificasset eos in vestitu suo praecepit eis dicens coquite carnes ante fores tabernaculi et ibi comedite eas panes quoque consecrationis edite qui positi sunt in canistro sicut praecepit mihi dicens Aaron et filii eius comedent eos*

And when he had sanctified them in their vestment, he commanded them, saying, "Cook *the* meat before *the* tabernacle's entrance and eat it there! Likewise, eat *the* loaves of consecration which are placed in *the* basket, as He commanded me, saying 'Aaron and his sons will eat it.'

8:32 *quicquid autem reliquum fuerit de carne et panibus ignis absumet*

"But whatever is left from *the* meat and bread will be taken away by fire.

8:33 *de ostio quoque tabernaculi non exibitis septem diebus usque ad diem quo conplebitur tempus consecrationis vestrae septem enim diebus finitur consecratio*

"Likewise, you will not go out of *the* tabernacle's door for seven days, until *the* day in which *the* time of your consecration will be completed. For *the* consecration is finished in seven days,

8:34 *sicut et inpraesentiarum factum est ut ritus sacrificii conpleretur*

"as also is done in *the* present circumstances, so *the* sacrificial rite may be completed.

8:35 *die ac nocte manebitis in tabernaculo observantes custodias Domini ne moriamini sic enim mihi praeceptum est*

"You will remain day and night, keeping *the* Lord's watches, so you will not die – for so He has commanded me."

8:36 *feceruntque Aaron et filii eius cuncta quae locutus est Dominus per manum Mosi*

And Aaron and his sons did all that *the* Lord had spoken through Moses' hand.

Preparation for the Lord's Appearance

Leviticus 9:1 *facto autem octavo die vocavit Moses Aaron et filios eius ac maiores natu Israhel dixitque ad Aaron*

But *the* eighth day come, Moses called Aaron and his sons and Israel's older born. And he said to Aaron,

9:2 *tolle de armento vitulum pro peccato et arietem in holocaustum utrumque inmaculatos et offer illos coram Domino*

"Take from *the* herd *a* calf for sin and *a* ram as *a* burnt offering, both without defect, and offer them before *the* Lord!

9:3 *et ad filios Israhel loqueris tollite hircum pro peccato et vitulum atque agnum anniculos et sine macula in holocaustum*

"And you will say to Israel's children, 'Take *a* he-goat for sin and *a* calf and *a* lamb, yearlings and without defect, as *a* burnt offering,

9:4 *bovem et arietem pro pacificis et immolate eos coram Domino in sacrificio singulorum similam oleo conspersam offerentes hodie enim Dominus apparebit vobis*

"'*an* ox and ram for peace offerings, and kill them before *the* Lord as *a* sacrifice, offering wheat flour sprinkled with oil with each one. For today *the* Lord will appear to you.'"

9:5 *tulerunt ergo cuncta quae iusserat Moses ad ostium tabernaculi ubi cum omnis staret multitudo*

Therefore, they took all that Moses had commanded to *the* tabernacle's entrance where, when *the* whole multitude stood,

9:6 *ait Moses iste est sermo quem praecepit Dominus facite et apparebit vobis gloria eius*

Moses said, "This is *the* work which *the* Lord commanded. Do *it*, and His glory will appear to you!"

9:7 *dixit et ad Aaron accede ad altare et immola pro peccato tuo offer holocaustum et deprecare pro te et pro populo cumque mactaveris hostiam populi ora pro eo sicut praecepit Dominus*

He said to Aaron, "Approach *the* altar and sacrifice for your sin! Offer *a* burnt offering and plead for you and for *the* people! And when you have killed *the* people's victim, pray for him as *the* Lord has commanded!

9:8 *statimque Aaron accedens ad altare immolavit vitulum pro peccato suo*

And Aaron, immediately coming near *the* altar, killed *the* calf for his sin,

9:9 *cuius sanguinem obtulerunt ei filii sui in quo tinguens digitum tetigit cornua altaris et fudit residuum ad basim eius*

whose blood his sons offered him. Dipping *a* finger in it, he touched *the* altar's horns and poured *the* rest at its base.

9:10 *adipemque et renunculos ac reticulum iecoris quae sunt pro peccato adolevit super altare sicut praeceperat Dominus Mosi*

And he burned on *the* altar *the* fat, and kidneys, and *the* liver's covering, which are for sin, as *the* Lord had commanded Moses.

9:11 *carnes vero et pellem eius extra castra conbusit igni*

But he burned its flesh and hide with fire outside *the* camps.

9:12 *immolavit et holocausti victimam obtuleruntque ei filii sui sanguinem eius quem fudit per altaris circuitum*

He also killed *the* burnt offering's victim. And his sons offered him its blood, which he poured around *the* altar,

9:13 *ipsam etiam hostiam in frusta concisam cum capite et membris singulis obtulerunt quae omnia super altare cremavit igni*

cutting *the* same victim also in pieces. They offered each of its members with its head, all of which he burned with fire on *the* altar,

9:14 *lotis prius aqua intestinis et pedibus*

after washing *the* intestines and feet with water.

9:15 *et pro peccato populi offerens mactavit hircum expiatoque altari*

And offering for *the* people's sin, he killed *the* he-goat.   And, *the* altar atoned for,

9:16 *fecit holocaustum*

he made *the* burnt offering,

9:17 *addens in sacrificio libamenta quae pariter offeruntur et adolens ea super altare absque caerimoniis holocausti matutini*

adding in sacrifice *the* libations which are offered together, and burning them on *the* altar, apart from *the* ceremonies of *the* morning's holocaust.

9:18 *immolavit et bovem atque arietem hostias pacificas populi obtuleruntque ei filii sui sanguinem quem fudit super altare in circuitu*

He killed also *the* ox and ram, *the* people's peace victims. And his sons

offered him *the* blood, which he poured out above, around *the* altar

9:19 *adipes autem bovis et caudam arietis renunculosque cum adipibus suis et reticulum iecoris*

But *the* ox's fat and *the* ram's tail and kidneys, with its fat and *the* liver's covering,

9:20 *posuerunt super pectora cumque cremati essent adipes in altari*

they placed on *the* breasts.   And when *the* fat was cremated on *the* altar,

9:21 *pectora eorum et armos dextros separavit Aaron elevans coram Domino sicut praeceperat Moses*

Aaron separated their breasts and right forequarters, lifting *them* before *the* Lord as Moses had commanded.

9:22 *et tendens manum contra populum benedixit eis sicque conpletis hostiis pro peccato et holocaustis et pacificis descendit*

And, stretching *his* hands toward *the* people, he blessed them. And thus completing *the* offerings for sin, and *the* holocausts, and *the* peace offerings, he came down.

9:23 *ingressi autem Moses et Aaron*

tabernaculum testimonii et deinceps egressi benedixerunt populo apparuitque gloria Domini omni multitudini

But Moses and Aaron, going into testimony's tabernacle and afterwards coming out, blessed *the* people. And *the* Lord's glory appeared to all *the* multitude.

9:24 *et ecce egressus ignis a Domino devoravit holocaustum et adipes qui erant super altare quod cum vidissent turbae laudaverunt Dominum ruentes in facies suas*

And, look! Fire coming out from *the* Lord devoured *the* holocaust and *the* fat that were on *the* altar. When *the* crowd had seen that, they praised *the* Lord, falling on their faces.

Nadab and Abiu
Die Before the Lord

Leviticus 10:1 *arreptisque Nadab et Abiu filii Aaron turibulis posuerunt ignem et incensum desuper offerentes coram Domino ignem alienum quod eis praeceptum non erat*

And Nadab and Abiu, Aaron's sons, taking censers, placed fire inside and incense above, offering before *the* Lord alien fire, which had not been commanded them.

10:2 *egressusque ignis a Domino devoravit eos et mortui sunt coram Domino*

And fire coming out from *the* Lord devoured them and they died before *the* Lord.

10:3 *dixitque Moses ad Aaron hoc est quod locutus est Dominus sanctificabor in his qui adpropinquant mihi et in conspectu omnis populi glorificabor quod audiens tacuit Aaron*

And Moses said to Aaron, "This is what *the* Lord has said: 'I will be sanctified in those who come near Me, and I will be glorified in all *the* people's sight.'"

Hearing this, Aaron was silent.

10:4 *vocatis autem Moses Misahel et Elsaphan filios Ozihel patrui*

Aaron ait ad eos ite et colligite fratres vestros de conspectu sanctuarii et asportate extra castra

But Moses, calling Misael and Elsaphan, sons of Oziel, Aaron's uncle, said to them, "Go and collect your brothers from *the* sanctuary's sight, and carry *them* outside *the* camps."

10:5 *confestimque pergentes tulerunt eos sicut iacebant vestitos lineis tunicis et eiecerunt foras ut sibi fuerat imperatum*

And going quickly, they took them as they fell, dressed in *the* linen tunics, and put them outside as had been commanded them.

10:6 *locutus est Moses ad Aaron et ad Eleazar atque Ithamar filios eius capita vestra nolite nudare et vestimenta nolite scindere ne forte moriamini et super omnem coetum oriatur indignatio fratres vestri et omnis domus Israhel plangant incendium quod Dominus suscitavit*

Moses said to Aaron and to Eleazar and Ithamar his sons, "Don't uncover your heads and don't tear your garments, unless perhaps you die, and indignation rise over all *the* assembly! Let your brothers and all Israel's house grieve over *the* fire which *the* Lord aroused!

10:7 *vos autem non egredimini fores*

tabernaculi alioquin peribitis oleum quippe sanctae unctionis est super vos qui fecerunt omnia iuxta praeceptum Mosi

"But you will not go outside *the* tabernacle. Otherwise, you will die, for *the* holy anointing oil is on you."

They did all according to Moses' commandment.

No Drunkenness in the Sanctuary

10:8 *dixit quoque Dominus ad Aaron*

The Lord also said to Aaron,

10:9 *vinum et omne quod inebriare potest non bibetis tu et filii tui quando intratis tabernaculum testimonii ne moriamini quia praeceptum est sempiternum in generationes vestras*

"You and your sons will not drink wine and all that can make drunk when you enter testimony's tabernacle, so you won't die, because it is commanded forever in your generations –

10:10 *et ut habeatis scientiam discernendi inter sanctum et profanum inter pollutum et mundum*

"and so you may have understanding to discern between holy and profane, between polluted and clean,

10:11 *doceatisque filios Israhel omnia legitima mea quae locutus est Dominus ad eos per manum Mosi*

"and you may teach Israel's children all My laws, which *the* Lord has spoken to them through Moses' hand."

Moses Commands
the Priests To Eat

10:12 *locutusque est Moses ad Aaron et ad Eleazar atque Ithamar filios eius qui residui erant tollite sacrificium quod remansit de oblatione Domini et comedite illud absque fermento iuxta altare quia sanctum sanctorum est*

Moses said to Aaron and to Eleazar and Ithamar, his sons who were left, "Take *the* sacrifice that remains from *the* Lord's offering, and eat it without yeast beside *the* altar, because *it* is holy of holies!

10:13 *comedetis autem in loco sancto quod datum est tibi et filiis tuis de oblationibus Domini sicut praeceptum est mihi*

"But you and your sons will eat what is given you from *the* Lord's offerings in *the* holy place, as was commanded me.

10:14 *pectusculum quoque quod oblatum est et armum qui separatus est edetis in loco mundissimo tu et filii tui ac filiae tuae tecum tibi enim*

ac liberis tuis reposita sunt de hostiis salutaribus filiorum Israhel

"Likewise, you and your sons and your daughters with you will eat *the* breast that is offered and *the* forequarter that is separated in *a* most clean place, for they are reserved for you and your children from *the* offerings for Israel's children's well-being –

10:15 *eo quod armum et pectus et adipes qui cremantur in altari elevaverint coram Domino et pertineant ad te et ad filios tuos lege perpetua sicut praecepit Dominus*

"because they have lifted up before *the* Lord *the* forequarter and breast and *the* fat portions which are burned on *the* altar, and they belong to you and your sons by *a* perpetual law, as *the* Lord commanded.

Aaron's Grief

10:16 *inter haec hircum qui oblatus fuerat pro peccato cum quaereret Moses exustum repperit iratusque contra Eleazar et Ithamar filios Aaron qui remanserant ait*

"When Moses sought among these *the* he-goat that was offered for sin, he found *it* burned up. And, angry with Eleazar and Ithamar, Aaron's sons who still lived, he said,

10:17 *cur non comedistis hostiam pro peccato in loco sancto quae*

sancta sanctorum est et data vobis ut portetis iniquitatem multitudinis et rogetis pro ea in conspectu Domini

"Why didn't you eat *the* offering for sin in *the* holy place? *The offering* is holy of holies and given to you so you can take away *the* multitude's treachery and pray for them in *the* Lord's sight –

10:18 *praesertim cum de sanguine illius non sit inlatum intra sancta et comedere eam debueritis in sanctuario sicut praeceptum est mihi*

"especially when none of its blood has been brought inside *the* holy *places*, and you ought to have eaten it in *the* sanctuary, as was commanded me!"

10:19 *respondit Aaron oblata est hodie victima pro peccato et holocaustum coram Domino mihi autem accidit quod vides quomodo potui comedere eam aut placere Domino in caerimoniis mente lugubri*

Aaron answered, "*The* victim for sin was offered today and *the* burnt offering before *the* Lord. But you saw what happened to me. How could I eat or please *the* Lord in *the* ceremonies with *a* grieving mind?"

10:20 *quod cum audisset Moses recepit satisfactionem*

When Moses heard that, he accepted satisfaction.

Dietary Laws
Leviticus 11:1 *locutus est Dominus ad Mosen et Aaron dicens*

The Lord spoke to Moses and Aaron, saying,

Concerning Land Animals
11:2 *dicite filiis Israhel haec sunt animalia quae comedere debetis de cunctis animantibus terrae*

"Say to Israel's children, 'These are *the* animals which you must eat, from all *the* land's animals.

11:3 *omne quod habet divisam ungulam et ruminat in pecoribus comedetis*

"'You will eat all that has *a* divided hoof and chews cud among *the* animals.

11:4 *quicquid autem ruminat quidem et habet ungulam sed non dividit eam sicut camelus et cetera non comedetis illud et inter inmunda reputabitis*

"'But anything that chews cud, for instance, and has *a* hoof, yet doesn't divide it, like *the* camel and others, you will not eat it. And you will consider it among *the* unclean.

11:5 *chyrogryllius qui ruminat ungulamque non dividit inmundus est*

"'*A* coney, which chews cud and doesn't divide *the* hoof is unclean;

11:6 *lepus quoque nam et ipse ruminat sed ungulam non dividit*

"'*a* rabbit, as well, for it also chews cud but doesn't divide *the* hoof;

11:7 *et sus qui cum ungulam dividat non ruminat*

"'and swine, with *the* hoof divided, does not chew cud.

11:8 *horum carnibus non vescemini nec cadavera contingetis quia inmunda sunt vobis*

"'You will not eat of their flesh or touch their dead bodies, because they are unclean to you.

Concerning Fish
11:9 *haec sunt quae gignuntur in aquis et vesci licitum est omne quod habet pinnulas et squamas tam in mari quam in fluminibus et stagnis comedetis*

"'These are those giving birth in waters and which it is permitted to eat: everything that has fins and scales, whether in *the* sea or in rivers and ponds, you will eat.

11:10 *quicquid autem pinnulas et squamas non habet eorum quae in aquis moventur et vivunt abominabile vobis*

"'But whatever does not have fins and scales of those that move in waters and live *is* detestable to you,

11:11 *et execrandum erit carnes eorum non comedetis et morticina vitabitis*

"'and their flesh will be refused. You will not eat *them* and will avoid those that died of themselves.

11:12 *cuncta quae non habent pinnulas et squamas in aquis polluta erunt*

"'All that do not have fins and scales in *the* waters will be polluted.

Concerning Birds

11:13 *haec sunt quae de avibus comedere non debetis et vitanda sunt vobis aquilam et grypem et alietum*

"'These are those among birds you must not eat and are to be avoided by you: eagle and griffin and osprey;

11:14 *milvum ac vulturem iuxta genus suum*

"'kite and vulture, according to their species;

11:15 *et omne corvini generis in similitudinem suam*

"'and every species of crow, in its likeness;

11:16 *strutionem et noctuam et larum et accipitrem iuxta genus suum*

"'ostrich and owl and gull and hawk, according to their species;

11:17 *bubonem et mergulum et ibin*

"'horned owl and small gull and ibis;

11:18 *cycnum et onocrotalum et porphirionem*

"'swan and pelican and coot;

11:19 *erodionem et charadrion iuxta genus suum opupam quoque et vespertilionem*

"'heron and yellow charadrion, according to their species; hoopoe as well, and bat.

Among Insects

11:20 *omne de volucribus quod graditur super quattuor pedes abominabile erit vobis*

"'Everything among flying *things* that goes on four feet will be detestable to you.

11:21 *quicquid autem ambulat quidem super quattuor pedes sed habet longiora retro crura per quae salit super terram*

"'But whatever walks, of course, on four legs but has longer legs behind by which it jumps on *the* ground

11:22 *comedere debetis ut est brucus in genere suo et attacus atque ophiomachus ac lucusta singula iuxta genus suum*

"'you may eat, as is wingless locust and cricket and larger locust, each according to its species.

11:23 *quicquid autem ex volucribus quattuor tantum habet pedes execrabile erit vobis*

"'But whatever from flying *things* has only four feet will be detestable to you.

11:24 *et quicumque morticina eorum tetigerit polluetur et erit inmundus usque ad vesperum*

"'And anyone who touches their dead bodies will be polluted, and will be unclean until *the* evening.

11:25 *et si necesse fuerit ut portet quippiam horum mortuum lavabit vestimenta sua et inmundus erit usque ad solis occasum*

"'And if it is necessary that he carry any of their dead bodies, he will wash his clothes and will be unclean until sunset.

General Restrictions
11:26 *omne animal quod habet quidem ungulam sed non dividit eam*

nec ruminat inmundum erit et quicquid tetigerit illud contaminabitur

"'Each animal that has, of course, *a* hoof, but doesn't divide it, nor chews cud, will be unclean. And whoever touches it will be contaminated.

11:27 *quod ambulat super manus ex cunctis animantibus quae incedunt quadrupedia inmundum erit qui tetigerit morticina eorum polluetur usque ad vesperum*

"'What walks on hands from all animals that go on four legs will be unclean. Who touches their dead bodies will be polluted until evening.

11:28 *et qui portaverit huiuscemodi cadavera lavabit vestimenta sua et inmundus erit usque ad vesperum quia omnia haec inmunda sunt vobis*

"'And who carries such dead bodies will wash his clothes, and will be unclean until evening, because all these are unclean to you.

11:29 *hoc quoque inter polluta reputabitur de his quae moventur in terra mustela et mus et corcodillus singula iuxta genus suum*

"'This, likewise, will be considered among *the* polluted, from those that move on land: weasel and mouse and crocodile, each according to its species;

11:30 *migale et cameleon et stelio ac lacerta et talpa*

"'shrew and chameleon and gecko and lizard and mole.

11:31 *omnia haec inmunda sunt qui tetigerit morticina eorum inmundus erit usque ad vesperum*

"'All these are unclean. Who touches their dead bodies will be unclean until evening.

11:32 *et super quod ceciderit quicquam de morticinis eorum polluetur tam vas ligneum et vestimentum quam pelles et cilicia et in quocumque fit opus tinguentur aqua et polluta erunt usque ad vesperum et sic postea mundabuntur*

"'And anything on which their dead bodies fall will be polluted, whether *a* wooden vessel or clothing from hide or hair, or whatever in *which* work is done. They will be dipped in water and will be polluted until evening, and so afterwards will be made clean.

11:33 *vas autem fictile in quo horum quicquam intro ceciderit polluetur et idcirco frangendum est*

"'But *an* earthenware vessel in which anything from them may fall will be polluted, and therefore must be broken.

11:34 *omnis cibus quem comeditis*

si fusa fuerit super eum aqua inmundus erit et omne liquens quod bibitur de universo vase inmundum erit

"'Any food that you eat, if water is poured over it *from such a vessel*, will be unclean. And any liquid which is drunk from any *such* vessel will be unclean.

11:35 *et quicquid de morticinis istiusmodi ceciderit super illud inmundum erit sive clibani sive cytropodes destruentur et inmundi erunt*

"'And whatever dead things of this type should fall on will be unclean. Whether *an* oven or *a* cook pot, they will be destroyed and will be unclean.

11:36 *fontes vero et cisternae et omnis aquarum congregatio munda erit qui morticinum eorum tetigerit polluetur*

"'But springs and cisterns and every gathering of water will be clean.

"'Who touches their dead bodies will be polluted.

11:37 *si ceciderint super sementem non polluent eam*

"'If they should fall on *a* seed, they won't pollute it.

11:38 *sin autem quispiam aqua*

sementem perfuderit et postea morticinis tacta fuerit ilico polluetur

"'But if anyone should pour water over seed and afterwards *the seed* be touched by dead things, it will immediately be polluted.

11:39 *si mortuum fuerit animal quod licet vobis comedere qui cadaver eius tetigerit inmundus erit usque ad vesperum*

"'If *an* animal which is permitted for you to eat should die, who touches its body will be unclean until evening.

11:40 *et qui comederit ex eo quippiam sive portaverit lavabit vestimenta sua et inmundus erit usque ad vesperum*

"'And who eats from it or even carries it will wash his clothes and be unclean until evening.

Reptiles and Crawling Things
11:41 *omne quod reptat super terram abominabile erit nec adsumetur in cibum*

"'Everything that crawls on *the* ground will be detestable, nor be taken up as food.

11:42 *quicquid super pectus quadrupes graditur et multos habet pedes sive per humum trahitur non comedetis quia abominabile est*

"'Whatever goes on its chest by four legs, or has many feet, or goes through dirt, you will not eat, because *it* is detestable.

Summary
11:43 *nolite contaminare animas vestras nec tangatis quicquam eorum ne inmundi sitis*

"'Don't contaminate your souls or touch anything of theirs, so you not be unclean,

11:44 *ego enim sum Dominus Deus vester sancti estote quoniam et ego sanctus sum ne polluatis animas vestras in omni reptili quod movetur super terram*

"'for I am *the* Lord your God. Be holy, because I also am holy. Do not pollute your souls in any crawling *thing* that moves over *the* ground.

11:45 *ego sum Dominus qui eduxi vos de terra Aegypti ut essem vobis in Deum sancti eritis quia et ego sanctus sum*

"'I am *the* Lord, who led you from Egypt's land so I might be as God to you. You will be holy because I am holy.

11:46 *ista est lex animantium et volucrum et omnis animae viventis quae movetur in aqua et reptat in terra*

"'This is *the* law of animals and flying *things* and all living souls that move on water or crawl on land,

11:47 *ut differentias noveritis mundi et inmundi et sciatis quid comedere et quid respuere debeatis*

"'so you may know *the* difference between clean and unclean, and understand what to eat and what you must refuse.'"

Purification
After Childbirth

Leviticus 12:1 *locutus est Dominus ad Mosen dicens*

The Lord spoke to Moses, saying,

12:2 *loquere filiis Israhel et dices ad eos mulier si suscepto semine pepererit masculum inmunda erit septem diebus iuxta dies separationis menstruae*

"Speak to Israel's children, and you will say to them, 'If *a* woman, receiving seed, births *a* male, she will be unclean seven days according to *the* days of menstrual separation.

12:3 *et die octavo circumcidetur infantulus*

"'And *the* infant will be circumcised *the* eighth day.

12:4 *ipsa vero triginta tribus diebus manebit in sanguine purificationis suae omne sanctum non tanget nec ingredietur sanctuarium donec impleantur dies purificationis eius*

"'She indeed will remain in her blood purification thirty-three days. She will not touch anything holy or go into *the* sanctuary until her days of purification are completed.

12:5 *sin autem feminam pepererit inmunda erit duabus ebdomadibus iuxta ritum fluxus menstrui et* *sexaginta ac sex diebus manebit in sanguine purificationis suae*

"'But if she births *a* female, she will be unclean two weeks, according to *the* rite of menstrual flux. And she will remain sixty-six days in her purification's blood.

12:6 *cumque expleti fuerint dies purificationis eius pro filio sive pro filia deferet agnum anniculum in holocaustum et pullum columbae sive turturem pro peccato ad ostium tabernaculi testimonii et tradet sacerdoti*

"'And when her purification's days are completed, whether for son or for daughter, she will bring *a* yearling lamb as *a* burnt offering and *a* young pigeon or dove for sin to *the* entrance of testimony's tabernacle. And she will give it to *the* priest,

12:7 *qui offeret illa coram Domino et rogabit pro ea et sic mundabitur a profluvio sanguinis sui ista est lex parientis masculum ac feminam*

"'who will offer them before *the* Lord and pray for her. And so she will be cleansed from her flowing forth of blood. This is *the* law for birthing male and female.

12:8 *quod si non invenerit manus eius nec potuerit offerre agnum sumet duos turtures vel duos pullos columbae unum in holocaustum et*

alterum pro peccato orabitque pro ea sacerdos et sic mundabitur

But if her hand can't find or can't offer *a* lamb, she will take two doves or two young pigeons, one as *a* burnt offering and *the* other for sin. And *the* priest will pray for her and so she will be cleansed.

Laws of Leprosy
Leviticus 13:1 *locutus est Dominus ad Mosen et Aaron dicens*

The Lord spoke to Moses and Aaron, saying,

13:2 *homo in cuius carne et cute ortus fuerit diversus color sive pustula aut quasi lucens quippiam id est plaga leprae adducetur ad Aaron sacerdotem vel ad unum quemlibet filiorum eius*

"*A* man in whose flesh and skin *a* strange color rises, whether *an* inflamed sore or something like light, it is *the* plague of leprosy. He will be brought to Aaron *the* priest or to any of his sons,

13:3 *qui cum viderit lepram in cute et pilos in album mutatos colorem ipsamque speciem leprae humiliorem cute et carne reliqua plaga leprae est et ad arbitrium eius separabitur*

who, when he sees *the* leprosy in *the* skin, and *the* hairs turned *the* color white, and *the* same place of leprosy lower than *the* skin and remaining flesh, it is *the* plague of leprosy and, at his judgment, he will be separated.

13:4 *sin autem lucens candor fuerit in cute nec humilior carne reliqua et pili coloris pristini recludet eum sacerdos septem diebus*

"But if *the* whiteness is shining in *the*

skin, nor lower than *the* rest of the flesh, and *the* hair color as at first, *the* priest will close him up seven days.

13:5 *et considerabit die septimo et siquidem lepra ultra non creverit nec transierit in cute priores terminos rursum includet eum septem diebus aliis*

"And he will consider on *the* seventh day, and if, accordingly, *the* leprosy has not grown further or crossed *its* prior limits in *the* skin, he will close him again seven further days.

13:6 *et die septimo contemplabitur si obscurior fuerit lepra et non creverit in cute mundabit eum quia scabies est lavabitque homo vestimenta sua et mundus erit*

"And he will examine on *the* seventh day. If *the* leprosy is darker and has not grown in *the* skin, he will declare him clean, because it is *the* itch. And *the* man will wash his clothes and will be clean.

13:7 *quod si postquam a sacerdote visus est et redditus munditiae iterum lepra creverit adducetur ad eum*

"But if, after he was seen by the priest and cleanness returned, *the* leprosy again grows, he will be brought to him

13:8 *et inmunditiae condemnabitur*

"and will be condemned as unclean.

13:9 *plaga leprae si fuerit in homine adducetur ad sacerdotem*

"If *the* plague of leprosy be in *a* man, he will be led to *the* priest.

13:10 *et videbit eum cumque color albus in cute fuerit et capillorum mutarit aspectum ipsa quoque caro viva apparuerit*

"And he will see him. And if *a* white color is in *the* skin and *the* hairs' aspect changed, likewise its flesh appears alive,

13:11 *lepra vetustissima iudicabitur atque inolita cuti contaminabit itaque eum sacerdos et non recludet quia perspicue inmunditia est*

it will be judged as *a* chronic leprosy and grown into *the* skin. So *the* priest will declare him contaminated and not close him in, because he is clearly unclean.

13:12 *sin autem effloruerit discurrens lepra in cute et operuerit omnem carnem a capite usque ad pedes quicquid sub aspectu oculorum cadit*

"But if *the* leprosy flourishes in *the* skin, running in different directions, and covers all *the* flesh, from *the* head even to *the* feet – whatever falls beneath *the* eyes' sight –

13:13 *considerabit eum sacerdos et teneri lepra mundissima iudicabit eo quod omnis in candorem versa sit et idcirco homo mundus erit*

"*the* priest will look at him, and will judge him to have *the* leprosy most clean, because everything is turned into whiteness. And therefore *the* man will be clean.

13:14 *quando vero caro vivens in eo apparuerit*

"When, indeed, living flesh appears in him,

13:15 *tunc sacerdotis iudicio polluetur et inter inmundos reputabitur caro enim viva si lepra aspergatur inmunda est*

"then, *the* priest judging, he will be polluted and will be considered among *the* unclean, for living flesh, if leprosy is scattered *in it*, is unclean.

13:16 *quod si rursum versa fuerit in alborem et totum hominem operuerit*

"But if again it is turned into whiteness, and covers *the* whole man,

13:17 *considerabit eum sacerdos et mundum esse decernet*

"*the* priest will look at him and discern *him* to be clean.

13:18 *caro et cutis in qua ulcus*

natum est et sanatum

"Flesh and skin in which *a* sore came forth and healed,

13:19 *et in loco ulceris cicatrix apparuerit alba sive subrufa adducetur homo ad sacerdotem*

"and in *the* sore's place *a* scar appeared, whether white or somewhat red, *the* man will be led to *the* priest,

13:20 *qui cum viderit locum leprae humiliorem carne reliqua et pilos versos in candorem contaminabit eum plaga enim leprae orta est in ulcere*

"who, when he sees *the* leprous place lower than *the* surrounding flesh and *the* hairs turned white, he will declare him contaminated, for *the* plague of leprosy has risen in *the* sore.

13:21 *quod si pilus coloris est pristini et cicatrix subobscura et vicina carne non est humilior recludet eum septem diebus*

"But if *the* hair color is as before, and *the* scar somewhat obscure, and it isn't lower than nearby flesh, he will close him up seven days.

13:22 *et siquidem creverit adiudicabit eum leprae*

"And if, accordingly, it grows, he will

judge him leprous.

13:23 *sin autem steterit in loco suo ulceris est cicatrix et homo mundus erit*

"But if *a* scar stands in *the* sore's place, *the* man will be clean.

13:24 *caro et cutis quam ignis exuserit et sanata albam sive rufam habuerit cicatricem*

"Skin and flesh which fire has burned and, healed, has *a* scar – whether white or red –

13:25 *considerabit eam sacerdos et ecce versa est in alborem et locus eius reliqua cute humilior contaminabit eum quia plaga leprae in cicatrice orta est*

"*the* priest will consider him, and, look, its place has turned white and is lower than *the* surrounding skin, he will declare him contaminated, because *the* plague of leprosy has risen in *the* scar.

13:26 *quod si pilorum color non fuerit inmutatus nec humilior plaga carne reliqua et ipsa leprae species fuerit subobscura recludet eum septem diebus*

"But if *the* hair color has not changed, and *the* diseased place is not lower than *the* surrounding flesh, and *the* appearance of *the* leprosy itself is somewhat obscure, he will close him in for seven days.

13:27 *et die septimo contemplabitur si creverit in cute lepra contaminabit eum*

and he will be examined on *the* seventh day. If *the* leprosy has grown in *the* skin, he will declare him contaminated.

13:28 *sin autem in loco suo candor steterit non satis clarus plaga conbustionis est et idcirco mundabitur quia cicatrix est conbusturae*

"But if whiteness stands in *the* place, not too clear, it is *a* sore of burning. And therefore he will be clean, because it is *a* burn scar.

13:29 *vir sive mulier in cuius capite vel barba germinarit lepra videbit eos sacerdos*

"*The* priest will examine them in whose head or beard leprosy springs up, whether man or woman.

13:30 *et siquidem humilior fuerit locus carne reliqua et capillus flavus solitoque subtilior contaminabit eos quia lepra capitis ac barbae est*

"And if, accordingly, *the* place is lower than *the* rest of *the* flesh and *the* hair is paler than usual, he will declare them contaminated, because

it is leprosy of *the* head or beard.

13:31 *sin autem viderit et locum maculae aequalem vicinae carni et capillum nigrum recludet eos septem diebus*

"But if he sees *the* place of *the* spot *the* same as *the* nearby flesh and *the* hair black, he will close them in seven days.

13:32 *et die septimo intuebitur si non creverit macula et capillus sui coloris est et locus plagae carni reliquae aequalis*

"On the seventh day he will consider. If *the* spot hasn't grown and its hair is *the* same color, and *the* place of *the* diseased flesh remains *the* same,

13:33 *radetur homo absque loco maculae et includetur septem diebus aliis*

"*the* man will be shaved away from *the* place of *the* spot and closed in seven more days.

13:34 *si die septimo visa fuerit stetisse plaga in loco suo nec humilior carne reliqua mundabit eum lotisque vestibus mundus erit*

"If on *the* seventh day it is seen that *the* wound has stayed in its place, nor is *it* lower than *the* remaining flesh, he will declare him clean. And, washing his clothes, he will be clean.

13:35 *sin autem post emundationem rursus creverit macula in cute*

"But if, after being declared clean, *the* spot again should grow in *the* skin,

13:36 *non quaeret amplius utrum capillus in flavum colorem sit commutatus quia aperte inmundus est*

"he will not seek further *that* other hair be changed into *a* paler color, because clearly he is unclean.

13:37 *porro si steterit macula et capilli nigri fuerint noverit hominem esse sanatum et confidenter eum pronuntiet mundum*

"Afterwards, if *the* spot stands and *the* hairs are black, *the* man will be known to be healthy, and he may confidently pronounce him clean.

13:38 *vir et mulier in cuius cute candor apparuerit*

"A man or woman in whose skin whiteness appears,

13:39 *intuebitur eos sacerdos si deprehenderit subobscurum alborem lucere in cute sciat non esse lepram sed maculam coloris candidi et hominem mundum*

"*the* priest will examine them. If he should find *a* shining of *a* somewhat obscure whiteness in *the* skin, he will know that it isn't leprous, but *a* spot of light color, and *the* man clean.

13:40 *vir de cuius capite capilli fluunt calvus ac mundus est*

"*A* man from whose head hair falls is bald and clean.

13:41 *et si a fronte ceciderint pili recalvaster et mundus est*

"And if hair should fall from his forehead, he is bald in front and clean.

13:42 *sin autem in calvitio sive in recalvatione albus vel rufus color fuerit exortus*

"But if, whether in baldness or being bald in front, a white or red color should come up,

13:43 *et hoc sacerdos viderit condemnabit eum haut dubiae leprae quae orta est in calvitio*

"and *the* priest sees this, he will condemn him without doubt as leprous, what came forth in baldness.

13:44 *quicumque ergo maculatus fuerit lepra et separatus ad arbitrium sacerdotis*

"And whoever, therefore, will be spotted by leprosy and separated at the priest's judgment,

13:45 *habebit vestimenta dissuta caput nudum os veste contectum contaminatum ac sordidum se clamabit*

"will have *an* unstitched garment, head uncovered, mouth covered, *the* contamination covered up, and will cry out *that* he is unclean.

13:46 *omni tempore quo leprosus est et inmundus solus habitabit extra castra*

"All *the* time that he is leprous and unclean, he will live alone outside *the* camps.

13:47 *vestis lanea sive linea quae lepram habuerit*

"*A* garment, whether woollen or linen, that has leprosy,

13:48 *in stamine atque subtemine aut certe pellis vel quicquid ex pelle confectum est*

"in warp or woof or, of course, hide, or anything that is made from hide,

13:49 *si alba aut rufa macula fuerit infecta lepra reputabitur ostendeturque sacerdoti*

"if it has *a* white or red spot, it will be considered infected with leprosy, and will be shown to *the* priest,

13:50 *qui consideratam recludet*

septem diebus

"who, having considered *it*, will close *it* in for seven days.

13:51 *et die septimo rursus aspiciens si crevisse deprehenderit lepra perseverans est pollutum iudicabit vestimentum et omne in quo fuerit inventa*

"And *the* seventh day, looking again, if he finds it to have grown, *the* leprosy is continuing. He will judge *the* garment and all that was found in it polluted.

13:52 *et idcirco conburetur flammis*

"And therefore it will be burned in flames.

13:53 *quod si eam viderit non crevisse*

"But if he sees it not to have grown,

13:54 *praecipiet et lavabunt id in quo lepra est recludetque illud septem diebus aliis*

"he will command and they will wash that in which *the* leprosy was. And he will close it in seven days more.

13:55 *et cum viderit faciem quidem pristinam non reversam nec tamen crevisse lepram inmundum iudicabit et igne conburet eo quod infusa sit in superficie vestimenti vel per totum* *lepra*

"And when he sees its appearance, indeed, not returned as before, nor yet *the* leprosy having increased, he will judge it unclean and it will be burned with fire, because it is permeated by leprosy, either in *the* garment's surface or throughout.

13:56 *sin autem obscurior fuerit locus leprae postquam vestis est lota abrumpet eum et a solido dividet*

"But if *the* leprous spot is less clear after *the* garment is washed, he will tear it and divide it from *the* rest.

13:57 *quod si ultra apparuerit in his locis quae prius inmaculata erant lepra volatilis et vaga debet igne conburi*

"But if it should appear further in those places which were spotless before, *it is a* volatile and roving leprosy. It must be burned with fire.

13:58 *si cessaverit lavabit ea quae pura sunt secundo et munda erunt*

"If it should cease, he will wash what *parts* are pure, and it will be clean."

13:59 *ista est lex leprae vestimenti lanei et linei staminis atque subteminis omnisque supellectilis pelliciae quomodo mundari debeat vel contaminari*

This is *the* law of leprous garments, woollen and linen, warp and woof, and all furnishings of hide, how they must be clean or contaminated.

Offerings for
a Cleansed Leper

Leviticus 14:1 *locutusque est Dominus ad Mosen dicens*

And *the* Lord spoke to Moses, saying,

14:2 *hic est ritus leprosi quando mundandus est adducetur ad sacerdotem*

"This is *the* leper's ritual when he is to be made clean. He will be led to *the* priest,

14:3 *qui egressus e castris cum invenerit lepram esse mundatam*

who, coming out from *the* camps, when he finds *the* leprosy to be cleansed,

14:4 *praecipiet ei qui purificatur ut offerat pro se duos passeres vivos quos vesci licitum est et lignum cedrinum vermiculumque et hysopum*

"he will command *the* one who may be purified that he offer for himself two live sparrows, which it is lawful to eat, and cedar wood, and violet *thread*, and hyssop.

14:5 *et unum e passeribus immolari iubebit in vase fictili super aquas viventes*

"And he will command one of *the* sparrows to be killed in *an* earthenware vessel, over living waters.

14:6 *alium autem vivum cum ligno cedrino et cocco et hysopo tinguet in sanguine passeris immolati*

"But he will dip *the* other *bird* alive, with *the* cedar wood and scarlet *thread* and hyssop, in *the* blood of *the* offered sparrow,

14:7 *quo asperget illum qui mundandus est septies ut iure purgetur et dimittet passerem vivum ut in agrum avolet*

"by which he will sprinkle him who will be made clean seven times, so he may be purged lawfully. And he will free *the* live sparrow, so it may fly into *the* field.

14:8 *cumque laverit homo vestimenta sua radet omnes pilos corporis et lavabitur aqua purificatusque ingredietur castra ita dumtaxat ut maneat extra tabernaculum suum septem diebus*

"And when *the* man has washed his clothes, he will shave all his body hair and will wash with *the* water of purification. And he will go into *the* camp to this extent: that he remains outside his tent for seven days.

14:9 *et die septimo radat capillos capitis barbamque et supercilia ac totius corporis pilos et lotis rursum* *vestibus et corpore*

"And *the* seventh day, he will shave *the* hair of his head and beard and eyebrows, and all *the* body's hair. And having washed clothes and body again,

14:10 *die octavo adsumet duos agnos inmaculatos et ovem anniculam absque macula et tres decimas similae in sacrificium quae conspersa sit oleo et seorsum olei sextarium*

"*the* eighth day he will take up two lambs without defect, and *a* yearling ewe without spot, and three tenths of fine flour in sacrifice, which is sprinkled with oil, and *a* sextarium of oil separately.

14:11 *cumque sacerdos purificans hominem statuerit eum et haec omnia coram Domino in ostio tabernaculi testimonii*

"And when *the* priest purifying *the* man stands him and all of these before *the* Lord, in *the* entrance of testimony's tabernacle,

14:12 *tollet agnum et offeret eum pro delicto oleique sextarium et oblatis ante Dominum omnibus*

"he will take *the* lamb and offer him for sin, and *the* sextarium of oil. And, offering all before *the* Lord,

14:13 *immolabit agnum ubi immolari solet hostia pro peccato et holocaustum id est in loco sancto sicut enim pro peccato ita et pro delicto ad sacerdotem pertinet hostia sancta sanctorum est*

"he will kill *the* lamb where victims are customarily offered for sin and holocaust – that is, in *the* holy place – for as for sin so also for offense, *the* victim belongs to *the* priest. *It* is holy of holies.

14:14 *adsumensque sacerdos de sanguine hostiae quae immolata est pro delicto ponet super extremum auriculae dextrae eius qui mundatur et super pollices manus dextrae et pedis*

"And *the* priest, taking up some of *the* victim's blood that was offered for offense, will put it on *the* earlobe of his right ear who was made clean, and on *the* thumbs of his right hand and foot.

14:15 *et de olei sextario mittet in manum suam sinistram*

"And he will pour some of *the* sextarium of oil in his left hand,

14:16 *tinguetque digitum dextrum in eo et asperget septies contra Dominum*

"and he will touch *the* right finger in it and sprinkle seven times toward *the* Lord.

14:17 *quod autem reliquum est olei in leva manu fundet super extremum auriculae dextrae eius qui mundatur et super pollices manus ac pedis dextri et super sanguinem qui fusus est pro delicto*

"But what is left from *the* oil he will pour out in *a* lifted hand over his right earlobe who was cleansed, and over *the* thumbs of his right hand and foot, and over *the* blood that was poured out for offense,

14:18 *et super caput eius*

"and over his head.

14:19 *rogabitque pro eo coram Domino et faciet sacrificium pro peccato tunc immolabit holocaustum*

"And he will pray for him before *the* Lord, and will make *a* sacrifice for sin. Then he will kill *the* burnt offering.

14:20 *et ponet illud in altari cum libamentis suis et homo rite mundabitur*

"And he will put it on *the* altar with its libations, and *the* man will be made clean by *the* rite.

Provision for the Poor
14:21 *quod si pauper est et non potest manus eius invenire quae*

dicta sunt adsumet agnum pro delicto ad oblationem ut roget pro eo sacerdos decimamque partem similae conspersae oleo in sacrificium et olei sextarium

"But if he is poor and his hand can't find those *things* that are commanded, he will take up *a* lamb for sin as *an* offering, so *the* priest will pray for him, and *a* tenth portion of flour sprinkled with oil as *a* sacrifice, and *a* sextarium of oil,

14:22 *duosque turtures sive duos pullos columbae quorum sit unus pro peccato et alter in holocaustum*

"and two doves or two young pigeons, one of which is for sin and *the* other as *a* burnt offering.

14:23 *offeretque ea die octavo purificationis suae sacerdoti ad ostium tabernaculi testimonii coram Domino*

"And he will offer them to *the* priest *the* eighth day of his purification at *the* door of testimony's tabernacle, before *the* Lord.

14:24 *qui suscipiens agnum pro delicto et sextarium olei levabit simul*

"*The priest,* taking *the* lamb for offense and *the* sextarium of oil, will lift them together

14:25 *immolatoque agno de sanguine eius ponet super extremum auriculae dextrae illius qui mundatur et super pollices manus eius ac pedis dextri*

"and, *the* lamb killed, he will put some of its blood on *the* right earlobe of *the* one who is cleansed, and over *the* thumbs of his right hand and foot.

14:26 *olei vero partem mittet in manum suam sinistram*

"And he will put part of *the* oil on his left hand,

14:27 *in quo tinguens digitum dextrae manus asperget septies contra Dominum*

"dipping *the* finger of his right hand in which, he will sprinkle seven times toward *the* Lord.

14:28 *tangetque extremum dextrae auriculae illius qui mundatur et pollices manus ac pedis dextri in loco sanguinis qui effusus est pro delicto*

"And he will touch *the* right earlobe of *the* one who is cleansed, and *the* thumbs of his right hand and feet, in *the same* place of *the* blood which is poured out for sin.

14:29 *reliquam autem partem olei quae est in sinistra manu mittet super caput purificati ut placet pro*

eo Dominum

"But he will pour *the* remaining part of *the* oil which is in *the* left hand over *the* purified one's head, so it may placate *the* Lord for him.

14:30 *et turturem sive pullum columbae offeret*

"And he will offer either *a* dove or young pigeon,

14:31 *unum pro delicto et alterum in holocaustum cum libamentis suis*

"one for offense and *the* other as *a* burnt offering, with its libations.

14:32 *hoc est sacrificium leprosi qui habere non potest omnia in emundationem sui*

"This is *the* leper's sacrifice who can't have all *things* for his cleansing."

Leprosy in Physical Objects
14:33 *locutus est Dominus ad Mosen et Aaron dicens*

The Lord spoke to Moses and Aaron, saying,

14:34 *cum ingressi fueritis terram Chanaan quam ego dabo vobis in possessionem si fuerit plaga leprae in aedibus*

"When you have come into Canaan's

land which I will give you as *a* possession, if leprosy's plague is in houses,

14:35 *ibit cuius est domus nuntians sacerdoti et dicet quasi plaga leprae videtur mihi esse in domo mea*

"*the* one whose house it is will go, telling *the* priest. And he will say, 'Something like *the* plague of leprosy seems to me to be in my house.'

14:36 *at ille praecipiet ut efferant universa de domo priusquam ingrediatur eam et videat utrum lepra sit ne inmunda fiant omnia quae in domo sunt intrabitque postea ut consideret domus lepram*

"And he will command that they carry out all from *the* house before he goes into it, so he may see whether leprosy is *there*, unless all that are in *the* house be unclean. And he will enter afterwards, so he can consider *the* house's leprosy.

14:37 *et cum viderit in parietibus illius quasi valliculas pallore sive rubore deformes et humiliores superficie reliqua*

"And when he sees in its walls something like small hollows, deformed by paleness or redness, and lower than *the* remaining surface,

14:38 *egredietur ostium domus et statim claudet eam septem diebus*

"he will go out *the* house's door and immediately close it for seven days.

14:39 *reversusque die septimo considerabit eam si invenerit crevisse lepram*

"And, coming back *the* seventh day, he will consider it. If he finds *the* leprosy to have grown,

14:40 *iubebit erui lapides in quibus lepra est et proici eos extra civitatem in loco inmundo*

"he will command *the* stones in which *the* leprosy is to be dug out, and to throw them away outside *the* city, in *an* unclean place;

14:41 *domum autem ipsam radi intrinsecus per circuitum et spargi pulverem rasurae extra urbem in loco inmundo*

"but to scrape that house all around, and to scatter *the* scraped dust outside *the* city in *an* unclean place;

14:42 *lapidesque alios reponi pro his qui ablati fuerint et luto alio liniri domum*

"and to place other stones for those that were taken away; and to plaster *the* house with other clay.

14:43 *sin autem postquam eruti sunt lapides et pulvis elatus et alia terra lita*

"But if, after *the* stones are taken away, and *the* dust carried off, and *the house* plastered with other clay,

14:44 *ingressus sacerdos viderit reversam lepram et parietes aspersos maculis lepra est perseverans et inmunda domus*

"*the* priest, going in, sees again *the* leprosy and *the* walls scattered with spots, *the* leprosy is ongoing and *the* house unclean.

14:45 *quam statim destruent et lapides eius ac ligna atque universum pulverem proicient extra oppidum in loco inmundo*

"They will destroy it immediately – both its stones and wood. And they will throw all *the* dust out, outside *the* town in *an* unclean place.

14:46 *qui intraverit domum quando clausa est inmundus erit usque ad vesperum*

"Who enters *the* house when it is closed up will be unclean until evening.

14:47 *et qui dormierit in ea et comederit quippiam lavabit vestimenta sua*

"And who sleeps in it and eats anything, will wash his clothes.

14:48 *quod si introiens sacerdos*

viderit lepram non crevisse in domo postquam denuo lita est purificabit eam reddita sanitate

"But if *the* priest, going in, sees *the* leprosy has not grown in *the* house after it was plastered again, he will purify it, wholeness *having* returned.

14:49 *et in purificationem eius sumet duos passeres lignumque cedrinum et vermiculum atque hysopum*

"And he will take in its purification two sparrows, and cedar wood, and purple *thread*, and hyssop.

14:50 *et immolato uno passere in vase fictili super aquas vivas*

"And, killing one sparrow in *an* earthenware vessel over living waters,

14:51 *tollet lignum cedrinum et hysopum et coccum et passerem vivum et intinguet omnia in sanguine passeris immolati atque in aquis viventibus et asperget domum septies*

"he will take *the* cedar wood and hyssop and purple *thread* and *the* live sparrow. And, dipping all in *the* blood of *the* offered sparrow and in *the* living waters too, he will sprinkle *the* house seven times.

14:52 *purificabitque eam tam in sanguine passeris quam in aquis* *viventibus et in passere vivo lignoque cedrino et hysopo atque vermiculo*

"And he will purify it as well in *the* sparrow's blood, as also in *the* living waters, and in *the* live sparrow, and *the* cedar wood, and *the* hyssop, and *the* purple *thread*.

14:53 *cumque dimiserit passerem avolare in agrum libere orabit pro domo et iure mundabitur*

"And when he has released *the* sparrow to fly free into *the* field, he will pray for *the* house and it will be made clean by law."

14:54 *ista est lex omnis leprae et percussurae*

This is *the* law for every leprosy and blow,

14:55 *leprae vestium et domorum*

leprosy of clothing and of houses,

14:56 *cicatricis et erumpentium papularum lucentis maculae et in varias species coloribus inmutatis*

of scars, and of sores erupting from *a* shining spot, and of colors changing into various different *kinds* –

14:57 *ut possit sciri quo tempore mundum quid vel inmundum sit*

so it may be known at *the* time what is clean or unclean.

Male Discharges

Leviticus 15:1 *locutusque est Dominus ad Mosen et Aaron dicens*

And *the* Lord spoke to Moses and Aaron, saying,

15:2 *loquimini filiis Israhel et dicite eis vir qui patitur fluxum seminis inmundus erit*

"Speak to Israel's children and say to them, '*A* man who suffers *a* flow of semen will be unclean.

15:3 *et tunc iudicabitur huic vitio subiacere cum per momenta singula adheserit carni illius atque concreverit foedus humor*

"'And then he will be judged to be under this vice when, at each moment, this foul liquid sticks to his flesh and thickens.

15:4 *omne stratum in quo dormierit inmundum erit et ubicumque sederit*

"'Every bed in which he sleeps and wherever he sits will be unclean.

15:5 *si quis hominum tetigerit lectum eius lavabit vestimenta sua et ipse lotus aqua inmundus erit usque ad vesperum*

"'If someone touches his bed, he will wash his clothes, and he himself, washed with water, will be unclean until evening.

15:6 *si sederit ubi ille sederat et ipse lavabit vestimenta sua et lotus aqua inmundus erit usque ad vesperum*

"'If he sits where he sat, he also will wash his clothes and, washed with water, will be unclean until evening.

15:7 *qui tetigerit carnem eius lavabit vestimenta sua et ipse lotus aqua inmundus erit usque ad vesperum*

"'Who touches his flesh will wash his clothes and he himself, washed with water, will be unclean until evening.

15:8 *si salivam huiuscemodi homo iecerit super eum qui mundus est lavabit vestem suam et lotus aqua inmundus erit usque ad vesperum*

"'If *a* man in this condition spits saliva on him who is clean, he will wash his garment and, washed with water, will be unclean until evening.

15:9 *sagma super quo sederit inmundum erit*

"'*A* saddle on which he sits will be unclean.

15:10 *et quicquid sub eo fuerit qui fluxum seminis patitur pollutum erit usque ad vesperum qui portaverit horum aliquid lavabit vestem suam et ipse lotus aqua inmundus erit usque ad vesperum*

"'And whatever has been under one who suffers *a* flow of semen will be polluted until evening. Who carries any of these will wash his garment and he himself, washed with water, will be unclean until evening.

15:11 *omnis quem tetigerit qui talis est non lotis ante manibus lavabit vestimenta sua et lotus aqua inmundus erit usque ad vesperum*

"'Everyone whom such *a* one touches, without washing hands before, will wash his clothes and, washed with water, will be unclean until evening.

15:12 *vas fictile quod tetigerit confringetur vas autem ligneum lavabitur aqua*

"'*An* earthenware vessel which he touches will be broken, but *a* wooden vessel will be washed with water.

15:13 *si sanatus fuerit qui huiuscemodi sustinet passionem numerabit septem dies post emundationem sui et lotis vestibus ac toto corpore in aquis viventibus erit mundus*

"If he who suffered *a* disease of this sort is healed, he will count seven days after his cleansing and, clothes and *the* whole body washed in living waters, he will be clean.

15:14 *die autem octavo sumet duos*

turtures aut duos pullos columbae et veniet in conspectu Domini ad ostium tabernaculi testimonii dabitque eos sacerdoti

"'But *the* eighth day, he will take two doves or two young pigeons, and will come into *the* Lord's sight, at *the* entrance of testimony's tabernacle. And he will give them to *the* priest,

15:15 *qui faciet unum pro peccato et alterum in holocaustum rogabitque pro eo coram Domino ut emundetur a fluxu seminis sui*

"'who will make one for sin and *the* other for *a* burnt offering. And he will pray for him before *the* Lord, that he may be made clean from his flow of semen.

Semen in Intercourse
15:16 *vir de quo egreditur semen coitus lavabit aqua omne corpus suum et inmundus erit usque ad vesperum*

"'*A* man from whom semen comes out during intercourse will wash all his body with water, and will be unclean until evening.

15:17 *vestem et pellem quam habuerit lavabit aqua et inmunda erit usque ad vesperum*

"'He will wash *the* cloth and hide which he has *on* and will be unclean until evening.

15:18 *mulier cum qua coierit lavabitur aqua et inmunda erit usque ad vesperum*

"*The* woman with whom he had intercourse will be washed with water, and she will be unclean until evening.

Menstrual Blood

15:19 *mulier quae redeunte mense patitur fluxum sanguinis septem diebus separabitur*

"*A* woman who suffers *a* flow of blood, returning monthly, will be separated for seven days.

15:20 *omnis qui tetigerit eam inmundus erit usque ad vesperum*

"'Everyone who touches her will be unclean until evening.

15:21 *et in quo dormierit vel sederit diebus separationis suae polluetur*

"And whatever she sleeps in or sits on during her days of separation will be polluted.

15:22 *qui tetigerit lectum eius lavabit vestimenta sua et ipse lotus aqua inmundus erit usque ad vesperum*

"'Who touches her bed will wash his clothes and he, washed with water, will be unclean until evening.

15:23 *omne vas super quo illa sederit quisquis adtigerit lavabit vestimenta sua et lotus aqua pollutus erit usque ad vesperum*

"'Anyone who touches any vessel on which she sits will wash his clothes and, washed with water, will be polluted until evening.

15:24 *si coierit cum ea vir tempore sanguinis menstrualis inmundus erit septem diebus et omne stratum in quo dormierit polluetur*

"'If *a* man has intercourse with her during *the* time of menstrual blood, he will be unclean for seven days. And every bed in which he sleeps will be polluted.

15:25 *mulier quae patitur multis diebus fluxum sanguinis non in tempore menstruali vel quae post menstruum sanguinem fluere non cessat quamdiu huic subiacet passioni inmunda erit quasi sit in tempore menstruo*

"'A woman who suffers *a* flow of blood many days not in *the* time of menstruation, or doesn't cease to flow after *the* menstrual blood, will be unclean as long as she subject to this disease, as if in *the* time of menstruation.

15:26 *omne stratum in quo dormierit et vas in quo sederit pollutum erit*

"Every bed in which she sleeps and vessel on which she sits will be polluted.

15:27 *quicumque tetigerit eam lavabit vestimenta sua et ipse lotus aqua inmundus erit usque ad vesperum*

"'Whoever touches her will wash his clothes and he, washed with water, will be unclean until evening.

15:28 *si steterit sanguis et fluere cessarit numerabit septem dies purificationis suae*

"'If *the* blood stands and ceases to flow, she will count seven days for her purification.

15:29 *et octavo die offeret pro se sacerdoti duos turtures vel duos pullos columbae ad ostium tabernaculi testimonii*

"'And *the* eighth day she will offer *the* priest for herself two doves or two young pigeons, at *the* entrance of testimony's tabernacle,

15:30 *qui unum faciet pro peccato et alterum in holocaustum rogabitque pro ea coram Domino et pro fluxu inmunditiae eius*

"'who will make one for sin and *the* other for *a* burnt offering. And he will pray for her before *the* Lord, and for her unclean flow.

15:31 *docebitis ergo filios Israhel ut caveant inmunditiam et non moriantur in sordibus suis cum polluerint tabernaculum meum quod est inter eos*

"'Therefore, you will teach Israel's children that they beware of uncleanness and they not die in their filth, when they pollute My tabernacle which is among them.'"

15:32 *ista est lex eius qui patitur fluxum seminis et qui polluitur coitu*

This is *the* law of him who suffers *a* flow of semen and who is polluted by intercourse;

15:33 *et quae menstruis temporibus separatur vel quae iugi fluit sanguine et hominis qui dormierit cum ea*

and *her* who is separated by times of menstruation or who flows continually with blood; and of *a* man who sleeps with her.

The Ritual for Entering
the Holy of Holies

Leviticus 16:1 *locutusque est Dominus ad Mosen post mortem duum filiorum Aaron quando offerentes ignem alienum interfecti sunt*

And *the* Lord spoke to Moses after *the* death of two of Aaron's sons when, offering strange fire, they were killed.

16:2 *et praecepit ei dicens loquere ad Aaron fratrem tuum ne omni tempore ingrediatur sanctuarium quod est intra velum coram propitiatorio quo tegitur arca ut non moriatur quia in nube apparebo super oraculum*

And He commanded him, saying, "Say to Aaron your brother that he may not go all *the* time into *the* sanctuary that is inside *the* veil, before *the* atonement seat that touches *the* ark, so he won't die – because I will appear in cloud over *the* oracle –

16:3 *nisi haec ante fecerit vitulum offeret pro peccato et arietem in holocaustum*

"unless he does these first. He will offer *a* calf for sin and *a* ram as *a* burnt offering.

16:4 *tunica linea vestietur feminalibus lineis verecunda celabit*

accingetur zona linea cidarim lineam inponet capiti haec enim vestimenta sunt sancta quibus cunctis cum lotus fuerit induetur

"He will dress in *the* linen tunic. He will hide *the* thighs modestly in linens. He will strap on *the* linen belt. He will put *the* linen head-dress on his head. For these are *the* holy vestments – all of which, when *he* has washed with water, he will put on.

16:5 *suscipietque ab universa multitudine filiorum Israhel duos hircos pro peccato et unum arietem in holocaustum*

"And he will accept from *the* whole multitude of Israel's children two he-goats for sin and one ram as *a* burnt offering.

16:6 *cumque obtulerit vitulum et oraverit pro se et pro domo sua*

"And when he has offered *the* calf and prayed for himself and for his house,

16:7 *duos hircos stare faciet coram Domino in ostio tabernaculi testimonii*

"he will make *the* two he-goats stand before *the* Lord, in *the* entrance of testimony's tabernacle.

16:8 *mittens super utrumque sortem unam Domino et alteram capro* *emissario*

"And, casting *a* lot over both– one for *the* Lord and *the* other for *the* goat-sent-out –

16:9 *cuius sors exierit Domino offeret illum pro peccato*

"*the* one whose lot will fall to *the* Lord, he will offer him for sin.

16:10 *cuius autem in caprum emissarium statuet eum vivum coram Domino ut fundat preces super eo et emittat illum in solitudinem*

"But *the* one as *the* goat-sent-out, he will stand him alive before *the* Lord, so he may pour out prayers over him. And he will send him out into *the* desert.

16:11 *his rite celebratis offeret vitulum et rogans pro se et pro domo sua immolabit eum*

"This rite celebrated, he will offer *the* calf and, praying for himself and his house, he will kill him.

16:12 *adsumptoque turibulo quod de prunis altaris impleverit et hauriens manu conpositum thymiama in incensum ultra velum intrabit in sancta*

"And taking up *a* censer which is filled with burning coals from *the* altar, and taking in hand composite powder as incense, he will go into *the* holy place beyond *the* veil,

16:13 *ut positis super ignem aromatibus nebula eorum et vapor operiat oraculum quod est super testimonium et non moriatur*

"so, placing *the* aromatic spices over *the* fire, *the* cloud and vapor will cover *the* oracle which is over *the* testimony, and he won't die.

16:14 *tollet quoque de sanguine vituli et asperget digito septies contra propitiatorium ad orientem*

"Likewise, he will take some of *the* calf's blood and sprinkle with *a* finger seven *times* before *the* atonement seat, to *the* east.

16:15 *cumque mactaverit hircum pro peccato populi inferet sanguinem eius intra velum sicut praeceptum est de sanguine vituli ut aspergat e regione oraculi*

"And when he has slaughtered *the* he-goat for *the* people's sin, he will carry its blood inside *the* veil, as was commanded of *the* calf's blood, so he can sprinkle *it* around *the* area of *the* oracle.

16:16 *et expiet sanctuarium ab inmunditiis filiorum Israhel et a praevaricationibus eorum cunctisque peccatis iuxta hunc ritum faciet tabernaculo testimonii quod fixum* *est inter eos in medio sordium habitationis eorum*

"And he will make atonement for *the* sanctuary from all *the* uncleanness of Israel's children, and from all their transgressions and their sins. He will work according to this rite in testimony's tabernacle, which is pitched among them, in *the* midst of their dwellings' filth.

16:17 *nullus hominum sit in tabernaculo quando pontifex ingreditur sanctuarium ut roget pro se et pro domo sua et pro universo coetu Israhel donec egrediatur*

"No man may be in *the* tabernacle when *the* high priest goes into *the* sanctuary until he comes out, so he can pray for himself, and for his house, and for *the* whole gathering of Israel.

16:18 *cum autem exierit ad altare quod coram Domino est oret pro se et sumptum sanguinem vituli atque hirci fundat super cornua eius per gyrum*

"But when he has gone out to *the* altar that is before *the* Lord, he will pray for himself and, taking *the* blood of *the* calf and he-goat, he will pour *it* over its horns all around.

16:19 *aspergensque digito septies expiet et sanctificet illud ab inmunditiis filiorum Israhel*

"And, sprinkling by finger seven *times*, he will atone for and make it holy from *the* uncleanness of Israel's children.

Confessing Israel's Sins

16:20 *postquam emundarit sanctuarium et tabernaculum et altare tunc offerat hircum viventem*

"After he has made *the* sanctuary and tabernacle and altar clean, then he may offer *the* living goat.

16:21 *et posita utraque manu super caput eius confiteatur omnes iniquitates filiorum Israhel et universa delicta atque peccata eorum quae inprecans capiti eius emittet illum per hominem paratum in desertum*

"And, placing both hands on its head, he will confess all Israel's children's treacheries, and all their offenses and sins, calling which down on its head, he will send it out by *a* prepared man into *the* desert.

16:22 *cumque portaverit hircus omnes iniquitates eorum in terram solitariam et dimissus fuerit in deserto*

"And when *the* goat has carried all their treacheries into *a* solitary place and been set free in *the* desert,

16:23 *revertetur Aaron in tabernaculum testimonii et depositis*

vestibus quibus prius indutus erat cum intraret sanctuarium relictisque ibi

"Aaron will go back into testimony's tabernacle. And, taking off *the* clothes which he dressed in before when he entered *the* sanctuary and leaving *them* there,

16:24 *lavabit carnem suam in loco sancto indueturque vestimentis suis et postquam egressus obtulerit holocaustum suum ac plebis rogabit tam pro se quam pro populo*

"he will wash his flesh in *the* holy place and put on his clothes. And after going out, he will offer his and *the* people's holocaust. He will pray for himself and for *the* people alike.

16:25 *et adipem qui oblatus est pro peccatis adolebit super altare*

"And he will burn *the* fat which is offered for sin on *the* altar.

16:26 *ille vero qui dimiserit caprum emissarium lavabit vestimenta sua et corpus aqua et sic ingredietur in castra*

"Indeed, he who released *the* goat-sent-out will wash his clothes and body with water, and so he will enter into *the* camps.

16:27 *vitulum autem et hircum qui pro peccato fuerant immolati et*

quorum sanguis inlatus est ut in sanctuario expiatio conpleretur asportabunt foras castra et conburent igni tam pelles quam carnes eorum et fimum

"But they will carry *the* calf and *the* goat which were killed for sin – whose blood was brought in so *the* sanctuary's atonement could be completed – outside *the* camps. And they will burn *them* with fire, their hides and flesh and excrement alike.

16:28 *et quicumque conbuserit ea lavabit vestimenta sua et carnem aqua et sic ingredietur in castra*

"And whoever burns them will wash his clothes and flesh with water, and so will come into *the* camps.

The Day of Atonement
16:29 *eritque hoc vobis legitimum sempiternum mense septimo decima die mensis adfligetis animas vestras nullumque facietis opus sive indigena sive advena qui peregrinatur inter vos*

"And this will be *an* everlasting law to you. *The* seventh month, *the* tenth day of *the* month, you will afflict your souls. And you will do no work, whether *the* native-born or *the* stranger who sojourns among you.

16:30 *in hac die expiatio erit vestri atque mundatio ab omnibus peccatis vestris coram Domino mundabimini*

"Atonement and cleansing will be yours on that day from all your sins. You will be made clean before *the* Lord,

16:31 *sabbatum enim requietionis est et adfligetis animas vestras religione perpetua*

"for *it* is *a* Sabbath of rest, and you will afflict your souls as *a* perpetual observance.

16:32 *expiabit autem sacerdos qui unctus fuerit et cuius initiatae manus ut sacerdotio fungatur pro patre suo indueturque stola linea et vestibus sanctis*

"But *the* priest who will be anointed and whose hand is initiated, so he can carry out priestly duties for his father, will make atonement. And he will be dressed in *the* linen stole and *the* holy vestments.

16:33 *et expiabit sanctuarium et tabernaculum testimonii atque altare sacerdotes quoque et universum populum*

"And he will atone for *the* sanctuary, and testimony's tabernacle, and *the* altars – *the* priests, likewise, and *the* whole people.

16:34 *eritque hoc vobis legitimum sempiternum ut oretis pro filiis Israhel et pro cunctis peccatis eorum semel in anno fecit igitur sicut*

praeceperat Dominus Mosi

"And this will be *an* everlasting law to you, so you may pray for Israel's children and for all their sins once *a* year."
He did so therefore, as *the* Lord had commanded Moses.

Regulations
Concerning Blood

Leviticus 17:1 *et locutus est Dominus ad Mosen dicens*

And *the* Lord spoke to Moses, saying,

17:2 *loquere Aaron et filiis eius et cunctis filiis Israhel et dices ad eos iste est sermo quem mandavit Dominus dicens*

"Speak to Aaron and his sons and all Israel's children. And you will say to them, 'This is *the* word which *the* Lord commanded, saying,

17:3 *homo quilibet de domo Israhel si occiderit bovem aut ovem sive capram in castris vel extra castra*

"'whatever man from Israel's house, if he kills *an* ox or sheep or goat, in *the* camps or outside *the* camps,

17:4 *et non obtulerit ad ostium tabernaculi oblationem Domino sanguinis reus erit quasi sanguinem fuderit sic peribit de medio populi sui*

"'and does not bring *it as an* offering to *the* Lord to *the* entrance of testimony's tabernacle, will be guilty of blood. As if he had poured out blood, so he will perish from among his people.

17:5 *ideo offerre debent sacerdoti filii Israhel hostias suas quas occidunt in agro ut sanctificentur*

Domino ante ostium tabernaculi testimonii et immolent eas hostias pacificas Domino

"'Therefore, Israel's children must offer *the* priests their victims which they kill in *the* field, so they may be made holy to *the* Lord before *the* entrance to testimony's tabernacle. And they may kill them *as* peace victims to *the* Lord.

17:6 *fundetque sacerdos sanguinem super altare Domini ad ostium tabernaculi testimonii et adolebit adipem in odorem suavitatis Domino*

"'And *the* priest will pour out *the* blood over *the* Lord's altar at *the* entrance to testimony's tabernacle. And he will burn *the* fat as *an* odor of smoothness to *the* Lord.

17:7 *et nequaquam ultra immolabunt hostias suas daemonibus cum quibus fornicati sunt legitimum sempiternum erit illis et posteris eorum*

"'And never more will they kill their victims to demons, with which they have fornicated. *This* will be *an* everlasting law to them and to their posterity.'

17:8 *et ad ipsos dices homo de domo Israhel et de advenis qui peregrinantur apud vos qui obtulerit holocaustum sive victimam*

"And you will say to them, '*A* man from Israel's house and from *the* strangers who sojourn with you who offers *a* burnt offering or victim,

17:9 *et ad ostium tabernaculi testimonii non adduxerit eam ut offeratur Domino interibit de populo suo*

"'and does not bring it to *the* entrance of testimony's tabernacle so it may be offered to *the* Lord, will die from his people.

17:10 *homo quilibet de domo Israhel et de advenis qui peregrinantur inter eos si comederit sanguinem obfirmabo faciem meam contra animam illius et disperdam eam de populo suo*

"'Whatever man from Israel's house and from *the* strangers who sojourn among them, if he eats blood, I will set My face against his soul and destroy it from his people –

17:11 *quia anima carnis in sanguine est et ego dedi illum vobis ut super altare in eo expietis pro animabus vestris et sanguis pro animae piaculo sit*

"'because *the* flesh's soul is in *the* blood. And I have given it to you so you may make atonement in it on *the* altar. And *the* blood may be *an* atoning rite for *the* soul.

17:12 *idcirco dixi filiis Israhel omnis anima ex vobis non comedet sanguinem nec ex advenis qui*

peregrinantur inter vos

"'Therefore I have said to Israel's children, No soul from among you will eat blood, nor from *the* strangers who sojourn among you.

17:13 *homo quicumque de filiis Israhel et de advenis qui peregrinantur apud vos si venatione atque aucupio ceperit feram vel avem quibus vesci licitum est fundat sanguinem eius et operiat illum terra*

"'Whatever man from Israel's children or from *the* strangers who sojourn with you, if he should take by hunting or bird-catching *a* wild animal *or* bird which is lawful to eat, let him pour out its blood and cover it with dirt.

17:14 *anima enim omnis carnis in sanguine est unde dixi filiis Israhel sanguinem universae carnis non comedetis quia anima carnis in sanguine est et quicumque comederit illum interibit*

"'For *the* soul of all flesh is in *the* blood, from which I have said to Israel's children, You will not eat *the* blood of all flesh. For *the* flesh's soul is in *the* blood, and whoever eats it will die.

17:15 *anima quae comederit morticinum vel captum a bestia tam de indigenis quam de advenis lavabit vestes suas et semet ipsum aqua et contaminatus erit usque ad vesperum* *et hoc ordine mundus fiet*

"'*A* soul that eats from *a* beast that died of itself or was taken, whether *he is* native born or stranger, will wash his clothes and himself with water, and will be contaminated until evening. And by this order he will be made clean.

17:16 *quod si non laverit vestimenta sua nec corpus portabit iniquitatem suam*

"'But if he does not wash his clothes or body, he will carry his treachery.

Keep the Lord's Commandments
Leviticus 18:1 *locutusque est Dominus ad Mosen dicens*

And *the* Lord spoke to Moses, saying,

18:2 *loquere filiis Israhel et dices ad eos ego Dominus Deus vester*

"Speak to Israel's children, and you will say to them, 'I *am the* Lord your God.

18:3 *iuxta consuetudinem terrae Aegypti in qua habitastis non facietis et iuxta morem regionis Chanaan ad quam ego introducturus sum vos non agetis nec in legitimis eorum ambulabitis*

"'You will not do according to *the* custom of Egypt's land in which you lived, and you will not act according to *the* manner of Canaan's region, into which I will bring you, nor will you walk in their laws.

18:4 *facietis iudicia mea et praecepta servabitis et ambulabitis in eis ego Dominus Deus vester*

"You will do My judgments, and serve *the* commandments, and walk in them. I *am the* Lord your God.

18:5 *custodite leges meas atque iudicia quae faciens homo vivet in eis ego Dominus*

"'Keep My laws and judgments,

working which, man will live in them!
I am *the* Lord.

Laws Concerning
Sexual Behavior

18:6 *omnis homo ad proximam
sanguinis sui non accedet ut revelet
turpitudinem eius ego Dominus*

"'No man will come near his
kinswoman by blood, so he may
reveal her nakedness. I *am the* Lord.

18:7 *turpitudinem patris et
turpitudinem matris tuae non
discoperies mater tua est non
revelabis turpitudinem eius*

"'You will not lay bare your father's
nakedness or your mother's
nakedness. She is your mother. You
will not reveal her nakedness.

18:8 *turpitudinem uxoris patris tui
non discoperies turpitudo enim
patris tui est*

"'You will not uncover your father's
wife's nakedness, for *it* is your
father's nakedness.

18:9 *turpitudinem sororis tuae ex
patre sive ex matre quae domi vel
foris genita est non revelabis*

"'You will not reveal your sister's
nakedness, whether from father or
mother, born in *the* home or outside.

18:10 *turpitudinem filiae filii tui vel
neptis ex filia non revelabis quia*

turpitudo tua est

"'You will not reveal *the* nakedness
of your son's daughter, or *a*
granddaughter from *your* daughter.
You will not reveal *it*, because *it* is
your nakedness.

18:11 *turpitudinem filiae uxoris
patris tui quam peperit patri tuo et
est soror tua non revelabis*

"'You will not reveal *the* nakedness
of your father's wife's daughter,
whom your father conceived, and she
is your sister.

18:12 *turpitudinem sororis patris tui
non discoperies quia caro est patris
tui*

"'You will not uncover *the* nakedness
of your father's sister, because she is
your father's flesh.

18:13 *turpitudinem sororis matris
tuae non revelabis eo quod caro sit
matris tuae*

"'You will not reveal *the* nakedness
of your mother's sister, because she
may be your mother's flesh.

18:14 *turpitudinem patrui tui non
revelabis nec accedes ad uxorem
eius quae tibi adfinitate coniungitur*

"'You will not reveal *the* nakedness
of your father's brother, nor come
near to his wife, who is joined to you
by marriage.

18:15 *turpitudinem nurus tuae non revelabis quia uxor filii tui est nec discoperies ignominiam eius*

"'You will not reveal your daughter-in-law's nakedness, because she is your son's wife, nor will you uncover her shame.

18:16 *turpitudinem uxoris fratris tui non revelabis quia turpitudo fratris tui est*

"'You will not reveal *the* nakedness of your brother's wife, because she is your brother's nakedness.

18:17 *turpitudinem uxoris tuae et filiae eius non revelabis filiam filii eius et filiam filiae illius non sumes ut reveles ignominiam eius quia caro illius sunt et talis coitus incestus est*

"'You will not reveal *the* nakedness of your wife and her daughter. You will not take up your son's daughter or his daughter's daughter so you reveal her shame, because they are his flesh and such intercourse is incest.

18:18 *sororem uxoris tuae in pelicatum illius non accipies nec revelabis turpitudinem eius adhuc illa vivente*

"'You will not receive your wife's sister into living together sexually, nor will you reveal her nakedness *while* she *is* still living.

18:19 *ad mulierem quae patitur menstrua non accedes nec revelabis foeditatem eius*

"'You will not come near *a* woman who suffers menstruation, nor reveal her filthiness.

18:20 *cum uxore proximi tui non coibis nec seminis commixtione maculaberis*

"'You will not have intercourse with your neighbor's wife, nor be stained by mixed semen.

18:21 *de semine tuo non dabis ut consecretur idolo Moloch nec pollues nomen Dei tui ego Dominus*

"'You will not give some of your semen so it may be consecrated to *the* idol Moloch, or pollute your God's name. I *am the* Lord.

18:22 *cum masculo non commisceberis coitu femineo quia abominatio est*

"'You will not be mixed together with *a* male as if having intercourse with *a* woman, because *it* is detestable.

18:23 *cum omni pecore non coibis nec maculaberis cum eo mulier non subcumbet iumento nec miscebitur ei quia scelus est*

"'You will not have intercourse with any animal, or be stained with it. *A* woman will not lie under cattle, nor be mixed with it, because *it* is *a* crime.

Do Not Be Polluted!

18:24 *ne polluamini in omnibus his quibus contaminatae sunt universae gentes quas ego eiciam ante conspectum vestrum*

"'Do not be polluted in all these *things* by which all *the* nations which I will throw out before your face are polluted,

18:25 *et quibus polluta est terra cuius ego scelera visitabo ut evomat habitatores suos*

"'and by which *the* land is polluted – whose crimes I will visit, so it may vomit out its inhabitants!

18:26 *custodite legitima mea atque iudicia et non faciat ex omnibus abominationibus istis tam indigena quam colonus qui peregrinatur apud vos*

"'Keep My laws and judgments, and do not act from any of these abominations – whether *the* native-born or *the* colonist who sojourns with you –

18:27 *omnes enim execrationes istas fecerunt accolae terrae qui fuerunt ante vos et polluerunt eam*

"'for all *the* land's inhabitants who were before you have done these terrible *things*, and polluted it!

18:28 *cavete ergo ne et vos similiter evomat cum paria feceritis sicut evomuit gentem quae fuit ante vos*

"'Take care, therefore, that it not likewise vomit you out when you have done accordingly, like it vomited out *the* nation which was before you!

18:29 *omnis anima quae fecerit de abominationibus his quippiam peribit de medio populi sui*

"'Every soul that does any of these abominations will perish from among his people.

18:30 *custodite mandata mea nolite facere quae fecerunt hii qui fuerunt ante vos et ne polluamini in eis ego Dominus Deus vester*

"'Keep My commandments! Don't do what those who were before you also did, unless you be polluted in them! I *am the* Lord your God.'"

Laws of Good Behavior
Leviticus 19:1 *locutus est Dominus ad Mosen dicens*

The Lord spoke to Moses, saying,

19:2 *loquere ad omnem coetum filiorum Israhel et dices ad eos sancti estote quia ego sanctus sum Dominus Deus vester*

"Speak to all Israel's children's gathering, and you will say to them, 'Be holy, because I, *the* Lord your God, am holy.

Fear Mother and Father
19:3 *unusquisque matrem et patrem suum timeat sabbata mea custodite ego Dominus Deus vester*

"'Let each one fear his mother and father! Keep My Sabbaths! I *am the* Lord your God.

Avoid Idols
19:4 *nolite converti ad idola nec deos conflatiles faciatis vobis ego Dominus Deus vester*

"'Do not be turned to idols or make yourselves cast-metal gods! I *am the* Lord your God.

Respect the Lord's Offerings
19:5 *si immolaveritis hostiam pacificorum Domino ut sit placabilis*

"'If you kill *a* peace victim to *the* Lord, that it may be atoning,

19:6 *eo die quo fuerit immolata comedetis eam et die altero quicquid autem residuum fuerit in diem tertium igne conburetis*

"'you will eat it on *the* day that it was killed and *the* day after. You will burn whatever will remain on *the* third day with fire.

19:7 *si quis post biduum comederit ex ea profanus erit et impietatis reus*

"'If someone should eat from it after two days, he will be profane and guilty of lawlessness.

19:8 *portabit iniquitatem suam quia sanctum Domini polluit et peribit anima illa de populo suo*

"'He will carry his treachery because he has polluted *the* Lord's holy place, and that soul will perish from his people.

Remember the Poor and Passer-by
19:9 *cum messueris segetes terrae tuae non tondebis usque ad solum superficiem terrae nec remanentes spicas colliges*

"'When you harvest your land's crops, you will not mow *the* field's surface to *the* ground, or collect *the* remaining heads *of grain.*

19:10 *neque in vinea tua racemos et grana decidentia congregabis sed pauperibus et peregrinis carpenda dimittes ego Dominus Deus vester*

"'And neither will you gather your vineyard's fallen clusters and grapes, but you will leave *them* for *the* poor and passers-by to gather. I *am the* Lord your God.

Be Truthful
19:11 *non facietis furtum non mentiemini nec decipiet unusquisque proximum suum*

"'You will not work theft. You will not lie, nor will anyone deceive his neighbor.

19:12 *non peierabis in nomine meo nec pollues nomen Dei tui ego Dominus*

"'You will not swear falsely in My name, nor pollute your God's name. I *am the* Lord.

19:13 *non facies calumniam proximo tuo nec vi opprimes eum non morabitur opus mercennarii apud te usque mane*

"'You will not work false accusation against your neighbor, or oppress him by force. *A* hired worker's work will not stay with you until morning.

Be Fair to the Disabled
19:14 *non maledices surdo nec coram caeco pones offendiculum sed timebis Deum tuum quia ego sum Dominus*

"'You will not curse *the* deaf or put *a* stumbling block before *the* blind, but you will fear your God, because I *am the* Lord.

Judge Fairly
19:15 *non facies quod iniquum est nec iniuste iudicabis nec consideres personam pauperis nec honores vultum potentis iuste iudica proximo tuo*

"'You will not do what is treacherous, nor judge unfairly, nor consider *a* poor person, nor honor *the* mighty's face. Judge your neighbor fairly!

Don't Stir Up Trouble
19:16 *non eris criminator et susurro in populis non stabis contra sanguinem proximi tui ego Dominus*

"'You will not be *an* accuser and whisperer among *the* people. You will not stand against your neighbor's blood. I *am the* Lord.

Don't Hate Your Brother
19:17 *ne oderis fratrem tuum in corde tuo sed publice argue eum ne habeas super illo peccatum*

"'You will not hate your brother in your heart. Yet accuse him publicly, lest you have sin concerning him!

19:18 *non quaeres ultionem nec memor eris iniuriae civium tuorum diliges amicum tuum sicut temet ipsum ego Dominus*

"'You will not seek revenge, nor will

you remember your fellow-citizen's injury. You will love your friend as yourself. I *am the* Lord.

Don't Mix Unnaturally
19:19 *leges meas custodite iumenta tua non facies coire cum alterius generis animantibus agrum non seres diverso semine veste quae ex duobus texta est non indueris*

"'Keep My laws! You will not make your cattle mate with another species of animals. You will not sow *a* field with different seed. You will not dress yourself with clothing woven from two fabrics.

Sexual Offense
19:20 *homo si dormierit cum muliere coitu seminis quae sit ancilla etiam nubilis et tamen pretio non redempta nec libertate donata vapulabunt ambo et non morientur quia non fuit libera*

"'If *a* man sleeps with *a* woman, conceiving by intercourse, she being *a* female slave and marriageable, and nevertheless neither bought by price nor given freedom, both will be beaten. And they will not die, because she was not free.

19:21 *pro delicto autem suo offeret Domino ad ostium tabernaculi testimonii arietem*

"'But he will offer *the* Lord *a* ram for his offense, at *the* entrance to testimony's tabernacle.

19:22 *orabitque pro eo sacerdos et pro delicto eius coram Domino et repropitiabitur ei dimitteturque peccatum*

"'And *the* priest will pray for him and for his offense before *the* Lord. And it will be atoned for on his behalf, and *the* sin will be forgiven.

Planting a Fruit Tree
19:23 *quando ingressi fueritis terram et plantaveritis in ea ligna pomifera auferetis praeputia eorum poma quae germinant inmunda erunt vobis nec edetis ex eis*

"'When you have gone into *the* land and you plant fruit trees in it, you will take away their foreskin. *The* fruits which germinate will be unclean to you, nor will you eat from them.

19:24 *quarto anno omnis fructus eorum sanctificabitur laudabilis Domino*

"'In *the* fourth year, all their fruit will be sanctified, praiseworthy to *the* Lord.

19:25 *quinto autem anno comedetis fructus congregantes poma quae proferunt ego Dominus Deus vester*

"'But *the* fifth year you will eat *the* produce, gathering *the* fruits which are put forth. I *am the* Lord your God.

Augury
19:26 *non comedetis cum sanguine non augurabimini nec observabitis somnia*

"'You will not eat *meat* with blood. You will not practice augury, or watch dreams.

Personal Grooming
19:27 *neque in rotundum adtondebitis comam nec radatis barbam*

"'You will not cut your hair smooth, or shave *the* beard.

No Tattoos
19:28 *et super mortuo non incidetis carnem vestram neque figuras aliquas et stigmata facietis vobis ego Dominus*

"'And you will not cut your flesh over *the* dead, or make other figures or marks on yourself. I *am the* Lord.

Prostitution and Crime
19:29 *ne prostituas filiam tuam et contaminetur terra et impleatur piaculo*

"'You may not prostitute your daughter and let *the* land be contaminated and filled with crime.

Sabbaths and Sanctuary
19:30 *sabbata mea custodite et sanctuarium meum metuite ego Dominus*

Keep My Sabbaths and fear My sanctuary! I *am the* Lord.

Magicians and Diviners
19:31 *ne declinetis ad magos nec ab ariolis aliquid sciscitemini ut polluamini per eos ego Dominus Deus vester*

"'You will not turn away to magicians or ask anything of diviners, that you be polluted through them. I *am the* Lord your God.

Honor the Elderly
19:32 *coram cano capite consurge et honora personam senis et time Deum tuum ego sum Dominus*

"Rise up before *a* gray head, and honor *an* elderly person, and fear your God! I *am the* Lord.

Newcomers in Your Land
19:33 *si habitaverit advena in terra vestra et moratus fuerit inter vos ne exprobretis ei*

"'If *a* newcomer lives in your land and will stay among you, you may not reproach him.

19:34 *sed sit inter vos quasi indigena et diligetis eum quasi vosmet ipsos fuistis enim et vos advenae in terra Aegypti ego Dominus Deus vester*

"'But let him be among you like *the* native-born. And you will delight in him as in yourselves, for you were newcomers in Egypt's land. I *am the* Lord your God.

Weights and Measures

19:35 *nolite facere iniquum aliquid in iudicio in regula in pondere in mensura*

Don't work any treachery: in judgment, in rule, in weight, in measure.

19:36 *statera iusta et aequa sint pondera iustus modius aequusque sextarius ego Dominus Deus vester qui eduxi vos de terra Aegypti*

"'Let *the* scales be fair and *the* weights equal, *the* peck just, and *the* sextarium *the* same. I *am the* Lord your God, who led you out of Egypt's land.

19:37 *custodite omnia praecepta mea et universa iudicia et facite ea ego Dominus*

"'Keep all My commandments and all *My* judgments, and do them! I *am the* Lord.'"

Laws Against Idolatry

Leviticus 20:1 *locutusque est Dominus ad Mosen dicens*

And *the* Lord spoke to Moses, saying,

Against Worshipers of Moloch

20:2 *haec loqueris filiis Israhel homo de filiis Israhel et de advenis qui habitant in Israhel si quis dederit de semine suo idolo Moloch morte moriatur populus terrae lapidabit eum*

"Say this to Israel's children: 'If *a* man from Israel's children and from *the* newcomers who live in Israel should give some of his seed to *the* idol Moloch, let him die by death. *The* land's people will stone him.

20:3 *et ego ponam faciem meam contra illum succidamque eum de medio populi sui eo quod dederit de semine suo Moloch et contaminaverit sanctuarium meum ac polluerit nomen sanctum meum*

"'And I will place My face against him and cut him down from among his people, because he gave Moloch some of his seed, and contaminated My sanctuary, and polluted My holy name.

20:4 *quod si neglegens populus terrae et quasi parvipendens imperium meum dimiserit hominem qui dederit de semine suo Moloch* *nec voluerit eum occidere*

"'But if *the* land's people, neglecting and, as if considering My decree unimportant, should let *the* man who gave some of his seed to Moloch go, and not want to kill him,

20:5 *ponam faciem meam super hominem illum et cognationem eius succidamque et ipsum et omnes qui consenserunt ei ut fornicarentur cum Moloch de medio populi sui*

"'I will place My face against that man and his kin. And I will cut down from among his people both him and all who joined him so they could fornicate with Moloch.

20:6 *anima quae declinaverit ad magos et ariolos et fornicata fuerit cum eis ponam faciem meam contra eam et interficiam illam de medio populi sui*

"'*A* soul that turns aside to magicians and fortune-tellers and fornicates with them, I will place My face against him. And I will kill him from among his people.

Be Holy
20:7 *sanctificamini et estote sancti quia ego Dominus Deus vester*

"'Be sanctified and be holy, because I *am the* Lord your God!

20:8 *custodite praecepta mea et facite ea ego Dominus qui sanctifico*

vos

"'Keep My commandments and do them. I *am the* Lord who makes you holy.

Cursing Father and Mother
20:9 *qui maledixerit patri suo et matri morte moriatur patri matrique maledixit sanguis eius sit super eum*

"'Let one who curses his father and mother die by death. He has cursed father and mother. His blood be on him!

More Laws
on Sexual Behavior
20:10 *si moechatus quis fuerit cum uxore alterius et adulterium perpetrarit cum coniuge proximi sui morte moriantur et moechus et adultera*

"'If someone should have sex with another's wife and perpetrate adultery with his neighbor's wife, let them die by death, both *the* adulterer and *the* adulteress.

20:11 *qui dormierit cum noverca sua et revelaverit ignominiam patris sui morte moriantur ambo sanguis eorum sit super eos*

"'Who sleeps with his stepmother and reveals his father's shame, let both die by death. Their blood be on them!

20:12 *si quis dormierit cum nuru*

sua uterque moriantur quia scelus operati sunt sanguis eorum sit super eos

"'If someone should sleep with his daughter-in-law, both will die, because they have worked *a* crime. Their blood be on them!

20:13 *qui dormierit cum masculo coitu femineo uterque operati sunt nefas morte moriantur sit sanguis eorum super eos*

"'Who sleeps with *a* male as if having intercourse with *a* woman, both have worked *a* violation of divine law. Let them die by death. Their blood be on them!

20:14 *qui supra uxorem filiam duxerit matrem eius scelus operatus est vivus ardebit cum eis nec permanebit tantum nefas in medio vestri*

"'Who in addition to *a* daughter should marry her mother has worked *a* crime. He will be burned alive with them, nor will such *a* violation of divine law remain among you.

20:15 *qui cum iumento et pecore coierit morte moriatur pecus quoque occidite*

"'Let who has intercourse with cattle or sheep die by death. Kill *the* animal as well!

20:16 *mulier quae subcubuerit*

cuilibet iumento simul interficietur cum eo sanguis eorum sit super eos

"'*A* woman who lies under whatever animal will be killed together with it. Their blood be on them!

20:17 *qui acceperit sororem suam filiam patris sui vel filiam matris suae et viderit turpitudinem eius illaque conspexerit fratris ignominiam nefariam rem operati sunt occidentur in conspectu populi sui eo quod turpitudinem suam mutuo revelarint et portabunt iniquitatem suam*

"'Who receives his sister, whether his father's daughter or his mother's daughter, and sees her nakedness, and she sees *the* brother's shame, they have worked *a* notorious thing. They will be killed in their people's sight, because they uncovered each other's nakedness. And they will carry their treachery.

20:18 *qui coierit cum muliere in fluxu menstruo et revelaverit turpitudinem eius ipsaque aperuerit fontem sanguinis sui interficientur ambo de medio populi sui*

"'Who has sex with *a* woman during *the* menstrual flow and reveals her nakedness, and she uncovers her blood's fountain, both will be killed from among their people.

20:19 *turpitudinem materterae tuae et amitae tuae non discoperies qui*

hoc fecerit ignominiam carnis suae
nudavit portabunt ambo iniquitatem
suam

"'You will not uncover *the* nakedness of your mother's sister or your father's sister. Who does this has stripped naked his flesh's shame. Both will carry their treachery.

20:20 *qui coierit cum uxore patrui*
vel avunculi sui et revelaverit
ignominiam cognationis suae
portabunt ambo peccatum suum
absque liberis morientur

"'Who has sex with *the* wife of his father's brother or his mother's brother, and reveals his kinsman's shame, both will carry their sin. They will die without children.

20:21 *qui duxerit uxorem fratris sui*
rem facit inlicitam turpitudinem
fratris sui revelavit absque filiis
erunt

"'Who marries his brother's wife has done *an* illegal act. He has revealed his brother's nakedness. They will be without children.

Keep My Laws

20:22 *custodite leges meas atque*
iudicia et facite ea ne et vos evomat
terra quam intraturi estis et
habitaturi

"'Keep My laws and judgments and do them, so *the* land which you will enter and live in may not vomit you

out also!

20:23 *nolite ambulare in legitimis*
nationum quas ego expulsurus sum
ante vos omnia enim haec fecerunt et
abominatus sum eos

"'Don't walk in *the* laws of *the* nations which I will expel before you, for they have done all these and I have detested them!

20:24 *vobis autem loquor possidete*
terram eorum quam dabo vobis in
hereditatem terram fluentem lacte et
melle ego Dominus Deus vester qui
separavi vos a ceteris populis

"'But I say to you – possess their land which I will give you as *an* inheritance, *a* land flowing with milk and honey! I *am the* Lord your God, who separated you from other peoples.

Separate Yourselves

20:25 *separate ergo et vos*
iumentum mundum ab inmundo et
avem mundam ab inmunda ne
polluatis animas vestras in pecore et
in avibus et cunctis quae moventur in
terra et quae vobis ostendi esse
polluta

"Therefore, you also separate clean cattle from unclean, and clean birds from unclean, unless you pollute your souls in cattle and in birds and in all that moves on *the* land, and which I have shown you to be polluted!

20:26 *eritis sancti mihi quia sanctus ego sum Dominus et separavi vos a ceteris populis ut essetis mei*

"'You will be holy to Me, because I, *the* Lord, am holy. And I separated you from other peoples, so you might be Mine.

Execute Magicians and Diviners

20:27 *vir sive mulier in quibus pythonicus vel divinationis fuerit spiritus morte moriantur lapidibus obruent eos sanguis eorum sit super illos*

"'Let *a* man or woman in whom is *a* spirit of magic or divination die by death. They will crush them with stones. Their blood be on them!

Laws for Priests

Leviticus 21:1 *dixit quoque Dominus ad Mosen loquere ad sacerdotes filios Aaron et dices eis ne contaminetur sacerdos in mortibus civium suorum*

Likewise, *the* Lord spoke to Moses, "Speak to *the* priests, Aaron's sons, and you will say to them, 'Let *a* priest not be contaminated in *the* deaths of his fellow citizens,

21:2 *nisi tantum in consanguineis ac propinquis id est super matre et patre et filio ac filia fratre quoque*

"'except only in his close blood relations – that is, over mother and father and son and daughter, brother, as well,

21:3 *et sorore virgine quae non est nupta viro*

"'and virgin sister, who is not married to *a* man.

21:4 *sed nec in principe populi sui contaminabitur*

"'Yet not even in his people's prince will he be contaminated.

21:5 *non radent caput nec barbam neque in carnibus suis facient incisuras*

"'They will not shave head or beard, or make cuts in their flesh.

21:6 *sancti erunt Deo suo et non polluent nomen eius incensum enim Domini et panes Dei sui offerunt et ideo sancti erunt*

"'They will be holy to their God and will not pollute His name, for they offer *the* Lord's incense and God's loaves – and therefore they will be holy.

Restrictions of Priestly Marriage

21:7 *scortum et vile prostibulum non ducet uxorem nec eam quae repudiata est a marito quia consecratus est Deo suo*

"'He will not marry *a* whore or *a* common prostitute, nor her who has been rejected by *a* husband, because he is consecrated to his God,

21:8 *et panes propositionis offert sit ergo sanctus quia et ego sanctus sum Dominus qui sanctifico vos*

"'and he offers *the* loaves of proposition. Therefore, let him be holy, because I also am holy – *the* Lord who makes you holy.

A Priest's Daughter

21:9 *sacerdotis filia si deprehensa fuerit in stupro et violaverit nomen patris sui flammis exuretur*

"'If *a* priest's daughter is caught in illicit sex and violates her father's name, she will be burned up by flames.

The High Priest

21:10 *pontifex id est sacerdos maximus inter fratres suos super cuius caput fusum est unctionis oleum et cuius manus in sacerdotio consecratae sunt vestitusque est sanctis vestibus caput suum non discoperiet vestimenta non scindet*

"'*The* high priest – that is, *the* greatest priest among his brothers – on whose head *the* anointing oil is poured out, and whose hands are consecrated in priesthood, and who is dressed in holy vestments, will not uncover his head or tear his clothes.

21:11 *et ad omnem mortuum non ingredietur omnino super patre quoque suo et matre non contaminabitur*

"'And he will not go in to any dead person at all. He will not be contaminated likewise over his father and mother,

21:12 *nec egredietur de sanctis ne polluat sanctuarium Domini quia oleum sanctae unctionis Dei sui super eum est ego Dominus*

"'nor will he go out from *the* holy *places*, so he not pollute *the* Lord's sanctuary, because God's holy anointing oil is on him. I *am the* Lord.

21:13 *virginem ducet uxorem*

"'He will marry *a* virgin *as* wife.

21:14 *viduam et repudiatam et sordidam atque meretricem non accipiet sed puellam de populo suo*

"'He will not accept *a* widow, or *one* rejected, or *a* filthy *one,* or *a* whore, but *a* young girl from his people.

21:15 *ne commisceat stirpem generis sui vulgo gentis suae quia ego Dominus qui sanctifico eum*

"'He will not mix *the* race of his birth with *the* common *stock* of his nation, because I *am the* Lord who makes him holy.'"

Disqualifications for Priestly Service

21:16 *locutusque est Dominus ad Mosen dicens*

And *the* Lord spoke to Moses, saying,

21:17 *loquere ad Aaron homo de semine tuo per familias qui habuerit maculam non offeret panes Deo suo*

"'Speak to Aaron, 'A man from your seed by families who has *a* defect will not offer *the* loaves to his God,

21:18 *nec accedet ad ministerium eius si caecus fuerit si claudus si vel parvo vel grandi et torto naso*

"'nor will he come near to His ministry if he is blind, if lame, if *having a* small or large or broken nose,

21:19 *si fracto pede si manu*

"'if broken in foot or hand,

21:20 *si gibbus si lippus si albuginem habens in oculo si iugem scabiem si inpetiginem in corpore vel hirniosus*

"'if malformed, if watery-eyed, if having *a* white spot in *the* eye, if joined to *the* itch, if *having a* skin eruption in *the* body, or ruptured.

21:21 *omnis qui habuerit maculam de semine Aaron sacerdotis non accedet offerre hostias Domino nec panes Deo suo*

"'Anyone who has *a* defect from Aaron *the* priest's seed will not come near to offer victims to *the* Lord, nor loaves to His God.

21:22 *vescetur tamen panibus qui offeruntur in sanctuario*

"'Nevertheless, he will eat *the* loaves which are offered in *the* sanctuary,

21:23 *ita dumtaxat ut intra velum non ingrediatur nec accedat ad altare quia maculam habet et contaminare non debet sanctuarium meum ego Dominus qui sanctifico eos*

"'so to this extent: that he may not go inside the veil, or come near *the* altar, because he has *a* defect. And he must not contaminate My sanctuary. I *am the* Lord who makes them holy.'"

21:24 *locutus est ergo Moses ad Aaron et filios eius et ad omnem Israhel cuncta quae sibi fuerant imperata*

Therefore, Moses spoke to Aaron and his sons and all Israel, all those *things* that were commanded them.

Priests Must
Offer Pure Gifts
Leviticus 22:1 *locutus quoque est Dominus ad Mosen dicens*

The Lord likewise spoke to Moses, saying,

22:2 *loquere ad Aaron et ad filios eius ut caveant ab his quae consecrata sunt filiorum Israhel et non contaminent nomen sanctificatorum mihi quae ipsi offerunt ego Dominus*

"Speak to Aaron and his sons, that they beware of those *gifts* of Israel's children that are set aside as holy, and they not contaminate *the* name of *the* holy *things* that they offer Me. I *am the* Lord.

22:3 *dic ad eos et ad posteros eorum omnis homo qui accesserit de stirpe vestra ad ea quae consecrata sunt et quae obtulerunt filii Israhel Domino in quo est inmunditia peribit coram Domino ego sum Dominus*

"Say to them and to their descendants, 'Any man from their race in whom is uncleanness, who comes near to those thing that are consecrated and that Israel's children offer to *the* Lord, will perish before *the* Lord. I am *the* Lord.

22:4 *homo de semine Aaron qui fuerit leprosus aut patiens fluxum seminis non vescetur de his quae sanctificata sunt mihi donec sanetur* *qui tetigerit inmundum super mortuo et ex quo egreditur semen quasi coitus*

"'*A* man from Aaron's seed who is leprous or *who* suffers from *a* flow of semen will not eat from those *things* that are sanctified to Me until he is healed. Who touches uncleanness concerning death, and concerning semen that comes out like in sex,

22:5 *et qui tangit reptile et quodlibet inmundum cuius tactus est sordidus*

"'and who touches *a* reptile or whatever unclean thing that is filthy to touch,

22:6 *inmundus erit usque ad vesperum et non vescetur his quae sanctificata sunt sed cum laverit carnem suam aqua*

"'will be unclean until evening, and will not eat those things that are sanctified. But when he has washed his flesh with water

22:7 *et occubuerit sol tunc mundatus vescetur de sanctificatis quia cibus illius est*

and *the* sun has set, then, made clean, he will eat from *the* holy things, for *that* is his food.

22:8 *morticinum et captum a bestia non comedent nec polluentur in eis ego sum Dominus*

"'They will not eat what died of itself or *was* taken by *a* wild animal, nor will they be polluted in them. I am *the* Lord.

22:9 *custodient praecepta mea ut non subiaceant peccato et moriantur in sanctuario cum polluerint illud ego Dominus qui sanctifico eos*

"'They will keep My commandments, so they not subject themselves to sin and die in *the* sanctuary, when they have polluted it. I *am the* Lord who makes them holy.

Who May Eat the Offerings

22:10 *omnis alienigena non comedet de sanctificatis inquilinus sacerdotis et mercennarius non vescentur ex eis*

"'No foreigner living in *a* priest's house will eat from *the* sanctified *things*, and *a* hired worker will not eat from them.

22:11 *quem autem sacerdos emerit et qui vernaculus domus eius fuerit hii comedent ex eis*

"'But whom *the* priest will buy, and who is domestic in his house, these will eat from them.

22:12 *si filia sacerdotis cuilibet ex populo nupta fuerit de his quae sanctificata sunt et de primitiis non vescetur*

"'If *a* priest's daughter should marry

anyone from *the* people, she will not eat from those things that are sanctified and from first fruits.

22:13 *sin autem vidua vel repudiata et absque liberis reversa fuerit ad domum patris sui sicut puella consuerat aletur cibis patris sui omnis alienigena comedendi ex eis non habet potestatem*

"'But if *a* widow or *a* divorced woman and without children should return to her father's house, she, like *a* girl customarily does, will be nourished by all her father's food. No foreign woman has power to eat from them.

22:14 *qui comederit de sanctificatis per ignorantiam addet quintam partem cum eo quod comedit et dabit sacerdoti in sanctuarium*

"'Who eats from sanctified food through ignorance will add *a* fifth part with that which he ate, and will give *it* to *the* priest in *the* sanctuary,

22:15 *nec contaminabunt sanctificata filiorum Israhel quae offerunt Domino*

"'nor will they contaminate Israel's children's holy *gifts*, which they offer *the* Lord,

22:16 *ne forte sustineant iniquitatem delicti sui cum sanctificata comederint ego Dominus qui sanctifico eos*

"'unless perhaps they suffer their offense's iniquity, when they have eaten *the* holy *things*. I *am the* Lord who makes them holy.'"

Laws for Giving to the Lord
22:17 *locutus est Dominus ad Mosen dicens*

The Lord spoke to Moses, saying,

22:18 *loquere ad Aaron et filios eius et ad omnes filios Israhel dicesque ad eos homo de domo Israhel et de advenis qui habitant apud vos qui obtulerit oblationem suam vel vota solvens vel sponte offerens quicquid illud obtulerit in holocaustum Domini*

"Speak to Aaron and his sons and to all Israel's children, and you will say to them, '*A* man from Israel's house and from *the* newcomers who live with you, who will bring his offering, whether releasing *a* promise or giving freely, whatever he will offer as *a* burnt offering to *the* Lord,

22:19 *ut offeratur per vos masculus inmaculatus erit ex bubus et ex ovibus et ex capris*

"'that he offer through you – *the* offering* will be *a* male without defect, from bulls and from sheep and from goats.

22:20 *si maculam habuerit non offeretis neque erit acceptabile*

"'You will not offer it if it has *a* defect, nor will *it* be acceptable.

22:21 *homo qui obtulerit victimam pacificorum Domino vel vota solvens vel sponte offerens tam de bubus quam de ovibus inmaculatum offeret ut acceptabile sit omnis macula non erit in eo*

"'*A* man who offers *the* Lord *a* peace victim – whether releasing *a* promise or offering freely, either from oxen or from sheep – will offer one without defect, so it may be acceptable to all. *There* will be no defect in it.

22:22 *si caecum fuerit si fractum si cicatricem habens si papulas aut scabiem vel inpetiginem non offeretis ea Domino neque adolebitis ex eis super altare Domini*

"'If *it* is blind, if broken, if having *a* scar, if pimpled or mangy or scaly-skinned, you will not offer them to *the* Lord, nor burn anything from them on *the* Lord's altar.

22:23 *bovem et ovem aure et cauda amputatis voluntarie offerre potes votum autem ex his solvi non potest*

"You can offer oxen or cattle, ear or tail amputated, as voluntary offerings. But gifts from these cannot unbind.

22:24 *omne animal quod vel contritis vel tunsis vel sectis ablatisque testiculis est non offeretis*

Domino et in terra vestra hoc omnino ne faciatis

"'You will not offer *the* Lord any soul that *is* either bruised, or worn out, or beaten, or *has its* testicles removed. And you will not do this in any part of your land.

22:25 *de manu alienigenae non offeretis panes Deo vestro et quicquid aliud dare voluerint quia corrupta et maculata sunt omnia non suscipietis ea*

You will not offer your God loaves from *a* stranger's hand, or any other *offerings* you want to give him that are corrupt and defective. You will not accept them.'"

Respecting the Offering

22:26 *locutusque est Dominus ad Mosen dicens*

And *the* Lord spoke to Moses, saying,

22:27 *bos ovis et capra cum genita fuerint septem diebus erunt sub ubere matris suae die autem octavo et deinceps offerri poterunt Domino*

"Ox, sheep, and goat, when they are born, will be seven days under their mothers' udder. But *the* eighth day and thereafter, they can be offered to *the* Lord.

22:28 *sive illa bos sive ovis non immolabuntur una die cum fetibus* *suis*

"Whether they be ox or sheep, they will not be killed *the* same day with their young.

22:29 *si immolaveritis hostiam pro gratiarum actione Domino ut possit esse placabilis*

"If you kill *a* victim for graces, by *the* Lord's process, so He may be placated,

22:30 *eodem die comedetis eam non remanebit quicquam in mane alterius diei ego Dominus*

"you will eat her *the* same day. Nothing will remain until morning *the* next day. I *am the* Lord.

Keep My Commandments
22:31 *custodite mandata mea et facite ea ego Dominus*

"Keep My commandments and do them! I *am the* Lord.

22:32 *ne polluatis nomen meum sanctum ut sanctificer in medio filiorum Israhel ego Dominus qui sanctifico vos*

"You will not pollute My holy name, so it may be treated as holy among Israel's children. I *am the* Lord who makes you holy.

22:33 *et eduxi de terra Aegypti ut essem vobis in Deum ego Dominus*

"And I led you out of Egypt's land so I could be as God to you. I *am the* Lord.

The Lord's Festivals
Leviticus 23:1 *locutus est Dominus ad Mosen dicens*

The Lord spoke to Moses, saying,

23:2 *loquere filiis Israhel et dices ad eos hae sunt feriae Domini quas vocabitis sanctas*

"Speak to Israel's children, and you will say to them, 'These are *the* Lord's festivals, which you will call holy.

The Sabbath
23:3 *sex diebus facietis opus dies septimus quia sabbati requies est vocabitur sanctus omne opus non facietis in eo sabbatum Domini est in cunctis habitationibus vestris*

"'You will do work six days, for *the* seventh day is *a* Sabbath of rest. It will be called holy. You will not do any work in it. *It* is *the* Lord's Sabbath in all your dwellings.

23:4 *hae sunt ergo feriae Domini sanctae quas celebrare debetis temporibus suis*

"'These, therefore, are *the* Lord's holy festivals, which you must celebrate in their seasons.

Passover
23:5 *mense primo quartadecima die mensis ad vesperum phase Domini est*

"'*The* Lord's Passover is *the* first month, *the* fourteenth day of *the* month, at evening.

23:6 *et quintadecima die mensis huius sollemnitas azymorum Domini est septem diebus azyma comedetis*

"'And *the* Lord's solemnity of unleavened *bread* is *the* fifteenth day of that month. You will eat unleavened *bread* seven days.

23:7 *dies primus erit vobis celeberrimus sanctusque omne opus servile non facietis in eo*

"'*The* first day will be most celebrated and holy to you. You will not do any servile work in it,

23:8 *sed offeretis sacrificium in igne Domino septem diebus dies autem septimus erit celebrior et sanctior nullumque servile opus fiet in eo*

"'but will offer *a* sacrifice to *the* Lord in fire for seven days. But *the* seventh day will be more celebrated and holier, and no servile work will be done in it.

The Festival of First Fruits
23:9 *locutusque est Dominus ad Mosen dicens*

And *the* Lord spoke to Moses, saying,

23:10 *loquere filiis Israhel et dices*

ad eos cum ingressi fueritis terram quam ego dabo vobis et messueritis segetem feretis manipulos spicarum primitias messis vestrae ad sacerdotem

"'Speak to Israel's children, and you will say to them, 'When you have come into *the* land which I will give you, and you harvest crops, you will bring bundles of grain, first fruits of your harvest, to *the* priest.

23:11 *qui elevabit fasciculum coram Domino ut acceptabile sit pro vobis altero die sabbati et sanctificabit illum*

The priest will lift up *the* bundle before *the* Lord *the* day after *the* Sabbath, so it may be acceptable for you, and he will sanctify it.

23:12 *atque in eodem die quo manipulus consecratur caedetur agnus inmaculatus anniculus in holocaustum Domini*

"'And on *the* same day that *the* bundle is consecrated, *a* yearling lamb without defect will be killed as *the* Lord's holocaust.

23:13 *et libamenta offerentur cum eo duae decimae similae conspersae oleo in incensum Domini odoremque suavissimum liba quoque vini quarta pars hin*

"'And libations will be offered with it: two tenths of wheat flour

sprinkled with oil, as *the* Lord's incense and *the* smoothest odor; likewise, *a* libation of wine, *a* fourth part of *a* hin.

23:14 *panem et pulentam et pultes non comedetis ex segete usque ad diem qua offeratis ex ea Deo vestro praeceptum est sempiternum in generationibus cunctisque habitaculis vestris*

"'You will not eat bread and roasted grain and meal from *the* crop until *the* day when you offer some of it to your God. *This* is *an* everlasting commandment in all your generations and dwellings.

The Festival of Pentecost

23:15 *numerabitis ergo ab altero die sabbati in quo obtulistis manipulum primitiarum septem ebdomadas plenas*

"'Therefore, you will number seven full weeks from *the* day after *the* Sabbath in which you offered *the* first fruits' bundles,

23:16 *usque ad alteram diem expletionis ebdomadae septimae id est quinquaginta dies et sic offeretis sacrificium novum Domino*

"'until *the* day after *the* completion of *the* seventh week – that is, fifty days. And so you will offer *a* new sacrifice to *the* Lord

23:17 *ex omnibus habitaculis vestris*

panes primitiarum duos de duabus decimis similae fermentatae quos coquetis in primitias Domini

"'from all your dwellings: two loaves of first fruits, from two tenths of leavened wheat flour, which you will bake as *the* Lord's first fruits.

23:18 *offeretisque cum panibus septem agnos inmaculatos anniculos et vitulum de armento unum et arietes duos et erunt in holocausto cum libamentis suis in odorem suavissimum Domino*

"'And you will offer with *the* loaves seven yearling lambs without defect, and one calf from *the* herd, and two rams. And they will be as *a* burnt offering with their libations, as *a* smoothest odor to *the* Lord.

23:19 *facietis et hircum pro peccato duosque agnos anniculos hostias pacificorum*

"'And you will make also *a* he-goat for sin and two yearling lambs as peace victims.

23:20 *cumque elevaverit eos sacerdos cum panibus primitiarum coram Domino cedent in usum eius*

"'And when *the* priest has lifted them with *the* first fruits' loaves before *the* Lord, they will grant *them* to his use.

23:21 *et vocabitis hunc diem celeberrimum atque sanctissimum*

omne opus servile non facietis in eo legitimum sempiternum erit in cunctis habitaculis et generationibus vestris

"'And that day will be called most celebrated and most holy. You will not do any servile work in it. *It* will be *an* everlasting law in all your dwellings and generations.

23:22 *postquam autem messueritis segetem terrae vestrae non secabitis eam usque ad solum nec remanentes spicas colligetis sed pauperibus et peregrinis dimittetis eas ego Dominus Deus vester*

"'But after you harvest your land's crops, you will not cut them down even to *the* soil, nor gather *the* remaining heads *of grain*, but will let them go for *the* poor and passers-by. I *am the* Lord your God.'"

**The Festival
of Sounding Trumpets**

23:23 *locutusque est Dominus ad Mosen dicens*

And *the* Lord spoke to Moses, saying,

23:24 *loquere filiis Israhel mense septimo prima die mensis erit vobis sabbatum memorabile clangentibus tubis et vocabitur sanctum*

"Speak to Israel's children: *the* seventh month, *the* first day of *the* month, will be *a* Sabbath of remembrance, with sounding trumpets. And it will be called holy.

23:25 *omne opus servile non facietis in eo et offeretis holocaustum Domino*

"'You will not do any servile work in it. And you will offer *the* Lord *a* burnt offering.'"

The Day of Atonement

23:26 *locutusque est Dominus ad Mosen dicens*

And the Lord spoke to Moses, saying,

23:27 *decimo die mensis huius septimi dies expiationum erit celeberrimus et vocabitur sanctus adfligetisque animas vestras in eo et offeretis holocaustum Domino*

"*The* tenth month, *the* seventh day of that month, *is the* day of atonement. It will be most celebrated. And it will be called holy, and you will afflict your souls in it. And you will offer *the* Lord *a* burnt offering.

23:28 *omne opus non facietis in tempore diei huius quia dies propitiationis est ut propitietur vobis Dominus Deus vester*

"'You will not do any work during that day's times, because it is *the* day of atonement, so *the* Lord your God may be made favorable to you.

23:29 *omnis anima quae adflicta non fuerit die hoc peribit de populis suis*

"'Any soul that is not afflicted on this day will perish from his people.

23:30 *et quae operis quippiam fecerit delebo eam de populo suo*

"'And who does any work, I will destroy him from his people.

23:31 *nihil ergo operis facietis in eo legitimum sempiternum erit vobis in cunctis generationibus et habitationibus vestris*

"'Therefore, you will do no work in it. This will be *an* everlasting law to you, in all your generations and dwellings.

23:32 *sabbatum requietionis est adfligetis animas vestras die nono mensis a vespero usque ad vesperum celebrabitis sabbata vestra*

"'*It* is *a* Sabbath of quiet reflection. You will afflict your souls *the* ninth day of *the* month. You will celebrate your Sabbaths from evening until evening.'"

The Festival of Tabernacles

23:33 *et locutus est Dominus ad Mosen dicens*

And *the* Lord spoke to Moses, saying,

23:34 *loquere filiis Israhel a quintodecimo die mensis huius septimi erunt feriae tabernaculorum septem diebus Domino*

"Speak to Israel's children: '*The* festivals of tabernacles will be from *the* fifteenth day of that seventh month, seven days to *the* Lord.

23:35 *dies primus vocabitur celeberrimus atque sanctissimus omne opus servile non facietis*

"'*The* first day will be called most celebrated and most holy. You will not do any servile work.

23:36 *et septem diebus offeretis holocausta Domino dies quoque octavus erit celeberrimus atque sanctissimus et offeretis holocaustum Domino est enim coetus atque collectae omne opus servile non facietis in eo*

"'And you will offer *the* Lord burnt offerings for seven days. Likewise, *the* eighth day will be most celebrated and most holy. And you will offer *the* Lord *a* burnt offering, for *it* is *the* gathering and contribution. You will not do any servile work in it.

23:37 *hae sunt feriae Domini quas vocabitis celeberrimas et sanctissimas offeretisque in eis oblationes Domino holocausta et libamenta iuxta ritum uniuscuiusque diei*

"'These are *the* Lord's festivals, which you will call most celebrated and most holy. And you will offer gifts in them to *the* Lord, burnt offerings and libations, according to *the* rite of each particular day,

23:38 *exceptis sabbatis Domini donisque vestris et quae offertis ex voto vel quae sponte tribuitis Domino*

"'apart from *the* Lord's Sabbaths, and your gifts, and what you offer from promise, or what you will give *the* Lord freely.

The Harvest Festival
23:39 *a quintodecimo ergo die mensis septimi quando congregaveritis omnes fructus terrae vestrae celebrabitis ferias Domini septem diebus die primo et die octavo erit sabbatum id est requies*

"'From *the* fifteenth day, therefore, of *the* seventh month, when you have gathered all your land's fruit, you will celebrate *the* Lord's festivals for seven days. *The* first day and *the* seventh day will be Sabbath – that is, rest.

23:40 *sumetisque vobis die primo fructus arboris pulcherrimae spatulasque palmarum et ramos ligni densarum frondium et salices de torrente et laetabimini coram Domino Deo vestro*

"'And *the* first day you will take up

the fruit of *the* most beautiful tree, and *the* branches of *the* widest palms, and *the* densest foliage of trees, and willows from *the* creek. And you will rejoice before *the* Lord your God.

23:41 *celebrabitisque sollemnitatem eius septem diebus per annum legitimum sempiternum erit in generationibus vestris mense septimo festa celebrabitis*

"'And you will celebrate its solemnity seven days each year. *It* will be *an* everlasting law in your generations. You will celebrate *the* feast in *the* seventh month.

23:42 *et habitabitis in umbraculis septem diebus omnis qui de genere est Israhel manebit in tabernaculis*

"'And you will live in shelters for seven days. All who are of Israel's stock will stay in tabernacles,

23:43 *ut discant posteri vestri quod in tabernaculis habitare fecerim filios Israhel cum educerem eos de terra Aegypti ego Dominus Deus vester*

"'so your descendants may learn that I made Israel's children live in tabernacles when I led them from Egypt's land. I *am the* Lord your God.'"

23:44 *locutusque est Moses super sollemnitatibus Domini ad filios*

Israhel

And Moses spoke concerning *the* Lord's solemnities to Israel's children.

The Tabernacle's Perishables
Leviticus 24:1 *et locutus est Dominus ad Mosen dicens*

And *the* Lord spoke to Moses, saying,

Oil for the Lamps
24:2 *praecipe filiis Israhel ut adferant tibi oleum de olivis purissimum ac lucidum ad concinnandas lucernas iugiter*

"Command Israel's children that they continually bring purest and clearest oil from olives, for preparing lamps.

24:3 *extra velum testimonii in tabernaculo foederis ponetque eas Aaron a vespere usque in mane coram Domino cultu rituque perpetuo in generationibus vestris*

"And Aaron will place them outside testimony's veil, in *the* Covenant Tabernacle before *the* Lord, from evening until morning, and *a* perpetual rite in your generations.

24:4 *super candelabro mundissimo ponentur semper in conspectu Domini*

"They will always be placed on *the* purest candelabra, in *the* Lord's sight.

The Bread of Propositions
24:5 *accipies quoque similam et coques ex ea duodecim panes qui singuli habebunt duas decimas*

"You will receive wheat flour likewise, and will bake from it twelve loaves, each one of which will have two tenths.

24:6 *quorum senos altrinsecus super mensam purissimam coram Domino statues*

"You will set each six of them on either side of *the* purest table before *the* Lord.

24:7 *et pones super eos tus lucidissimum ut sit panis in monumentum oblationis Domini*

"And you will place on them *the* clearest incense, so *the* bread may be as *a* memorial of *the* Lord's offering.

24:8 *per singula sabbata mutabuntur coram Domino suscepti a filiis Israhel foedere sempiterno*

"They will be changed out before *the* Lord each Sabbath, received from Israel's children as *an* everlasting covenant.

24:9 *eruntque Aaron et filiorum eius ut comedant eos in loco sancto quia sanctum sanctorum est de sacrificiis Domini iure perpetuo*

"And they will be for Aaron and his sons, so they may eat them in *the* holy place, because *it* is holy of holies from *the* Lord's sacrifices, *an* enduring law.

A Case of Blasphemy

24:10 *ecce autem egressus filius mulieris israhelitis quem pepererat de viro aegyptio inter filios Israhel iurgatus est in castris cum viro israhelite*

But look, coming out, *an* Israelite woman's son, whom she birthed to *an* Egyptian man among Israel's children, quarreled with *an* Israelite man in *the* camps.

24:11 *cumque blasphemasset nomen et maledixisset ei adductus est ad Mosen vocabatur autem mater eius Salumith filia Dabri de tribu Dan*

And when he had blasphemed *the* name and cursed him, he was brought to Moses. But his mother was called Salumith, Dabri's daughter, from Dan's tribe.

24:12 *miseruntque eum in carcerem donec nossent quid iuberet Dominus*

And they put him in custody until they knew what *the* Lord would command,

24:13 *qui locutus est ad Mosen*

who spoke to Moses,

24:14 *dicens educ blasphemum extra castra et ponant omnes qui audierunt manus suas super caput eius et lapidet eum populus universus*

saying, "Take *the* blasphemer outside *the* camps, and let all who heard him put their hands on his head. And let *the* whole people stone him.

24:15 *et ad filios Israhel loqueris homo qui maledixerit Deo suo portabit peccatum suum*

"And you will say to Israel's children, '*A* man who curses his God will carry his sin,

24:16 *et qui blasphemaverit nomen Domini morte moriatur lapidibus opprimet eum omnis multitudo sive ille civis seu peregrinus fuerit qui blasphemaverit nomen Domini morte moriatur*

"'and let *one* who blasphemes *the* Lord's name die by death. *The* whole multitude will crush him with stones, whether he is *a* citizen or sojourner. Let who blasphemes *the* Lord's name die by death.

24:17 *qui percusserit et occiderit hominem morte moriatur*

"'Let who strikes and kills *a* man die by death.

24:18 *qui percusserit animal reddat vicarium id est animam pro anima*

"'Let who strikes *an* animal repay in kind – that is, animal for animal.

24:19 *qui inrogaverit maculam cuilibet civium suorum sicut fecit fiet* *ei*

"'Who imposes any mark whatsoever on his fellow-citizens, as he did, it will be done to him.

24:20 *fracturam pro fractura oculum pro oculo dentem pro dente restituet qualem inflixerit maculam talem sustinere cogetur*

"'He will repay fracture for fracture, eye for eye, tooth for tooth. Whatever mark he inflicted, he will be forced to sustain.

24:21 *qui percusserit iumentum reddet aliud qui percusserit hominem punietur*

"'Who strikes *a* cow will repay another. Who strikes *a* man will be punished.

24:22 *aequum iudicium sit inter vos sive peregrinus sive civis peccaverit quia ego sum Dominus Deus vester*

"'Let judgment be equal among you, whether *a* sojourner or citizen sins, because I am *the* Lord your God.'"

24:23 *locutusque est Moses ad filios Israhel et eduxerunt eum qui blasphemaverat extra castra ac lapidibus oppresserunt feceruntque filii Israhel sicut praeceperat Dominus Mosi*

And Moses spoke to Israel's children, and they led him who blasphemed outside *the* camps. And Israel's children crushed him with stones, and did as *the* Lord had commanded Moses.

The Sabbath Year

Leviticus 25:1 *locutusque est Dominus ad Mosen in monte Sinai dicens*

And *the* Lord spoke to Moses on Mount Sinai, saying,

25:2 *loquere filiis Israhel et dices ad eos quando ingressi fueritis terram quam ego dabo vobis sabbatizet sabbatum Domini*

"Speak to Israel's children, and you will say to them: 'When you have come into *the* land which I will give you, you will observe *the* Lord's Sabbath.

25:3 *sex annis seres agrum tuum et sex annis putabis vineam tuam colligesque fructus eius*

"'You will sow your field for six years, and care for your vineyard for six years, and collect its fruit.

25:4 *septimo autem anno sabbatum erit terrae requietionis Domini agrum non seres et vineam non putabis*

"'But *the* seventh year will be *the* land's Sabbath, *the* Lord's rest. You will not sow *the* field or care for *the* vineyard.

25:5 *quae sponte gignit humus non metes et uvas primitiarum tuarum non colliges quasi vindemiam annus enim requietionis terrae est*

"'You will not reap what *the* soil sprouts freely, and you will not collect your first fruits' grapes like produce, for *it* is *the* year of *the* land's rest.

25:6 *sed erunt vobis in cibum tibi et servo tuo ancillae et mercennario tuo et advenae qui peregrinantur apud te*

"'But they will be as food to you – to you and your slave, your slave woman and hired helper, and *the* newcomers who sojourn with you.

25:7 *iumentis tuis et pecoribus omnia quae nascuntur praebebunt cibum*

"'All that will grow will supply food to your cattle and animals.

The Year of Release

25:8 *numerabis quoque tibi septem ebdomades annorum id est septem septies quae simul faciunt annos quadraginta novem*

"'You will number likewise to yourself seven weeks of years – that is, seven sevens, which together make forty-nine years.

25:9 *et clanges bucina mense septimo decima die mensis propitiationis tempore in universa terra vestra*

"'And you will blow *the* horn *the* seventh month, *the* tenth day of *the* month, at *the* time of atonement in all your land.

25:10 *sanctificabisque annum quinquagesimum et vocabis remissionem cunctis habitatoribus terrae tuae ipse est enim iobeleus revertetur homo ad possessionem suam et unusquisque rediet ad familiam pristinam*

"'And you will make *the* fiftieth year holy, and call it *the* year of release in all your land's dwelling places, for *it* is *the* Jubilee year. *A* man will return to his possession, and each one will go back to his original family.

25:11 *quia iobeleus est et quinquagesimus annus non seretis neque metetis sponte in agro nascentia et primitias vindemiae non colligetis*

"'Because *it* is Jubilee and *the* fiftieth year, you will not sow or reap what comes up freely in *the* field. And you will not gather *the* vineyard's first fruits,

25:12 *ob sanctificationem iobelei sed statim ablata comedetis*

"'because of *the* Jubilee's holiness. Instead, as soon *as it is* given, you will eat.

25:13 *anno iobelei redient omnes ad possessiones suas*

"'All will return to their possessions in *the* Jubilee year.

25:14 *quando vendes quippiam civi tuo vel emes ab eo ne contristes fratrem tuum sed iuxta numerum annorum iobelei emes ab eo*

"'When you sell anything to your fellow citizen or buy from him, you will not sadden your brother. But you will buy from him according to *the* number of years to *the* Jubilee.

25:15 *et iuxta supputationem frugum vendet tibi*

"'And he will sell to you according to *the* calculated crops.

25:16 *quanto plus anni remanserint post iobeleum tanto crescet et pretium et quanto minus temporis numeraveris tanto minoris et emptio constabit tempus enim frugum vendet tibi*

"'*The* more years that remain after *the* Jubilee, *the* more *the* price will increase as well. And *the* fewer seasons you count, *the* smaller also *the* price will correspond, for he will sell you *the* time's crops.

25:17 *nolite adfligere contribules vestros sed timeat unusquisque Deum suum quia ego Dominus Deus vester*

"'Don't afflict your fellow tribesmen, but let each one fear his God, for I *am the* Lord your God!

Do My Commandments

25:18 *facite praecepta mea et iudicia custodite et implete ea ut habitare possitis in terra absque ullo pavore*

"'Do My commandments and keep *the* judgments and fulfill them, so you can live in *the* land without any fear!

25:19 *et gignat vobis humus fructus suos quibus vescamini usque ad saturitatem nullius impetum formidantes*

"'And may *the* soil bear you its fruits, which you may eat until satisfaction, fearing no assaults!

Answering Anxious Questions

25:20 *quod si dixeritis quid comedemus anno septimo si non seruerimus neque collegerimus fruges nostras*

"But if you say, 'What will we eat *the* seventh year, if we neither sow nor gather our crops?' –

25:21 *dabo benedictionem meam vobis anno sexto et faciet fructus trium annorum*

"'I will give you My blessing *the* sixth year, and it will make *a* three-year crop.

25:22 *seretisque anno octavo et comedetis veteres fruges usque ad nonum annum donec nova nascantur*

edetis vetera

"'And you will sow *the* eighth year and eat *the* old crops until *the* ninth year. You will eat *the* old until *the* new ones are born.

Land Ownership

25:23 *terra quoque non veniet in perpetuum quia mea est et vos advenae et coloni mei estis*

"'Likewise, *the* land will not come *to be sold in* perpetuity, because it is Mine – and you are newcomers and colonists to me.

25:24 *unde cuncta regio possessionis vestrae sub redemptionis condicione vendetur*

From this, *the* whole region of your possession will be sold under condition of redemption.

25:25 *si adtenuatus frater tuus vendiderit possessiunculam suam et voluerit propinquus eius potest redimere quod ille vendiderat*

"'If your brother, stretched out, should sell his small property, and his neighbor wants it, he can redeem what he sold.

25:26 *sin autem non habuerit proximum et ipse pretium ad redimendum potuerit invenire*

"'But if he doesn't have *a* neighbor, and he himself can find *the* money to buy it back,

25:27 *conputabuntur fructus ex eo tempore quo vendidit et quod reliquum est reddet emptori sicque recipiet possessionem suam*

"'*the* crop will be estimated from *the* time which he sold it. And he will return what is left to *the* seller. And he will receive his possession.

25:28 *quod si non invenerit manus eius ut reddat pretium habebit emptor quod emerat usque ad annum iobeleum in ipso enim omnis venditio redit ad dominum et ad possessorem pristinum*

"'And if his hand cannot find enough so he can pay *the* price, *the* buyer will have what he bought until *the* Jubilee year, for in it, everything sold returns to its master, and to its original possessor.

Urban Property
25:29 *qui vendiderit domum intra urbis muros habebit licentiam redimendi donec unus impleatur annus*

"'Who sells *a* house inside city walls has right to redeem *it* until *a* year is completed.

25:30 *si non redemerit et anni circulus fuerit evolutus emptor possidebit eam et posteri eius in perpetuum et redimi non poterit etiam in iobeleo*

"'If he does not buy it back and *the* year's circle is turned, *the* buyer and his descendants will possess it in perpetuity. And it cannot be bought back, even in *the* Jubilee.

25:31 *sin autem in villa fuerit domus quae muros non habet agrorum iure vendetur si ante redempta non fuerit in iobeleo revertetur ad dominum*

"'But if *the* house is in *a* village that has no walls, it will be sold under *the* law of *the* fields. If it is not bought back before, it reverts to its master in *the* Jubilee.

Levitical Property
25:32 *aedes Levitarum quae in urbibus sunt semper possunt redimi*

The Levites' houses which are in cities can always be bought back.

25:33 *si redemptae non fuerint in iobeleo revertentur ad dominos quia domus urbium leviticarum pro possessionibus sunt inter filios Israhel*

"'If they aren't bought back, they will revert to *the* masters in *the* Jubilee, because *the* Levites' urban houses are for their possessions among Israel's children.

25:34 *suburbana autem eorum non venient quia possessio sempiterna est*

"'But their suburban houses will not come *to sale*, because it is *an* everlasting possession.

Helping a Brother

25:35 *si adtenuatus fuerit frater tuus et infirmus manu et susceperis eum quasi advenam et peregrinum et vixerit tecum*

"'If your brother is stretched out and with *a* weak hand, and you receive him as newcomer and sojourner, and he lives with you,

25:36 *ne accipias usuras ab eo nec amplius quam dedisti time Deum tuum ut vivere possit frater tuus apud te*

"'you will not accept usuries from him, nor more than he has given. Fear your God, so your brother may live with you!

25:37 *pecuniam tuam non dabis ei a d u s u r a m e t f r u g u m superabundantiam non exiges*

"'You will not give your money to him at usury, and not demand *an* overabundant crop.

25:38 *ego Dominus Deus vester qui eduxi vos de terra Aegypti ut darem vobis terram Chanaan et essem vester Deus*

"'I am *the* Lord your God who led you out of Egypt's land, so I could give you Canaan's land and be your God.

An Enslaved Brother

25:39 *si paupertate conpulsus vendiderit se tibi frater tuus non eum opprimes servitute famulorum*

"'If, compelled by poverty, your brother should sell himself to you, you will not push him down by base servitude –

25:40 *sed quasi mercennarius et colonus erit usque ad annum iobeleum operabitur apud te*

"'but he will be like *a* hired man or colonist. He will work with you until *the* Jubilee year.

25:41 *et postea egredietur cum liberis suis et revertetur ad cognationem et ad possessionem patrum suorum*

"'And afterward, he will go out with his children, and return to his kin and to their fathers' possession.

25:42 *mei enim servi sunt et ego eduxi eos de terra Aegypti non venient condicione servorum*

"'For they are My slaves, and I led them out of Egypt's land. They will not come into *a* state of slavery.

25:43 *ne adfligas eum per potentiam sed metuito Deum tuum*

"'You will not afflict him by force, but fear your God!

25:44 *servus et ancilla sint vobis de nationibus quae in circuitu vestro sunt*

Let *a* slave and slave woman be yours from *the* nations which are around you,

25:45 *et de advenis qui peregrinantur apud vos vel qui ex his nati fuerint in terra vestra hos habebitis famulos*

"'and from *the* newcomers who stay with you, or those who are born from them in your land. You will have servants from these.

25:46 *et hereditario iure transmittetis ad posteros ac possidebitis in aeternum fratres autem vestros filios Israhel ne opprimatis per potentiam*

"'And you will pass *them* on by legal inheritance to descendants, and you will possess *them* in eternity. But you will not oppress your brothers, Israel's children, by force.

25:47 *si invaluerit apud vos manus advenae atque peregrini et adtenuatus frater tuus vendiderit se ei aut cuiquam de stirpe eius*

"'If *a* newcomer or sojourner's hand should be strengthened among you, and, stretched out, your brother should sell himself to him, or to anyone of his kind,

25:48 *post venditionem potest redimi qui voluerit ex fratribus suis redimet eum*

"'after *the* sale, he can be redeemed. Who wishes among his brothers will buy him back –

25:49 *et patruus et patruelis et consanguineus et adfinis sin autem et ipse potuerit redimet se*

"'either father's uncle, or cousin, or blood relation, or relation by marriage. But if he can, he will buy himself back –

25:50 *supputatis dumtaxat annis a tempore venditionis suae usque ad annum iobeleum et pecunia qua venditus fuerat iuxta annorum numerum et rationem mercennarii supputata*

"'adding up to this extent: *the* years from *the* time of his sale until *the* Jubilee year; and *the* price for which he was sold, according to *the* number of years, and *a* hired *person's* calculated pay rate.

25:51 *si plures fuerint anni qui remanent usque ad iobeleum secundum hos reddet et pretium*

"'If many years remain until *the* Jubilee, he will repay *the* money according to them

25:52 *si pauci ponet rationem cum eo iuxta annorum numerum et reddet emptori quod reliquum est annorum*

"'If few, he will set *the* pay rate with him according to *the* number of years, and will repay to *the* buyer what years are left.

25:53 *quibus ante servivit mercedibus inputatis non adfliget eum violenter in conspectu tuo*

"'considering *the* value of that which he served before. You will not afflict him violently in your sight.

25:54 *quod si per haec redimi non potuerit anno iobeleo egredietur cum liberis suis*

"'But if he can't be redeemed through these, he will go out in *the* Jubilee with his children.

25:55 *mei sunt enim servi filii Israhel quos eduxi de terra Aegypti*

"'For Israel's children are My slaves, whom I led out of Egypt's land.'"

Blessings of Obedience

Leviticus 26:1 *ego Dominus Deus vester non facietis vobis idolum et sculptile nec titulos erigetis nec insignem lapidem ponetis in terra vestra ut adoretis eum ego enim sum Dominus Deus vester*

"'I *am the* Lord your God. You will not make yourselves idols or images, nor will you set up titles, nor place *an* eminent stone on your land so you may worship it, for I am *the* Lord your God.

26:2 *custodite sabbata mea et pavete ad sanctuarium meum ego Dominus*

"'Keep My Sabbaths and have fear toward My sanctuary. I *am the* Lord.

26:3 *si in praeceptis meis ambulaveritis et mandata mea custodieritis et feceritis ea dabo vobis pluvias temporibus suis*

"'If you walk in My precepts and keep My commandments and do them, I will give you rains in their seasons,

26:4 *et terra gignet germen suum et pomis arbores replebuntur*

"'and land will sprout its seed, and trees will be filled with fruit.

26:5 *adprehendet messium tritura vindemiam et vindemia occupabit* *sementem et comedetis panem vestrum in saturitatem et absque pavore habitabitis in terra vestra*

"'*The* harvest's threshing will catch *the* grape-gathering, and *the* grape-gathering will occupy *the* sowing. And you will eat your bread to fullness, and will live in your land without fear.

26:6 *dabo pacem in finibus vestris dormietis et non erit qui exterreat auferam malas bestias et gladius non transibit terminos vestros*

"'I will give peace in your borders. You will sleep, and *there* will be no one who terrifies. I will take away harmful beasts, and *the* sword will not pass through your boundaries.

26:7 *persequemini inimicos vestros et corruent coram vobis*

"'You will pursue your enemies, and they will fall before you.

26:8 *persequentur quinque de vestris centum alienos et centum ex vobis decem milia cadent inimici vestri in conspectu vestro gladio*

"Five of yours will pursue *a* hundred foreigners, and *a* hundred of you will cut down ten thousand of your enemies, in your sword's sight.

26:9 *respiciam vos et crescere faciam multiplicabimini et firmabo pactum meum vobiscum*

"'I will look on you, and make you increase. You will be multiplied, and I will affirm My pact with you.

26:10 *comedetis vetustissima veterum et vetera novis supervenientibus proicietis*

"'You will eat *the* oldest of *the* old, and, *the* new coming on, you will throw out *the* old.

26:11 *ponam tabernaculum meum in medio vestri et non abiciet vos anima mea*

"'I will place My tabernacle among you, and My soul will not abandon you.

26:12 *ambulabo inter vos et ero vester Deus vosque eritis populus meus*

"'I will walk among you, and will be your God. And you will be My people.

26:13 *ego Dominus Deus vester qui eduxi vos de terra Aegyptiorum ne serviretis eis et qui confregi catenas cervicum vestrarum ut incederetis erecti*

"'I am *the* Lord your God, who led you out of *the* Egyptians' land, that you might not slave for them, and who shattered *the* yokes on your necks, so you might walk upright.

Curses of Disobedience

26:14 *quod si non audieritis me nec feceritis omnia mandata mea*

"'But if you won't hear Me or do all My commandments,

26:15 *si spreveritis leges meas et iudicia mea contempseritis ut non faciatis ea quae a me constituta sunt et ad irritum perducatis pactum meum*

"'if you scorn My laws and have contempt for My judgments so you do not do those *things* that were constituted by Me, and you bring My pact to nothing,

26:16 *ego quoque haec faciam vobis visitabo vos velociter in egestate et ardore qui conficiat oculos vestros et consumat animas frustra seretis sementem quae ab hostibus devorabitur*

"'I likewise will do these to you. I will visit you quickly in need and burning, which may finish off your eyes and consume souls. You will sow seed in vain that will be eaten by enemies.

26:17 *ponam faciem meam contra vos et corruetis coram hostibus vestris et subiciemini his qui oderunt vos fugietis nemine persequente*

"'I will set My face against you, and you will run before your enemies, and be subject to those who hated you.

You will flee, no one pursuing.

26:18 *sin autem nec sic oboedieritis mihi addam correptiones vestras septuplum propter peccata vestra*

"'But if even so you won't obey Me, I will add seven-fold *to* your rebukes concerning your sins,

26:19 *et conteram superbiam duritiae vestrae daboque caelum vobis desuper sicut ferrum et terram aeneam*

"'and I will shatter your harshness's pride. And I will give you *a* sky above like iron and *a* land *like* bronze.

26:20 *consumetur in cassum labor vester non proferet terra germen nec arbores poma praebebunt*

"'Your labor will be consumed in futility. *The* land will not bring forth *a* crop, nor *the* trees fruit.

26:21 *si ambulaveritis ex adverso mihi nec volueritis audire me addam plagas vestras usque in septuplum propter peccata vestra*

"'If you walk against Me, nor want to hear Me, I will add even seven-fold to your blows, because of your sins.

26:22 *emittamque in vos bestias agri quae consumant et vos et pecora vestra et ad paucitatem cuncta* *redigant desertaeque fiant viae vestrae*

"'And I will send in among you *the* field's beasts, who will consume both you and your herds. And they may drive all back to scarcity, and your ways be made deserted.

26:23 *quod si nec sic volueritis recipere disciplinam sed ambulaveritis ex adverso mihi*

"'But if even so you don't want to accept discipline, but walk against Me,

26:24 *ego quoque contra vos adversus incedam et percutiam vos septies propter peccata vestra*

"'I likewise will march against you, and strike you seven *times* because of your sins.

26:25 *inducamque super vos gladium ultorem foederis mei cumque confugeritis in urbes mittam pestilentiam in medio vestri et trademini hostium manibus*

"'And I will lead in over you My covenant's avenging sword. And when you have fled into cities, I will send pestilence in among you, and you will be handed over into *the* hands of enemies.

26:26 *postquam confregero baculum panis vestri ita ut decem mulieres in uno clibano coquant*

panes et reddant eos ad pondus et comedetis et non saturabimini

"'Afterwards I will shatter your bread's staff, so that ten women may bake bread in one oven, and return them to *the* scale. And you will eat and not be satisfied.

26:27 *sin autem nec per haec audieritis me sed ambulaveritis contra me*

"'But if you won't hear Me even through these, but will walk against Me,

26:28 *et ego incedam adversum vos in furore contrario et corripiam vos septem plagis propter peccata vestra*

"'I also will march against you in *an* opposing fury. And I will rebuke you with seven blows because of your sins,

26:29 *ita ut comedatis carnes filiorum et filiarum vestrarum*

"'so that you may eat your sons and your daughters' flesh.

26:30 *destruam excelsa vestra et simulacra confringam cadetis inter ruinas idolorum vestrorum et abominabitur vos anima mea*

"'I will destroy your high *places* and shatter your images. You will fall among your idols' ruins, and My soul will detest you –

26:31 *in tantum ut urbes vestras redigam in solitudinem et deserta faciam sanctuaria vestra nec recipiam ultra odorem suavissimum*

"'so much so that I return your cities to wasteland and make your sanctuaries desert. Nor will I accept further *the* smoothest odor.

26:32 *disperdamque terram vestram et stupebunt super ea inimici vestri cum habitatores illius fuerint*

"'And I will destroy your land, and your enemies will be stupefied over it, when they are its inhabitants.

26:33 *vos autem dispergam in gentes et evaginabo post vos gladium eritque terra vestra deserta et civitates dirutae*

"'But I will scatter you among nations, and unsheathe *a* sword after you. And your land will be desert and its cities pulled down.

26:34 *tunc placebunt terrae sabbata sua cunctis diebus solitudinis suae quando fueritis*

"'Then *the* land will enjoy its Sabbaths all *the* days of its solitude, when you have gone

26:35 *in terra hostili sabbatizabit et requiescet in sabbatis solitudinis suae eo quod non requieverit in sabbatis vestris quando habitabatis in ea*

"'into *a* hostile land. It will keep its Sabbaths, and rest in its solitude's Sabbaths, because it did not rest in your Sabbaths when you lived in it.

26:36 *et qui de vobis remanserint dabo pavorem in cordibus eorum in regionibus hostium terrebit eos sonitus folii volantis et ita fugient quasi gladium cadent nullo sequente*

"'And I will give fear in their hearts who remain from among you. In *an* enemy's land, *the* sound of *a* blowing leaf will terrify them. And so, they will flee as if *from the* sword. They will fall, no one pursuing.

26:37 *et corruent singuli super fratres suos quasi bella fugientes nemo vestrum inimicis audebit resistere*

"'And each will fall over their brothers, as if fleeing war. No one of yours will dare to resist enemies.

26:38 *peribitis inter gentes et hostilis vos terra consumet*

"'You will perish among nations, and *a* hostile land will consume you.

26:39 *quod si et de his aliqui remanserint tabescent in iniquitatibus suis in terra inimicorum suorum et propter peccata patrum suorum et sua adfligentur*

"'But if even from these some

remain, they will be silent in their treacheries, in their enemies' land. And they will be afflicted because of their fathers' sins and their own,

26:40 *donec confiteantur iniquitates suas et maiorum suorum quibus praevaricati sunt in me et ambulaverunt ex adverso mihi*

"'until they confess their and their elders' treacheries, by which they transgressed against Me and walked opposed to Me.

A Promise of Repentance
26:41 *ambulabo igitur et ego contra eos et inducam illos in terram hostilem donec erubescat incircumcisa mens eorum tunc orabunt pro impietatibus suis*

"'Therefore, I also will walk opposed to them, and lead them into *a* hostile land, until their uncircumcised mind is ashamed. Then they will pray over their lawlessness,

26:42 *et recordabor foederis mei quod pepigi cum Iacob et Isaac et Abraham terrae quoque memor ero*

"'and I will remember My covenant which I struck with Jacob and Isaac and Abraham. Likewise, I will be mindful of *the* land,

26:43 *quae cum relicta fuerit ab eis conplacebit sibi in sabbatis suis patiens solitudinem propter illos ipsi vero rogabunt pro peccatis suis eo*

quod abiecerint iudicia mea et leges meas despexerint

"'which, when it has been abandoned by them, will please itself in its Sabbaths, enduring solitude because of them. They, indeed, will pray over their sins, because they threw away My judgments and despised My laws.

26:44 *et tamen etiam cum essent in terra hostili non penitus abieci eos neque sic despexi ut consumerentur et irritum facerem pactum meum cum eis ego enim sum Dominus Deus eorum*

"'Yet nevertheless, I have not thrown them away completely, even when they were in *a* hostile land. Nor have I despised them so that they are consumed and I made My pact with them void – for I am *the* Lord their God.

26:45 *et recordabor foederis mei pristini quando eduxi eos de terra Aegypti in conspectu gentium ut essem Deus eorum ego Dominus Deus haec sunt praecepta atque iudicia et leges quas dedit Dominus inter se et inter filios Israhel in monte Sinai per manum Mosi*

"'And I will remember My original Covenant, when I led them out of Egypt's land in *the* nations' sight, so I might be their God. I *am the* Lord God.'"

These are *the* precepts and judgments

and laws which *the* Lord gave between Him and between Israel's children on Mount Sinai, by Moses' hand.

The Price of One's Soul

Leviticus 27:1 *locutusque est Dominus ad Mosen dicens*

And *the* Lord spoke to Moses, saying,

27:2 *loquere filiis Israhel et dices ad eos homo qui votum fecerit et spoponderit Deo animam suam sub aestimatione dabit pretium*

"Speak to Israel's children, and you will say to them, '*A* man who made *a* promise and pledged his soul to God will give *the* price according to *the* estimation.

27:3 *si fuerit masculus a vicesimo usque ad sexagesimum annum dabit quinquaginta siclos argenti ad mensuram sanctuarii*

"'If he is male, from twenty up to sixty years old, he will give fifty silver shekels, *according* to *the* sanctuary's measure,

27:4 *si mulier triginta*

"'thirty if *a* woman;

27:5 *a quinto autem anno usque ad vicesimum masculus dabit viginti siclos femina decem*

"'but *a* male from five years up to twenty will give twenty shekels, *a* female ten;

27:6 *ab uno mense usque ad annum*

*quintum pro masculo dabuntur
quinque sicli pro femina tres*

"'from one month up to five years,
five shekels will be given for *a* male,
three for a female;

27:7 *sexagenarius et ultra masculus
dabit quindecim siclos femina decem*

"'sixty *years old* and up, *a* male will
give fifteen shekels, a female ten.

27:8 *si pauper fuerit et
aestimationem reddere non valebit
stabit coram sacerdote et quantum
ille aestimaverit et viderit eum posse
reddere tantum dabit*

"'But if he is poor and can't repay
the estimation, he will stand before
the priest. And whatever he
estimates and sees that he is able to
repay, he will give that much.

Don't Change
What You Promised

27:9 *animal autem quod immolari
potest Domino si quis voverit
sanctum erit*

"'But if someone should promise *an*
animal that can be offered to *the*
Lord, it will be holy,

27:10 *et mutari non poterit id est
nec melius malo nec peius bono
quod si mutaverit et ipsum quod
mutatum est et illud pro quo
mutatum est consecratum erit
Domino*

"'and it may not be exchanged – that
is, neither best for worse, nor poorest
for better. But if it is exchanged,
both what was exchanged and that
for which it was exchanged will be
consecrated to *the* Lord.

27:11 *animal inmundum quod
immolari Domino non potest si quis
voverit adducetur ante sacerdotem*

"'If someone should promise *an*
unclean animal that cannot be offered
to *the* Lord, it will be led before *the*
priest,

27:12 *qui diiudicans utrum bonum
an malum sit statuet pretium*

"'who, judging whether *it* is good
and bad, will set *the* price,

27:13 *quod si dare voluerit is qui
offert addet supra aestimationis
quintam partem*

"'to which, if he who is offering
wants to give it, he will add *a* fifth
part over *the* estimation.

Promising a House

27:14 *homo si voverit domum suam
et sanctificaverit Domino
considerabit eam sacerdos utrum
bona an mala sit et iuxta pretium
quod ab eo fuerit constitutum
venundabitur*

"'If *a* man promises his house and
sanctifies *it* to *the* Lord, *the* priest
will consider it – whether it be good

or bad – and it will be sold according to *the* price that he will set for it.

27:15 *sin autem ille qui voverat voluerit redimere eam dabit quintam partem aestimationis supra et habebit domum*

"'But if he who promised wants to buy it back, he will give *a* fifth part over *the* estimation, and will have *the* house.

Promising a Field
27:16 *quod si agrum possessionis suae voverit et consecraverit Domino iuxta mensuram sementis aestimabitur pretium si triginta modiis hordei seritur terra quinquaginta siclis veniet argenti*

"'But if he promises *a* field of his possession and consecrates it to *the* Lord, *the* price will be estimated according to *the* measure of seed. If *the* land is sown with thirty measures of barley, it will come to fifty shekels.

27:17 *si statim ab anno incipientis iobelei voverit agrum quanto valere potest tanto aestimabitur*

"'If he promises *the* field immediately at *the* beginning of *the* Jubilee year, it will be estimated for as much as it is worth.

27:18 *sin autem post aliquantum temporis supputabit sacerdos pecuniam iuxta annorum qui reliqui sunt numerum usque ad iobeleum et*

detrahetur ex pretio

"'But if after some time, *the* priest will calculate *the* money according to *the* number of years that remain until *the* Jubilee. And *it* will be deducted from *the* price.

27:19 *quod si voluerit redimere agrum ille qui voverat addet quintam partem aestimatae pecuniae et possidebit eum*

"'But if he who promised wants to buy *the* field back, he will add *a* fifth part to *the* estimate's money, and he will possess it.

27:20 *sin autem noluerit redimere sed alteri cuilibet fuerit venundatus ultra eum qui voverat redimere non poterit*

"'But if he doesn't want to redeem it, but will sell it to any other, he who promised *it* can't buy *it* back further,

27:21 *quia cum iobelei venerit dies sanctificatus erit Domino et possessio consecrata ad ius pertinet sacerdotum*

"'because when *the* Jubilee comes, *the* holy day, it will be to *the* Lord. And *the* consecrated possession by law will belong to *the* priest.

27:22 *si ager emptus et non de possessione maiorum sanctificatus fuerit Domino*

"'If it is *a* purchased field, and not from *the* elders' possession, it will be sanctified to *the* Lord.

27:23 *supputabit sacerdos iuxta annorum numerum usque ad iobeleum pretium et dabit ille qui voverat eum Domino*

"'*The* priest will calculate *the* price according to *the* number of years until *the* Jubilee, and he who promised it to *the* Lord will give *it*.

27:24 *in iobeleo autem revertetur ad priorem dominum qui vendiderat eum et habuerat in sortem possessionis suae*

"'But in *the* Jubilee it will revert to its prior master who sold it, and had it by his possession's lot.

The Legal Value of Money
27:25 *omnis aestimatio siclo sanctuarii ponderabitur siclus viginti obolos habet*

"'Every estimation will be weighed out by *the* sanctuary's shekel. *The* shekel has twenty obolos.

Don't Give the Lord
What Is Already His
27:26 *primogenita quae ad Dominum pertinent nemo sanctificare poterit et vovere sive bos sive ovis fuerit Domini sunt*

"'No one can sanctify or promise *the* firstborn that belong to the Lord.

Whether it is oxen or sheep, they are *the* Lord's.

27:27 *quod si inmundum est animal redimet qui obtulit iuxta aestimationem tuam et addet quintam partem pretii si redimere noluerit vendetur alteri quantocumque a te fuerit aestimatum*

"'But if *an* animal is unclean, he who offered *it* will buy *it* back according to your estimation, and he will add *a* fifth part to *the* price. If he doesn't want to buy it back, it will be sold to another, and for whatever *the* estimation will be by you.

27:28 *omne quod Domino consecratur sive homo fuerit sive animal sive ager non veniet nec redimi poterit quicquid semel fuerit consecratum sanctum sanctorum erit Domino*

"'Everything that is made holy to *the* Lord, whether it be man or animal or field, will not come *up for sale* or be able to be bought back. Whatever is once consecrated will be holy of holies to *the* Lord.

27:29 *et omnis consecratio quae offertur ab homine non redimetur sed morte morietur*

"'And every consecrated *thing* that is offered by man will not be redeemed, but will die by being killed.

27:30 *omnes decimae terrae sive de*

frugibus sive de pomis arborum Domini sunt et illi sanctificantur

"'All *the* land's tenths – whether from crops or from trees' fruit – are *the* Lord's, and will be made holy to Him.

27:31 *si quis autem voluerit redimere decimas suas addet quintam partem earum*

"'But if someone wants to buy back his tenths, he will add *a* fifth part to them.

27:32 *omnium decimarum boves et oves et caprae quae sub pastoris virga transeunt quicquid decimum venerit sanctificabitur Domino*

"'Of all *the* tenths of oxen and sheep and goats that pass under *the* shepherd's rod, whatever comes tenth will be sanctified to *the* Lord.

27:33 *non eligetur nec bonum nec malum nec altero commutabitur si quis mutaverit et quod mutatum est et pro quo mutatum est sanctificabitur Domino et non redimetur*

"'Neither *the* good nor *the* bad will be chosen, nor *one* exchanged for another. If someone should exchange *something*, both what was exchanged and that which was exchanged for it will be sanctified to *the* Lord, and it will not be bought back.'"

27:34 *haec sunt praecepta quae mandavit Dominus Mosi ad filios Israhel in monte Sinai*

These are *the* precepts which *the* Lord commanded Moses for Israel's children on Mount Sinai.

The Latin Torah, 486

Numbers

Numbers 1:1 *locutusque est Dominus ad Mosen in deserto Sinai in tabernaculo foederis prima die mensis secundi anno altero egressionis eorum ex Aegypto dicens*

And *the* Lord spoke to Moses in *the* Sinai desert, in *the* Covenant Tabernacle, *the* first day of *the* second month, *the* year after their going out of Egypt, saying,

1:2 *tollite summam universae congregationis filiorum Israhel per cognationes et domos suas et nomina singulorum quicquid sexus est masculini*

"Take *a* sum of *the* whole congregation of Israel's children, by their families and houses, and each one's names, whatever is of masculine sex,

1:3 *a vicesimo anno et supra omnium virorum fortium ex Israhel et numerabitis eos per turmas suas tu et Aaron*

"twenty years and above, all of *the* strong men from Israel. And you and Aaron will number them by their companies.

1:4 *eruntque vobiscum principes tribuum ac domorum in cognationibus suis*

"And *the* princes of tribes and houses and clans will be with you,

1:5 *quorum ista sunt nomina de Ruben Elisur filius Sedeur*

"whose names are these: from Reuben, Elisur, Sedeur's son;

1:6 *de Symeon Salamihel filius Surisaddai*

"from Simeon, Salamiel, Surisaddai's son;

1:7 *de Iuda Naasson filius Aminadab*

"from Judah, Naasson, Aminadab's son;

1:8 *de Isachar Nathanahel filius Suar*

"from Issachar, Nathanael, Suar's son;

1:9 *de Zabulon Heliab filius Helon*

"from Zebulon, Heliab, Helon's son;

1:10 *filiorum autem Ioseph de Ephraim Helisama filius Ammiud de Manasse Gamalihel filius Phadassur*

"but of Joseph's children, from Ephraim, Helisama, Amniud's son; from Manasseh, Gamaliel, Phadassur's son;

1:11 *de Beniamin Abidan filius Gedeonis*

"from Benjamin, Abidan, Gideon's

son;

1:12 *de Dan Ahiezer filius Amisaddai*

"from Dan, Ahiezer, Amisaddai's son;

1:13 *de Aser Phegihel filius Ochran*

"from Asher, Phegiel, Ochran's son;

1:14 *de Gad Heliasaph filius Duhel*

"from Gad, Heliasaph, Duel's son;

1:15 *de Nepthali Ahira filius Henan*

"from Napthali, Ahira, Henan's son."

1:16 *hii nobilissimi principes multitudinis per tribus et cognationes suas et capita exercitus Israhel*

These *are the* multitude's noblest princes, by their tribes and clans, and *the* heads of Israel's army,

1:17 *quos tulerunt Moses et Aaron cum omni vulgi multitudine*

whom Moses and Aaron took with all *the* multitude of common people.

1:18 *et congregaverunt primo die mensis secundi recensentes eos per cognationes et domos ac familias et capita et nomina singulorum a vicesimo anno et supra*

And they gathered together *the* first day of *the* second month, counting them by clans and houses and families and heads and *the* names of each, from twenty years old and up,

1:19 *sicut praeceperat Dominus Mosi numeratique sunt in deserto Sinai*

as *the* Lord had commanded Moses. And they were numbered in *the* Sinai desert.

Reuben
1:20 *de Ruben primogenito Israhelis per generationes et familias ac domos suas et nomina capitum singulorum omne quod sexus est masculini a vicesimo anno et supra procedentium ad bellum*

From Reuben, Israel's firstborn, by his generations and families and houses and *the* names of each one's head, all that is of masculine sex, from twenty years old and over, proceeding to war,

1:21 *quadraginta sex milia quingenti*

forty-six thousand, five hundred.

Simeon
1:22 *de filiis Symeon per generationes et familias ac domos cognationum suarum recensiti sunt per nomina et capita singulorum omne quod sexus est masculini a vicesimo anno et supra procedentium*

ad bellum

From Simeon's children were counted by their clans' generations and families and houses, by names and by each one's heads, all that is masculine sex from twenty years old and above, proceeding to war,

1:23 *quinquaginta novem milia trecenti*

fifty-nine thousand, three hundred.

Gad
1:24 *de filiis Gad per generationes et familias ac domos cognationum suarum recensiti sunt per nomina singulorum a viginti annis et supra omnes qui ad bella procederent*

From Gad's children were counted by their clans' generations and families and houses, by each one's names, from twenty years old and above, all who could go out to war,

1:25 *quadraginta quinque milia sescenti quinquaginta*

forty-five thousand, six hundred fifty.

Judah
1:26 *de filiis Iuda per generationes et familias ac domos cognationum suarum per nomina singulorum a vicesimo anno et supra omnes qui poterant ad bella procedere*

From Judah's children by their clans' generations and families and houses,

by each one's names, from twenty years old and over, all who could go out to war,

1:27 *recensiti sunt septuaginta quattuor milia sescenti*

seventy-four thousand, six hundred were counted.

Issachar
1:28 *de filiis Isachar per generationes et familias ac domos cognationum suarum per nomina singulorum a vicesimo anno et supra omnes qui ad bella procederent*

From Issachar's children by their clans' generations and families and houses, by each one's names, from twenty years old and over, all who could go out to war,

1:29 *recensiti sunt quinquaginta quattuor milia quadringenti*

forty-four thousand, four hundred were counted.

Zebulon
1:30 *de filiis Zabulon per generationes et familias ac domos cognationum suarum recensiti sunt per nomina singulorum a vicesimo anno et supra omnes qui poterant ad bella procedere*

From Zebulon's children were counted by their clans' generations and families and houses, by each one's names, from twenty years old and above, all who could go out to war,

1:31 *quinquaginta septem milia quadringenti*

fifty-seven thousand, four hundred.

Ephraim
1:32 *de filiis Ioseph filiorum Ephraim per generationes et familias ac domos cognationum suarum recensiti sunt per nomina singulorum a vicesimo anno et supra omnes qui poterant ad bella procedere*

From Joseph's children, Ephraim's children were counted by their clans' generations and families and houses, by each one's names, from twenty years old and above, all who could go out to war,

1:33 *quadraginta milia quingenti*

forty-four thousand, five hundred.

Manasseh
1:34 *porro filiorum Manasse per generationes et familias ac domos cognationum suarum recensiti sunt per nomina singulorum a viginti annis et supra omnes qui poterant ad bella procedere*

Then Manasseh's children were counted by their clans' generations and families and houses, by each one's names, from twenty years old and above, all who could go out to battle,

1:35 *triginta duo milia ducenti*

thirty-two thousand, two hundred.

Benjamin
1:36 *de filiis Beniamin per generationes et familias ac domos cognationum suarum recensiti sunt nominibus singulorum a vicesimo anno et supra omnes qui poterant ad bella procedere*

From Benjamin's children were counted by their clans' generations and families and houses, by each one's names, from twenty years old and above, who could go out to war,

1:37 *triginta quinque milia quadringenti*

thirty-five thousand, four hundred.

Dan
1:38 *de filiis Dan per generationes et familias ac domos cognationum suarum recensiti sunt nominibus singulorum a vicesimo anno et supra omnes qui poterant ad bella procedere*

From Dan's children were counted by their clans' generations and families and houses, by each one's names, from twenty years old and above, who could go out to war,

1:39 *sexaginta duo milia septingenti*

sixty-two thousand, seven hundred.

Asher

1:40 *de filiis Aser per generationes et familias ac domos cognationum suarum recensiti sunt per nomina singulorum a vicesimo anno et supra omnes qui poterant ad bella procedere*

From Asher's children were counted by their clans' generations and families and houses, by each one's names, from twenty years old and above, all who could go out to war,

1:41 *quadraginta milia et mille quingenti*

forty-one thousand, five hundred.

Napthali

1:42 *de filiis Nepthali per generationes et familias ac domos cognationum suarum recensiti sunt nominibus singulorum a vicesimo anno et supra omnes qui poterant ad bella procedere*

From Napthali's children were counted by their clans' generations and families and houses, by each one's names, from twenty years old and above, who could go out to war,

1:43 *quinquaginta tria milia quadringenti*

fifty-three thousand, four hundred.

The Total Count

1:44 *hii sunt quos numeraverunt Moses et Aaron et duodecim principes Israhel singulos per domos cognationum suarum*

These are those whom Moses and Aaron and Israel's twelve princes counted, each one by their clans' houses.

1:45 *fueruntque omnes filiorum Israhel per domos et familias suas a vicesimo anno et supra qui poterant ad bella procedere*

And all Israel's children, by their houses and families, from twenty years old and above, who could go out to war, were

1:46 *sescenta tria milia virorum quingenti quinquaginta*

six hundred three thousand, five hundred fifty men.

Levi

1:46 *Levitae autem in tribu familiarum suarum non sunt numerati cum eis*

But *the* Levites in their families' tribe were not counted with them.

1:48 *locutusque est Dominus ad Mosen dicens*

And *the* Lord spoke to Moses, saying,

1:49 *tribum Levi noli numerare neque ponas summam eorum cum filiis Israhel*

"Do not number Levi's tribe, or put their sum with Israel's children.

1:50 *sed constitue eos super tabernaculum testimonii cuncta vasa eius et quicquid ad caerimonias pertinet ipsi portabunt tabernaculum et omnia utensilia eius et erunt in ministerio ac per gyrum tabernaculi metabuntur*

"But set them up over testimony's tabernacle, all its vessels, and whatever pertains to its ceremonies. These will carry *the* tabernacle and all its utensils. And they will be in ministry, and be measured off around *the* tabernacle.

1:51 *cum proficiscendum fuerit deponent Levitae tabernaculum cum castra metanda erigent quisquis externorum accesserit occidetur*

"When *Israel* sets out, *the* Levites will take down *the* tabernacle. When marking off camps, they will set *it* up. Whoever comes close from outsiders will be killed.

1:52 *metabuntur autem castra filii Israhel unusquisque per turmas et cuneos atque exercitum suum*

"But Israel's children will mark off *the* camps, each one by their companies and wedges and armies.

1:53 *porro Levitae per gyrum tabernaculi figent tentoria ne fiat indignatio super multitudinem filiorum Israhel et excubabunt in custodiis tabernaculi testimonii*

"Afterwards, *the* Levites will fix tents around *the* tabernacle, so indignation may not be over Israel's children's multitude. And they will keep watch as keepers of testimony's tabernacle."

1:54 *fecerunt ergo filii Israhel iuxta omnia quae praeceperat Dominus Mosi*

Therefore, Israel's children did according to all that *the* Lord had commanded Moses.

How Israel Will Camp

Numbers 2:1 *locutusque est Dominus ad Mosen et Aaron dicens*

And *the* Lord spoke to Moses and Aaron, saying,

2:2 *singuli per turmas signa atque vexilla et domos c o g n a t i o n u m   s u a r u m castrametabuntur filiorum Israhel per gyrum tabernaculi foederis*

"Each of Israel's children will make camp around *the* Covenant Tabernacle by their clans' companies, signs and banners and houses.

Judah

2:3 *ad orientem Iudas figet tentoria per turmas exercitus sui eritque princeps filiorum eius Naasson filius Aminadab*

"Judah will pitch tents to *the* east by its army's companies, and its children's prince will be Naasson, Aminadab's son.

2:4 *et omnis de stirpe eius summa pugnantium septuaginta quattuor milia sescentorum*

And all of its race, *the* sum of fighting men, *was* seventy-four thousand, six hundred.

Issachar

2:5 *iuxta eum castrametati sunt de tribu Isachar quorum princeps fuit Nathanahel filius Suar*

"Beside him they will encamp from Issachar's tribe, whose prince was Nathanael, Suar's son.

2:6 *et omnis numerus pugnatorum eius quinquaginta quattuor milia quadringenti*

"And all his fighting men's number *was* fifty-four thousand, four hundred.

Zebulon

2:7 *in tribu Zabulon princeps fuit Heliab filius Helon*

"*The* prince in Zebulon's tribe was Heliab, Helon's son.

2:8 *omnis de stirpe eius exercitus pugnatorum quinquaginta septem milia quadringenti*

"All from his race, *the* fighting men's army, *was* fifty-seven thousand, four hundred.

2:9 *universi qui in castris Iudae adnumerati sunt fuerunt centum octoginta sex milia quadringenti et per turmas suas primi egredientur*

"All who were numbered in Judah's camps were one hundred eighty-six thousand, four hundred. And they will go out first by their columns.

Reuben

2:10 *in castris filiorum Ruben ad meridianam plagam erit princeps Elisur filius Sedeur*

"In Reuben's children's camps, to *the* southern quarter, Elisur, Sedeur's son, will be prince.

2:11 *et cunctus exercitus pugnatorum eius qui numerati sunt quadraginta sex milia quingenti*

"And all his fighting men's army who were counted *were* forty-six thousand, five hundred.

Simeon
2:12 *iuxta eum castrametati sunt de tribu Symeon quorum princeps fuit Salamihel filius Surisaddai*

"Beside him, they camped from Simeon's tribe, whose prince was Salamiel, Surisaddai's son.

2:13 *et cunctus exercitus pugnatorum eius qui numerati sunt quinquaginta novem milia trecenti*

"And all his fighting men's army who were counted *were* fifty-nine thousand, three hundred.

Gad
2:14 *in tribu Gad princeps fuit Heliasaph filius Duhel*

Heliasaph, Duel's son, was prince in Gad's tribe.

2:15 *et cunctus exercitus pugnatorum eius qui numerati sunt quadraginta quinque milia sescenti quinquaginta*

"And all his fighting men's army who were counted *were* forty-five thousand, six hundred fifty.

2:16 *omnes qui recensiti sunt in castris Ruben centum quinquaginta milia et mille quadringenti quinquaginta per turmas suas in secundo loco proficiscentur*

"All who were included in *the* census in Reuben's camps were one hundred fifty-one thousand, four hundred fifty, by their columns. They will set out in second place.

Levi
2:17 *levabitur autem tabernaculum testimonii per officia Levitarum et turmas eorum quomodo erigetur ita et deponetur singuli per loca et ordines suos proficiscentur*

"But testimony's tabernacle will be lifted by *the* Levites' office and their columns. As it will be set up, so also it will be set down. Each will set out by their places and directions.

Ephraim
2:18 *ad occidentalem plagam erunt castra filiorum Ephraim quorum princeps fuit Helisama filius Ammiud*

"To *the* western quarter will be Ephraim's children's camps, whose prince was Helisama, Ammiud's son.

2:19 *cunctus exercitus pugnatorum eius qui numerati sunt quadraginta* *milia quingenti*

"All his fighting men's army who were numbered *were* forty thousand, five hundred.

Manasseh

2:20   *et cum eis tribus filiorum Manasse quorum princeps fuit Gamalihel filius Phadassur*

"And Manasseh's children's tribe *was* with them, whose prince was Gamaliel, Phadassur's son.

2:21   *cunctus exercitus pugnatorum eius qui numerati sunt triginta duo milia ducenti*

"And his fighting men's army who were numbered *were* thirty-two thousand, two hundred.

Benjamin

2:22   *in tribu filiorum Beniamin princeps fuit Abidan filius Gedeonis*

"In Benjamin's children's tribe, Abidan, Gideon's son, was prince.

2:23   *et cunctus exercitus pugnatorum eius qui recensiti sunt triginta quinque milia quadringenti*

"And all his fighting men's army who were counted in *the* census *were* thirty-five thousand, four hundred.

2:24   *omnes qui numerati sunt in castris Ephraim centum octo milia centum per turmas suas tertii*

proficiscentur

"All who were numbered in Ephraim's camps *were* one hundred eight thousand, by their columns. They will set out third.

Dan

2:25   *ad aquilonis partem castrametati sunt filii Dan quorum princeps fuit Ahiezer filius Amisaddai*

"On *the* northern quarter Dan's children camped, whose prince was Ahiezer, Amisaddai's son.

2:26   *cunctus exercitus pugnatorum eius qui numerati sunt sexaginta duo milia septingenti*

"All his fighting men's army who were numbered *were* sixty-two thousand, seven hundred.

Asher

2:27   *iuxta eum fixere tentoria de tribu Aser quorum princeps fuit Phegihel filius Ochran*

"Beside him, tents were pitched from Asher's tribe, whose prince was Phegiel, Ochran's son.

2:28   *cunctus exercitus pugnatorum eius qui numerati sunt quadraginta milia et mille quingenti*

"All his fighting men's army who were numbered *were* forty-one thousand, five hundred.

Napthali

2:29 *de tribu filiorum Nepthalim princeps fuit Ahira filius Henan*

"From Napthali's children's tribe, Ahira, Henan's son, was prince.

2:30 *cunctus exercitus pugnatorum eius quinquaginta tria milia quadringenti*

"All his fighting men's army *was* fifty-three thousand, four hundred.

2:31 *omnes qui numerati sunt in castris Dan fuerunt centum quinquaginta septem milia sescenti et novissimi proficiscentur*

"All who were numbered in Dan's camp were one hundred fifty-seven thousand, six hundred. And they will set out last."

2:32 *hic numerus filiorum Israhel per domos cognationum suarum et turmas divisi exercitus sescenta tria milia quingenti quinquaginta*

This is *the* number of Israel's children, *the* army divided by their clans' houses and columns – six hundred three thousand, five hundred fifty.

2:33 *Levitae autem non sunt numerati inter filios Israhel sic enim praecepit Dominus Mosi*

But *the* Levites were not numbered among Israel's children, for so *the* Lord had commanded Moses.

2:34 *feceruntque filii Israhel iuxta omnia quae mandaverat Dominus castrametati sunt per turmas suas et profecti per familias ac domos patrum suorum*

And Israel's children did according to all that *the* Lord had commanded. They camped by their columns and set out by their fathers' families and houses.

Aaron's Children

Numbers 3:1 *haec sunt generationes Aaron et Mosi in die qua locutus est Dominus ad Mosen in monte Sinai*

These are Aaron and Moses' generations, on *the* day when *the* Lord spoke to Moses on Mount Sinai.

3:2 *et haec nomina filiorum Aaron primogenitus eius Nadab dein Abiu et Eleazar et Ithamar*

And these are Aaron's sons' names: his firstborn, Nadab, then Abiu, and Eleazar, and Ithamar.

3:3 *haec nomina filiorum Aaron sacerdotum qui uncti sunt et quorum repletae et consecratae manus ut sacerdotio fungerentur*

These are *the* names of Aaron *the* priest's sons, who were anointed and whose hands were filled and consecrated so they could carry out priestly duties:

3:4 *mortui sunt Nadab et Abiu cum offerrent ignem alienum in conspectu Domini in deserto Sinai absque liberis functique sunt sacerdotio Eleazar et Ithamar coram Aaron patre suo*

Nadab and Abiu died without children when they offered strange fire in *the* Lord's sight, in Sinai's desert. And Eleazar and Ithamar performed priestly duties before Aaron their father.

Aaron and His Sons
Set Aside as Priests

3:5 *locutus est Dominus ad Mosen dicens*

And *the* Lord spoke to Moses, saying,

3:6 *adplica tribum Levi et fac stare in conspectu Aaron sacerdotis ut ministrent ei et excubent*

"Bring Levi's tribe, and make *it* stand in Aaron's *the* priest's sight, so they may minister to him, and be attentive,

3:7 *et observent quicquid ad cultum pertinet multitudinis coram tabernaculo testimonii*

"and watch over whatever pertains to *the* multitude's worship before testimony's tabernacle,

3:8 *et custodiant vasa tabernaculi servientes in ministerio eius*

"and keep *the* tabernacle's vessels, serving in its ministry.

3:9 *dabisque dono Levitas*

"And you will give *the* Levites *as a* gift

3:10 *Aaron et filiis eius quibus traditi sunt a filiis Israhel Aaron autem et filios eius constitues super* *cultum sacerdotii externus qui ad ministrandum accesserit morietur*

"to Aaron and his sons – to whom they are given by Israel's children. But you will appoint Aaron and his sons over *the* priesthood's worship. *An* outsider who comes near to minister will die."

Why God Took the Levites

3:11 *locutusque est Dominus ad Mosen dicens*

And *the* Lord spoke to Moses, saying,

3:12 *ego tuli Levitas a filiis Israhel pro omni primogenito qui aperit vulvam in filiis Israhel eruntque Levitae mei*

"I took *the* Levites from Israel's children in place of every firstborn who opens *a* vulva among Israel's children, and *the* Levites will be Mine.

3:13 *meum est enim omne primogenitum ex quo percussi primogenitos in terra Aegypti sanctificavi mihi quicquid primum nascitur in Israhel ab homine usque ad pecus mei sunt ego Dominus*

"For every firstborn is Mine, because I struck down *the* firstborn in Egypt's land. I have sanctified to Me anything that is born first in Israel. From men even to cattle, they are Mine. I *am the* Lord.

Count the Levites

3:14 *locutus est Dominus ad Mosen in deserto Sinai dicens*

The Lord spoke to Moses in Sinai's desert, saying,

3:15 *numera filios Levi per domos patrum suorum et familias omnem masculum ab uno mense et supra*

"Count Levi's sons by their fathers' houses and families, every male from one month old and above."

3:16 *numeravit Moses ut praeceperat Dominus*

Moses counted as *the* Lord had commanded.

3:17 *et inventi sunt filii Levi per nomina sua Gerson et Caath et Merari*

And Levi's sons were found by their names: Gerson and Caath and Merari.

3:18 *filii Gerson Lebni et Semei*

Gerson's sons *were* Lebni and Semei.

3:19 *filii Caath Amram et Iessaar Hebron et Ozihel*

Caath's sons *were* Amram and Iessaar, Hebron and Oziel.

3:20 *filii Merari Mooli et Musi*

Merari's sons *were* Mooli and Musi.

The Gersonites

3:21 *de Gerson fuere familiae duae lebnitica et semeitica*

Two families were from Gerson: *the* Lebnites and *the* Semeites.

3:22 *quarum numeratus est populus sexus masculini ab uno mense et supra septem milia quingentorum*

whose people was numbered, masculine sex from one month and above, seven thousand five hundred.

3:23 *hii post tabernaculum metabuntur ad occidentem*

These will make *camp* behind *the* tabernacle, to *the* west,

3:24 *sub principe Eliasaph filio Lahel*

under Eliasaph, Lael's son, *their* prince.

3:25 *et habebunt excubias in tabernaculo foederis*

And they will keep watch in *the* Covenant Tabernacle,

3:26 *ipsum tabernaculum et operimentum eius tentorium quod trahitur ante fores tecti foederis et cortinas atrii tentorium quoque quod adpenditur in introitu atrii tabernaculi et quicquid ad ritum*

altaris pertinet funes tabernaculi et omnia utensilia eius

of *the* tabernacle itself and its covering; *the* partition which is drawn before *the* covenant roof's entrance; *the* partition, likewise, that is hung in *the* entrance to *the* tabernacle's courtyard; and whatever pertains to *the* altar's ritual – *the* tabernacle's ties and all its utensils.

The Caathites

3:27 *cognatio Caath habebit populos Amramitas et Iessaaritas et Hebronitas et Ozihelitas hae sunt familiae Caathitarum recensitae per nomina sua*

Caath's clan had *as* peoples *the* Amramites, and Iessaarites, and Hebronites, and Ozielites. These are *the* Caathite families, counted by their names.

3:28 *omnes generis masculini ab uno mense et supra octo milia sescenti habebunt excubias sanctuarii*

All of male gender from one month old and above *were* eight thousand six hundred. They will have watch over *the* sanctuary,

3:29 *et castrametabuntur ad meridianam plagam*

and camp to *the* southern quarter.

3:30 *princepsque eorum erit*

Elisaphan filius Ozihel

And their prince will be Elisaphan Oziel's son.

3:31 *et custodient arcam mensamque et candelabrum altaria et vasa sanctuarii in quibus ministratur et velum cunctamque huiuscemodi supellectilem*

And they will keep *the* ark, and table, and candelabra; *the* altars, and *the* sanctuary's vessels in which it is administered, and *the* veil, and all furnishings of this kind.

The Prince of Levi's Princes
3:32 *princeps autem principum Levitarum Eleazar filius Aaron sacerdotis erit super excubitores custodiae sanctuarii*

But *the* prince of *the* Levites' princes *is* Eleazar, Aaron *the* priest's son. He will be over *the* keepers of *the* sanctuary's guardians.

The Merarites
3:33 *at vero de Merari erunt populi Moolitae et Musitae recensiti per nomina sua*

And indeed from Merari will be *the* Moolite and Musite peoples, counted by their names,

3:34 *omnes generis masculini ab uno mense et supra sex milia ducenti*

All of masculine gender from one

month old and above *are* six thousand two hundred.

3:35 *princeps eorum Surihel filius Abiahihel in plaga septentrionali castrametabuntur*

Their prince *is* Suriel, Abiahiel's son. They will camp in *the* northern quarter.

3:36 *erunt sub custodia eorum tabulae tabernaculi et vectes et columnae ac bases earum et omnia quae ad cultum huiuscemodi pertinent*

Under their care will be *the* tabernacle's boards and poles; and *the* columns and their bases, and all that pertains to this kind of ritual;

3:37 *columnaeque atrii per circuitum cum basibus suis et paxilli cum funibus*

and *the* courtyard's columns around with their bases; and *the* tent pegs with their ties.

Moses and the Priests
3:38 *castrametabuntur ante tabernaculum foederis id est ad orientalem plagam Moses et Aaron cum filiis suis habentes custodiam sanctuarii in medio filiorum Israhel quisquis alienus accesserit morietur*

Moses and Aaron and their children will camp before *the* Covenant Tabernacle – that is, to *the* eastern quarter – having *the* sanctuary's custody among Israel's children. Whatever stranger comes near will die.

3:39 *omnes Levitae quos numeraverunt Moses et Aaron iuxta praeceptum Domini per familias suas in genere masculino a mense uno et supra fuerunt viginti duo milia*

All *the* Levites whom Moses and Aaron counted, according *the* Lord's commandment – by their families, of masculine gender, from one month old and above – were twenty-two thousand.

The Census of Israel's Firstborn

3:40 *et ait Dominus ad Mosen numera primogenitos sexus masculini de filiis Israhel a mense uno et supra et habebis summam eorum*

And *the* Lord said to Moses, "Count *the* firstborn of masculine sex from Israel's children, from one month old and above, and you will have their number!

3:41 *tollesque Levitas mihi pro omni primogenito filiorum Israhel ego sum Dominus et pecora eorum pro universis primogenitis pecoris filiorum Israhel*

"And you will take *the* Levites to me in place of every firstborn of Israel's

children – I *am the* Lord – and their cattle for all *the* firstborn cattle of Israel's children."

3:42 *recensuit Moses sicut praeceperat Dominus primogenitos filiorum Israhel*

And Moses took *a* census of Israel's children's firstborn, as *the* Lord had commanded.

3:43 *et fuerunt masculi per nomina sua a mense uno et supra viginti duo milia ducenti septuaginta tres*

And *there* were twenty-two thousand, two hundred seventy-three males, by their names, from one month old and above.

3:44 *locutusque est Dominus ad Mosen*

And *the* Lord spoke to Moses,

3:45 *tolle Levitas pro primogenitis filiorum Israhel et pecora Levitarum pro pecoribus eorum eruntque Levitae mei ego sum Dominus*

"Take *the* Levites in place of Israel's children's firstborn, and *the* Levites' cattle for their cattle, and *the* Levites will be Mine! I am *the* Lord.

3:46 *in pretio autem ducentorum septuaginta trium qui excedunt numerum Levitarum de primogenitis filiorum Israhel*

"But as *the* price for *the* two hundred seventy-three who exceed *the* number of Levites among Israel's children's firstborn,

3:47 *accipies quinque siclos per singula capita ad mensuram sanctuarii siclus habet obolos viginti*

"you will accept five shekels for each head, by *the* sanctuary's measure. (A shekel has twenty obolos.)

3:48 *dabisque pecuniam Aaron et filiis eius pretium eorum qui supra sunt*

"And you will give Aaron and his sons *the* money, *the* price of those who are above."

3:49 *tulit igitur Moses pecuniam eorum qui fuerant amplius et quos redemerant a Levitis*

Therefore, Moses took *the* money for those who were above, and who had been bought back from *the* Levites

3:50 *pro primogenitis filiorum Israhel mille trecentorum sexaginta quinque siclorum iuxta pondus sanctuarii*

in place of Israel's children's firstborn – one thousand three hundred sixty-five shekels, according to *the* sanctuary's scale.

3:51 *et dedit eam Aaroni et filiis eius iuxta verbum quod praeceperat sibi Dominus*

And he gave it to Aaron and his sons, according to *the* word which *the* Lord Himself had commanded.

Arrangements for Moving
the Tabernacle

Numbers 4:1 *locutusque est Dominus ad Mosen et Aaron dicens*

And *the* Lord spoke to Moses and Aaron, saying,

4:2 *tolle summam filiorum Caath de medio Levitarum per domos et familias suas*

"Take *the* sum of Caath's children from *the* Levites' midst, by their houses and families,

4:3 *a tricesimo anno et supra usque ad quinquagesimum annum omnium qui ingrediuntur ut stent et ministrent in tabernaculo foederis*

"from *the* thirtieth year and above, until *the* fiftieth year, of all who go in so they may stand and minister in *the* Covenant Tabernacle.

4:4 *hic est cultus filiorum Caath tabernaculum foederis et sanctum sanctorum*

"This is *the* rite of Caath's children: *the* Covenant Tabernacle and *the* holy of holies.

4:5 *ingredientur Aaron et filii eius quando movenda sunt castra et deponent velum quod pendet ante fores involventque eo arcam testimonii*

"Aaron and his sons will go in when *the* camps must be moved, and will take down *the* veil that hangs before *the* entrance. And they will wrap testimony's ark in it,

4:6 *et operient rursum velamine ianthinarum pellium extendentque desuper pallium totum hyacinthinum et inducent vectes*

"and will cover *it* again with *the* veil of violet-colored hides. And they will stretch out over *it as* covering all *the* blue-colored *curtains*. And they will put in *its* poles.

4:7 *mensam quoque propositionis involvent hyacinthino pallio et ponent cum ea turibula et mortariola cyatos et crateras ad liba fundenda panes semper in ea erunt*

"Likewise, they will wrap *the* table of propositions with *a* violet-colored covering. And they will put with it *the* censers and small mortars, *the* wine-ladles and mixing bowls, cast for libations. And *the* loaves will always be in it.

4:8 *extendentque desuper pallium coccineum quod rursum operient velamento ianthinarum pellium et inducent vectes*

"And they will stretch out over *it the* scarlet covering, that again they will cover by *a* veil of violet-colored hides. And they will put in *its* poles.

4:9 *sument et pallium hyacinthinum quo operient candelabrum cum lucernis et forcipibus suis et emunctoriis et cunctis vasis olei quae ad concinnandas lucernas necessaria sunt*

"They will also take up *a* violet-colored covering, by which they will cover *the* candelabra with *the* lamps, and its tongs and snuffers, and all *the* vessels of oil which are necessary for servicing *the* lamps.

4:10 *et super omnia ponent operimentum ianthinarum pellium et inducent vectes*

"And they will put *a* covering of violet-colored hides over all, and put in *their* poles.

4:11 *nec non et altare aureum involvent hyacinthino vestimento et extendent desuper operimentum ianthinarum pellium inducentque vectes*

"In addition, they will wrap *the* golden altar also in *a* blue vestment, and stretch over *it* *a* covering of violet-colored hides, and put in *its* poles.

4:12 *omnia vasa quibus ministratur in sanctuario involvent hyacinthino pallio et extendent desuper operimentum ianthinarum pellium inducentque vectes*

"They will wrap in *a* blue covering all *the* vessels by which *the Lord* is served in *the* sanctuary. And they will extend over *them* *a* covering of violet-colored hides, and put in *their* poles.

4:13 *sed et altare mundabunt cinere et involvent illud purpureo vestimento*

"But they will clean *the* altar of ashes and wrap it in *a* purple vestment.

4:14 *ponentque cum eo omnia vasa quibus in ministerio eius utuntur id est ignium receptacula fuscinulas ac tridentes uncinos et vatilla cuncta vasa altaris operient simul velamine ianthinarum pellium et inducent vectes*

"And they will put with it all *the* vessels that are used in its ministry – that is, *the* fire receptacles, flesh hooks and three-pronged forks, hooks and coal shovels, all *the* altar's vessels. They will cover them together with *a* veil of violet-colored hides, and put in *the* poles.

4:15 *cumque involverint Aaron et filii eius sanctuarium et omnia vasa eius in commotione castrorum tunc intrabunt filii Caath ut portent involuta et non tangant vasa sanctuarii ne moriantur ista sunt onera filiorum Caath in tabernaculo foederis*

"And when Aaron and his sons have wrapped up *the* sanctuary and all its vessels for moving *the* camps, then Caath's sons will enter, so they can carry *the* wrapped *things*. And they may not touch *the* sanctuary's vessels, so they not die. These are Caath's children's burdens in *the* Covenant Tabernacle.

4:16 *super quos erit Eleazar filius Aaron sacerdotis ad cuius pertinet curam oleum ad concinnandas lucernas et conpositionis incensum et sacrificium quod semper offertur et oleum unctionis et quicquid ad cultum tabernaculi pertinet omniumque vasorum quae in sanctuario sunt*

"Eleazar, Aaron *the* priest's son, will be over them, to whose care belongs *the* oil for preparing *the* lamps, and *the* composite incense, and *the* sacrifice that is always offered, and *the* anointing oil, and whatever else pertains to *the* tabernacle's ritual and all *the* vessels that are in *the* sanctuary.

4:17 *locutusque est Dominus ad Mosen et Aaron dicens*

And *the* Lord spoke to Moses, saying,

4:18 *nolite perdere populum Caath de medio Levitarum*

"Don't destroy Caath's people from

among *the* Levites,

4:19 *sed hoc facite eis ut vivant et non moriantur si tetigerint sancta sanctorum Aaron et filii eius intrabunt ipsique disponent opera singulorum et divident quid portare quis debeat*

"but do this for them, so they may live and not die if they touch holy of holies! Aaron and his sons will go in, and they will arrange each one's works, and divide what one must carry.

4:20 *alii nulla curiositate videant quae sunt in sanctuario priusquam involvantur alioquin morientur*

"Let others by no curiosity see what *things* are in *the* sanctuary before they are wrapped. Otherwise, they will die."

Gerson
4:21 *locutus est Dominus ad Mosen dicens*

The Lord spoke to Moses, saying,

4:22 *tolle summam etiam filiorum Gerson per domos ac familias et cognationes suas*

"Take *a* sum also of Gerson's children, by their houses and families and clans,

4:23 *a triginta annis et supra usque*

ad annos quinquaginta numera omnes qui ingrediuntur et ministrant in tabernaculo foederis

"from thirty years old and above, up to fifty years old! Number all who go in and minister in *the* Covenant Tabernacle!

4:24 *hoc est officium familiae Gersonitarum*

"This is *the* Gersonite families' office:

4:25 *ut portent cortinas tabernaculi et tectum foederis operimentum aliud et super omnia velamen ianthinum tentoriumque quod pendet in introitu foederis tabernaculi*

"that they carry *the* tabernacle's curtains and *the* covenant roof, and *the* other covering, and *the* violet-colored veil over all, and *the* partition that hangs in *the* Covenant Tabernacle's entrance;

4:26 *cortinas atrii et velum in introitu quod est ante tabernaculum omnia quae ad altare pertinent funiculos et vasa ministerii*

"*the* courtyard's curtains, and *the* veil in *the* entrance that is before *the* tabernacle; all *the* ties and ministerial vessels that pertain to *the* altar.

4:27 *iubente Aaron et filiis eius portabunt filii Gerson et scient*

singuli cui debeant oneri mancipari

"Aaron and his sons commanding, Gerson's children will carry, and each one will know what burdens they ought to move.

4:28 *hic est cultus familiae Gersonitarum in tabernaculo foederis eruntque sub manu Ithamar filii Aaron sacerdotis*

"This is *the* rite of *the* Gersonites' family in *the* Covenant Tabernacle, and they will be under *the* hand of Ithamar, Aaron *the* priest's son.

Merari
4:29 *filios quoque Merari per familias et domos patrum suorum recensebis*

"You will likewise take *a* census of Merari's children, by their fathers' families and houses,

4:30 *a triginta annis et supra usque ad annos quinquaginta omnes qui ingrediuntur ad officium ministerii sui et cultum foederis testimonii*

"from thirty years old and above, up to fifty years old, all who come into their ministerial office and testimony's tabernacle's ritual.

4:31 *haec sunt onera eorum portabunt tabulas tabernaculi et vectes eius columnas et bases earum*

"These are their burdens. They will carry *the* tabernacle's boards and its poles, *the* columns and their bases;

4:32 *columnas quoque atrii per circuitum cum basibus et paxillis et funibus suis omnia vasa et supellectilem ad numerum accipient sicque portabunt*

"likewise *the* courtyard's columns all around, with their bases and tent pegs and ties. They will receive all *the* vessels and furnishings to count, and so they will carry *them*.

4:33 *hoc est officium familiae Meraritarum et ministerium in tabernaculo foederis eruntque sub manu Ithamar filii Aaron sacerdotis*

"This is *the* Merarites' family duty and ministry in *the* Covenant Tabernacle, and they will be under *the* hand of Ithamar, Aaron *the* priest's son."

Moses and Aaron
Count the Caathites

4:34 *recensuerunt igitur Moses et Aaron et principes synagogae filios Caath per cognationes et domos patrum suorum*

Therefore, Moses and Aaron and *the* gathering's princes took *a* census of Caath's children, by their fathers' clans and houses,

4:35 *a triginta annis et supra usque*

ad annum quinquagesimum omnes qui ingrediuntur ad ministerium tabernaculi foederis

from thirty years old and above, up to *the* fiftieth year, all who go in to *the* Covenant Tabernacle's ministry.

4:36 *et inventi sunt duo milia septingenti quinquaginta*

And two thousand, seven hundred fifty were found.

4:37 *hic est numerus populi Caath qui intrat tabernaculum foederis hos numeravit Moses et Aaron iuxta sermonem Domini per manum Mosi*

This is *the* number of Caath's people who enter *the* Covenant Tabernacle. Moses counted them, and Aaron, according to *the* Lord's word by Moses' hand.

Gersonites Counted

4:38 *numerati sunt et filii Gerson per cognationes et domos patrum suorum*

Gerson's sons also were numbered by their fathers' clans and houses,

4:39 *a triginta annis et supra usque ad annum quinquagesimum omnes qui ingrediuntur ut ministrent in tabernaculo foederis*

from thirty years old and above, up to *the* fiftieth year – all who go in so they could minister in *the* Covenant Tabernacle.

4:40 *et inventi sunt duo milia sescenti triginta*

And two thousand six hundred thirty were found.

4:41 *hic est populus Gersonitarum quos numeraverunt Moses et Aaron iuxta verbum Domini*

This is *the* Gersonites' people, which Moses and Aaron counted according to *the* Lord's word.

Merarites Counted

4:42 *numerati sunt et filii Merari per cognationes et domos patrum suorum*

Merari's children also were numbered by their fathers' clans and houses,

4:43 *a triginta annis et supra usque ad annum quinquagesimum omnes qui ingrediuntur ad explendos ritus tabernaculi foederis*

from thirty years and above, up to *the* fiftieth year – all who go in to fulfill testimony's tabernacle's ritual.

4:44 *et inventi sunt tria milia ducenti*

And three thousand two hundred were found.

4:45 *hic est numerus filiorum Merari quos recensuerunt Moses et Aaron iuxta imperium Domini per manum Mosi*

This is *the* number of Merari's children whom Moses and Aaron counted in census, according to *the* Lord's decree by Moses' hand.

4:46 *omnes qui recensiti sunt de Levitis et quos fecit ad nomen Moses et Aaron et principes Israhel per cognationes et domos patrum suorum*

All who were counted from *the* Levites and whom Moses made by name – and Aaron and Israel's princes – by their fathers' clans and houses,

4:47 *a triginta annis et supra usque ad annum quinquagesimum ingredientes ad ministerium tabernaculi et onera portanda*

from thirty years old and above, until *the* fiftieth year, going in to *the* tabernacle's ministry and carrying burdens,

4:48 *fuerunt simul octo milia quingenti octoginta*

were eight thousand, five hundred eighty together.

4:49 *iuxta verbum Domini recensuit eos Moses unumquemque iuxta* *officium et onera sua sicut praeceperat ei Dominus*

Moses counted them according to *the* Lord's word, each one according to their office and burdens, as *the* Lord had commanded him.

Eject the Ritually Unclean

Numbers 5:1 *locutusque est Dominus ad Mosen dicens*

And *the* Lord spoke to Moses, saying,

5:2 *praecipe filiis Israhel ut eiciant de castris omnem leprosum et qui semine fluit pollutusque est super mortuo*

"Command Israel's children that they eject from *the* camps every leper, and *one* who has *a* flow of semen, and *one who* is polluted over *the* dead.

5:3 *tam masculum quam feminam eicite de castris ne contaminent ea cum habitaverim vobiscum*

"Whether male or female, eject them from *the* camps so they do not contaminate them, when I live with you."

5:4 *feceruntque ita filii Israhel et eiecerunt eos extra castra sicut locutus erat Dominus Mosi*

And Israel's children did so, and they ejected them outside *the* camps as *the* Lord had spoken to Moses.

Confessing and Being Forgiven

5:5 *locutus est Dominus ad Mosen dicens*

The Lord spoke to Moses, saying,

5:6 *loquere ad filios Israhel vir sive mulier cum fecerint ex omnibus peccatis quae solent hominibus accidere et per neglegentiam transgressi fuerint mandatum Domini atque deliquerint*

"Speak to Israel's children, whether man or woman, when they do any of all *the* sins which humans are accustomed to do, and by negligence violate *the* Lord's command and fall short,

5:7 *confitebuntur peccatum suum et reddent ipsum caput quintamque partem desuper ei in quem peccaverint*

"they will confess their sins, and will repay *the* head itself, and *a* fifth part above to him in whom they have sinned.

5:8 *sin autem non fuerit qui recipiat dabunt Domino et erit sacerdotis excepto ariete qui offertur pro expiatione ut sit placabilis hostia*

"But if *there* is no one who may receive *it*, they will give to *the* Lord and it will be *the* priest's, except for *the* ram which is offered for atonement, so it may be *a* pleasing victim.

5:9 *omnes quoque primitiae quas offerunt filii Israhel ad sacerdotem pertinent*

"Likewise, all *the* first fruits which Israel's children offer belong to *the* priest.

5:10 *et quicquid in sanctuarium offertur a singulis et traditur manibus sacerdotis ipsius erit*

"And whatever is offered in *the* sanctuary by each one, and is handed into *the* priest's hands, will be his.

The Test of Infidelity
5:11 *locutus est Dominus ad Mosen dicens*

The Lord spoke to Moses, saying,

5:12 *loquere ad filios Israhel et dices ad eos vir cuius uxor erraverit maritumque contemnens*

"Speak to Israel's children, and you will say to them, '*A* man whose wife wanders and, condemning *the* husband,

5:13 *dormierit cum altero viro et hoc maritus deprehendere non quiverit sed latet adulterium et testibus argui non potest quia non est inventa in stupro*

"'sleeps with another man, and this husband can not catch them, but she hides *the* adultery, and it cannot be proven by witnesses, because she is not found in *the* act of illicit sex;

5:14 *si spiritus zelotypiae*

concitaverit virum contra uxorem suam quae vel polluta est vel falsa suspicione appetitur

"'if *a* jealous spirit agitates *a* man against his wife, who, whether she is polluted or is grasped by false suspicion,

5:15 *adducet eam ad sacerdotem et offeret oblationem pro illa decimam partem sati farinae hordiaciae non fundet super eam oleum nec inponet tus quia sacrificium zelotypiae est et oblatio investigans adulterium*

"'he will lead her to *the* priest. And he will offer as *an* oblation for her *a* tenth portion of flour of sown barley. He will not pour oil over it and put incense on *it*, because *it* is *a* sacrifice of jealousy, and *an* offering investigating adultery.

5:16 *offeret igitur eam sacerdos et statuet coram Domino*

"'Therefore *the* priest will offer it, and stand *it* before *the* Lord,

5:17 *adsumetque aquam sanctam in vase fictili et pauxillum terrae de pavimento tabernaculi mittet in eam*

"'and take up sanctified water in *an* earthenware vessel. And he will put *a* little dirt in it from *the* tabernacle's pavement.

5:18 *cumque steterit mulier in*

conspectu Domini discoperiet caput eius et ponet super manus illius sacrificium recordationis et oblationem zelotypiae ipse autem tenebit aquas amarissimas in quibus cum execratione maledicta congessit

"'And when *the* woman stands in *the* Lord's sight, she will uncover her head and put her hands on *the* sacrifice of remembering, and *the* offering of jealousy. But he will hold *the* bitterest waters, in which he has amassed curses with rebuke.

5:19 *adiurabitque eam et dicet si non dormivit vir alienus tecum et si non polluta es deserto mariti toro non te nocebunt aquae istae amarissimae in quas maledicta congessi*

"And he will make her swear and say, 'If *a* different man has not slept with you, and if you are not polluted by *a* man's forsaken erection, these most bitter waters in which I have amassed curses will not harm you.

5:20 *sin autem declinasti a viro tuo atque polluta es et concubuisti cum altero*

"'But if you have turned aside from your husband, and are polluted, and have had sex with another,

5:21 *his maledictionibus subiacebis det te Dominus in maledictionem exemplumque cunctorum in populo*

suo putrescere faciat femur tuum et tumens uterus disrumpatur

"'these curses will expose you. May *the* Lord give you *as a* curse and *an* example to all among His people! May He cause your thigh to rot, and may your swelling uterus burst open!

5:22 *ingrediantur aquae maledictae in ventrem tuum et utero tumescente putrescat femur et respondebit mulier amen amen*

"'Let cursing's waters go into your womb and, *the* uterus swelling, may *the* thigh rot!'"

"And *the* woman will answer, 'Amen, Amen.'

5:23 *scribetque sacerdos in libello ista maledicta et delebit ea aquis amarissimis in quas maledicta congessit*

"And *the* priest will write these curses in *a* book, and erase them by *the* bitterest waters, in which he has amassed curses.

5:24 *et dabit ei bibere quas cum exhauserit*

"And he will give *them* to her to drink which, when she has drunk,

5:25 *tollet sacerdos de manu eius sacrificium zelotypiae et elevabit illud coram Domino inponetque*

super altare ita dumtaxat ut prius

"*the* priest will take from his hand *the* sacrifice of jealousy and lift it before *the* Lord. And he will put it on *the* altar so to this extent: that before,

5:26 *pugillum sacrificii tollat de eo quod offertur et incendat super altare et sic potum det mulieri aquas amarissimas*

"he may take *a* handful of *the* sacrifice from what is offered, and burn *it* on *the* altar. And so he may give *the* woman *a* drink from *the* bitterest waters.

5:27 *quas cum biberit si polluta est et contempto viro adulterii rea pertransibunt eam aquae maledictionis et inflato ventre conputrescet femur eritque mulier in maledictionem et in exemplum omni populo*

"When she has drunk them, if she is polluted and, despising *the* husband, *is* guilty of adultery, cursing's waters will pass through her. And, *the* womb swollen, *the* thigh will rot. And *the* woman will be as *a* curse and as *an* example to *the* whole people.

5:28 *quod si polluta non fuerit erit innoxia et faciet liberos*

"But if she is not polluted, she will be unharmed and will make children.

5:29 *ista est lex zelotypiae si declinaverit mulier a viro suo et si polluta fuerit*

"'This is *the* law of jealousy, if *a* woman has turned aside from her husband, and if she is polluted,

5:30 *maritusque zelotypiae spiritu concitatus adduxerit eam in conspectu Domini et fecerit ei sacerdos iuxta omnia quae scripta sunt*

and *the* husband, struck by *a* jealous spirit, will bring her into *the* Lord's sight, and *the* priest will do to her according to all *the words* that are written.

5:31 *maritus absque culpa erit et illa recipiet iniquitatem suam*

The husband will be without guilt, and she will recover her treachery.'"

Rules for Consecrating Oneself to the Lord

Numbers 6:1 *locutus est Dominus ad Mosen dicens*

The Lord spoke to Moses, saying,

6:2 *loquere ad filios Israhel et dices ad eos vir sive mulier cum fecerit votum ut sanctificentur et se voluerint Domino consecrare*

"Speak to Israel's children, and you will say to them, 'Whether *a* man or *a* woman makes *a* promise that they may be sanctified, and they want to consecrate themselves to *the* Lord,

6:3 *vino et omni quod inebriare potest abstinebunt acetum ex vino et ex qualibet alia potione et quicquid de uva exprimitur non bibent uvas recentes siccasque non comedent*

"'they will abstain from wine and all that can inebriate, vinegar from wine, and from whatever other drink. And they will not drink whatever is squeezed from grapes, and will not eat fresh or dried grapes,

6:4 *cunctis diebus quibus ex voto Domino consecrantur quicquid ex vinea esse potest ab uva passa usque ad acinum non comedent*

"'all *the* days which they are consecrated to *the* Lord by promise. They will not eat whatever can be from *the* vineyard, from grape spread even to seed.

6:5 *omni tempore separationis suae novacula non transibit super caput eius usque ad conpletum diem quo Domino consecratur sanctus erit crescente caesarie capitis eius*

"'*A* razor will not pass through his head all *the* time of his separation, even to *the* day of completion. *The one* who is consecrated to *the* Lord will be holy, his head's hair growing freely.

6:6 *omni tempore consecrationis suae super mortuum non ingredietur*

"'He will not go in over *the* dead all *the* time of his consecration.

6:7 *nec super patris quidem et matris et fratris sororisque funere contaminabitur quia consecratio Dei sui super caput eius est*

"He will not be contaminated by burial even over father or mother or brother or sister, because God's consecration is on his head.

6:8 *omnes dies separationis suae sanctus erit Domino*

"'He will be holy to *the* Lord all the days of his separation.

6:9 *sin autem mortuus fuerit subito quispiam coram eo polluetur caput consecrationis eius quod radet ilico*

et in eadem die purgationis suae et rursum septima

"'But if someone should die suddenly before him, his consecration's head will be polluted, which he will shave at once, and in *the* same day of his purification, and again *the* seventh *day.*

6:10 *in octavo autem die offeret duos turtures vel duos pullos columbae sacerdoti in introitu foederis testimonii*

"'But on *the* eighth day, he will offer *the* priest two doves or two young pigeons, at *the* entrance to *the* covenant's testimony.

6:11 *facietque sacerdos unum pro peccato et alterum in holocaustum et deprecabitur pro eo quia peccavit super mortuo sanctificabitque caput eius in die illo*

"'And *the* priest will make one for sin and *the* other as *a* burnt offering. And he will pray for him, because he sinned over *the* dead. And he will sanctify his head on that day.

6:12 *et consecrabit Domino dies separationis illius offerens agnum anniculum pro peccato ita tamen ut dies priores irriti fiant quoniam polluta est sanctificatio eius*

"And he will consecrate his days of separation to *the* Lord, offering *a* yearling lamb so for sin, that nevertheless *the* prior days be made void because his sanctification was polluted.

6:13 *ista est lex consecrationis cum dies quos ex voto decreverat conplebuntur adducet eum ad ostium tabernaculi foederis*

"'This is *the* law of consecration. When *the* days which he had settled by promise are completed, he will bring him to *the* door of testimony's tabernacle,

6:14 *et offeret oblationem eius Domino agnum anniculum inmaculatum in holocaustum et ovem anniculam inmaculatam pro peccato et arietem inmaculatum hostiam pacificam*

"'and will offer to *the* Lord *as* his oblation *a* yearling lamb without defect as *a* burnt offering; and *a* spotless yearling ewe for sin; and *a* ram without defect as *a* peace offering;

6:15 *canistrum quoque panum azymorum qui conspersi sunt oleo et lagana absque fermento uncta oleo ac libamina singulorum*

"'a basket of unleavened bread, likewise, which is sprinkled with oil; and cakes without yeast smeared with oil; and each ones' libations,

6:16 *quae offeret sacerdos coram Domino et faciet tam pro peccato quam in holocaustum*

"'which *the* priest will offer before *the* Lord. And he will do alike for *the* sin *offering* as for *the* burnt offering.

6:17 *arietem vero immolabit hostiam pacificam Domino offerens simul canistrum azymorum et libamenta quae ex more debentur*

"'And he will kill *the* ram as *a* peace victim to *the* Lord, offering together *the* basket of unleavened *loaves* and *the* libations which by custom are owed.

6:18 *tunc radetur nazareus ante ostium tabernaculi foederis caesarie consecrationis suae tolletque capillos eius et ponet super ignem qui est subpositus sacrificio pacificorum*

"'Then *the* Nazarite will be shaved of his consecration's hair before *the* opening of testimony's tabernacle. And *the priest* will take his hair and put it on *the* fire which *is* placed under *the* peace sacrifice,

6:19 *et armum coctum arietis tortamque absque fermento unam de canistro et laganum azymum unum et tradet in manibus nazarei postquam rasum fuerit caput eius*

"'and *the* ram's cooked forequarter, and one loaf without yeast from *the* basket, and one unleavened cake, and will put it into *the* Nazarite's hand after his head is shaved.

6:20 *susceptaque rursum ab eo elevabit in conspectu Domini et sanctificata sacerdotis erunt sicut pectusculum quod separari iussum est et femur post haec potest bibere nazareus vinum*

"'And, taking them again from him, he will lift them up before *the* Lord, and they will sanctified to *the* priest, like *the* breast and thigh that are commanded to be set aside. After this, *the* Nazarite can drink wine.

6:21 *ista est lex nazarei cum voverit oblationem suam Domino tempore consecrationis suae exceptis his quae invenerit manus eius iuxta quod mente devoverat ita faciet ad perfectionem sanctificationis suae*

"'This is *the* law of *the* Nazarite, when he promises his offering to *the* Lord during his consecration's time, except for those which his hand finds. According to what mind has promised, so he will do to his sanctification's completion.'"

The Priestly Blessing

6:22 *locutus est Dominus ad Mosen dicens*

The Lord spoke to Moses, saying,

6:23 *loquere Aaron et filiis eius sic benedicetis filiis Israhel et dicetis eis*

"Speak to Aaron and his sons: 'You will bless Israel's children so, and will say to them,

6:24 *benedicat tibi Dominus et custodiat te*

"'*The* Lord bless you and keep you.

6:25 *ostendat Dominus faciem suam tibi et misereatur tui*

"'*The* Lord show His face to you, and be merciful to you.

6:26 *convertat Dominus vultum suum ad te et det tibi pacem*

"'*The* Lord turn His attention to you, and give you peace.'

6:27 *invocabunt nomen meum super filios Israhel et ego benedicam eis*

"They will invoke My name over Israel's children, and I will bless them."

Israel's Leaders Bring Gifts

Numbers 7:1 *factum est autem in die qua conplevit Moses tabernaculum et erexit illud unxitque et sanctificavit cum omnibus vasis suis altare similiter et vasa eius*

But it happened that in *the* day when Moses completed *the* tabernacle and set it up, and anointed and sanctified it with all its vessels, *the* altar as well and its vessels,

7:2 *obtulerunt principes Israhel et capita familiarum qui erant per singulas tribus praefecti eorum qui numerati fuerant*

Israel's princes and *the* heads of families, who were their officers through each of *the* tribes that were numbered, brought

7:3 *munera coram Domino sex plaustra tecta cum duodecim bubus unum plaustrum obtulere duo duces et unum bovem singuli obtuleruntque ea in conspectu tabernaculi*

gifts before *the* Lord: six covered wagons with twelve oxen. Two dukes offered one wagon, and each one *an* ox. And they offered them in *the* tabernacle's presence.

7:4 *ait autem Dominus ad Mosen*

But *the* Lord said to Moses,

7:5 *suscipe ab eis ut serviant in ministerio tabernaculi et tradas ea Levitis iuxta ordinem ministerii sui*

"Receive *all* from them, so they may serve in *the* tabernacle's ministry. And you will give them to *the* Levites according to their ministry's order."

7:6 *itaque cum suscepisset Moses plaustra et boves tradidit eos Levitis*

And so, when Moses had received *the* wagons and oxen, he gave them to *the* Levites.

7:7 *duo plaustra et quattuor boves dedit filiis Gerson iuxta id quod habebant necessarium*

He gave two wagons and four oxen to Gerson's children, according to that which they had need of.

7:8 *quattuor alia plaustra et octo boves dedit filiis Merari secundum officia et cultum suum sub manu Ithamar filii Aaron sacerdotis*

He gave four other wagons and eight oxen to Merari's children, according to their office and rite under *the* hand of Ithamar, Aaron *the* priest's son.

7:9 *filiis autem Caath non dedit plaustra et boves quia in sanctuario serviunt et onera propriis portant umeris*

But he did not give wagons and oxen to Caath's children, because they serve in *the* sanctuary and carry burdens on *their* own shoulders.

7:10 *igitur obtulerunt duces in dedicationem altaris die qua unctum est oblationem suam ante altare*

Therefore, *the* dukes offered their oblation before *the* altar, on *the* day of *the* altar's dedication, which was anointed.

Each Tribe Brings Gifts

7:11 *dixitque Dominus ad Mosen singuli duces per singulos dies offerant munera in dedicationem altaris*

And *the* Lord said to Moses, "Let each of *the* dukes offer gifts for each day in *the* altar's dedication."

Judah's Gift

7:12 *primo die obtulit oblationem suam Naasson filius Aminadab de tribu Iuda*

The first day, Naasson, Aminadab's son, from Judah's tribe, brought his oblation.

7:13 *fueruntque in ea acetabulum argenteum pondo centum triginta siclorum fiala argentea habens septuaginta siclos iuxta pondus sanctuarii utrumque plenum simila conspersa oleo in sacrificium*

And in it were *a* silver cup, weighing one hundred thirty shekels; *a* silver drinking cup having seventy shekels according to *the* sanctuary's weight; and both full of wheat flour sprinkled with oil, as *a* sacrifice;

7:14 *mortariolum ex decem siclis aureis plenum incenso*

a small mortar of ten golden shekels, filled with incense;

7:15 *bovem et arietem et agnum anniculum in holocaustum*

an ox, and *a* ram, and *a* yearling lamb as *a* burnt offering;

7:16 *hircumque pro peccato*

and *a* he-goat for sin;

7:17 *et in sacrificio pacificorum boves duos arietes quinque hircos quinque agnos anniculos quinque haec est oblatio Naasson filii Aminadab*

and as *a* peace sacrifice, two oxen, five rams, five he-goats, *and* five yearling lambs. This is Naasson, Aminadab's son's, offering.

Issachar

7:18 *secundo die obtulit Nathanahel filius Suar dux de tribu Isachar*

The second day, Nathanael, Suar's son, duke of Issachar's tribe, offered

7:19 *acetabulum argenteum*

adpendens centum triginta siclos fialam argenteam habentem septuaginta siclos iuxta pondus sanctuarii utrumque plenum simila conspersa oleo in sacrificium

a silver cup weighing one hundred thirty shekels; *a* silver drinking bowl having seventy shekels, according to *the* sanctuary's measure; and both full of wheat flour sprinkled with oil as *a* sacrifice;

7:20 *mortariolum aureum habens decem siclos plenum incenso*

a small, golden mortar, having ten shekels, filled with incense;

7:21 *bovem de armento et arietem et agnum anniculum in holocaustum*

an ox from *the* herd, and *a* ram, and *a* yearling lamb as *a* burnt offering;

7:22 *hircumque pro peccato*

a he-goat for sin;

7:23 *et in sacrificio pacificorum boves duos arietes quinque hircos quinque agnos anniculos quinque haec fuit oblatio Nathanahel filii Suar*

and as *a* peace sacrifice, five oxen, five rams, five he-goats, *and* five yearling lambs. This was Nathanael, Suar's son's, offering.

Zebulon

7:24 *tertio die princeps filiorum Zabulon Heliab filius Helon*

The third day, *the* prince of Zebulon's children, Heliab, Helon's son,

7:25 *obtulit acetabulum argenteum adpendens centum triginta siclos fialam argenteam habentem septuaginta siclos ad pondus sanctuarii utrumque plenum simila conspersa oleo in sacrificium*

offered *a* silver cup weighing one hundred thirty shekels; *a* silver drinking cup having seventy shekels, according to *the* sanctuary's measure; and both full of wheat flour sprinkled with oil as *a* sacrifice;

7:26 *mortariolum aureum adpendens decem siclos plenum incenso*

a small, golden mortar weighing ten shekels, full of incense;

7:27 *bovem de armento et arietem et agnum anniculum in holocaustum*

an ox from *the* herd, and *a* ram, and *a* yearling lamb as *a* burnt offering;

7:28 *hircumque pro peccato*

a he-goat for sin;

7:29 *et in sacrificio pacificorum*

boves duos arietes quinque hircos quinque agnos anniculos quinque haec est oblatio Heliab filii Helon

and as *a* peace sacrifice two oxen, five rams, five he-goats, *and* five yearling lambs. This is *the* oblation of Heliab, Helon's son.

Reuben

7:30 *die quarto princeps filiorum Ruben Helisur filius Sedeur*

The fourth day, Reuben's children's prince, Helisur, Seduer's son,

7:31 *obtulit acetabulum argenteum adpendens centum triginta siclos fialam argenteam habentem septuaginta siclos ad pondus sanctuarii utrumque plenum simila conspersa oleo in sacrificium*

offered *a* silver cup weighing one hundred thirty shekels; *a* silver drinking cup having seventy shekels by *the* sanctuary's weight; and both full of wheat flour sprinkled with oil as *a* sacrifice;

7:32 *mortariolum aureum adpendens decem siclos plenum incenso*

a small, golden mortar weighing ten shekels, filled with incense;

7:33 *bovem de armento et arietem et agnum anniculum in holocaustum*

an ox from *the* herd, and *a* ram, and *a* yearling lamb as *a* burnt offering;

7:34 *hircumque pro peccato*

a he-goat for sin;

7:35 *et in hostias pacificorum boves duos arietes quinque hircos quinque agnos anniculos quinque haec fuit oblatio Helisur filii Sedeur*

and as peace victims two oxen, five rams, five he-goats, and five yearling lambs. This was Helisur, Sedeur's son's, offering.

Simeon

7:36 *die quinto princeps filiorum Symeon Salamihel filius Surisaddai*

The fifth day, Salamiel, Surisaddai's son, prince of Simeon's children,

7:37 *obtulit acetabulum argenteum adpendens centum triginta siclos fialam argenteam habentem septuaginta siclos ad pondus sanctuarii utrumque plenum simila conspersa oleo in sacrificium*

offered *a* silver cup weighing one hundred thirty shekels; *a* silver drinking cup having seventy shekels by *the* sanctuary's weight; and both full of wheat flour sprinkled with oil as *a* sacrifice;

7:38 *mortariolum aureum adpendens decem siclos plenum*

incenso

a small, golden mortar weighing ten shekels, filled with incense;

7:39 *bovem de armento et arietem et agnum anniculum in holocaustum*

an ox from *the* herd, and *a* ram, and *a* yearling lamb as *a* burnt offering;

7:40 *hircumque pro peccato*

a he-goat for sin;

7:41 *et in hostias pacificorum boves duos arietes quinque hircos quinque agnos anniculos quinque haec fuit oblatio Salamihel filii Surisaddai*

and as peace victims two oxen, five rams, five he-goats, and five yearling lambs. This was Salamiel, Surisaddai's son's, offering.

Gad
7:42 *die sexto princeps filiorum Gad Heliasaph filius Duhel*

The sixth day, Heliasaph, Duel's son, Gad's children's prince,

7:43 *obtulit acetabulum argenteum adpendens centum triginta siclos fialam argenteam habentem septuaginta siclos ad pondus sanctuarii utrumque plenum simila conspersa oleo in sacrificium*

offered *a* silver cup weighing one

hundred thirty shekels; *a* silver drinking cup having seventy shekels by *the* sanctuary's weight; and both full of wheat flour sprinkled with oil as *a* sacrifice;

7:44 *mortariolum aureum adpendens siclos decem plenum incenso*

a small, golden mortar weighing ten shekels, filled with incense;

7:45 *bovem de armento et arietem et agnum anniculum in holocaustum*

an ox from *the* herd, and *a* ram, and *a* yearling lamb as *a* burnt offering;

7:46 *hircumque pro peccato*

a he-goat for sin;

7:47 *et in hostias pacificorum boves duos arietes quinque hircos quinque agnos anniculos quinque haec fuit oblatio Heliasaph filii Duhel*

and as peace victims two oxen, five rams, five he-goats, and five yearling lambs. This was Heliasaph, Duel's son's, offering.

Ephraim
7:48 *die septimo princeps filiorum Ephraim Helisama filius Ammiud*

The seventh day, Helisama, Ammiud's son, Ephraim's children's prince,

7:49 *obtulit acetabulum argenteum adpendens centum triginta siclos fialam argenteam habentem septuaginta siclos ad pondus sanctuarii utrumque plenum simila conspersa oleo in sacrificium*

offered *a* silver cup weighing one hundred thirty shekels; *a* silver drinking cup having seventy shekels by *the* sanctuary's weight; and both full of wheat flour sprinkled with oil as *a* sacrifice;

7:50 *mortariolum aureum adpendens decem siclos plenum incenso*

a small, golden mortar weighing ten shekels, filled with incense;

7:51 *bovem de armento et arietem et agnum anniculum in holocaustum*

an ox from *the* herd, and *a* ram, and *a* yearling lamb as *a* burnt offering;

7:52 *hircumque pro peccato*

a he-goat for sin;

7:53 *et in hostias pacificas boves duos arietes quinque hircos quinque agnos anniculos quinque haec fuit oblatio Helisama filii Ammiud*

and as peace victims two oxen, five rams, five he-goats, and five yearling lambs. This was Helisama, Ammiud's son's, offering

Manasseh

7:54 *die octavo princeps filiorum Manasse Gamalihel filius Phadassur*

The eighth, Gamaliel, Phadassur's son, prince of Manasseh's children,

7:55 *obtulit acetabulum argenteum adpendens centum triginta siclos fialam argenteam habentem septuaginta siclos ad pondus sanctuarii utrumque plenum simila conspersa oleo in sacrificium*

offered *a* silver cup weighing one hundred thirty shekels; *a* silver drinking cup having seventy shekels by *the* sanctuary's weight; and both full of wheat flour sprinkled with oil as *a* sacrifice;

7:56 *mortariolum aureum adpendens decem siclos plenum incenso*

a small, golden mortar weighing ten shekels, filled with incense;

7:57 *bovem de armento et arietem et agnum anniculum in holocaustum*

an ox from *the* herd, and *a* ram, and *a* yearling lamb as *a* burnt offering;

7:58 *hircumque pro peccato*

a he-goat for sin;

7:59 *et in hostias pacificorum boves duos arietes quinque hircos quinque* *agnos anniculos quinque haec fuit oblatio Gamalihel filii Phadassur*

and as peace victims two oxen, five rams, five he-goats, and five yearling lambs. This was Gamaliel, Phadassur's son's, offering.

Benjamin

7:60 *die nono princeps filiorum Beniamin Abidan filius Gedeonis*

The ninth day, Abidan, Gideon's son, prince of Benjamin's children,

7:61 *obtulit acetabulum argenteum adpendens centum triginta siclos fialam argenteam habentem septuaginta siclos ad pondus sanctuarii utrumque plenum simila conspersa oleo in sacrificium*

offered *a* silver cup weighing one hundred thirty shekels; *a* silver drinking cup having seventy shekels by *the* sanctuary's weight; and both full of wheat flour sprinkled with oil as *a* sacrifice;

7:62 *mortariolum aureum adpendens decem siclos plenum incenso*

a small, golden mortar weighing ten shekels, filled with incense;

7:63 *bovem de armento et arietem et agnum anniculum in holocaustum*

an ox from *the* herd, and *a* ram, and

a yearling lamb as *a* burnt offering;

7:64 *hircumque pro peccato*

a he-goat for sin;

7:65 *et in hostias pacificorum boves duos arietes quinque hircos quinque agnos anniculos quinque haec fuit oblatio Abidan filii Gideonis*

and as peace victims two oxen, five rams, five he-goats, and five yearling lambs. This was Abidan, Gideon's son's, offering.

Dan

7:66 *die decimo princeps filiorum Dan Ahiezer filius Amisaddai*

The tenth day, Ahiezer, Amisaddai's son, Dan's children's prince,

7:67 *obtulit acetabulum argenteum adpendens centum triginta siclos fialam argenteam habentem septuaginta siclos ad pondus sanctuarii utrumque plenum simila conspersa oleo in sacrificium*

offered *a* silver cup weighing one hundred thirty shekels; *a* silver drinking cup having seventy shekels by *the* sanctuary's weight; and both full of wheat flour sprinkled with oil as *a* sacrifice;

7:68 *mortariolum aureum adpendens decem siclos plenum incenso*

a small, golden mortar weighing ten shekels, filled with incense;

7:69 *bovem de armento et arietem et agnum anniculum in holocaustum*

an ox from *the* herd, and *a* ram, and *a* yearling lamb as *a* burnt offering;

7:70 *hircumque pro peccato*

a he-goat for sin;

7:71 *et in hostias pacificorum boves duos arietes quinque hircos quinque agnos anniculos quinque haec fuit oblatio Ahiezer filii Amisaddai*

and as peace victims two oxen, five rams, five he-goats, and five yearling lambs.   This   was   Ahiezer, Amisaddai's son's, offering.

Asher
7:72   *die   undecimo   princeps filiorum   Aser   Phagaihel   filius Ochran*

The eleventh day, Phagaiel, Ochran's son, Asher's children's prince,

7:73 *obtulit acetabulum argenteum adpendens centum triginta siclos fialam   argenteam   habentem septuaginta   siclos   ad   pondus sanctuarii utrumque plenum simila conspersa oleo in sacrificium*

offered *a* silver cup weighing one hundred thirty shekels; *a* silver

drinking cup having seventy shekels by *the* sanctuary's weight; and both full of wheat flour sprinkled with oil as *a* sacrifice;

7:74   *mortariolum   aureum adpendens   decem   siclos   plenum incenso*

a small, golden mortar weighing ten shekels, filled with incense;

7:75 *bovem de armento et arietem et agnum anniculum in holocaustum*

an ox from *the* herd, and *a* ram, and *a* yearling lamb as *a* burnt offering;

7:76 *hircumque pro peccato*

a he-goat for sin;

7:77 *et in hostias pacificorum boves duos arietes quinque hircos quinque agnos anniculos quinque haec fuit oblatio Phagaihel filii Ochran*

and as peace victims two oxen, five rams, five he-goats, and five yearling lambs. This was Phagaiel, Ochran's son's, offering.

Napthali
7:78   *die   duodecimo   princeps filiorum   Nepthalim   Achira   filius Henan*

The twelfth day, Achira, Henan's son, prince of Napthali's children,

7:79 *obtulit acetabulum argenteum adpendens centum triginta siclos fialam argenteam habentem septuaginta siclos ad pondus sanctuarii utrumque plenum simila conspersa oleo in sacrificium*

offered *a* silver cup weighing one hundred thirty shekels; *a* silver drinking cup having seventy shekels by *the* sanctuary's weight; and both full of wheat flour sprinkled with oil as *a* sacrifice;

7:80 *mortariolum aureum adpendens decem siclos plenum incenso*

a small, golden mortar weighing ten shekels, filled with incense;

7:81 *bovem de armento et arietem et agnum anniculum in holocaustum*

an ox from *the* herd, and *a* ram, and *a* yearling lamb as *a* burnt offering;

7:82 *hircumque pro peccato*

a he-goat for sin;

7:83 *et in hostias pacificorum boves duos arietes quinque hircos quinque agnos anniculos quinque haec fuit oblatio Achira filii Henan*

and as peace victims two oxen, five rams, five he-goats, and five yearling lambs. This was Achira, Henan's son's, offering.

Summary of the Gifts

7:84 *haec in dedicatione altaris oblata sunt a principibus Israhel in die qua consecratum est acetabula argentea duodecim fialae argenteae duodecim mortariola aurea duodecim*

These were given by Israel's princes in *the* altar's dedication, on *the* day that it was consecrated: twelve silver cups, twelve silver drinking cups, twelve small, golden mortars;

7:85 *ita ut centum triginta argenti siclos haberet unum acetabulum et septuaginta siclos una fiala id est in commune vasorum omnium ex argento sicli duo milia quadringenti pondere sanctuarii*

so that one cup had one hundred thirty shekels, and seventy shekels for one drinking cup – that is, in common, all *the* vessels from silver *were* two thousand, four hundred shekels, by *the* sanctuary's measure;

7:86 *mortariola aurea duodecim plena incenso denos siclos adpendentia pondere sanctuarii id est simul auri sicli centum viginti*

twelve small, golden mortars full of incense, weighing ten shekels by *the* sanctuary's measure – that is, *the* gold together *weighing* one hundred twenty shekels;

7:87 *boves de armento in*

holocaustum duodecim arietes duodecim agni anniculi duodecim et libamenta eorum hirci duodecim pro peccato

twelve oxen from *the* herd as burnt offerings, twelve rams, twelve yearling lambs, and their libations; twelve he-goats for sin;

7:88 *hostiae pacificorum boves viginti quattuor arietes sexaginta hirci sexaginta agni anniculi sexaginta haec oblata sunt in dedicatione altaris quando unctum est*

twenty-four oxen, sixty rams, sixty he-goats, *and* sixty yearling lambs as peace victims. These were given at *the* altar's dedication, when *it* was anointed.

7:89 *cumque ingrederetur Moses tabernaculum foederis ut consuleret oraculum audiebat vocem loquentis ad se de propitiatorio quod erat super arcam testimonii inter duos cherubin unde et loquebatur ei*

And when Moses went into *the* Covenant Tabernacle so he could consult *the* oracle, he heard *the* Voice speaking to him from *the* atonement seat which was over testimony's ark, between *the* two cherubim. And from there He spoke to him.

**Lighting the Lamps
in the Tabernacle**
Numbers 8:1 *locutus est Dominus ad Mosen dicens*

The Lord spoke to Moses, saying,

8:2 *loquere Aaroni et dices ad eum cum posueris septem lucernas contra eam partem quam candelabrum respicit lucere debebunt*

"Speak to Aaron, and you will say to him, 'When you set *the* seven lamps, they must be lit beside that part which *the* candelabra faces. '"

8:3 *fecitque Aaron et inposuit lucernas super candelabrum ut praeceperat Dominus Mosi*

And Aaron did *it*, and put *the* lamps on *the* candelabra, as *the* Lord had commanded Moses.

8:4 *haec autem erat factura candelabri ex auro ductili tam medius stipes quam cuncta ex utroque calamorum latera nascebantur iuxta exemplum quod ostendit Dominus Mosi ita operatus est candelabrum*

But this was *the* candelabra's manufacture: from formed gold – as in *the* center post, so all *the* branches on either side that came forth. According to *the* example that *the* Lord showed Moses, so *the* candelabra was made.

Purify the Levites

8:5 *et locutus est Dominus ad Mosen dicens*

And *the* Lord spoke to Moses, saying,

8:6 *tolle Levitas de medio filiorum Israhel et purificabis eos*

"Take *the* Levites from among Israel's children! And you will purify them

8:7 *iuxta hunc ritum aspergantur aqua lustrationis et radant omnes pilos carnis suae cumque laverint vestimenta sua et mundati fuerint*

"according to this rite. Let them be sprinkled by cleansing's water, and let them shave all their flesh's hair. And when they have washed their clothes and are clean,

8:8 *tollant bovem de armentis et libamentum eius similam oleo conspersam bovem autem alterum de armento tu accipies pro peccato*

"let them take *an* ox from *the* herd and its libation, wheat flour sprinkled with oil. But you will receive another ox from *the* herd for sin.

8:9 *et adplicabis Levitas coram tabernaculo foederis convocata omni multitudine filiorum Israhel*

"And you will set *the* Levites before

the Covenant Tabernacle, calling together all *the* multitude of Israel's children.

8:10 *cumque Levitae fuerint coram Domino ponent filii Israhel manus suas super eos*

"And when *the* Levites are before *the* Lord, Israel's children will place their hands on them.

8:11 *et offeret Aaron Levitas munus in conspectu Domini a filiis Israhel ut serviant in ministerio eius*

"And Aaron will offer *the* Levites *as a* gift from Israel's children in *the* Lord's sight, so they may serve in His ministry.

8:12 *Levitae quoque ponent manus suas super capita boum e quibus unum facies pro peccato et alterum in holocaustum Domini ut depreceris pro eis*

"*The* Levites likewise will place their hands on *the* oxen's heads, from which you will make one for sin and *the* other as *the* Lord's burnt offering, so you may pray for them.

8:13 *statuesque Levitas in conspectu Aaron et filiorum eius et consecrabis oblatos Domino*

"And you will stand *the* Levites in Aaron and his sons' sight. And you will consecrate *them as* gifts to *the*

Lord,

8:14 *ac separabis de medio filiorum Israhel ut sint mei*

"and separate *them* from among Israel's children, that they may be Mine.

8:15 *et postea ingrediantur tabernaculum foederis ut serviant mihi sicque purificabis et consecrabis eos in oblationem Domini quoniam dono donati sunt mihi a filiis Israhel*

"And afterwards, they may go into *the* Covenant Tabernacle so they can serve Me. So also you will purify and consecrate them as *the* Lord's offering, because they were given to Me as *a* gift from Israel's children.

8:16 *pro primogenitis quae aperiunt omnem vulvam in Israhel accepi eos*

"I have accepted them in place of *the* firstborn who open every vulva in Israel.

8:17 *mea sunt omnia primogenita filiorum Israhel tam ex hominibus quam ex iumentis ex die quo percussi omnem primogenitum in terra Aegypti sanctificavi eos mihi*

"All Israel's children's firstborn are Mine, from humans as well as from cattle. I have sanctified them to Me from *the* day when I struck all *the*

firstborn in Egypt's land.

8:18 *et tuli Levitas pro cunctis primogenitis filiorum Israhel*

"And I have taken *the* Levites in place of all Israel's children's firstborn.

8:19 *tradidique eos dono Aaroni et filiis eius de medio populi ut serviant mihi pro Israhel in tabernaculo foederis et orent pro eis ne sit in populo plaga si ausi fuerint accedere ad sanctuarium*

"And I have given them as *a* gift to Aaron and his sons from among *the* people, so they may serve Me in Israel's place in *the* Covenant Tabernacle. And they may pray for them, so there be no plague among *the* people if they are presumptuous in coming to *the* sanctuary."

8:20 *feceruntque Moses et Aaron et omnis multitudo filiorum Israhel super Levitas quae praeceperat Dominus Mosi*

And Moses and Aaron and *the* whole multitude of Israel's children did what *the* Lord had commanded Moses concerning *the* Levites.

8:21 *purificatique sunt et laverunt vestimenta sua elevavitque eos Aaron in conspectu Domini et oravit pro eis*

And they were purified and washed their clothes, and Aaron lifted them up in *the* Lord's sight. And he prayed for them,

8:22 *ut purificati ingrederentur ad officia sua in tabernaculum foederis coram Aaron et filiis eius sicut praeceperat Dominus Mosi de Levitis ita factum est*

that, purified, they could go into their office in *the* Covenant Tabernacle before Aaron and his sons. As *the* Lord had commanded Moses concerning *the* Levites, so it was done.

Terms of Levitical Service

8:23 *locutus est Dominus ad Mosen dicens*

The Lord spoke to Moses, saying,

8:24 *haec est lex Levitarum a viginti quinque annis et supra ingredientur ut ministrent in tabernaculo foederis*

"This is *the* law of *the* Levites. From twenty-five years old and above, they will go in so they may minister in *the* Covenant Tabernacle.

8:25 *cumque quinquagesimum annum aetatis impleverint servire cessabunt*

"And when they complete *the* fiftieth year of age, they will cease to serve.

8:26 *eruntque ministri fratrum suorum in tabernaculo foederis ut custodiant quae sibi fuerint commendata opera autem ipsa non faciant sic dispones Levitas in custodiis suis*

"And they will be their brothers' ministers in *the* Covenant Tabernacle, so they may keep what *things* are entrusted to them – but they may not do those works. So you will appoint *the* Levites to their keeping."

The Second Passover

Numbers 9:1 *locutus est Dominus ad Mosen in deserto Sinai anno secundo postquam egressi sunt de terra Aegypti mense primo dicens*

The Lord spoke to Moses in *the* Sinai desert, *the* second year after they had come out of Egypt's land, *the* first month, saying,

9:2 *faciant filii Israhel phase in tempore suo*

"Let Israel's children make *the* Passover at its time,

9:3 *quartadecima die mensis huius ad vesperam iuxta omnes caerimonias et iustificationes eius*

"*the* fourteenth day this month, at evening, according to all its ceremonies and justifications."

9:4 *praecepitque Moses filiis Israhel ut facerent phase*

And Moses commanded Israel's children that they make *the* Passover.

9:5 *qui fecerunt tempore suo quartadecima die mensis ad vesperam in monte Sinai iuxta omnia quae mandaverat Dominus Mosi fecerunt filii Israhel*

They made *it* at its time, *the* fourteenth day of *the* month at evening, on Mount Sinai. According to all that *the* Lord had commanded Moses, Israel's children made *it*.

Question of Those Unclean for Passover

9:6 *ecce autem quidam inmundi super animam hominis qui non poterant facere pascha in die illo accedentes ad Mosen et Aaron*

But look, some *who were* unclean over a man's soul, who couldn't make *the* Passover on that day, coming to Moses and Aaron,

9:7 *dixerunt eis inmundi sumus super animam hominis quare fraudamur ut non valeamus offerre oblationem Domino in tempore suo inter filios Israhel*

said to them, "We are unclean over *a* man's soul. Why are we cheated so we can't offer *the* Lord *the* oblation at its time among Israel's children?"

9:8 *quibus respondit Moses state ut consulam quid praecipiat Dominus de vobis*

Moses answered them, "Stand here, so I can take counsel what *the* Lord may command about you."

9:9 *locutusque est Dominus ad Mosen dicens*

And *the* Lord spoke to Moses, saying,

9:10 *loquere filiis Israhel homo qui fuerit inmundus super anima sive in via procul in gente vestra faciat phase Domino*

"Speak to Israel's children: *a* man who is unclean concerning a soul or on *the* road far away among your people may make *the* Passover to *the* Lord.

9:11 *mense secundo quartadecima die mensis ad vesperam cum azymis et lactucis agrestibus comedent illud*

"They will eat it *the* second month, *the* fourteenth day, at evening, with unleavened bread and wild leaves.

9:12 *non relinquent ex eo quippiam usque mane et os eius non confringent omnem ritum phase observabunt*

"They will not leave anything from it until morning, and they will not break its bones. They will observe every rite.

9:13 *si quis autem et mundus est et in itinere non fuit et tamen non fecit phase exterminabitur anima illa de populis suis quia sacrificium Domino non obtulit tempore suo peccatum suum ipse portabit*

"But if someone is both clean and was not on *the* road and, nevertheless, did not make *the* Passover, that soul will be exterminated from his people, because he did not offer sacrifice to *the* Lord at its time. He will carry his sin.

9:14 *peregrinus quoque et advena si fuerit apud vos faciet phase Domini iuxta caerimonias et iustificationes eius praeceptum idem erit apud vos tam advenae quam indigenae*

"Likewise, if *a* sojourner and newcomer is with you, he will make *the* Lord's Passover, according to its ceremonies and justifications. It will be *the* same law with you, whether for newcomer or for native-born."

Cloud and Fire

9:15 *igitur die qua erectum est tabernaculum operuit illud nubes a vespere autem super tentorium erat quasi species ignis usque mane*

Therefore, *the* day that *the* tabernacle was set up, *a* cloud covered it. But at night, *something* like *a* type of fire was over *the* partition until morning.

9:16 *sic fiebat iugiter per diem operiebat illud nubes et per noctem quasi species ignis*

It happened so continually. By day *a* cloud covered it, and by night *something* like *a* type of fire.

9:17 *cumque ablata fuisset nubes quae tabernaculum protegebat tunc proficiscebantur filii Israhel et in* *loco ubi stetisset nubes ibi castrametabantur*

And when *the* cloud that protected *the* tabernacle was taken away, then Israel's children set out. And in *the* place where *the* cloud stood, there they camped.

9:18 *ad imperium Domini proficiscebantur et ad imperium illius figebant tabernaculum cunctis diebus quibus stabat nubes super tabernaculum manebant in eodem loco*

They set out at *the* Lord's command, and they set up *the* tabernacle at His command. All the days that *the* cloud stood over *the* tabernacle, they stayed in *the* same place.

9:19 *et si evenisset ut multo tempore maneret super illud erant filii Israhel in excubiis Domini et non proficiscebantur*

And if it happened that it stayed *a* long time over it, Israel's children were in *the* Lord's vigil, and did not set out

9:20 *quotquot diebus fuisset nubes super tabernaculum ad imperium Domini erigebant tentoria et ad imperium illius deponebant*

however many days *the* cloud was over *the* tabernacle. They set up tents at *the* Lord's command, and

took them down at His command.

9:21 *si fuisset nubes a vespere usque mane et statim diluculo tabernaculum reliquisset proficiscebantur et si post diem et noctem recessisset dissipabant tentoria*

If *the* cloud was from evening until morning and, immediately at daybreak it left *the* tabernacle, they set out. And if it withdrew after *a* day and night they took down *the* tents.

9:22 *si biduo aut uno mense vel longiori tempore fuisset super tabernaculum manebant filii Israhel in eodem loco et non proficiscebantur statim autem ut recessisset movebant castra*

"If it was over *the* tabernacle two days or one month or *a* longer time, Israel's children stayed in *the* same place and didn't set out. But as soon as it moved, they moved *the* camps.

9:23 *per verbum Domini figebant tentoria et per verbum illius proficiscebantur erantque in excubiis Domini iuxta imperium eius per manum Mosi*

At *the* Lord's word they pitched tents, and at His word they set out. And they were in *the* Lord's vigil, according to His command by Moses' hand.

Trumpets for Signaling
the Camps

Numbers 10:1 *locutus est Dominus ad Mosen dicens*

The Lord spoke to Moses, saying,

10:2 *fac tibi duas tubas argenteas ductiles quibus convocare possis multitudinem quando movenda sunt castra*

"Make yourself two trumpets of formed silver, by which you can call *the* multitude together when *the* camps must be moved!

10:3 *cumque increpueris tubis congregabitur ad te omnis turba ad ostium foederis tabernaculi*

"And when you have sounded *the* trumpets, *the* whole crowd will come together before you at *the* opening of *the* Covenant Tabernacle.

10:4 *si semel clangueris venient ad te principes et capita multitudinis Israhel*

"If you blow once, Israel's multitude's princes and heads will come to you.

10:5 *sin autem prolixior atque concisus clangor increpuerit movebunt castra primi qui sunt ad orientalem plagam*

"But if you sound it longer and in staccato *form*, *the* camps will move. *The* first *will be* those who are toward *the* eastern quarter.

10:6 *in secundo autem sonitu et pari ululatu tubae levabunt tentoria qui habitant ad meridiem et iuxta hunc modum reliqui facient ululantibus tubis in profectione*

"But at *the* second sound, and *the* trumpets wailing together, those who live toward *the* south will lift up *the* tents. And *the* rest will make their setting out according to this mode, *the* trumpets wailing.

10:7 *quando autem congregandus est populus simplex tubarum clangor erit et non concise ululabunt*

"But when *the* people must be gathered, *the* trumpets' sound will be simple, and they will not wail staccato.

10:8 *filii Aaron sacerdotes clangent tubis eritque hoc legitimum sempiternum in generationibus vestris*

"Aaron *the* priest's sons will sound *the* trumpets, and this will be *an* everlasting law in your generations.

10:9 *si exieritis ad bellum de terra vestra contra hostes qui dimicant adversum vos clangetis ululantibus tubis et erit recordatio vestri coram Domino Deo vestro ut eruamini de* *manibus inimicorum vestrorum*

"If you go out to war from your land against enemies who fight against you, you will sound by wailing trumpets. And your memory will be before *the* Lord your God, so you may be rescued from your enemies' hands.

10:10 *si quando habebitis epulum et dies festos et kalendas canetis tubis super holocaustis et pacificis victimis ut sint vobis in recordationem Dei vestri ego Dominus Deus vester*

"And whenever you have *a* feast and festival days and days of proclamation, you will sound *the* trumpets over burnt offerings and peace victims, that they may be for *a* memory of your God. I *am the* Lord your God."

Israel's Order of March

10:11 *anno secundo mense secundo vicesima die mensis elevata est nubes de tabernaculo foederis*

The second year, *the* second month, *the* twentieth day of *the* month, *the* cloud was taken up from *the* Covenant Tabernacle.

10:12 *profectique sunt filii Israhel per turmas suas de deserto Sinai et recubuit nubes in solitudine Pharan*

Israel's children set out by their columns from *the* Sinai desert, and *the* cloud rested again in Pharan's wasteland.

10:13 *moveruntque castra primi iuxta imperium Domini in manu Mosi*

And *the* first camps moved, according to *the* Lord's command by Moses' hand,

10:14 *filii Iuda per turmas suas quorum princeps erat Naasson filius Aminadab*

were Judah's children by their columns, whose prince was Naasson, Aminadad's son.

10:15 *in tribu filiorum Isachar fuit princeps Nathanahel filius Suar*

Nathanael, Suar's son, was prince in Issachar's children's tribe.

10:16 *in tribu Zabulon erat princeps Heliab filius Helon*

Heliab, Helon's son, was prince in Zebulon's tribe.

10:17 *depositumque est tabernaculum quod portantes egressi sunt filii Gerson et Merari*

The tabernacle was taken down, carrying which Gerson and Merari's children set out.

10:18 *profectique sunt et filii Ruben per turmas et ordinem suum quorum princeps erat Helisur filius Sedeur*

Reuben's children, whose prince was Helisur, Sedeur's son, also set out by their columns and order.

10:19 *in tribu autem filiorum Symeon princeps fuit Salamihel filius Surisaddai*

But Salamiel, Surisaddai's son, was prince in Simeon's tribe.

10:20 *porro in tribu Gad erat princeps Heliasaph filius Duhel*

Further, Heliasaph, Duel's son, was prince in Gad's tribe.

10:21 *profectique sunt et Caathitae portantes sanctuarium tamdiu tabernaculum portabatur donec venirent ad erectionis locum*

And *the* Caathites also set out, carrying *the* sanctuary as long as *the* tabernacle was carried, until they came to *the* place to set *it* up.

10:22 *moverunt castra et filii Ephraim per turmas suas in quorum exercitu princeps erat Helisama filius Ammiud*

And Ephraim's children moved camps by their columns, in whose army Helisama, Ammud's son, was prince.

10:23 *in tribu autem filiorum Manasse princeps fuit Gamalihel filius Phadassur*

But Gamaliel, Phadassur's son, was prince in Manasseh's children's tribe.

10:24 *et in tribu Beniamin dux Abidan filius Gedeonis*

And Abidan, Gideon's son, was duke in Benjamin's tribe.

10:25 *novissimi castrorum omnium profecti sunt filii Dan per turmas suas in quorum exercitu princeps fuit Ahiezer filius Amisaddai*

The last camps of all, Dan's children set out by their columns, in whose army Ahiezer, Amisaddai's son, was prince.

10:26 *in tribu autem filiorum Aser erat princeps Phagaihel filius Ochran*

But in Asher's children's tribe, Phagaiel, Ochran's son, was prince.

10:27 *et in tribu filiorum Nepthalim princeps Achira filius Henan*

And in Napthali's children's tribe, Achira, Henan's son, was prince.

10:28 *haec sunt castra et profectiones filiorum Israhel per turmas suas quando egrediebantur*

These are Israel's children's camps and orders of march, by their columns, when they set out.

Moses Asks Hobab
to Go with Them

10:29 *dixitque Moses Hobab filio Rahuhel Madianiti cognato suo proficiscimur ad locum quem Dominus daturus est nobis veni nobiscum ut benefaciamus tibi quia Dominus bona promisit Israheli*

And Moses said to Hobab, Rahuel *the* Midianite's son, his kinsman, "We are setting out to *the* place which *the* Lord will give us. Come with us so we may bless you, because *the* Lord has promised good *things* to Israel!"

10:30 *cui ille respondit non vadam tecum sed revertar in terram meam in qua natus sum*

He answered him, "I will not go with you, but will go back into my land, in which I was born.

10:31 *et ille noli inquit nos relinquere tu enim nosti in quibus locis per desertum castra ponere debeamus et eris ductor noster*

And he said, "Don't leave! For you know in which places we ought to place *the* camps through *the* desert. And you will be our guide.

10:32 *cumque nobiscum veneris*

quicquid optimum fuerit ex opibus quas nobis traditurus est Dominus dabimus tibi

"And when you come with us, we will give you whatever is best from *the* riches which *the* Lord will hand over to us."

10:33 *profecti sunt ergo de monte Domini via trium dierum arcaque foederis Domini praecedebat eos per dies tres providens castrorum locum*

So they set out from *the* Lord's mountain, *a* three-day journey. *The* ark of *the* Lord's covenant went before them for three days, providing *their* camps' location.

10:34 *nubes quoque Domini super eos erat per diem cum incederent*

Likewise, *the* Lord's cloud was over them by day when they marched.

10:35 *cumque elevaretur arca dicebat Moses surge Domine et dissipentur inimici tui et fugiant qui oderunt te a facie tua*

And when *the* ark was lifted up, Moses said, "Rise up, Lord, and scatter your enemies, and may those who hated You flee from Your face!"

10:36 *cum autem deponeretur aiebat revertere Domine ad multitudinem exercitus Israhel*

But when it was set down, he said, "Return, Lord, to *the* multitude of Israel's army!"

A Fire Kindled

Numbers 11:1 *interea ortum est murmur populi quasi dolentium pro labore contra Dominum quod cum audisset iratus est et accensus in eos ignis Domini devoravit extremam castrorum partem*

Meanwhile, *the* people's complaint against *the* Lord sprung up, like those suffering from hard work. When He had heard this, He was angry. And *the* Lord's fire, kindled among them, burned up *the* extreme part of *the* camps.

11:2 *cumque clamasset populus ad Mosen oravit Moses Dominum et absortus est ignis*

And when *the* people had cried to Moses, Moses prayed to *the* Lord and *the* fire was swallowed up.

11:3 *vocavitque nomen loci illius Incensio eo quod succensus fuisset contra eos ignis Domini*

And he called that place's name Burning, because *the* Lord's fire was kindled against them.

The People Complain About Food

11:4 *vulgus quippe promiscuum quod ascenderat cum eis flagravit desiderio sedens et flens iunctis sibi pariter filiis Israhel et ait quis dabit nobis ad vescendum carnes*

The common mob, of course, which had come up with them, burned with desire, sitting and weeping, joined together with Israel's children. And they said, "Who will give us meat to eat?"

11:5 *recordamur piscium quos comedebamus in Aegypto gratis in mentem nobis veniunt cucumeres et pepones porrique et cepae et alia*

"We remember *the* fish which we ate for free in Egypt. Cucumbers and melons and leeks and onions and others come into our minds.

11:6 *anima nostra arida est nihil aliud respiciunt oculi nostri nisi man*

"Our soul is dry. Our eyes see nothing except manna!"

11:7 *erat autem man quasi semen coriandri coloris bdellii*

But manna was like coriander seed, *the* gum tree's color.

11:8 *circuibatque populus et colligens illud frangebat mola sive terebat in mortario coquens in olla et faciens ex eo tortulas saporis quasi panis oleati*

And *the* people walked around and *were* gathering it, crushing at *the* millstone or grinding in small mortars, cooking in *an* oven and making small cakes from it tasting

like bread with oil.

Moses Asks for Help

11:9 *cumque descenderet nocte super castra ros descendebat pariter et man*

And when night came, dew descended together over *the* camps, and manna.

11:10 *audivit ergo Moses flentem populum per familias singulos per ostia tentorii sui iratusque est furor Domini valde sed et Mosi intoleranda res visa est*

Therefore, Moses heard *the* people weeping through each of *the* families, at *the* tents' openings. And *the* Lord's fury was great, and to Moses *the* affair seemed intolerable.

11:11 *et ait ad Dominum cur adflixisti servum tuum quare non invenio gratiam coram te et cur inposuisti pondus universi populi huius super me*

And he said to *the* Lord, "Why have you afflicted Your slave? Why do I not find grace before you? And why have you put all this people's weight on me?

11:12 *numquid ego concepi omnem hanc multitudinem vel genui eam ut dicas mihi porta eos in sinu tuo sicut portare solet nutrix infantulum et defer in terram pro qua iurasti* *patribus eorum*

"I didn't conceive this whole multitude or birth them, did I, that You say to me, 'Carry them on your breast like *a* nurse carries *a* little baby, and take them to *the* land for which I swore to their fathers!?

11:13 *unde mihi carnes ut dem tantae multitudini flent contra me dicentes da nobis carnes ut comedamus*

"Where *is* meat for me so I can give it to all this crowd? They are crying against me, saying, 'Give us meat so we can eat!'

11:14 *non possum solus sustinere omnem hunc populum quia gravis mihi est*

"I can't sustain all this people alone, because it is too heavy for me!

11:15 *sin aliter tibi videtur obsecro ut interficias me et inveniam gratiam in oculis tuis ne tantis adficiar malis*

"If it seems otherwise to You, I pray that you kill me. And I will find grace in Your eyes, that I not suffer so many harms!"

11:16 *et dixit Dominus ad Mosen congrega mihi septuaginta viros de senibus Israhel quos tu nosti quod senes populi sint ac magistri et duces eos ad ostium tabernaculi foederis*

faciesque ibi stare tecum

And *the* Lord said to Moses, "Gather to Me seventy men from Israel's elders, whom you know that are *the* people's elders and teachers! And you will lead them to *the* opening of *the* Covenant Tabernacle, and will make them stand there with you,

11:17 *ut descendam et loquar tibi et auferam de spiritu tuo tradamque eis ut sustentent tecum onus populi et non tu solus graveris*

"so I will come down and speak to You. And I will take from your spirit and will give it to them, so they can sustain *the* people's burden with you and you won't be weighed down alone.

11:18 *populo quoque dices sanctificamini cras comedetis carnes ego enim audivi vos dicere quis dabit nobis escas carnium bene nobis erat in Aegypto ut det vobis Dominus carnes et comedatis*

"Likewise, you will say to *the* people, 'Sanctify yourselves! Tomorrow you will eat flesh, for I have heard you say, 'Who will give us meat meals? It was better for us in Egypt!' So *the* Lord may give you flesh, and you may eat,

11:19 *non uno die nec duobus vel quinque aut decem nec viginti quidem*

"'not one day or two or five or ten or even twenty,

11:20 *sed usque ad mensem dierum donec exeat per nares vestras et vertatur in nausiam eo quod reppuleritis Dominum qui in medio vestri est et fleveritis coram eo dicentes quare egressi sumus ex Aegypto*

"'but up to *a* month's days, until it comes out your nostrils and turns to nausea – because you have rejected *the* Lord who is among you, and wept before Him saying, 'Why did we come out of Egypt?'"

11:21 *et ait Moses sescenta milia peditum huius populi sunt et tu dicis dabo eis esum carnium mense integro*

And Moses said, "This people's foot soldiers are six hundred thousand, and you say, 'I will give them meat meals *a* whole month'?

11:22 *numquid ovium et boum multitudo caedetur ut possit sufficere ad cibum vel omnes pisces maris in unum congregabuntur ut eos satient*

"Should *a* multitude of sheep and oxen be cut down, so it is sufficient for food, or all *the* sea's fish be gathered as one, so they may be satisfied?"

11:23 *cui respondit Dominus*

numquid manus Domini invalida est iam nunc videbis utrum meus sermo opere conpleatur

The Lord answered him, "Is *the* Lord's hand already weak? Now you will see whether My word may be completed in work!'"

Moses Calls the Elders
11:24 *venit igitur Moses et narravit populo verba Domini congregans septuaginta viros de senibus Israhel quos stare fecit circa tabernaculum*

So Moses came and told *the* people *the* Lord's words, gathering seventy men from Israel's elders, who he made stand around *the* tabernacle.

11:25 *descenditque Dominus per nubem et locutus est ad eum auferens de spiritu qui erat in Mosen et dans septuaginta viris cumque requievisset in eis spiritus prophetaverunt nec ultra cessarunt*

And *the* Lord came down in *the* cloud and spoke to him, taking from *the* spirit that was in Moses and giving it to *the* seventy men. And when *the* spirit had rested in them, they prophesied, nor did they cease further.

11:26 *remanserant autem in castris duo viri quorum unus vocabatur Heldad et alter Medad super quos requievit spiritus nam et ipsi descripti fuerant et non exierant ad* *tabernaculum*

But two men remained in *the* camps, one named Heldad and *the* other Medad, on whom *the* spirit rested. For they also were called, yet had not gone to *the* tabernacle.

11:27   *cumque prophetarent in castris cucurrit puer et nuntiavit Mosi dicens Heldad et Medad prophetant in castris*

And when they prophesied in *the* camps, *a* boy ran and told Moses, saying , "Heldad and Medad are prophesying in *the* camps!"

11:28   *statim Iosue filius Nun minister Mosi et electus e pluribus ait domine mi Moses prohibe eos*

Immediately Joshua, Nun's son, Moses' minister and *one* chosen from many, said, "My Lord Moses, forbid them!"

11:29   *at ille quid inquit aemularis pro me quis tribuat ut omnis populus prophetet et det eis Dominus spiritum suum*

And he said, "Why are you jealous for me? Who may give that all *the* people prophesy, and *the* Lord give them His spirit?"

11:30   *reversusque est Moses et maiores natu Israhel in castra*

And Moses and Israel's older born went back into *the* camps.

11:31   *ventus autem egrediens a Domino arreptas trans mare coturnices detulit et dimisit in castra itinere quantum uno die confici potest ex omni parte castrorum per circuitum volabantque in aere duobus cubitis altitudine super terram*

But *a* wind coming from *the* Lord, taking quail across *the* sea, carried *them* and left *them* in *the* camps. *The people* could collect them from every part of *the* camps around, as much as *a* day's journey. And they flew in *the* air two cubits height above *the* ground.

11:32   *surgens ergo populus toto die illo et nocte ac die altero congregavit coturnicum qui parum decem choros et siccaverunt eas per gyrum castrorum*

So *the* people, rising up all that day and night and *the* next day, gathered quail, *the* smallest taking ten chores. And they dried them around *the* camps.

11:33   *adhuc carnes erant in dentibus eorum nec defecerat huiuscemodi cibus et ecce furor Domini concitatus in populum percussit eum plaga magna nimis*

The meat was still in their teeth,

neither had that type of food run short, and look, *the* Lord's fury, stirred up against *the* people, struck them with *an* overwhelmingly great plague.

11:34 *vocatusque est ille locus sepulchra Concupiscentiae ibi enim sepelierunt populum qui desideraverat egressi autem de sepulchris Concupiscentiae venerunt in Aseroth et manserunt ibi*

And that place was called Lusting's graves, for there they buried *the* people who lusted. But going on from Lusting's graves, they came to Aseroth and stayed there.

Mary and Aaron Criticize Moses Numbers 12:1 *locutaque est Maria et Aaron contra Mosen propter uxorem eius aethiopissam*

And Mary and Aaron spoke against Moses because of his wife, *an* Ethiopian.

12:2 *et dixerunt num per solum Mosen locutus est Dominus nonne et nobis similiter est locutus quod cum audisset Dominus*

And they said, "Has *the* Lord only spoken through Moses? Hasn't he also spoken to us as well?"

When *the* Lord had heard that,

12:3 *erat enim Moses vir mitissimus super omnes homines qui morabantur in terra*

(for Moses was *the* most humble man of all *the* men who lived on earth)

12:4 *statim locutus est ad eum et ad Aaron et Mariam egredimini vos tantum tres ad tabernaculum foederis cumque fuissent egressi*

He immediately said to him, and to Aaron and Mary, "You three alone go out to *the* Covenant Tabernacle!"

And when they had gone out,

12:5 *descendit Dominus in columna nubis et stetit in introitu tabernaculi* *vocans Aaron et Mariam qui cum issent*

the Lord came down in *a* column of cloud and stood at *the* tabernacle's entrance, calling Aaron and Mary, who, when they had come,

12:6 *dixit ad eos audite sermones meos si quis fuerit inter vos propheta Domini in visione apparebo ei vel per somnium loquar ad illum*

He said to them, "Listen to My words! If someone is *the* Lord's prophet among you, I will appear to him in *a* vision, or speak to him through *a* dream.

12:7 *at non talis servus meus Moses qui in omni domo mea fidelissimus est*

"Yet *it is* not so with My slave Moses, who is most faithful in all My house.

12:8 *ore enim ad os loquor ei et palam non per enigmata et figuras Dominum videt quare igitur non timuistis detrahere servo meo Mosi*

"For I speak to him mouth to mouth, and he sees *the* Lord clearly, not by enigmas and figures. How, then, were you not afraid to tear down My slave Moses?"

12:9 *iratusque contra eos abiit*

And, angry with them, He went away.

12:10 *nubes quoque recessit quae erat super tabernaculum et ecce Maria apparuit candens lepra quasi nix cumque respexisset eam Aaron et vidisset perfusam lepra*

Likewise, *the* cloud which was over *the* tabernacle withdrew and, look, Mary appeared white with leprosy, like snow. And when Aaron had looked at her and seen *the* leprosy overspread,

12:11 *ait ad Mosen obsecro domine mi ne inponas nobis hoc peccatum quod stulte commisimus*

he said to Moses, "I pray, my lord, do not place this sin on us, which we committed foolishly,

12:12 *ne fiat haec quasi mortua et ut abortivum quod proicitur de vulva matris suae ecce iam medium carnis eius devoratum est lepra*

"so she may not be like *the* dead, or like *an* abortion that is thrown away from her mother's vulva! Look, already half her flesh is eaten up by leprosy!"

12:13 *clamavitque Moses ad Dominum dicens Deus obsecro sana eam*

And Moses cried out to *the* Lord,

saying, "God, I pray, heal her!"

12:14 *cui respondit Dominus si pater eius spuisset in faciem illius nonne debuerat saltem septem dierum rubore suffundi separetur septem diebus extra castra et postea revocabitur*

The Lord answered him, "If her father had spit in her face, wouldn't she at least have been covered with shame seven days? Let her be separated seven days outside *the* camps, and afterwards she will be called back."

12:15 *exclusa est itaque Maria extra castra septem diebus et populus non est motus de loco illo donec revocata est Maria*

And so Mary was excluded seven days outside *the* camps. And *the* people was not moved from that place until Mary was called back.

Spies Sent to Consider Canaan
Numbers 13:1 *profectus est de Aseroth fixis tentoriis in deserto Pharan*

The people set out from Aseroth, pitching tents in Pharan's desert.

13:2 *ibi locutus est Dominus ad Mosen dicens*

The Lord spoke to Moses there, saying,

13:3 *mitte viros qui considerent terram Chanaan quam daturus sum filiis Israhel singulos de singulis tribubus ex principibus*

"Send men who can consider Canaan's land, which I will give to Israel's children – one from each of *the* tribes, from *the* princes!"

13:4 *fecit Moses quod Dominus imperarat de deserto Pharan mittens principes viros quorum ista sunt nomina*

Moses did what *the* Lord had commanded, sending important men from Pharan's desert, whose names were these:

13:5 *de tribu Ruben Semmua filium Zecchur*

from Reuben's tribe, Semmua, Zecchur's son;

13:6 *de tribu Symeon Saphat filium Huri*

from Simeon's tribe, Saphat, Huri's son;

13:7 *de tribu Iuda Chaleb filium Iepphonne*

from Judah's tribe, Caleb, Iepphone's son;

13:8 *de tribu Isachar Igal filium Ioseph*

from Issachar's tribe, Igal, Joseph's son;

13:9 *de tribu Ephraim Osee filium Nun*

from Ephraim's tribe, Hosea, Nun's son;

13:10 *de tribu Beniamin Phalti filium Raphu*

from Benjamin's tribe, Phalti, Raphu's son;

13:11 *de tribu Zabulon Geddihel filium Sodi*

from Zebulon's tribe, Geddiel, Sodi's son;

13:12 *de tribu Ioseph sceptri Manasse Gaddi filium Susi*

from Joseph's tribe, Manasseh's scepter, Gaddi, Susi's son;

13:13 *de tribu Dan Ammihel filium Gemalli*

from Dan's tribe, Ammiel, Gemalli's son;

13:14 *de tribu Aser Sthur filium Michahel*

from Asher's tribe, Sthur, Michael's son;

13:15 *de tribu Nepthali Naabbi filium Vaphsi*

from Napthali's tribe, Naabbi, Vaphsi's son;

13:16 *de tribu Gad Guhel filium Machi*

from Gad's tribe, Guel, Machi's son.

13:17 *haec sunt nomina virorum quos misit Moses ad considerandam terram vocavitque Osee filium Nun Iosue*

These are *the* men's names whom Moses sent to consider *the* land. And he called Hosea, Nun's son, Joshua.

Moses' Instructions

13:18 *misit ergo eos Moses ad considerandam terram Chanaan et dixit ad eos ascendite per meridianam plagam cumque* *veneritis ad montes*

So Moses sent them to consider Canaan's land, and he said to them, "Go up through *the* southern quarter. And when you come to *the* mountains,

13:19 *considerate terram qualis sit et populum qui habitator est eius utrum fortis sit an infirmus pauci numero an plures*

"consider *the* land, how it is, and *the* people who are its inhabitants, whether they are strong or weak, few in number or many;

13:20 *ipsa terra bona an mala urbes quales muratae an absque muris*

the land itself good or bad; *the* cities, whether walled or without walls;

13:21 *humus pinguis an sterilis nemorosa an absque arboribus confortamini et adferte nobis de fructibus terrae erat autem tempus quando iam praecoquae uvae vesci possunt*

the soil fat or sterile, wooded or without trees. Be strengthened, and bring us some of *the* land's fruit."

The Spies Explore the Land
But it was already time when they could eat *the* precooked grapes.

13:22 *cumque ascendissent*

exploraverunt terram a deserto Sin usque Roob intrantibus Emath

And when they had climbed up, they explored *the* land – from Sin's desert to Rohob, going into Emath.

13:23 *ascenderuntque ad meridiem et venerunt in Hebron ubi erant Ahiman et Sisai et Tholmai filii Enach nam Hebron septem annis ante Tanim urbem Aegypti condita est*

And they climbed up to *the* south and came to Hebron, where Ahiman, and Sisai, and Tholmai, Enach's son's, were, for Hebron was restored seven years before *the* Egyptian city *of* Tanis.

13:24 *pergentesque usque ad torrentem Botri absciderunt palmitem cum uva sua quem portaverunt in vecte duo viri de malis quoque granatis et de ficis loci illius tulerunt*

And coming even to Botrus brook, they cut down *a* branch with its grapes, which two men carried on *a* pole. They also took some pomegranates and figs from that place,

13:25 *qui appellatus est Neelescol id est torrens Botri eo quod botrum inde portassent filii Israhel*

which was called Neelescol – that is,

Botrus brook – because Israel's children had carried a cluster *of grapes* from there.

13:26 *reversique exploratores terrae post quadraginta dies omni regione circuita*

And *the* land's explorers, coming back after forty days around all *the* region,

13:27 *venerunt ad Mosen et Aaron et ad omnem coetum filiorum Israhel in desertum Pharan quod est in Cades locutique eis et omni multitudini ostenderunt fructus terrae*

came to Moses and Aaron and all Israel's children's gathering in Pharan's desert, which is in Kadesh. And, speaking to them and all *the* multitude, they showed *the* land's fruit.

The Spies Report
13:28 *et narraverunt dicentes venimus in terram ad quam misisti nos quae re vera fluit lacte et melle ut ex his fructibus cognosci potest*

And they told them, saying, "We came into *the* land to which you sent us, which thing truly flows with milk and honey, as can be known from these fruits.

13:29 *sed cultores fortissimos habet et urbes grandes atque muratas*

stirpem Enach vidimus ibi

"But it has *the* mightiest farmers, and *the* cities *are* large and walled. We saw Enach's race there.

13:30 *Amalech habitat in meridie Hettheus et Iebuseus et Amorreus in montanis Chananeus vero moratur iuxta mare et circa fluenta Iordanis*

"Amalek lives in *the* south, *the* Hittite and Jebusite and Amorite in *the* mountains, and *the* Canaanite lives alongside *the* sea and around *the* Jordan's floods.

Caleb Encourages the People
13:31 *inter haec Chaleb conpescens murmur populi qui oriebatur contra Mosen ait ascendamus et possideamus terram quoniam poterimus obtinere eam*

While this was happening, Caleb, restraining *the* people's complaint that had sprung up against Moses, said, "Let's go up and possess *the* land, because we will be able to take it!"

13:32 *alii vero qui fuerant cum eo dicebant nequaquam ad hunc populum valemus ascendere quia fortior nobis est*

The others who were with him, though, said, "By no means can we go up to this people, because it is stronger than us!"

13:33 *detraxeruntque terrae quam inspexerant apud filios Israhel dicentes terram quam lustravimus devorat habitatores suos populum quem aspeximus procerae staturae est*

And they criticized *the* land which they had inspected among Israel's children, saying, "*The* land which we walked around devours its inhabitants. *The* people whom we saw are of great stature.

13:34 *ibi vidimus monstra quaedam filiorum Enach de genere giganteo quibus conparati quasi lucustae videbamur*

"We saw monsters there like Enach's children, from *a* race of giants, compared to whom we seemed like locusts."

The People Cry Out

Numbers 14:1 *igitur vociferans omnis turba flevit nocte illa*

Therefore, all *the* crowd, shouting, wept that night.

14:2 *et murmurati sunt contra Mosen et Aaron cuncti filii Israhel dicentes*

And all Israel's children complained against Moses and Aaron, saying,

14:3 *utinam mortui essemus in Aegypto et non in hac vasta solitudine utinam pereamus et non inducat nos Dominus in terram istam ne cadamus gladio et uxores ac liberi nostri ducantur captivi nonne melius est reverti in Aegyptum*

"Better we had died in Egypt and not in this vast wasteland! Better we had perished and *the* Lord had not led us into this land, unless we fall by *the* sword and our wives and children be led away captive! It is better that we go back to Egypt!"

14:4 *dixeruntque alter ad alterum constituamus nobis ducem et revertamur in Aegyptum*

And they said one to another, "Let's set up *a* leader for ourselves and go back to Egypt,"

14:5 *quo audito Moses et Aaron ceciderunt proni in terram coram*

omni multitudine filiorum Israhel

hearing which, Moses and Aaron fell face down on *the* ground before all Israel's children's multitude.

Joshua and Caleb
Plead with Israel

14:6 *at vero Iosue filius Nun et Chaleb filius Iepphonne qui et ipsi lustraverant terram sciderunt vestimenta sua*

And indeed Joshua, Nun's son, and Caleb, Iepphone's son, who also had walked around *the* land, tore their clothes

14:7 *et ad omnem multitudinem filiorum Israhel locuti sunt terram quam circuivimus valde bona est*

and said to all Israel's children's multitude, "*The* land we walked around is very good!

14:8 *si propitius fuerit Dominus inducet nos in eam et tradet humum lacte et melle manantem*

"If *the* Lord is favorably inclined, He will lead us into it and hand over soil flowing with milk and honey.

14:9 *nolite rebelles esse contra Dominum neque timeatis populum terrae huius quia sicut panem ita eos possumus devorare recessit ab illis omne praesidium Dominus nobiscum est nolite metuere*

"Don't be rebels against *the* Lord, or fear that land's people, because we can eat them up like bread is eaten up! *The* Lord takes away every protection from them. He is with us. Don't be afraid!"

The Lord's Glory Appears

14:10 *cumque clamaret omnis multitudo et lapidibus eos vellet opprimere apparuit gloria Domini super tectum foederis cunctis filiis Israhel*

And when all *the* multitude had shouted and wanted to crush them with stones, *the* Lord's glory appeared to all Israel's children over *the* covenant roof.

14:11 *et dixit Dominus ad Mosen usquequo detrahet mihi populus iste quousque non credent mihi in omnibus signis quae feci coram eis*

And *the* Lord said to Moses, "How long will this people criticize Me? How long will they not believe Me in all *the* signs that I have done before them?

14:12 *feriam igitur eos pestilentia atque consumam te autem faciam principem super gentem magnam et fortiorem quam haec est*

"Therefore, I will bring pestilence and consume them, but I will make you prince over *a* great nation, and mightier than this one is.

Moses Pleads with the Lord

14:13 *et ait Moses ad Dominum ut audiant Aegyptii de quorum medio eduxisti populum istum*

And Moses said to *the* Lord, "But *the* Egyptians may hear, from whose midst You led this people out –

14:14 *et habitatores terrae huius qui audierunt quod tu Domine in populo isto sis et facie videaris ad faciem et nubes tua protegat illos et in columna nubis praecedas eos per diem et in columna ignis per noctem*

"and *this* land's inhabitants, who have heard that You, Lord, are among that people, and are seen face-to-face, and protect them by Your cloud, and go before them in *a* column of cloud by day and in *a* column of fire by night –

14:15 *quod occideris tantam multitudinem quasi unum hominem et dicant*

"that You have killed so great *a* multitude as one man. And they may say,

14:16 *non poterat introducere populum in terram pro qua iuraverat idcirco occidit eos in solitudine*

'He couldn't bring *the* people into *the* land for which He swore. For this reason He killed them in *the* wasteland.'

14:17 *magnificetur ergo fortitudo Domini sicut iurasti dicens*

"Therefore, let *the* Lord's strength be magnified, as You swore, saying,

14:18 *Dominus patiens et multae misericordiae auferens iniquitatem et scelera nullumque innoxium derelinquens qui visitas peccata patrum in filios in tertiam et quartam generationem*

"'*The* Lord is patient and of many mercies, taking away treachery and crimes, and leaving behind no one innocent.'

"You who visit *the* fathers' sins on children to *the* third and fourth generation,

14:19 *dimitte obsecro peccatum populi tui huius secundum magnitudinem misericordiae tuae sicut propitius fuisti egredientibus de Aegypto usque ad locum istum*

"let go, I pray, this Your people's sin, according to Your great mercy, as you have been favorable bringing them out of Egypt, even to this place!"

The Lord Forgives and Condemns

14:20 *dixitque Dominus dimisi iuxta verbum tuum*

And *the* Lord said, "I have forgiven,

according to your word.

14:21 *vivo ego et implebitur gloria Domini universa terra*

"I live, and *the* whole land will be filled by *the* Lord's glory!

14:22 *attamen omnes homines qui viderunt maiestatem meam et signa quae feci in Aegypto et in solitudine et temptaverunt me iam per decem vices nec oboedierunt voci meae*

"Nevertheless, all *the* men who saw My majesty and *the* signs I did in Egypt and in *the* wasteland, and have tempted Me already ten times and not obeyed My voice,

14:23 *non videbunt terram pro qua iuravi patribus eorum nec quisquam ex illis qui detraxit mihi intuebitur eam*

"will not see *the* land for which I swore to their fathers – nor will anyone else go into it who tore Me down among them!

14:24 *servum meum Chaleb qui plenus alio spiritu secutus est me inducam in terram hanc quam circuivit et semen eius possidebit eam*

"My slave Caleb who, full of *a* different spirit, has followed me, I will lead into this land which he walked around, and his seed will possess it.

14:25 *quoniam Amalechites et Chananeus habitant in vallibus cras movete castra et revertimini in solitudinem per viam maris Rubri*

"Because *the* Amalekites and Canaanites live in *the* valleys, tomorrow you will move *the* camps and go back into *the* wasteland by way of *the* Red Sea.

The Lord Predicts
Forty Years of Wandering

14:26 *locutusque est Dominus ad Mosen et Aaron dicens*

And *the* Lord spoke to Moses and Aaron, saying,

14:27 *usquequo multitudo haec pessima murmurat contra me querellas filiorum Israhel audivi*

"How long will this dismal multitude gripe against Me? I have heard Israel's children's complaints.

14:28 *dic ergo eis vivo ego ait Dominus sicut locuti estis audiente me sic faciam vobis*

"Therefore, say to them, 'I live,' *the* Lord says. 'As you have spoken, Me hearing, so I will do to you.

14:29 *in solitudine hac iacebunt cadavera vestra omnes qui numerati estis a viginti annis et supra et* *murmurastis contra me*

"'They will lay down your dead bodies in this wasteland, all of you who were numbered – from twenty years old and above – and who griped against Me.

14:30 *non intrabitis terram super quam levavi manum meam ut habitare vos facerem praeter Chaleb filium Iepphonne et Iosue filium Nun*

"'You will not go into *the* land over which I lifted up My hand that I would make you live there, except Caleb, Iepphone's son, and Joshua, Nun's son.

14:31 *parvulos autem vestros de quibus dixistis quod praedae hostibus forent introducam ut videant terram quae vobis displicuit*

"'But your little ones, about whom you said that they would be *the* enemies' prey, I will bring them in, that they may see *the* land that displeased you.

14:32 *vestra cadavera iacebunt in solitudine*

"'They will lay down your dead bodies in *the* wasteland.

14:33 *filii vestri erunt vagi in deserto annis quadraginta et portabunt fornicationem vestram donec consumantur cadavera patrum*

in deserto

"'Your children will be wanderers in *the* desert for forty years. And they will carry your fornication, until *the* fathers' dead bodies are consumed in *the* desert.

14:34 *iuxta numerum quadraginta dierum quibus considerastis terram annus pro die inputabitur et quadraginta annis recipietis iniquitates vestras et scietis ultionem meam*

"'*A* year will be imputed for *a* day, according to *the* number of *the* forty days in which you considered *the* land. And you will receive your treacheries for forty years, and will know My revenge.

14:35 *quoniam sicut locutus sum ita faciam omni multitudini huic pessimae quae consurrexit adversum me in solitudine hac deficiet et morietur*

"'For as I have spoken, so I will do to all this dismal multitude which rose up against Me. They will falter and die in this wasteland.'"

The Spies' Fate

14:36 *igitur omnes viri quos miserat Moses ad contemplandam terram et qui reversi murmurare fecerant contra eum omnem multitudinem detrahentes terrae quod esset mala*

Therefore, all *the* men whom Moses sent to consider *the* land, and who, coming back, made all *the* multitude gripe against him – criticizing *the* land, that it was bad –

14:37 *mortui sunt atque percussi in conspectu Domini*

died and were struck down in *the* Lord's sight.

14:38 *Iosue autem filius Nun et Chaleb filius Iepphonne vixerunt ex omnibus qui perrexerant ad considerandam terram*

But Joshua, Nun's son, and Caleb, Iepphone's son, lived – out of all who had gone out to consider *the* land.

The People Disobey Again
14:39 *locutusque est Moses universa verba haec ad omnes filios Israhel et luxit populus nimis*

And Moses spoke all these words to all Israel's children, and *the* people grieved overwhelmingly.

14:40 *et ecce mane primo surgentes ascenderunt verticem montis atque dixerunt parati sumus ascendere ad locum de quo Dominus locutus est quia peccavimus*

And, look, getting up at first light, they climbed up *the* mountain peaks and said, "We have prepared to go up to *the* place of which *the* Lord has spoken, because we have sinned."

14:41 *quibus Moses cur inquit transgredimini verbum Domini quod vobis non cedet in prosperum*

Moses said to them, "Why are you violating *the* Lord's word, which won't submit to you in prosperity?

14:42 *nolite ascendere non enim est Dominus vobiscum ne corruatis coram inimicis vestris*

"Don't go up, for *the* Lord isn't with you – unless you fall before your enemies!

14:43 *Amalechites et Chananeus ante vos sunt quorum gladio corruetis eo quod nolueritis adquiescere Domino nec erit Dominus vobiscum*

"*The* Amalekites and Canaanites are before you, by whose sword you will fall, because you didn't submit to *the* Lord – nor will *the* Lord be with you!"

14:44 *at illi contenebrati ascenderunt in verticem montis arca autem testamenti Domini et Moses non recesserunt de castris*

Yet they, being blinded, climbed up onto *the* mountain top. But *the* ark of *the* Lord's testimony and Moses did not go out of *the* camps.

14:45 *descenditque Amalechites et Chananeus qui habitabant in monte et percutiens eos atque concidens persecutus est usque Horma*

And *the* Amalekites and Canaanites who lived on *the* mountain came down and, striking and cutting them down, pursued them to Horma.

Rules for Offerings
Numbers 15:1 *locutus est Dominus ad Mosen dicens*

The Lord spoke to Moses, saying,

15:2 *loquere ad filios Israhel et dices ad eos cum ingressi fueritis terram habitationis vestrae quam ego dabo vobis*

"Speak to Israel's children, and you will say to them, 'When you come into your habitation's land which I will give you,

15:3 *et feceritis oblationem Domino in holocaustum aut victimam vota solventes vel sponte offerentes munera aut in sollemnitatibus vestris adolentes odorem suavitatis Domino de bubus sive de ovibus*

"'and you make *an* offering to *the* Lord, as *a* holocaust, or *a* victim releasing *a* promise, or offering *a* gift freely, or in your solemnities – burning *an* odor of smoothness to *the* Lord, whether from bulls or from sheep –

15:4 *offeret quicumque immolaverit victimam sacrificium similae decimam partem oephi conspersae oleo quod mensuram habebit quartam partem hin*

"'whoever will offer *it*, will kill *the* sacrificial victim, with *a* tenth part of *an* ephah of wheat flour, sprinkled with oil, which will have *the* measure of *a* quarter part of *a* hin.

15:5 *et vinum ad liba fundenda eiusdem mensurae dabit in holocausto sive in victima per agnos singulos*

"'And he will give wine as *a* libation poured out in *the* same measure, whether for *a* burnt offering or for *a* peace victim, for each of *the* lambs.

15:6 *et arietis erit sacrificium similae duarum decimarum quae conspersa sit oleo tertiae partis hin*

"'And *a* ram's sacrifice will be two tenths of wheat flour, which is sprinkled with three parts of *a* hin of oil.

15:7 *et vinum ad libamentum tertiae partis eiusdem mensurae offeret in odorem suavitatis Domino*

"'And he will offer three parts of *the* same measure of wine as *a* libation, in *an* odor of smoothness to *the* Lord.

15:8 *quando vero de bubus feceris holocaustum aut hostiam ut impleas votum vel pacificas victimas*

"'When indeed you will make *a* burnt offering or victim from bulls, so you may fulfill *a* promise or *give* peace victims,

15:9 *dabis per singulos boves similae tres decimas conspersae oleo quod habeat medium mensurae hin*

"'you will give for each of *the* oxen three tenths of wheat flour sprinkled with oil, which has half *a* hin's measure,

15:10 *et vinum ad liba fundenda eiusdem mensurae in oblationem suavissimi odoris Domino*

"'and wine as *a* libation poured out of *the* same measure, in *an* oblation of *the* smoothest odor to *the* Lord.

15:11 *sic facietis*

"'So you will do

15:12 *per singulos boves et arietes et agnos et hedos*

"'for each of *the* oxen and rams and lambs and goats.

15:13 *tam indigenae quam peregrini*

"'Whether native-born or *a* sojourner,

15:14 *eodem ritu offerent sacrificia*

"'they will offer sacrifices by *the* same ritual.

15:15 *unum praeceptum erit atque iudicium tam vobis quam advenis terrae*

"'*There* will be one precept and judgment, whether for you or for *the* land's newcomers.'"

Instructions on First Fruits

15:16 *locutus est Dominus ad Mosen dicens*

The Lord spoke to Moses, saying,

15:17 *loquere filiis Israhel et dices ad eos*

"Speak to Israel's children, and you will say to them,

15:18 *cum veneritis in terram quam dabo vobis*

"'When you come into *the* land which I will give you,

15:19 *et comederitis de panibus regionis illius separabitis primitias Domino*

"'and you eat from those regions' loaves, you will separate first fruits to *the* Lord

15:20 *de cibis vestris sicut de areis primitias separatis*

"'from your food. As you will separate first fruits from your threshing floors,

15:21 *ita et de pulmentis dabitis primitiva Domino*

"'so also you will give *the* Lord first fruits of your meals.

Atoning for Sins of Ignorance

15:22 *quod si per ignorantiam praeterieritis quicquam horum quae locutus est Dominus ad Mosen*

"'But if through ignorance you pass over any of these which *the* Lord has spoken to Moses

15:23 *et mandavit per eum ad vos a die qua coepit iubere et ultra*

"'and commanded through him to you, from *the* day when He began to order and beyond,

15:24 *oblitaque fuerit facere multitudo offeret vitulum de armento holocaustum in odorem suavissimum Domino et sacrificium eius ac liba ut caerimoniae postulant hircumque pro peccato*

"'and *the* multitude has forgotten to do *it*, it will offer *a* calf from *the* herd *as a* burnt offering, as *the* smoothest odor to *the* Lord, and its sacrifice and libations as *the* ceremonies require; and *a* he-goat for sin.

15:25 *et rogabit sacerdos pro omni multitudine filiorum Israhel et dimittetur eis quoniam non sponte peccaverunt nihilominus offerentes incensum Domino pro se et pro peccato atque errore suo*

"'And *the* priest will pray for all *the* multitude of Israel's children, and it will be forgiven them because they did not sin willingly. Nevertheless, offering *the* Lord incense for itself and for its sin and error,

15:26 *et dimittetur universae plebi filiorum Israhel et advenis qui peregrinantur inter vos quoniam culpa est omnis populi per ignorantiam*

"'it also will be forgiven *the* whole people of Israel's children, and *the* newcomers who sojourn among them, because *the* whole people is guilty through ignorance.

15:27 *quod si anima una nesciens peccaverit offeret capram anniculam pro peccato suo*

"'But if one soul should sin unknowing, he will offer *a* yearling goat for his sin.

15:28 *et deprecabitur pro ea sacerdos quod inscia peccaverit coram Domino inpetrabitque ei veniam et dimittetur illi*

"'And *the* priest will plead for him, that he sinned without knowledge before *the* Lord. And he will obtain pardon for him, and it will be forgiven him.

15:29 *tam indigenis quam advenis una lex erit omnium qui peccaverint*

ignorantes

"'Whether for native-born or newcomers, one law will be for all who sin without knowing.

Those Who Sin Knowingly
15:30 *anima vero quae per superbiam aliquid commiserit sive civis sit ille sive peregrinus quoniam adversum Dominum rebellis fuit peribit de populo suo*

"'Yet *a* soul that through pride commits something will perish from his people, whether he be *a* citizen or *a* sojourner, because he has rebelled against *the* Lord.

15:31 *verbum enim Domini contempsit et praeceptum illius fecit irritum idcirco delebitur et portabit iniquitatem suam*

"'For he has held *the* Lord's word in contempt, and made His precept void. Therefore, he will be destroyed, and will carry his iniquity.'"

Case of One Found Breaking the Sabbath
15:32 *factum est autem cum essent filii Israhel in solitudine et invenissent hominem colligentem ligna in die sabbati*

But it happened *that* when Israel's children were in *the* wasteland, and they had found *a* man gathering wood on *the* Sabbath day,

15:33 *obtulerunt eum Mosi et Aaron et universae multitudini*

they brought him to Moses and Aaron and *the* whole multitude,

15:34 *qui recluserunt eum in carcerem nescientes quid super eo facere deberent*

who closed him up in custody, not knowing what they should do about him.

15:35 *dixitque Dominus ad Mosen morte moriatur homo iste obruat eum lapidibus omnis turba extra castra*

And *the* Lord said to Moses, "Let that man die by death. Let *the* whole crowd crush him with stones outside *the* camps."

15:36 *cumque eduxissent eum foras obruerunt lapidibus et mortuus est sicut praeceperat Dominus*

And when they had led him outside, they crushed *him* with stones and he died, as *the* Lord had commanded.

15:37 *dixit quoque Dominus ad Mosen*

The Lord likewise said to Moses,

15:38 *loquere filiis Israhel et dices*

ad eos ut faciant sibi fimbrias per angulos palliorum ponentes in eis vittas hyacinthinas

"Speak to Israel's children, and you will say to them that they should make themselves fringes on their coverings' corners, putting violet threads inside them.

15:39 *quas cum viderint recordentur omnium mandatorum Domini nec sequantur cogitationes suas et oculos per res varias fornicantes*

"When they see them, they may remember all *the* Lord's commandments, nor follow their thoughts and eyes, fornicating through various affairs.

15:40 *sed magis memores praeceptorum Domini faciant ea sintque sancti Deo suo*

"But, remembering rather *the* Lord's precepts, they may do them and be holy to their God.

15:41 *ego Dominus Deus vester qui eduxi vos de terra Aegypti ut essem vester Deus*

"'I *am the* Lord your God, who led you out of Egypt's land so I could be your God.'"

Core, Dathan, and Abiram Rebel
Numbers 16:1 *ecce autem Core filius Isaar filii Caath filii Levi et Dathan atque Abiram filii Heliab Hon quoque filius Pheleth de filiis Ruben*

But look, Core, Isaar's son, Caath's son, Levi's son, and Dathan and Abiram, Heliab's son, as well as Hon, Pheleth's son, from Reuben's children,

16:2 *surrexerunt contra Mosen aliique filiorum Israhel ducenti quinquaginta viri proceres synagogae et qui tempore concilii per nomina vocabantur*

rose up against Moses, and two hundred fifty others of Israel's children, leading men of *the* gathering, and who were called by name at *the* time of assembly.

16:3 *cumque stetissent adversum Mosen et Aaron dixerunt sufficiat vobis quia omnis multitudo sanctorum est et in ipsis est Dominus cur elevamini super populum Domini*

And when they had stood against Moses and Aaron, they said, "Let it be sufficient to you that all *the* multitude is holy, and that *the* Lord is among them. Why do you lift yourselves up over *the* Lord's people?"

16:4 *quod cum audisset Moses*

cecidit pronus in faciem

When Moses had heard this, he fell face-down,

16:5 *locutusque ad Core et ad omnem multitudinem mane inquit notum faciet Dominus qui ad se pertineant et sanctos adplicabit sibi et quos elegerit adpropinquabunt ei*

and he spoke to Core and to *the* whole multitude. "In *the* morning," he said, "*the* Lord will make known who belongs to Him, and He will attach *the* holy *ones* to Himself. And those whom He has chosen will come near Him.

16:6 *hoc igitur facite tollat unusquisque turibula sua tu Core et omne concilium tuum*

"Therefore, do this! Let each one take his censer – you, Core, and all your council –

16:7 *et hausto cras igne ponite desuper thymiama coram Domino et quemcumque elegerit ipse erit sanctus multum erigimini filii Levi*

"and drawing out fire, tomorrow put incense on them before *the* Lord. And whomever He will chose, he will be holy. You have stirred up many, Levi's children!"

16:8 *dixitque rursum ad Core audite filii Levi*

And he said again to Core, "Listen, Levi's children!

16:9 *num parum vobis est quod separavit vos Deus Israhel ab omni populo et iunxit sibi ut serviretis ei in cultu tabernaculi et staretis coram frequentia populi et ministraretis ei*

"Isn't it enough to you that Israel's God separated you from all *the* people, and anointed you so you could serve Him in *the* tabernacle's ritual, and stand before *the* people who come, and minister to Him?

16:10 *idcirco ad se fecit accedere te et omnes fratres tuos filios Levi ut vobis etiam sacerdotium vindicetis*

"Therefore, He made you and all your brothers, Levi's children, come near Him. So are you even claiming *the* priesthood,

16:11 *et omnis globus tuus stet contra Dominum quid est enim Aaron ut murmuretis contra eum*

"and is all your crowd standing against *the* Lord – for what is Aaron that you complain about him?

16:12 *misit ergo Moses ut vocaret Dathan et Abiram filios Heliab qui responderunt non venimus*

Therefore, Moses sent so he could call Dathan and Abiram, Heliab's children, who answered, "We won't come!

16:13 *numquid parum est tibi quod eduxisti nos de terra quae lacte et melle manabat ut occideres in deserto nisi et dominatus fueris nostri*

"Isn't it enough to you that you led us from *a* land that flowed with milk and honey so you could kill *us* in *the* desert? Do you have to be our lord?

16:14 *re vera induxisti nos in terram quae fluit rivis lactis et mellis et dedisti nobis possessiones agrorum et vinearum an et oculos nostros vis eruere non venimus*

"Did you really lead us into *a* land that flows with rivers of milk and honey, and give us possessions of fields and vineyards? Do you want to pull our eyes out too? We won't come!"

16:15 *iratusque Moses valde ait ad Dominum ne respicias sacrificia eorum tu scis quod ne asellum quidem umquam acceperim ab eis nec adflixerim quempiam eorum*

And Moses was very angry. He said to *the* Lord, "Don't look on their sacrifices! You know that I didn't take even one little donkey from them, nor did I afflict anyone of theirs!"

16:16 *dixitque ad Core tu et omnis*

congregatio tua state seorsum coram Domino et Aaron die crastino separatim

And he said to Core, "You and all your gathering stand apart tomorrow before *the* Lord, and Aaron separately.

16:17 *tollite singuli turibula vestra et ponite super ea incensum offerentes Domino ducenta quinquaginta turibula Aaron quoque teneat turibulum suum*

"Each of you take your censers and put incense on them, offering to *the* Lord two hundred fifty censers. Aaron likewise will have his censer."

16:18 *quod cum fecissent stantibus Mosen et Aaron*

When they had done it, Moses and Aaron standing

16:19 *et coacervassent adversum eos omnem multitudinem ad ostium tabernaculi apparuit cunctis gloria Domini*

and all *the* multitude amassed against them at *the* tabernacle's opening, *the* Lord's glory appeared to all.

16:20 *locutusque Dominus ad Mosen et Aaron ait*

And *the* Lord spoke to Moses and Aaron. He said,

16:21 *separamini de medio congregationis huius ut eos repente disperdam*

"Move away from among this crowd, so I can quickly destroy them!

16:22 *qui ceciderunt proni in faciem atque dixerunt fortissime Deus spirituum universae carnis num uno peccante contra omnes tua ira desaeviet*

They fell face down and said, "Mightiest God of all flesh's spirits, will Your anger rage, one sinning against all?"

16:23 *et ait Dominus ad Mosen*

And *the* Lord said to Moses,

16:24 *praecipe universo populo ut separetur a tabernaculis Core et Dathan et Abiram*

"Command all *the* people that they move away from Core and Dathan and Abiram's tents!"

16:25 *surrexitque Moses et abiit ad Dathan et Abiram et sequentibus eum senioribus Israhel*

And Moses got up and went to Dathan and Abiram, and Israel's elders *were* following him.

16:26 *dixit ad turbam recedite a tabernaculis hominum impiorum et* *nolite tangere quae ad eos pertinent ne involvamini in peccatis eorum*

And he said to *the* crowd, "Move back from *these* lawless men's tents! And don't touch *things* that belong to them, so you not involve yourselves in their sins!"

16:27 *cumque recessissent a tentoriis eorum per circuitum Dathan et Abiram egressi stabant in introitu papilionum suorum cum uxoribus et liberis omnique frequentia*

And when they had moved back from their tents all around, Dathan and Abiram, coming out, stood at *the* entrance to their dwellings with their wives and children and all visitors.

16:28 *et ait Moses in hoc scietis quod Dominus miserit me ut facerem universa quae cernitis et non ex proprio ea corde protulerim*

And Moses said, "You will know in this that *the* Lord sent me so I could do all that you discern – and I did not bring them forward from my own heart!

16:29 *si consueta hominum morte interierint et visitaverit eos plaga qua et ceteri visitari solent non misit me Dominus*

"If these are destroyed by death in *the* usual human manner, and blows visit them that usually visit others, *the* Lord has not sent me.

16:30 *sin autem novam rem fecerit Dominus ut aperiens terra os suum degluttiat eos et omnia quae ad illos pertinent descenderintque viventes in infernum scietis quod blasphemaverint Dominum*

"But if *the* Lord does *a* new thing – that *the* land, opening its mouth, swallows them and all that belongs to them, and they go down living into *the* inferno – you will know that they blasphemed *the* Lord.

Dathan and Abiram Destroyed
16:31 *confestim igitur ut cessavit loqui disrupta est terra sub pedibus eorum*

As soon, therefore, as he stopped speaking, *the* ground was disrupted under their feet.

16:32 *et aperiens os suum devoravit illos cum tabernaculis suis et universa substantia*

And, opening its mouth, it devoured them with their tents and all their substance.

16:33 *descenderuntque vivi in infernum operti humo et perierunt de medio multitudinis*

And they went down alive into *the* inferno, *the* dirt covering *them*, and they perished from among *the* multitude.

16:34 *at vero omnis Israhel qui stabat per gyrum fugit ad clamorem pereuntium dicens ne forte et nos terra degluttiat*

And indeed all Israel which stood around fled from *the* cry of *the* dying, saying, "Unless perhaps *the* ground also swallow us!"

The Two Hundred Fifty Men Destroyed

16:35 *sed et ignis egressus a Domino interfecit ducentos quinquaginta viros qui offerebant incensum*

Yet fire also, coming out from *the* Lord, killed *the* two hundred fifty men who offered incense.

Gather the Censers

16:36 *locutusque est Dominus ad Mosen dicens*

And *the* Lord commanded Moses, saying,

16:37 *praecipe Eleazaro filio Aaron sacerdotis ut tollat turibula quae iacent in incendio et ignem huc illucque dispergat quoniam sanctificata sunt*

"Command Eleazar, Aaron *the* priest's son, that he take *the* censers that lie in *the* burning, and scatter *the*

fire here and there, because they are made holy

16:38 *in mortibus peccatorum producatque ea in lamminas et adfigat altari eo quod oblatum sit in eis incensum Domino et sanctificata sint ut cernant ea pro signo et monumento filii Israhel*

"in *the* sinners' death. And let him make them into metal plates, and attach *them* to *the* altar, because *the* Lord's incense is offered in them and they are made holy – so Israel's children may understand them as *a* sign and monument!"

16:39 *tulit ergo Eleazar sacerdos turibula aenea in quibus obtulerant hii quos incendium devoravit et produxit ea in lamminas adfigens altari*

So Eleazar *the* priest took *the* bronze censers, in which those whom *the* fire devoured had made offerings. And he made them into plates, attaching *them* to *the* altar,

16:40 *ut haberent postea filii Israhel quibus commonerentur ne quis accedat alienigena et qui non est de semine Aaron ad offerendum incensum Domino ne patiatur sicut passus est Core et omnis congregatio eius loquente Domino ad Mosen*

so Israel's children would have them afterwards, by which they would be warned, so someone who is *a* stranger and who is not of Aaron's seed may not come near to offer incense to *the* Lord – unless they suffer what happened to Core and all his gathering, spoken by *the* Lord to Moses.

Israel Rebels Further

16:41 *murmuravit autem omnis multitudo filiorum Israhel sequenti die contra Mosen et Aaron dicens vos interfecistis populum Domini*

But all *the* multitude of Israel's children complained against Moses and Aaron *the* following day, saying, "You killed *the* Lord's people!"

16:42 *cumque oreretur seditio et tumultus incresceret*

And when sedition had begun and *the* tumult had increased,

16:43 *Moses et Aaron fugerunt ad tabernaculum foederis quod postquam ingressi sunt operuit nubes et apparuit gloria Domini*

Moses and Aaron fled to *the* Covenant Tabernacle. After they went into it, *the* cloud covered *it* and *the* Lord's glory appeared.

16:44 *dixitque Dominus ad Mosen*

And *the* Lord said to Moses,

16:45 *recedite de medio huius multitudinis etiam nunc delebo eos cumque iacerent in terra*

"Back away from among this multitude, for now I will destroy them!"

And when they had thrown themselves onto *the* ground,

16:46 *dixit Moses ad Aaron tolle turibulum et hausto igne de altari mitte incensum desuper pergens cito ad populum ut roges pro eis iam enim egressa est ira a Domino et plaga desaevit*

Moses said to Aaron, "Take *a* censer and, carrying fire from *the* altar, put incense above – going quickly to *the* people so you can pray for them! For anger has already gone out from *the* Lord, and *the* plague is raging!"

16:47 *quod cum fecisset Aaron et cucurrisset ad mediam multitudinem quam iam vastabat incendium obtulit thymiama*

When Aaron had done this, and had run into *the* middle of *the* multitude which *the* fire was already destroying, he offered *the* incense.

16:48 *et stans inter mortuos ac viventes pro populo deprecatus est et plaga cessavit*

And, standing between *the* dead and *the* living, he pleaded for *the* people and *the* plague ceased.

16:49 *fuerunt autem qui percussi sunt quattuordecim milia hominum et septingenti absque his qui perierant in seditione Core*

But those who were struck down were fourteen thousand, seven hundred men, apart from those who perished in Core's sedition.

16:50 *reversusque est Aaron ad Mosen ad ostium tabernaculi foederis postquam quievit interitus*

And Aaron went back to Moses at *the* Covenant Tabernacle's entrance after *the* destruction was calmed.

Israel's Tribes' Rods Before the Lord

Numbers 17:1 *et locutus est Dominus ad Mosen dicens*

And *the* Lord spoke to Moses, saying,

17:2 *loquere ad filios Israhel et accipe ab eis virgas singulas per cognationes suas a cunctis principibus tribuum virgas duodecim et uniuscuiusque nomen superscribes virgae suae*

"Speak to Israel's children, and accept rods from them for each of their clans, from all *the* tribes' princes – twelve rods. And you will write each one's name on his rod.

17:3 *nomen autem Aaron erit in tribu Levi et una virga cunctas eorum familias continebit*

"But Aaron's name will be on *that of* Levi's tribe, and one rod will contain all their families.

17:4 *ponesque eas in tabernaculo foederis coram testimonio ubi loquar ad te*

"And you will place them in *the* Covenant Tabernacle, before *the* testimony, where I speak to you.

17:5 *quem ex his elegero germinabit virga eius et cohibebo a me querimonias filiorum Israhel quibus* *contra vos murmurant*

"*The* one whom I choose from among them, his staff will germinate. And I will curb from me Israel's children's complaints, by which they gripe against you."

Moses Brings Out the Rods

17:6 *locutusque est Moses ad filios Israhel et dederunt ei omnes principes virgas per singulas tribus fueruntque virgae duodecim absque virga Aaron*

And Moses spoke to Israel's children, and all *the* princes gave him rods for each of *the* tribes. And there were twelve rods, apart from Aaron's rod,

17:7 *quas cum posuisset Moses coram Domino in tabernaculo testimonii*

which, when Moses had placed them before *the* Lord in testimony's tabernacle,

17:8 *sequenti die regressus invenit germinasse virgam Aaron in domo Levi et turgentibus gemmis eruperant flores qui foliis dilatatis in amigdalas deformati sunt*

coming back *the* following day, he found Aaron's rod had germinated for Levi's house. And buds swelling had erupted into flowers, which were shaped through spreading leaves into

almonds.

17:9 *protulit ergo Moses omnes virgas de conspectu Domini ad cunctos filios Israhel videruntque et receperunt singuli virgas suas*

So Moses brought all *the* rods out from *the* Lord's sight to all Israel's children. And each saw and received *back* their rods.

17:10 *dixitque Dominus ad Mosen refer virgam Aaron in tabernaculum testimonii ut servetur ibi in signum rebellium filiorum et quiescant querellae eorum a me ne moriantur*

And *the* Lord said to Moses, "Take Aaron's rod back into testimony's tabernacle, so it can be saved there as *a* sign of *the* children's rebellion. And their complaints against Me may be quieted, so they not die.

17:11 *fecitque Moses sicut praeceperat Dominus*

And Moses did as *the* Lord had commanded.

Israel's Children's Fear

17:12 *dixerunt autem filii Israhel ad Mosen ecce consumpti sumus omnes perivimus*

But Israel's children said to Moses, "Look, we are burned up! All *of us* have perished!

17:13 *quicumque accedit ad tabernaculum Domini moritur num usque ad internicionem cuncti delendi sumus*

"Whoever comes near *the* Lord's tabernacle dies! Will all of us be destroyed, even to extermination?"

Aaron's Custody
of the Tabernacle Affirmed

Numbers 18:1 *dixitque Dominus ad Aaron tu et filii tui et domus patris tui tecum portabitis iniquitatem sanctuarii et tu et filii tui simul sustinebitis peccata sacerdotii vestri*

And *the* Lord said to Aaron, "You and your sons and your father's house with you will carry *the* sanctuary's treachery, and you and your sons together will bear your priests' sins.

18:2 *sed et fratres tuos de tribu Levi et sceptro patris tui sume tecum praestoque sint et ministrent tibi tu autem et filii tui ministrabitis in tabernaculo testimonii*

"Yet take up with you also your brothers from Levi's tribe and, by your father's scepter, let them be available, and let them minister to you. But you and your sons will minister in testimony's tabernacle.

18:3 *excubabuntque Levitae ad praecepta tua et ad cuncta opera tabernaculi ita dumtaxat ut ad vasa sanctuarii et altare non accedant ne et illi moriantur et vos pereatis simul*

"And *the* Levites will keep watch at your commands, and at all *the* tabernacle's works, to this extent only: that they may not come near *the* sanctuary's vessels and altar, so they may not die, and you perish together.

18:4 *sint autem tecum et excubent in custodiis tabernaculi et in omnibus caerimoniis eius alienigena non miscebitur vobis*

"But let them be with you and keep watch in *the* tabernacle's keeping, and in all its ceremonies. *A* stranger will not be mixed with you.

18:5 *excubate in custodia sanctuarii et in ministerio altaris ne oriatur indignatio super filios Israhel*

"Keep watch in *the* sanctuary's care and in *the* altar's ministry, so indignation may not spring up against Israel's children!

18:6 *ego dedi vobis fratres vestros Levitas de medio filiorum Israhel et tradidi donum Domino ut serviant in ministeriis tabernaculi eius*

"I have given you your brothers, *the* Levites, from among Israel's children, and I handed them over as *a* gift by *the* Lord, so they may serve in His tabernacle's ministries.

18:7 *tu autem et filii tui custodite sacerdotium vestrum et omnia quae ad cultum altaris pertinent et intra velum sunt per sacerdotes administrabuntur si quis externus accesserit occidetur*

"But you and your sons – keep your

priesthood! And all *things* that pertain to *the* altar's ritual, and that are inside *the* veil, will be administered through *the* priests. If *an* outsider comes near, he will be killed.

Custody of All Offerings
18:8 *locutus est Dominus ad Aaron ecce dedi tibi custodiam primitiarum mearum omnia quae sanctificantur a filiis Israhel tibi tradidi et filiis tuis pro officio sacerdotali legitima sempiterna*

The Lord spoke to Aaron, "Look, I have given you custody of My first fruits. I have given you and your sons all *gifts* that are sanctified by Israel's children for *the* priestly office, *an* everlasting law.

18:9 *haec ergo accipies de his quae sanctificantur et oblata sunt Domino omnis oblatio et sacrificium et quicquid pro peccato atque delicto redditur mihi et cedet in sancta sanctorum tuum erit et filiorum tuorum*

"Therefore, you will receive these from those that are sanctified and are given to *the* Lord. Every offering and sacrifice, and whatever is paid Me for sin and offense and will go into the holy of holies will be yours and your sons.

18:10 *in sanctuario comedes illud mares tantum edent ex eo quia* *consecratum est tibi*

"You will eat it in *the* sanctuary. Only males will eat from it, for *it* is consecrated to you.

18:11 *primitias autem quas voverint et obtulerint filii Israhel tibi dedi et filiis ac filiabus tuis iure perpetuo qui mundus est in domo tua vescetur eis*

"But I have given you and your sons and daughters *the* first fruits, which Israel's children pay back and offer Me, as *a* perpetual law. Who is clean in your house will eat them.

18:12 *omnem medullam olei et vini ac frumenti quicquid offerunt primitiarum Domino tibi dedi*

"Every essence of oil and wine and grain – whatever they offer as first fruits to *the* Lord – I have given you.

18:13 *universa frugum initia quas gignit humus et Domino deportantur cedent in usus tuos qui mundus est in domo tua vescetur eis*

"All *the* first ripe fruit that *the* soil bears and they carry to *the* Lord will go to your uses. Who is clean in your house will eat them.

18:14 *omne quod ex voto reddiderint filii Israhel tuum erit*

"Everything that Israel's children pay

back from *a* promise will be yours.

18:15 *quicquid primum erumpet e vulva cunctae carnis quam offerunt Domino sive ex hominibus sive de pecoribus fuerit tui iuris erit ita dumtaxat ut pro hominis primogenito pretium accipias et omne animal quod inmundum est redimi facias*

"Whatever breaks forth first from *the* vulva of all flesh they offer to *the* Lord – whether from men or animals – is yours, to this extent so: that you will receive *the* price for firstborn men; and every animal that is unclean, you will cause to be bought back –

18:16 *cuius redemptio erit post unum mensem siclis argenti quinque pondere sanctuarii siclus viginti obolos habet*

"whose redemption will be five silver shekels after one month, by the sanctuary's weight. *(A* shekel has twenty obolos.)

18:17 *primogenitum autem bovis et ovis et caprae non facies redimi quia sanctificata sunt Domino sanguinem tantum eorum fundes super altare et adipes adolebis in suavissimum odorem Domino*

But you will not cause *the* firstborn ox or sheep or goat to be redeemed, because they are sanctified to *the* Lord. You will pour out their blood only over *the* altar, and you will burn their fat as *the* smoothest odor to *the* Lord.

18:18 *carnes vero in usum tuum cedent sicut pectusculum consecratum et armus dexter tua erunt*

"Indeed, *the* flesh will go to your use, as *the* consecrated breast and right forequarter will be yours.

18:19 *omnes primitias sanctuarii quas offerunt filii Israhel Domino tibi dedi et filiis ac filiabus tuis iure perpetuo pactum salis est sempiternum coram Domino tibi ac filiis tuis*

"I have given to you and your sons and daughters all *the* sanctuary's first fruits which Israel's children offer *the* Lord, *as an* enduring law. *It* is *an* everlasting pact of salt before *the* Lord, to you and your sons."

The Lord Is Aaron's Portion

18:20 *dixitque Dominus ad Aaron in terra eorum nihil possidebitis nec habebitis partem inter eos ego pars et hereditas tua in medio filiorum Israhel*

And *the* Lord said to Aaron, "You will possess nothing in their land, nor have *a* portion among them. I *will be* your portion and inheritance among Israel's children.

18:21 *filiis autem Levi dedi omnes decimas Israhelis in possessionem pro ministerio quo serviunt mihi in tabernaculo foederis*

"But I have given Levi's children all Israel's tithes as *a* possession for ministry, for those who serve Me in *the* Covenant Tabernacle,

18:22 *ut non accedant ultra filii Israhel ad tabernaculum nec committant peccatum mortiferum*

"so Israel's children may not come near *the* tabernacle further, nor commit *a* death-dealing sin –

18:23 *solis filiis Levi mihi in tabernaculo servientibus et portantibus peccata populi legitimum sempiternum erit in generationibus vestris nihil aliud possidebunt*

"Levi's children alone serving Me in *the* tabernacle, and carrying *the* people's sins. *It* will be an everlasting law in your generations. They will possess nothing else,

18:24 *decimarum oblatione contenti quas in usus eorum et necessaria separavi*

"content in *the* offering's tithes, which I have separated in their use and necessities.

A Tithe of the Tithes

18:25 *locutusque est Dominus ad Mosen dicens*

And *the* Lord spoke to Moses, saying,

18:26 *praecipe Levitis atque denuntia cum acceperitis a filiis Israhel decimas quas dedi vobis primitias earum offerte Domino id est decimam partem decimae*

"Command *the* Levites and tell them, 'When you receive tithes from Israel's children, which I have given you, you will offer their first fruits to *the* Lord – that is, *a* tenth part of *a* tenth –

18:27 *ut reputetur vobis in oblationem primitivorum tam de areis quam de torcularibus*

"so it may be reputed to you as *an* oblation of first fruits, whether from rams or from *the* winepresses.

18:28 *et universis quorum accipitis primitias offerte Domino et date Aaron sacerdoti*

"And of all *things* from which you receive, offer first fruits to *the* Lord, and give *them* to Aaron *the* priest!

The Best of the Gifts

18:29 *omnia quae offertis ex decimis et in donaria Domini separatis optima et electa erunt*

"You will separate all *the* best of *the things* that are offered as *the* Lord's tithes and gifts, and they will be chosen.

18:30 *dicesque ad eos si praeclara et meliora quaeque obtuleritis ex decimis reputabitur vobis quasi de area et torculari dederitis primitias*

"And you will say to them, 'If whatever you offer from *the* tithes is splendid and superior, it will be reputed to you as if you have given first fruits from *the* threshing floor and winepress.

18:31 *et comedetis eas in omnibus locis vestris tam vos quam familiae vestrae quia pretium est pro ministerio quo servitis in tabernaculo testimonii*

"'And you will eat them in all of your places, whether you or your families, because *it* is *the* price of your ministry, by which you serve in testimony's tabernacle.

18:32 *et non peccabitis super hoc egregia vobis et pinguia reservantes ne polluatis oblationes filiorum Israhel et moriamini*

"And you will not sin over this, reserving *the* superior and fat ones for yourselves, so you do not pollute Israel's children's offerings, and you die."

Ceremony of the Red Heifer
Numbers 19:1 *locutusque est Dominus ad Mosen et Aaron dicens*

And *the* Lord spoke to Moses and Aaron, saying,

19:2 *ista est religio victimae quam constituit Dominus praecipe filiis Israhel ut adducant ad te vaccam rufam aetatis integrae in qua nulla sit macula nec portaverit iugum*

"This is *the* binding rite of *the* victim, which *the* Lord appointed. Command Israel's children that they bring you *a* red cow, of full age, in which is no defect, nor has it carried *a* yoke.

19:3 *tradetisque eam Eleazaro sacerdoti qui eductam extra castra immolabit in conspectu omnium*

"And you will hand her to Eleazar *the* priest, who, leading *her* outside *the* camps, will kill *her* in *the* sight of all.

19:4 *et tinguens digitum in sanguine eius asperget contra fores tabernaculi septem vicibus*

"And, dipping *a* finger in her blood, he will sprinkle *it* seven times against *the* tabernacle's doors.

19:5 *conburetque eam cunctis videntibus tam pelle et carnibus eius quam sanguine et fimo flammae*

traditis

"And he will burn her, all watching, handing over to flames her hide and flesh as well as her blood and excrement.

19:6 *lignum quoque cedrinum et hysopum coccumque bis tinctum sacerdos mittet in flammam quae vaccam vorat*

"*The* priest likewise will throw cedar wood, and hyssop, *and* scarlet *thread* twice dyed, into *the* flames that consume *the* cow.

19:7 *et tunc demum lotis vestibus et corpore suo ingredietur in castra commaculatusque erit usque ad vesperam*

"And then, finally, washing his clothes and body, he will go into *the* camps, and will be deeply defiled until evening.

19:8 *sed et ille qui conbuserit eam lavabit vestimenta sua et corpus et inmundus erit usque ad vesperam*

"Yet he also who burned her will wash his clothes and body, and will be unclean until evening.

19:9 *colliget autem vir mundus cineres vaccae et effundet eos extra castra in loco purissimo ut sint multitudini filiorum Israhel in custodiam et in aquam aspersionis* *quia pro peccato vacca conbusta est*

"But *a ritually* clean man will gather *the* cow's ashes and pour them out outside *the* camps in *the* purest place, so they may be in keeping for Israel's children's multitude, and for *the* water of sprinkling, because *the* cow was burned for sin.

19:10 *cumque laverit qui vaccae portaverat cineres vestimenta sua inmundus erit usque ad vesperum habebunt hoc filii Israhel et advenae qui habitant inter eos sanctum iure perpetuo*

"And when he who carried *the* cow's ashes has washed his clothes, he will be unclean until evening. Israel's children and *the* newcomers who live among them will have this *as* holy, *an* enduring law.

19:11 *qui tetigerit cadaver hominis et propter hoc septem diebus fuerit inmundus*

Who touches *a* human body and, because of this, is unclean for seven days,

19:12 *aspergetur ex hac aqua die tertio et septimo et sic mundabitur si die tertio aspersus non fuerit septimo non poterit emundari*

will be sprinkled from this water *the* third day and *the* seventh, and so will be made clean. If he is not sprinkled

the third day, he cannot be made clean *the* seventh day.

19:13 *omnis qui tetigerit humanae animae morticinum et aspersus hac commixtione non fuerit polluet tabernaculum Domini et peribit ex Israhel quia aqua expiationis non est aspersus inmundus erit et manebit spurcitia eius super eum*

Everyone who touches *the* dead body of *a* human soul, and is not sprinkled with this mixture, will pollute *the* Lord's tabernacle, and will perish from Israel, because *the* water of atonement is not sprinkled. He will be unclean and his filth will remain on him."

Dealing with the Dead
19:14 *ista est lex hominis qui moritur in tabernaculo omnes qui ingrediuntur tentorium illius et universa vasa quae ibi sunt polluta erunt septem diebus*

"This is *the* law of *a* man who dies inside *a* tent. All who go into his partition and all *the* vessels that are there will be polluted for seven days.

19:15 *vas quod non habuerit operculum nec ligaturam desuper inmundum erit*

"*A* vessel that has neither *a* cover nor *a* binding on top *of it* will be unclean.

19:16 *si quis in agro tetigerit*

cadaver occisi hominis aut per se mortui sive os illius vel sepulchrum inmundus erit septem diebus

"If one touches in *a* field *the* body *of a* man killed, or who died of himself, or his bone or grave, he will be unclean for seven days.

19:17 *tollent de cineribus conbustionis atque peccati et mittent aquas vivas super eos in vas*

"They will take some of *the* ashes of burning and sin, and put living waters over them in *a* vessel.

19:18 *in quibus cum homo mundus tinxerit hysopum asperget eo omne tentorium et cunctam supellectilem et homines huiuscemodi contagione pollutos*

"When *a ritually* clean man has dipped hyssop in it, he will sprinkle with it all *the* partition, and all *the* furnishings, and all those men polluted by *the* contagion.

19:19 *atque hoc modo mundus lustrabit inmundum tertio et septimo die expiatusque die septimo lavabit et se et vestimenta sua et mundus erit ad vesperam*

"*The ritually* clean one will purify *the* unclean in this manner *the* third and seventh day. And, atoned for on *the* seventh day, he will wash both himself and his clothes, and will be clean at evening.

19:20 *si quis hoc ritu non fuerit expiatus peribit anima illius de medio ecclesiae quia sanctuarium Domini polluit et non est aqua lustrationis aspersus*

"If someone is not atoned for by this rite, his soul will perish from among *the* gathering, because he pollutes *the* Lord's sanctuary and is not sprinkled with *the* water of purification.

19:21 *erit hoc praeceptum legitimum sempiternum ipse quoque qui aspergit aquas lavabit vestimenta sua omnis qui tetigerit aquas expiationis inmundus erit usque ad vesperam*

"This will be *a* binding, everlasting commandment. He likewise who sprinkles *the* waters will wash his clothes. Everyone who touches *the* waters of atonement will be unclean until evening.

19:22 *quicquid tetigerit inmundus inmundum faciet et anima quae horum quippiam tetigerit inmunda erit usque ad vesperum*

"Whatever *the* unclean one touches, he makes unclean. And *a* soul who touches any of these will be unclean until evening."

Mary, Moses' Sister, Dies in Kadesh

Numbers 20:1 *veneruntque filii Israhel et omnis multitudo in desertum Sin mense primo et mansit populus in Cades mortuaque est ibi Maria et sepulta in eodem loco*

And Israel's children and all *the* multitude came into Sin's desert *the* first month, and *the* people stayed in Kadesh. And Mary died there, and *was* buried in *the* same place.

Contradiction's Waters

20:2 *cumque indigeret aqua populus coierunt adversum Mosen et Aaron*

And when *the* people lacked water, they came together against Moses and Aaron.

20:3 *et versi in seditionem dixerunt utinam perissemus inter fratres nostros coram Domino*

And turning to sedition, they said, "If only we had died among our brothers before *the* Lord!

20:4 *cur eduxistis ecclesiam Domini in solitudinem ut et nos et nostra iumenta moriantur*

"Why have you led *the* Lord's assembly into *a* wasteland? So we and our cattle can die?

20:5 *quare nos fecistis ascendere de Aegypto et adduxistis in locum istum pessimum qui seri non potest qui nec ficum gignit nec vineas nec mala granata insuper et aquam non habet ad bibendum*

"Why did you make us come up out of Egypt, and lead us into this dismal place, which can't be sown, nor produces figs or vines or pomegranates above, and has no water to drink?"

20:6 *ingressusque Moses et Aaron dimissa multitudine tabernaculum foederis corruerunt proni in terram et apparuit gloria Domini super eos*

And Moses and Aaron, dismissing *the* multitude and going into *the* Covenant Tabernacle, fell face-down on *the* ground. And *the* Lord's glory appeared over them.

20:7 *locutusque est Dominus ad Mosen dicens*

And *the* Lord spoke to Moses, saying,

20:8 *tolle virgam et congrega populum tu et Aaron frater tuus et loquimini ad petram coram eis et illa dabit aquas cumque eduxeris aquam de petra bibet omnis multitudo et iumenta eius*

"Take *the* staff and gather *the* people – you, and Aaron your brother – and speak to *the* rock before them, and it will give you waters! And when you have led water from *the* rock, all *the* multitude will drink, and their cattle."

20:9 *tulit igitur Moses virgam quae erat in conspectu Domini sicut praeceperat ei*

So Moses took *the* staff which was in *the* Lord's sight, as He had commanded him.

20:10 *congregata multitudine ante petram dixitque eis audite rebelles et increduli num de petra hac vobis aquam poterimus eicere*

When the multitude gathered before *the* rock, he said to them, "Listen, rebels and unbelievers! Should we drive water from this rock for you?

20:11 *cumque elevasset Moses manum percutiens virga bis silicem egressae sunt aquae largissimae ita ut et populus biberet et iumenta*

And when Moses had lifted up *his* hand, striking *the* rock twice with *the* staff, *the* greatest waters came out, so that *the* people and cattle could drink.

20:12 *dixitque Dominus ad Mosen et Aaron quia non credidistis mihi ut sanctificaretis me coram filiis Israhel non introducetis hos populos in terram quam dabo eis*

And *the* Lord said to Moses and Aaron, "Because you did not believe

Me, so you might sanctify Me before Israel's children, you will not lead these peoples into *the* land which I will give them."

20:13 *haec est aqua Contradictionis ubi iurgati sunt filii Israhel contra Dominum et sanctificatus est in eis*

This was Contradiction's waters, where Israel's children argued against *the* Lord, and He was sanctified among them.

Moses Sends Messengers to Edom

20:14 *misit interea nuntios Moses de Cades ad regem Edom qui dicerent haec mandat frater tuus Israhel nosti omnem laborem qui adprehendit nos*

Meanwhile, Moses sent messengers from Kadesh to Edom's king, who said, "May your brother Israel command this. You have known all *the* labor that has overtaken us;

20:15 *quomodo descenderint patres nostri in Aegyptum et habitaverimus ibi multo tempore adflixerintque nos Aegyptii et patres nostros*

"how our fathers went down into Egypt, and we lived there *a* long time, and *the* Egyptians afflicted us and our fathers;

20:16 *et quomodo clamaverimus ad Dominum et exaudierit nos* *miseritque angelum qui eduxerit nos de Aegypto ecce in urbe Cades quae est in extremis finibus tuis positi*

"and how we cried out to *the* Lord, and He heard us, and sent *an* angel who led us from Egypt. Look, *we are* in *the* city of Kadesh, which is placed in your farthest borders!

20:17 *obsecramus ut nobis transire liceat per terram tuam non ibimus per agros nec per vineas non bibemus aquas de puteis tuis sed gradiemur via publica nec ad dextram nec ad sinistram declinantes donec transeamus terminos tuos*

"We pray that it may be lawful for us to pass through your land. We will not go through fields or vineyards. We will not drink water from your wells, but will go down *the* public road, turning aside neither to *the* right nor to *the* left until we pass through your boundaries."

Edom Refuses
20:18 *cui respondit Edom non transibis per me alioquin armatus occurram tibi*

Edom answered them, "You will not pass through me. Otherwise I will meet you armed."

20:19 *dixeruntque filii Israhel per tritam gradiemur viam et si biberimus aquas tuas nos et pecora nostra dabimus quod iustum est*

nulla erit in pretio difficultas tantum velociter transeamus

And Israel's children said, "We will go down *the* well-traveled road. And if we drink your waters, we and our animals, we will give what is fair. Nothing will be difficult in price. Only may we cross through quickly!

20:20 *at ille respondit non transibis statimque egressus est obvius cum infinita multitudine et manu forti*

And he answered, "You will not pass through."

And immediately, he came out to meet them with *a* limitless multitude and *a* strong hand,

20:21 *nec voluit adquiescere deprecanti ut concederet transitum per fines suos quam ob rem devertit ab eo Israhel*

nor did he acquiesce to *their* pleas that he concede passage through his borders. Because of this, Israel turned aside from him.

Aaron's Death
20:22 *cumque castra movissent de Cades venerunt in montem Or qui est in finibus terrae Edom*

And when *the* camps had moved from Kadesh they came to Mount Hor, which is on *the* borders of Edom's land,

20:23 *ubi locutus est Dominus ad Mosen*

where *the* Lord spoke to Moses.

20:24 *pergat inquit Aaron ad populos suos non enim intrabit terram quam dedi filiis Israhel eo quod incredulus fuerit ori meo ad aquas Contradictionis*

"Let Aaron go," He said, "to his peoples, for he will not enter *the* land which I have given to Israel's children, because he disbelieved My mouth at Contradiction's waters.

20:25 *tolle Aaron et filium eius cum eo et duces eos in montem Or*

"Take Aaron and his son with him, and you will lead them to Mount Hor.

20:26 *cumque nudaveris patrem veste sua indues ea Eleazarum filium eius et Aaron colligetur et morietur ibi*

"And when you have stripped *the* father of his vestment, you will put it on Eleazar his son. And Aaron will be gathered and will die there."

20:27 *fecit Moses ut praeceperat Dominus et ascenderunt in montem Or coram omni multitudine*

Moses did as *the* Lord had commanded. And they climbed up onto Mount Hor before all *the* multitude.

20:28 *cumque Aaron spoliasset vestibus suis induit eis Eleazarum filium eius*

And when he had stripped Aaron of his vestments , he put them on Eleazar, his son.

20:29 *illo mortuo in montis supercilio descendit cum Eleazaro*

Aaron dying on *the* mountain's brow, *Moses* came down with Eleazar.

20:30 *omnis autem multitudo videns occubuisse Aaron flevit super eo triginta diebus per cunctas familias suas*

But all *the* multitude, seeing Aaron lay dead, wept over him thirty days through all their families.

Defeating Arad at Horma

Numbers 21:1 *quod cum audisset Chananeus rex Arad qui habitabat ad meridiem venisse scilicet Israhel per exploratorum viam pugnavit contra illum et victor existens duxit ex eo praedam*

When Arad, *a* Canaanite king who lived toward *the* south, heard that Israel had come, of course, by *the* spies' way, he fought against him. And, being *the* victor, he took plunder from him.

21:2 *at Israhel voto se Domino obligans ait si tradideris populum istum in manu mea delebo urbes eius*

And Israel, binding itself by promise to *the* Lord, said, "If you will hand this people into my hand, I will destroy their cities."

21:3 *exaudivitque Dominus preces Israhel et tradidit Chananeum quem ille interfecit subversis urbibus eius et vocavit nomen loci illius Horma id est anathema*

And *the* Lord heard Israel's pleas and handed over *the* Canaanite, whom he killed, overthrowing his cities. And he called that place's name Horma – that is, curse.

Fire-Causing Snakes

21:4 *profecti sunt autem et de monte Or per viam quae ducit ad mare Rubrum ut circumirent terram Edom et taedere coepit populum itineris ac laboris*

But they set out also from Mount Hor by *the* road that leads to *the* Red Sea, so they could walk around Edom's land. And *the* people began to tire from *the* journey and *the* work.

21:5 *locutusque contra Deum et Mosen ait cur eduxisti nos de Aegypto ut moreremur in solitudine deest panis non sunt aquae anima nostra iam nausiat super cibo isto levissimo*

And, speaking against God and Moses, he said, "Why did you lead us out from Egypt so we could die in *the* wasteland? Bread is lacking! *There* are no waters! Our soul is already nauseated over this trifling food!"

21:6 *quam ob rem misit Dominus in populum ignitos serpentes ad quorum plagas et mortes plurimorum*

Because of this, *the* Lord sent fire-causing snakes among *the* people, from whose wounds also many died.

21:7 *venerunt ad Mosen atque dixerunt peccavimus quia locuti sumus contra Dominum et te ora ut tollat a nobis serpentes oravit Moses pro populo*

They came to Moses and said, "We

have sinned, because we spoke against *the* Lord. And I pray you that He take *the* snakes away from us!"

Moses prayed for *the* people,

21:8 *et locutus est Dominus ad eum fac serpentem et pone eum pro signo qui percussus aspexerit eum vivet*

and *the* Lord said to him, "Make *a* snake and place it as *a* sign. Who, struck, looks at it, will live."

21:9 *fecit ergo Moses serpentem aeneum et posuit pro signo quem cum percussi aspicerent sanabantur*

So Moses made *a* brass snake, and placed it as *a* sign. When one who was struck looked *at it*, they were healed.

Further Travels in the Desert
21:10 *profectique filii Israhel castrametati sunt in Oboth*

And Israel's children, setting out, camped in Oboth.

21:11 *unde egressi fixere tentoria in Hieabarim in solitudine quae respicit Moab contra orientalem plagam*

Going out from there, they fixed tents in Hieabarim, in *the* wasteland that looks on Moab, against *the* eastern quarter.

21:12 *et inde moventes venerunt ad torrentem Zared*

And, moving from there, they came to Zared brook,

21:13 *quem relinquentes castrametati sunt contra Arnon quae est in deserto et prominet in finibus Amorrei siquidem Arnon terminus est Moab dividens Moabitas et Amorreos*

leaving which, they camped beside Arnon, which is in *the* desert and sticks out into *the* Amorite's borders. Accordingly, Arnon is Moab's boundary, dividing Moabites and Amorites,

21:14 *unde dicitur in libro bellorum Domini sicut fecit in mari Rubro sic faciet in torrentibus Arnon*

from which it is said in *the* book of *the* Lord's wars,
"As He did at *the* Red Sea,
so He will do in Arnon's brooks.

21:15 *scopuli torrentium inclinati sunt ut requiescerent in Ar et recumberent in finibus Moabitarum*

"*The* torrents' rocks bent down
so they could rest in Ar
and lie down
in *the* Moabites' borders."

A New Song in Ar
21:16 *ex eo loco apparuit puteus*

super quo locutus est Dominus ad Mosen congrega populum et dabo ei aquam

A well appeared from that place, over which *the* Lord said to Moses, "Gather *the* people, and I will give him water!"

21:17 *tunc cecinit Israhel carmen istud ascendat puteus concinebant*

Then Israel sang this song, "May *the* well go up," which they sang together.

21:18 *puteus quem foderunt principes et paraverunt duces multitudinis in datore legis et in baculis suis de solitudine Matthana*

"*This is the* well which *the* princes dug and *the* multitude's dukes prepared, at *the* law-giver's *command*, and by their sticks."

From Matthana's wasteland *they marched–*

21:19 *de Matthana Nahalihel de Nahalihel in Bamoth*

from Matthana to Nahaliel; from Nahaliel to Bamoth;

21:20 *de Bamoth vallis est in regione Moab in vertice Phasga et quod respicit contra desertum*

from Bamoth valley, *which* is in Moab's region, to Pisgah's height, and which looks across *the* desert.

The Conquest Begins with Sihon
21:21 *misit autem Israhel nuntios ad Seon regem Amorreorum dicens*

But Israel sent messengers to Sihon, *the* Amorites' king, saying,

21:22 *obsecro ut transire mihi liceat per terram tuam non declinabimus in agros et vineas non bibemus aquas ex puteis via regia gradiemur donec transeamus terminos tuos*

"I pray that it may be lawful for me to cross through your land. We will not turn aside into your fields and vineyards. We will not drink waters from *the* wells. We will go down *the* king's road until we pass through your boundaries.

21:23 *qui concedere noluit ut transiret Israhel per fines suos quin potius exercitu congregato egressus est obviam in desertum et venit in Iasa pugnavitque contra eum*

He didn't concede that Israel could pass through his borders. More than that, gathering *an* army, he came out to meet him in *the* desert. And he came to Iasa and fought against him,

21:24 *a quo percussus est in ore gladii et possessa est terra eius ab*

Arnon usque Iebboc et filios Ammon quia forti praesidio tenebantur termini Ammanitarum

by whom he was struck down by *the* sword's mouth. And his land was taken, from Arnon even to *the* Jabbok and Ammon's children – for they had *a* strong garrison on *the* Ammonites' borders.

21:25 *tulit ergo Israhel omnes civitates eius et habitavit in urbibus Amorrei in Esebon scilicet et viculis eius*

So Israel took all his cities, and lived in *the* Amorite's cities – in Heshbon, of course, and its villages.

21:26 *urbs Esebon fuit regis Seon Amorrei qui pugnavit contra regem Moab et tulit omnem terram quae dicionis illius fuerat usque Arnon*

Heshbon city was Sihon's, *the* Amorite king, who fought against Moab's king and took all *the* land that was under his authority, even to Arnon.

21:27 *idcirco dicitur in proverbio venite in Esebon aedificetur et construatur civitas Seon*

For this reason it is said in *a* proverb,
"Come to Heshbon!
It will be built,
and may Sihon's city be constructed!

21:28 *ignis egressus est de Esebon flamma de oppido Seon et devoravit Ar Moabitarum et habitatores excelsorum Arnon*

"Fire came out from Heshbon,
flame from Sihon's town,
and it devoured the Moabites' Ar,
and *the* inhabitants
of Arnon's high *places*.

21:29 *vae tibi Moab peristi popule Chamos dedit filios eius in fugam et filias in captivitatem regi Amorreorum Seon*

"Woe to you, Moab!
You have perished,
Chemosh's people!
He gave his sons to flight,
and *the* daughters of Sihon,
the Amorites' king, to captivity!

21:30 *iugum ipsorum disperiit ab Esebon usque Dibon lassi pervenerunt in Nophe et usque Medaba*

"Their yoke was destroyed
from Heshbon even to Dibon.
The weak came through
to Nophe and even to Medaba.

21:31 *habitavit itaque Israhel in terra Amorrei*

And so Israel lived in *the* Amorite's land.

Iazer Captured

21:31 *misitque Moses qui explorarent Iazer cuius ceperunt viculos et possederunt habitatores*

And Moses sent some who explored Iazer, who captured villages and possessed *the* inhabitants.

War with Og, Bashan's King

21:33 *verteruntque se et ascenderunt per viam Basan et occurrit eis Og rex Basan cum omni populo suo pugnaturus in Edrai*

And they turned themselves and climbed up by *the* road to Bashan. And Og, Bashan's king, met them with all his people, to fight in Edrai.

21:34 *dixitque Dominus ad Mosen ne timeas eum quia in manu tua tradidi illum et omnem populum ac terram eius faciesque illi sicut fecisti Seon regi Amorreorum habitatori Esebon*

And *the* Lord said to Moses, "Don't fear him, because I have given him and all his people and land into your hand! And you will do to him as you did to Sihon, *the* Amorites' king, Heshbon's inhabitants.

21:35 *percusserunt igitur et hunc cum filiis suis universumque populum eius usque ad internicionem et possederunt terram illius*

Therefore, they struck him down with his sons and all his people, even to extermination, and they possessed his land.

Balak Panics Before Israel

Numbers 22:1 *profectique castrametati sunt in campestribus Moab ubi trans Iordanem Hierichus sita est*

And setting out, they camped in Moab's plains, where Jericho sits across *the* Jordan.

22:2 *videns autem Balac filius Sepphor omnia quae fecerat Israhel Amorreo*

But Balak, Sepphor's son, seeing all that Israel had done to *the* Amorite,

22:3 *et quod pertimuissent eum Moabitae et impetum eius ferre non possent*

and that *the* Moabites feared him greatly, and could not resist his strength,

22:4 *dixit ad maiores natu Madian ita delebit hic populus omnes qui in nostris finibus commorantur quomodo solet bos herbas usque ad radices carpere ipse erat eo tempore rex in Moab*

said to Midian's older-born, "So this people will destroy all who live in our borders *the* way *the* ox is accustomed to destroy grass – grazing even to *the* roots!"

He was king in Moab at that time.

Messengers Sent to Balaam

22:5 *misit ergo nuntios ad Balaam filium Beor ariolum qui habitabat super flumen terrae filiorum Ammon ut vocarent eum et dicerent ecce egressus est populus ex Aegypto qui operuit superficiem terrae sedens contra me*

Therefore, he sent messengers to Balaam, Beor's son, *a* diviner who lived above *the* river in Ammon's children's land, so they could call him and say, "Look, *a* people has come out from Egypt who cover *the* land's face, sitting against me."

22:6 *veni igitur et maledic populo huic quia fortior me est si quo modo possim percutere et eicere eum de terra mea novi enim quod benedictus sit cui benedixeris et maledictus in quem maledicta congesseris*

"Come, then, and curse this people, because it is mightier than me – if somehow I might strike *him* down and throw him out of my land! For I know that whom you bless is blessed, and whom you consign to curses is cursed."

Balaam Hesitates

22:7 *perrexerunt seniores Moab et maiores natu Madian habentes divinationis pretium in manibus cumque venissent ad Balaam et narrassent ei omnia verba Balac*

Moab's elders and Midian's older-born got up, having *the* divination's price in *their* hands. And when they had come to Balaam and told him all Balak's words,

22:8 *ille respondit manete hic nocte et respondebo quicquid mihi dixerit Dominus manentibus illis apud Balaam venit Deus et ait ad eum*

he answered, "Stay here tonight and I will tell you whatever *the* Lord may say to me."

While they *were* staying with Balaam, God came and said to him,

22:9 *quid sibi volunt homines isti apud te*

"What do these men want with you?"

22:10 *respondit Balac filius Sepphor rex Moabitarum misit ad me*

He answered, "Balak, Sepphor's son, *the* Moabites' king, sent to me,

22:11 *dicens ecce populus qui egressus est de Aegypto operuit superficiem terrae veni et maledic ei si quo modo possim pugnans abicere eum*

"saying, 'Look, *a* people who came out of Egypt has covered *the* land's face! Come and curse him, if somehow I, fighting, can throw him out!'"

22:11 *dixitque Deus ad Balaam noli ire cum eis neque maledicas populo quia benedictus est*

And God said to Balaam, "Don't go with them! Nor will you curse *the* people, for it is blessed."

22:13 *qui mane consurgens dixit ad principes ite in terram vestram quia prohibuit me Deus venire vobiscum*

He, getting up early, said to the princes, "Go to your land, because God wouldn't let me go with you!"

Balak Tries Again
22:14 *reversi principes dixerunt ad Balac noluit Balaam venire nobiscum*

Going back, *the* princes said to Balak, "Balaam wouldn't come with us."

22:15 *rursum ille multo plures et nobiliores quam ante miserat misit*

He sent again, many others and nobler than *those* he had sent before.

22:16 *qui cum venissent ad Balaam dixerunt sic dicit Balac filius Sepphor ne cuncteris venire ad me*

They, when they had come to Balaam, said, "Balak, Sepphor's son, speaks so: 'Don't hesitate to come to me!

22:17 *paratum honorare te et quicquid volueris dare veni et maledic populo isti*

"'I am prepared to honor you, and whatever you want to give. Come and curse this people!'"

22:18 *respondit Balaam si dederit mihi Balac plenam domum suam argenti et auri non potero inmutare verbum Domini Dei mei ut vel plus vel minus loquar*

Balaam answered, "If Balak should give me his house full of silver and gold, I couldn't change *the* Lord my God's word, so I could say either more or less!

22:19 *obsecro ut hic maneatis etiam hac nocte et scire queam quid mihi rursum respondeat Dominus*

"I pray that you stay here this night too, and I'll be able to know again what *the* Lord may respond to me."

22:20 *venit ergo Deus ad Balaam nocte et ait ei si vocare te venerunt homines isti surge et vade cum eis ita dumtaxat ut quod tibi praecepero facias*

So God came to Balaam by night and said to him, "If these men came to call you, get up and go with them, to this extent only: that you do what I will command you!"

Balaam Goes to Balak

22:21 *surrexit Balaam mane et strata asina profectus est cum eis*

Balaam got up early and, saddling *a* donkey, set out with them.

22:22 *et iratus est Deus stetitque angelus Domini in via contra Balaam qui sedebat asinae et duos pueros habebat secum*

And God was angry. And *the* Lord's Angel stood in *the* way against Balaam, who sat on *the* donkey and had two servants with him.

Balaam's Donkey
Sees the Lord's Angel

22:23 *cernens asina angelum stantem in via evaginato gladio avertit se de itinere et ibat per agrum quam cum verberaret Balaam et vellet ad semitam reducere*

The donkey, discerning *the* Angel standing in *the* way, sword unsheathed, turned aside from *the* road and went into *a* field. When Balaam had beaten her, and wanted to go back to *the* road,

22:24 *stetit angelus in angustiis duarum maceriarum quibus vineae cingebantur*

the Angel stood in *a* tight spot between two walls by which vineyards were closed in.

22:25 *quem videns asina iunxit se parieti et adtrivit sedentis pedem at ille iterum verberabat*

Seeing Him, *the* donkey pressed herself to *the* wall and bumped against *the* rider's foot. And he again beat *her*.

22:26 *et nihilominus angelus ad locum angustum transiens ubi nec ad dextram nec ad sinistram poterat deviari obvius stetit*

And nevertheless, *the* Angel, moving to *a* tight place where one couldn't turn away either to *the* right or to *the* left, stood in *the* way.

22:27 *cumque vidisset asina stantem angelum concidit sub pedibus sedentis qui iratus vehementius caedebat fuste latera*

And when *the* donkey saw *the* Angel standing, she fell down under *the* feet of *the* one sitting *on her*, who, angry, beat her sides fiercely with *a* stick.

22:28 *aperuitque Dominus os asinae et locuta est quid feci tibi cur percutis me ecce iam tertio*

And *the* Lord opened *the* donkey's mouth, and she said, "What have I done to you? Why are you beating me – look, three times already?"

22:29 *respondit Balaam quia commeruisti et inlusisti mihi utinam*

haberem gladium ut te percuterem

Balaam answered, "Because you earned *it* and you've mocked me! If only I had *a* sword so I could kill you!"

22:30 *dixit asina nonne animal tuum sum cui semper sedere consuesti usque in praesentem diem dic quid simile umquam fecerim tibi at ille ait numquam*

The donkey said, "Aren't I your animal whom you always sit on, even to *the* present day? Tell *me* when I have ever done anything like that to you?"

And he said, "Never."

Balaam Sees the Angel
22:31 *protinus aperuit Dominus oculos Balaam et vidit angelum stantem in via evaginato gladio adoravitque eum pronus in terram*

At once *the* Lord opened Balaam's eyes, and he saw *the* Angel standing in *the* way, sword unsheathed. And he paid homage to Him, face-down on *the* ground.

22:32 *cui angelus cur inquit tertio verberas asinam tuam ego veni ut adversarer tibi quia perversa est via tua mihique contraria*

The Angel said to him, "Why are you beating your donkey three times? I came so I could oppose you, because your way is perverted and against Me.

22:33 *et nisi asina declinasset de via dans locum resistenti te occidissem et illa viveret*

"And if *the* donkey hadn't turned aside from *the* way, giving place and resisting, I would have killed you and she would have lived."

22:34 *dixit Balaam peccavi nesciens quod tu stares contra me et nunc si displicet tibi ut vadam revertar*

Balaam said, "I have sinned, not knowing that You stood against me. And now, if it is displeasing to You that I go, I will turn back."

22:35 *ait angelus vade cum istis et cave ne aliud quam praecepero tibi loquaris ivit igitur cum principibus*

The Angel said, "Go with them. And take care that you not say anything other than what I command you."

So he went with *the* princes.

Balak Comes to Balaam
22:36 *quod cum audisset Balac egressus est in occursum eius in oppido Moabitarum quod situm est in extremis finibus Arnon*

When Balak had heard that *Balaam had come*, he came out to meet him in *a* Moabite town that sat in Arnon's farthest borders.

22:37 *dixitque ad Balaam misi nuntios ut vocarent te cur non statim venisti ad me an quia mercedem adventui tuo reddere nequeo*

And he said to Balaam, "I sent messengers so they could call you. Why didn't you come to me immediately? Could it be that I can't pay *the* price at your coming?"

22:38 *cui ille respondit ecce adsum numquid loqui potero aliud nisi quod Deus posuerit in ore meo*

Balaam answered him, "Look, I'm here! I can't say anything except what God puts in my mouth, can I?"

22:39 *perrexerunt ergo simul et venerunt in urbem quae in extremis regni eius finibus erat*

Therefore, they got up together and came into *a* city that was in *the* farthest part of his kingdom.

22:40 *cumque occidisset Balac boves et oves misit ad Balaam et principes qui cum eo erant munera*

And when Balak had killed oxen and sheep, he sent gifts to Balaam and *the* princes who were with him.

22:41 *mane autem facto duxit eum ad excelsa Baal et intuitus est* *extremam partem populi*

But, morning come, he led him to Baal's high places, and he saw *the* last portion of *Israel's* people.

Balaam's First Prophecy

Numbers 23:1 *dixitque Balaam ad Balac aedifica mihi hic septem aras et para totidem vitulos eiusdemque numeri arietes*

And Balaam said to Balak, "Build me here seven altars, and prepare for each calves and *the* same number of rams!"

23:2 *cumque fecisset iuxta sermonem Balaam inposuerunt simul vitulum et arietem super aram*

And when he had done according to Balaam's word, they placed *a* calf and *a* ram together on *the* altar.

23:3 *dixitque Balaam ad Balac sta paulisper iuxta holocaustum tuum donec vadam si forte occurrat mihi Dominus et quodcumque imperaverit loquar tibi*

And Balaam said to Balak, "Stand *a* little while beside your burnt offering, until I go – if, perhaps, *the* Lord may meet me. And whatever He commands, I will tell you."

23:4 *cumque abisset velociter occurrit ei Deus locutusque ad eum Balaam septem inquit aras erexi et inposui vitulum et arietem desuper*

And when he had gone, God met him quickly and spoke to him. Balaam said, "I set up seven altars and put *a* calf and ram on *each*."

23:5 *Dominus autem posuit verbum in ore eius et ait revertere ad Balac et haec loqueris*

But *the* Lord put *a* word in his mouth and said, "Go back to Balak, and you will say this!"

23:6 *reversus invenit stantem Balac iuxta holocaustum suum et omnes principes Moabitarum*

Going back, he found Balak standing beside his burnt offering, and all *the* Moabites' princes.

23:7 *adsumptaque parabola sua dixit de Aram adduxit me Balac rex Moabitarum de montibus orientis veni inquit et maledic Iacob propera et detestare Israhel*

And taking up his parable, he said, "Balak, *the* Moabites' king, took me from Aram, from *the* eastern mountains. 'Come,' he said, 'and curse Jacob! Hurry and detest Israel!'

23:8 *quomodo maledicam cui non maledixit Deus qua ratione detester quem Dominus non detestatur*

"How will I curse
whom God has not cursed?
For what reason may I detest
whom *the* Lord has not detested?

23:9 *de summis silicibus videbo eum et de collibus considerabo illum*

populus solus habitabit et inter gentes non reputabitur

"I will see him
from *the* mountains' heights,
and will consider him
from *the* hills.
The people will live alone,
and will not be considered
among nations.

23:10 *quis dinumerare possit pulverem Iacob et nosse numerum stirpis Israhel moriatur anima mea morte iustorum et fiant novissima mea horum similia*

"Who can count Jacob's dust,
and know Israel's offspring's number?
May my soul die
the death of *the* fair *ones*,
and my last moments
be like theirs!"

23:11 *dixitque Balac ad Balaam quid est hoc quod agis ut malediceres inimicis vocavi te et tu e contrario benedicis eis*

And Balak said to Balaam, "What is this that you are doing, since I called you to curse enemies – and to *the* contrary, you bless them!"

23:12 *cui ille respondit num aliud possum loqui nisi quod iusserit Dominus*

He answered him, "Can I say

anything except what *the* Lord has commanded?"

Balak Tries Again

23:13 *dixit ergo Balac veni mecum in alterum locum unde partem Israhelis videas et totum videre non possis inde maledicito ei*

So Balak said, "Come with me to another place where you can see part of Israel, and you can't see all. Curse him from there!"

23:14 *cumque duxisset eum in locum sublimem super verticem montis Phasga aedificavit Balaam septem aras et inpositis supra vitulo atque ariete*

And when he had led him to *a* high place on *the* peak of Mount Pisgah, Balaam built seven altars and, putting *a* calf and ram *on each,*

23:15 *dixit ad Balac sta hic iuxta holocaustum tuum donec ego pergam obvius*

he said to Balak, "Stand here beside your burnt offering until I come to meet *you!*"

23:16 *cui cum Dominus occurrisset posuissetque verbum in ore eius ait revertere ad Balac et haec loqueris ei*

When *the* Lord had met him and put *a* word in his mouth, He said, "Go back to Balak, and you will say this to him!"

23:17 *reversus invenit eum stantem iuxta holocaustum suum et principes Moabitarum cum eo ad quem Balac quid inquit locutus est Dominus*

Coming back, he found him standing beside his burnt offering, and *the* Moabites' princes with him. Balak said to him, "What has *the* Lord said?"

23:18 *at ille adsumpta parabola sua ait sta Balac et ausculta audi fili Sepphor*

And he, taking up his parable, said, "Stand, Balak, and hear! Listen, Sepphor's son!

23:19 *non est Deus quasi homo ut mentiatur nec ut filius hominis ut mutetur dixit ergo et non faciet locutus est et non implebit*

"God is not like man that He should lie, nor like man's son, that He should be changed. He spoke, therefore, and will He not work? He gave *a* word, and will He not fulfill *it*?

23:20 *ad benedicendum adductus sum benedictionem prohibere non valeo*

"I am led out to bless, *a* blessing I cannot prohibit.

23:21 *non est idolum in Iacob nec videtur simulacrum in Israhel Dominus Deus eius cum eo est et clangor victoriae regis in illo*

"*There* is no idol in Jacob, nor is *an* image seen in Israel. *The* Lord his God is with him, and *the* King's victory shout *sounds* among him.

23:22 *Deus eduxit eum de Aegypto cuius fortitudo similis est rinocerotis*

"God led him from Egypt, whose strength is like *the* rhinoceros.

23:23 *non est augurium in Iacob nec divinatio in Israhel temporibus suis dicetur Iacob et Israheli quid operatus sit Deus*

"*There* is no augury in Jacob, nor divination in Israel. It will be said of Jacob and Israel in their times what God may do.

23:24 *ecce populus ut leaena consurget et quasi leo erigetur non accubabit donec devoret praedam et occisorum sanguinem bibat*

"Look, *the* people will rise up like *a* lioness and roar like *a* lion! He will not lie down until he devours *the* prey and drinks *the* blood of *the* slain!"

23:25 *dixitque Balac ad Balaam nec maledicas ei nec benedicas*

And Balak said to Balaam, "Neither curse nor bless him!"

23:26 *et ille nonne ait dixi tibi quod quicquid mihi Deus imperaret hoc facerem*

And he said, "Didn't I say to you that whatever God commanded me, this I would do?"

Balak Tries Yet Again
23:27 *et ait Balac ad eum veni et ducam te ad alium locum si forte placeat Deo ut inde maledicas eis*

And Balak said to him, "Come, and I will lead you to another place, if perhaps it may please God that you curse them from there!"

23:28 *cumque duxisset eum super verticem montis Phogor qui respicit solitudinem*

And when he had led him to Mount Phogor's top, which looks on *the* wasteland,

23:29 *dixit ei Balaam aedifica mihi hic septem aras et para totidem vitulos eiusdemque numeri arietes*

Balaam said to him, "Build me here seven altars, and prepare calves for each, and *the* same number of rams!"

23:30 *fecit Balac ut Balaam dixerat inposuitque vitulos et arietes per singulas aras*

Balak did as Balaam had said, and he put *the* calves and rams on each of *the* altars.

Balaam's Third Blessing

Numbers 24:1 *cumque vidisset Balaam quod placeret Domino ut benediceret Israheli nequaquam abiit ut ante perrexerat ut augurium quaereret sed dirigens contra desertum vultum suum*

And when Balaam had seen that it pleased *the* Lord that he bless Israel, he no longer went out as he went before – to seek *an* oracle. Instead, directing his attention toward *the* desert,

24:2 *et elevans oculos vidit Israhel in tentoriis commorantem per tribus suas et inruente in se spiritu Dei*

and, lifting eyes, he saw Israel living in *its* tents by their tribes. And, God's spirit rushing in on him,

24:3 *adsumpta parabola ait dixit Balaam filius Beor dixit homo cuius obturatus est oculus*

taking up *a* parable, he said,
"Balaam, Beor's son, spoke.
A man whose eye is closed spoke.

24:4 *dixit auditor sermonum Dei qui visionem Omnipotentis intuitus est qui cadit et sic aperiuntur oculi eius*

"God's word's hearer,
who understands
the Omnipotent's vision,
who has fallen
and so his eyes are open,

said,

24:5 *quam pulchra tabernacula tua Iacob et tentoria tua Israhel*

"'How beautiful
your tabernacles are, Jacob,
and your tents, Israel!

24:6 *ut valles nemorosae ut horti iuxta fluvios inrigui ut tabernacula quae fixit Dominus quasi cedri propter aquas*

"'Like well-wooded valleys,
like gardens watered by rivers,
as tabernacles that *the* Lord
has set up –
like cedars beside waters!

24:7 *fluet aqua de situla eius et semen illius erit in aquas multas tolletur propter Agag rex eius et auferetur regnum illius*

"Water will flow
from its basin,
and his seed will be
in many waters!
He will be destroyed
because of Agag, his king,
and his kingdom
will be taken away!

24:8 *Deus eduxit illum de Aegypto cuius fortitudo similis est rinocerotis devorabunt gentes hostes illius ossaque eorum confringent et perforabunt sagittis*

"God led him from Egypt,
whose strength is like *the* rhinoceros.
They will devour nations –
His enemies –
and shatter their bones,
and shoot *them* with arrows.

24:9 *accubans dormivit ut leo et quasi leaena quam suscitare nullus audebit qui benedixerit tibi erit ipse benedictus qui maledixerit in maledictione reputabitur*

"Lying down,
he has slept like *a* lion
and like *a* lioness,
whom no one will dare to rouse!
Who blesses you
will himself be blessed.
Who curses you
will be considered as cursed."

Balak Dismisses Balaam in Fury
24:10 *iratusque Balac contra Balaam conplosis manibus ait ad maledicendum inimicis meis vocavi te quibus e contrario tertio benedixisti*

And Balak, furious with Balaam, striking his hands together, said, "I called you to curse enemies who, on *the* contrary, you have blessed three times!

24:11 *revertere ad locum tuum decreveram quidem magnifice honorare te sed Dominus privavit te honore disposito*

"Go back to your place! I had decided indeed to honor you magnificently, but *the* Lord has deprived you of *the* appointed honor!"

Balaam Foretells the Future

24:12 *respondit Balaam ad Balac nonne nuntiis tuis quos misisti ad me dixi*

Balaam responded to Balak, "Didn't I say to your messengers whom you sent to me,

24:13 *si dederit mihi Balac plenam domum suam argenti et auri non potero praeterire sermonem Domini Dei mei ut vel boni quid vel mali proferam ex corde meo sed quicquid Dominus dixerit hoc loquar*

"'If Balak should give me his house full of silver and gold, I cannot go beyond *the* Lord my God's word, so I may bring out from my heart whether for good or for harm. But whatever *the* Lord may speak, this I will say?'

24:14 *verumtamen pergens ad populum meum dabo consilium quid populus tuus huic populo faciat extremo tempore*

"Nevertheless, I will give counsel, going to my people, what your people may do to this people at *the* end of time."

24:15 *sumpta igitur parabola rursum ait dixit Balaam filius Beor dixit homo cuius obturatus est oculus*

Therefore, again taking up *a* parable, he said,
"Balaam speaks, Beor's son.
A man whose eye is closed speaks.

24:16 *dixit auditor sermonum Dei qui novit doctrinam Altissimi et visiones Omnipotentis videt qui cadens apertos habet oculos*

"*The* hearer of God's word,
who has known
the Most High's doctrine
and seen visions
of *the* Omnipotent,
who, falling, has eyes opened,
speaks:

24:17 *videbo eum sed non modo intuebor illum sed non prope orietur stella ex Iacob et consurget virga de Israhel et percutiet duces Moab vastabitque omnes filios Seth*

"I will see him, yet not by measure.
I will consider him, yet not nearby.
A star will arise from Jacob,
and *a* staff rise up from Israel.
And he will strike Moab's dukes,
and lay waste all Seth's children.

24:18 *et erit Idumea possessio eius hereditas Seir cedet inimicis suis Israhel vero fortiter aget*

"And Idumea

will be his possession.
Seir's inheritance will fall
to his enemies.
Israel, indeed,
will act mightily.

24:19 *de Iacob erit qui dominetur et perdat reliquias civitatis*

"One who will
dominate and destroy
the city's remains
will be from Jacob."

Concerning Amalekites
24:20 *cumque vidisset Amalech adsumens parabolam ait principium gentium Amalech cuius extrema perdentur*

And when he had seen Amalek, taking up *a* parable, he said, "The nations' beginning, Amalek, whose ends will be destroyed!"

Concerning the Kenites
24:21 *vidit quoque Cineum et adsumpta parabola ait robustum est quidem habitaculum tuum sed si in petra posueris nidum tuum*

Likewise, he saw *the* Kenites and, taking up *a* parable, said,
"Your dwelling
is mighty indeed!
Yet even if you put
your nest in a rock,

24:22 *et fueris electus de stirpe Cain quamdiu poteris permanere*

Assur enim capiet te

"and are chosen
from Cain's race,
how long can you endure –
for Assur will capture you!"

Prophecy of Coming Destruction
24:23 *adsumptaque parabola iterum locutus est heu quis victurus est quando ista faciet Deus*

And, taking up *the* parable again, he said,
"Oh, who will survive
when God will do those *things*?

24:24 *venient in trieribus de Italia superabunt Assyrios vastabuntque Hebraeos et ad extremum etiam ipsi peribunt*

"They will come
in warships from Italy.
They will overcome *the* Assyrians
and lay waste *the* Hebrews.
And they also will perish
even to *the* end!"

24:25 *surrexitque Balaam et reversus est in locum suum Balac quoque via qua venerat rediit*

And Balaam got up and went back to his place. Balak likewise returned by the way he had come.

Israel Fornicates
with Moab's Daughters

Numbers 25:1 *morabatur autem eo tempore Israhel in Setthim et fornicatus est populus cum filiabus Moab*

But Israel lived at that time in Setthim. And *the* people fornicated with Moab's daughters,

25:2 *quae vocaverunt eos ad sacrificia sua at illi comederunt et adoraverunt deos earum*

who called them to their sacrifices. And they ate and worshiped their gods.

25:3 *initiatusque est Israhel Beelphegor et iratus Dominus*

And Israel was initiated at Beelphegor. And *the* Lord, angry,

25:4 *ait ad Mosen tolle cunctos principes populi et suspende eos contra solem in patibulis ut avertatur furor meus ab Israhel*

said to Moses, "Take all *the* people's princes and hang them toward *the* sun on gibbets, so My fury may be turned away from Israel.

25:5 *dixitque Moses ad iudices Israhel occidat unusquisque proximos suos qui initiati sunt Beelphegor*

And Moses said to Israel's judges, "Let each one kill his neighbors who were initiated at Beelphegor!"

Phineas Discourages Prostitution

25:6 *et ecce unus de filiis Israhel intravit coram fratribus suis ad scortum madianitin vidente Mose et omni turba filiorum Israhel qui flebant ante fores tabernaculi*

And, look, one of Israel's sons entered before his brothers to *a* Midianite whore, in sight of Moses and *the* whole crowd of Israel's children, who wept outside *the* tabernacle.

25:7 *quod cum vidisset Finees filius Eleazari filii Aaron sacerdotis surrexit de medio multitudinis et arrepto pugione*

When Phineas, Eleazar's brother, Aaron *the* priest's son, had seen this, he got up from among *the* multitude. And, grabbing *a* dagger,

25:8 *ingressus est post virum israhelitem in lupanar et perfodit ambos simul virum scilicet et mulierem in locis genitalibus cessavitque plaga a filiis Israhel*

he went in after *the* Israelite man in *the* brothel. And he stabbed through both together – *the* man, of course, and *the* woman, in *the* place of their genitalia. And *the* plague ceased among Israel's children.

25:9 *et occisi sunt viginti quattuor milia homines*

And twenty-four thousand men were killed.

The Lord Blesses Phineas
25:10 *dixitque Dominus ad Mosen*

And *the* Lord said to Moses,

25:11 *Finees filius Eleazari filii Aaron sacerdotis avertit iram meam a filiis Israhel quia zelo meo commotus est contra eos ut non ipse delerem filios Israhel in zelo meo*

"Phineas, Eleazar's brother, Aaron *the* priest's son, has turned My anger away from Israel's children, because he was moved by My zeal against them – that I might not destroy Israel's children in My zeal.

25:12 *idcirco loquere ad eos ecce do ei pacem foederis mei*

"Therefore, say to them, 'Look, I give My covenant's peace to him.

25:13 *et erit tam ipsi quam semini illius pactum sacerdotii sempiternum quia zelatus est pro Deo suo et expiavit scelus filiorum Israhel*

"And it will be *an* everlasting pact of priesthood with him and his seed alike – because he was zealous for his

God, and he atoned for Israel's children's crime."

25:14 *erat autem nomen viri israhelitae qui occisus est cum Madianitide Zambri filius Salu dux de cognatione et tribu Symeonis*

But *the* Israelite man's name who was killed with *the* Midianite was Zambri, Salu's son, leader of Simeon's clan and tribe.

25:15 *porro mulier madianitis quae pariter interfecta est vocabatur Chozbi filia Sur principis nobilissimi Madianitarum*

Further, *the* Midianite woman who was killed with him was called Chozbi, Sur's daughter, of *the* Midianites' noblest prince.

25:16 *locutusque est Dominus ad Mosen dicens*

And *the* Lord spoke to Moses, saying,

25:17 *hostes vos sentiant Madianitae et percutite eos*

"Let *the* Midianites consider you enemies, and strike them down –

25:18 *quia et ipsi hostiliter egerunt contra vos et decepere insidiis per idolum Phogor et Chozbi filiam ducis Madian sororem suam quae percussa est in die plagae pro*

sacrilegio Phogor

"because they also acted with hostility against you, and deceived you with traps through their idol Phogor, and Chozbi, daughter of Midian's duke, their sister, who was killed in *the* day of *the* plague for Phogor's sacrilege.

The Second Census

Numbers 26:1 *postquam noxiorum sanguis effusus est dixit Dominus ad Mosen et Eleazarum filium Aaron sacerdotem*

After *the* guilty ones' blood was poured out, *the* Lord said to Moses and Eleazar, Aaron *the* priest's son,

26:2 *numerate omnem summam filiorum Israhel a viginti annis et supra per domos et cognationes suas cunctos qui possunt ad bella procedere*

"Number all *the* sum of Israel's children, from twenty years old and above, by their houses and clans – all who can go out to war!"

26:3 *locuti sunt itaque Moses et Eleazar sacerdos in campestribus Moab super Iordanem contra Hierichum ad eos qui erant*

So Moses and Eleazar *the* priest spoke in Moab's plains, on *the* Jordan across from Jericho, to those who were *present*,

26:4 *a viginti annis et supra sicut Dominus imperarat quorum iste est numerus*

from twenty years old and above, as *the* Lord had commanded, of whom this is *the* number.

Reuben

26:5 *Ruben primogenitus Israhel huius filius Enoch a quo familia Enochitarum et Phallu a quo familia Phalluitarum*

Reuben *was* Israel's firstborn, whose son *was* Enoch, from whom came *the* Enochites' family; and Phallu, from whom *the* Phalluites' family;

26:6 *et Esrom a quo familia Esromitarum et Charmi a quo familia Charmitarum*

and Esrom, from whom *the* Esromites's family; and Charmi, from whom *the* Charmitites' family.

26:7 *hae sunt familiae de stirpe Ruben quarum numerus inventus est quadraginta tria milia et septingenti triginta*

These are Reuben's stock's families, whose number was found *to be* forty-three thousand, seven hundred thirty.

26:8 *filius Phallu Heliab*

Phallu's son *was* Heliab,

26:9 *huius filii Namuhel et Dathan et Abiram isti sunt Dathan et Abiram principes populi qui surrexerunt contra Mosen et Aaron in seditione Core quando adversum Dominum rebellaverunt*

whose sons were Namuel and Dathan and Abiram. These are *the* Dathan and Abiram, *the* people's princes, who rose up against Moses and Aaron in Core's sedition, when they rebelled against *the* Lord.

26:10 *et aperiens terra os suum devoravit Core morientibus plurimis quando conbusit ignis ducentos quinquaginta viros et factum est grande miraculum*

And *the* ground, opening its mouth, devoured Core, many dying – when fire burned up two hundred fifty men, and *a* great miracle happened,

26:11 *ut Core pereunte filii illius non perirent*

that, Core perishing, his children did not perish.

Simeon

26:12 *filii Symeon per cognationes suas Namuhel ab hoc familia Namuhelitarum Iamin ab hoc familia Iaminitarum Iachin ab hoc familia Iachinitarum*

Simeon's children by their clans *were* Namuel (from him *came the* Namuelites' family); Iamin (from him *the* Iaminites' family); Iachin (from him Iachinites' family);

26:13 *Zare ab hoc familia Zareitarum Saul ab hoc familia Saulitarum*

Zare (from him *the* Zareites' family); Saul (from him *the* Saulites' family).

26:14 *hae sunt familiae de stirpe Symeon quarum omnis numerus fuit viginti duo milia ducentorum*

These are *the* families of Simeon's stock, whose whole number was twenty-two thousand, two hundred.

Gad
26:15 *filii Gad per cognationes suas Sephon ab hoc familia Sephonitarum Aggi ab hoc familia Aggitarum Suni ab hoc familia Sunitarum*

Gad's children by their clans *were* Sephon (from him *the* Sephonites' family); Aggi (from him *the* Aggitites' family); Suni (from him *the* Sunites' family);

26:16 *Ozni ab hoc familia Oznitarum Heri ab hoc familia Heritarum*

Ozni (from him *the* Oznites' family); Heri (from him *the* Herites' family);

26:17 *Arod ab hoc familia Aroditarum Arihel ab hoc familia Arihelitarum*

Arod (from him *the* Arodites' family); Ariel (from him *the* Arielites' family);

26:18 *istae sunt familiae Gad quarum omnis numerus fuit*

quadraginta milia quingentorum

These are Gad's families, whose whole number was forty thousand, five hundred.

Judah
26:19 *filii Iuda Her et Onan qui ambo mortui sunt in terra Chanaan*

Judah's sons were Er and Onan, both of whom died in Canaan's land.

26:20 *fueruntque filii Iuda per cognationes suas Sela a quo familia Selanitarum Phares a quo familia Pharesitarum Zare a quo familia Zareitarum*

And Judah's children by their tribes were Selah (from him *the* Selanites' family); Phares (from him *the* Pharesites' family); Zare (from him *the* Zareites' family);

26:21 *porro filii Phares Esrom a quo familia Esromitarum et Amul a quo familia Amulitarum*

Afterwards, Phares's sons *were* Esrom (from him *the* Esromites' family); and Amul (from him *the* Amulites' family).

26:22 *istae sunt familiae Iuda quarum omnis numerus fuit septuaginta milia quingentorum*

These are Judah's families, whose number was seventy thousand, five hundred.

Issachar

26:23 *filii Isachar per cognationes suas Thola a quo familia Tholaitarum Phua a quo familia Phuaitarum*

Issachar's children by their clans *were* Thola (from him *the* Tholaites' family); Phua (from him *the* Phuaites' family);

26:24 *Iasub a quo familia Iasubitarum Semran a quo familia Semranitarum*

Iasub (from him *the* Iasubites' family); Semran (from him *the* Semranites' family).

26:25 *hae sunt cognationes Isachar quarum numerus fuit sexaginta quattuor milia trecentorum*

These are Issachar's clans, whose number was sixty-four thousand, three hundred.

Zebulon

26:26 *filii Zabulon per cognationes suas Sared a quo familia Sareditarum Helon a quo familia Helonitarum Ialel a quo familia Ialelitarum*

Zebulon's children by their clans *were* Sared (from him *the* Saredites' family); Helon (from him *the* Helonites' family); Ialel (from him

the Ialelites' family).

26:27 *hae sunt cognationes Zabulon quarum numerus fuit sexaginta milia quingentorum*

These are Zebulon's clans, whose number was sixty thousand, five hundred.

Joseph

26:28 *filii Ioseph per cognationes suas Manasse et Ephraim*

Joseph's children by their clans *were* Manasseh and Ephraim.

Manasseh

26:29 *de Manasse ortus est Machir a quo familia Machiritarum Machir genuit Galaad a quo familia Galaaditarum*

From Manasseh, Machir was born (from him *the* Machirites' family). Machir fathered Galaad (from him *the* Galaadites' family).

26:30 *Galaad habuit filios Hiezer a quo familia Hiezeritarum et Elec a quo familia Elecarum*

Galaad had sons: Hiezer (from him *the* Hiezerites' family); and Elec (from him *the* Elecites' family);

26:31 *et Asrihel a quo familia Asrihelitarum et Sechem a quo familia Sechemitarum*

and Asriel (from him *the* Asrielites' family); and Shechem (from him *the* Shechemites' family);

26:32 *et Semida a quo familia Semidatarum et Epher a quo familia Epheritarum*

and Semida (from him *the* Semidates' family); and Epher (from him *the* Epherites' family);

26:33 *fuit autem Epher pater Salphaad qui filios non habebat sed tantum filias quarum ista sunt nomina Maala et Noa et Egla et Melcha et Thersa*

But Epher was Salphaad's father, who did not have sons, but only daughters. Their names were Maala, and Noa, and Egla, and Melcha, and Thersa.

26:34 *hae sunt familiae Manasse et numerus earum quinquaginta duo milia septingentorum*

These are Manasseh's families, and their number *was* fifty-two thousand, seven hundred.

Ephraim
26:35 *filii autem Ephraim per cognationes suas fuerunt hii Suthala a quo familia Suthalitarum Becher a quo familia Becheritarum Tehen a quo familia Tehenitarum*

But Ephraim's children by their clans

were these: Suthala (from him *the* Suthalites' family); Becher (from him *the* Becherites' family); Tehen (from him *the* Tehenites' family).

26:36 *porro filius Suthala fuit Heran a quo familia Heranitarum*

After, Suthala's son was Heran (from him *the* Heranites' family).

26:37 *hae sunt cognationes filiorum Ephraim quarum numerus triginta duo milia quingentorum*

These are Ephraim's children's clans, whose number was thirty-two thousand, five hundred.

26:38 *isti sunt filii Ioseph per familias suas filii Beniamin in cognationibus suis Bale a quo familia Baleitarum Azbel a quo familia Azbelitarum Ahiram a quo familia Ahiramitarum*

These are Joseph's children by their families.

Benjamin
Benjamin's sons in their clans *were* Bale (from him *the* Baleites' family); Azbel (from him *the* Azbelites' family); Ahiram (from him *the* Ahiramites' family);

26:39 *Supham a quo familia Suphamitarum Hupham a quo familia Huphamitarum*

Supham (from him *the* Suphamites' family); Hupham (from him *the* Huphamites' family).

26:40 *filii Bale Hered et Noeman de Hered familia Hereditarum de Noeman familia Noemitarum*

Bale's sons *were* Hered and Noeman. From Hered *came the* Heredites' family; from Noeman, *the* Noemanites' family.

26:41 *hii sunt filii Beniamin per cognationes suas quorum numerus quadraginta quinque milia sescentorum*

These are Benjamin's children, by their clans, whose number was forty-five thousand, six hundred.

Dan

26:42 *filii Dan per cognationes suas Suham a quo familia Suhamitarum hae cognationes Dan per familias suas*

Dan's children by their clans *were* Suham (from him *the* Suhamites' family). These *were* Dan's clans, by their families.

26:43 *omnes fuere Suhamitae quorum numerus erat sexaginta quattuor milia quadringentorum*

All were Suhamites, whose number was sixty-four thousand, four hundred.

Asher

26:44 *filii Aser per cognationes suas Iemna a quo familia Iemnaitarum Iessui a quo familia Iessuitarum Brie a quo familia Brieitarum*

Asher's children by their families were Iemna (from him *the* Iemnaites' family); Iessui (from him *the* Iessuites' family); Brie (from him *the* Brieites' family).

26:45 *filii Brie Haber a quo familia Haberitarum et Melchihel a quo familia Melchihelitarum*

Brie's children were Haber (from him *the* Haberites' family); and Melchiel (from him *the* Melchielites' family).

26:46 *nomen autem filiae Aser fuit Sara*

But Asher's daughter's name was Sara.

26:47 *hae cognationes filiorum Aser et numerus eorum quinquaginta tria milia quadringentorum*

These *are the* clans of Asher's children, and their number *was* fifty-three thousand, four hundred.

Napthali

26:48 *filii Nepthalim per cognationes suas Iessihel a quo familia Iessihelitarum Guni a quo familia Gunitarum*

Napthali's children by their clans were Iessiel (from him *the* Iessielites' family); Guni (from him *the* Gunites' family);

26:49 *Iesser a quo familia Iesseritarum Sellem a quo familia Sellemitarum*

Iesser (from him *the* Iesserites' family); Sellem (from him *the* Sellemites' family);

26:50 *hae sunt cognationes filiorum Nepthalim per familias suas quorum numerus quadraginta quinque milia quadringentorum*

These are *the* clans of Napthali's children, by their families, whose number was forty-five thousand, four hundred.

The Sum of Israel's Children

26:51 *ista est summa filiorum Israhel qui recensiti sunt sescenta milia et mille septingenti triginta*

This is *the* sum of Israel's children, who were counted: six hundred one thousand, seven hundred thirty.

Divide the Land by Lots

26:52 *locutusque est Dominus ad Mosen dicens*

And *the* Lord spoke to Moses, saying,

26:53 *istis dividetur terra iuxta*

numerum vocabulorum in possessiones suas

"*The* land will be divided among these, according to *the* number of those called, as their possessions.

26:54 *pluribus maiorem partem dabis et paucioribus minorem singulis sicut nunc recensiti sunt tradetur possessio*

"You will give *a* larger portion to more, and *a* smaller to fewer. Possession will be handed to each as now they have been counted,

26:55 *ita dumtaxat ut sors terram tribubus dividat et familiis*

"to this extent: that *the* land may be divided by lots among tribes and families.

26:56 *quicquid sorte contigerit hoc vel plures accipient vel pauciores*

"Whatever falls by lot, this they will receive, whether more or fewer.

Levi

26:57 *hic quoque est numerus filiorum Levi per familias suas Gerson a quo familia Gersonitarum Caath a quo familia Caathitarum Merari a quo familia Meraritarum*

This, likewise, is *the* number of Levi's children, by their families: Gerson (from him *the* Gersonites' family); Caath (from him *the* Caathites' family); Merari (from him *the* Merarites' family).

26:58 *hae sunt familiae Levi familia Lobni familia Hebroni familia Mooli familia Musi familia Cori at vero Caath genuit Amram*

These are Levi's families: *the* Lobni family; *the* Hebroni family; *the* Mooli family; *the* Musi family; *the* Cori family.

And, indeed, Caath fathered Amram,

26:59 *qui habuit uxorem Iochabed filiam Levi quae nata est ei in Aegypto haec genuit viro suo Amram filios Aaron et Mosen et Mariam sororem eorum*

who had *as* wife Jochabed, Levi's daughter. She was born to him in Egypt. She birthed sons to Amram, her husband: Aaron, and Moses, and Mary, their sister.

Aaron's Descendants
26:60 *de Aaron orti sunt Nadab et Abiu et Eleazar et Ithamar*

From Aaron, Nadab, and Abiu, and Eleazar, and Ithamar were born,

26:61 *quorum Nadab et Abiu mortui sunt cum obtulissent ignem alienum coram Domino*

of whom Nadab and Abiu died when

they offered strange fire before *the* Lord.

26:62 *fueruntque omnes qui numerati sunt viginti tria milia generis masculini ab uno mense et supra quia non sunt recensiti inter filios Israhel nec eis cum ceteris data possessio*

And all who were numbered were twenty-three thousand, of male gender, from one month old and above – for they were not counted among Israel's children, nor *a* possession given them among *the* others.

Numbers Summarizing God's Judgment
26:63 *hic est numerus filiorum Israhel qui descripti sunt a Mosen et Eleazaro sacerdote in campestribus Moab supra Iordanem contra Hiericho*

This is *the* number of Israel's children, who were described by Moses and Eleazar *the* priest, in Moab's plains on *the* Jordan, across from Jericho.

26:64 *inter quos nullus fuit eorum qui ante numerati sunt a Mose et Aaron in deserto Sinai*

No one remained among them of those who were counted by Moses and Aaron before, in Sinai's desert,

26:65 *praedixerat enim Dominus quod omnes morerentur in solitudine nullusque remansit ex eis nisi Chaleb filius Iepphonne et Iosue filius Nun*

for *the* Lord had commanded that all would die in *the* wasteland. And no one remained from them except Caleb, Iepphonne's son, and Joshua, Nun's son.

Salphaad's Daughters

Numbers 27:1 *accesserunt autem filiae Salphaad filii Epher filii Galaad filii Machir filii Manasse qui fuit filius Ioseph quarum sunt nomina Maala et Noa et Egla et Melcha et Thersa*

But *the* daughters of Salphaad, Epher's son, Galaad's son, Machir's son, Manasseh's son, who was Joseph's son, came near, whose names were Maala, and Noa, and Egla, and Melcha, and Thersa.

27:2 *steteruntque coram Mosen et Eleazaro sacerdote et cunctis principibus populi ad ostium tabernaculi foederis atque dixerunt*

And they stood before Moses and Eleazar *the* priest and all *the* people's princes, at *the* entrance to *the* Covenant Tabernacle. And they said,

27:3 *pater noster mortuus est in deserto nec fuit in seditione quae concitata est contra Dominum sub Core sed in peccato suo mortuus est hic non habuit mares filios cur tollitur nomen illius de familia sua quia non habet filium date nobis possessionem inter cognatos patris nostri*

"Our father died in *the* desert. He wasn't in *the* sedition that was stirred up against *the* Lord under Core, but died in his *own* sin. He had no male children here. Why is his name taken away from his family because he has no son? Give us *a* possession among our father's kinsmen!"

Laws of Inheritance

27:4 *rettulitque Moses causam earum ad iudicium Domini*

And Moses took their cause to *the* Lord's judgment,

27:5 *qui dixit ad eum*

who said to him,

27:6 *iustam rem postulant filiae Salphaad da eis possessionem inter cognatos patris sui et ei in hereditate succedant*

"Salphaad's daughters are asking *a* fair judgment. Give them *a* possession among their father's kin, and let them follow him in *the* inheritance!

27:7 *ad filios autem Israhel loqueris haec*

"But you will say this to Israel's children:

27:8 *homo cum mortuus fuerit absque filio ad filiam eius transibit hereditas*

"'*The* inheritance of *a* man who dies without *a* son will pass to his daughter.

27:9 *si filiam non habuerit habebit successores fratres suos*

"'If he has no daughter, he will have his brothers as heirs.

27:10 *quod si et fratres non fuerint dabitis hereditatem fratribus patris eius*

"'But if he also has no brothers, he will give *the* inheritance to his father's brothers.

27:11 *sin autem nec patruos habuerit dabitur hereditas his qui ei proximi sunt eritque hoc filiis Israhel sanctum lege perpetua sicut praecepit Dominus Mosi*

"'But if he has no paternal uncles, *the* inheritance will be given to those who are close to him. This will be *an* enduring holy law to Israel's children, as *the* Lord commanded Moses.'"

The Lord Commands Moses to Prepare for Death

27:12 *dixit quoque Dominus ad Mosen ascende in montem istum Abarim et contemplare inde terram quam daturus sum filiis Israhel*

The Lord likewise said to Moses, "Climb up onto this mountain, Abarim, and look from there on *the* land which I will give to Israel's children!

27:13 *cumque videris eam ibis et tu ad populum tuum sicut ivit frater tuus Aaron*

"And when you have seen it, you also will go to your people, as your brother Aaron went –

27:14 *quia offendistis me in deserto Sin in contradictione multitudinis nec sanctificare me voluistis coram ea super aquas hae sunt aquae Contradictionis in Cades deserti Sin*

because you offended Me in Sin's desert, in *the* multitude's contradiction, nor did you want to sanctify Me before them over *the* waters."

(These are Contradiction's waters in Kadesh, in Sin's desert.)

Moses Asks God
to Provide a Successor
27:15 *cui respondit Moses*

Moses answered Him,

27:16 *provideat Dominus Deus spirituum omnis carnis hominem qui sit super multitudinem hanc*

"May *the* Lord, God of *the* spirits of all flesh, provide *a* man who may be over this multitude,

27:17 *et possit exire et intrare ante eos et educere illos vel introducere ne sit populus Domini sicut oves absque pastore*

"and may go out and come in before them, and lead them or bring them in – so *the* Lord's people may not be like sheep without *a* shepherd."

27:18 *dixitque Dominus ad eum tolle Iosue filium Nun virum in quo est spiritus et pone manum tuam super eum*

And *the* Lord said to him, "Take Joshua, Nun's son, *a* man in whom is spirit, and place your hand on him –

27:19 *qui stabit coram Eleazaro sacerdote et omni multitudine*

"who will stand before Eleazar *the* priest and all *the* multitude.

27:20 *et dabis ei praecepta cunctis videntibus et partem gloriae tuae ut audiat eum omnis synagoga filiorum Israhel*

"And you will give him commandments, all seeing, and part of your glory, so all Israel's children's gathering may listen to him.

27:21 *pro hoc si quid agendum erit Eleazar sacerdos consulet Dominum ad verbum eius egredietur et ingredietur ipse et omnes filii Israhel cum eo et cetera multitudo*

"Whatever must be done, Eleazar *the*

priest will consult *the* Lord for him. At his word, he, and all Israel's children with him, and *the* rest of *the* multitude will go out and come in."

Moses Ordains Joshua

27:22 *fecit Moses ut praeceperat Dominus cumque tulisset Iosue statuit eum coram Eleazaro sacerdote et omni frequentia populi*

Moses did as *the* Lord had commanded. And when he had taken Joshua, he stood him before Eleazar *the* priest and all *the* people's crowd.

27:23 *et inpositis capiti eius manibus cuncta replicavit quae mandaverat Dominus*

And, laying hands on his head, he repeated all that *the* Lord had commanded.

The Ongoing Sacrifices

Numbers 28:1 *dixit quoque Dominus ad Mosen*

The Lord likewise said to Moses,

28:2 *praecipe filiis Israhel et dices ad eos oblationem meam et panes et incensum odoris suavissimi offerte per tempora sua*

"Command Israel's children, and you will say to them: 'You will offer my oblation, and loaves, and incense as *the* smoothest odor, at their times.

28:3 *haec sunt sacrificia quae offerre debetis agnos anniculos inmaculatos duos cotidie in holocaustum sempiternum*

"'These are *the* sacrifices that you must offer: two yearling lambs without defect, daily, as *an* everlasting burnt offering.

28:4 *unum offeretis mane et alterum ad vesperam*

"'You will offer one in *the* morning and *the* other at evening;

28:5 *decimam partem oephi similae quae conspersa sit oleo purissimo et habeat quartam partem hin*

"'*a* tenth part of *an* ephah of wheat flour, which is sprinkled with purest oil, and has *a* quarter part of *a* hin.

28:6 *holocaustum iuge est quod obtulistis in monte Sinai in odorem suavissimum incensi Domini*

"'It is *the* continuing holocaust which you offered on Mount Sinai, as *the* smoothest odor, *the* Lord's incense.

28:7 *et libabitis vini quartam partem hin per agnos singulos in sanctuario Domini*

"'And you will make *a* libation of wine, *a* quarter part of *a* hin for each of *the* lambs, in *the* Lord's sanctuary.

28:8 *alterumque agnum similiter offeretis ad vesperam iuxta omnem ritum sacrificii matutini et libamentorum eius oblationem suavissimi odoris Domino*

"'You will offer *the* other lamb and its libations similarly at evening, according to all *the* morning sacrifice's ritual, *an* offering of *the* smoothest odor to *the* Lord.

Sabbath Offerings
28:9 *die autem sabbati offeretis duos agnos anniculos inmaculatos et duas decimas similae oleo conspersae in sacrificio et liba*

"'But *the* Sabbath day you will offer two yearling lambs without defect, and two tenths of wheat flour sprinkled with oil, as *a* sacrifice and libation,

28:10 *quae rite funduntur per singula sabbata in holocausto sempiterno*

"'which are poured out by ritual for each Sabbath, as *an* everlasting holocaust.

At the Beginning of the Month
28:11 *in kalendis autem id est in mensuum exordiis offeretis holocaustum Domino vitulos de armento duos arietem unum agnos anniculos septem inmaculatos*

"'On *the* day of proclamation – that is, *the* months' beginnings – you will offer *the* Lord *a* holocaust of two calves from *the* herd, one ram, seven yearling lambs without defect;

28:12 *et tres decimas similae oleo conspersae in sacrificio per singulos vitulos et duas decimas similae oleo conspersae per singulos arietes*

"'and three tenths of wheat flour sprinkled with oil in sacrifice for each of *the* calves, and two tenths of wheat flour sprinkled with oil for each of *the* rams;

28:13 *et decimam decimae similae ex oleo in sacrificio per agnos singulos holocaustum suavissimi odoris atque incensi est Domino*

"'and *a* tenth tenths of wheat flour without oil, in sacrifice for each of *the* lambs. It is *a* holocaust of *the* smoothest odor and incense to *the* Lord.

28:14 *libamenta autem vini quae per singulas fundenda sunt victimas ista erunt media pars hin per vitulos singulos tertia per arietem quarta per agnum hoc erit holocaustum per omnes menses qui sibi anno vertente succedunt*

"'But *the* libations of wine which will be poured out for each of those victims will be *a* half part of *a* hin for each of *the* calves; *a* third for *the* ram; *a* fourth for *the* lamb. This will be *the* burnt offering for all *the* months that follow each other as *the* year turns.

Sin Offerings

28:15 *hircus quoque offeretur Domino pro peccatis in holocaustum sempiternum cum libamentis suis*

"'*A* he-goat, likewise, with its libations will be offered to *the* Lord for sin as *an* everlasting holocaust.

Passover

28:16 *mense autem primo quartadecima die mensis phase Domini erit*

"'But *the* first month, *the* fourteenth day of *the* month, will be *the* Lord's Passover,

28:17 *et quintadecima die sollemnitas septem diebus vescentur*

azymis

"'and *the* fifteenth day *a* solemn observance. Unleavened *loaves* will be eaten for seven days,

28:18 *quarum dies prima venerabilis et sancta erit omne opus servile non facietis in ea*

"'whose first day will be most honored and holy. You will do no servile work in it.

28:19 *offeretisque incensum holocaustum Domino vitulos de armento duos arietem unum agnos anniculos inmaculatos septem*

"'And you will offer *as* incense *the* Lord's holocaust: two calves from *the* herd, one ram, seven yearling lambs without defect;

28:20 *et sacrificia singulorum ex simila quae conspersa sit oleo tres decimas per singulos vitulos et duas decimas per arietem*

"'and each ones' sacrifices from wheat flour that is sprinkled with oil – three tenths for each of *the* calves, and two tenths for *the* ram,

28:21 *et decimam decimae per agnos singulos id est per septem agnos*

"'and *a* tenth tenth for each of *the* lambs – that is, for seven lambs –

28:22 *et hircum pro peccato unum ut expietur pro vobis*

"'and one he-goat for sin, so it may be atoned for on your behalf,

28:23 *praeter holocaustum matutinum quod semper offertis*

"'in addition to *the* morning holocaust which you always offer.

28:24 *ita facietis per singulos dies septem dierum in fomitem ignis et in odorem suavissimum Domino qui surget de holocausto et de libationibus singulorum*

"'You will do so for each of *the* seven days as *the* fire's kindling, which will rise up from *the* holocaust and from each ones' libations as *the* smoothest odor to *the* Lord.

28:25 *dies quoque septimus celeberrimus et sanctus erit vobis omne opus servile non facietis in eo*

"*The* seventh day also will be most observed and holy to you. You will do no servile work in it.

Festival of First Fruits
28:26 *dies etiam primitivorum quando offertis novas fruges Domino expletis ebdomadibus venerabilis et sancta erit omne opus servile non facietis in ea*

"'Also, *the* days of first fruits, when

you offer new crops to *the* Lord, *the* weeks *being* completed, will be most honored and holy. You will do no servile work in it.

28:27 *offeretisque holocaustum in odorem suavissimum Domino vitulos de armento duos arietem unum et agnos anniculos inmaculatos septem*

"'And you will offer two calves from *the* herd, one ram, and seven yearling lambs without defect *as a* burnt offering, as *the* smoothest odor to *the* Lord;

28:28 *atque in sacrificiis eorum similae oleo conspersae tres decimas per singulos vitulos per arietes duas*

and in their sacrifices wheat flour sprinkled with oil: three tenths for each of *the* calves, two for *the* rams,

28:29 *per agnos decimam decimae qui simul sunt agni septem hircum quoque*

a tenth tenths for *the* lambs which, together, are seven lambs; *the* ram, likewise,

28:30 *qui mactatur pro expiatione praeter holocaustum sempiternum et liba eius*

which is killed as *an* atonement along with *the* everlasting holocaust and its libations.

28:31 *inmaculata offeretis omnia cum libationibus suis*

"'You will offer all without defect, with their libations.'"

Trumpets

Numbers 29:1 *mensis etiam septimi prima dies venerabilis et sancta erit vobis omne opus servile non facietis in ea quia dies clangoris est et tubarum*

"'*The* first day of *the* seventh month also will be most honored and holy to you. You will do no servile work in it, because it is *the* day of blasts and trumpets.

29:2 *offeretisque holocaustum in odorem suavissimum Domino vitulum de armento unum arietem unum agnos anniculos inmaculatos septem*

"'And you will offer *the* Lord *as a* burnt offering one calf from *the* herd, one ram, *and* seven yearling lambs without defect;

29:3 *et in sacrificiis eorum similae oleo conspersae tres decimas per singulos vitulos duas decimas per arietem*

"'and wheat flour sprinkled with oil in their sacrifices: three tenths for each of *the* calves, two tenths for *the* ram,

29:4 *unam decimam per agnum qui simul sunt agni septem*

"'one tenth for *the* lamb, which are seven lambs together;

29:5 *et hircum pro peccato qui offertur in expiationem populi*

"'and *a* he-goat for sin, which is offered as *the* people's atonement,

29:6 *praeter holocaustum kalendarum cum sacrificiis suis et holocaustum sempiternum cum libationibus solitis hisdem caerimoniis offeretis in odorem suavissimum incensum Domino*

"'alongside *the* holocaust of *the* month's beginning, with its sacrifices, and *the* everlasting holocaust with its libations. You will offer *them* according to their customary ceremonies as *a* smoothest odor, incense to *the* Lord.

The Day of Atonement
29:7 *decima quoque dies mensis huius septimi erit vobis sancta atque venerabilis et adfligetis animas vestras omne opus servile non facietis in ea*

"'*The* tenth day of this seventh month likewise will be holy and most honored to you, and you will afflict your souls. You will do no servile work in it.

29:8 *offeretisque holocaustum Domino in odorem suavissimum vitulum de armento unum arietem unum agnos anniculos inmaculatos septem*

"'And you will offer to *the* Lord *as a* holocaust, as *the* smoothest odor, one calf from *the* herd, one ram, seven yearling lambs without defect;

29:9 *et in sacrificiis eorum similae oleo conspersae tres decimas per vitulos singulos duas decimas per arietem*

"'and wheat flour sprinkled with oil in their sacrifices: three tenths for each of *the* calves, two tenths for *the* ram,

29:10 *decimam decimae per agnos singulos qui sunt simul septem agni*

"'*a* tenth tenths for each of *the* lambs, which are seven rams together;

29:11 *et hircum pro peccato absque his quae offerri pro delicto solent in expiationem et holocaustum sempiternum in sacrificio et libaminibus eorum*

"'and *a* he-goat for sin, apart from those which are customarily offered for offense as *an* atonement, and *the* everlasting holocaust as *a* sacrifice, and their libations.

Eight Days of Offerings
The First Day
29:12 *quintadecima vero die mensis septimi quae vobis erit sancta atque venerabilis omne opus servile non facietis in ea sed celebrabitis sollemnitatem Domino septem diebus*

"'Indeed, *the* fifteenth day of *the* seventh month, which will be holy and honored to you, you will do no servile work in it – but will celebrate *a* solemnity to *the* Lord for seven days.

29:13 *offeretisque holocaustum in odorem suavissimum Domino vitulos de armento tredecim arietes duos agnos anniculos quattuordecim inmaculatos*

"'And you will offer to *the* Lord *as a* holocaust of *the* smoothest odor thirteen calves from *the* herd, two rams, fourteen yearling lambs without defect;

29:14 *et in libamentis eorum similae oleo conspersae tres decimas per vitulos singulos qui sunt simul vituli tredecim et duas decimas arieti uno id est simul arietibus duobus*

"'and wheat flour sprinkled with oil in their libations: three tenths for each of *the* calves, who together are thirteen calves; and two tenths per ram (that is, two rams together);

29:15 *et decimam decimae agnis singulis qui sunt simul agni quattuordecim*

"'and *a* tenth tenths for each of *the* lambs, which are fourteen lambs together;

29:16 *et hircum pro peccato absque*

holocausto sempiterno et sacrificio et libamine eius

"'and *a* he-goat for sin, apart from *the* everlasting holocaust and its sacrifice and libation.

The Second Day
29:17 *in die altero offeres vitulos de armento duodecim arietes duos agnos anniculos inmaculatos quattuordecim*

"'On *the* following day, you will offer twelve calves from *the* herd, two rams, *and* fourteen yearling lambs without defect.

29:18 *sacrificiaque et libamina singulorum per vitulos et arietes et agnos rite celebrabis*

"'And you will celebrate by ritual *the* sacrifices and libations for each of *the* calves and rams and lambs,

29:19 *et hircum pro peccato absque holocausto sempiterno sacrificioque eius et libamine*

"'and *a* he-goat for sin, apart from *the* everlasting holocaust, and its sacrifice and libation.

The Third Day
29:20 *die tertio offeres vitulos undecim arietes duos agnos anniculos inmaculatos quattuordecim*

"'*The* third day, you will offer eleven calves, two rams, *and* fourteen yearling lambs without defect

29:21 *sacrificiaque et libamina singulorum per vitulos et arietes et agnos rite celebrabis*

"'And you will celebrate by ritual *the* sacrifices and libations for each of *the* calves and rams and lambs;

29:22 *et hircum pro peccato absque holocausto sempiterno et sacrificio et libamine eius*

"'and *a* he-goat for sin, apart from *the* everlasting holocaust and its sacrifice and libation.

The Fourth Day
29:23 *die quarto offeres vitulos decem arietes duos agnos anniculos inmaculatos quattuordecim*

"'*The* fourth day, you will offer ten calves, two rams, *and* fourteen yearling lambs without defect.

29:24 *sacrificiaque eorum et libamina singulorum per vitulos et arietes et agnos rite celebrabis*

"'And you will celebrate by ritual their sacrifices and libations for each of *the* calves and rams and lambs;

29:25 *et hircum pro peccato absque holocausto sempiterno sacrificioque eius et libamine*

"'and *a* he-goat for sin, apart from *the* everlasting holocaust and its sacrifice and libation.

The Fifth Day
29:26 *die quinto offeres vitulos novem arietes duos agnos anniculos inmaculatos quattuordecim*

"'*The* fifth day, you will offer nine calves, two rams, *and* fourteen yearling lambs.

29:27 *sacrificiaque et libamina singulorum per vitulos et arietes et agnos rite celebrabis*

"'And you will celebrate by ritual *the* sacrifices and libations for each of *the* calves and rams and lambs;

29:28 *et hircum pro peccato absque holocausto sempiterno sacrificioque eius et libamine*

"'and *a* he-goat for sin, apart from *the* everlasting holocaust and its sacrifice and libation.

The Sixth Day
29:29 *die sexto offeres vitulos octo arietes duos agnos anniculos inmaculatos quattuordecim*

"'*The* sixth day, you will offer eight calves, two rams, *and* fourteen yearling lambs without defect.

29:30 *sacrificiaque et libamina singulorum per vitulos et arietes et* *agnos rite celebrabis*

"'And you will celebrate by ritual *the* sacrifices and libations for each of *the* calves and rams and lambs;

29:31 *et hircum pro peccato absque holocausto sempiterno sacrificioque eius et libamine*

"'and *a* he-goat for sin, apart from *the* everlasting holocaust and its sacrifice and libation.

The Seventh Day
29:32 *die septimo offeres vitulos septem arietes duos agnos anniculos inmaculatos quattuordecim*

"'*The* seventh day, you will offer seven calves, two rams, *and* fourteen yearling lambs without defect.

29:33 *sacrificiaque et libamina singulorum per vitulos et arietes et agnos rite celebrabis*

"'And you will celebrate by ritual *the* sacrifices and libations for each of *the* calves and rams and lambs;

29:34 *et hircum pro peccato absque holocausto sempiterno sacrificioque eius et libamine*

"'and *a* he-goat for sin, apart from *the* everlasting holocaust and its sacrifice and libation.

The Eighth Day
29:35 *die octavo qui est celeberrimus omne opus servile non facietis*

"'*The* eighth day, which is most honored, you will do no servile work,

29:36 *offerentes holocaustum in odorem suavissimum Domino vitulum unum arietem unum agnos anniculos inmaculatos septem*

"'offering *as a* holocaust of *the* smoothest odor to *the* Lord one calf, one ram, *and* seven yearling lambs without defect.

29:37 *sacrificiaque et libamina singulorum per vitulos et arietes et agnos rite celebrabis*

"'And you will celebrate by ritual *the* sacrifices and libations for each of *the* calves and rams and lambs;

29:38 *et hircum pro peccato absque holocausto sempiterno sacrificioque eius et libamine*

"'and *a* he-goat for sin, apart from *the* everlasting holocaust and its sacrifice and libation.

29:39 *haec offeretis Domino in sollemnitatibus vestris praeter vota et oblationes spontaneas in holocausto in sacrificio in libamine et in hostiis pacificis*

"'You will offer these to *the* Lord in your solemnities, along with promises and spontaneous offerings, in holocaust, in sacrifice, in libation, and in peace victims.'"

Promises and Oaths

Numbers 30:1 *narravitque Moses filiis Israhel omnia quae ei Dominus imperarat*

And Moses told Israel's children all that *the* Lord had commanded him.

30:2 *et locutus est ad principes tribuum filiorum Israhel iste est sermo quem praecepit Dominus*

And he spoke to *the* princes of Israel's children's tribes. "This is *the* word which *the* Lord commanded.

A Man's Promise

30:3 *si quis virorum votum Domino voverit aut se constrinxerit iuramento non faciet irritum verbum suum sed omne quod promisit implebit*

"If one of *the* men should promise *a* vow to *the* Lord or bind himself by oath, he will not make his word void. But all that he promised, he will fulfill.

A Woman's Promise

30:4 *mulier si quippiam voverit et se constrinxerit iuramento quae est in domo patris sui et in aetate adhuc puellari si cognoverit pater votum quod pollicita est et iuramentum quo obligavit animam suam et tacuerit voti rea erit*

"*A* woman who is in her father's house and still in *the* age of girlhood, if she promises anything or binds herself by oath, if *the* father knows *the* vow which she promised and *the* oath by which she obligated her soul and he remains silent, it will be *a* genuine promise.

30:5 *quicquid pollicita est et iuravit opere conplebit*

"Whatever she has promised and sworn, she will complete by work.

30:6 *sin autem statim ut audierit contradixerit pater et vota et iuramenta eius irrita erunt nec obnoxia tenebitur sponsioni eo quod contradixerit pater*

"But if, as soon as he hears, *the* father contradicts *it*, both her promise and oath will be void, nor will she be held guilty by *the* promise, because *the* father contradicted her.

30:7 *si maritum habuerit et voverit aliquid et semel verbum de ore eius egrediens animam illius obligaverit iuramento*

"If she has *a* husband and promises something, and *the* word once going out of her mouth obligates her soul by oath,

30:8 *quo die audierit vir et non contradixerit voti rea erit reddet quodcumque promiserat*

"that day *the* man hears and does not

contradict *it*, it will be *a* genuine promise. She will repay whatever she has promised.

30:9 *sin autem audiens statim contradixerit et irritas fecerit pollicitationes eius verbaque quibus obstrinxerat animam suam propitius ei erit Dominus*

"But, if hearing, he immediately contradicts and makes void her promises and *the* word by which she bound her soul, *the* Lord will be propitiated toward her.

30:10 *vidua et repudiata quicquid voverint reddent*

"Whatever *a* widow or *a* divorced woman promise, they will repay.

30:11 *uxor in domo viri cum se voto constrinxerit et iuramento*

"*A* wife in *a* husband's house, when she binds herself by promise and oath,

30:12 *si audierit vir et tacuerit nec contradixerit sponsioni reddet quodcumque promiserat*

"if *the* husband should hear and be silent, nor contradict *the* promise, she will repay whatever she had promised.

30:13 *sin autem extemplo contradixerit non tenebitur*

promissionis rea quia maritus contradixit et Dominus ei propitius erit

"But if forthwith he contradicts, she will not be held by *the* promise's guilt, because *the* husband contradicted it. And *the* Lord will be propitiated toward her.

30:14 *si voverit et iuramento se constrinxerit ut per ieiunium vel ceterarum rerum abstinentiam adfligat animam suam in arbitrio viri erit ut faciat sive non faciat*

"If she promises and binds herself by oath that she may afflict her soul by fasting or by abstinence from other things, it will be at *the* man's judgment that she does *it* or does not do *it*.

30:15 *quod si audiens vir tacuerit et in alteram diem distulerit sententiam quicquid voverat atque promiserat reddet quia statim ut audivit tacuit*

"But, if hearing, *the* man is silent and postpones *the* sentence to another day, whatever she vowed and promised she will repay, because as soon as he heard, he was silent.

30:16 *sin autem contradixerit postquam rescivit portabit ipse iniquitatem eius*

"But if he should contradict after he has learned, he will carry her

treachery."

30:17 *istae sunt leges quas constituit Dominus Mosi inter virum et uxorem inter patrem et filiam quae in puellari adhuc aetate est vel quae manet in parentis domo*

These are *the* laws which *the* Lord appointed for Moses between husband and wife, *and* between father and *a* daughter who is still in *the* age of girlhood, or who remains in *the* parent's home.

Revenge Against the Midianites
Numbers 31:1 *locutusque est Dominus ad Mosen dicens*

And *the* Lord spoke to Moses, saying,

31:2 *ulciscere prius filios Israhel de Madianitis et sic colligeris ad populum tuum*

"Avenge first Israel's children against *the* Midianites, and so you will be gathered to your people!"

31:3 *statimque Moses armate inquit ex vobis viros ad pugnam qui possint ultionem Domini expetere de Madianitis*

And Moses immediately said, "Arm men to fight from among you, who can demand *the* Lord's revenge from *the* Midianites!

31:4 *mille viri de singulis tribubus eligantur Israhel qui mittantur ad bellum*

Let *a* thousand men be chosen from each of Israel's tribes, who can be sent to war.

31:5 *dederuntque millenos de cunctis tribubus id est duodecim milia expeditorum ad pugnam*

And they gave *the* thousands from all *the* tribes – that is, twelve thousand foot soldiers to battle –

31:6 *quos misit Moses cum Finees filio Eleazari sacerdotis vasa quoque sancta et tubas ad clangendum tradidit ei*

whom Moses sent with Phineas, Eleazar *the* priest's son. He also handed over to him holy vessels and trumpets for sounding.

31:7 *cumque pugnassent contra Madianitas atque vicissent omnes mares occiderunt*

And when they had fought against *the* Midianites and conquered them, they killed all *the* men

31:8 *et reges eorum Evi et Recem et Sur et Ur et Rebe quinque principes gentis Balaam quoque filium Beor interfecerunt gladio*

and their kings, Evi, and Recem, and Sur, and Ur, and Rebe, five of *the* people's princes. They also killed Balaam, Beor's son, with *the* sword.

31:9 *ceperuntque mulieres eorum et parvulos omniaque pecora et cunctam supellectilem quicquid habere potuerant depopulati sunt*

And they captured their women and little ones and all *the* cattle and all goods. Whatever they could have was plundered.

31:10 *tam urbes quam viculos et castella flamma consumpsit*

The army consumed cities and towns and strongholds alike by fire.

31:11 *et tulerunt praedam et universa quae ceperant tam ex hominibus quam ex iumentis*

And they took *the* plunder and all that they captured, from humans and cattle alike,

31:12 *et adduxerunt ad Mosen et Eleazarum sacerdotem et ad omnem multitudinem filiorum Israhel reliqua etiam utensilia portaverunt ad castra in campestribus Moab iuxta Iordanem contra Hiericho*

and brought them to Moses and Eleazar *the* priest, and to all *the* multitude of Israel's children. And they carried *the* rest of *the* utensils to *the* camps in Moab's plains beside *the* Jordan, across from Jericho.

Moses Angry

31:13 *egressi sunt autem Moses et Eleazar sacerdos et omnes principes synagogae in occursum eorum extra castra*

But Moses and Eleazar *the* priest and all *the* gathering's leaders went out to meet them outside *the* camps.

31:14 *iratusque Moses principibus exercitus tribunis et centurionibus qui venerant de bello*

And Moses, angry with *the* army's

princes, tribunes, and centurions who came from *the* battle,

31:15 *ait cur feminas reservastis*

said, "Why have you kept *the* females?

31:16 *nonne istae sunt quae deceperunt filios Israhel ad suggestionem Balaam et praevaricari vos fecerunt in Domino super peccato Phogor unde et percussus est populus*

"Aren't they *the* ones who deceived Israel's children at Balaam's suggestion, and made you transgress against *the* law under Phogor's sin, from which also *the* people was struck down?

31:17 *ergo cunctos interficite quicquid est generis masculini etiam in parvulis et mulieres quae noverunt viros in coitu iugulate*

"Therefore, kill all – whatever is of masculine sex, even among little ones! And slit *the* throats of women who have known men in sex!

31:18 *puellas autem et omnes feminas virgines reservate vobis*

"But reserve for yourselves girls and all virgin females!

31:19 *et manete extra castra septem diebus qui occiderit hominem vel* *occisum tetigerit lustrabitur die tertio et septimo*

"And stay outside the camps seven days. Who killed *a* man or touched one killed will be purified ceremonially *the* third day and *the* seventh.

31:20 *et de omni praeda sive vestimentum fuerit sive vas et aliquid in utensilia praeparatum de caprarum pellibus et pilis et ligno expiabitur*

"And it will be atonement for all *the* plunder, whether it is clothing, or *a* vessel, or anything as *a* utensil for preparing goat hide and hair, or wood."

Eleazar Speaks to the Troops

31:21 *Eleazar quoque sacerdos ad viros exercitus qui pugnaverant sic locutus est hoc est praeceptum legis quod mandavit Dominus Mosi*

Eleazar *the* priest likewise spoke so to the army's men, who had fought: "This is *the* precept of *the* law that *the* Lord commanded Moses.

31:22 *aurum et argentum et aes et ferrum et stagnum et plumbum*

"Gold, and silver, and bronze, and iron, and tin, and lead,

31:23 *et omne quod potest transire per flammas igne purgabitur*

quicquid autem ignem non potest sustinere aqua expiationis sanctificabitur

"and all that can pass through flames will be purged by fire. But whatever can't sustain fire will be sanctified by *the* water of atonement.

31:24 *et lavabitis vestimenta vestra die septimo et purificati postea castra intrabitis*

"And you will wash your clothes *the* seventh day, and, after being purified, you will enter *the* camps."

Divide the Plunder Fairly

31:25 *dixitque Dominus ad Mosen*

And *the* Lord said to Moses,

31:26 *tollite summam eorum quae capta sunt ab homine usque ad pecus tu et Eleazar sacerdos et principes vulgi*

"Take their number who were captured, from humans even to cattle – you, and Eleazar *the* priest, and *the* crowd's princes.

31:27 *dividesque ex aequo praedam inter eos qui pugnaverunt et egressi sunt ad bellum et inter omnem reliquam multitudinem*

"And you will divide *the* plunder equally among those who fought and went out to war, and between all *the* rest of *the* multitude.

31:28 *et separabis partem Domino ab his qui pugnaverunt et fuerunt in bello unam animam de quingentis tam ex hominibus quam ex bubus et asinis et ovibus*

"And you will separate *a* portion to *the* Lord from those who fought and went to war – one soul from five hundred, whether from humans or from oxen and donkeys and sheep.

31:29 *et dabis eam Eleazaro sacerdoti quia primitiae Domini sunt*

"And you will give them to Eleazar *the* priest, because they are *the* Lord's first fruits.

31:30 *ex media quoque parte filiorum Israhel accipies quinquagesimum caput hominum et boum et asinorum et ovium cunctarumque animantium et dabis ea Levitis qui excubant in custodiis tabernaculi Domini*

"And you will receive from among Israel's children's portion *the* fiftieth head of human and ox and donkeys and sheep, and all *the* souls. And you will give them to *the* Levites who watch in *the* sanctuary's keeping."

31:31 *feceruntque Moses et Eleazar sicut praeceperat Dominus*

And Moses and Eleazar did as *the* Lord had commanded.

Catalog of the Plunder

31:32 *fuit autem praeda quam exercitus ceperat ovium sescenta septuaginta quinque milia*

But all *the* plunder that *the* army captured was six hundred seventy-five thousand sheep,

31:33 *boum septuaginta duo milia*

seventy-two thousand oxen,

31:34 *asinorum sexaginta milia et mille*

sixty-one thousand donkeys,

31:35 *animae hominum sexus feminei quae non cognoverant viros triginta duo milia*

and thirty-two thousand human souls of female gender, who had not known men.

31:36 *dataque est media pars his qui in proelio fuerant ovium trecenta triginta septem milia quingenta*

And *a* half portion was given to those who had gone to battle: three hundred thirty-seven thousand, five hundred sheep,

31:37 *e quibus in partem Domini supputatae sunt oves sescentae septuaginta quinque*

from which six hundred seventy-five sheep were counted as *the* Lord's portion;

31:38 *et de bubus triginta sex milibus boves septuaginta duo*

and from thirty-six thousand oxen, seventy-two oxen;

31:39 *de asinis triginta milibus quingentis asini sexaginta unus*

and from thirty thousand, five hundred donkeys, sixty-one donkeys.

31:40 *de animabus hominum sedecim milibus cesserunt in partem Domini triginta duae animae*

From sixteen thousand human souls, they granted as *the* Lord's portion thirty-two souls.

31:41 *tradiditque Moses numerum primitiarum Domini Eleazaro sacerdoti sicut ei fuerat imperatum*

And Moses handed over *the* number of *the* Lord's first fruits to Eleazar *the* priest, as had been commanded him,

31:42 *ex media parte filiorum Israhel quam separaverat his qui in proelio fuerant*

from half of Israel's children's portion, which he had set aside from those who went to battle;

31:43 *de media vero parte quae contigerat reliquae multitudini id est de ovium trecentis triginta septem milibus quingentis*

and from half *the* portion that fell to the rest of *the* multitude – that is, from *the* three hundred thirty-seven thousand, five hundred sheep,

31:44 *et de bubus triginta sex milibus*

and from *the* thirty-six thousand oxen;

31:45 *et de asinis triginta milibus quingentis*

and from *the* thirty thousand, five hundred donkeys;

31:46 *et de hominibus sedecim milibus*

and from *the* sixteen thousand humans.

31:47 *tulit Moses quinquagesimum caput et dedit Levitis qui excubant in tabernaculo Domini sicut praeceperat Dominus*

Moses took *the* fiftieth head and gave *them* to *the* Levites who kept watch in *the* Lord's tabernacle, as *the* Lord had commanded.

The Army's Gratitude
to the Lord

31:48 *cumque accessissent principes exercitus ad Mosen et tribuni centurionesque dixerunt*

And when *the* army's princes had come with *the* tribunes and centurions to Moses, they said,

31:49 *nos servi tui recensuimus numerum pugnatorum quos habuimus sub manu nostra et ne unus quidem defuit*

"We, your slaves, have counted *the* number of fighters who we had under our hand, and not even one of them is missing.

31:50 *ob hanc causam offerimus in donariis Domini singuli quod in praeda auri potuimus invenire periscelides et armillas anulos et dextralia ac murenulas ut depreceris pro nobis Dominum*

"For this reason, we are offering as *the* Lord's gifts what gold each of us could find among *the* plunder – anklets and armbands, rings and bracelets and necklaces – so you may pray to *the* Lord for us."

31:51 *susceperuntque Moses et Eleazar sacerdos omne aurum in diversis speciebus*

And Moses and Eleazar *the* priest received all *the* gold in its different varieties,

31:52 *pondo sedecim milia septingentos quinquaginta siclos a tribunis et centurionibus*

weighing sixteen thousand, seven hundred fifty shekels, from *the* tribunes and centurions.

31:53 *unusquisque enim quod in praeda rapuerat suum erat*

For that which was taken in *the* plunder was each one's,

31:54 *et susceptum intulerunt in tabernaculum testimonii in monumentum filiorum Israhel coram Domino*

and, *being* received, they brought it into testimony's tabernacle as Israel's children's monument before *the* Lord.

Reuben and Gad
Ask to Remain Beyond
the Jordan

Numbers 32:1 *filii autem Ruben et Gad habebant pecora multa et erat illis in iumentis infinita substantia cumque vidissent Iazer et Galaad aptas alendis animalibus*

But Reuben and Gad's children had many herds, and *a* limitless substance in cattle was theirs. And when they had seen Iazer and Galaad suitable for feeding animals,

32:2 *venerunt ad Mosen et ad Eleazarum sacerdotem et principes multitudinis atque dixerunt*

they came to Moses, and to Eleazar *the* priest, and *the* multitude's leaders. And they said,

32:3 *Atharoth et Dibon et Iazer et Nemra Esbon et Eleale et Sabam et Nebo et Beon*

"Atharoth, and Dibon, and Iazer, and Nemra, Heshbon, and Eleale, and Sabam, and Nebo, and Beon –

32:4 *terram quam percussit Dominus in conspectu filiorum Israhel regionis uberrimae est ad pastum animalium et nos servi tui habemus iumenta plurima*

"*the* land which *the* Lord struck down in *the* sight of Israel's children – is *a* most abundant region for feeding animals. And we, your slaves, have many herds.

32:5 *precamurque si invenimus gratiam coram te ut des nobis famulis tuis eam in possessionem ne facias nos transire Iordanem*

"We pray, if we have found grace before you, that you give it to us, your servants, as *a* possession, nor make us cross over *the* Jordan."

Moses Rebukes Reuben and Gad

32:6 *quibus respondit Moses numquid fratres vestri ibunt ad pugnam et vos hic sedebitis*

Moses answered them, "Your brothers won't go to fight, and you sit here, will they?

32:7 *cur subvertitis mentes filiorum Israhel ne transire audeant in locum quem eis daturus est Dominus*

"Why are you subverting Israel's children's minds, so they won't dare to cross over into *the* place which *the* Lord will give them?

32:8 *nonne ita egerunt patres vestri quando misi de Cadesbarne ad explorandam terram*

"Didn't your fathers act so when I sent from Kadesh Barnea to explore *the* land?

32:9 *cumque venissent usque ad*

vallem Botri lustrata omni regione subverterunt cor filiorum Israhel ut non intrarent fines quos eis Dominus dedit

"And when they had come even to Botrus valley, passing through all *the* region, they subverted Israel's children's heart, so they didn't enter *the* borders which *the* Lord had given them.

32:10 *qui iratus iuravit dicens*

"*The Lord* swore in anger, saying,

32:11 *si videbunt homines isti qui ascenderunt ex Aegypto a viginti annis et supra terram quam sub iuramento pollicitus sum Abraham Isaac et Iacob et noluerunt sequi me*

"'These men who came up out of Egypt, from twenty years old and above, won't see *the* land which I have sworn under oath to Abraham, Isaac, and Jacob – and they didn't follow Me –

32:12 *praeter Chaleb filium Iepphonne Cenezeum et Iosue filium Nun isti impleverunt voluntatem meam*

"'except Caleb, Iepphone *the* Kenezite's son, and Joshua, Nun's son! These fulfilled My will.'

32:13 *iratusque Dominus adversum Israhel circumduxit eum per*

desertum quadraginta annis donec consumeretur universa generatio quae fecerat malum in conspectu eius

"And *the* Lord, angry against Israel, led him through *the* desert forty years, until *the* whole generation that had done harm in His sight was consumed.

32:14 *et ecce inquit vos surrexistis pro patribus vestris incrementa et alumni hominum peccatorum ut augeretis furorem Domini contra Israhel*

"And look," he said, "you have risen up in your fathers' places, increased and nourished by sinful men, so you may increase *the* Lord's fury against Israel –

32:15 *qui si nolueritis sequi eum in solitudine populum derelinquet et vos causa eritis necis omnium*

"who, if you won't follow Him, will abandon *the* people in *the* wasteland. And you will be *the* cause of *the* death of all!"

Reuben and Gad Promise
to Fight for Their Brothers
32:16 *at illi prope accedentes dixerunt caulas ovium fabricabimus et stabula iumentorum parvulis quoque nostris urbes munitas*

And they, coming near, said, "We

will build folds for *the* sheep and stables for cattle, and fortified cities as well for our little ones.

32:17 *nos autem ipsi armati et accincti pergemus ad proelium ante filios Israhel donec introducamus eos ad loca sua parvuli nostri et quicquid habere possumus erunt in urbibus muratis propter habitatorum insidias*

"But we ourselves will go armed and girded to battle before Israel's children, until we can bring them to their places. Our little ones and whatever we can have will be in walled cities, because of *the* inhabitants' plots.

32:18 *non revertemur in domos nostras usquequo possideant filii Israhel hereditatem suam*

"We will not go back to our homes until Israel's children possess their inheritance.

32:19 *nec quicquam quaeremus trans Iordanem quia iam habemus possessionem nostram in orientali eius plaga*

"Nor will we seek anything across *the* Jordan, because we already have our possession in its eastern quarter."

Moses Sets Terms
for Reuben and Gad
32:20 *quibus Moses ait si facitis*

quod promittitis expediti pergite coram Domino ad pugnam

Moses said to them, "If you do as you promise, go out armed before *the* Lord to battle!

32:21 *et omnis vir bellator armatus Iordanem transeat donec subvertat Dominus inimicos suos*

"And let every armed warrior cross *the* Jordan until *the* Lord has overthrown His enemies,

32:22 *et subiciatur ei omnis terra tunc eritis inculpabiles et apud Dominum et apud Israhel et obtinebitis regiones quas vultis coram Domino*

and all *the* land be subjected to Him. Then you will be guiltless also with *the* Lord and with Israel. And you will obtain *the* regions which you want before *the* Lord.

32:23 *sin autem quod dicitis non feceritis nulli dubium quin peccetis in Dominum et scitote quoniam peccatum vestrum adprehendet vos*

"But if you will not do what you say, without doubt you will sin against *the* Lord. And know that your sin will capture you!

32:24 *aedificate ergo urbes parvulis vestris et caulas ac stabula ovibus ac iumentis et quod polliciti estis* *implete*

"Build, then, cities for your little ones, and folds and stables for sheep and cattle. And fulfill what you have promised!"

Gad and Reuben Accept

32:25 *dixeruntque filii Gad et Ruben ad Mosen servi tui sumus faciemus quod iubet dominus noster*

And Gad's children and Reuben said to Moses, "We are your slaves. We will do what our lord commands.

32:26 *parvulos nostros et mulieres et pecora ac iumenta relinquemus in urbibus Galaad*

"We will leave our little ones and women and flocks and herds in Galaad's cities.

32:27 *nos autem famuli tui omnes expediti pergemus ad bellum sicut tu domine loqueris*

"But all of us, your servants, will go out armed to war, as you, lord, have said."

Moses Commands Israel Concerning Gad and Reuben

32:28 *praecepit ergo Moses Eleazaro sacerdoti et Iosue filio Nun et principibus familiarum per tribus Israhel et dixit ad eos*

So Moses commanded Eleazar *the*

priest, and Joshua, Nun's son, and *the* princes of families throughout Israel's tribes. And he said to them,

32:29 *si transierint filii Gad et filii Ruben vobiscum Iordanem omnes armati ad bellum coram Domino et vobis fuerit terra subiecta date eis Galaad in possessionem*

"If Gad's children and Reuben's children cross *the* Jordan with you, all armed for war before *the* Lord, and *the* land be subject to you, give them Galaad as *a* possession.

32:30 *sin autem noluerint transire vobiscum in terram Chanaan inter vos habitandi accipiant loca*

"But if they won't cross over with you into Canaan's land, let them receive places to live among you."

32:31 *responderuntque filii Gad et filii Ruben sicut locutus est Dominus servis suis ita faciemus*

And Gad's children and Reuben's children said, "As the Lord has spoken to His slaves, so we will do.

32:32 *ipsi armati pergemus coram Domino in terram Chanaan et possessionem iam suscepisse nos confitemur trans Iordanem*

"We will go armed before *the* Lord into Canaan's land. And we acknowledge that we have already received our possession across *the* Jordan."

Moses Gives Them the Land

32:33 *dedit itaque Moses filiis Gad et Ruben et dimidiae tribui Manasse filii Ioseph regnum Seon regis Amorrei et regnum Og regis Basan et terram eorum cum urbibus suis per circuitum*

So Moses gave *the* children of Gad and Reuben, and half *the* tribe of Manasseh, Joseph's son, *the* kingdom of Sihon, *the* Amorite king, and *the* kingdom of Og, Bashan's king, and their land, with their surrounding cities.

Gad's Territory

32:34 *igitur extruxerunt filii Gad Dibon et Atharoth et Aroer*

Therefore, Gad's children built Dibon and Atharoth and Aroer,

32:35 *Etrothsophan et Iazer Iecbaa*

Etrothsophan and Iazer, Iecbaa

32:36 *et Bethnemra et Betharan urbes munitas et caulas pecoribus suis*

and Bethnemra and Betharan, fortified cities and their sheepfolds.

Reuben's Territory

32:37 *filii vero Ruben aedificaverunt Esbon et Eleale et*

Cariathaim

Reuben's children indeed built Heshbon and Eleale and Cariathaim,

32:38 *et Nabo et Baalmeon versis nominibus Sabama quoque inponentes vocabula urbibus quas extruxerant*

and Nabo and Baalmeon, changing *the* names, and Sabama too, putting designations on *the* cities which they built.

Manasseh's Territory

32:39 *porro filii Machir filii Manasse perrexerunt in Galaad et vastaverunt eam interfecto Amorreo habitatore eius*

Afterwards, *the* children of Machir, Manasseh's son, went into Galaad and devastated it, killing its inhabitant, *the* Amorite.

32:40 *dedit ergo Moses terram Galaad Machir filio Manasse qui habitavit in ea*

Therefore, Moses gave Galaad's land to Machir, Manasseh's son, who lived in it.

32:41 *Iair autem filius Manasse abiit et occupavit vicos eius quos appellavit Avothiair id est villas Iair*

But Jair, Manasseh's son, went out and occupied its villages, which he called Avothjair – that is, Jair's estate.

32:42 *Nobe quoque perrexit et adprehendit Canath cum viculis suis vocavitque eam ex nomine suo Nobe*

Nobe also went in and took Canath with its villages. And he called it after his name, Nobe.

Numbers 33:1 *hae sunt mansiones filiorum Israhel qui egressi sunt de Aegypto per turmas suas in manu Mosi et Aaron*

These are *the* lodgings of Israel's children, who went out of Egypt by their companies under Moses' and Aaron's hand,

33:2 *quas descripsit Moses iuxta castrorum loca quae Domini iussione mutabant*

which Moses described, according to *the* camps' location, which they changed at *the* Lord's order.

33:3 *profecti igitur de Ramesse mense primo quintadecima die mensis primi altera die phase filii Israhel in manu excelsa videntibus cunctis Aegyptiis*

Setting out, therefore, from Ramesses, *the* first month, fifteenth day of *the* first month, *the* day after Passover, Israel's children, under *a* lifted up hand, all *the* Egyptians seeing,

33:4 *et sepelientibus primogenitos quos percusserat Dominus nam et in diis eorum exercuerat ultionem*

and burying *the* firstborn, whom *the* Lord had struck down, for he had enforced revenge also against *their* gods,

33:5 *castrametati sunt in Soccoth*

camped in Soccoth.

33:6 *et de Soccoth venerunt in Aetham quae est in extremis finibus solitudinis*

And from Soccoth, they came to Etham, which is in *the* farthest borders of *the* wasteland.

33:7 *inde egressi venerunt contra Phiahiroth quae respicit Beelsephon et castrametati sunt ante Magdolum*

Going out from there, they came beside Phiahiroth, which looks on Baalsephon, and they camped before Magdolum.

33:8 *profectique de Phiahiroth transierunt per medium mare in solitudinem et ambulantes tribus diebus per desertum Aetham castrametati sunt in Mara*

And setting out from Phiahiroth, they passed through *the* middle of *the* sea into *the* wasteland. And walking three days through Etham's desert, they camped in Mara.

33:9 *profectique de Mara venerunt in Helim ubi erant duodecim fontes aquarum et palmae septuaginta ibique castrametati sunt*

And setting out from Mara, they came to Elim, where there were twelve springs of water. And seventy palm trees *were* there.

33:10 *sed et inde egressi fixere tentoria super mare Rubrum profectique de mari Rubro*

Yet going out from there also, they pitched tents on *the* Red Sea. And setting out from *the* Red Sea,

33:11 *castrametati sunt in deserto Sin*

they camped in Sin's desert.

33:12 *unde egressi venerunt in Dephca*

Going out from there, they came into Dephca.

33:13 *profectique de Dephca castrametati sunt in Alus*

And setting out from Dephca, they camped in Alus.

33:14 *egressi de Alus Raphidim fixere tentoria ubi aqua populo defuit ad bibendum*

Going out from Alus, they pitched tents in Raphidim, where *the* people lacked water to drink.

33:15 *profectique de Raphidim castrametati sunt in deserto Sinai*

Setting out from Raphidim, they

camped in *the* Sinai desert.

33:16 *sed et de solitudine Sinai egressi venerunt ad sepulchra Concupiscentiae*

Yet also going out from Sinai's wasteland, they came to Lusting's graves.

33:17 *profectique de sepulchris Concupiscentiae castrametati sunt in Aseroth*

And setting out from Lusting's graves, they camped in Aseroth.

33:18 *et de Aseroth venerunt in Rethma*

And from Aseroth they came into Rethma.

33:19 *profectique de Rethma castrametati sunt in Remmonphares*

And setting out from Rethma, they camped in Remmonphares.

33:20 *unde egressi venerunt in Lebna*

Leaving from there, they came to Lebna.

33:21 *et de Lebna castrametati sunt in Ressa*

And from Lebna they camped in Ressa.

33:22 *egressi de Ressa venerunt in Ceelatha*

Going out of Ressa, they came to Ceelatha.

33:23 *unde profecti castrametati sunt in monte Sepher*

Setting out from there, they camped on Mount Sepher.

33:24 *egressi de monte Sepher venerunt in Arada*

Leaving from Mount Sepher, they came to Arada.

33:25 *inde proficiscentes castrametati sunt in Maceloth*

Setting out from there, they camped in Maceloth.

33:26 *profectique de Maceloth venerunt in Thaath*

And setting out from Maceloth, they came to Thaath.

33:27 *de Thaath castrametati sunt in Thare*

From Thaath they camped in Thare.

33:28 *unde egressi fixerunt tentoria in Methca*

Leaving from there, they fixed tents in Methca.

33:29 *et de Methca castrametati sunt in Esmona*

And from Methca they camped in Esmona.

33:30 *profectique de Esmona venerunt in Moseroth*

And setting out from Esmona, they came to Moseroth.

33:31 *et de Moseroth castrametati sunt in Baneiacan*

And from Moseroth they camped in Baneiacan.

33:32 *egressique de Baneiacan venerunt in montem Gadgad*

Leaving from Baneiacan, they came to Mount Gadgad.

33:33 *unde profecti castrametati sunt in Hietebatha*

Setting out from there, they camped in Hietebatha.

33:34 *et de Hietebatha venerunt in Ebrona*

And from Hietebatha they came to Ebrona.

33:35 *egressique de Ebrona castrametati sunt in Asiongaber*

And going out from Ebrona, they camped in Asiongaber.

33:36 *inde profecti venerunt in desertum Sin haec est Cades*

Setting out from there, they came into Sin's desert, that is, Kadesh.

33:37 *egressique de Cades castrametati sunt in monte Hor in extremis finibus terrae Edom*

And going out of Kadesh, they camped on Mount Hor, on *the* farthest boundaries of Edom's land.

Aaron's Death on Mount Hor

33:38 *ascenditque Aaron sacerdos montem Hor iubente Domino et ibi mortuus est anno quadragesimo egressionis filiorum Israhel ex Aegypto mense quinto prima die mensis*

And Aaron *the* priest climbed up Mount Hor at *the* Lord's command, and he died there in *the* fortieth year of Israel's children's exodus from Egypt, *the* fifth month, *the* first day of *the* month –

33:39 *cum esset annorum centum viginti trium*

when he was one hundred twenty-three years old.

33:40 *audivitque Chananeus rex Arad qui habitabat ad meridiem in terra Chanaan venisse filios Israhel*

And *the* Canaanite king Arad, who lived toward *the* south, heard that Israel's children had come to Canaan's land.

The Journey Continues

33:41 *et profecti de monte Hor castrametati sunt in Salmona*

And setting out from Mount Hor, they camped in Salmona.

33:42 *unde egressi venerunt in Phinon*

Going out from there, they came to Phinon.

33:43 *profectique de Phinon castrametati sunt in Oboth*

And setting out from Phinon, they camped in Oboth.

33:44 *et de Oboth venerunt in Ieabarim quae est in finibus Moabitarum*

And from Oboth they came to Ieabarim, which is on *the* Moabites' borders.

33:45 *profectique de Ieabarim fixere tentoria in Dibongad*

And setting out from Ieabaraim, they pitched tents in Dibongad.

33:46 *unde egressi castrametati sunt in Elmondeblathaim*

Going out from there, they camped in Elmondeblathaim.

33:47 *egressi de Elmondeblathaim venerunt ad montes Abarim contra Nabo*

Going out from Elmondeblathaim, they came to *the* Abarim mountains, across from Nabo.

33:48 *profectique de montibus Abarim transierunt ad campestria Moab super Iordanem contra Hiericho*

And setting out from *the* Abarim mountains, they passed through Moab's plains on *the* Jordan, across from Jericho.

The Lord Warns Israel to Destroy the Canaanites

33:49 *ibique castrametati sunt de Bethsimon usque ad Belsattim in planioribus locis Moabitarum*

And they camped there from Bethsimon even to Belsattim, in *the* Moabites' flat places,

33:50 *ubi locutus est Dominus ad Mosen*

where *the* Lord said to Moses,

33:51 *praecipe filiis Israhel et dic ad eos quando transieritis Iordanem intrantes terram Chanaan*

"Command Israel's children and say to them, 'When you have crossed *the* Jordan, entering Canaan's land,

33:52 *disperdite cunctos habitatores regionis illius confringite titulos et statuas comminuite atque omnia excelsa vastate*

"'destroy all that region's inhabitants! Break down their titles, and smash their statues, and lay waste all *the* high *places,*

33:53 *mundantes terram et habitantes in ea ego enim dedi vobis illam in possessionem*

"'cleansing *the* land and living in it! For I have given it to you as *a* possession,

33:54 *quam dividetis vobis sorte pluribus dabitis latiorem et paucis angustiorem singulis ut sors ceciderit ita tribuetur hereditas per tribus et familias possessio dividetur*

"'which you will divide among yourselves by lot. You will give more to *the* larger and less to *the* smaller. As *the* lot falls to each one, so *the* inheritance will be given. *The* possession will be divided through *the* tribes and families.

33:55 *sin autem nolueritis interficere habitatores terrae qui remanserint erunt vobis quasi clavi in oculis et lanceae in lateribus et*

adversabuntur vobis in terra habitationis vestrae

"'But if you won't kill *the* land's inhabitants, they who remain will be like nails in *the* eye and lances in *the* side to you . And they will oppose you in your habitation's land.

33:56 *et quicquid illis facere cogitaram vobis faciam*

"'And whatever I had thought to do to them, I will do to you.'"

Canaan's Borders
Numbers 34:1 *locutus est Dominus ad Mosen*

And *the* Lord said to Moses,

34:2 *praecipe filiis Israhel et dices ad eos cum ingressi fueritis terram Chanaan et in possessionem vobis sorte ceciderit his finibus terminabitur*

"Command Israel's children, and you will say to them, 'When you have come into Canaan's land, and it has fallen to you by lot, it will be bounded by these borders:

34:3 *pars meridiana incipiet a solitudine Sin quae est iuxta Edom et habebit terminos contra orientem mare Salsissimum*

"'*The* southern part will begin from Sin's wasteland, which is beside Edom, and will have boundaries beside *the* Saltiest sea on *the* east.

34:4 *qui circumibunt australem plagam per ascensum Scorpionis ita ut transeant Senna et perveniant in meridiem usque ad Cadesbarne unde egredientur confinia ad villam nomine Addar et tendent usque Asemona*

"'*They* will circle *the* southern quarter by Scorpion ridge, so that they pass through Senna and come through in the south even to Kadesh

Barnea. From there they will go out to *the* confines of *a* village named Addar, and stretch to Asemona.

34:5 *ibitque per gyrum terminus ab Asemona usque ad torrentem Aegypti et maris Magni litore finietur*

"'And there *the* border will finish by turn from Asemona to *the* brook of Egypt and shore of *the* Great sea.

34:6 *plaga autem occidentalis a mari Magno incipiet et ipso fine cludetur*

But *the* western quarter will begin from *the* Great sea, and will be finished on *the* same border.

34:7 *porro ad septentrionalem plagam a mari Magno termini incipient pervenientes usque ad montem Altissimum*

Afterwards, *the* borders to *the* northern quarter will begin from *the* Great sea, coming through to *the* Highest mountain.

34:8 *a quo venies in Emath usque ad terminos Sedada*

"'You will go from there to Emath, even to Sedada's borders.

34:9 *ibuntque confinia usque Zephrona et villam Henan hii erunt termini in parte aquilonis*

"*The* confines will go to Zephrona and Henan village. These will be *the* boundaries in *the* northern portion.

34:10 *inde metabuntur fines contra orientalem plagam de villa Henan usque Sephama*

"'From there, *the* borders will pass across *the* eastern quarter from Henan village to Sephama.

34:11 *et de Sephama descendent termini in Rebla contra fontem inde pervenient contra orientem ad mare Chenereth*

"'And *the* frontiers will come down from Sephama to Rebla, beside *the* spring. From there, they will come through across *the* east to Chenereth sea.

34:12 *et tendent usque Iordanem et ad ultimum Salsissimo cludentur mari hanc habebitis terram per fines suos in circuitu*

"'And they will stretch to *the* Jordan and be closed in at last by *the* Saltiest sea. You will have this land through its boundaries all around.

Moses Tells the People
34:13 *praecepitque Moses filiis Israhel dicens haec erit terra quam possidebitis sorte et quam iussit dari Dominus novem tribubus et dimidiae tribui*

And Moses commanded Israel's children, saying, "This will be *the* land that you will possess by lot, and that *the* Lord commanded to be given to nine tribes and half *a* tribe.

34:14 *tribus enim filiorum Ruben per familias suas et tribus filiorum Gad iuxta cognationum numerum media quoque tribus Manasse*

"For Reuben's children's tribe by its families, and Gad's children's tribe according to *the* number of its clans, and half of Manasseh's tribe" –

34:15 *id est duae semis tribus acceperunt partem suam trans Iordanem contra Hiericho ad orientalem plagam*

– that is, two and *a* half tribes – "received their portion across *the* Jordan, facing Jericho to *the* eastern quarter."

Those Who Will Divide the Land
34:16 *et ait Dominus ad Mosen*

And *the* Lord said to Moses,

34:17 *haec sunt nomina virorum qui terram vobis divident Eleazar sacerdos et Iosue filius Nun*

"These are *the* men's names who will divide *the* land for you: Eleazar *the* priest, and Joshua, Nun's son,

34:18 *et singuli principes de*

tribubus singulis

"and each of *the* princes from each of *the* tribes,

34:19 *quorum ista sunt vocabula de tribu Iuda Chaleb filius Iepphonne*

"whose names are these: from Judah's tribe, Caleb, Iepphonne's son;

34:20 *de tribu Symeon Samuhel filius Ammiud*

"from Simeon's tribe, Samuel, Ammiud's son;

34:21 *de tribu Beniamin Helidad filius Chaselon*

"from Benjamin's tribe, Helidad, Chaselon's son'

34:22 *de tribu filiorum Dan Bocci filius Iogli*

"from Dan's children's tribe, Bocci, Iogli's son;

34:23 *filiorum Ioseph de tribu Manasse Hannihel filius Ephod*

"of Joseph's children, from Manasseh's tribe, Hanniel, Ephod's son;

34:24 *de tribu Ephraim Camuhel filius Sephtan*

"from Ephraim's tribe, Camuel, Sephtan's son;

34:25 *de tribu Zabulon Elisaphan filius Pharnach*

"from Zebulon's tribe, Elisaphan, Pharnach's son;

34:26 *de tribu Isachar dux Faltihel filius Ozan*

"from Issachar's tribe, Duke Faltiel, Ozan's son;

34:27 *de tribu Aser Ahiud filius Salomi*

"from Asher's tribe, Ahiud, Salomi's son;

34:28 *de tribu Nepthali Phedahel filius Ameiud*

"from Napthali's tribe, Phedael, Ameiud's son."

34:29 *hii sunt quibus praecepit Dominus ut dividerent filiis Israhel terram Chanaan*

These are *those* whom *the* Lord commanded, that they divide Canaan's land for Israel's children.

Provision for the Levites

Numbers 35:1 *haec quoque locutus est Dominus ad Mosen in campestribus Moab super Iordanem contra Hiericho*

The Lord said this to Moses as well, in Moab's plains on *the* Jordan, across from Jericho.

35:2 *praecipe filiis Israhel ut dent Levitis de possessionibus suis*

"Command Israel's children that they give to *the* Levites from their possessions:

35:3 *urbes ad habitandum et suburbana earum per circuitum ut ipsi in oppidis maneant et suburbana sint pecoribus ac iumentis*

"cities to live in and their cultivated fields around, so they may stay in *the* towns, and *the* cultivated fields may be for sheep and cattle –

35:4 *quae a muris civitatum forinsecus per circuitum mille passuum spatio tendentur*

which will stretch *the* space of *a* thousand steps around on *the* outside of *the* cities' walls.

35:5 *contra orientem duo milia erunt cubiti et contra meridiem similiter duo milia ad mare quoque quod respicit occidentem eadem mensura erit et septentrionalis plaga*

aequali termino finietur eruntque urbes in medio et foris suburbana

"Two thousand cubits will be facing east, and two thousand similarly facing south. *The* same measure will be toward *the* sea, as well, which looks west, and *the* southern will be bounded by equal limits. And *the* cities will be in *the* middle and *the* cultivated fields outside.

35:6 *de ipsis autem oppidis quae Levitis dabitis sex erunt in fugitivorum auxilia separata ut fugiat ad ea qui fuderit sanguinem exceptis his alia quadraginta duo oppida*

"But six of *the* same towns which you will give *the* Levites will be set aside to help fugitives, so one who sheds blood may flee to them, except for those forty-two other towns –

35:7 *id est simul quadraginta octo cum suburbanis suis*

"that is, forty-eight together, with their cultivated fields.

35:8 *ipsaeque urbes quae dabuntur de possessionibus filiorum Israhel ab his qui plus habent plures auferentur et qui minus pauciores singuli iuxta mensuram hereditatis suae dabunt oppida Levitis*

"More of these same cities which will be given from Israel's children's possessions will be taken from those who have more, and from those who have less fewer. Each will give towns to *the* Levites according to *the* measure of his inheritance."

Cities of Refuge
35:9 *ait Dominus ad Mosen*

The Lord said to Moses,

35:10 *loquere filiis Israhel et dices ad eos quando transgressi fueritis Iordanem in terram Chanaan*

"Speak to Israel's children, and you will say to them: 'When you have crossed *the* Jordan into Canaan's land,

35:11 *decernite quae urbes esse debeant in praesidia fugitivorum qui nolentes sanguinem fuderint*

"decide which cities must be for *the* protection of fugitives who shed blood unwillingly.

35:12 *in quibus cum fuerit profugus cognatus occisi eum non poterit occidere donec stet in conspectu multitudinis et causa illius iudicetur*

"When *a* fugitive is in them, *the* killed one's kin cannot kill him until he stands in *the* multitude's sight and his cause is judged.

35:13 *de ipsis autem urbibus quae ad fugitivorum subsidia separantur*

"From *the* same cities that are separated for *the* relief of fugitives,

35:14 *tres erunt trans Iordanem et tres in terra Chanaan*

"three will be across *the* Jordan, and three in Canaan's land,

35:15 *tam filiis Israhel quam advenis atque peregrinis ut confugiat ad eas qui nolens sanguinem fuderit*

"so one who sheds blood unwillingly may flee to them – whether from Israel's children or *the* newcomers and sojourners.

Definitions of Murder
35:16 *si quis ferro percusserit et mortuus fuerit qui percussus est reus erit homicidii et ipse morietur*

"If one will strike by iron and he who was struck dies, he is guilty of homicide, and he will die.

35:17 *si lapidem iecerit et ictus occubuerit similiter punietur*

"If he will throw *a* rock and *the* one struck lies dead, he will be punished similarly.

35:18 *si ligno percussus interierit percussoris sanguine vindicabitur*

"If one struck by wood should die, he will be avenged by *the* murderer's blood.

35:19 *propinquus occisi homicidam interficiet statim ut adprehenderit eum percutiet*

"*The* next of kin of *the* one killed will kill *the* murderer. As soon as he catches him, he will strike down.

35:20 *si per odium quis hominem inpulerit vel iecerit quippiam in eum per insidias*

"If through hate one should push *a* man or throw anything at him through plots,

35:21 *aut cum esset inimicus manu percusserit et ille mortuus fuerit percussor homicidii reus erit cognatus occisi statim ut invenerit eum iugulabit*

"or, when he was *an* enemy, should strike by hand, and he will die, *the* one who struck will be guilty of homicide. *A* kinsman of the *one* killed will slit *his* throat as soon as he finds him.

Cases of Accidental Death

35:22 *quod si fortuito et absque odio*

"But if by chance and without hatred

35:23 *et inimicitiis quicquam horum fecerit*

"or hostility he does any of these *things*,

35:24 *et hoc audiente populo fuerit conprobatum atque inter percussorem et propinquum sanguinis quaestio ventilata*

"and this be proven, *the* people hearing, and *the* dispute between *the* killer and *the* blood's next of kin aired,

35:25 *liberabitur innocens de ultoris manu et reducetur per sententiam in urbem ad quam confugerat manebitque ibi donec sacerdos magnus qui oleo sancto unctus est moriatur*

"*the* innocent will be freed from *the* avenger's hand, and be brought back through *the* sentence into *the* city to which he had fled. And he will stay there until *the* high priest, who is anointed by holy oil, dies.

35:26 *si interfector extra fines urbium quae exulibus deputatae sunt*

"If *the* killer, outside *the* boundaries of *the* cities which are designated for exiles,

35:27 *fuerit inventus et percussus ab eo qui ultor est sanguinis absque noxa erit qui eum occiderit*

"will be found and struck down by him who is avenger of blood, *the one* who killed him will be without guilt;

35:28 *debuerat enim profugus usque*

ad mortem pontificis in urbe residere postquam autem ille obierit homicida revertetur in terram suam

"for *the* fugitive ought to have stayed in *the* city until *the* high priest's death. But after he dies, *the* killer will go back to his land.

35:29 *haec sempiterna erunt et legitima in cunctis habitationibus vestris*

"These will be everlasting and laws in all your habitations.

More Than One Witness Needed

35:30 *homicida sub testibus punietur ad unius testimonium nullus condemnabitur*

"*A* murderer will be punished under witnesses. No one will be condemned at *the* testimony of one.

35:31 *non accipietis pretium ab eo qui reus est sanguinis statim et ipse morietur*

"You will not accept *a* price from him who is guilty of blood. He also will die immediately.

35:32 *exules et profugi ante mortem pontificis nullo modo in urbes suas reverti poterunt*

"Exiles and fugitives by no means may go back to their cities before *the* high priest's death.

35:33 *ne polluatis terram habitationis vestrae quae insontium cruore maculatur nec aliter expiari potest nisi per eius sanguinem qui alterius sanguinem fuderit*

"You may not pollute your habitation's land, which is stained by innocent murder; nor can it be atoned for otherwise, except by his blood who shed *the* other's blood.

35:34 *atque ita emundabitur vestra possessio me commorante vobiscum ego enim sum Dominus qui habito inter filios Israhel*

"And so your possession will be made clean, Me living with you, for I am *the* Lord, who lives among Israel's children.

More on Salphaad's Daughters
Numbers 36:1 *accesserunt autem et principes familiarum Galaad filii Machir filii Manasse de stirpe filiorum Ioseph locutique sunt Mosi coram principibus Israhel atque dixerunt*

But *the* princes of *the* family of Galaad, Machir's son, Manasseh's son, of Joseph's children's stock, also came near and spoke to Moses before Israel's princes. And they said,

36:2 *tibi domino nostro praecepit Dominus ut terram sorte divideres filiis Israhel et ut filiabus Salphaad fratris nostri dares possessionem debitam patri*

"*The* Lord commanded you, our lord, that you divide *the* land by lot among Israel's children, and that you give to *the* daughters of Salphaad, our brother, *the* possession owed *the* father.

36:3 *quas si alterius tribus homines uxores acceperint sequetur possessio sua et translata ad aliam tribum de nostra hereditate minuetur*

"But if men from another tribe receive these women as wives, their possession will follow. And, being transferred to another tribe, it will be reduced from our inheritance.

36:4 *atque ita fiet ut cum iobeleus*

id est quinquagesimus annus remissionis advenerit confundatur sortium distributio et aliorum possessio ad alios transeat

"And so it will be that, when *the* Jubilee (that is, *the* fiftieth year of remission) comes, *the* lots' distribution may be confounded, and their possession may pass over to others."

36:5 *respondit Moses filiis Israhel et Domino praecipiente ait recte tribus filiorum Ioseph locuta est*

Moses answered Israel's children and, *the* Lord commanding, said, "Joseph's children's tribe has spoken rightly.

36:6 *et haec lex super filiabus Salphaad a Domino promulgata est nubant quibus volunt tantum ut suae tribus hominibus*

"And this law is promulgated from *the* Lord concerning Salphaad's daughters. They may marry whomever they want, only that *they* be from their tribe's men.

36:7 *ne commisceatur possessio filiorum Israhel de tribu in tribum omnes enim viri ducent uxores de tribu et cognatione sua*

"Let Israel's children's possession not be mixed together from tribe to tribe, for men will take wives from their tribe and clan.

36:8 *et cunctae feminae maritos de eadem tribu accipient ut hereditas permaneat in familiis*

"And all females will accept husbands from *the* same tribe, so *the* inheritance may remain in families.

36:9 *nec sibi misceantur tribus sed ita maneant*

"Let *the* tribes not be mixed among themselves, yet let them remain so,

36:10 *ut a Domino separatae sunt feceruntque filiae Salphaad ut fuerat imperatum*

"as they were set apart to *the* Lord."

And Salphaad's daughters did as was commanded.

36:11 *et nupserunt Maala et Thersa et Egla et Melcha et Noa filiis patrui sui*

And Maala, and Thersa, and Egla, and Melcha, and Noa were married among their uncles' sons,

36:12 *de familia Manasse qui fuit filius Ioseph et possessio quae illis fuerat adtributa mansit in tribu et familia patris earum*

from Manasseh's family, who was Joseph's son. And *the* possession that was distributed to them remained in *the* tribe and family of their father.

36:13 *haec sunt mandata atque iudicia quae praecepit Dominus per manum Mosi ad filios Israhel in campestribus Moab super Iordanem contra Hiericho*

These are *the* mandates and judgments that *the* Lord commanded through Moses' hand to Israel's children, in Moab's plains on *the* Jordan, across from Jericho.

Deuteronomy

Moses Addresses the People

Deuteronomy 1:1 *haec sunt verba quae locutus est Moses ad omnem Israhel trans Iordanem in solitudine campestri contra mare Rubrum inter Pharan et Thophel et Laban et Aseroth ubi auri est plurimum*

These are *the* words which Moses spoke to all Israel, across *the* Jordan in *the* desert flat-land, against *the* Red Sea, between Pharan and Thophel and Laban and Aseroth, where gold is plentiful,

1:2 *undecim diebus de Horeb per viam montis Seir usque Cadesbarne*

eleven days from Horeb by way of Mount Seir, even to Kadesh-Barnea.

1:3 *quadragesimo anno undecimo mense prima die mensis locutus est Moses ad filios Israhel omnia quae praeceperat illi Dominus ut diceret eis*

The fortieth year, eleventh month, first day of *the* month, Moses spoke to Israel's children all that *the* Lord had commanded in advance, so he could tell them –

1:4 *postquam percussit Seon regem Amorreorum qui habitavit in Esebon et Og regem Basan qui mansit in Aseroth et in Edrai*

after He struck down Sihon, *the* Amorites' king, who lived in Heshbon, and Og, Bashan's king, who stayed in Aseroth and in Edrai.

1:5 *trans Iordanem in terra Moab coepitque Moses explanare legem et dicere*

And across *the* Jordan, in Moab's land, Moses began to explain *the* law. And he said,

1:6 *Dominus Deus noster locutus est ad nos in Horeb dicens sufficit vobis quod in hoc monte mansistis*

The Lord our God spoke to us in Horeb, saying, "What you've spent on this mountain is enough for you.

1:7 *revertimini et venite ad montem Amorreorum et ad cetera quae ei proxima sunt campestria atque montana et humiliora loca contra meridiem et iuxta litus maris terram Chananeorum et Libani usque ad flumen magnum Eufraten*

"Turn back and come into *the* Amorites' mountains and to *the* others that are close to them – fields and mountains and low places on *the* south, and along *the* seashore – *the* Canaanites' land and Lebanon, even to *the* great river Euphrates.

God Commands

1:8 *en inquit tradidi vobis ingredimini et possidete eam super qua iuravit Dominus patribus vestris Abraham et Isaac et Iacob ut daret*

illam eis et semini eorum post eos

"Look," *He* said, "I have given it to you. Go in and take it, over which *the* Lord of your fathers' Abraham and Isaac and Jacob has sworn, that He will give it to them and to their seed after them."

The People Choose Leaders

1:9 *dixique vobis illo in tempore*

And I said to them at that time,

1:10 *non possum solus sustinere vos quia Dominus Deus vester multiplicavit vos et estis hodie sicut stellae caeli plurimae*

"I can't support you alone, because *the* Lord your God has multiplied you. And you today are like *the* sky's many stars.

1:11 *Dominus Deus patrum vestrorum addat ad hunc numerum multa milia et benedicat vobis sicut locutus est*

"May *the* Lord, God of your fathers, add to this number many thousands, and may He bless you, as He said!

1:12 *non valeo solus vestra negotia sustinere et pondus ac iurgia*

"I am not able to bear your business, and weight, and arguments alone.

1:13 *date e vobis viros sapientes et*

gnaros et quorum conversatio sit probata in tribubus vestris ut ponam eos vobis principes

"Give from among yourselves wise, experienced men, whose conversation is approved among your tribes, so you can appoint them as leaders for yourselves."

1:14 *tunc respondistis mihi bona res est quam vis facere*

Then you responded to me, "*The* thing which you want to do is good."

1:15 *tulique de tribubus vestris viros sapientes et nobiles et constitui eos principes tribunos et centuriones et quinquagenarios ac decanos qui docerent vos singula*

And I took wise and noble men from among your tribes. And I appointed them leaders of courts, and commanders of *a* hundred, and commanders of fifty, and of ten, who can teach you individually.

1:16 *praecepique eis dicens audite illos et quod iustum est iudicate sive civis sit ille sive peregrinus*

I commanded them in advance, saying, "Listen to them, and judge what is fair, whether it be *a* citizen or *a* foreigner!

1:17 *nulla erit distantia personarum ita parvum audietis ut magnum nec* *accipietis cuiusquam personam quia Dei iudicium est quod si difficile vobis aliquid visum fuerit referte ad me et ego audiam*

"There will be no distance between persons. You will listen alike to small and great, nor will you accept whoever's person, because judgment is God's. If something should seem difficult to you, refer it to me and I will hear."

1:18 *praecepique omnia quae facere deberetis*

And I have taught all that you must do.

Israel Doubts the Lord

1:19 *profecti autem de Horeb transivimus per heremum terribilem et maximam quam vidistis per viam montis Amorrei sicut praeceperat Dominus Deus noster nobis cumque venissemus in Cadesbarne*

But setting out from Horeb, we crossed through terrible and extreme desert, which you saw on *the* way to *the* Amorites' mountains, as *the* Lord our God had commanded us. And once we had come to Kadesh Barnea,

1:20 *dixi vobis venistis ad montem Amorrei quem Dominus Deus noster daturus est nobis*

I said to you, "Go to *the* Amorites' mountain, which *the* Lord our God will give us!

1:21 *vide terram quam Dominus Deus tuus dat tibi ascende et posside eam sicut locutus est Dominus Deus patribus tuis noli metuere nec quicquam paveas*

"Look at *the* land which *the* Lord your God is giving you! Go up and possess it, as *the* Lord, God of your fathers, has said! Do not be afraid or terrified in *the* least!"

1:22 *et accessistis ad me omnes atque dixistis mittamus viros qui considerent terram et renuntient per quod iter debeamus ascendere et ad quas pergere civitates*

And all of you came to me and said, "Send men who can look over *the* land. And they can tell by which road we ought to go up, and which cities to go on to."

1:23 *cumque mihi sermo placuisset misi e vobis duodecim viros singulos de tribubus suis*

And when *the* word seemed pleasing to me, I sent twelve men from you, one from each of *the* tribes.

1:24 *qui cum perrexissent et ascendissent in montana venerunt usque ad vallem Botri et considerata terra*

who, when they had gone through

and climbed up into *the* mountains, they came even to Botrus valley, and looked over *the* land.

1:25 *sumentes de fructibus eius ut ostenderent ubertatem adtulerunt ad nos atque dixerunt bona est terra quam Dominus Deus noster daturus est nobis*

Taking some of its fruits so they could show its bounty, they brought them to us and said, "*The* land which *the* Lord our God will give us is good."

1:26 *et noluistis ascendere sed increduli ad sermonem Domini Dei nostri*

And you didn't want to go up, but disbelieved *the* Lord our God's word.

1:27 *murmurati estis in tabernaculis vestris atque dixistis odit nos Dominus et idcirco eduxit nos de terra Aegypti ut traderet in manu Amorrei atque deleret*

You griped in your tents, and you said, "*The* Lord hates us, and led us out of Egypt's land for this reason – so He could give us into *the* Amorites' hands and annihilate *us*."

1:28 *quo ascendemus nuntii terruerunt cor nostrum dicentes maxima multitudo est et nobis in statura procerior urbes magnae et ad*

caelum usque munitae filios Enacim vidimus ibi

"Where should we go? *The* messengers have terrified our heart, saying, '*There* is *a* great multitude, and larger than us in stature. *There are* great cities, and their fortifications *stretch* even up to the sky. We saw *the* Enacim's children there."

1:29 *et dixi vobis nolite metuere nec timeatis eos*

And I said to you, "Don't be afraid or terrified of them!

1:30 *Dominus Deus qui ductor est vester pro vobis ipse pugnabit sicut fecit in Aegypto videntibus cunctis*

"*The* Lord God, who is your leader, He will fight for you as He did in Egypt, which all saw.

1:31 *et in solitudine ipse vidisti portavit te Dominus Deus tuus ut solet homo gestare parvulum filium suum in omni via per quam ambulasti donec veniretis ad locum istum*

"And you saw that *the* Lord your God carried you in *the* desert, as *a* man carries his small child, in all *the* ways down which you walked, until you came to this place.

1:32 *et nec sic quidem credidistis*

Domino Deo vestro

"Yet even so, haven't you believed *the* Lord your God –

1:33 *qui praecessit vos in via et metatus est locum in quo tentoria figere deberetis nocte ostendens vobis iter per ignem et die per columnam nubis*

"who went before you on *the* way, and marked out *the* place where you ought to stake your tents – by night showing you *the* way through fire, and by day through *a* column of cloud?"

1:34 *cumque audisset Dominus vocem sermonum vestrorum iratus iuravit et ait*

And when *the* Lord heard your words' voice, *He was* angry. He swore and said,

1:35 *non videbit quispiam de hominibus generationis huius pessimae terram bonam quam sub iuramento pollicitus sum patribus vestris*

"Not one of *the* men of this dismal generation will see *the* good land I promised under oath to their fathers,

1:36 *praeter Chaleb filium Iepphonne ipse enim videbit eam et ipsi dabo terram quam calcavit et filiis eius quia secutus est Dominum*

"except Caleb, Iepphone's son. For he will see it, and I will give him and his children *the* land which he walked on, because He has followed *the* Lord."

The Lord Judges Moses
1:37 *nec miranda indignatio in populum cum mihi quoque iratus Dominus propter vos dixerit nec tu ingredieris illuc*

Not wondering *about* indignation with *the* people, *the* Lord also *was* angry with me because of you. He said, "Nor will you go in there.

1:38 *sed Iosue filius Nun minister tuus ipse intrabit pro te hunc exhortare et robora et ipse terram sorte dividat Israheli*

"But Joshua, Nun's son, your minister, he will go in, in your place. So encourage and strengthen him, and he will divide *the* land for Israel!'

1:39 *parvuli vestri de quibus dixistis quod captivi ducerentur et filii qui hodie boni ac mali ignorant distantiam ipsi ingredientur et ipsis dabo terram et possidebunt eam*

"Your little ones, about whom you said that they would be led away captive, and *the* children who today do not know *the* distance between good and harm – they will go in. And I will give them *the* land, and they will possess it.

1:40 *vos autem revertimini et abite in solitudinem per viam maris Rubri*

"But you, turn around and go back into *the* wasteland, by way of *the* Red Sea!"

1:41 *et respondistis mihi peccavimus Domino ascendemus atque pugnabimus sicut praecepit Dominus Deus noster cumque instructi armis pergeretis in montem*

Yet you said to me, "We have sinned against *the* Lord. We will climb up and fight, like *the* Lord our God commanded."
And when arms were ready, you went up into *the* mountain.

1:42 *ait mihi Dominus dic ad eos nolite ascendere neque pugnetis non enim sum vobiscum ne cadatis coram inimicis vestris*

The Lord said to me, "Speak to them! Do not go up or fight, for I am not with you, or you may fall before your enemies!"

1:43 *locutus sum et non audistis sed adversantes imperio Domini et tumentes superbia ascendistis in montem*

I spoke, and you did not hear, but opposing *the* Lord's command and swollen with pride, you climbed up onto *the* mountain.

1:44 *itaque egressus Amorreus qui habitabat in montibus et obviam veniens persecutus est vos sicut solent apes persequi et cecidit de Seir usque Horma*

And so, *the* Amorite who lived in *the* land came out into *the* mountains. And coming on *the* way, he followed you the way bees follow. And he chopped *you* down, from Seir even to Horma.

1:45 *cumque reversi ploraretis coram Domino non audivit vos nec voci vestrae voluit adquiescere*

And when you came back, you cried before *the* Lord, but He did not hear you, nor did He care to assent to your voice.

1:46 *sedistis ergo in Cadesbarne multo tempore*

Therefore you sat in Kadesh Barnea *a* long time.

Wandering in the Desert

Deuteronomy 2:1 *profectique inde venimus in solitudinem quae ducit ad mare Rubrum sicut mihi dixerat Dominus et circumivimus montem Seir longo tempore*

And going forth from there, we came into *the* wasteland that leads to *the* Red Sea, as *the* Lord had said to me. And we wandered around Mount Seir *a* long time.

Spare Esau

2:2 *dixitque Dominus ad me*

And *the* Lord said to me,

2:3 *sufficit vobis circumire montem istum ite contra aquilonem*

"It is enough for you wandering around this mountain. Go to *the* north!

2:4 *et populo praecipe dicens transibitis per terminos fratrum vestrorum filiorum Esau qui habitant in Seir et timebunt vos*

"And command *the* people, saying, You will go around *the* borders of your brother Esau's children, who live in Seir, and they will fear you.

2:5 *videte ergo diligenter ne moveamini contra eos neque enim dabo vobis de terra eorum quantum potest unius pedis calcare vestigium quia in possessionem Esau dedi*

montem Seir

"So watch carefully that you do not move against them, for I will not give you from their land even as much as *the* sole of one foot can step on, because I gave Mount Seir to Esau as *a* possession.

2:6 *cibos emetis ab eis pecunia et comedetis aquam emptam haurietis et bibetis*

"You will buy food from them with money, and eat. You will draw up bought water, and drink."

2:7 *Dominus Deus tuus benedixit tibi in omni opere manuum tuarum novit iter tuum quomodo transieris solitudinem hanc magnam per quadraginta annos habitans tecum Dominus Deus tuus et nihil tibi defuit*

The Lord your God has blessed you in every work of your hands. He has known your way, how you have passed for forty years through this great wasteland, *the* Lord your God living with you. And nothing has been lacking to you.

Spare Moab

2:8 *cumque transissemus fratres nostros filios Esau qui habitabant in Seir per viam campestrem de Helath et de Asiongaber venimus ad iter quod ducit in desertum Moab*

And when we had passed our brothers, Esau's children, who lived in Seir, we came by *the* plain's road from Helath and from Asiongaber to *the* way which leads into Moab's desert.

2:9 *dixitque Dominus ad me non pugnes contra Moabitas nec ineas adversum eos proelium non enim dabo tibi quicquam de terra eorum quia filiis Loth tradidi Ar in possessionem*

And *the* Lord said to me, "Do not fight against *the* Moabites, nor enter battle against them. For I will not give you any of their land, because I gave Ar to Lot's children as *a* possession."

2:10 *Emim primi fuerunt habitatores eius populus magnus et validus et tam excelsus ut de Enacim stirpe*

The Emim were its first inhabitants, *a* great and mighty people and very tall, like *the* Enacim's stock.

2:11 *quasi gigantes crederentur et essent similes filiorum Enacim denique Moabitae appellant eos Emim*

They were considered like giants, and were like *the* Enacim's children. Indeed, *the* Moabites call them Emim.

2:12 *in Seir autem prius habitaverunt Horim quibus expulsis atque deletis habitaverunt filii Esau sicut fecit Israhel in terra possessionis suae quam dedit ei Dominus*

But *the* Horites lived in Seir first, who *were* expelled and destroyed. *Then,* Esau's children lived there, like Israel did in *the* land of his possession, which *the* Lord gave him.

2:13 *surgentes ergo ut transiremus torrentem Zared venimus ad eum*

Getting up, then, so we could cross *the* brook of Zared, we came to it.

2:14 *tempus autem quo ambulavimus de Cadesbarne usque ad transitum torrentis Zared triginta octo annorum fuit donec consumeretur omnis generatio hominum bellatorum de castris sicut iuraverat Dominus*

But *the* time which we walked around from Kadesh Barnea even to *the* ford of the brook of Zared was thirty-eight years, until *the* whole generation of men of war from *the* camps was consumed, as *the* Lord had sworn –

2:15 *cuius manus fuit adversum eos ut interirent de castrorum medio*

whose hand was against them, so they could die out from *the* camps' midst.

Spare Ammon

2:16 *postquam autem universi ceciderunt pugnatores*

But after all *the* warriors had fallen,

2:17 *locutus est Dominus ad me dicens*

the Lord spoke to me, saying,

2:18 *tu transibis hodie terminos Moab urbem nomine Ar*

"You will cross Moab's borders today, *a* city named Ar.

2:19 *et accedens in vicina filiorum Ammon cave ne pugnes contra eos nec movearis ad proelium non enim dabo tibi de terra filiorum Ammon quia filiis Loth dedi eam in possessionem*

"And, coming into *the* neighborhood of Ammon's children, take care that you not fight against them, nor move to battle. For I will not give you any of *the* land of Ammon's children, because I gave it to Lot's children as *a* possession."

2:20 *terra gigantum reputata est et in ipsa olim habitaverunt gigantes quos Ammanitae vocant Zomzommim*

It was considered *a* land of giants, and at one time giants lived in it,

whom *the* Ammonites called Zomzommim –

2:21 *populus magnus et multus et procerae longitudinis sicut Enacim quos delevit Dominus a facie eorum et fecit illos habitare pro eis*

a great and numerous people, and of great height like *the* Enacim, whom *the* Lord destroyed before their face, and made them live *there* in their place,

2:22 *sicut fecerat filiis Esau qui habitant in Seir delens Horreos et terram eorum illis tradens quam possident usque in praesens*

as He had done for Esau's children, who live in Seir, destroying *the* Horites and giving their land to them, who possess it even to *the* present.

2:23 *Eveos quoque qui habitabant in Aserim usque Gazam Cappadoces expulerunt qui egressi de Cappadocia deleverunt eos et habitaverunt pro illis*

The Cappadocians, who had come from Cappadocia, likewise expelled *the* Hevites, who lived in Aserim even to Gaza. They destroyed them and lived in their place.

The Conquest Begins

2:24 *surgite et transite torrentem Arnon ecce tradidi in manu tua Seon regem Esebon Amorreum et terram*

eius incipe possidere et committe
adversum eum proelium

"Go up and cross *the* brook at
Arnon. Look, I have given Sihon,
the Amorites' king in Heshbon, into
your hand. Begin to take possession
of his land, and commit to battle
against him.

2:25 *hodie incipiam mittere*
terrorem atque formidinem tuam in
populos qui habitant sub omni caelo
ut audito nomine tuo paveant et in
morem parturientium contremescant
et dolore teneantur

"Today I will begin to send your
terror and even fear into *the* peoples
who live under all *the* sky, that they
may tremble at *the* hearing of your
name, and they may shake like one
giving birth, and possess sorrow."

2:26 *misi ergo nuntios de solitudine*
Cademoth ad Seon regem Esebon
verbis pacificis dicens

So, I sent messengers from *the*
wasteland at Cademoth to Sihon,
Heshbon's king, speaking peaceful
words.

2:27 *transibimus per terram tuam*
publica gradiemur via non
declinabimus neque ad dextram
neque ad sinistram

"We will pass openly through your
land. We will go by *the* way. We

will not turn aside either to *the* right
or to *the* left.

2:28 *alimenta pretio vende nobis ut*
vescamur aquam pecunia tribue et
sic bibemus tantum est ut nobis
concedas transitum

"Sell us food at *a* price, so we can
eat. Assign water for money, and so
we will drink. It only is that you may
allow us passage,

2:29 *sicut fecerunt filii Esau qui*
habitant in Seir et Moabitae qui
morantur in Ar donec veniamus ad
Iordanem et transeamus in terram
quam Dominus Deus noster daturus
est nobis

"like Esau's children did, who live in
Seir, and *the* Moabites, who dwell in
Ar, until we come to *the* Jordan and
cross through into *the* land which *the*
Lord our God will give us."

Sihon Opposes Israel
2:30 *noluitque Seon rex Esebon*
dare nobis transitum quia
induraverat Dominus Deus tuus
spiritum eius et obfirmaverat cor
illius ut traderetur in manus tuas
sicut nunc vides

Yet Sihon, Heshbon's king, didn't
want to give us passage, because *the*
Lord your God had hardened his
spirit and locked his heart, so he
could be handed over into your
hands, as you now see.

2:31 *dixitque Dominus ad me ecce coepi tradere tibi Seon et terram eius incipe possidere eam*

And *the* Lord said to me, "Look, I have begun to give Sihon and his land to you. Start to possess it!"

2:32 *egressusque est Seon obviam nobis cum omni populo suo ad proelium in Iesa*

And Sihon came out on *the* road to battle against us in Iesa, with all his people.

2:33 *et tradidit eum Dominus Deus noster nobis percussimusque eum cum filiis et omni populo suo.*

And *the* Lord our God handed him over, and we struck him down with *his* sons and all his people.

2:34 *cunctasque urbes in tempore illo cepimus interfectis habitatoribus earum viris ac mulieribus et parvulis non reliquimus in eis quicquam*

And we captured all *his* cities at that time, killing their inhabitants – men and women and little ones. We did not leave anyone among them,

2:35 *absque iumentis quae in partem venere praedantium et spoliis urbium quas cepimus*

apart from cattle which came as part of *the* plunder, and spoils from those

cities which we captured.

2:36 *ab Aroer quae est super ripam torrentis Arnon oppido quod in valle situm est usque Galaad non fuit vicus et civitas quae nostras effugeret manus omnes tradidit Dominus Deus noster nobis*

From Aroer, which is on *the* bank of *the* brook of Arnon, *a* town which is located in *the* valley, even to Galaad. *There* was not *a* town or city which escaped from our hands. *The* Lord our God gave all of them over to us –

2:37 *absque terra filiorum Ammon ad quam non accessimus et cunctis quae adiacent torrenti Ieboc et urbibus montanis universisque locis a quibus nos prohibuit Dominus Deus noster*

except for Ammon's children's land, to which we did not go up, and all that was by Jabbok brook, and *the* mountain cities, and all *the* places which the Lord our God prohibited to us.

Og Opposes Israel

Deuteronomy 3:1 *itaque conversi ascendimus per iter Basan egressusque est Og rex Basan in occursum nobis cum populo suo ad bellandum in Edrai*

Then, turning back, we went up by *the* road to Bashan. And Og, Bashan's king, came out to meet us with his people, to make war in Edrai.

3:2 *dixitque Dominus ad me ne timeas eum quia in manu tua traditus est cum omni populo ac terra sua faciesque ei sicut fecisti Seon regi Amorreorum qui habitavit in Esebon*

And *the* Lord said to me, "Do not fear him, because he is given into your hand, with all his people and land. And you will do to him what you did to Sihon, *the* Amorites' king, who lived in Heshbon."

3:3 *tradidit ergo Dominus Deus noster in manibus nostris etiam Og regem Basan et universum populum eius percussimusque eos usque ad internicionem*

Therefore, *the* Lord our God gave into our hands even Og, Bashan's king, and all his people. And we struck them down even to annihilation,

3:4 *vastantes cunctas civitates illius uno tempore non fuit oppidum quod*

nos effugeret sexaginta urbes omnem regionem Argob regni Og in Basan

laying waste all those cities at one time. *There* was no town which escaped us, sixty cities of all *the* Argob region, Og's kingdom in Bashan.

3:5 *cunctae urbes erant munitae muris altissimis portisque et vectibus absque oppidis innumeris quae non habebant muros*

All *the* cities were fortified with high walls and gates and bars, apart from innumerable towns which had no walls.

3:6 *et delevimus eos sicut feceramus Seon regi Esebon disperdentes omnem civitatem virosque ac mulieres et parvulos*

And we destroyed them like we did to Sihon, Heshbon's king, massacring every town – men and women and little ones.

3:7 *iumenta autem et spolia urbium diripuimus*

But *the* cattle and plunder we kept apart.

Moses Divides
the Captured Lands

3:8 *tulimusque illo in tempore terram de manu duorum regum Amorreorum qui erant trans*

Iordanem a torrente Arnon usque ad montem Hermon

And we took that land at that time, from *the* hands of *the* two Amorite kings who were across *the* Jordan, from *the* brook of Arnon even to Mount Hermon,

3:9 *quem Sidonii Sarion vocant et Amorrei Sanir*

which *the* Sidonians called Sarion, and *the* Amorites Sanir –

3:10 *omnes civitates quae sitae sunt in planitie et universam terram Galaad et Basan usque Selcha et Edrai civitates regni Og in Basan*

all *the* cities which were located in *the* plain, and all *the* land of Galaad and Bashan, even Selcha and Edrai, cities of Og's kingdom in Bashan.

3:11 *solus quippe Og rex Basan restiterat de stirpe gigantum monstratur lectus eius ferreus qui est in Rabbath filiorum Ammon novem cubitos habens longitudinis et quattuor latitudinis ad mensuram cubiti virilis manus*

Only Og, Bashan's king, had remained from *the* stock of giants. His iron bed is displayed, which is in Rabbath of Ammon's children, having nine cubits length and four of width, at *the* measure of *a* man's hand.

3:12 *terramque possedimus in tempore illo ab Aroer quae est super ripam torrentis Arnon usque ad mediam partem montis Galaad et civitates illius dedi Ruben et Gad*

And we possessed *the* land at that time, from Aroer, which is on *the* bank of *the* brook of Arnon, even to half part Mount Galaad. And I gave those cities to Reuben and Gad.

3:13 *reliquam autem partem Galaad et omnem Basan regni Og tradidi mediae tribui Manasse omnem regionem Argob cuncta Basan vocatur terra gigantum*

But *the* remaining part of Galaad and all of Bashan, Og's kingdom, I handed to half of Manasseh's tribe – all *the* Argob region, together with Bashan, called *the* land of giants.

3:14 *Iair filius Manasse possedit omnem regionem Argob usque ad terminos Gesuri et Machathi vocavitque ex nomine suo Basan Avothiair id est villas Iair usque in praesentem diem*

Jair, Manasseh's son, possessed all *the* Argob region, even to *the* borders of Gesuri and Machathi. And he called Bashan by his name, Avoth-Jair, which is "Jair's Estate," even to *the* present day.

3:15 *Machir quoque dedi Galaad*

I likewise gave Galaad to Machir.

3:16 *et tribubus Ruben et Gad dedi terram Galaad usque ad torrentem Arnon medium torrentis et finium usque ad torrentem Ieboc qui est terminus filiorum Ammon*

And I gave *the* land of Galaad to *the* tribes of Reuben and Gad, even to *the* brook of Arnon, half *the* flow, and from *the* border even to *the* Jabbok brook, which is *the* border of Ammon's children –

3:17 *et planitiem solitudinis atque Iordanem et terminos Chenereth usque ad mare Deserti quod est Salsissimum ad radices montis Phasga contra orientem*

and *the* desert plateau to *the* Jordan, and Chenereth's borders, even to *the* Desert sea, which is *the* Salt *Sea*, to *the* roots of Mount Pisgah on *the* east.

Don't Abandon Your Brothers
3:18 *praecepique vobis in tempore illo dicens Dominus Deus vester dat vobis terram hanc in hereditatem expediti praecedite fratres vestros filios Israhel omnes viri robusti*

And I commanded you at that time, saying, "*The* Lord your God gives you this land as *an* inheritance. Go ready before your brothers, Israel's children, all strong men,

3:19 *absque uxoribus et parvulis ac iumentis novi enim quod plura habeatis pecora et in urbibus remanere debebunt quas tradidi vobis*

apart from wives and little ones and cattle! For I knew that you have many herds. And they must stay behind in the cities which I gave you,

3:20 *donec requiem tribuat Dominus fratribus vestris sicut vobis tribuit et possideant etiam ipsi terram quam daturus est eis trans Iordanem tunc revertetur unusquisque in possessionem suam quam dedi vobis*

until *the* Lord gives rest to your brothers, like He gave to you, and they possess even *the* land which He will give them across *the* Jordan. Then each one will turn back into his possession, which I gave you.

3:21 *Iosue quoque in tempore illo praecepi dicens oculi tui viderunt quae fecit Dominus Deus vester duobus his regibus sic faciet omnibus regnis ad quae transiturus es*

I commanded Joshua likewise at that time, saying, "Your eyes have seen what *the* Lord your God did to those two kings. So He will do to all *the* kingdoms to which you will cross over.

Moses Asks to Cross the Jordan

3:22 *ne timeas eos Dominus enim Deus vester pugnabit pro vobis*

"Do not fear them, because *the* Lord your God will fight for you!"

3:23 *precatusque sum Dominum in tempore illo dicens*

And I prayed to *the* Lord at that time, saying,

3:24 *Domine Deus tu coepisti ostendere servo tuo magnitudinem tuam manumque fortissimam neque enim est alius Deus vel in caelo vel in terra qui possit facere opera tua et conparari fortitudini tuae*

"Lord God, You have begun to show Your greatness and Your mighty hand to Your slave. For neither is there another God, either in sky or in land, who can do Your works, or who compares to Your strengths.

3:25 *transibo igitur et videbo terram hanc optimam trans Iordanem et montem istum egregium et Libanum*

"Therefore, I will cross over and see this choice land across *the* Jordan, and this exceptional mountain, and Lebanon."

3:26 *iratusque est Dominus mihi propter vos nec exaudivit me sed dixit mihi sufficit tibi nequaquam*

ultra loquaris de hac re ad me

And *the* Lord was angry with me because of you, nor did He hear me. But He said to me, "*This* is enough for you. Don't speak to Me further about this thing.

3:27 *ascende cacumen Phasgae et oculos tuos circumfer ad occidentem et aquilonem austrumque et orientem et aspice nec enim transibis Iordanem istum*

"Climb up Pisgah's peak, and cast your eyes to *the* west and north and south and east, and look, for you will not cross over this Jordan.

3:28 *praecipe Iosue et corrobora eum atque conforta quia ipse praecedet populum istum et dividet eis terram quam visurus es*

"Command Joshua and confirm him and strengthen, because he will lead this people. And he will divide for them *the* land which you will see."

3:29 *mansimusque in valle contra fanum Phogor*

And we stayed in *the* valley, alongside Phogor's temple.

Hear the Commandments!

Deuteronomy 4:1 *et nunc Israhel audi praecepta et iudicia quae ego doceo te ut faciens ea vivas et ingrediens possideas terram quam Dominus Deus patrum vestrorum daturus est vobis*

And now, Israel, hear *the* commandments and judgments which I am teaching you, that, doing them, you may live, and, going in, you may possess *the* land which *the* Lord, God of your fathers, will give you.

4:2 *non addetis ad verbum quod vobis loquor neque auferetis ex eo custodite mandata Domini Dei vestri quae ego praecipio vobis*

You will not add to *the* word which I am speaking to you, or take away from it. Keep *the* Lord your God's commandments, which I am teaching you.

Your Eyes Have Seen

4:3 *oculi vestri viderunt omnia quae fecit Dominus contra Beelphegor quomodo contriverit omnes cultores eius de medio vestri*

Your eyes have seen all that *the* Lord did against Beelphegor, how He destroyed all its worshipers from among you.

4:4 *vos autem qui adheretis Domino Deo vestro vivitis universi usque in praesentem diem*

But you who stayed close to *the* Lord your God, all *of you* are living even to *the* present day.

4:5 *scitis quod docuerim vos praecepta atque iustitias sicut mandavit mihi Dominus Deus meus sic facietis ea in terra quam possessuri estis*

You know that I have taught you commandments and justices, as *the* Lord my God commanded me. So you will do them in *the* land which you will possess.

4:6 *et observabitis et implebitis opere haec est enim vestra sapientia et intellectus coram populis ut audientes universa praecepta haec dicant en populus sapiens et intellegens gens magna*

And you will observe and fulfill them in practice, for this is your wisdom and understanding before peoples, that, hearing all these precepts, they may say among people, "Look, *a* wise and understanding people, *a* great nation!"

4:7 *nec est alia natio tam grandis quae habeat deos adpropinquantes sibi sicut Dominus Deus noster adest cunctis obsecrationibus nostris*

Nor is another nation so great, which has gods close to itself, like *the* Lord our God is near to all our acts of prayer.

4:8 *quae est enim alia gens sic inclita ut habeat caerimonias iustaque iudicia et universam legem quam ego proponam hodie ante oculos vestros*

For what is another nation so celebrated, that it has ceremonies, rights, judgments, and *the* whole law, which I today set forth before your eyes?

Moses Recounts
God's Appearance at Sinai

4:9 *custodi igitur temet ipsum et animam tuam sollicite ne obliviscaris verborum quae viderunt oculi tui et ne excedant de corde tuo cunctis diebus vitae tuae docebis ea filios ac nepotes tuos*

Therefore, keep yourselves and your souls with anxious care! Do not forget *the* words which your eyes have seen, nor let them fade away from your hearts all *the* days of your life! Teach them to your children and grandchildren –

4:10 *diem in quo stetisti coram Domino Deo tuo in Horeb quando Dominus locutus est mihi dicens congrega ad me populum ut audiat sermones meos et discat timere me omni tempore quo vivit in terra doceantque filios suos*

the day in which you stood before *the* Lord your God on Horeb, when *the* Lord spoke to me, saying, "Gather *the* people to Me, that they may hear My words and learn to fear Me – all *the* time which he lives in *the* land, and teaching his children."

4:11 *et accessistis ad radices montis qui ardebat usque ad caelum erantque in eo tenebrae nubes et caligo*

And you came to *the* mountain's bases, which burned even to *the* sky. And shadows, clouds, and gloom were in it.

4:12 *locutusque est Dominus ad vos de medio ignis vocem verborum eius audistis et formam penitus non vidistis*

And *the* Lord spoke to you from *the* middle of *the* fire. You heard *the* voice of His words, yet you did not see *a* figure within.

4:13 *et ostendit vobis pactum suum quod praecepit ut faceretis et decem verba quae scripsit in duabus tabulis lapideis*

And He showed you His pact, which He commanded that you do, and *the* ten words which He wrote in two stone tables.

4:14 *mihique mandavit in illo tempore ut docerem vos caerimonias et iudicia quae facere deberetis in terra quam possessuri estis*

And He commanded me at that time, that I teach you ceremonies and judgments which you must do in *the* land which you will possess.

Guard Your Souls!

4:15 *custodite igitur sollicite animas vestras non vidistis aliquam similitudinem in die qua locutus est Dominus vobis in Horeb de medio ignis*

Guard your souls, then, with anxious care. You did not see any likeness on *the* day which *the* Lord spoke to you on Horeb from *the* midst of fire –

4:16 *ne forte decepti faciatis vobis sculptam similitudinem aut imaginem masculi vel feminae*

unless, perhaps, deceived, you will make yourselves *a* sculpted likeness or image, masculine or feminine –

4:17 *similitudinem omnium iumentorum quae sunt super terram vel avium sub caelo volantium*

a likeness of all cattle which are on *the* land, or birds flying beneath *the* sky –

4:18 *atque reptilium quae moventur in terra sive piscium qui sub terra morantur in aquis*

or reptiles which move on *the* land, or fish which live in waters under *the* land.

4:19 *ne forte oculis elevatis ad caelum videas solem et lunam et omnia astra caeli et errore deceptus adores ea et colas quae creavit Dominus Deus tuus in ministerium cunctis gentibus quae sub caelo sunt*

Unless, perhaps, you lift your eye to *the* sky, *and* you may see sun and moon and all *the* sky's stars and, deceived by error, you adore them, and worship what *the* Lord your God has created in ministry to all nations which are under *the* sky.

4:20 *vos autem tulit Dominus et eduxit de fornace ferrea Aegypti ut haberet populum hereditarium sicut est in praesenti die*

But *the* Lord took you and led you out of *the* iron-smelting furnace, Egypt, that He might have *a* people of inheritance, as *it* is in *the* present day.

4:21 *iratusque est Dominus contra me propter sermones vestros et iuravit ut non transirem Iordanem nec ingrederer terram optimam quam daturus est vobis*

And *the* Lord was angry against me because of your words. And He swore that I would not cross Jordan, nor go into *the* choice land which He will give you.

4:22 *ecce morior in hac humo non transibo Iordanem vos transibitis et possidebitis terram egregiam*

Look, I am dying in this soil! I will not cross over Jordan. You will cross over and possess *this* exceptional land.

Don't Forget the Lord

4:23 *cave nequando obliviscaris pacti Domini Dei tui quod pepigit tecum et facias tibi sculptam similitudinem eorum quae fieri Dominus prohibuit*

Take care that you never forget *the* Lord your God's pact – which He agreed on with you – and you make yourselves those sculpted images which *the* Lord prohibited *you* to make –

4:24 *quia Dominus Deus tuus ignis consumens est Deus aemulator*

for *the* Lord your God is *a* consuming fire, *a* jealous God!

4:25 *si genueritis filios ac nepotes et morati fueritis in terra deceptique feceritis vobis aliquam similitudinem patrantes malum coram Domino Deo vestro ut eum ad iracundiam provocetis*

If you bear children or grandchildren and will live in *the* land, and, deceived, you make yourselves some sort of image, accomplishing harm

before *the* Lord your God, so that you provoke Him to anger,

4:26 *testes invoco hodie caelum et terram cito perituros vos esse de terra quam transito Iordane possessuri estis non habitabitis in ea longo tempore sed delebit vos Dominus*

I invoke today sky and land as witnesses. You will be destroyed quickly from *the* land you will possess across *the* Jordan. You will not live in it *a* long time, but *the* Lord will destroy you.

4:27 *atque disperget in omnes gentes et remanebitis pauci in nationibus ad quas vos ducturus est Dominus*

And He will scatter *you* among all nations, and you will remain few among *the* nations to which the Lord will lead you.

4:28 *ibique servietis diis qui hominum manu fabricati sunt ligno et lapidi qui non vident non audiunt non comedunt non odorantur*

And you will serve there gods of wood and stone, whom human hands have made – who cannot see or hear or eat or smell.

The Lord Will Not Forget You

4:29 *cumque quaesieris ibi Dominum Deum tuum invenies eum*

si tamen toto corde quaesieris et tota tribulatione animae tuae

Yet when you have sought *the* Lord your God there, you will find Him, if nevertheless you seek with all your heart and all your soul's tribulation.

4:30 *postquam te invenerint omnia quae praedicta sunt novissimo tempore reverteris ad Dominum Deum tuum et audies vocem eius*

After all that is predicted has found you, at *the* end time you will turn back to *the* Lord your God, and will hear His voice.

4:31 *quia Deus misericors Dominus Deus tuus est non dimittet te nec omnino delebit neque obliviscetur pacti in quo iuravit patribus tuis*

For *the* Lord your God is *a* merciful God. He will not let you go, or destroy *you* completely. Nor will He forget *the* pact which He swore to your fathers.

Sinai's Uniqueness

4:32 *interroga de diebus antiquis qui fuerunt ante te ex die quo creavit Deus hominem super terram a summo caeli usque ad summum eius si facta est aliquando huiuscemodi res aut umquam cognitum est*

Question from ancient days which were before you, from *the* day in which God created man on *the* land,

from *the* sky's summit even to its summit – if something like this has happened, or such *a* thing was known –

4:33 *ut audiret populus vocem Dei loquentis de medio ignis sicut tu audisti et vixisti*

that *a* people heard its God's voice speaking from fire's midst, like you have heard and seen –

4:34 *si fecit Deus ut ingrederetur et tolleret sibi gentem de medio nationum per temptationes signa atque portenta per pugnam et robustam manum extentumque brachium et horribiles visiones iuxta omnia quae fecit pro vobis Dominus Deus vester in Aegypto videntibus oculis tuis*

if God did *it*, that He went in and took out for Himself *a* nation from *the* midst of other nations, through trials, signs, and portents, through battle and *a* mighty hand and *a* stretched-out arm and terrifying visions, along with all *the* Lord your God has done for you in Egypt, which your eyes see –

4:35 *ut scires quoniam Dominus ipse est Deus et non est alius praeter unum*

that you may know that *the* Lord, He is God, and *there* is no other but One alone!

4:36 *de caelo te fecit audire vocem suam ut doceret te et in terra ostendit tibi ignem suum maximum et audisti verba illius de medio ignis*

From *the* sky, He caused you to hear His voice, so He could teach you. And He showed you His great fire in *the* land, and you heard His words from *the* fire's midst.

4:37 *quia dilexit patres tuos et elegit semen eorum post eos eduxitque te praecedens in virtute sua magna ex Aegypto*

For He delighted in your fathers, and chose their seed after them. And He led you out, going before *you* in His great strength from Egypt,

4:38 *ut deleret nationes maximas et fortiores te in introitu tuo et introduceret te daretque tibi terram earum in possessionem sicut cernis in praesenti die*

so He could destroy great nations and mightier than you by your coming in. And He might lead you in and give you their land as *a* possession, as you see in *the* present day.

4:39 *scito ergo hodie et cogitato in corde tuo quod Dominus ipse sit Deus in caelo sursum et in terra deorsum et non sit alius*

Know, therefore, today, and consider in your heart that *the* Lord, He is God in sky above and in land below, and there is no other.

4:40 *custodi praecepta eius atque mandata quae ego praecipio tibi ut bene sit tibi et filiis tuis post te et permaneas multo tempore super terram quam Dominus Deus tuus daturus est tibi*

Keep His precepts and commandments which I am commanding you, that it may be well with you and your children after you, and you may remain much time on *the* land which *the* Lord your God will give you.

Cities of Refuge

4:41 *tunc separavit Moses tres civitates trans Iordanem ad orientalem plagam*

Then Moses set apart three cities across *the* Jordan, to *the* eastern quarter,

4:42 *ut confugiat ad eas qui occiderit nolens proximum suum nec fuerit inimicus ante unum et alterum diem et ad harum aliquam urbium possit evadere*

so one who killed his neighbor unintentionally, nor was *an* enemy one or another day before, could flee to them, and in one of these cities might escape:

4:43 *Bosor in solitudine quae sita est in terra campestri de tribu Ruben et Ramoth in Galaad quae est in tribu Gad et Golam in Basan quae est in tribu Manasse*

Bosor, in *the* desert, which is located in *the* flat land of *the* tribe of Reuben; and Ramoth in Galaad, which is in *the* tribe of Gad; and Golam in Bashan, which is in *the* tribe of Manasseh.

The Law Set Forth

4:44 *ista est lex quam proposuit Moses coram filiis Israhel*

This is *the* law which Moses set forth before Israel's children.

4:45 *et haec testimonia et caerimoniae atque iudicia quae locutus est ad filios Israhel quando egressi sunt de Aegypto*

And these are *the* testimonies and ceremonies and judgments which he spoke to Israel's children, when they had come out of Egypt,

4:46 *trans Iordanem in valle contra fanum Phogor in terra Seon regis Amorrei qui habitavit in Esebon quem percussit Moses filii quoque Israhel egressi ex Aegypto*

across *the* Jordan, in *the* valley beside Phogor's temple, in *the* land of Sihon, *the* Amorite king, who lived in Heshbon, whom Moses struck down

and Israel's children as well, coming out of Egypt.

4:47 *possederunt terram eius et terram Og regis Basan duorum regum Amorreorum qui erant trans Iordanem ad solis ortum*

They possessed his land and Og, Bashan's king's land, two Amorite kings who were across *the* Jordan toward *the* rising sun –

4:48 *ab Aroer quae sita est super ripam torrentis Arnon usque ad montem Sion qui est et Hermon*

from Aroer, which is located on *the* bank of *the* brook of Arnon, even to Mount Sion, which is Hermon –

4:49 *omnem planitiem trans Iordanem ad orientalem plagam usque ad mare Solitudinis et usque ad radices montis Phasga*

all *the* plain across *the* Jordan to *the* eastern quarter, even to *the* sea of Solitude, and even to *the* roots of Mount Pisgah.

The Ten Commandments

Deuteronomy 5:1 *vocavitque Moses omnem Israhelem et dixit ad eum audi Israhel caerimonias atque iudicia quae ego loquor in auribus vestris hodie discite ea et opere conplete*

And Moses called all Israel and said to him, "Hear, Israel, *the* ceremonies and judgments which I am speaking in your ears today! Learn them and do them completely!"

5:2 *Dominus Deus noster pepigit nobiscum foedus in Horeb*

The Lord our God made *a* pact with us on Horeb.

5:3 *non cum patribus nostris iniit pactum sed nobiscum qui inpraesentiarum sumus et vivimus*

He did not make *the* pact with our fathers, but with us who are present here and living.

5:4 *facie ad faciem locutus est nobis in monte de medio ignis*

He spoke to us face to face on *the* mountain, from *the* middle of fire.

5:5 *ego sequester et medius fui inter Dominum et vos in tempore illo ut adnuntiarem vobis verba eius timuistis enim ignem et non ascendistis in montem et ait*

I was *the* go-between and mediator between *the* Lord and you at that time, so I could tell you His words – for you feared *the* fire and did not climb up *the* mountain. And He said,

5:6 *ego Dominus Deus tuus qui eduxi te de terra Aegypti de domo servitutis*

"I *am the* Lord your God, who led you out of Egypt's land, out of slavery's house.

I

5:7 *non habebis deos alienos in conspectu meo*

"You will not have alien gods in My sight.

II

5:8 *non facies tibi sculptile nec similitudinem omnium quae in caelo sunt desuper et quae in terra deorsum et quae versantur in aquis sub terra*

"You will not make yourself *a* sculpted image or likeness of all *the* things which are in sky above, and which are on land below, and which move around in waters below *the* land.

5:9 *non adorabis ea et non coles ego enim sum Dominus Deus tuus Deus aemulator reddens iniquitatem patrum super filios in tertiam et*

quartam generationem his qui oderunt me

"You will not adore them and will not worship, for I am *the* Lord your God, a jealous God, paying back *a* father's treachery over children to *the* third and fourth generation of those who hated Me –

5:10 *et faciens misericordiam in multa milia diligentibus me et custodientibus praecepta mea*

"and working mercy among many thousands delighting in Me, and keeping My commandments.

III
5:11 *non usurpabis nomen Domini Dei tui frustra quia non erit inpunitus qui super re vana nomen eius adsumpserit*

"Do not seize on *the* Lord your God's name without purpose, for he will not be unpunished who takes up His name over vain *things.*

IV
5:12 *observa diem sabbati ut sanctifices eum sicut praecepit tibi Dominus Deus tuus*

"Keep *the* Sabbath day, so you can make it holy, like *the* Lord your God commanded you.

5:13 *sex diebus operaberis et facies omnia opera tua*

"You will work six days and do all your business.

5:14 *septimus dies sabbati est id est requies Domini Dei tui non facies in eo quicquam operis tu et filius tuus et filia servus et ancilla et bos et asinus et omne iumentum tuum et peregrinus qui est intra portas tuas ut requiescat servus et ancilla tua sicut et tu*

"The seventh day – it is Sabbath. It is *the* Lord your God's rest. Do not do any business in it – you, or your son, or your daughter, slave, or slave woman, or ox, or ass, or all your cattle, or *the* stranger who is in your gates – so *a* slave can rest, and your slave woman, just like you.

5:15 *memento quod et ipse servieris in Aegypto et eduxerit te inde Dominus Deus tuus in manu forti et brachio extento idcirco praecepit tibi ut observares diem sabbati*

"Remember that even you slaved in Egypt, and *the* Lord your God led you out of there by *a* mighty hand and *a* stretched-out arm. For this reason He commanded you that you observe *the* Sabbath Day.

V
5:16 *honora patrem tuum et matrem sicut praecepit tibi Dominus Deus tuus ut longo vivas tempore et bene sit tibi in terra quam Dominus Deus tuus daturus est tibi*

"Honor your father and mother as *the* Lord your God commanded you, so you can live *a* long time, and it may be well with you in *the* land which *the* Lord your God will give you.

VI
5:17 *non occides*

"You will not kill,

VII
5:18 *neque moechaberis*

"nor will you commit adultery,

VIII
5:19 *furtumque non facies*

"and you will not work theft.

IX
5:20 *nec loqueris contra proximum tuum falsum testimonium*

"You will not speak lying testimony against your neighbor.

X
5:21 *non concupisces uxorem proximi tui non domum non agrum non servum non ancillam non bovem non asinum et universa quae illius sunt*

"You will not lust after your neighbor's wife, or house, or field, or slave, or slave girl, or ox, or ass, or all that are his."

Israel Fears God's Voice
5:22 *haec verba locutus est Dominus ad omnem multitudinem vestram in monte de medio ignis et nubis et caliginis voce magna nihil addens amplius et scripsit ea in duabus tabulis lapideis quas tradidit mihi*

The Lord spoke these words to all your multitude on *the* mountain, from *the* middle of fire and cloud and gloom, adding nothing more. And He wrote them in two stone tables, which He gave me.

5:23 *vos autem postquam audistis vocem de medio tenebrarum et montem ardere vidistis accessistis ad me omnes principes tribuum et maiores natu atque dixistis*

But after you heard *the* voice from *the* middle of darkness, and saw *the* mountain burning, all your tribes' princes and older born came to me, and you said,

5:24 *ecce ostendit nobis Dominus Deus noster maiestatem et magnitudinem suam vocem eius audivimus de medio ignis et probavimus hodie quod loquente Deo cum homine vixerit homo*

"Look, *the* Lord God has shown us His majesty and greatness, and we have heard His voice from fire's midst, and we have proved today that, God speaking with man, man could live.

5:25 *cur ergo morimur et devorabit nos ignis hic maximus si enim audierimus ultra vocem Domini Dei nostri moriemur*

"Why then are we dying, and will this tremendous fire devour us? For if we hear *the* Lord our God's voice more, we will die.

5:26 *quid est omnis caro ut audiat vocem Dei viventis qui de medio ignis loquitur sicut nos audivimus et possit vivere*

"What is all flesh that it should hear *the* living God's voice, who speaks from *the* fire's midst – like we have heard – and we may live?

5:27 *tu magis accede et audi cuncta quae dixerit Dominus Deus noster tibi loquerisque ad nos et nos audientes faciemus ea*

"Better you go and hear all that *the* Lord our God will speak to you. And you speak to us, and we, hearing, will do them."

God Agrees to Israel's Request

5:28 *quod cum audisset Dominus ait ad me audivi vocem verborum populi huius quae locuti sunt tibi bene omnia sunt locuti*

Which, when *the* Lord heard, He said to me, "I have heard *the* voice of this people's words, which they have spoken to you. All they said is good.

5:29 *quis det talem eos habere mentem ut timeant me et custodiant universa mandata mea in omni tempore ut bene sit eis et filiis eorum in sempiternum*

"Who may grant them to have such awareness, so they fear Me and keep all My commandments in every season, so it may be well with them and their children in eternity?

5:30 *vade et dic eis revertimini in tentoria vestra*

"Go and say to them, 'Go back into your tents!'

5:31 *tu vero hic sta mecum et loquar tibi omnia mandata et caerimonias atque iudicia quae docebis eos ut faciant ea in terra quam dabo illis in possessionem*

"You, though, stand here with Me, and I will tell you all My commandments and ceremonies and judgments, which you will teach them, so they can do them in *the* land which I will give them as *a* possession."

5:32 *custodite igitur et facite quae praecepit Dominus Deus vobis non declinabitis neque ad dextram neque ad sinistram*

Keep, therefore, and do what *the* Lord your God has commanded you! Don't turn away, either to *the* right or to *the* left!

5:33 *sed per viam quam praecepit Dominus Deus vester ambulabitis ut vivatis et bene sit vobis et protelentur dies in terra possessionis vestrae*

But you will walk by *the* path which *the* Lord your God commanded, so you can live, and it may be well with you, and your days may be prolonged in *the* land of your possession.

Keep and Do the Commandments

Deuteronomy 6:1 *haec sunt praecepta et caerimoniae atque iudicia quae mandavit Dominus Deus vester ut docerem vos et faciatis ea in terra ad quam transgredimini possidendam*

These are *the* commandments and ceremonies and judgments which *the* Lord your God commanded that I teach you, that you may do them in *the* land which you are crossing over to possess –

6:2 *ut timeas Dominum Deum tuum et custodias omnia mandata et praecepta eius quae ego praecipio tibi et filiis ac nepotibus tuis cunctis diebus vitae tuae ut prolongentur dies tui*

so you may fear *the* Lord your God and keep all His commandments and precepts, which I am teaching you, and your children and your grandchildren, all your life's days, so your days may be prolonged.

6:3 *audi Israhel et observa ut facias et bene sit tibi et multipliceris amplius sicut pollicitus est Dominus Deus patrum tuorum tibi terram lacte et melle manantem*

Hear, Israel, and observe, so you may work, and it may be well with you, and you may be multiplied more, since *the* Lord, your fathers' God, has promised you *a* land flowing with milk and honey.

6:4 *audi Israhel Dominus Deus noster Dominus unus est*

Hear, Israel: *the* Lord our God is one Lord.

6:5 *diliges Dominum Deum tuum ex toto corde tuo et ex tota anima tua et ex tota fortitudine tua*

You will delight in *the* Lord your God from all your heart and from all your soul and from all your strength.

Pass the Law On

6:6 *eruntque verba haec quae ego praecipio tibi hodie in corde tuo*

And these words which I am teaching you today will be in your heart.

6:7 *et narrabis ea filiis tuis et meditaberis sedens in domo tua et ambulans in itinere dormiens atque consurgens*

And you will tell them to your children, and you will reflect, sitting in your house and walking in *the* way, sleeping and getting up.

6:8 *et ligabis ea quasi signum in manu tua eruntque et movebuntur inter oculos tuos*

And you will bind them like *a* sign. And they will be in your hand, and

move between your eyes.

6:9 *scribesque ea in limine et ostiis domus tuae*

And you will write them on your house's entry and doorposts.

6:10 *cumque introduxerit te Dominus Deus tuus in terram pro qua iuravit patribus tuis Abraham Isaac et Iacob et dederit tibi civitates magnas et optimas quas non aedificasti*

And when *the* Lord your God has brought you into *the* land which He swore to your fathers, Abraham, Isaac, and Jacob, and has given you great and fine cities which you did not build,

6:11 *domos plenas cunctarum opum quas non extruxisti cisternas quas non fodisti vineta et oliveta quae non plantasti*

houses full of wealth which you didn't build, wells which you didn't dig, vineyards and olive groves which you didn't plant –

6:12 *et comederis et saturatus fueris*

and you eat and are full,

6:13 *cave diligenter ne obliviscaris Domini qui eduxit te de terra Aegypti de domo servitutis Dominum Deum tuum timebis et ipsi servies ac per* *nomen illius iurabis*

take diligent care that you not forget *the* Lord, who led you out of Egypt's land, out of slavery's house! You will fear *the* Lord your God and serve Him, and will swear by His name.

6:14 *non ibitis post deos alienos cunctarum gentium quae in circuitu vestro sunt*

You will not go after *the* alien gods of all *the* nations who are around you,

6:15 *quoniam Deus aemulator Dominus Deus tuus in medio tui nequando irascatur furor Domini Dei tui contra te et auferat te de superficie terrae*

for *the* Lord your God *is a* jealous God among you, unless *the* Lord your God's fury be angered against you, and He take you away from *the* land's face!

6:16 *non temptabis Dominum Deum tuum sicut temptasti in loco temptationis*

You will not test *the* Lord your God, as you tested Him in temptation's place.

6:17 *custodi praecepta Domini Dei tui ac testimonia et caerimonias quas praecepit tibi*

Keep *the* Lord your God's commandments and testimonies and ceremonies, which He commanded you!

Remember God, Even in Prosperity

6:18 *et fac quod placitum est et bonum in conspectu Domini ut bene sit tibi et ingressus possideas terram optimam de qua iuravit Dominus patribus tuis*

And do what is pleasing and good in *the* Lord's sight, that it may be well with you and, going in, you will possess *the* choice land, over which *the* Lord has sworn to your fathers,

6:19 *ut deleret omnes inimicos tuos coram te sicut locutus est*

that He may destroy all your enemies before you, as He said.

Israel's Identity

6:20 *cum interrogaverit te filius tuus cras dicens quid sibi volunt testimonia haec et caerimoniae atque iudicia quae praecepit Dominus Deus noster nobis*

Tomorrow, when your child asks you, saying, 'What do these testimonies and ceremonies and judgments want in themselves, which *the* Lord our God has commanded us?' –

6:21 *dices ei servi eramus*

Pharaonis in Aegypto et eduxit nos Dominus de Aegypto in manu forti

you will say to him, 'We were Pharaoh's slaves in Egypt, and *the* Lord led us out from Egypt by *a* mighty hand.

6:22 *fecitque signa atque prodigia magna et pessima in Aegypto contra Pharaonem et omnem domum illius in conspectu nostro*

'And He worked great and terrible signs and wonders in Egypt against Pharaoh and all His house in our sight.

6:23 *et eduxit nos inde ut introductis daret terram super qua iuravit patribus nostris*

'And He led us out of there, so, bringing *us* in, He could give us *the* land over which He had sworn to our fathers.

6:24 *praecepitque nobis Dominus ut faciamus omnia legitima haec et timeamus Dominum Deum nostrum et bene sit nobis cunctis diebus vitae nostrae sicut est hodie*

'And *the* Lord commanded us that we do all these laws, and we fear *the* Lord our God, and it may be well with us all our life's days, as it is today.

6:25 *eritque nostri misericors si*

custodierimus et fecerimus omnia praecepta eius coram Domino Deo nostro sicut mandavit nobis

'And He will be mercy to us if we keep and do all His precepts before *the* Lord our God, as He has commanded us.'

No Mercy
in Conquering Canaan

Deuteronomy 7:1 *cum introduxerit te Dominus Deus tuus in terram quam possessurus ingredieris et deleverit gentes multas coram te Hettheum et Gergeseum et Amorreum Chananeum et Ferezeum et Eveum et Iebuseum septem gentes multo maioris numeri quam tu es et robustiores te*

When *the* Lord your God has brought you into *the* land which you are entering to possess, and has destroyed many nations before you – Hittites and Girgashites and Amorites, Canaanites and Pherezites and Hivites and Jebusites, seven nations much larger in number than you and mightier than you –

7:2 *tradideritque eas Dominus Deus tuus tibi percuties eas usque ad internicionem non inibis cum eis foedus nec misereberis earum*

and *the* Lord your God has handed them over to you, strike them down even to extermination! You will not enter into agreements with them or have pity on them.

7:3 *neque sociabis cum eis coniugia filiam tuam non dabis filio eius nec filiam illius accipies filio tuo*

And you will not join with them. You will not give your daughter in marriage to his son, or accept his

daughter for your son.

7:4 *quia seducet filium tuum ne sequatur me et ut magis serviat diis alienis irasceturque furor Domini et delebit te cito*

For she will seduce your son, so he won't follow Me, and that he serve alien gods more. And *the* Lord's fury will be enraged and He will destroy you quickly.

7:5 *quin potius haec facietis eis aras eorum subvertite confringite statuas lucosque succidite et sculptilia conburite*

Rather, do this to them: overthrow their altars, smash to pieces *their* statues, cut down *their* sacred groves, and burn *their* idols –

7:6 *quia populus sanctus es Domino Deo tuo te elegit Dominus Deus tuus ut sis ei populus peculiaris de cunctis populis qui sunt super terram*

for you are holy people to *the* Lord your God. *The* Lord your God chose you, so you could be for Him *a* peculiar people from among all *the* peoples who are on *the* land's face.

Why God Chose Israel

7:7 *non quia cunctas gentes numero vincebatis vobis iunctus est Dominus et elegit vos cum omnibus sitis populis pauciores*

Not because you surpassed all nations in numerical strength is *the* Lord alongside you and has chosen you – when you were fewer than all peoples –

7:8 *sed quia dilexit vos Dominus et custodivit iuramentum quod iuravit patribus vestris eduxitque vos in manu forti et redemit de domo servitutis de manu Pharaonis regis Aegypti*

but because *the* Lord delighted in you, and He kept *the* oath which He swore to your fathers. And He led you out by *a* mighty hand, and bought you back from slavery's house, from Pharaoh king of Egypt's hand.

7:9 *et scies quia Dominus Deus tuus ipse est Deus fortis et fidelis custodiens pactum et misericordiam diligentibus se et his qui custodiunt praecepta eius in mille generationes*

And you will know that *the* Lord your God, He is *the* mighty and faithful God, keeping covenant and mercy with those delighting in Him and those who keep His precepts, in *a* thousand generations –

7:10 *et reddens odientibus se statim ita ut disperdat eos et ultra non differat protinus eis restituens quod merentur*

and quickly paying back those who

hate him, so that He may destroy them, and not give them further respite, immediately giving what they deserve.

The Reward
of Keeping the Law

7:12 *custodi ergo praecepta et caerimonias atque iudicia quae ego mando tibi hodie ut facias*

Keep, then, *the* precepts and ceremonies and judgments which I am commanding you today, that you do *them*.

7:12 *si postquam audieris haec iudicia custodieris ea et feceris custodiet et Dominus Deus tuus tibi pactum et misericordiam quam iuravit patribus tuis*

If after you hear these judgments, you will keep and do them, *the* Lord your God also will keep covenant and mercy with you, which He swore to your fathers.

7:13 *et diliget te ac multiplicabit benedicetque fructui ventris tui et fructui terrae tuae frumento tuo atque vindemiae oleo et armentis gregibus ovium tuarum super terram pro qua iuravit patribus tuis ut daret eam tibi*

And He will delight in you, and multiply and bless your womb's fruit and your land's fruit, your grain and grapes, oil and herds, your sheep flocks on *the* land over which He swore to your fathers, that He would give it to you.

7:14 *benedictus eris inter omnes populos non erit apud te sterilis utriusque sexus tam in hominibus quam in gregibus tuis*

You will be blessed among all peoples. No sterile one of either sex will be with you, either among people or in your flocks.

7:15 *auferet Dominus a te omnem languorem et infirmitates Aegypti pessimas quas novisti non inferet tibi sed cunctis hostibus tuis*

The Lord will take away from you all weakness. And Egypt's dreadful sicknesses, which you have known, he will afflict not on you, but on all your enemies.

7:16 *devorabis omnes populos quos Dominus Deus tuus daturus est tibi non parcet eis oculus tuus nec servies diis eorum ne sint in ruinam tui*

You will devour all *the* peoples whom *the* Lord your God is giving you. Your eye will not spare them, nor will you serve their gods, so they may not be your ruin.

Don't Fear the Nations
7:17 *si dixeris in corde tuo plures sunt gentes istae quam ego quomodo*

potero delere eas

If you say in your heart, 'These nations are larger than I am. How can I destroy them? –

7:18 *noli metuere sed recordare quae fecerit Dominus Deus tuus Pharaoni et cunctis Aegyptiis*

do not be afraid, but remember what *the* Lord your God did to Pharaoh and all *the* Egyptians –

7:19 *plagas maximas quas viderunt oculi tui et signa atque portenta manumque robustam et extentum brachium ut educeret te Dominus Deus tuus sic faciet cunctis populis quos metuis*

the great plagues which your eyes saw, and *the* signs and wonders and mighty hand and stretched-out arm, so *the* Lord your God could lead you out. So He will do to all *the* peoples whom you fear.

7:20 *insuper et crabrones mittet Dominus Deus tuus in eos donec deleat omnes atque disperdat qui te fugerint et latere potuerint*

In addition, *the* Lord your God will send hornets also among them, until He can destroy all. And He will destroy even *the* ones who escape you and are able to hide.

7:21 *non timebis eos quia Dominus*

Deus tuus in medio tui est Deus magnus et terribilis

You will not fear them, because *the* Lord your God among you is *a* great and terrifying God.

7:22 *ipse consumet nationes has in conspectu tuo paulatim atque per partes non poteris delere eas pariter ne forte multiplicentur contra te bestiae terrae*

He will consume these nations in your sight, little by little and by parts. You will not be able to destroy them at once, unless perhaps *the* land's beasts be multiplied against you.

7:23 *dabitque eos Dominus Deus tuus in conspectu tuo et interficiet illos donec penitus deleantur*

And *the* Lord your God will give them *over* in your sight, and will kill them until they are destroyed inside.

7:24 *tradet reges eorum in manus tuas et disperdes nomina eorum sub caelo nullus poterit resistere tibi donec conteras eos*

He will hand their kings over into your hand, and you will destroy their name under *the* sky. No one will be able to resist you until you have destroyed them.

7:25 *sculptilia eorum igne conbures non concupisces argentum et aurum*

de quibus facta sunt neque adsumes ex eis tibi quicquam ne offendas propter ea quia abominatio est Domini Dei tui

You will burn their sculpted idols with fire. Do not lust after *the* silver and gold from which they were made, or take up anything for yourselves from them, so you don't offend because of them – for *it* is an abomination to *the* Lord your God!

7:26 *nec inferes quippiam ex idolo in domum tuam ne fias anathema sicut et illud est quasi spurcitiam detestaberis et velut inquinamentum ac sordes abominationi habebis quia anathema est*

You will not bring anything from *an* idol into your house, that you not become *a* curse, even as it is. You will detest it like filth, and you will consider it *an* abomination, as if it were dung-covered or soiled, because *it* is *a* curse.

Remember the Long Journey
Deuteronomy 8:1 *omne mandatum quod ego praecipio tibi hodie cave diligenter ut facias ut possitis vivere et multiplicemini ingressique possideatis terram pro qua iuravit Dominus patribus vestris*

Every commandment which I am teaching you today, take diligent care that you do, so you can live and be multiplied, and going in, you may possess *the* land over which *the* Lord swore to your fathers!

8:2 *et recordaberis cuncti itineris per quod adduxit te Dominus Deus tuus quadraginta annis per desertum ut adfligeret te atque temptaret et nota fierent quae in tuo animo versabantur utrum custodires mandata illius an non*

And you will remember all *the* routes by which *the* Lord your God has led you forty years through *the* desert, so He could afflict you and even test you, so *the* thoughts which turn in your soul might be made known, whether you will keep His commandments or not.

8:3 *adflixit te penuria et dedit tibi cibum manna quem ignorabas tu et patres tui ut ostenderet tibi quod non in solo pane vivat homo sed in omni verbo quod egreditur ex ore Domini*

He afflicted you with need, and He gave you food – manna, which you did not know or your fathers – so He could show you that man does not live by bread only, but by every word which comes forth from *the* Lord's mouth.

8:4 *vestimentum tuum quo operiebaris nequaquam vetustate defecit et pes tuus non est subtritus en quadragesimus annus est*

Your clothes with which you covered yourself did not fall apart from age, and your foot was not blistered – and this is *the* fortieth year –

8:5 *ut recogites in corde tuo quia sicut erudit homo filium suum sic Dominus Deus tuus erudivit te*

so you may recognize in your heart that as man teaches his son, so *the* Lord your God has taught you –

8:6 *ut custodias mandata Domini Dei tui et ambules in viis eius et timeas eum*

so you may keep *the* Lord your God's commandments, and walk in His ways, and fear Him.

God Will Guide You
8:7 *Dominus enim Deus tuus introducet te in terram bonam terram rivorum aquarumque et fontium in cuius campis et montibus erumpunt fluviorum abyssi*

For *the* Lord your God will bring you

into *a* good land, *a* land of streams and waters and springs, in whose fields and mountains *the* abyss's floods burst forth –

8:8 *terram frumenti hordei vinearum in qua ficus et mala granata et oliveta nascuntur terram olei ac mellis*

a land of grain, barley, and vines, in which fig and pomegranate and olive are born, *a* land of oil and honey,

8:9 *ubi absque ulla penuria comedes panem tuum et rerum omnium abundantia perfrueris cuius lapides ferrum sunt et de montibus eius aeris metalla fodiuntur*

where, apart from any lack, you will eat your bread and enjoy *the* abundance of all things – whose stones are iron, and from its mountains copper metal is mined.

8:10 *ut cum comederis et satiatus fueris benedicas Domino Deo tuo pro terra optima quam dedit tibi*

So when you have eaten and are full, you may bless *the* Lord your God for *the* choice land which He has given you.

Don't Let Prosperity Blind You!
8:11 *observa et cave nequando obliviscaris Domini Dei tui et neglegas mandata eius atque iudicia et caerimonias quas ego praecipio*

tibi hodie

Watch and take care, so you don't forget *the* Lord your God and neglect His commandments and judgments and ceremonies, which I am teaching you today –

8:12 *ne postquam comederis et satiatus domos pulchras aedificaveris et habitaveris in eis*

unless, after you have eaten are full, have built beautiful houses and live in them,

8:13 *habuerisque armenta et ovium greges argenti et auri cunctarumque rerum copiam*

and have herds and flocks of sheep, silver and gold, and all things abundantly,

8:14 *elevetur cor tuum et non reminiscaris Domini Dei tui qui eduxit te de terra Aegypti de domo servitutis*

your heart be lifted up, and you not remember *the* Lord your God, who led you from Egypt's land, from slavery's house!

8:15 *et ductor tuus fuit in solitudine magna atque terribili in qua erat serpens flatu adurens et scorpio ac dipsas et nullae omnino aquae qui eduxit rivos de petra durissima*

And He was your leader in *that* great and terrible wasteland, in which were snakes snorting fire, and scorpions, and snakes of thirst, and no water at all – *the Lord,* who brought rivers out of hardest rock.

8:16 *et cibavit te manna in solitudine quod nescierunt patres tui et postquam adflixit ac probavit ad extremum misertus est tui*

And He fed you manna in *the* wasteland, which your fathers had not known. And after He had afflicted and tested you to *the* extreme, He was merciful to you.

Credit Where Credit Is Due
8:17 *ne diceres in corde tuo fortitudo mea et robur manus meae haec mihi omnia praestiterunt*

Do not say in your heart, 'All these things are supplied to me by my strength and my hand's force' –

8:18 *sed recorderis Domini Dei tui quod ipse tibi vires praebuerit ut impleret pactum suum super quo iuravit patribus tuis sicut praesens indicat dies*

but remember *the* Lord your God, that He supplied strengths to you, so He could fulfill His covenant, over which He swore to your fathers, as *the* present day indicates!

8:19 *sin autem oblitus Domini Dei*

tui secutus fueris alienos deos coluerisque illos et adoraveris ecce nunc praedico tibi quod omnino dispereas

But if, forgetting *the* Lord your God, you follow alien gods and serve them and worship, look! I tell you now that you will be destroyed completely.

8:20 *sicut gentes quas delevit Dominus in introitu tuo ita et vos peribitis si inoboedientes fueritis voci Domini Dei vestri*

Like *the* nations which *the* Lord destroyed in your entry, so you also will perish, if you are disobedient to *the* Lord your God's voice.

Crossing into the Enemy's Land
Deuteronomy 9:1 *audi Israhel tu transgredieris hodie Iordanem ut possideas nationes maximas et fortiores te civitates ingentes et ad caelum usque muratas*

Listen Israel! You are crossing *the* Jordan today so you can possess great nations and mightier than you, huge cities and walled even to *the* sky –

9:2 *populum magnum atque sublimem filios Enacim quos ipse vidisti et audisti quibus nullus potest ex adverso resistere*

a great and eminent people, *the* Enacim's children, whom you saw and heard, against whom no one is able to resist.

9:3 *scies ergo hodie quod Dominus Deus tuus ipse transibit ante te ignis devorans atque consumens qui conterat eos et deleat atque disperdat ante faciem tuam velociter sicut locutus est tibi*

You will know, then, today, that *the* Lord your God, He will go before you in *a* devouring and consuming fire, who will quickly crush and destroy and even scatter them before your face, as He promised you.

9:4 *ne dicas in corde tuo cum deleverit eos Dominus Deus tuus in conspectu tuo propter iustitiam*

meam introduxit me Dominus ut terram hanc possiderem cum propter impietates suas istae deletae sint nationes

Do not say in your heart when *the* Lord your God has destroyed them in your sight, 'Because of my fairness, *the* Lord brought me into this land so I could posses it,' when because of their lawlessness these nations are destroyed.

9:5 *neque enim propter iustitias tuas et aequitatem cordis tui ingredieris ut possideas terras eorum sed quia illae egerunt impie te introeunte deletae sunt et ut conpleret verbum suum Dominus quod sub iuramento pollicitus est patribus tuis Abraham Isaac et Iacob*

You are not going in to take over their land because of your fairness or your heart's equity. They are destroyed at your entry because they acted harmfully, and so *the* Lord may fulfill His word which He promised on oath to your fathers Abraham, Isaac, and Jacob.

God Has No Illusions
About Israel
9:6 *scito igitur quod non propter iustitias tuas Dominus Deus tuus dederit tibi terram hanc optimam in possessionem cum durissimae cervicis sis populus*

Know, therefore, that *the* Lord your

God is not giving you this choice land as *a* possession on account of your fairness, when you are *a* most hard-necked people.

9:7 *memento et ne obliviscaris quomodo ad iracundiam provocaveris Dominum Deum tuum in solitudine ex eo die quo es egressus ex Aegypto usque ad locum istum semper adversum Dominum contendisti*

Remember, and do not forget, how you provoked *the* Lord your God to anger in *the* wasteland, from *the* day you came out of Egypt even to this place! You have always wrestled against *the* Lord.

9:8 *nam et in Horeb provocasti eum et iratus delere te voluit*

For even in Horeb you provoked Him, and, in anger, He wanted to destroy you,

9:9 *quando ascendi in montem ut acciperem tabulas lapideas tabulas pacti quod pepigit vobiscum Dominus et perseveravi in monte quadraginta diebus ac noctibus panem non comedens et aquam non bibens*

when I climbed up onto *the* mountain so I could receive *the* stone tables, *the* covenant's tables which *the* Lord made with you. And I stayed on *the* mountain forty days and nights, not eating bread and not drinking water.

9:10 *deditque mihi Dominus duas tabulas lapideas scriptas digito Dei et continentes omnia verba quae vobis in monte locutus est de medio ignis quando contio populi congregata est*

And *the* Lord gave me two stone tables, written by God's finger and containing all *the* words which He spoke to you on *the* mountain from *the* fire's midst, when *the* people's assembly was gathered.

9:11 *cumque transissent quadraginta dies et totidem noctes dedit mihi Dominus duas tabulas lapideas tabulas foederis*

And when forty days and as many nights had passed, *the* Lord gave me two stone tables, *the* pact's tables.

9:12 *dixitque mihi surge et descende hinc cito quia populus tuus quos eduxisti de Aegypto deseruerunt velociter viam quam demonstrasti eis feceruntque sibi conflatile*

And He said to me, "Get up and climb down quickly from here, because your people, whom I led out of Egypt, has quickly deserted *the* way which you showed them. And they have made themselves *a* cast idol."

Moses Pleads for Israel

9:13 *rursumque ait Dominus ad me cerno quod populus iste durae cervicis sit*

And *the* Lord said to me again, "I discern that this is a hard-necked people.

9:14 *dimitte me ut conteram eum et deleam nomen eius sub caelo et constituam te super gentem quae hac maior et fortior sit*

"Let Me go so I can crush him and destroy his name under *the* sky! And I will appoint you over *a* nation which will be greater and stronger than this one."

9:15 *cumque de monte ardente descenderem et duas tabulas foederis utraque tenerem manu*

And when I had climbed down from *the* burning mountain, and had *the* pact's two tables in either hand,

9:16 *vidissemque vos peccasse Domino Deo vestro et fecisse vobis vitulum conflatilem ac deseruisse velociter viam eius quam vobis ostenderat*

and I saw that you had sinned against *the* Lord your God, and made yourselves *a* cast-metal calf, and had quickly deserted His way, which He had shown you,

9:17 *proieci tabulas de manibus meis confregique eas in conspectu vestro*

I threw down *the* tables from my hands and broke them in your sight.

9:18 *et procidi ante Dominum sicut prius quadraginta diebus et noctibus panem non comedens et aquam non bibens propter omnia peccata vestra quae gessistis contra Dominum et eum ad iracundiam provocastis*

And I fell prostrate before *the* Lord as before, forty days and nights, not eating bread and not drinking water, because of all your sins which you carried on against *the* Lord. And you provoked Him to anger.

9:19 *timui enim indignationem et iram illius qua adversum vos concitatus delere vos voluit et exaudivit me Dominus etiam hac vice*

For I feared His indignation and wrath, which was stirred up against you. He wanted to destroy you, yet *the* Lord heard me even by this exchange.

9:20 *adversum Aaron quoque vehementer iratus voluit eum conterere et pro illo similiter deprecatus sum*

Likewise greatly angered against Aaron, He wanted to crush him. And I pleaded for him as well.

9:21 *peccatum autem vestrum quod feceratis id est vitulum arripiens igne conbusi et in frusta comminuens omninoque in pulverem redigens proieci in torrentem qui de monte descendit*

But taking your sin which you made – it was *the* calf – I burned *it* with fire. And cutting *it* in pieces, mixing *it* entirely, grinding *it* into powder, I threw *it* into *the* stream which came down from *the* mountain.

9:22 *in Incendio quoque et in Temptatione et in sepulchris Concupiscentiae provocastis Dominum*

You likewise provoked *the* Lord in Fire and in Testing and in Lusting's tombs.

9:23 *et quando misit vos de Cadesbarne dicens ascendite et possidete terram quam dedi vobis et contempsistis imperium Domini Dei vestri et non credidistis ei neque vocem eius audire voluistis*

And when He sent you from Kadesh-Barnea, saying, "Go up and take over *the* land which I have given you," you also scorned *the* Lord your God's rule and did not believe Him, nor did you want to hear His voice.

Always Rebels
9:24 *sed semper fuistis rebelles a die qua nosse vos coepi*

But you were always rebels, from *the* day that I began to know you.

9:25 *et iacui coram Domino quadraginta diebus ac noctibus quibus eum suppliciter deprecabar ne deleret vos ut fuerat comminatus*

And I lay prostrate before *the* Lord forty days and nights, in which I humbly prayed that He not destroy you, as He had threatened.

9:26 *et orans dixi Domine Deus ne disperdas populum tuum et hereditatem tuam quam redemisti in magnitudine tua quos eduxisti de Aegypto in manu forti*

And praying, I said, "Lord God, do not destroy Your people and Your inheritance, which You bought back in your greatness, whom You led out of Egypt by *a* mighty hand!

9:27 *recordare servorum tuorum Abraham Isaac et Iacob ne aspicias duritiam populi huius et impietatem atque peccatum*

"Remember your slaves – Abraham, Isaac, and Jacob! Do not look on this people's hardness and lawlessness and sin –

9:28 *ne forte dicant habitatores terrae de qua eduxisti nos non poterat Dominus introducere eos in terram quam pollicitus est eis et oderat illos idcirco eduxit ut* *interficeret eos in solitudine*

"unless, perhaps, *the* inhabitants of *the* land to which you have led us say, '*The* Lord wasn't able to bring them into *the* land He promised them, and He hated them. Therefore He led them out, so He could kill them in *the* wasteland'!

9:29 *qui sunt populus tuus et hereditas tua quos eduxisti in fortitudine tua magna et in brachio tuo extento*

"*They* are Your people and Your inheritance, whom You led out by Your great strength and by Your stretched-out arm."

Two Stone Tablets

Deuteronomy 10:1 *in tempore illo dixit Dominus ad me dola tibi duas tabulas lapideas sicut priores fuerunt et ascende ad me in montem faciesque arcam ligneam*

At that time, *the* Lord said to me, "Cut out two stone tables, as were before, and climb up to Me on *the* mountain. And you will make *a* wooden box.

10:2 *et scribam in tabulis verba quae fuerunt in his quas ante confregisti ponesque eas in arca*

"And I will write on *the* tables *the* words which were on those which you broke before. And you will put them in *the* box.

The Covenant Ark

10:3 *feci igitur arcam de lignis setthim cumque dolassem duas tabulas lapideas instar priorum ascendi in montem habens eas in manibus*

Then I made *the* box of acacia wood. And when I had carved two stone tables like *the* first, I climbed onto *the* mountain, having them in hand.

10:4 *scripsitque in tabulis iuxta id quod prius scripserat verba decem quae locutus est Dominus ad vos in monte de medio ignis quando populus congregatus est et dedit eas mihi*

And He wrote on *the* tables according to what He had written before – ten words which *the* Lord spoke to you on *the* mountain, from *the* fire's midst, when *the* people was gathered. And He gave them to me.

10:5 *reversusque de monte descendi et posui tabulas in arcam quam feceram quae hucusque ibi sunt sicut mihi praecepit Dominus*

And turning back from *the* mountain, I climbed down and put *the* tables into *the* box which I had made, which are there to this day, as *the* Lord had commanded me.

Aaron's Death

10:6 *filii autem Israhel castra moverunt ex Beroth filiorum Iacan in Musera ubi Aaron mortuus ac sepultus est pro quo sacerdotio functus est filius eius Eleazar*

But Israel's children's camp moved from Beeroth of Iacan's children, to Musera, where Aaron died and was buried. His son Eleazar served as priest in his place.

10:7 *inde venerunt in Gadgad de quo loco profecti castrametati sunt in Ietabatha in terra aquarum atque torrentium*

From there, they went into Gadgad, setting out from which place they camped in Ietabatha, in *a* land of waters and brooks.

Levi Set Apart

10:8 *eo tempore separavit tribum Levi ut portaret arcam foederis Domini et staret coram eo in ministerio ac benediceret in nomine illius usque in praesentem diem*

At that time, He separated Levi's tribe, so it could carry *the* Lord's covenant's box, and stand before Him in ministry, and bless in His name even to *the* present day.

10:9 *quam ob rem non habuit Levi partem neque possessionem cum fratribus suis quia ipse Dominus possessio eius est sicut promisit ei Dominus Deus tuus*

For which reason, Levi had no portion or possession with his brothers, because *the* Lord is his possession, as *the* Lord your God promised him.

10:10 *ego autem steti in monte sicut prius quadraginta diebus ac noctibus exaudivitque me Dominus etiam hac vice et te perdere noluit*

But I stood on *the* mountain as before, forty days and nights. And *the* Lord heard me even by this exchange, and did not want to destroy you.

10:11 *dixitque mihi vade et praecede populum ut ingrediatur et possideat terram quam iuravi patribus eorum ut traderem eis*

And He said to me, "Go, and go before *the* people, so they can go in and possess *the* land which I swore to their fathers, that I would give it to them!"

What Does the Lord Want from You?

10:12 *et nunc Israhel quid Dominus Deus tuus petit a te nisi ut timeas Dominum Deum tuum et ambules in viis eius et diligas eum ac servias Domino Deo tuo in toto corde tuo et in tota anima tua*

And now, Israel, what does *the* Lord your God ask of you, except that you fear *the* Lord your God, and walk in His ways, and delight in and serve *the* Lord your God in all your heart and in all your soul?

10:13 *custodiasque mandata Domini et caerimonias eius quas ego hodie praecipio ut bene sit tibi*

And you will keep *the* Lord's commandments and His ceremonies which I am teaching you today, so it may be well with you.

The Wonder of Israel's Election

10:14 *en Domini Dei tui caelum est et caelum caeli terra et omnia quae in ea sunt*

See! *The* sky is *the* Lord your God's, and *the* sky's sky, *the* land and all *things* that are in it.

10:15 *et tamen patribus tuis conglutinatus est Dominus et amavit eos elegitque semen eorum post eos id est vos de cunctis gentibus sicut hodie conprobatur*

Yet nevertheless, *the* Lord was joined to your fathers and loved them. And He chose their seed after them – it is you – from all nations, as today is proven.

Care for the Newcomer

10:16 *circumcidite igitur praeputium cordis vestri et cervicem vestram ne induretis amplius*

Circumcise your heart's foreskin, then, and do not harden your neck further!

10:17 *quia Dominus Deus vester ipse est Deus deorum et Dominus dominantium Deus magnus et potens et terribilis qui personam non accipit nec munera*

For *the* Lord your God, He is *the* gods' God and *the* lords' Lord, *a* great and mighty and terrifying God, who favors neither person nor bribes.

10:18 *facit iudicium pupillo et viduae amat peregrinum et dat ei victum atque vestitum*

He works judgment for orphan and widow. He loves *the* stranger and gives him food and clothing.

10:19 *et vos ergo amate peregrinos quia et ipsi fuistis advenae in terra Aegypti*

And you, therefore, love *the* strangers, because even you were newcomers in Egypt's land!

10:20 *Dominum Deum tuum timebis et ei servies ipsi adherebis iurabisque in nomine illius*

You will fear *the* Lord your God and serve Him. You will hold on to Him, and swear in His name.

10:21 *ipse est laus tua et Deus tuus qui fecit tibi haec magnalia et terribilia quae viderunt oculi tui*

He is your praise and your God, who worked these mighty and terrifying *works* for you, which your eyes have seen.

10:22 *in septuaginta animabus descenderunt patres tui in Aegyptum et ecce nunc multiplicavit te Dominus Deus tuus sicut astra caeli*

Your fathers went down into Egypt as seventy souls, and now, look! *The* Lord your God has multiplied you like *the* sky's stars.

**Remember What
You Have Seen!**
Deuteronomy 11:1 *ama itaque Dominum Deum tuum et observa praecepta eius et caerimonias iudicia atque mandata omni tempore*

Therefore, love *the* Lord your God, and keep His precepts and ceremonies, judgments and commandments, all *the* time!

11:2 *cognoscite hodie quae ignorant filii vestri qui non viderunt disciplinam Domini Dei vestri magnalia eius et robustam manum extentumque brachium*

Understand today what your children do not know, who have not seen *the* Lord your God's discipline, His great *works* and mighty hand and stretched-out arm –

11:3 *signa et opera quae fecit in medio Aegypti Pharaoni regi et universae terrae eius*

signs and works which He did in Egypt's midst to King Pharaoh and all his land,

11:4 *omnique exercitui Aegyptiorum et equis ac curribus quomodo operuerint eos aquae Rubri maris cum vos persequerentur et deleverit eos Dominus usque in praesentem diem*

and all *the* Egyptians' army and

horses and chariots, how *the* Red Sea's waters covered them when they pursued you – and *the* Lord destroyed them, even to *the* present day –

11:5 *vobisque quae fecerit in solitudine donec veniretis ad hunc locum*

– what He did for you in the desert, until you had come to this place –

11:6 *et Dathan atque Abiram filiis Heliab qui fuit filius Ruben quos aperto ore suo terra absorbuit cum domibus et tabernaculis et universa substantia eorum quam habebant in medio Israhelis*

– and to Dathan and Abiram, Heliab's children, who was Reuben's child, whom *the* ground, opening its mouth, swallowed with their houses and tents and all their substance, which they had among *the* Israelites.

11:7 *oculi vestri viderunt omnia opera Domini magna quae fecit*

Your eyes have seen all *the* Lord's great works, which He did,

11:8 *ut custodiatis universa mandata illius quae ego hodie praecipio vobis et possitis introire et possidere terram ad quam ingredimini*

so you can keep all His commandments, which I am teaching you today, and you may enter and take over *the* land into which you are going.

11:9 *multoque in ea vivatis tempore quam sub iuramento pollicitus est Dominus patribus vestris et semini eorum lacte et melle manantem*

And you may live *a* long time in it, which *the* Lord swore under oath to your fathers and their seed – flowing with milk and honey.

Canaan Not Like Egypt
11:10 *terra enim ad quam ingredieris possidendam non est sicut terra Aegypti de qua existi ubi iacto semine in hortorum morem aquae ducuntur inriguae*

For *the* land which you are going in to take over is not like Egypt's land, from which you left, where, planting seed in *the* manner of gardens, waters are led in to irrigate *it*.

11:11 *sed montuosa est et campestris de caelo expectans pluvias*

But it is mountainous, and *its* plains expecting rain from *the* sky –

11:12 *quam Dominus Deus tuus semper invisit et oculi illius in ea sunt a principio anni usque ad finem eius*

which *the* Lord your God always watches over, and His eyes are on it from *the* year's beginning even to its end.

11:13 *si ergo oboedieritis mandatis meis quae hodie praecipio vobis ut diligatis Dominum Deum vestrum et serviatis ei in toto corde vestro et in tota anima vestra*

If, then, you obey my commandments which I am teaching you today, so you delight in *the* Lord your God and serve Him in all your heart and in all your soul,

11:14 *dabo pluviam terrae vestrae temporivam et serotinam ut colligatis frumentum et vinum et oleum*

I will give your land early and late rain, so you may gather grain and wine and oil,

11:15 *faenum ex agris ad pascenda iumenta et ut ipsi comedatis ac saturemini*

hay from *the* fields to feed cattle, and so you yourselves may eat and be satisfied.

11:16 *cavete ne forte decipiatur cor vestrum et recedatis a Domino serviatisque diis alienis et adoretis eos*

Take care, unless perhaps your heart be deceived and you turn away from *the* Lord, and you serve alien gods and adore them –

11:17 *iratusque Dominus claudat caelum et pluviae non descendant nec terra det germen suum pereatisque velociter de terra optima quam Dominus daturus est vobis*

and *the* Lord, angry, may close *the* sky and *the* rain not fall, nor *the* land give its bud, and you perish quickly from *the* choice land which *the* Lord will give you!

Put These Words in Your Hearts!
11:18 *ponite haec verba mea in cordibus et in animis vestris et suspendite ea pro signo in manibus et inter vestros oculos conlocate*

Put these, my words, in your hearts and souls, and hang them as *a* sign in *your* hands, and place them between your eyes!

11:19 *docete filios vestros ut illa meditentur quando sederis in domo tua et ambulaveris in via et accubueris atque surrexeris*

Teach your children, so they reflect on them when you sit in your house and walk in *the* way, when you lie down and when you get up!

11:20 *scribes ea super postes et ianuas domus tuae*

Write them on your houses' posts and doors,

11:21 *ut multiplicentur dies tui et filiorum tuorum in terra quam iuravit Dominus patribus tuis ut daret eis quamdiu caelum inminet terrae*

so your days and your children's may be multiplied in *the* land which *the* Lord swore to your fathers that He would give them, as long as sky hangs over land!

Blessings of Obedience
11:22 *si enim custodieritis mandata quae ego praecipio vobis et feceritis ea ut diligatis Dominum Deum vestrum et ambuletis in omnibus viis eius adherentes ei*

For if you keep *the* commandments which I am teaching you, and you do them, so you delight in the Lord your God and walk in all His ways, sticking close to Him,

11:23 *disperdet Dominus omnes gentes istas ante faciem vestram et possidebitis eas quae maiores et fortiores vobis sunt*

the Lord will destroy all these nations before your face, and you will take over those who are larger and stronger than you!

11:24 *omnis locus quem calcaverit pes vester vester erit a deserto et*

Libano a flumine magno Eufraten usque ad mare occidentale erunt termini vestri

Every place in which your foot steps will be yours, from *the* desert and Lebanon to *the* great river Euphrates, even to *the* eastern sea. These will be your borders.

11:25 *nullus stabit contra vos terrorem vestrum et formidinem dabit Dominus Deus vester super omnem terram quam calcaturi estis sicut locutus est vobis*

No one will stand against you. *The* Lord your God will give your terror and fear over all *the* land on which you will step, as He said to you.

Ritual of Blessing and Curse
11:26 *en propono in conspectu vestro hodie benedictionem et maledictionem*

Look! I am placing today blessing and curse in your sight –

11:27 *benedictionem si oboedieritis mandatis Domini Dei vestri quae ego praecipio vobis*

blessing if you obey *the* Lord your God's commandments which I am teaching you;

11:28 *maledictionem si non audieritis mandata Domini Dei vestri sed recesseritis de via quam* *ego nunc ostendo vobis et ambulaveritis post deos alienos quos ignoratis*

curse, if you won't hear *the* Lord your God's commandments, but turn back from *the* way which I am showing you now, and walk after strange gods whom you haven't known.

11:29 *cum introduxerit te Dominus Deus tuus in terram ad quam pergis habitandam pones benedictionem super montem Garizim maledictionem super montem Hebal*

When *the* Lord your God has brought you into *the* land which you are entering to inhabit, you will place blessing on Mount Gerizim, cursing on Mount Hebal,

11:30 *qui sunt trans Iordanem post viam quae vergit ad solis occubitum in terra Chananei qui habitat in campestribus contra Galgalam quae est iuxta vallem tendentem et intrantem procul*

which are across *the* Jordan, after *the* way which inclines to *the* setting sun, in *the* Canaanites' land who live in *the* plains around Gilgal, which is alongside *the* Valley of Tents and reaching far away.

11:31 *vos enim transibitis Iordanem ut possideatis terram quam Dominus Deus vester daturus est vobis et*

habeatis ac possideatis illam

For you will cross *the* Jordan, so you can take over *the* land which the Lord your God will give you. And you will have and possess it.

11:32 *videte ergo ut impleatis caerimonias atque iudicia quae ego hodie ponam in conspectu vestro*

See, then, that you fulfill *the* ceremonies and judgments which I am placing in your sight today!

Dealing with Idols

Deuteronomy 12:1 *haec sunt praecepta atque iudicia quae facere debetis in terra quam Dominus Deus patrum tuorum daturus est tibi ut possideas eam cunctis diebus quibus super humum gradieris*

These are *the* precepts and judgments which you must do in *the* land which *the* Lord God of your fathers will give you, so you may possess it all *the* days which you live on *the* soil.

12:2 *subvertite omnia loca in quibus coluerunt gentes quas possessuri estis deos suos super montes excelsos et colles et subter omne lignum frondosum*

Overturn every place in which *the* nations which you will possess served their gods – on mountains' heights and hills and under every leafing tree!

12:3 *dissipate aras earum et confringite statuas lucos igne conburite et idola comminuite disperdite nomina eorum de locis illis*

Scatter their altars and smash statues! Burn groves with fire and break up their idols! Destroy their names from that place!

God Will Choose a Place

12:4 *non facietis ita Domino Deo vestro*

You will not do so for *the* Lord your God.

12:5 *sed ad locum quem elegerit Dominus Deus vester de cunctis tribubus vestris ut ponat nomen suum ibi et habitet in eo venietis*

But you will come to *the* place which *the* Lord your God chooses from all your tribes, to put His name there and live in it.

12:6 *et offeretis in illo loco holocausta et victimas vestras decimas et primitias manuum vestrarum et vota atque donaria primogenita boum et ovium*

And you will offer in that place your burnt offerings and victims, tithes and your hands' first fruits and vows, and gifts of firstborn oxen and sheep.

12:7 *et comedetis ibi in conspectu Domini Dei vestri ac laetabimini in cunctis ad quae miseritis manum vos et domus vestrae in quibus benedixerit vobis Dominus Deus vester*

And you will eat there in *the* Lord your God's sight, and will be happy in all your hand and your house will send out, in which *the* Lord your God has blessed you.

12:8 *non facietis ibi quae nos hic facimus hodie singuli quod sibi rectum videtur*

You will not do there what we do here for ourselves today, each one what seems right to him,

12:9 *neque enim usque in praesens tempus venistis ad requiem et possessionem quam Dominus Deus daturus est vobis*

for even to *the* present day you have not come to *the* rest and possession which *the* Lord God will give you.

12:10 *transibitis Iordanem et habitabitis in terram quam Dominus Deus vester daturus est vobis ut requiescatis a cunctis hostibus per circuitum et absque ullo timore habitetis*

You will cross *the* Jordan and live in *the* land which *the* Lord your God will give you, so you may rest from all your enemies around, and you will live apart from any fear,

12:11 *in loco quem elegerit Dominus Deus vester ut sit nomen eius in eo illuc omnia quae praecipio conferetis holocausta et hostias ac decimas et primitias manuum vestrarum et quicquid praecipuum est in muneribus quae vovistis Domino*

in *the* place which *the* Lord your God will choose, that His name may be in it. You will bring there all that I am commanding – burnt offerings and victims and tithes and your hands'

first fruits and whatever is commanded, as gifts which you have promised to *the* Lord.

12:12 *ibi epulabimini coram Domino Deo vestro vos filii ac filiae vestrae famuli et famulae atque Levites qui in vestris urbibus commorantur neque enim habet aliam partem et possessionem inter vos*

You will feast there before *the* Lord your God, you, your sons and daughters, male and female slaves and *the* Levites who live in your towns. For he has no other portion or possession among you.

Making Your Offering
12:13 *cave ne offeras holocausta tua in omni loco quem videris*

Take care that you not offer your burnt offerings in every place which you see –

12:14 *sed in eo quem elegerit Dominus in una tribuum tuarum offeres hostias et facies quaecumque praecipio tibi*

but in *the* place which *the* Lord will choose from one of your tribes, you will offer victims, and you will do whatever I teach you.

Eating Meat
12:15 *sin autem comedere volueris et te esus carnium delectarit occide*

et comede iuxta benedictionem Domini Dei tui quam dedit tibi in urbibus tuis sive inmundum fuerit hoc est maculatum et debile sive mundum hoc est integrum et sine macula quod offerri licet sicut capream et cervum comedes

But if you want to eat and eating meat delights you, kill and eat according to *the* Lord your God's blessing, which He gave you in your towns: whether it be unclean (that is, flawed and weak), or whether clean (that is, whole and without defect, what it is permitted to offer, like goats and deer), you will eat –

12:16   *absque esu dumtaxat sanguinis quod super terram quasi aquam effundes*

without eating blood to this extent, that you pour it out over *the* ground like water.

Coming Before the Lord

12:17   *non poteris comedere in oppidis tuis decimam frumenti et vini et olei tui primogenita armentorum et pecorum et omnia quae voveris et sponte offerre volueris et primitias manuum tuarum*

You cannot eat in your towns *the* tithe of grain and wine and oil, *the* first fruits of your cattle and sheep, and all that you promise, and *the* free-will offerings you want, and your hands' first fruits.

12:18   *sed coram Domino Deo tuo comedes ea in loco quem elegerit Dominus Deus tuus tu et filius tuus ac filia servus et famula atque Levites qui manet in urbibus tuis et laetaberis et reficieris coram Domino Deo tuo in cunctis ad quae extenderis manum tuam*

But you will eat them before *the* Lord your God, in *the* place which *the* Lord your God will choose – you and your son and your daughter, male and female slaves, and Levites who stay in your towns. And you will be happy and be restored before *the* Lord your God in all things to which you extend your hand.

12:19   *cave ne derelinquas Leviten omni tempore quo versaris in terra*

Take care that you not abandon *the* Levites all *the* time that you move about in *the* land.

12:20   *quando dilataverit Dominus Deus tuus terminos tuos sicut locutus est tibi et volueris vesci carnibus quas desiderat anima tua*

When *the* Lord your God has broadened your borders, as He has spoken to you, and you want to eat *the* meat which your soul desires,

12:21   *locus autem quem elegerit Dominus Deus tuus ut sit nomen eius ibi si procul fuerit occides de armentis et pecoribus quae habueris*

sicut praecepi tibi et comedes in oppidis tuis ut tibi placet

but *the* place is far away which *the* Lord your God has chosen that His name may be, kill from your herds and flocks which you have, as I have taught you, and eat in your towns what pleases you.

12:22 *sicut comeditur caprea et cervus ita vesceris eis et mundus et inmundus in commune vescentur*

As goat and deer are eaten, so you will eat them. And clean and unclean alike you will eat.

12:23 *hoc solum cave ne sanguinem comedas sanguis enim eorum pro anima est et idcirco non debes animam comedere cum carnibus*

This only take care: that you not eat blood. For their blood is for *the* soul, and therefore, you must not eat it with *the* meat,

12:24 *sed super terram fundes quasi aquam*

but pour it on *the* ground like water –

12:25 *ut sit tibi bene et filiis tuis post te cum feceris quod placet in conspectu Domini*

that it may be well with you and your children after you, when you do what

is pleasing in *the* Lord's sight.

Bring Your Offering

12:26 *quae autem sanctificaveris et voveris Domino tolles et venies ad locum quem elegerit Dominus*

But what you have made holy and promised to *the* Lord, take *it* and come to *the* place which *the* Lord has chosen.

12:27 *et offeres oblationes tuas carnem et sanguinem super altare Domini Dei tui sanguinem hostiarum fundes in altari carnibus autem ipse vesceris*

And you will offer your offerings – flesh and blood – on *the* Lord your God's altar. You will pour *the* victims' blood on *the* altar, but you may eat *the* meat.

Don't Imitate Idol Worshipers

12:28 *observa et audi omnia quae ego praecipio tibi ut bene sit tibi et filiis tuis post te in sempiternum cum feceris quod bonum est et placitum in conspectu Domini Dei tui*

Keep and hear all that I am teaching you, that it may be well with you and your children after you forever, when you do what is good and pleasing in *the* Lord your God's sight!

12:29 *quando disperderit Dominus Deus tuus ante faciem tuam gentes ad quas ingredieris possidendas et* *possederis eas atque habitaveris in terra earum*

When *the* Lord has destroyed nations before your face, whom you are going in to possess, and you take them over and live in their land,

12:30 *cave ne imiteris eas postquam te fuerint introeunte subversae et requiras caerimonias earum dicens sicut coluerunt gentes istae deos suos ita et ego colam*

take care that you not imitate them, after they have been overthrown by your entry, and you seek their ceremonies, saying, 'As these nations served their gods, so also I will serve.'

12:31 *non facies similiter Domino Deo tuo omnes enim abominationes quas aversatur Dominus fecerunt diis suis offerentes filios et filias et conburentes igne*

You will not do that to *the* Lord your God, for all *the* abominations which *the* Lord turns away from in disgust they have done for their gods – offering sons and daughters and burning them with fire.

12:32 *quod praecipio tibi hoc tantum facito Domino nec addas quicquam nec minuas*

What I am commanding you, this much you will do for *the* Lord. You will neither add anything nor take away.

Testing Prophets

Deuteronomy 13:1 *si surrexerit in medio tui prophetes aut qui somnium vidisse se dicat et praedixerit signum atque portentum*

If *a* prophet, or one who claims to see dreams, should rise up among you who tells or predicts *a* sign or wonder,

13:2 *et evenerit quod locutus est et dixerit tibi eamus et sequamur deos alienos quos ignoras et serviamus eis*

and what he said should happen, and he should say to you, "Let us go and follow strange gods, which you have not known, and let us serve them,"

13:3 *non audies verba prophetae illius aut somniatoris quia temptat vos Dominus Deus vester ut palam fiat utrum diligatis eum an non in toto corde et in tota anima vestra*

do not listen to that prophet or dreamer's words, because *the* Lord your God is testing you, that it may be made plain whether you will delight in Him or not in all your heart and in all your soul!

13:4 *Dominum Deum vestrum sequimini et ipsum timete mandata illius custodite et audite vocem eius ipsi servietis et ipsi adherebitis*

Follow *the* Lord your God, and fear Him! Keep His commandments and listen to His voice! You will serve Him and stick close to him.

13:5 *propheta autem ille aut fictor somniorum interficietur quia locutus est ut vos averteret a Domino Deo vestro qui eduxit vos de terra Aegypti et redemit de domo servitutis ut errare te faceret de via quam tibi praecepit Dominus Deus tuus et auferes malum de medio tui*

But *that* prophet or author of dreams will be killed, because he has spoken that he may turn you from *the* Lord your God, who led you from Egypt's land and bought you back from slavery's house, so he can make you wander from *the* way which *the* Lord your God has taught you. And you will take harm away from your midst.

Cost of Turning Away

13:6 *si tibi voluerit persuadere frater tuus filius matris tuae aut filius tuus vel filia sive uxor quae est in sinu tuo aut amicus quem diligis ut animam tuam clam dicens eamus et serviamus diis alienis quos ignoras tu et patres tui*

If your brother, your mother's son, or your son or daughter, whether *the* wife who is in your breast, or *a* friend whom you love like your soul, says secretly, "Let us go and serve alien gods, whom you or your fathers have not known,

13:7 *cunctarum in circuitu gentium*

quae iuxta vel procul sunt ab initio usque ad finem terrae

"from all *the* nations around which are near or far, from *the* land's beginning even to *its* end,"

13:8 *non adquiescas ei nec audias neque parcat ei oculus tuus ut misereris et occultes eum*

do not give in to him or listen! And do not let your eye spare him, so you can have pity or hide him!

13:9 *sed statim interficies sit primum manus tua super eum et post te omnis populus mittat manum*

But you will kill him quickly. Let your hand be first against him, and after you let *the* whole people cast *a* hand.

13:10 *lapidibus obrutus necabitur quia voluit te abstrahere a Domino Deo tuo qui eduxit te de terra Aegypti de domo servitutis*

Let him be killed by crushing stones, because he wanted to take you from *the* Lord your God, who led you from Egypt's land, from slavery's house –

13:11 *ut omnis Israhel audiens timeat et nequaquam ultra faciat quippiam huius rei simile*

so all Israel, hearing, may fear, and never again do something like this!

13:12 *si audieris in una urbium tuarum quas Dominus Deus tuus dabit tibi ad habitandum dicentes aliquos*

If you should hear some saying, in one of your towns which *the* Lord your God will give you to live in,

13:13 *egressi sunt filii Belial de medio tui et averterunt habitatores urbis tuae atque dixerunt eamus et serviamus diis alienis quos ignoratis*

"Belial's children have gone out from among you, and have turned your town's inhabitants away, and they say, 'Let us go and serve strange gods whom you do not know,'"

13:14 *quaere sollicite et diligenter rei veritate perspecta si inveneris certum esse quod dicitur et abominationem hanc opere perpetratam*

investigate *the* thing anxiously and diligently, by truthful evidence. If you find it true what is said, and this abomination was carried through,

13:15 *statim percuties habitatores urbis illius in ore gladii et delebis eam omniaque quae in illa sunt usque ad pecora*

you will strike that town's inhabitants down immediately by *the* sword's mouth, and destroy it and all that are in it, even to cattle!

13:16 *quicquid etiam supellectilis fuerit congregabis in medium platearum eius et cum ipsa civitate succendes ita ut universa consumas Domino Deo tuo et sit tumulus sempiternus non aedificabitur amplius*

And even any furniture *that* is there, you will pile up in *the* middle of its streets. And you will burn it with this city, so you consume all by *the* Lord your God, and it may be *an* everlasting tomb. It will not be built again.

13:17 *et non adherebit de illo anathemate quicquam in manu tua ut avertatur Dominus ab ira furoris sui et misereatur tui multiplicetque te sicut iuravit patribus tuis*

And nothing from that cursed *place* will stick to your hand, so *the* Lord may turn from His anger's fury, and have mercy on you, and multiply you, as He swore to your fathers.

13:18 *quando audieris vocem Domini Dei tui custodiens omnia praecepta eius quae ego praecipio tibi hodie ut facias quod placitum est in conspectu Domini Dei tui*

When *you* hear the Lord your God's voice, *continue* keeping all His precepts which I am teaching you today, that you do what is pleasing in *the* Lord your God's sight!

Don't Cut Yourselves

Deuteronomy 14:1 *filii estote Domini Dei vestri non vos incidetis nec facietis calvitium super mortuo*

Be *the* Lord your God's children! You will not cut yourselves or make yourselves bald over *the* dead,

14:2 *quoniam populus sanctus es Domino Deo tuo et te elegit ut sis ei in populum peculiarem de cunctis gentibus quae sunt super terram*

for you are holy people to *the* Lord your God, and He chose you so you could be *a* peculiar people for Him, from all *the* nations which are on *the* land.

Clean and Unclean Meat

14:3 *ne comedatis quae inmunda sunt*

You will not eat what is unclean.

14:4 *hoc est animal quod comedere debetis bovem et ovem et capram*

This is *the kind of* animal which you will eat: cattle and sheep and deer,

14:5 *cervum capream bubalum tragelaphum pygargon orygem camelopardalum*

stag, wild goat, antelope, bearded goat, white-tail deer, wild ox, giraffe.

14:6 *omne animal quod in duas partes ungulam findit et ruminat comedetis*

Every animal that divides *the* hoof in two parts and chews cud you will eat.

14:7 *de his autem quae ruminant et ungulam non findunt haec comedere non debetis camelum leporem choerogyllium quia ruminant et non dividunt ungulam inmunda erunt vobis*

But from all that chew cud and don't divide *the* hoof, these you must not eat. Camel, hare, rabbit, because they chew cud and do not divide *the* hoof, will be unclean to you.

14:8 *sus quoque quoniam dividit ungulam et non ruminat inmunda erit carnibus eorum non vescemini et cadavera non tangetis*

Swine, likewise, because it divides *the* hoof and does not chew cud, will be unclean. You will not eat their meat or touch their dead bodies.

14:9 *haec comedetis ex omnibus quae morantur in aquis quae habent pinnulas et squamas comedite*

These you will eat from all which live in *the* waters. Those that have fins and scales, eat!

14:10 *quae absque pinnulis et squamis sunt ne comedatis quia* *inmunda sunt*

Those that are without fins and scales you will not eat, because they are unclean.

14:11 *omnes aves mundas comedite*

All clean birds, eat.

14:12 *inmundas ne comedatis aquilam scilicet et grypem et alietum*

You will not eat *the* unclean: eagles, of course, griffins and ospreys,

14:13 *ixon et vulturem ac milvum iuxta genus suum*

ringtails and vultures and kites, according to its type,

14:14 *et omne corvini generis*

and all families of crows –

14:15 *strutionem ac noctuam et larum atque accipitrem iuxta genus suum*

ostrich and owl and gull, and hawks, according to its type –

14:16 *herodium et cycnum et ibin*

stork and swan and ibis –

14:17 *ac mergulum porphirionem et nycticoracem*

and small gull, purple coot, and night raven –

14:18 *onocrotalum et charadrium singula in genere suo upupam quoque et vespertilionem*

pelican and yellowfish bird, each in its type, hoopoe likewise and bat.

14:19 *et omne quod reptat et pinnulas habet inmundum erit nec comedetur*

And everything that crawls and has wings will be unclean, nor will it be eaten.

14:20 *omne quod mundum est comedite*

All that is clean, eat.

14:21 *quicquid morticinum est ne vescamini ex eo peregrino qui intra portas tuas est da ut comedat aut vende ei quia tu populus sanctus Domini Dei tui es non coques hedum in lacte matris suae*

You will not eat from whatever is dead without slaughter. Give it to the stranger who is in your gates, or sell it, because you are holy people to the Lord your God. You will not cook *a* young goat in its mother's milk.

Giving a Tenth
14:22 *decimam partem separabis de*

cunctis frugibus tuis quae nascuntur in terra per annos singulos

You will set aside *a* tenth part of all your crops, which will grow in *the* land each year.

14:23 *et comedes in conspectu Domini Dei tui in loco quem elegerit ut in eo nomen illius invocetur decimam frumenti tui et vini et olei et primogenita de armentis et ovibus tuis ut discas timere Dominum Deum tuum omni tempore*

And you will eat *them* in *the* Lord your God's sight, in *the* place which He will choose, that His name may be invoked in it – *a* tenth of your grain and wine and oil, and first fruits of your cattle and sheep, so you may learn to fear *the* Lord your God at all times.

14:24 *cum autem longior fuerit via et locus quem elegerit Dominus Deus tuus tibique benedixerit nec potueris ad eum haec cuncta portare*

But when *the* way is long, and He has blessed you, and you aren't able to carry all these things to *the* place which *the* Lord your God has chosen,

14:25 *vendes omnia et in pretium rediges portabisque manu tua et proficisceris ad locum quem elegerit Dominus Deus tuus*

you will sell all *of it,* and reduce *it* to

money, and take *it* in your hand. And you will set out for *the* place which *the* Lord your God has chosen.

14:26 *et emes ex eadem pecunia quicquid tibi placuerit sive ex armentis sive ex ovibus vinum quoque et siceram et omne quod desiderat anima tua et comedes coram Domino Deo tuo et epulaberis tu et domus tua*

And you will buy from it for money whatever pleases you, whether from cattle or from sheep, wine likewise and liquor, and all that you soul wants. And you will eat before *the* Lord your God, and you will feast and your house.

14:27 *et Levita qui intra portas tuas est cave ne derelinquas eum quia non habet aliam partem in possessione tua*

And *the* Levite who is in your gates, take care that you not neglect him, for he has no other portion in your possession.

Every Third Year for the Poor
14:28 *anno tertio separabis aliam decimam ex omnibus quae nascuntur tibi eo tempore et repones intra ianuas tuas*

The third year you will separate another tenth from all that grows for you at that time, and you will store *it* inside your doors.

14:29 *venietque Levites qui aliam non habet partem nec possessionem tecum et peregrinus et pupillus ac vidua qui intra portas tuas sunt et comedent et saturabuntur ut benedicat tibi Dominus Deus tuus in cunctis operibus manuum tuarum quae feceris*

And *the* Levite will come, who has no other portion or possession with you, and *the* stranger and orphan and widow who are in your gates. And they will eat and be filled, so *the* Lord your God can bless you in all *the* works which your hands will do.

The Year of Releasing
Deuteronomy 15:1 *septimo anno facies remissionem*

The seventh year you will make *a* releasing,

15:2 *quae hoc ordine celebrabitur cui debetur aliquid ab amico vel proximo ac fratre suo repetere non poterit quia annus remissionis est Domini*

which will be performed in this order: one who is owed something by his friend or neighbor or brother will not be able to demand repayment, because *it* is *the* Lord's year of release.

15:3 *a peregrino et advena exiges civem et propinquum repetendi non habes potestatem*

You will require payment from traveler and newcomer. You do not have power to demand *repayment* from citizen or neighbor.

15:4 *et omnino indigens et mendicus non erit inter vos ut benedicat tibi Dominus in terra quam traditurus est tibi in possessionem*

And there will not be among you at all *a* poor person or beggar, so *the* Lord may bless you in *the* land which He will give to you as possession.

15:5 *si tamen audieris vocem*

Domini Dei tui et custodieris universa quae iussit et quae ego hodie praecipio tibi benedicet tibi ut pollicitus est

If indeed you will hear *the* Lord your God's voice, and keep all which He has commanded, and which I am teaching you today, He will bless you as He promised.

15:6 *fenerabis gentibus multis et ipse a nullo accipies mutuum dominaberis nationibus plurimis et tui nemo dominabitur*

You will lend to many nations and will borrow from no one. You will dominate many nations, and no one will dominate you.

Remember Your Poor Brother
15:7 *si unus de fratribus tuis qui morantur intra portas civitatis tuae in terra quam Dominus Deus tuus daturus est tibi ad paupertatem venerit non obdurabis cor tuum nec contrahes manum*

If one of your brothers who lives in your city's gates, in *the* land which *the* Lord your God will give you, should come to poverty, you will not harden your heart or close *your* hand.

15:8 *sed aperies eam pauperi et dabis mutuum quod eum indigere perspexeris*

But you will open it to *the* poor and give help, what you have known him to need.

15:9 *cave ne forte subripiat tibi impia cogitatio et dicas in corde tuo adpropinquat septimus annus remissionis et avertas oculos a paupere fratre tuo nolens ei quod postulat mutuum commodare ne clamet contra te ad Dominum et fiat tibi in peccatum*

Take care, unless *a* lawless thought steal you away, and you say in your heart, '*The* seventh year of release is near,' and you turn your eyes away from your poor brother, not wanting to accommodate him in what help he asks! May he not cry out to *the* Lord against you and *it* become *a* sin to you.

15:10 *sed dabis ei nec ages quippiam callide in eius necessitatibus sublevandis ut benedicat tibi Dominus Deus tuus in omni tempore et in cunctis ad quae manum miseris*

But you will give to him, and not carry on something deceptively in assisting his needs, so *the* Lord your God may bless you at all times and in all which your hand will send out.

15:11 *non deerunt pauperes in terra habitationis tuae idcirco ego praecipio tibi ut aperias manum fratri tuo egeno et pauperi qui tecum versatur in terra*

The poor will not be abandoned in your habitation's land. Therefore I am commanding you that you open your hand to your needy brother, and to *the* poor who goes around with you in *the* land.

Rules for Slaves

15:12 *cum tibi venditus fuerit frater tuus hebraeus aut hebraea et sex annis servierit tibi in septimo anno dimittes eum liberum*

When your Hebrew brother or sister has been sold to you, and has served you six years, in *the* seventh year, you will set him free.

15:13 *et quem libertate donaveris nequaquam vacuum abire patieris*

And one whom you have given freedom, you by no means will allow to go away empty.

15:14 *sed dabis viaticum de gregibus et de area et torculari tuo quibus Dominus Deus tuus benedixerit tibi*

But you will give provision from flocks and from threshing floors, and your winepress, by which *the* Lord your God has blessed you.

15:15 *memento quod et ipse servieris in terra Aegypti et liberaverit te Dominus Deus tuus et idcirco ego nunc praecipiam tibi*

Remember that you also slaved in Egypt's land, and *the* Lord your God freed you, and for this reason I will command you now!

15:16 *sin autem dixerit nolo egredi eo quod diligat te et domum tuam et bene sibi apud te esse sentiat*

But if he should say, 'I do not want to go away,' that he loves you and your house, and he feels well being with you,

15:17 *adsumes subulam et perforabis aurem eius in ianua domus tuae et serviet tibi usque in aeternum ancillae quoque similiter facies*

you will take *a* shoemaker's awl and pierce his ear in your house's doorway, and he will slave for you even in eternity. Likewise, you will do *the* same for your slave woman.

15:18 *non avertes ab eis oculos tuos quando dimiseris eos liberos quoniam iuxta mercedem mercennarii per sex annos servivit tibi ut benedicat tibi Dominus Deus tuus in cunctis operibus quae agis*

You will not turn your eyes away from them when you send them away free, for he has served you according to *the* price of six years' wages, so *the* Lord your God may bless you in all *the* works which you carry on.

First Fruits

15:19 *de primogenitis quae nascuntur in armentis et ovibus tuis quicquid sexus est masculini sanctificabis Domino Deo tuo non operaberis in primogenito bovis et non tondebis primogenita ovium*

From *the* first which are born among your cattle and sheep – whatever is masculine sex – you will make holy to *the* Lord your God. You will not work with *the* firstborn ox or shear *the* firstborn sheep.

15:20 *in conspectu Domini Dei tui comedes ea per annos singulos in loco quem elegerit Dominus tu et domus tua*

You will eat them each year in *the* Lord your God's sight, in the place which *the* Lord has chosen – you and your house.

15:21 *sin autem habuerit maculam et vel claudum fuerit vel caecum aut in aliqua parte deforme vel debile non immolabitur Domino Deo tuo*

But if one should have *a* blemish, or be lame, or blind, or in some part deformed or weak, you will not burn it to *the* Lord your God.

15:22 *sed intra portas urbis tuae comedes illud tam mundus quam inmundus similiter vescentur eis quasi caprea et cervo*

But you will eat it inside your city's gates. Clean and unclean alike will be eaten by them, like goat and deer.

15:23 *hoc solum observabis ut sanguinem eorum non comedas sed effundas in terram quasi aquam*

You will observe this only, that you not eat their blood, but you pour *it* out on *the* ground like water.

Passover

Deuteronomy 16:1 *observa mensem novarum frugum et verni primum temporis ut facias phase Domino Deo tuo quoniam in isto mense eduxit te Dominus Deus tuus de Aegypto nocte*

Keep *the* month of new fruit and *the* first times of spring, so you work *the* Lord your God's Passover, for in this month *the* Lord your God led you by night out of Egypt.

16:2 *immolabisque phase Domino Deo tuo de ovibus et de bubus in loco quem elegerit Dominus Deus tuus ut habitet nomen eius ibi*

And you will offer *the* Passover to *the* Lord your God, from sheep and oxen, in *the* place which *the* Lord your God will choose, so His name may live there.

16:3 *non comedes in eo panem fermentatum septem diebus comedes absque fermento adflictionis panem quoniam in pavore egressus es de Aegypto ut memineris diei egressionis tuae de Aegypto omnibus diebus vitae tuae*

You will not eat fermented bread in it. For seven days, you will eat affliction's bread without yeast, because you came out of Egypt in fear, so you can remember *the* day of your coming out of Egypt all your life's days.

16:4 *non apparebit fermentum in omnibus terminis tuis septem diebus et non manebit de carnibus eius quod immolatum est vesperi in die primo mane*

Yeast will not appear in all your borders for seven days. Nothing will remain from its meat which was offered, from evening to *the* day's first light.

16:5 *non poteris immolare phase in qualibet urbium tuarum quas Dominus Deus tuus daturus est tibi*

You cannot offer *the* Passover in whichever of your cities which *the* Lord your God will give you.

16:6 *sed in loco quem elegerit Dominus Deus tuus ut habitet nomen eius ibi immolabis phase vesperi ad solis occasum quando egressus es de Aegypto*

But in *the* place which *the* Lord you God will choose so His name can inhabit, there you will offer *the* Passover at evening, at sunset, when you came out of Egypt.

16:7 *et coques et comedes in loco quem elegerit Dominus Deus tuus maneque consurgens vades in tabernacula tua*

And you will cook and eat *it* in *the* place which *the* Lord your God will choose. And rising up early, you will go into your tents.

16:8 *sex diebus comedes azyma et in die septimo quia collecta est Domini Dei tui non facies opus*

Six days you will eat uncorrupted bread, and on *the* seventh day you will do no work, because it is *the* Lord your God's gathering.

The Feast of Weeks

16:9 *septem ebdomadas numerabis tibi ab ea die qua falcem in segetem miseris*

You will count out seven weeks for yourself from that day in which you will send *the* sickle into *the* grain field.

16:10 *et celebrabis diem festum ebdomadarum Domino Deo tuo oblationem spontaneam manus tuae quam offeres iuxta benedictionem Domini Dei tui*

And you will celebrate *the* day of *the* feast of weeks to *the* Lord your God. You will offer by your hand *a* free offering, according to *the* Lord your God's blessing.

16:11 *et epulaberis coram Domino Deo tuo tu et filius tuus et filia tua et servus tuus et ancilla et Levites qui est intra portas tuas et advena ac pupillus et vidua qui morantur vobiscum in loco quem elegerit Dominus Deus tuus ut habitet nomen*

eius ibi

And you will feast before *the* Lord your God, and your son and your daughter and your slave and slave woman, and *the* Levite who is in your gates, and *the* newcomer and orphan and widow who live with you, in *the* place which *the* Lord your God will choose, so His name may live there.

16:12 *et recordaberis quoniam servus fueris in Aegypto custodiesque ac facies quae praecepta sunt*

And you will remember that you were *a* slave in Egypt, and you will keep and do *those things* that are commanded.

The Observance of Tents

16:13 *sollemnitatem quoque tabernaculorum celebrabis per septem dies quando collegeris de area et torculari fruges tuas*

Likewise, you will celebrate *the* solemnity of tents for seven days, when you gather your crops from threshing floor and winepress.

16:14 *et epulaberis in festivitate tua tu et filius tuus et filia et servus tuus et ancilla Levites quoque et advena et pupillus ac vidua qui intra portas tuas sunt*

And you will feast in your

celebration, you and your son and daughter, and your slave and slave woman, *the* Levite likewise and newcomer and widow who are in your gates.

Celebrating the Feasts
16:15 *septem diebus Domino Deo tuo festa celebrabis in loco quem elegerit Dominus benedicetque tibi Dominus Deus tuus in cunctis frugibus tuis et in omni opere manuum tuarum erisque in laetitia*

You will celebrate *the* feasts to *the* Lord your God seven days, in *the* place which *the* Lord will choose. And *the* Lord your God will bless you in all your crops, and in every work of your hand. And you will be in happiness.

16:16 *tribus vicibus per annum apparebit omne masculinum tuum in conspectu Domini Dei tui in loco quem elegerit in sollemnitate azymorum et in sollemnitate ebdomadarum et in sollemnitate tabernaculorum non apparebit ante Dominum vacuus*

Each of your males will appear three times *a* year *in* the Lord your God's sight, in *the* place which the Lord your God will choose: in *the* solemnity of uncorrupted *bread*, and in *the* solemnity of weeks, and in *the* solemnity of tents. He will not appear empty-handed before *the* Lord.

16:17 *sed offeret unusquisque secundum quod habuerit iuxta benedictionem Domini Dei sui quam dederit ei*

But each one will offer according to what he has, along with *the* blessing which *the* Lord his God has given him.

Judges and Officials
16:18 *iudices et magistros constitues in omnibus portis tuis quas Dominus Deus tuus dederit tibi per singulas tribus tuas ut iudicent populum iusto iudicio*

You will appoint judges and magistrates in all your gates which *the* Lord your God will give you, for each of your tribes, so they can judge *the* people with fair judgment.

16:19 *nec in alteram partem declinent non accipies personam nec munera quia munera excaecant oculos sapientium et mutant verba iustorum*

They may not turn away into another part, nor will you favor person or bribes, because bribes blind wise men's eyes and change fair men's words.

16:20 *iuste quod iustum est persequeris ut vivas et possideas terram quam Dominus Deus tuus dederit tibi*

Fairly, you will seek what is fair, so you can live and possess *the* land which *the* Lord your God will give you.

Laws for Worship
16:21 *non plantabis lucum et omnem arborem iuxta altare Domini Dei tui*

You will not plant *a* sacred grove and every tree beside *the* Lord your God's altar.

16:22 *nec facies tibi atque constitues statuam quae odit Dominus Deus tuus*

You will not make for yourself or set up *a* statue, which *the* Lord your God hates.

An Unblemished Offering
Deuteronomy 17:1 *non immolabis Domino Deo tuo bovem et ovem in quo est macula aut quippiam vitii quia abominatio est Domini Dei tui*

You will not offer to *the* Lord your God *an* ox or sheep in which *there* is any blemish or defect, because *it* is *an* abomination to the Lord your God.

Covenant Breakers
17:2 *cum repperti fuerint apud te intra unam portarum tuarum quas Dominus Deus tuus dabit tibi vir aut mulier qui faciant malum in conspectu Domini Dei tui et transgrediantur pactum illius*

When men or women who do harm in *the* Lord your God's sight and violate His pact are found among you, in one of your gates which *the* Lord your God will give you,

17:3 *ut vadant et serviant diis alienis et adorent eos solem et lunam et omnem militiam caeli quae non praecepi*

so they go and serve alien gods and adore them – sun and moon and all *the* sky's soldiers, which I have not commanded –

17:4 *et hoc tibi fuerit nuntiatum audiensque inquisieris diligenter et verum esse reppereris et abominatio facta est in Israhel*

and this is told you, and, hearing, you inquire carefully and find *it* to be true, and *an* abomination has happened in Israel,

17:5 *educes virum ac mulierem qui rem sceleratissimam perpetrarunt ad portas civitatis tuae et lapidibus obruentur*

you will lead *the* man or woman who perpetrated this most criminal act to your city's gates, and crush them *with* stones.

17:6 *in ore duorum aut trium testium peribit qui interficietur nemo occidatur uno contra se dicente testimonium*

He who will be executed will die at *the* mouth of two or three witnesses. Let no one be killed by only one giving testimony against him.

17:7 *manus testium prima interficiet eum et manus reliqui populi extrema mittetur ut auferas malum de medio tui*

The witnesses' hands will kill him first, and *the* hands of *the* rest of *the* people will cast *stones* to *the* end, so you can take away harm from among you.

Difficult Cases

17:8 *si difficile et ambiguum apud te iudicium esse perspexeris inter sanguinem et sanguinem causam et*

causam lepram et non lepram et iudicum intra portas tuas videris verba variari surge et ascende ad locum quem elegerit Dominus Deus tuus

If judgment should seem difficult and ambiguous where you are – between blood and blood, cause and cause, leprosy and not leprosy – and you see that *the* judges' words in your gates vary, get up and go up to *the* place which *the* Lord your God will choose.

17:9 *veniesque ad sacerdotes levitici generis et ad iudicem qui fuerit illo tempore quaeresque ab eis qui indicabunt tibi iudicii veritatem*

And come to *the* line of Levitical priests, and to *the* judge who is *serving* at that time. And you will ask them, who will tell you *the* judgment's truth.

17:10 *et facies quodcumque dixerint qui praesunt loco quem elegerit Dominus et docuerint te*

And you will do whatever *those* who are in charge in *the* place which *the* Lord your God will choose tell you. And they will teach you.

17:11 *iuxta legem eius sequeris sententiam eorum nec declinabis ad dextram vel ad sinistram*

You will follow their sentence

according to His law, nor will you turn away to *the* right or to *the* left.

17:12 *qui autem superbierit nolens oboedire sacerdotis imperio qui eo tempore ministrat Domino Deo tuo et decreto iudicis morietur homo ille et auferes malum de Israhel*

But one who will be proud, not wanting to obey *the* priest's decree who ministers to *the* Lord your God at that time, and *the* judge's decree – that man will die. And you will take away harm from Israel.

17:13 *cunctusque populus audiens timebit ut nullus deinceps intumescat superbia*

And all *the* people, hearing, will fear, and no one thereafter will swell with pride.

Qualifications for Kings
17:14 *cum ingressus fueris terram quam Dominus Deus tuus dabit tibi et possederis eam habitaverisque in illa et dixeris constituam super me regem sicut habent omnes per circuitum nationes*

When you have come into *the* land which *the* Lord your God will give you, and you possess it and live in it, and you say, 'I will appoint *a* king over me, like all *the* nations around have,'

17:15 *eum constitues quem*

Dominus Deus tuus elegerit de numero fratrum tuorum non poteris alterius gentis hominem regem facere qui non sit frater tuus

you will appoint one whom *the* Lord your God will choose, from your brothers' number. You cannot appoint *a* man from another nation, to make one who is not your brother king.

17:16 *cumque fuerit constitutus non multiplicabit sibi equos nec reducet populum in Aegyptum equitatus numero sublevatus praesertim cum Dominus praeceperit vobis ut nequaquam amplius per eandem viam revertamini*

And when he has been appointed, he will not multiply horses for himself, or return *the* people to Egypt, lifted up by *the* number of *his* cavalry – particularly when *the* Lord has commanded you that you never more return by that road.

17:17 *non habebit uxores plurimas quae inliciant animum eius neque argenti et auri inmensa pondera*

He will not have many wives who may entice his soul, or immense weights of silver and gold.

17:18 *postquam autem sederit in solio regni sui describet sibi deuteronomium legis huius in volumine accipiens exemplar a* *sacerdotibus leviticae tribus*

But after he has sat down on his royal throne, he will write out for himself *the* restatement of this law in *a* book, accepting *the* copy of *the* Levitical tribe's priests.

17:19 *et habebit secum legetque illud omnibus diebus vitae suae ut discat timere Dominum Deum suum et custodire verba et caerimonias eius quae lege praecepta sunt*

And he will have it with him, and will read it all his life's days, so he may learn to fear *the* Lord his God, and to keep His words and ceremonies, which are taught in the law.

17:20 *nec elevetur cor eius in superbiam super fratres suos neque declinet in partem dextram vel sinistram ut longo tempore regnet ipse et filii eius super Israhel*

And let his heart not be lifted up in pride over his brothers, nor let him turn away to *the* right portion or left, so he and his son may reign *a* long time over Israel.

Priests and Levites Don't Inherit
Deuteronomy 18:1 *non habebunt sacerdotes et Levitae et omnes qui de eadem tribu sunt partem et hereditatem cum reliquo Israhel quia sacrificia Domini et oblationes eius comedent*

Priests and Levites and all who are from their tribe will not have part or inheritance with *the* rest of Israel, because they will eat *the* Lord's sacrifices and offerings.

18:2 *et nihil aliud accipient de possessione fratrum suorum Dominus enim ipse est hereditas eorum sicut locutus est illis*

And they will receive nothing else from their brothers' possession, for *the* Lord Himself is their inheritance, as He has spoken to them.

18:3 *hoc erit iudicium sacerdotum a populo et ab his qui offerunt victimas sive bovem sive ovem immolaverint dabunt sacerdoti armum ac ventriculum*

This will be *the* priests' judgment from *the* people, and from those who are offering victims, whether ox or sheep, so they may be burned. They will give *the* priest *the* forequarter and breast,

18:4 *primitias frumenti vini et olei et lanarum partem ex ovium tonsione*

first fruits of grain, wine, and oil, and part of *the* wool from *the* sheep's shearing.

18:5 *ipsum enim elegit Dominus Deus tuus de cunctis tribubus tuis ut stet et ministret nomini Domini ipse et filii eius in sempiternum*

For *the* Lord your God chose him from all your tribes, so he can stand and minister in *the* Lord's name, and his children, forever.

18:6 *si exierit Levites de una urbium tuarum ex omni Israhel in qua habitat et voluerit venire desiderans locum quem elegerit Dominus*

If *a* Levite from one of your cities in which he lives, of all Israel, should come out, and wants to go, desiring *the* place which the Lord will choose,

18:7 *ministrabit in nomine Dei sui sicut omnes fratres eius Levitae qui stabunt eo tempore coram Domino*

he will minister in his God's name like all his brothers, Levites who stand before *the* Lord at that time.

18:8 *partem ciborum eandem accipiet quam et ceteri excepto eo quod in urbe sua ex paterna ei successione debetur*

He will receive *the* same portion of food that *the* others also *do*, except that which is owed him by succession

in his city from his father.

Don't Worship Like a Canaanite
18:9 *quando ingressus fueris terram quam Dominus Deus tuus dabit tibi cave ne imitari velis abominationes illarum gentium*

When you have come into *the* land which *the* Lord your God will give you, take care that you not imitate *the* abominations of those nations!

18:10 *nec inveniatur in te qui lustret filium suum aut filiam ducens per ignem aut qui ariolos sciscitetur et observet somnia atque auguria ne sit maleficus*

Let no one be found among you who purifies his son or daughter, leading them through fire, or who consults seers, or watches dreams and auguries, or is *a* wizard,

18:11 *ne incantator ne pythones consulat ne divinos et quaerat a mortuis veritatem*

or consults enchanters or snake-slayers or diviners, and seeks truth from *the* dead.

18:12 *omnia enim haec abominatur Dominus et propter istiusmodi scelera delebit eos in introitu tuo*

For *the* Lord despises all of these, and, because of such crimes, He will destroy them at your entry.

18:13 *perfectus eris et absque macula cum Domino Deo tuo*

You will be perfect and without stain with *the* Lord your God.

The Lord Will Stir Up a Prophet
18:14 *gentes istae quarum possidebis terram augures et divinos audiunt tu autem a Domino Deo tuo aliter institutus es*

These nations whose land you will take over listen to augurs and diviners, but you were set up differently by *the* Lord your God.

18:15 *prophetam de gente tua et de fratribus tuis sicut me suscitabit tibi Dominus Deus tuus ipsum audies*

The Lord your God will stir up for you from your nation and your brothers *a* prophet like me. You will listen to him,

18:16 *ut petisti a Domino Deo tuo in Horeb quando contio congregata est atque dixisti ultra non audiam vocem Domini Dei mei et ignem hunc maximum amplius non videbo ne moriar*

as you begged *the* Lord your God on Horeb, when *the* assembly was gathered and you said, 'I will not hear *the* Lord my God's voice further, and I will not see this overwhelming fire any more, so I won't die.'

18:17 *et ait Dominus mihi bene omnia sunt locuti*

And *the* Lord said to me, "They have spoken all things well.

18:18 *prophetam suscitabo eis de medio fratrum suorum similem tui et ponam verba mea in ore eius loqueturque ad eos omnia quae praecepero illi*

"I will stir up *a* prophet for them like you from among their brothers, and I will put My words in his mouth. And he will speak to them all that I will command him.

18:19 *qui autem verba eius quae loquetur in nomine meo audire noluerit ego ultor existam*

"But I will prove to be avenger *to* one who does not want to hear *the* words which he will speak in My name.

18:20 *propheta autem qui arrogantia depravatus voluerit loqui in nomine meo quae ego non praecepi illi ut diceret aut ex nomine alienorum deorum interficietur*

"But *a* prophet who arrogantly wants to speak depravity in My name, which I did not command him that he say, or in *the* name of strange gods, will be killed

Proving Genuine Prophets

18:21 *quod si tacita cogitatione responderis quomodo possum intellegere verbum quod non est locutus Dominus*

"If by silent thought you respond, 'How can I understand *a* word which *the* Lord has not spoken?'

18:22 *hoc habebis signum quod in nomine Domini propheta ille praedixerit et non evenerit hoc Dominus non locutus est sed per tumorem animi sui propheta confinxit et idcirco non timebis eum*

"you will have this sign: what that prophet predicts in *the* Lord's name but does not happen, this *the* Lord has not spoken. But *the* prophet, by his swollen soul, has fabricated *it*. And therefore, you will not fear him.

Cities of Refuge in Canaan

Deuteronomy 19:1 *cum disperderit Dominus Deus tuus gentes quarum tibi traditurus est terram et possederis eam habitaverisque in urbibus eius et in aedibus*

When *the* Lord your God has destroyed *the* nations whose land He will give you, and you take it over and live in its cities and houses,

19:2 *tres civitates separabis tibi in medio terrae quam Dominus Deus tuus dabit tibi in possessionem*

you will set aside for yourself three cities in *the* midst of *the* land which *the* Lord your God will give you as *a* possession.

19:3 *sternens diligenter viam et in tres aequaliter partes totam terrae tuae provinciam divides ut habeat e vicino qui propter homicidium profugus est quo possit evadere*

And, laying *the* way out carefully, you will divide all *the* province of your land in three equal parts, so he who has fled because of killing *a* man may have *one city* close by where he can escape.

Involuntary Manslaughter

19:4 *haec erit lex homicidae fugientis cuius vita servanda est qui percusserit proximum suum nesciens et qui heri et nudius tertius nullum contra eum habuisse odium* *conprobatur*

This will be *the* law of one fleeing from killing *a* man, whose life must be spared. One who will strike down his neighbor unknowingly, and who *it* can be proved had no hatred against him yesterday and *the* day before,

19:5 *sed abisse simpliciter cum eo in silvam ad ligna caedenda et in succisione lignorum securis fugerit manu ferrumque lapsum de manubrio amicum eius percusserit et occiderit hic ad unam supradictarum urbium confugiet et vivet*

but simply went with him into *the* forest to chop wood, and, in chopping wood, *the* ax escaped *the* hand, and, *the* iron slipping from *the* handle, he struck his friend and killed him. He will flee to one of *the* aforesaid cities and will live.

19:6 *ne forsitan proximus eius cuius effusus est sanguis dolore stimulatus persequatur et adprehendat eum si longior via fuerit et percutiat animam eius qui non est reus mortis quia nullum contra eum qui occisus est odium prius habuisse monstratur*

Unless, perhaps, *the* next of kin of him whose blood was spilled, moved by pain, may go after and catch him, if *the* way is longer, and may strike his soul who is not liable to death, because he can be shown to have had no prior hatred against *the* one who

was killed.

19:7 *idcirco praecipio tibi ut tres civitates aequalis inter se spatii dividas*

Therefore, I am commanding you that you divide up equally among *the* space three cities.

19:8 *cum autem dilataverit Dominus Deus tuus terminos tuos sicut iuravit patribus tuis et dederit tibi cunctam terram quam eis pollicitus est*

But when *the* Lord your God will broaden your borders, as He swore to your fathers, and He gives you all *the* land which He promised to them,

19:9 *si tamen custodieris mandata eius et feceris quae hodie praecipio tibi ut diligas Dominum Deum tuum et ambules in viis eius omni tempore addes tibi tres alias civitates et supradictarum trium urbium numerum duplicabis*

if nevertheless you will keep His commandments and do what I am commanding you today, that you delight in *the* Lord your God and walk in His ways all *the* time, you will add for yourself three other cities, and will duplicate *the* number of *the* aforesaid three cities,

19:10 *ut non effundatur sanguis innoxius in medio terrae quam*

Dominus Deus tuus dabit tibi possidendam nec sis sanguinis reus

so innocent blood may not be poured out in *the* middle of *the* land which *the* Lord your God will give you to possess, nor may you be guilty of blood.

Murder

19:11 *si quis autem odio habens proximum suum insidiatus fuerit vitae eius surgensque percusserit illum et mortuus fuerit fugeritque ad unam de supradictis urbibus*

But if someone having his neighbor in hatred will plot against his life and, rising up, will strike him and he be dead, and he will flee to one of *the* aforesaid cities,

19:12 *mittent seniores civitatis illius et arripient eum de loco effugii tradentque in manu proximi cuius sanguis effusus est et morietur*

his city's elders will send and take him from *the* place of escape and, handing him into *the* hands of *the* next of kin of *the* one whose blood was spilled, he will die.

19:13 *nec misereberis eius et auferes innoxium sanguinem de Israhel ut bene sit tibi*

Nor will you pity him, and you will take away innocent blood from Israel, so it may be well with you.

Respect Property Lines

19:14 *non adsumes et transferes terminos proximi tui quos fixerunt priores in possessione tua quam Dominus Deus tuus dabit tibi in terra quam acceperis possidendam*

You will not take up and move your neighbor's boundaries, which were laid down by those before *you* in your possession, which *the* Lord your God will give you in *the* land which you will receive to possess.

Multiple Witnesses

19:15 *non stabit testis unus contra aliquem quicquid illud peccati et facinoris fuerit sed in ore duorum aut trium testium stabit omne verbum*

One witness will not stand against another, whatever his sin or crime might be. But every word will stand in *the* testimony of two or three mouths.

Lying Witnesses

19:16 *si steterit testis mendax contra hominem accusans eum praevaricationis*

If *a* lying witness should stand against *a* man, accusing him of *an* offense,

19:17 *stabunt ambo quorum causa est ante Dominum in conspectu sacerdotum et iudicum qui fuerint in diebus illis*

both of those whose cause *it* is will stand before *the* Lord in *the* priests' and judges' sight, who serve at that time.

19:18 *cumque diligentissime perscrutantes invenerint falsum testem dixisse contra fratrem suum mendacium*

And when they, carefully investigating, have found that he spoke false testimony against his brother, lying,

19:19 *reddent ei sicut fratri suo facere cogitavit et auferes malum de medio tui*

they will pay to him as he plotted to do to his brother, and you will take harm away from your midst,

19:20 *ut audientes ceteri timorem habeant et nequaquam talia audeant facere*

so others, hearing, will have fear, and they may not dare to do such things again.

19:21 *non misereberis eius sed animam pro anima oculum pro oculo dentem pro dente manum pro manu pedem pro pede exiges*

You will not pity him, but will weigh out soul for soul, eye for eye, tooth for tooth, hand for hand, foot for foot.

Laws of War

Deuteronomy 20:1 *si exieris ad bellum contra hostes tuos et videris equitatum et currus et maiorem quam tu habes adversarii exercitus multitudinem non timebis eos quia Dominus Deus tuus tecum est qui eduxit te de terra Aegypti*

If you go out to battle against your enemies, and you see cavalry and chariots, and *the* multitude of *the* enemy's army greater than you have, you will not fear them, because *the* Lord your God is with you, who led you from Egypt's land.

20:2 *adpropinquante autem iam proelio stabit sacerdos ante aciem et sic loquetur ad populum*

But, *the* battle already coming close, *the* priest will stand before *the* line and will speak so to *the* people:

20:3 *audi Israhel vos hodie contra inimicos vestros pugnam committitis non pertimescat cor vestrum nolite metuere nolite cedere nec formidetis eos*

"Listen, Israel. Today you join *the* battle against your enemies. Let your heart not be terrified! Do not fear! Do not yield or be afraid of them!

20:4 *quia Dominus Deus vester in medio vestri est et pro vobis contra adversarios dimicabit ut eruat vos de periculo*

"For *the* Lord your God is among you, and will fight for you against adversaries, so He can rescue you from danger."

20:5 *duces quoque per singulas turmas audiente exercitu proclamabunt quis est homo qui aedificavit domum novam et non dedicavit eam vadat et revertatur in domum suam ne forte moriatur in bello et alius dedicet illam*

Likewise, *the* leaders through each squadron will proclaim in *the* army's hearing, "Who is *a* man who has built *a* new house and not dedicated it? Let him go and turn back to his house, unless perhaps he die in battle and another dedicate it.

20:6 *quis est homo qui plantavit vineam et necdum eam fecit esse communem et de qua vesci omnibus liceat vadat et revertatur in domum suam ne forte moriatur in bello et alius homo eius fungatur officio*

"Who is *a* man who has planted *a* vineyard and not yet made it be shared, from which everyone is permitted to eat? Let him go and turn back to his house, unless perhaps he die in battle and another man enjoy his service.

20:7 *quis est homo qui despondit uxorem et non accepit eam vadat et revertatur in domum suam ne forte moriatur in bello et alius homo*

accipiat eam

"Who is *a* man who has engaged *a* wife and not received her? Let him go and turn back to his house, unless perhaps he die in battle and another man receive her.

20:8 *his dictis addent reliqua et loquentur ad populum quis est homo formidolosus et corde pavido vadat et revertatur in domum suam ne pavere faciat corda fratrum suorum sicut ipse timore perterritus est*

This said, let them add to *the* rest and say to *the* people, "Who is *a* frightened man with *a* terrified heart? Let him go and turn back to his house, so he does not make his brothers' heart terrified, like he himself is terrified.

20:9 *cumque siluerint exercitus duces et finem loquendi fecerint unusquisque suos ad bellandum cuneos praeparabit*

And when *the* army's leaders grow silent and have made *an* end to speaking, each one of them will prepare *the* battalions for war.

First Offer Peace
20:10 *si quando accesseris ad expugnandam civitatem offeres ei primum pacem*

When you come to fight against *a* city, first you will offer them peace.

20:11 *si receperit et aperuerit tibi portas cunctus populus qui in ea est salvabitur et serviet tibi sub tributo*

If they accept *it* and open *the* gates to you, all *the* people who are in it will be spared and will serve you under tribute.

20:12 *sin autem foedus inire noluerint et receperint contra te bellum obpugnabis eam*

But if they don't want to go into *a* treaty *with you,* and undertake war against you, you will attack it.

20:13 *cumque tradiderit Dominus Deus tuus illam in manu tua percuties omne quod in ea generis masculini est in ore gladii*

And when *the* Lord your God has handed it into your hand, you will strike by *the* sword's mouth all in it who are males,

20:14 *absque mulieribus et infantibus iumentis et ceteris quae in civitate sunt omnem praedam exercitui divides et comedes de spoliis hostium tuorum quae Dominus Deus tuus dederit tibi*

apart from women and children, cattle and others who are in *the* city. You will divide all *the* plunder for *the* army, and you will eat from your enemies' spoils, which *the* Lord your God will give you.

20:15 *sic facies cunctis civitatibus quae a te procul valde sunt et non sunt de his urbibus quas in possessionem accepturus es*

So you will do to all *the* cities which are very far from you, and are not from those cities which you will be given as *a* possession.

No Peace for Near Neighbors
20:16 *de his autem civitatibus quae dabuntur tibi nullum omnino permittes vivere*

But from those cities which will be given you, you will permit nothing at all to live.

20:17 *sed interficies in ore gladii Hettheum videlicet et Amorreum et Chananeum Ferezeum et Eveum et Iebuseum sicut praecepit tibi Dominus Deus tuus*

But you will kill by *the* sword's mouth *the* Hittite, clearly, and Amorite and Canannite, Ferezite and Hivite and Jebusite, as *the* Lord your God has commanded you,

20:18 *ne forte doceant vos facere cunctas abominationes quas ipsi operati sunt diis suis et peccetis in Dominum Deum vestrum*

unless, perhaps, they teach you to do all *the* abominations which they have done for their gods, and you sin against *the* Lord your God.

Sieges

20:19 *quando obsederis civitatem multo tempore et munitionibus circumdederis ut expugnes eam non succides arbores de quibus vesci potest nec securibus per circuitum debes vastare regionem quoniam lignum est et non homo nec potest bellantium contra te augere numerum*

When you will lay siege to *a* city for *a* long time, and surround it by walls so you can fight against it, you will not cut down trees from which it is possible to eat, nor do you have to destroy *the* surrounding region by axes, because *it* is wood and not man. It cannot increase *the* number of those fighting against you.

20:20 *si qua autem ligna non sunt pomifera sed agrestia et in ceteros apta usus succide et extrue machinas donec capias civitatem quae contra te dimicat*

But if *the* trees are not fruit-bearing but wild, and in other ways apt for use, cut *them* down and build machines, until you capture *the* city which fights against you.

Investigating Murder

Deuteronomy 21:1 *quando inventum fuerit in terra quam Dominus Deus tuus daturus est tibi hominis cadaver occisi et ignoratur caedis reus*

When *a* killed human corpse will be found in *the* land which *the* Lord your God will give you, and *the* one guilty of murder is not known,

21:2 *egredientur maiores natu et iudices tui et metientur a loco cadaveris singularum per circuitum spatia civitatum*

the older born and your judges will go out and measure from *the* body's place *the* distance to each of *the* cities around.

21:3 *et quam viciniorem ceteris esse perspexerint seniores civitatis eius tollent vitulam de armento quae non traxit iugum nec terram scidit vomere*

And after they have seen which of *the* others is closest, *that* city's elders will take *a* calf from *the* herd, which has not drawn a yoke or torn *the* land with *a* plow.

21:4 *et ducent eam ad vallem asperam atque saxosam quae numquam arata est nec sementem recepit et caedent in ea cervices vitulae*

And they will lead it to *an* uneven and stony valley, which has not been plowed or received seed. And they will chop off *the* calf's head in it.

21:5 *accedentque sacerdotes filii Levi quos elegerit Dominus Deus tuus ut ministrent ei et benedicant in nomine eius et ad verbum eorum omne negotium et quicquid mundum vel inmundum est iudicetur*

And priests, Levi's children, will come, whom *the* Lord your God has chosen so they can minister to Him and bless in His name, and every affair and whatever is clean or unclean will be judged by their word.

21:6 *et maiores natu civitatis illius ad interfectum lavabuntque manus suas super vitulam quae in valle percussa est*

And *the* older born of that city *closest* to *the* killed one will wash their hands over *the* calf which was struck down in *the* valley.

21:6 *et dicent manus nostrae non effuderunt hunc sanguinem nec oculi viderunt*

And they will say, "Our hands have not poured out this blood, nor have *our* eyes seen."

21:8 *propitius esto populo tuo Israhel quem redemisti Domine et non reputes sanguinem innocentem*

in medio populi tui Israhel et auferetur ab eis reatus sanguinis

"Be favorable toward your people Israel, Lord, whom You bought back, and do not repute innocent blood among your people, Israel."

And blood guilt will be taken away from them.

21:9 *tu autem alienus eris ab innocentis cruore qui fusus est cum feceris quod praecepit Dominus*

But you will be *a* stranger from *the* innocent's gore, which was poured out, when you have done what *the* Lord commanded.

A Captive Woman

21:10 *si egressus fueris ad pugnam contra inimicos tuos et tradiderit eos Dominus Deus tuus in manu tua captivosque duxeris*

If you go out to fight against your enemies, and *the* Lord your God hands them over into your hand, and you lead them captive,

21:11 *et videris in numero captivorum mulierem pulchram et adamaveris eam volueris que habere uxorem*

and you see in *the* captives' number *a* beautiful woman, and you lust for her and want to have her as wife,

21:12 *introduces in domum tuam quae radet caesariem et circumcidet ungues*

you will bring her into your house. *She* will shave her flowing hair and cut her nails.

21:13 *et deponet vestem in qua capta est sedensque in domo tua flebit patrem et matrem suam uno mense et postea intrabis ad eam dormiesque cum illa et erit uxor tua*

And she will take off *the* clothes in which she was captured, and, sitting in your house, will mourn her father and mother one month. And after, you will enter into her and sleep with her, and she will be your wife.

21:14 *sin autem postea non sederit animo tuo dimittes eam liberam nec vendere poteris pecunia nec opprimere per potentiam quia humiliasti eam*

But if afterward she does not sit well with your soul, you will set her free. You cannot sell her for money or oppress her through force, because you have humiliated her.

Firstborn Rights
21:15 *si habuerit homo uxores duas unam dilectam et alteram odiosam genuerintque ex eo liberos et fuerit filius odiosae primogenitus*

If *a* man has two wives, one loved

and *the* other hated, and they give birth to children from him, and *the* hated one's son be firstborn,

21:16 *volueritque substantiam inter filios suos dividere non poterit filium dilectae facere primogenitum et praeferre filio odiosae*

and he wants to divide his substance among his children, he cannot make *the* loved one's son firstborn and prefer him over *the* hated one's son.

21:17 *sed filium odiosae agnoscet primogenitum dabitque ei de his quae habuerit cuncta duplicia iste est enim principium liberorum eius et huic debentur primogenita*

But he will recognize *the* hated one's son *as* firstborn. He will give him *a* two-fold share from all that he has. For he is his children's beginning, and *the* firstborn's rights are owed him.

Disobedient Children
21:18 *si genuerit homo filium contumacem et protervum qui non audiat patris aut matris imperium et coercitus oboedire contempserit*

If *a* man bears *a* disobedient and violent son, who does not listen to father or mother's rule, and, being corrected, will despise obeying,

21:19 *adprehendent eum et ducent ad seniores civitatis illius et ad portam iudicii*

they will take him and lead him to that city's elders, and to judgement's gate.

21:20 *dicentque ad eos filius noster iste protervus et contumax est monita nostra audire contemnit comesationibus vacat et luxuriae atque conviviis*

And they will say to them, "This our son is violent and disobedient. He despises listening to our warnings. He is idle in feasting and extravagance and partying."

21:21 *lapidibus eum obruet populus civitatis et morietur ut auferatis malum de medio vestri et universus Israhel audiens pertimescat*

The city's people will crush him with stones and he will die, so you may take away harm from among you. And all Israel, hearing, will fear.

Hangings
21:22 *quando peccaverit homo quod morte plectendum est et adiudicatus morti adpensus fuerit in patibulo*

When *a* man has sinned so that he will be punished by death, and, condemned to death, is hung on *a* gibbet,

21:23 *non permanebit cadaver eius in ligno sed in eadem die sepelietur quia maledictus a Deo est qui pendet in ligno et nequaquam contaminabis*

terram tuam quam Dominus Deus tuus dederit tibi in possessionem

you will not leave his body on *the* tree. But he will be buried that same day, because one who is hung on *a* tree is cursed by God. And you will by no means contaminate your land, which *the* Lord your God will give you as *a* possession.

My Brother's Keeper

Deuteronomy 22:1 *non videbis bovem fratris tui aut ovem errantem et praeteribis sed reduces fratri tuo*

You will not see your brother's ox or sheep lost and pass by. But you will lead them back to your brother.

22:2 *etiam si non est propinquus tuus frater nec nosti eum duces in domum tuam et erunt apud te quamdiu quaerat ea frater tuus et recipiat*

Even if your brother isn't close, or you don't know him, you will lead *them* to your house, and they will be with you until your brother looks for them and receives *them.*

22:3 *similiter facies de asino et de vestimento et de omni re fratris tui quae perierit si inveneris eam ne neglegas quasi alienam*

You will do likewise with donkey and clothing and everything that your brother will lose. If you find them, do not neglect them like *a* stranger.

22:4 *si videris asinum fratris tui aut bovem cecidisse in via non despicies sed sublevabis cum eo*

If you see your brother's donkey or ox fallen in *the* road, do not look down, but lift *it* up with him.

Social Roles

22:5 *non induetur mulier veste virili nec vir utetur veste feminea abominabilis enim apud Deum est qui facit haec*

A woman will not be dressed in man's clothing, nor *a* man use woman's clothing, for one who does this is detestable with God.

Preserving Life

22:6 *si ambulans per viam in arbore vel in terra nidum avis inveneris et matrem pullis vel ovis desuper incubantem non tenebis eam cum filiis*

If, walking in *the* road, you find *a* bird nest in *a* tree or on *the* ground, and *the* mother with young, or over eggs incubating, you will not take her with her young.

22:7 *sed abire patieris captos tenens filios ut bene sit tibi et longo vivas tempore*

But you will let *her* go, having *the* children captive, so it may be well with you and you may live *a* long time.

At Home

22:8 *cum aedificaveris domum novam facies murum tecti per circuitum ne effundatur sanguis in domo tua et sis reus labente alio et in praeceps ruente*

When you build *a* new house, you will make *a* walled roof around *it*. Do not let blood be poured out in your house, and let guilt be, another slipping and falling headfirst.

In Your Fields

22:9 *non seres vineam tuam altero semine ne et sementis quam sevisti et quae nascuntur ex vinea pariter sanctificentur*

You will not sow your vineyard with different seed, lest both what *grows* from *the* seed you have sown and what will grow from *the* vine will be sanctified together.

22:10 *non arabis in bove simul et asino*

You will not plow with ox and donkey at once.

Clothing

22:11 *non indueris vestimento quod ex lana linoque contextum est*

You will not put on clothing which is woven together from wool and linen.

22:12 *funiculos in fimbriis facies per quattuor angulos pallii tui quo operieris*

You will make thin cords into fringes for *the* four corners of *the* cloak you cover yourself with.

Slandering Israel's Virgin Daughters

22:13 *si duxerit vir uxorem et postea eam odio habuerit*

If *a* man takes *a* wife and after has her in hatred,

22:14 *quaesieritque occasiones quibus dimittat eam obiciens ei nomen pessimum et dixerit uxorem hanc accepi et ingressus ad eam non inveni virginem*

and he looks for occasions by which he can let her go, throwing *the* lowest name at her, and says, "I received this wife and, going into her, I did not find *her a* virgin,"

22:15 *tollent eam pater et mater eius et ferent secum signa virginitatis eius ad seniores urbis qui in porta sunt*

her father and mother will take her, and bring with them signs of her virginity to *the* city's elders, who are in *the* gate.

22:16 *et dicet pater filiam meam dedi huic uxorem quam quia odit*

And *the* father will say, "I have given my daughter *as* wife to this *man*, who, because he hates,

22:17 *inponet ei nomen pessimum ut dicat non inveni filiam tuam virginem et ecce haec sunt signa*

virginitatis filiae meae expandent vestimentum coram senibus civitatis

"will inflict *the* lowest name on her, so he says, 'I did not find your daughter *a* virgin.' And look, these are signs of my daughter's virginity."

They will spread out *the* clothing before *the* city's elders.

22:18 *adprehendentque senes urbis illius virum et verberabunt illum*

And that city's elders will take *the* man and beat him.

22:19 *condemnantes insuper centum siclis argenti quos dabit patri puellae quoniam diffamavit nomen pessimum super virginem Israhel habebitque eam uxorem et non poterit dimittere omni tempore vitae suae*

condemning in addition one hundred silver shekels, which he will give to the girl's father, because he made public *the* lowest name against Israel's young woman. And he will have her *as* wife, and will not be able to let her go all his lifetime.

Adultery

22:20 *quod si verum est quod obicit et non est in puella inventa virginitas*

But if what he presents is true, and virginity is not found in *the* girl,

22:21 *eicient eam extra fores domus patris sui et lapidibus obruent viri civitatis eius et morietur quoniam fecit nefas in Israhel ut fornicaretur in domo patris sui et auferes malum de medio tui*

they will throw her outside *the* doors of her father's house, and her city's men will crush her with stones, and she will die, because she worked *a* violation of divine law in Israel, that she fornicated in her father's house. And you will take away harm from among you.

22:22 *si dormierit vir cum uxore alterius uterque morientur id est adulter et adultera et auferes malum de Israhel*

If *a* man sleeps with another's wife, each will die, that is, adulterer and adulteress, and you will take away harm from Israel.

22:23 *si puellam virginem desponderit vir et invenerit eam aliquis in civitate et concubuerit cum illa*

If *a* man will get engaged to *a* virgin in marriage, and another man will find her in *the* city and have sex with her,

22:24 *educes utrumque ad portam civitatis illius et lapidibus obruentur puella quia non clamavit cum esset in civitate vir quia humiliavit uxorem*

proximi sui et auferes malum de medio tui

you will lead both to that city's gate and crush them with stones: *the* girl, because she did not cry out when she was in *the* city; *the* man, because he humiliated his neighbor's wife. And you will take away harm from among you.

22:25 *sin autem in agro reppererit vir puellam quae desponsata est et adprehendens concubuerit cum illa ipse morietur solus*

But if *a* man finds in *a* field *a* girl who is engaged to be married and, taking her, has sex with her, he only will die.

22:26 *puella nihil patietur nec est rea mortis quoniam sicut latro consurgit contra fratrem suum et occidit animam eius ita et puella perpessa est*

The girl will suffer nothing, nor is liable to death, because as *a* thief rises up against his brother and kills his soul, so also *the* girl has suffered.

22:27 *sola erat in agro clamavit et nullus adfuit qui liberaret eam*

She was alone in *the* field. She called out, and no one who could free her came out.

22:28 *si invenerit vir puellam*

virginem quae non habet sponsum et adprehendens concubuerit cum ea et res ad iudicium venerit

If *a* man finds *a* virgin girl who has no fiancee, and, taking her, has sex with her, and *the* matter comes to judgment,

22:29 *dabit qui dormivit cum ea patri puellae quinquaginta siclos argenti et habebit eam uxorem quia humiliavit illam non poterit dimittere cunctis diebus vitae suae*

the one who slept with her will give *the* girl's father fifty silver shekels, and he will have her *as* wife, because he has humiliated her. He cannot let *her* go all his life's days.

22:30 *non accipiet homo uxorem patris sui nec revelabit operimentum eius*

A man will not receive his father's wife, or lift up his covering.

Assembly

Deuteronomy 23:1 *non intrabit eunuchus adtritis vel amputatis testiculis et absciso veretro ecclesiam Domini*

A eunuch, testicles worn away or amputated, and one whose penis is cut off, will not enter *the* Lord's assembly.

23:2 *non ingredietur mamzer hoc est de scorto natus in ecclesiam Domini usque ad decimam generationem*

An unmarried mother's child, that is, one born from *a* prostitute, will not go into *the* Lord's assembly, even to *the* tenth generation.

23:3 *Ammanites et Moabites etiam post decimam generationem non intrabunt ecclesiam Domini in aeternum*

Ammonites and Moabites, even after *the* tenth generation, will not enter *the* Lord's assembly in eternity,

23:4 *quia noluerunt vobis occurrere cum pane et aqua in via quando egressi estis de Aegypto et quia conduxerunt contra te Balaam filium Beor de Mesopotamiam Syriae ut malediceret tibi*

because they didn't want to meet you with bread and water in *the* road, when you came out of Egypt, and

because they hired against you Balaam, son of Beor, of Syrian Mesopotamia, so he could curse you.

23:5 *et noluit Dominus Deus tuus audire Balaam vertitque maledictionem eius in benedictionem tuam eo quod diligeret te*

And *the* Lord your God did not want to hear Balaam. And He turned his curse into blessing, because He delighted in you.

23:6 *non facies cum eis pacem nec quaeres eis bona cunctis diebus vitae tuae in sempiternum*

You will not make peace with them, or seek good for them, all your life's days, forever.

Brotherhood

23:7 *non abominaberis Idumeum quia frater tuus est nec Aegyptium quia advena fuisti in terra eius*

You will not detest *an* Edomite, because he is your brother, or *an* Egyptian, because you were *a* newcomer in his land.

23:8 *qui nati fuerint ex eis tertia generatione intrabunt ecclesiam Domini*

Those who are born from them in *the* third generation will enter *the* Lord's assembly.

Laws of War

23:9 *quando egressus fueris adversus hostes tuos in pugnam custodies te ab omni re mala*

When you go out against your enemies to fight, you will keep yourself from every harmful thing.

23:10 *si fuerit inter vos homo qui nocturno pollutus sit somnio egredietur extra castra*

If *there* is *a* man among you who is polluted by *a* night dream, he will go out of *the* camp.

23:11 *et non revertetur priusquam ad vesperam lavetur aqua et post solis occasum regredietur in castra*

And he will not come back in before he will wash with water at evening. And, after sunset, he will come back into camp.

23:12 *habebis locum extra castra ad quem egrediaris ad requisita naturae*

You will have *a* place outside *the* camp which you will go out to for nature's requirements.

23:13 *gerens paxillum in balteo cumque sederis fodies per circuitum et egesta humo operies*

And when you sit, taking *a* stake in *your* belt, you will dig around *it*, and will cover *the* discharge with soil

23:14 *quo relevatus es Dominus enim Deus tuus ambulat in medio castrorum ut eruat te et tradat tibi inimicos tuos ut sint castra tua sancta et nihil in eis appareat foeditatis nec derelinquat te*

where you relieve yourself, for *the* Lord your God walks among *the* camps, so he can rescue you and hand your enemies over to you – so let your camps be holy. And let nothing vile appear, so He does not abandon you.

Fugitive Slaves

23:15 *non trades servum domino suo qui ad te confugerit*

Do not hand *a* slave who has fled to you over to his master.

23:16 *habitabit tecum in loco qui ei placuerit et in una urbium tuarum requiescet nec contristes eum*

He will live with you in *a* place that pleases him, and he will rest in one of your cities, nor will you sadden him.

Prostitution

23:17 *non erit meretrix de filiabus Israhel neque scortator de filiis Israhel*

There will be no female prostitute among Israel's daughters, nor *a* whore's customer among Israel's sons.

23:18 *non offeres mercedem prostibuli nec pretium canis in domum Domini Dei tui quicquid illud est quod voverint quia abominatio est utrumque apud Dominum Deum tuum*

You will not offer *a* prostitute's pay or *a* dog's price in *the* Lord your God's house, whatever it is that they have promised, because either is disgusting to *the* Lord your God.

Lending Money
23:19 *non fenerabis fratri tuo ad usuram pecuniam nec fruges nec quamlibet aliam rem*

You will not lend money, or crops, or whatever other thing at usury to your brother,

23:20 *sed alieno fratri autem tuo absque usura id quod indiget commodabis ut benedicat tibi Dominus Deus tuus in omni opere tuo in terra ad quam ingredieris possidendam*

but to *a* stranger. But you will lend to your brother without usury that which he needs, so *the* Lord your God may bless you in all your works, in *the* land which you will go in to take over.

23:21 *cum voveris votum Domino Deo tuo non tardabis reddere quia requiret illud Dominus Deus tuus et si moratus fueris reputabit tibi in*

peccatum

When you make *a* promise to *the* Lord your God, you will not wait to pay, because *the* Lord your God will require it. And if you have delayed, *it* will be considered as sin for you.

Making Promises
23:22 *si nolueris polliceri absque peccato eris*

If you do not make promises, you will be without sin.

23:23 *quod autem semel egressum est de labiis tuis observabis et facies sicut promisisti Domino Deo tuo et propria voluntate et ore tuo locutus es*

But you will observe what once has come out of your lips, and will do as you promised *the* Lord your God, and have spoken of *your* own will and by your *own* mouth.

Limits of Sharing
23:24 *ingressus vineam proximi tui comede uvas quantum tibi placuerit foras autem ne efferas tecum*

Going in to your neighbor's vineyard, eat however many grapes may please you, but you will not take them out with you.

23:25 *si intraveris in segetem amici tui franges spicas et manu conteres falce autem non metes*

If you go into your friend's grain field, you will break *the* heads and crush them by hand, but you will not put in *the* sickle.

Marriage

Deuteronomy 24:1 *si acceperit homo uxorem et habuerit eam et non invenerit gratiam ante oculos eius propter aliquam foeditatem scribet libellum repudii et dabit in manu illius et dimittet eam de domo sua*

If *a* man receives a wife and has her, and she does not find favor before his eyes because of some vileness, he will write *a* rejection letter and put it in her hand, and let her go from his house.

24:2 *cumque egressa alterum maritum duxerit*

And when, going out, she marries another,

24:3 *et ille quoque oderit eam dederitque ei libellum repudii et dimiserit de domo sua vel certe mortuus fuerit*

and he, likewise, will hate her and give her *a* rejection letter and send her from his house, or, at least, has died,

24:4 *non poterit prior maritus recipere eam in uxorem quia polluta est et abominabilis facta est coram Domino ne peccare facias terram tuam quam Dominus Deus tuus tibi tradiderit possidendam*

her former husband may not receive her as wife, because she is polluted and has become *an* abomination before *the* Lord. You will not cause *the* land which *the* Lord your God will give you to possess to sin.

24:5 *cum acceperit homo nuper uxorem non procedet ad bellum nec ei quippiam necessitatis iniungetur publicae sed vacabit absque culpa domui suae ut uno anno laetetur cum uxore sua*

When *a* man has recently received *a* wife, he will not go out to war, nor have any public necessity imposed on him. But he will be free in his house, without blame, so he can be happy one year with his wife.

Pledges
24:6 *non accipies loco pignoris inferiorem et superiorem molam quia animam suam adposuit tibi*

You will not receive in place of *a* pledge *a* lower and upper millstone, because he has set his soul before you.

Selling Out
24:7 *si deprehensus fuerit homo sollicitans fratrem suum de filiis Israhel et vendito eo accipiens pretium interficietur et auferes malum de medio tui*

If *a* man is discovered disturbing his brother from Israel's children and, selling him, receiving *the* price, he will be killed. And you will take

away harm from among you.

Leprosy
24:8 *observa diligenter ne incurras in plagam leprae sed facies quaecumque docuerint te sacerdotes levitici generis iuxta id quod praecepi eis et imple sollicite*

Watch carefully that you not meet with *the* plague of leprosy! But you will do whatever *the* line of Levitical priests teach you, according to what I have commanded them. And fulfill *it* anxiously!

24:9 *mementote quae fecerit Dominus Deus vester Mariae in via cum egrederemini de Aegypto*

Remember what *the* Lord your God did to Mary in *the* way, when you came out of Egypt.

Respect
24:10 *cum repetes a proximo tuo rem aliquam quam debet tibi non ingredieris domum eius ut pignus auferas*

When you demand from your neighbor something which he owes you, you will not go into his house so you can take away *a* pledge.

24:11 *sed stabis foris et ille tibi proferet quod habuerit*

But you will stand outside, and he will bring out to you what he has.

24:12 *sin autem pauper est non pernoctabit apud te pignus*

But if he is poor, *the* pledge will not pass *the* night with you;

24:13 *sed statim reddes ei ante solis occasum ut dormiens in vestimento suo benedicat tibi et habeas iustitiam coram Domino Deo tuo*

yet you will return *it* to him quickly, before sunset, so, sleeping in his clothing, he may bless you, and you have fairness before *the* Lord your God.

Paying Workers
24:14 *non negabis mercedem indigentis et pauperis fratris tui sive advenae qui tecum moratur in terra et intra portas tuas est*

You will not hold back *the* needy's wages and *the* poor's, whether *from* your brother or *a* newcomer who lives with you in *the* land, and is in your gates;

24:15 *sed eadem die reddes ei pretium laboris sui ante solis occasum quia pauper est et ex eo sustentat animam suam ne clamet contra te ad Dominum et reputetur tibi in peccatum*

yet that same day you will pay him his labor's price, before sunset, because he is poor and sustains his soul from it. Let him not cry out to

the Lord against you, and *it* be considered as sin to you.

Individual Responsibility
24:16 *non occidentur patres pro filiis nec filii pro patribus sed unusquisque pro suo peccato morietur*

Fathers will not be killed in place of children, or children in place of fathers, but each one will die for his own sin.

Protecting the Defenseless
24:17 *non pervertes iudicium advenae et pupilli nec auferes pignoris loco viduae vestimentum*

You will not pervert judgment against newcomer or orphan, nor will you take away *a* widow's clothing in place of *a* pledge.

24:18 *memento quod servieris in Aegypto et eruerit te Dominus Deus tuus inde idcirco praecipio tibi ut facias hanc rem*

Remember that you slaved in Egypt, and *the* Lord your God rescued you from there! For this reason, I am commanding you that you do this thing.

24:19 *quando messueris segetem in agro tuo et oblitus manipulum reliqueris non reverteris ut tollas eum sed advenam et pupillum et viduam auferre patieris ut benedicat* *tibi Dominus Deus tuus in omni opere manuum tuarum*

When you have harvested grain in your field and, forgetting, you leave behind *a* bundle, you will not go back so you can take it. But you will allow *the* newcomer and orphan and widow to take it, so *the* Lord your God may bless you in all your hands' works.

24:20 *si fruges colliges olivarum quicquid remanserit in arboribus non reverteris ut colligas sed relinques advenae pupillo ac viduae*

When you gather *the* olives' fruit, you will not go back so you can collect whatever remains in *the* trees. But you will leave it for newcomer, orphan, and widow.

24:21 *si vindemiaveris vineam tuam non colliges remanentes racemos sed cedent in usus advenae pupilli ac viduae*

When you harvest your vineyard, you will not gather *the* remaining clusters. But they will be granted for use by newcomer, orphan, and widow.

24:22 *memento quod et tu servieris in Aegypto et idcirco praecipiam tibi ut facias hanc rem*

Remember that you also slaved in Egypt, and for this reason I will command you that you do this thing!

Judges to Judge Fairly
Deuteronomy 25:1 *si fuerit causa inter aliquos et interpellaverint iudices quem iustum esse perspexerint illi iustitiae palmam dabunt quem impium condemnabunt impietatis*

If there is *a* cause between some, and they call in judges, they will give fairness's palm to *the* one whom they find to be fair. They will condemn *the* lawless one for lawlessness.

25:2 *sin autem eum qui peccavit dignum viderint plagis prosternent et coram se facient verberari pro mensura peccati erit et plagarum modus*

But if they see that *the* one who sinned *is* worthy of *a* beating, they will lay him down and will cause him to be beaten before them. *The* punishment's manner will be according to *the* sin's measure –

25:2 *ita dumtaxat ut quadragenarium numerum non excedant ne foede laceratus ante oculos tuos abeat frater tuus*

so only to this extent, that *the* number may not exceed forty, so that you brother not go away before your eyes, mangled shamelessly.

Workers' Rights
25:4 *non ligabis os bovis terentis in area fruges tuas*

You will not bind up *the* ox's mouth treading your grain in *the* threshing floor.

A Dead Brother's Legacy

25:5 *quando habitaverint fratres simul et unus ex eis absque liberis mortuus fuerit uxor defuncti non nubet alteri sed accipiet eam frater eius et suscitabit semen fratris sui*

When brothers are living together, and one of them will die without children, *the* dead man's wife will not marry another. Instead, his brother will receive her, and raise up seed for his brother.

25:6 *et primogenitum ex ea filium nomine illius appellabit ut non deleatur nomen eius ex Israhel*

And he will call *the* firstborn son from her by his name, so his name not be destroyed from Israel.

25:7 *sin autem noluerit accipere uxorem fratris sui quae ei lege debetur perget mulier ad portam civitatis et interpellabit maiores natu dicetque non vult frater viri mei suscitare nomen fratris sui in Israhel nec me in coniugium sumere*

But if he doesn't want to receive his brother's wife, who by law is obligated to him, *the* woman will go to *the* city's gate and appeal to *the* elder born, and say, "My husband's brother doesn't want to raise up his brother's name in Israel, or receive me in marriage."

25:8 *statimque accersiri eum facient et interrogabunt si responderit nolo eam uxorem accipere*

And they will immediately make him be summoned and will question him. If he should respond, "I don't want to receive her as wife,"

25:9 *accedet mulier ad eum coram senioribus et tollet calciamentum de pede eius spuetque in faciem illius et dicet sic fit homini qui non aedificat domum fratris sui*

the woman will come to him before *the* elders, and will take *the* shoe from his foot, and will spit in his face. And she will say, "So may *it* be to *a* man be who does not build his brother's house!"

25:10 *et vocabitur nomen illius in Israhel domus Disculciati*

And his name in Israel will be called "house of *the* Unshoed."

Interfering in a Fight

25:11 *si habuerint inter se iurgium viri et unus contra alterum rixari coeperit volensque uxor alterius eruere virum suum de manu fortioris miserit manum et adprehenderit verenda eius*

If men have *a* fight among

themselves, and one begins to brawl violently against *the* other, and *the* other's wife, wanting to rescue her husband from *a* stronger hand, sticks out *a* hand and grabs his privates,

25:12 *abscides manum illius nec flecteris super eam ulla misericordia*

you will cut off her hand, nor will you soften any mercy over her.

Fair Weights and Measures

25:13 *non habebis in sacculo diversa pondera maius et minus*

You will not have in *the* sack different weights, greater and less,

25:14 *nec erit in domo tua modius maior et minor*

nor will there be in your house *a* greater and less dry measure.

25:15 *pondus habebis iustum et verum et modius aequalis et verus erit tibi ut multo vivas tempore super terram quam Dominus Deus tuus dederit tibi*

You will have fair and true weights, and *an* equal and true dry measure will be with you, so you can live *a* long time on *the* land which *the* Lord your God will give you –

25:16 *abominatur enim Dominus eum qui facit haec et aversatur omnem iniustitiam*

for *the* Lord detests one who does this, and He turns away in disgust from every unfairness.

Remember the Amalekites

25:17 *memento quae fecerit tibi Amalech in via quando egrediebaris ex Aegypto*

Remember what Amalek did to you in *the* way, when you came out of Egypt,

25:18 *quomodo occurrerit tibi et extremos agminis tui qui lassi residebant ceciderit quando tu eras fame et labore confectus et non timuerit Deum*

how he came against you and your column's rear. He chopped down those who sat down exhausted, when you were spent by hunger and hard work, and he did not fear God.

25:19 *cum ergo Dominus Deus tuus dederit tibi requiem et subiecerit cunctas per circuitum nationes in terra quam tibi pollicitus est delebis nomen eius sub caelo cave ne obliviscaris*

Therefore, when *the* Lord your God gives you peace, and throws down all *the* surrounding nations in *the* land which He has promised you, you will destroy his name under *the* sky. Take care that you not forget!

Offering First Fruits

Deuteronomy 26:1 *cumque intraveris terram quam Dominus Deus tuus tibi daturus est possidendam et obtinueris eam atque habitaveris in illa*

And when you cross into *the* land which *the* Lord your God will give you to possess, and you attain it, and live in it,

26:2 *tolles de cunctis frugibus primitias et pones in cartallo pergesque ad locum quem Dominus Deus tuus elegerit ut ibi invocetur nomen eius*

you will take from all first fruits, and put them in *a* basket, and go to *the* place which *the* Lord your God will choose, so His name may be invoked there.

26:3 *accedesque ad sacerdotem qui fuerit in diebus illis et dices ad eum profiteor hodie coram Domino Deo tuo quod ingressus sim terram pro qua iuravit patribus nostris ut daret eam nobis*

And you will come to *the* priest who *serves* in that day, and you will say to him, "I declare today before *the* Lord your God, so I may come into *the* land for which He swore to our fathers, that He would give it to us."

26:4 *suscipiensque sacerdos cartallum de manu eius ponet ante*

altare Domini Dei tui

And, *the* priest, taking *the* basket from his hand, will put it before *the* Lord your God's altar.

26:5 *et loqueris in conspectu Domini Dei tui Syrus persequebatur patrem meum qui descendit in Aegyptum et ibi peregrinatus est in paucissimo numero crevitque in gentem magnam et robustam et infinitae multitudinis*

And you will say in *the* Lord your God's sight, "A Syrian pursued my father, who went down to Egypt. And he wandered there as *an* alien, very few in number. And he grew into *a* great and mighty people, and *an* infinite multitude.

26:6 *adflixeruntque nos Aegyptii et persecuti sunt inponentes onera gravissima*

"And *the* Egyptians afflicted and persecuted us, laying on *us the* heaviest loads.

26:7 *et clamavimus ad Dominum Deum patrum nostrorum qui exaudivit nos et respexit humilitatem nostram et laborem atque angustias*

"And we cried out to *the* Lord, our fathers' God, who heard us and saw our humiliation and hard work, and anguish.

26:8 *et eduxit nos de Aegypto in manu forti et brachio extento in ingenti pavore in signis atque portentis*

"And He led us out of Egypt by *a* mighty hand and *a* stretched-out arm, in inordinate fear, in signs and wonders.

26:9 *et introduxit ad locum istum et tradidit nobis terram lacte et melle manantem*

"And He led us to this place, and handed *this* land flowing with milk and honey over to us.

26:10 *et idcirco nunc offero primitias frugum terrae quam dedit Dominus mihi et dimittes eas in conspectu Domini Dei tui adorato Domino Deo tuo*

"And therefore, now I offer first fruits from *the* land which *the* Lord gave me."

And you will leave them in *the* Lord your God's sight. Adore *the* Lord your God,

26:11 *et epulaberis in omnibus bonis quae Dominus Deus tuus dederit tibi et domui tuae tu et Levites et advena qui tecum est*

and you will feast in all good things which the Lord your God will give you and your house – you and *the* Levite and *the* newcomer who is with you.

26:12 *quando conpleveris decimam cunctarum frugum tuarum anno decimarum tertio dabis Levitae et advenae et pupillo et viduae ut comedant intra portas tuas et saturentur*

When you have supplied *a* tenth of your crop, in *the* third year of tenths, you will give to *the* Levite and newcomer and widow and orphan, so they can eat inside your gates and be filled.

26:13 *loquerisque in conspectu Domini Dei tui abstuli quod sanctificatum est de domo mea et dedi illud Levitae et advenae pupillo et viduae sicut iussisti mihi non praeterivi mandata tua nec sum oblitus imperii*

And you will say in *the* Lord your God's sight, "I have taken what was holy from my house, and given it to *the* Levite and newcomer, orphan and widow, like You commanded me. I have not neglected your commandment or forgotten your authority.

26:14 *non comedi ex eis in luctu meo nec separavi ea in qualibet inmunditia nec expendi ex his quicquam in re funebri oboedivi voci Domini Dei mei et feci omnia sicut praecepisti mihi*

"I have not eaten from it in my grief, or divided it in whatever uncleanness, or spent anything from it in *a* matter of funeral rites. I have obeyed *the* Lord my God's voice, and done all that You commanded me.

26:15 *respice de sanctuario tuo de excelso caelorum habitaculo et benedic populo tuo Israhel et terrae quam dedisti nobis sicut iurasti patribus nostris terrae lacte et melle mananti*

"Look down from Your holy place, *Your* dwelling in *the* highest skies, and bless your people Israel, and *the* land which You gave us, as You swore to our fathers – *a* land flowing with milk and honey!"

26:16 *hodie Dominus Deus tuus praecepit tibi ut facias mandata haec atque iudicia et custodias et impleas ex toto corde tuo et ex tota anima tua*

Today *the* Lord your God taught you, so you may do His commandments and judgments, and guard and fulfill *them,* from all your heart and from all your soul.

26:17 *Dominum elegisti hodie ut sit tibi Deus et ambules in viis eius et custodias caerimonias illius et mandata atque iudicia et oboedias eius imperio*

You have chosen *the* Lord today, that He be God to you. And you will walk in His ways, and keep His ceremonies and commandments and judgments, and you will obey His authority.

26:18 *et Dominus elegit te hodie ut sis ei populus peculiaris sicut locutus est tibi et custodias omnia praecepta eius*

And *the* Lord chose you today, that *you* be *a* peculiar people to Him, as He said to you. And you will keep all His precepts.

26:19 *et faciat te excelsiorem cunctis gentibus quas creavit in laudem et nomen et gloriam suam ut sis populus sanctus Domini Dei tui sicut locutus est*

And may He make you *the* highest of all nations which He created, in His praise and name and glory, that you be *a* holy people to *the* Lord your God, as He said!

Building the Lord's Altar

Deuteronomy 27:1 *praecepit autem Moses et seniores Israhel populo dicentes custodite omne mandatum quod praecipio vobis hodie*

But Moses and *the* elders commanded Israel's people, saying, "Keep every commandment that I am teaching you today!"

27:2 *cumque transieritis Iordanem in terram quam Dominus Deus tuus dabit tibi eriges ingentes lapides et calce levigabis eos*

And when you pass over *the* Jordan into *the* land which *the* Lord your God will give you, you will set up giant stones and smooth them with stone,

27:3 *ut possis in eis scribere omnia verba legis huius Iordane transmisso ut introeas terram quam Dominus Deus tuus dabit tibi terram lacte et melle manantem sicut iuravit patribus tuis*

so, *the* Jordan crossed, you can write on them all *the* words of this law, so you can enter *the* land which *the* Lord your God will give you – *a* land flowing with milk and honey, like He swore to your fathers.

27:4 *quando ergo transieritis Iordanem erige lapides quos ego hodie praecipio vobis in monte Hebal et levigabis calce*

When, therefore, you have crossed *the* Jordan, set up *the* stones which I am commanding you today on Mount Ebal! And you will smooth them with stone.

27:5 *et aedificabis ibi altare Domino Deo tuo de lapidibus quos ferrum non tetigit*

And you will build *an* altar there to *the* Lord you God, from stones which iron has not touched,

27:6 *et de saxis informibus et inpolitis et offeres super eo holocausta Domino Deo tuo*

and from unformed and rough rocks. And you will offer burnt offerings to *the* Lord your God on it.

27:7 *et immolabis hostias pacificas comedesque ibi et epulaberis coram Domino Deo tuo*

And you will burn peace-making sacrifices and will eat there. And you will feast before *the* Lord your God.

27:8 *et scribes super lapides omnia verba legis huius plane et lucide*

And you will write on stones all of this law's words, plainly and clearly.

Moses and the Elders Address the People

27:9 *dixeruntque Moses et sacerdotes levitici generis ad omnem*

Israhelem adtende et audi Israhel hodie factus es populus Domini Dei tui

And Moses and *the* line of Levitical priests said to all Israel, "Pay attention and hear, Israel! Today you have become *a* people to *the* Lord your God.

27:10 *audies vocem eius et facies mandata atque iustitias quas ego praecipio tibi*

"You will listen to His voice and do His commandments and fairnesses, which I am teaching you today."

The Ritual of Curses
and Blessings

27:11 *praecepitque Moses populo in die illo dicens*

And Moses commanded *the* people on that day, saying,

27:12 *hii stabunt ad benedicendum Domino super montem Garizim Iordane transmisso Symeon Levi Iudas Isachar Ioseph et Beniamin*

"These will stand to blessing *the* Lord on Mount Gerizim, *the* Jordan crossed: Simeon, Levi, Judah, Issachar, Joseph, and Benjamin.

27:13 *et e regione isti stabunt ad maledicendum in monte Hebal Ruben Gad et Aser Zabulon Dan et Nepthalim*

"And from *that* region, these will stand to cursing on Mount Ebal: Reuben, Gad and Asher, Zebulon, Dan, and Napthali.

The Curses
27:14 *et pronuntiabunt Levitae dicentque ad omnes viros Israhel excelsa voce*

"And *the* Levites will pronounce and say to all Israel's men in *a* lifted up voice,

27:15 *maledictus homo qui facit sculptile et conflatile abominationem Domini opus manuum artificum ponetque illud in abscondito et respondebit omnis populus et dicet amen*

"'*A* man who makes *a* sculpted image and idol, *the* Lord's abomination, work of *a* practiced hand, and puts it in *a* hidden place, *is* cursed.'

"And all *the* people will respond and say, 'Amen.'

27:16 *maledictus qui non honorat patrem suum et matrem et dicet omnis populus amen*

"'One who does not honor his father and mother *is* cursed.'

"And all the people will say, 'Amen.'

27:17 *maledictus qui transfert terminos proximi sui et dicet omnis*

populus amen

"'One who moves his neighbors' boundaries *is* cursed.'

'And all *the* people will say, 'Amen.'

27:18 *maledictus qui errare facit caecum in itinere et dicet omnis populus amen*

"'One who makes *the* blind get lost on *the* way *is* cursed.'

"And all *the* people will say, 'Amen.'

27:19 *maledictus qui pervertit iudicium advenae pupilli et viduae et dicet omnis populus amen*

"'One who perverts judgment against newcomer, orphan, and widow, *is* cursed.'

"And all *the* people will say, 'Amen.'

27:20 *maledictus qui dormit cum uxore patris sui et revelat operimentum lectuli eius et dicet omnis populus amen*

"'One who sleeps with his father's wife, and uncovers his bed's covering, *is* cursed.'

"And all *the* people will say, 'Amen.'

27:21 *maledictus qui dormit cum omni iumento et dicet omnis populus amen*

"'One who sleeps with any animal *is* cursed.'

"And all the people will say, 'Amen.'

27:22 *maledictus qui dormit cum sorore sua filia patris sui sive matris suae et dicet omnis populus amen*

"'One who sleeps with his sister, whether his father's daughter or his mother's, *is* cursed.'

"And all *the* people will say, 'Amen.'

27:23 *maledictus qui dormit cum socru sua et dicet omnis populus amen*

"'One who sleeps with his mother-in-law *is* cursed.'

"And all the people will say, 'Amen.'

27:24 *maledictus qui clam percusserit proximum suum et dicet omnis populus amen*

"'One who will strike his neighbor in secret *is* cursed.'

"And all *the* people will say, 'Amen.'

27:25 *maledictus qui accipit munera ut percutiat animam sanguinis innocentis et dicet omnis populus amen*

"'One who accepts *a* bribe so he can strike *a* soul of innocent blood, *is* cursed,'

"And all *the* people will say, 'Amen.'

27:26 *maledictus qui non permanet in sermonibus legis huius nec eos opere perficit et dicet omnis populus amen*

"'One who does not remain in this law's teachings, or complete them by work, *is* cursed.'

"And all *the* people will say, 'Amen.'"

Blessings

Deuteronomy 28:1 *sin autem audieris vocem Domini Dei tui ut facias atque custodias omnia mandata eius quae ego praecipio tibi hodie faciet te Dominus Deus tuus excelsiorem cunctis gentibus quae versantur in terra*

But if you will hear *the* Lord your God's voice, so you will do and keep all His commandments which I am teaching you today, *the* Lord your God will make you higher than all *the* nations which move around in *the* land.

28:2 *venientque super te universae benedictiones istae et adprehendent te si tamen praecepta eius audieris*

And all these blessings will come over you and will catch you, if still you will listen to His precepts.

28:3 *benedictus tu in civitate et benedictus in agro*

You *will be* blessed in *the* city and blessed in *the* field.

28:4 *benedictus fructus ventris tui et fructus terrae tuae fructusque iumentorum tuorum greges armentorum et caulae ovium tuarum*

Your womb's fruit and your land's fruit *will be* blessed, and your cattle's fruit, cattle's herds and sheep of your flock.

28:5 *benedicta horrea tua et benedictae reliquiae tuae*

Your barns *will be* blessed and your savings blessed.

28:6 *benedictus eris et ingrediens et egrediens*

You will be blessed both coming in and going out.

28:7 *dabit Dominus inimicos tuos qui consurgunt adversum te corruentes in conspectu tuo per unam viam venient contra te et per septem fugient a facie tua*

The Lord will give *you* your enemies, who will rise up against you, falling in your sight. They will come against you by one road, and will run away from your face by seven.

28:8 *emittet Dominus benedictionem super cellaria tua et super omnia opera manuum tuarum benedicetque tibi in terra quam acceperis*

The Lord will send out blessing over your storehouses, and over all your hands' works. And He will bless you in *the* land which you will receive.

28:9 *suscitabit te Dominus sibi in populum sanctum sicut iuravit tibi si custodieris mandata Domini Dei tui et ambulaveris in viis eius*

The Lord will raise you up for Himself as *a* holy people, as He swore to you, if you will keep *the* Lord your God's commandments and walk in His ways.

28:10 *videbuntque omnes terrarum populi quod nomen Domini invocatum sit super te et timebunt te*

And *the* people of all lands will see that *the* Lord's name is invoked over you, and they will fear you.

28:11 *abundare te faciet Dominus omnibus bonis fructu uteri tui et fructu iumentorum tuorum fructu terrae tuae quam iuravit Dominus patribus tuis ut daret tibi*

The Lord will make you prosper in all good things – your womb's fruit and your cattle's fruit, your land's fruit, which *the* Lord swore to your fathers that He would give you.

28:12 *aperiet Dominus thesaurum suum optimum caelum ut tribuat pluviam terrae tuae in tempore suo benedicet cunctis operibus manuum tuarum et fenerabis gentibus multis et ipse a nullo fenus accipies*

The Lord will open His choice treasury, *the* sky, so He can give your land rain in its season. He will bless all your hands' works, and you will lend to many nations and accept loans from none.

28:13 *constituet te Dominus in caput et non in caudam et eris semper supra et non subter si audieris mandata Domini Dei tui quae ego praecipio tibi hodie et custodieris et feceris*

The Lord will place you at *the* head and not at *the* tail, and you will always be above and not below, if you listen to *the* Lord your God's commandments which I am teaching you today, so you keep and do *them*.

28:14 *ac non declinaveris ab eis nec ad dextram nec ad sinistram nec secutus fueris deos alienos neque colueris eos*

And you will not turn away from them either to *the* right or left, nor will you follow strange gods or serve them.

The Curses

28:15 *quod si audire nolueris vocem Domini Dei tui ut custodias et facias omnia mandata eius et caerimonias quas ego praecipio tibi hodie venient super te omnes maledictiones istae et adprehendent te*

If you won't to listen to *the* Lord your God's voice, so you keep and do all His commandments and ceremonies which I am teaching you today, all these curses will come over you and capture you.

28:16 *maledictus eris in civitate maledictus in agro*

You will be cursed in *the* city, cursed in *the* field.

28:17 *maledictum horreum tuum et maledictae reliquiae tuae*

Your barn *will be* cursed and your savings cursed.

28:18 *maledictus fructus ventris tui et fructus terrae tuae armenta boum tuorum et greges ovium tuarum*

Your womb's fruit and your land's fruit, your ox herds and your sheep flocks *will be* cursed.

28:19 *maledictus eris ingrediens et maledictus egrediens*

You will be cursed coming in and cursed going out.

28:20 *mittet Dominus super te famem et esuriem et increpationem in omnia opera tua quae facies donec conterat te et perdat velociter propter adinventiones tuas pessimas in quibus reliquisti me*

The Lord will send hunger and thirst and rebuke against you, in all your works which you do, until He has destroyed you. And He will destroy quickly, because of your dismal inventions in which you abandoned Me.

28:21 *adiungat Dominus tibi pestilentiam donec consumat te de terra ad quam ingredieris possidendam*

May *the* Lord yoke pestilence to you, until He has consumed you from *the* land which you are going in to take over!

28:22 *percutiat te Dominus egestate febri et frigore ardore et aestu et aere corrupto ac robigine et persequatur donec pereas*

May *the* Lord strike you with poverty, fever, and cold, fire and seething and rusted bronze and mildew, and pursue *you* until you perish!

28:23 *sit caelum quod supra te est aeneum et terra quam calcas ferrea*

May *the* sky which is above you be copper, and *the* land which you walk on iron!

28:24 *det Dominus imbrem terrae tuae pulverem et de caelo descendat super te cinis donec conteraris*

May *the* Lord give dust *as* your land's rain, and may ashes descend over you from *the* sky, until you are destroyed!

28:25 *tradat te Dominus corruentem ante hostes tuos per unam viam egrediaris contra eos et per septem*

fugias et dispergaris per omnia regna terrae

May *the* Lord hand you over, falling before your enemies! You will come against them by one route, and flee by seven. And you will be scattered through all *the* land's kingdoms.

28:26 *sitque cadaver tuum in escam cunctis volatilibus caeli et bestiis terrae et non sit qui abigat*

And may your body be as food to all *the* sky's birds and *the* land's beasts, and *there* be no one who drives *them* away!

28:27 *percutiat te Dominus ulcere Aegypti et parte corporis per quam stercora digeruntur scabie quoque et prurigine ita ut curari nequeas*

May *the* Lord strike you with Egypt's ulcer, and *the* body's part by which excrement is expelled with rot, likewise, and itch, so that you cannot be healed!

28:28 *percutiat te Dominus amentia et caecitate ac furore mentis*

May *the* Lord strike you with insanity and blindness and mind's fury!

28:29 *et palpes in meridie sicut palpare solet caecus in tenebris et non dirigas vias tuas omnique tempore calumniam sustineas et opprimaris violentia nec habeas qui* *liberet te*

May you grope in midday, like *a* blind man is used to groping in shadows, and may you not direct your way! May you sustain abuse and be oppressed by violence, nor have anyone who can free you!

28:30 *uxorem accipias et alius dormiat cum ea domum aedifices et non habites in ea plantes vineam et non vindemies eam*

May you accept *a* wife and another sleep with her! May you build *a* house and not live in it! May you plant *a* vineyard, yet not make wine from it!

28:31 *bos tuus immoletur coram te et non comedas ex eo asinus tuus rapiatur in conspectu tuo et non reddatur tibi oves tuae dentur inimicis tuis et non sit qui te adiuvet*

May your ox be sacrificed before you, and you not eat from it! May your donkey be taken away in your sight, and not be returned to you! May your sheep be given to your enemies, and there be no one who helps you!

28:32 *filii tui et filiae tuae tradantur alteri populo videntibus oculis tuis et deficientibus ad conspectum eorum tota die et non sit fortitudo in manu tua*

May your son and your daughter be handed over to other people, your eyes seeing, and passing away in their sight all day, and *there* be no strength in your hand!

28:33 *fructus terrae tuae et omnes labores tuos comedat populus quem ignoras et sis semper calumniam sustinens et oppressus cunctis diebus*

May *a* people whom you do not know eat your land's fruit and all your labors, and you always sustain abuse and be oppressed all days,

28:34 *et stupens ad terrorem eorum quae videbunt oculi tui*

and frightened to terror at what your eyes will see!

28:35 *percutiat te Dominus ulcere pessimo in genibus et in suris sanarique non possis a planta pedis usque ad verticem tuum*

May *the* Lord strike your knees and calves with *a* dismal ulcer, and you not be able to be healed, from your foot's sole even to *the* top of your head!

28:36 *ducet Dominus te et regem tuum quem constitueris super te in gentem quam ignoras tu et patres tui et servies ibi diis alienis ligno et lapidi*

May *the* Lord lead you and *the* king

whom you will set up over you *to* a nation whom you and your fathers do not know! And you will serve alien gods of wood and stone there.

28:37 *et eris perditus in proverbium ac fabulam omnibus populis ad quos te introduxerit Dominus*

And you will be ruined, *a* proverb and fable for all *the* peoples to whom *the* Lord will bring you.

28:38 *sementem multam iacies in terram et modicum congregabis quia lucustae omnia devorabunt*

You will cast much seed on *the* land, and gather little, because locusts will devour all.

28:39 *vineam plantabis et fodies et vinum non bibes nec colliges ex ea quippiam quoniam vastabitur vermibus*

You will plant *a* vineyard and dig, yet you will not drink wine or gather anything from it, because it will be wasted by worms.

28:40 *olivas habebis in omnibus terminis tuis et non ungueris oleo quia defluent et peribunt*

You will have olives in all your boundaries, yet will not anoint with oil, because they will fall off and rot.

28:41 *filios generabis et filias et*

non frueris eis quoniam ducentur in captivitatem

You will parent sons and daughters, yet you will not enjoy them, because they will be led into captivity.

28:42 *omnes arbores tuas et fruges terrae tuae robigo consumet*

Blight will consume all your trees and your land's fruit.

28:43 *advena qui tecum versatur in terra ascendet super te eritque sublimior tu autem descendes et eris inferior*

A newcomer who moves around in *the* land with you will climb up over you, and he will be higher. But you will go down, and you will be inferior.

28:44 *ipse fenerabit tibi et tu non fenerabis ei ipse erit in caput et tu eris in caudam*

He will lend to you, and you won't lend to him. He will be at *the* head, and you will be at *the* tail.

28:45 *et venient super te omnes maledictiones istae et persequentes adprehendent te donec intereas quia non audisti vocem Domini Dei tui nec servasti mandata eius et caerimonias quas praecepit tibi*

And all these curses will come over

you, and, pursuing, they will capture you until you are destroyed, because you did not listen to *the* Lord your God's voice, or serve His commandments and ceremonies, which He commanded you.

28:46 *et erunt in te signa atque prodigia et in semine tuo usque in sempiternum*

And signs and wonders will be among you and your seed, even in everlasting years.

28:47 *eo quod non servieris Domino Deo tuo in gaudio cordisque laetitia propter rerum omnium abundantiam*

If, therefore, you will not serve *the* Lord your God in joy and with *a* happy heart, because of *the* abundance of all things,

28:48 *servies inimico tuo quem inmittet Dominus tibi in fame et siti et nuditate et omnium penuria et ponet iugum ferreum super cervicem tuam donec te conterat*

you will serve your enemy, whom *the* Lord will send in among you, in hunger and thirst and nakedness and every poverty. And he will put *an* iron yoke on your neck, until he destroys you.

28:49 *adducet Dominus super te gentem de longinquo et de extremis finibus terrae in similitudinem*

aquilae volantis cum impetu cuius linguam intellegere non possis

The Lord will lead against you *a* nation from far away, and from *the* land's limits, like *an* eagle flying with force, whose tongue you won't be able to understand –

28:50 *gentem procacissimam quae non deferat seni nec misereatur parvulo*

a pushing nation, which won't honor age or pity *the* small.

28:51   *et devoret fructum iumentorum tuorum ac fruges terrae tuae donec intereas et non relinquat tibi triticum vinum et oleum armenta boum et greges ovium donec te disperdat*

And it will devour your cattle's offspring and your land's fruit, until you are destroyed. And it will not leave you wheat, wine, or oil, cattle, oxen, or flocks of sheep, until it destroys you.

28:52 *et conterat in cunctis urbibus tuis et destruantur muri tui firmi atque sublimes in quibus habebas fiduciam in omni terra tua obsideberis intra portas tuas in omni terra quam dabit tibi Dominus Deus tuus*

And it will destroy in all your cities, and your strong and high walls in which you had faith will be destroyed, in all your land. And you will be besieged in your gates, in all *the* land which *the* Lord your God will give you.

28:53 *et comedes fructum uteri tui et carnes filiorum et filiarum tuarum quas dedit tibi Dominus Deus tuus in angustia et vastitate qua opprimet te hostis tuus*

And you will eat your uterus's fruit, and *the* flesh of your sons and daughters whom *the* Lord your God gave you, in *the* anguish and devastation with which your enemy will oppress you.

28:54 *homo delicatus in te et luxuriosus valde invidebit fratri suo et uxori quae cubat in sinu suo*

A delicate and very pampered man will begrudge you and your brother and *the* wife who sleeps in his embrace.

28:55 *ne det eis de carnibus filiorum suorum quas comedet eo quod nihil habeat aliud in obsidione et penuria qua vastaverint te inimici tui intra omnes portas tuas*

He will not give part of his children's flesh which he is eating, because he will have nothing else, in *the* siege and poverty with which your enemies will devastate you inside all your gates.

28:56 *tenera mulier et delicata quae super terram ingredi non valebat nec pedis vestigium figere propter mollitiem et teneritudinem nimiam invidebit viro suo qui cubat in sinu eius super filii et filiae carnibus*

A fragile and delicate woman, who couldn't walk on *the* ground, or leave behind footprints because of softness and great fragility, will begrudge her husband, who sleeps in her embrace, *her* sons and daughters' flesh,

28:57 *et inluvie secundarum quae egrediuntur de medio feminum eius et super liberis qui eadem hora nati sunt comedent enim eos clam propter rerum omnium penuriam in obsidione et vastitate qua opprimet te inimicus tuus intra portas tuas*

and over *the* afterbirth filth which goes out from her female parts, and over *the* children who are born that same hour. For they will eat them secretly, because of all things' poverty, in *the* siege and devastation with which your enemy will oppress you in your gates.

28:58 *nisi custodieris et feceris omnia verba legis huius quae scripta sunt in hoc volumine et timueris nomen eius gloriosum et terribile hoc est Dominum Deum tuum*

Unless you keep and do all this law's words – those which are written in this volume – and fear His famous and terrifying name – this is *the* Lord your God –

28:59 *augebit Dominus plagas tuas et plagas seminis tui plagas magnas et perseverantes infirmitates pessimas et perpetuas*

the Lord will increase your wounds and your offsprings' wounds, great wounds and continuing, dismal, endless sicknesses.

28:60 *et convertet in te omnes adflictiones Aegypti quas timuisti et adherebunt tibi*

And He will turn back to you all of Egypt's afflictions, which you feared, and they will stick to you.

28:61 *insuper et universos languores et plagas quae non sunt scriptae in volumine legis huius inducet Dominus super te donec te conterat*

And in addition, *the* Lord will lead in against you all *the* weaknesses and wounds which are not written in this law's book, until He destroys you.

28:62 *et remanebitis pauci numero qui prius eratis sicut astra caeli prae multitudine quoniam non audisti vocem Domini Dei tui*

And you will remain few in number, who before were like *the* sky's stars for multitude, because you have not

listened to *the* Lord your God's voice.

28:63 *et sicut ante laetatus est Dominus super vos bene vobis faciens vosque multiplicans sic laetabitur disperdens vos atque subvertens ut auferamini de terra ad quam ingredieris possidendam*

And as before *the* Lord was happy over you, doing well for you and multiplying you, so He will be happy scattering and subverting you, so you can be taken away from *the* land which you are going in to take over.

28:64 *disperget te Dominus in omnes populos a summitate terrae usque ad terminos eius et servies ibi diis alienis quos et tu ignoras et patres tui lignis et lapidibus*

The Lord will scatter you among all peoples, from *the* land's height even to its limits. And you will serve alien gods there, whom neither you nor your fathers know, *gods* of wood and stone.

28:65 *in gentibus quoque illis non quiesces neque erit requies vestigio pedis tui dabit enim tibi Dominus ibi cor pavidum et deficientes oculos et animam maerore consumptam*

Likewise, you will not be quiet among those nations, nor will your footsteps be in peace. For *the* Lord will give you there *a* fearful heart and failing eyes and *a* soul consumed by grief.

28:66 *et erit vita tua quasi pendens ante te timebis nocte et die et non credes vitae tuae*

And your life will be as if hanging before you. You will fear by night and day, and will not trust your life.

28:67 *mane dices quis mihi det vesperum et vespere quis mihi det mane propter cordis tui formidinem qua terreberis et propter ea quae tuis videbis oculis*

You will say at morning, "Who will grant me evening?", and at evening, "Who will grant me morning?" – because of *the* terror which you will fear, and because of that which your eyes will see.

28:68 *reducet te Dominus classibus in Aegyptum per viam de qua dixi tibi ut eam amplius non videres ibi venderis inimicis tuis in servos et ancillas et non erit qui emat*

The Lord will bring you back by groups to Egypt, by *the* route which I have said to you that you will not see it further. You will be sold there to your enemies as slaves and slave women, and *there* will be no one who buys.

**A Summary Restatement
of the Pact**
Deuteronomy 29:1 *haec sunt verba foederis quod praecepit Dominus Mosi ut feriret cum filiis Israhel in terra Moab praeter illud foedus quod cum eis pepigit in Horeb*

These are *the* words of *the* agreement which *the* Lord commanded Moses to strike with Israel's children in Moab's land, after that agreement which He made with them in Horeb.

29:2 *vocavitque Moses omnem Israhelem et dixit ad eos vos vidistis universa quae fecit Dominus coram vobis in terra Aegypti Pharaoni et omnibus servis eius universaeque terrae illius*

And Moses called all Israel and said to them, You have see all that *the* Lord has done before you in Egypt's land, to Pharaoh and all his slaves and all his land –

29:3 *temptationes magnas quas viderunt oculi tui signa illa portentaque ingentia*

great temptations which your eyes have seen, those gigantic signs and wonders.

29:4 *et non dedit Dominus vobis cor intellegens et oculos videntes et aures quae possint audire usque in praesentem diem*

And *the* Lord has not given you *an* understanding heart, or seeing eyes, or ears that can hear, even to *the* present day.

29:5 *adduxi vos quadraginta annis per desertum non sunt adtrita vestimenta vestra nec calciamenta pedum tuorum vetustate consumpta sunt*

I have led you forty years through *the* desert. Your clothes have not worn out, nor have *the* shoes on your feet been consumed by age.

29:6 *panem non comedistis vinum et siceram non bibistis ut sciretis quia ego sum Dominus Deus vester*

You haven't eaten bread, or drunk wine or liquor, so you could know that I am *the* Lord your God.

29:7 *et venistis ad locum hunc egressusque est Seon rex Esebon et Og rex Basan occurrens nobis ad pugnam et percussimus eos*

And you came to this place, and Sihon, Heshbon's king, came out, and Og, Bashan's king, coming to you to fight. And we struck them down.

29:8 *et tulimus terram eorum ac tradidimus possidendam Ruben et Gad et dimidiae tribui Manasse*

And we took their land, and gave it as possession to Reuben and Gad, and half of Manasseh's tribe.

29:9 *custodite ergo verba pacti huius et implete ea ut intellegatis universa quae facitis*

Therefore, keep this agreement's words and fulfill them, so you may understand all that you do!

29:10 *vos statis hodie cuncti coram Domino Deo vestro principes vestri ac tribus et maiores natu atque doctores omnis populus Israhel*

All of you are standing today before *the* Lord your God – your princes and tribes and older born and teachers, all Israel's people;

29:11 *liberi et uxores vestrae et advena qui tecum moratur in castris exceptis lignorum caesoribus et his qui conportant aquas*

children, and your wives, and *the* newcomer who lives with you in your camps, except those who cut your wood and carry your water –

29:12 *ut transeas in foedere Domini Dei tui et in iureiurando quod hodie Dominus Deus tuus percutit tecum*

so you may cross over into *the* Lord your God's agreement, and into *the* sworn oath that *the* Lord your God strikes with you today –

29:13 *ut suscitet te sibi in populum et ipse sit Deus tuus sicut locutus est tibi et sicut iuravit patribus tuis Abraham Isaac et Iacob*

so He may stir you up to Himself today as *a* people, and He may be your God, as He has spoken to you, and as He swore to your fathers, Abraham, Isaac, and Jacob.

29:14 *nec vobis solis ego hoc foedus ferio et haec iuramenta confirmo*

I am not striking this agreement and confirming these oaths with you only,

29:15 *sed cunctis praesentibus et absentibus*

but with all – *those* present and *those* absent.

29:16 *vos enim nostis ut habitaverimus in terra Aegypti et quomodo transierimus per medium nationum quas transeuntes*

For you have known how we lived in Egypt's land, and how we crossed through *the* midst of *the* nations which we passed.

29:17 *vidistis abominationes et sordes id est idola eorum lignum et lapidem argentum et aurum quae colebant*

You have seen abominations and filth – that is, their idols of wood and

stone, silver and gold, which they worshiped –

29:18 *ne forte sit inter vos vir aut mulier familia aut tribus cuius cor aversum est hodie a Domino Deo vestro ut vadat et serviat diis illarum gentium et sit inter vos radix germinans fel et amaritudinem*

unless perhaps *there* be among you *a* man or woman, family or tribe, whose heart is turned away today from *the* Lord your God, that it go and serve those nations' gods, and *there* be among you *a* root sprouting up bile and bitterness.

29:19 *cumque audierit verba iuramenti huius benedicat sibi in corde suo dicens pax erit mihi et ambulabo in pravitate cordis mei et adsumat ebria sitientem*

And when he has heard this oath's words, he bless himself in his heart, saying, "Peace will be with me, and I will walk in my heart's twistedness," and he take up thirsting like *a* drunk.

29:20 *et Dominus non ignoscat ei sed tunc quam maxime furor eius fumet et zelus contra hominem illum et sedeant super eo omnia maledicta quae scripta sunt in hoc volumine et deleat nomen eius sub caelo*

And *the* Lord may not forgive him, but then His anger and jealousy may fume greatly against that man, and

He may settle down over him all *the* curses which are written in this volume, and destroy his name under *the* sky.

29:21 *et consumat eum in perditionem ex omnibus tribubus Israhel iuxta maledictiones quae in libro legis huius ac foederis continentur*

And He may consume him in loss out of all Israel's tribes, according to *the* curses which are contained in *the* book of this law and agreement.

29:22 *dicetque sequens generatio et filii qui nascentur deinceps et peregrini qui de longe venerint videntes plagas terrae illius et infirmitates quibus eam adflixerit Dominus*

And *the* following generation, and children who will be born thereafter, and strangers who will come from far away, will say, seeing this land's wounds and sicknesses, with which *the* Lord has afflicted it –

29:23 *sulphure et salis ardore conburens ita ut ultra non seratur nec virens quippiam germinet in exemplum subversionis Sodomae et Gomorrae Adamae et Seboim quas subvertit Dominus in ira et furore suo*

burning sulphur and flaming salt, so it can no longer be sown, nor any green

thing spring up, in *the* example of Sodom and Gomorrah, Adamah and Seboim's destruction, which *the* Lord destroyed in His anger and fury –

29:24 *et dicent omnes gentes quare sic fecit Dominus terrae huic quae est haec ira furoris eius inmensa*

and all nations will say, "Why has *the* Lord done so to this land? What is this immense anger of His fury?"

29:25 *et respondebunt quia dereliquerunt pactum Domini quod pepigit cum patribus eorum quando eduxit eos de terra Aegypti*

And they will answer, "Because they abandoned *the* Lord's agreement which He made with their fathers, when He led them from Egypt's land.

29:26 *et servierunt diis alienis et adoraverunt eos quos nesciebant et quibus non fuerant adtributi*

"And they served alien gods and adored them, whom they didn't know, and to whom they had not been subjected.

29:27 *idcirco iratus est furor Domini contra terram istam ut induceret super eam omnia maledicta quae in hoc volumine scripta sunt*

"Therefore, *the* Lord's fury was angered against this land, so he led in over it all *the* curses which are written in this volume.

29:28 *et eiecit eos de terra sua in ira et furore et indignatione maxima proiecitque in terram alienam sicut hodie conprobatur*

"And He threw them out of His land in anger and fury and extreme indignation, and threw them into *a* strange land, as is clear today."

29:29 *abscondita Domino Deo nostro quae manifesta sunt nobis et filiis nostris usque in aeternum ut faciamus universa legis huius*

Things hidden by *the* Lord our God *are* what are manifest to us and our children even in eternity, so we can do all this law.

Deuteronomy 30:1 *cum ergo venerint super te omnes sermones isti benedictio sive maledictio quam proposui in conspectu tuo et ductus paenitudine cordis tui in universis gentibus in quas disperserit te Dominus Deus tuus*

When, therefore, all these words come over you which I have placed in your sight, whether blessing or curse, and they lead your heart to repentance among all *the* nations to which *the* Lord your God has scattered you,

30:2 *reversus fueris ad eum et oboedieris eius imperiis sicut ego hodie praecipio tibi cum filiis tuis in toto corde tuo et in tota anima tua*

you will turn back to Him and obey His decrees, as I am commanding you today with your children, in all your heart and in all your soul.

30:3 *reducet Dominus Deus tuus captivitatem tuam ac miserebitur tui et rursum congregabit te de cunctis populis in quos te ante dispersit*

The Lord your God will turn back your captivity and be merciful to you. And He will gather you again from all *the* peoples among whom He scattered you before.

30:4 *si ad cardines caeli fueris dissipatus inde te retrahet Dominus Deus tuus*

If you are scattered to *the* sky's poles, *the* Lord your God will bring you back from there.

30:5 *et adsumet atque introducet in terram quam possederunt patres tui et obtinebis eam et benedicens tibi maioris numeri esse te faciet quam fuerunt patres tui*

And He will take you up and bring you into *the* land which your fathers possessed, and you will obtain it. And, blessing you, he will make your number greater than your fathers were.

30:6 *circumcidet Dominus Deus tuus cor tuum et cor seminis tui ut diligas Dominum Deum tuum in toto corde tuo et in tota anima tua et possis vivere*

The Lord your God will circumcise your heart and your seed's heart, so you will delight in *the* Lord your God in all your heart and in all your soul, and you may live.

30:7 *omnes autem maledictiones has convertet super inimicos tuos et eos qui oderunt te et persequuntur*

But He will turn all these curses against your enemies, and those who hated you and pursue *you.*

30:8 *tu autem reverteris et audies vocem Domini Dei tui faciesque universa mandata quae ego*

praecipio tibi hodie

But you will turn back and listen to *the* Lord your God's voice, and do all *the* commandments which I am teaching you today.

30:9 *et abundare te faciet Dominus Deus tuus in cunctis operibus manuum tuarum in subole uteri tui et in fructu iumentorum tuorum in ubertate terrae tuae et in rerum omnium largitate revertetur enim Dominus ut gaudeat super te in omnibus bonis sicut gavisus est in patribus tuis*

And *the* Lord your God will make you prosper in all your hand's works, in your womb's offspring, and in your cattle's fruit, in your land's richness, and in all things' abundance. For *the* Lord will turn back, so He may rejoice over you in all good, as He was glad in your fathers,

30:10 *si tamen audieris vocem Domini Dei tui et custodieris praecepta eius et caerimonias quae in hac lege conscriptae sunt et revertaris ad Dominum Deum tuum in toto corde tuo et in tota anima tua*

if still you will hear *the* Lord your God's voice, and keep His precepts and ceremonies which are written in this law, and will turn back to *the* Lord your God in all your heart and in all your soul.

No Excuses

30:11 *mandatum hoc quod ego praecipio tibi hodie non supra te est neque procul positum*

This mandate which I am commanding you today is not above you or placed far away,

30:12 *nec in caelo situm ut possis dicere quis nostrum ad caelum valet conscendere ut deferat illud ad nos et audiamus atque opere conpleamus*

nor *is it* placed in *the* sky, so you can say, "Who can climb up from us to *the* sky, so he can bring it down to us, and we can hear *it* and fulfill *it* by work?"

30:13 *neque trans mare positum ut causeris et dicas quis e nobis transfretare poterit mare et illud ad nos usque deferre ut possimus audire et facere quod praeceptum est*

Nor *is it* placed across *the* sea, so you can allege and say, "Who among us can cross *the* sea and bring it even to us, so we can hear and do what is commanded?"

30:14 *sed iuxta te est sermo valde in ore tuo et in corde tuo ut facias illum*

But *the* word is very close to you, in your mouth and in your heart, so you may do it.

Choose!

30:15 *considera quod hodie proposuerim in conspectu tuo vitam et bonum et e contrario mortem et malum*

Consider what I have placed in your sight today – life and good, and, on *the* other hand, death and harm –

30:16 *ut diligas Dominum Deum tuum et ambules in viis eius et custodias mandata illius et caerimonias atque iudicia et vivas ac multiplicet te benedicatque tibi in terra ad quam ingredieris possidendam*

so you may delight in *the* Lord your God, and walk in His ways, and keep His commandments and ceremonies and judgments, and you may live and He may multiply and bless you in *the* land which you are going in to take over.

30:17 *sin autem aversum fuerit cor tuum et audire nolueris atque errore deceptus adoraveris deos alienos et servieris eis*

But if your heart will be turned back, and you don't want to listen and, deceived by error, you adore strange gods and serve them,

30:18 *praedico tibi hodie quod pereas et parvo tempore moreris in terra ad quam Iordane transmisso ingredieris possidendam*

I tell you beforehand today that you will perish, and will live *only a* little time in that land which, *the* Jordan crossed, you will go in to possess.

The Covenant's Witnesses

30:19 *testes invoco hodie caelum et terram quod proposuerim vobis vitam et mortem bonum et malum benedictionem et maledictionem elige ergo vitam ut et tu vivas et semen tuum*

I invoke today sky and land *as* witnesses, that I have placed before you life and death, good and harm, blessing and curse. Choose life, therefore, so both you and your seed may live,

30:20 *et diligas Dominum Deum tuum atque oboedias voci eius et illi adhereas ipse est enim vita tua et longitudo dierum tuorum ut habites in terra pro qua iuravit Dominus patribus tuis Abraham Isaac et Iacob ut daret eam illis*

and you may delight in *the* Lord your God, and obey His voice, and stick close to Him! For He is your life and your days' length, so you may live in *the* land for which *the* Lord swore to your fathers, Abraham, Isaac, and Jacob, that He would give it to them.

Moses Affirms Joshua

Deuteronomy 31:1 *abiit itaque Moses et locutus est omnia verba haec ad universum Israhel*

So Moses went out and spoke all these words to all Israel.

31:2 *et dixit ad eos centum viginti annorum sum hodie non possum ultra egredi et ingredi praesertim cum et Dominus dixerit mihi non transibis Iordanem istum*

And he said to them, "I am one hundred twenty years old today. I can't go out and come in further, particularly when *the* Lord has said to me, 'You will not cross this Jordan.'

31:3 *Dominus ergo Deus tuus transibit ante te ipse delebit omnes gentes has in conspectu tuo et possidebis eas et Iosue iste transibit ante te sicut locutus est Dominus*

"Therefore, *the* Lord your God will go across before you. He will destroy all these nations in your sight, and you will possess them. And Joshua, he will go across before you, as *the* Lord said.

31:4 *facietque Dominus eis sicut fecit Seon et Og regibus Amorreorum et terrae eorum delebitque eos*

"And *the* Lord will do to them like

He did to Sihon and Og, *the* Amorites' kings, and to their land. And He will destroy them.

31:5 *cum ergo et hos tradiderit vobis similiter facietis eis sicut praecepi vobis*

"And when, therefore, He has handed them over to you, you will do *the* same to them, like I commanded you.

31:6 *viriliter agite et confortamini nolite timere nec paveatis a conspectu eorum quia Dominus Deus tuus ipse est ductor tuus et non dimittet nec derelinquet te*

"Live manfully and be strengthened! Do not fear them or be frightened in their sight, because *the* Lord your God, He is your leader! And He will not let *you* go or abandon you.

31:7 *vocavitque Moses Iosue et dixit ei coram omni Israhel confortare et esto robustus tu enim introduces populum istum in terram quam daturum se patribus eorum iuravit Dominus et tu eam sorte divides*

And Moses called Joshua and said to him before all Israel, "Be strengthened and be strong! For you will lead this people into *the* land which *the* Lord swore to their fathers would be given, and you will divide it by lot.

31:8 *et Dominus qui ductor vester*

est ipse erit tecum non dimittet nec derelinquet te noli timere nec paveas

"And *the* Lord, who is your leader, He will be with you. He will not let *you* go or abandon you. Do not fear or be frightened!"

Moses Writes the Law

31:9 *scripsit itaque Moses legem hanc et tradidit eam sacerdotibus filiis Levi qui portabant arcam foederis Domini et cunctis senioribus Israhelis*

So Moses wrote this law, and gave it to *the* priests, Levi's children, who carried *the* Lord's covenant's box, and to all Israel's elders.

31:10 *praecepitque eis dicens post septem annos anno remissionis in sollemnitate tabernaculorum*

And he commanded them, saying, "After seven years, in *the* year of release, in *the* Feast of Tabernacles,

31:11 *convenientibus cunctis ex Israhel ut appareant in conspectu Domini Dei tui in loco quem elegerit Dominus leges verba legis huius coram omni Israhel audientibus eis*

"all from Israel coming together so they may appear in *the* Lord your God's sight, in *the* place which *the* Lord will choose, you will read this law's words before all Israel, them listening.

31:12 *et in unum omni populo congregato tam viris quam mulieribus parvulis et advenis qui sunt intra portas tuas ut audientes discant et timeant Dominum Deum vestrum et custodiant impleantque omnes sermones legis huius*

"And all *the* people gathering as one, men and women alike, little ones and newcomers who are in your gates, so that, hearing, they may learn, and may fear *the* Lord your God, and keep and fulfill all this law's teachings.

30:13 *filii quoque eorum qui nunc ignorant audire possint et timeant Dominum Deum suum cunctis diebus quibus versantur in terra ad quam vos Iordane transito pergitis obtinendam*

"Their children, likewise, who now do not know, may be able to hear and may fear *the* Lord their God, all *the* days in which they move around in *the* land which you, Jordan crossed, will go in to obtain.

The Lord Speaks Through Moses
31:14 *et ait Dominus ad Mosen ecce prope sunt dies mortis tuae voca Iosue et state in tabernaculo testimonii ut praecipiam ei abierunt ergo Moses et Iosue et steterunt in tabernaculo testimonii*

And *the* Lord said to Moses, "Look, your days of death are near. Call Joshua and stand him in *the* tent of testimony, so I can command him."

Therefore, Moses and Joshua went and stood in *the* tent of testimony.

31:15 *apparuitque Dominus ibi in columna nubis quae stetit in introitu tabernaculi*

And *the* Lord appeared there in *a* column of cloud, which stood at *the* tent's entrance.

31:16 *dixitque Dominus ad Mosen ecce tu dormies cum patribus tuis et populus iste consurgens fornicabitur post deos alienos in terra ad quam ingredietur et habitabit in ea ibi derelinquet me et irritum faciet foedus quod pepigi cum eo*

And *the* Lord said to Moses, "Look, you will sleep with your fathers, and this people, rising up, will fornicate after strange gods in *the* land to which it is going. And he will live in it. He will abandon Me there, and will make *the* covenant which I agreed on with him void.

31:17 *et irascetur furor meus contra eum in die illo et derelinquam eum et abscondam faciem meam ab eo et erit in devorationem invenient eum omnia mala et adflictiones ita ut dicat in illo die vere quia non est Deus mecum invenerunt me haec mala*

"And My fury will be angered against him on that day, and I will abandon him and hide My face from him. And he will be for devouring. Every harm and affliction will find him, so that he may say on that day, 'Truly, these harms have found me because God is not with me.'

31:18 *ego autem abscondam et celabo faciem meam in die illo propter omnia mala quae fecit quia secutus est deos alienos*

"But I will hide and conceal My face on that day, because of all *the* harms which he did, because he followed after strange gods.

31:19 *nunc itaque scribite vobis canticum istud et docete filios Israhel ut memoriter teneant et ore decantent et sit mihi carmen istud pro testimonio inter filios Israhel*

"Now, therefore, write yourselves this song and teach it to Israel's children, so they have it memorized and sing it by mouth. And this song may be *a* witness for Me among Israel's children.

31:20 *introducam enim eum in terram pro qua iuravi patribus eius lacte et melle manantem cumque comederint et saturati crassique fuerint avertentur ad deos alienos et servient eis et detrahent mihi et irritum facient pactum meum*

"For I will bring him into *the* land for which I swore to his fathers – flowing with milk and honey. And when they have eaten and, filled, become fat, they will turn aside to strange gods, and will serve them and abandon Me. And they will make My pact void.

31:21 *postquam invenerint eum mala multa et adflictiones respondebit ei canticum istud pro testimonio quod nulla delebit oblivio ex ore seminis tui scio enim cogitationes eius quae facturus sit hodie antequam introducam eum in terram quam ei pollicitus sum*

"After many harms and afflictions have found him, this song will answer him for testimony, because no forgetfulness will destroy *it* from your offspring's mouth. For I know his thoughts, what may be done today, before I lead him into *the* land which I promised him."

31:22 *scripsit ergo Moses canticum et docuit filios Israhel*

So Moses wrote *the* song and taught Israel's children.

31:23 *praecepitque Iosue filio Nun et ait confortare et esto robustus tu enim introduces filios Israhel in terram quam pollicitus sum et ego ero tecum*

And he commanded Joshua, Nun's

son, and said, "Be strengthened and be strong, for you will lead Israel's children into *the* land which I have promised! And I will be with you."

31:24 *postquam ergo scripsit Moses verba legis huius in volumine atque conplevit*

Then, after Moses had written this law's words in *a* volume, and completed it,

31:25 *praecepit Levitis qui portabant arcam foederis Domini dicens*

he commanded *the* Levites, who carried *the* Lord's covenant box, saying,

31:26 *tollite librum istum et ponite eum in latere arcae foederis Domini Dei vestri ut sit ibi contra te in testimonio*

"Take this book and put it inside *the* Lord your God's covenant box, so it may be there as witness against you.

31:27 *ego enim scio contentionem tuam et cervicem tuam durissimam adhuc vivente me et ingrediente vobiscum semper contentiose egistis contra Dominum quanto magis cum mortuus fuero*

"For I know your argument and your hardest neck. You have always carried on stubbornly against the Lord, me still living and going with you. How much more when I am dead!

31:28 *congregate ad me omnes maiores natu per tribus vestras atque doctores et loquar audientibus eis sermones istos et invocabo contra eos caelum et terram*

"Gather to me all *the* older born from your tribes, and *the* teachers, and I will speak these teachings, them hearing. And I will invoke sky and land against you.

31:29 *novi enim quod post mortem meam inique agetis et declinabitis cito de via quam praecepi vobis et occurrent vobis mala in extremo tempore quando feceritis malum in conspectu Domini ut inritetis eum per opera manuum vestrarum*

"For I have known that, after my death, you will carry on treacherously and quickly turn away from the way I have taught you. And harms will meet you in *the* end time, when you have done harm in *the* Lord's sight, so you exasperate Him by your hands' work."

31:30 *locutus est ergo Moses audiente universo coetu Israhel verba carminis huius et ad finem usque conplevit*

Therefore Moses spoke this song's words to all Israel's gathering, *them* hearing, and he completed *it* even to *the* end.

Moses' Song

Deuteronomy 32:1 *audite caeli quae loquor audiat terra verba oris mei*

Listen to what I say, skies! Let land hear my mouth's words!

32:2 *concrescat in pluvia doctrina mea fluat ut ros eloquium meum quasi imber super herbam et quasi stillae super gramina*

May my teaching condense into rain, my eloquence flow like dew – like rain on grass, and like drops on pasture –

32:3 *quia nomen Domini invocabo date magnificentiam Deo nostro*

for I will invoke *the* Lord's name! Give magnificence to our God!

32:4 *Dei perfecta sunt opera et omnes viae eius iudicia Deus fidelis et absque ulla iniquitate iustus et rectus*

God's works are complete, and all His ways *are* judgments. God *is* faithful and without any treachery, fair and straightforward.

32:5 *peccaverunt ei non filii eius in sordibus generatio prava atque perversa*

They sinned against him. They *are* not His children, in filth – *a* twisted and perverse generation.

32:6 *haecine reddis Domino popule stulte et insipiens numquid non ipse est pater tuus qui possedit et fecit et creavit te*

Is this what you return to *the* Lord, foolish and mindless people? Is He not your Father, who possessed and made and created you?

32:7 *memento dierum antiquorum cogita generationes singulas interroga patrem tuum et adnuntiabit tibi maiores tuos et dicent tibi*

Remember ancient days! Think about each generation! Ask your father, and he will tell you, your elders, and they will speak to you!

32:8 *quando dividebat Altissimus gentes quando separabat filios Adam constituit terminos populorum iuxta numerum filiorum Israhel*

When *the* Most High divided nations, when He separated Adam's children, He set *the* peoples' boundaries, according to Israel's children's number.

32:9 *pars autem Domini populus eius Iacob funiculus hereditatis eius*

But *the* Lord's portion *is* His people, Jacob, His inheritance's cord.

32:10 *invenit eum in terra deserta in*

loco horroris et vastae solitudinis circumduxit eum et docuit et custodivit quasi pupillam oculi sui

He found him in *a* desert land, in *a* place of dread, and led him around *a* vast wasteland. And He taught and guarded Him, like His eye's pupil.

32:11 *sicut aquila provocans ad volandum pullos suos et super eos volitans expandit alas suas et adsumpsit eum atque portavit in umeris suis*

Like *an* eagle provoking her chicks to flight and flying over them, He spread out His wings, and took him up, and carried him on His shoulders.

32:12 *Dominus solus dux eius fuit et non erat cum eo deus alienus*

The Lord alone was his leader, and no alien god was with Him.

32:13 *constituit eum super excelsam terram ut comederet fructus agrorum ut sugeret mel de petra oleumque de saxo durissimo*

He set him up over *the* land's heights, so he could eat *the* fields' fruit, so he could take in honey from *a* rock and oil from hardest stone –

32:14 *butyrum de armento et lac de ovibus cum adipe agnorum et arietum filiorum Basan et hircos cum medulla tritici et sanguinem* *uvae biberet meracissimum*

butter from *the* herd and milk from sheep, with *the* lambs' fat, and Bashan's children's rams, and goats, and wheat's marrow. And he may drink *the* grape's blood undiluted.

32:15 *incrassatus est dilectus et recalcitravit incrassatus inpinguatus dilatatus dereliquit Deum factorem suum et recessit a Deo salutari suo*

The delighted *one* grew fat, and, fattened, sleek, and widened, he rebelled. He abandoned God, his Maker, and turned back from *the* God of his security.

32:16 *provocaverunt eum in diis alienis et in abominationibus ad iracundiam concitaverunt*

They provoked Him in alien gods, and stirred Him up to anger in abominations.

32:17 *immolaverunt daemonibus et non Deo diis quos ignorabant novi recentesque venerunt quos non coluerunt patres eorum*

They sacrificed to demons and not God, gods whom they didn't know, new and recent. They came to those their fathers did not serve.

32:18 *Deum qui te genuit dereliquisti et oblitus es Domini creatoris tui*

You have abandoned God who birthed you, and forgotten *the* Lord your Creator.

32:19 *vidit Dominus et ad iracundiam concitatus est quia provocaverunt eum filii sui et filiae*

The Lord saw and was stirred up to anger, because His sons and daughters provoked Him.

32:20 *et ait abscondam faciem meam ab eis et considerabo novissima eorum generatio enim perversa est et infideles filii*

And He said, "I will hide My face from them, and I will consider their end, for *the* generation is perverse and *the* children unfaithful.

32:21 *ipsi me provocaverunt in eo qui non erat Deus et inritaverunt in vanitatibus suis et ego provocabo eos in eo qui non est populus et in gente stulta inritabo illos*

"They provoked Me in one who was not God, and exasperated *Me* in their vanities. And I will provoke them in one who is not *a* people, and will exasperate them in *a* foolish nation.

32:22 *ignis succensus est in furore meo et ardebit usque ad inferni novissima devorabitque terram cum germine suo et montium fundamenta conburet*

"Fire is kindled in My fury, and it will burn even to *the* inferno's end. And it will devour land with its seed, and burn *the* mountains' foundations.

32:23 *congregabo super eos mala et sagittas meas conplebo in eis*

"I will gather harm against them, and will fill up among them by my arrows.

32:24 *consumentur fame et devorabunt eos aves morsu amarissimo dentes bestiarum inmittam in eos cum furore trahentium super terram atque serpentium*

"They will be consumed by hunger, and birds will devour them with *a* most bitter bite. I will send beasts' teeth in among them, with *the* fury of those crawling over *the* ground, and *with* snakes.

32:25 *foris vastabit eos gladius et intus pavor iuvenem simul ac virginem lactantem cum homine sene*

"*A* sword will lay them waste outside, and fear inside – young man and young woman alike, *a* nursing child with *an* old man.

32:26 *dixi ubinam sunt cessare faciam ex hominibus memoriam eorum*

"For I have said, 'Wherever they are,

I will make their memory cease from among men.'

32:27 *sed propter iram inimicorum distuli ne forte superbirent hostes eorum et dicerent manus nostra excelsa et non Dominus fecit haec omnia*

"But, because of *the* enemies' anger, I have kept waiting, so their enemies wouldn't be proud and they say, 'Our highest hand, and not *the* Lord, has done all this.'

32:28 *gens absque consilio est et sine prudentia*

"*The* nation *is* without counsel and without prudence.

32:29 *utinam saperent et intellegerent ac novissima providerent*

"If only they would be wise and understand and make provision for *the* end!

32:30 *quomodo persequatur unus mille et duo fugent decem milia nonne ideo quia Deus suus vendidit eos et Dominus conclusit illos*

"How can one pursue *a* thousand, or two chase ten thousand? Isn't it because his God sold them and *the* Lord closed them in?

32:31 *non enim est Deus noster ut*

deus eorum et inimici nostri sunt iudices

"For our God is not like their god, and our enemies are judges.

32:32 *de vinea Sodomorum vinea eorum et de suburbanis Gomorrae uva eorum uva fellis et botri amarissimi*

"Their vine *is* from Sodom's vines, and from Gomorrah's surroundings. Their grape *is a* poison grape and *a* most bitter cluster.

32:33 *fel draconum vinum eorum et venenum aspidum insanabile*

"Their wine *is* dragon's bile and asps' venom, incurable.

32:34 *nonne haec condita sunt apud me et signata in thesauris meis*

"Aren't these things preserved with Me, and stamped in My treasury?

32:35 *mea est ultio et ego retribuam in tempore ut labatur pes eorum iuxta est dies perditionis et adesse festinant tempora*

"Revenge is Mine, and I will repay in time, so their foot may slip and fall. Destruction's day is near, and *the* seasons hurry to come near.

32:36 *iudicabit Dominus populum suum et in servis suis miserebitur*

videbit quod infirmata sit manus et clausi quoque defecerint residuique consumpti sint

"*The* Lord will judge His people, and will have mercy on His slaves. He will see that his hand is weak, and *the* closed up likewise will falter, and *the* survivors be consumed.

32:37 *et dicet ubi sunt dii eorum in quibus habebant fiduciam*

"And he will say, 'Where are their gods, in whom they had faith,

32:38 *de quorum victimis comedebant adipes et bibebant vinum libaminum surgant et opitulentur vobis et in necessitate vos protegant*

'from whose offerings they ate fat and drank first fruits' wine? Let them rise up and bring you help, and protect you in need!

32:39 *videte quod ego sim solus et non sit alius deus praeter me ego occidam et ego vivere faciam percutiam et ego sanabo et non est qui de manu mea possit eruere*

"See that I only exist, and *there* will be no other god beside me! I will kill and cause to live. I will strike and I will heal. And there is no one who can rescue from My hand.

32:40 *levabo ad caelum manum*

meam et dicam vivo ego in aeternum

"I will raise My hand to *the* sky and say, 'I live in eternity.'

32:41 *si acuero ut fulgur gladium meum et arripuerit iudicium manus mea reddam ultionem hostibus meis et his qui oderunt me retribuam*

"If I will sharpen My sword like lightning and take judgment into My hand, I will return revenge to My enemies, and pay back those who hate Me.

32:42 *inebriabo sagittas meas sanguine et gladius meus devorabit carnes de cruore occisorum et de captivitate nudati inimicorum capitis*

"I will make My arrows drunk with blood, and My sword will devour *the* flesh of slayers of blood, and of captivity, and of *the* enemies' bare heads.

32:43 *laudate gentes populum eius quia sanguinem servorum suorum ulciscetur et vindictam retribuet in hostes eorum et propitius erit terrae populi sui*

"Praise His people, nations, because He will avenge His slaves' blood, and repay revenge among their enemies. And He will be favorable to His people's land."

32:44 *venit ergo Moses et locutus est omnia verba cantici huius in auribus populi ipse et Iosue filius Nun*

Then Moses came and spoke all this song's words in *the* people's ears, he and Joshua, Nun's son.

32:45 *conplevitque omnes sermones istos loquens ad universum Israhel*

And he completed all these teachings, speaking to all Israel.

32:46 *et dixit ad eos ponite corda vestra in omnia verba quae ego testificor vobis hodie ut mandetis ea filiis vestris custodire et facere et implere universa quae scripta sunt legis huius*

And he said to them, "Set your hearts on all *the* words which I testify to you today, so you can command them to your children, to keep and do and fulfill all that is written in this law,

32:47 *quia non in cassum praecepta sunt vobis sed ut singuli in eis viverent quae facientes longo perseveretis tempore in terra ad quam Iordane transmisso ingredimini possidendam*

"because they are not commanded to you in vain, but that everyone may live in them! Doing which, you will stay *a* long time in *the* land which, *the* Jordan crossed, you will go in to possess."

The Lord Commands
Moses' Death

32:48 *locutusque est Dominus ad Mosen in eadem die dicens*

And *the* Lord spoke to Moses that same day, saying,

32:49 *ascende in montem istum Abarim id est transituum in montem Nebo qui est in terra Moab contra Hiericho et vide terram Chanaan quam ego tradam filiis Israhel obtinendam et morere in monte*

"Climb up onto this mountain, Abarim, that is *the* passage to Mount Nebo, which is in Moab's land across from Jericho, to look at Canaan's land, which I am handing over to Israel's children to obtain, and to die on *the* mountain,

32:50 *quem conscendens iungeris populis tuis sicut mortuus est Aaron frater tuus in monte Hor et adpositus populis suis*

"which, climbing up, you will be joined to your people, like Aaron your brother died on Mount Hor and was placed with his people –

32:51 *quia praevaricati estis contra me in medio filiorum Israhel ad aquas Contradictionis in Cades deserti Sin et non sanctificastis me inter filios Israhel*

"because you transgressed against me among Israel's children at *the* waters of Contradiction in Kadesh, in Sin's desert, and did not sanctify Me among Israel's children.

32:52 *e contra videbis terram et non ingredieris in eam quam ego dabo filiis Israhel*

"And you will see *the* land across, and will not go into it, which I will give to Israel's children."

Moses Blesses Israel

Deuteronomy 33:1 *haec est benedictio qua benedixit Moses homo Dei filiis Israhel ante mortem suam*

This is *the* blessing with which Moses, God's man, blessed Israel's children before his death.

33:2 *et ait Dominus de Sina venit et de Seir ortus est nobis apparuit de monte Pharan et cum eo sanctorum milia in dextera eius ignea lex*

And he said, "*The* Lord came from Sinai, and has risen for us from Seir. He appeared from Mount Pharan, and with him thousands of holy ones – in His right hand, *the* burning law.

33:3 *dilexit populos omnes sancti in manu illius sunt et qui adpropinquant pedibus eius accipient de doctrina illius*

"He has delighted in the peoples. All *the* holy *ones* are in His hand. And those who approach His feet will receive from His teaching.

33:4 *legem praecepit nobis Moses hereditatem multitudinis Iacob*

Moses commanded us *a* law, *the* inheritance of Jacob's multitude.

33:5 *erit apud rectissimum rex congregatis principibus populi cum tribubus Israhel*

He will be King with *the* most right, to *the* people's leaders' gathering, with Israel's tribes.

33:6 *vivat Ruben et non moriatur et sit parvus in numero*

"May Reuben live and not die, and be small in number!"

33:7 *haec est Iudae benedictio audi Domine vocem Iudae et ad populum suum introduc eum manus eius pugnabunt pro eo et adiutor illius contra adversarios eius erit*

This is Judah's blessing. "Hear, Lord, Judah's voice, and bring him to His people. His hands will fight for him, and He will be his helper against his enemies."

33:8 *Levi quoque ait perfectio tua et doctrina tua viro sancto tuo quem probasti in Temptatione et iudicasti ad aquas Contradictionis*

To Levi likewise, he said, "Your perfection and your teaching *are* to Your holy man, whom You proved in Temptation, and You judged at Contradiction's waters,

33:9 *qui dixit patri suo et matri suae nescio vos et fratribus suis ignoro illos et nescierunt filios suos hii custodierunt eloquium tuum et pactum tuum servaverunt*

"who said to his father and his

mother, 'I do not know you,' and to his brothers, 'I do not know them,' and did not know his sons – those who kept your eloquence and served your pact,

33:10 *iudicia tua o Iacob et legem tuam o Israhel ponent thymiama in furore tuo et holocaustum super altare tuum*

"your judgment, O Jacob, and your law, O Israel. They will place incense in your fury, and *a* burnt offering on your altar.

33:11 *benedic Domine fortitudini eius et opera manuum illius suscipe percute dorsa inimicorum eius et qui oderunt eum non consurgant*

"Bless *the* Lord in His might, and sustain His hands' works! Strike His enemies' backs, and let those who hated Him not rise!"

33:12 *et Beniamin ait amantissimus Domini habitabit confidenter in eo quasi in thalamo tota die morabitur et inter umeros illius requiescet*

And to Benjamin he said, "*The* Lord's most loved will live confidently in Him. He will live as in *a* marriage bed all day, and will rest between His shoulders.

33:13 *Ioseph quoque ait de benedictione Domini terra eius de pomis caeli et rore atque abysso*

subiacente

To Joseph, likewise, he said, "His land be from *the* Lord's blessing, from sky's fruit and dew and abyss beneath,

33:14 *de pomis fructuum solis ac lunae*

"from apples, sun and moon's fruit,

33:15 *de vertice antiquorum montium de pomis collium aeternorum*

"from ancient mountains' crown, from fruit of eternal hills,

33:16 *et de frugibus terrae et plenitudine eius benedictio illius qui apparuit in rubo veniat super caput Ioseph et super verticem nazarei inter fratres suos*

"and from *the* land's fruit and its plenty. May His blessing who appeared in the bush, come over Joseph's head, and over *the* neck of *the* Nazarite among his brothers.

33:17 *quasi primogeniti tauri pulchritudo eius cornua rinocerotis cornua illius in ipsis ventilabit gentes usque ad terminos terrae hae sunt multitudines Ephraim et haec milia Manasse*

"His beauty *is* like *the* firstborn bull, his horn like *the* rhinoceros's horn.

He will gore nations with it even to *the* land's end. These are Ephraim's multitudes and these are Manasseh's thousands."

33:18 *et Zabulon ait laetare Zabulon in exitu tuo et Isachar in tabernaculis tuis*

And to Zebulon he said, "Rejoice, Zebulon, in your success, and Issachar, in your tents!

33:19 *populos ad montem vocabunt ibi immolabunt victimas iustitiae qui inundationem maris quasi lac sugent et thesauros absconditos harenarum*

"They will call peoples to *the* mountain. There you will offer fairness's sacrifices, who will drink up *the* sea's flood like milk, and *the* sand's hidden treasures."

33:20 *et Gad ait benedictus in latitudine Gad quasi leo requievit cepitque brachium et verticem*

And to Gad he said, "Gad is blessed in broadness. Like *a* lion he rested, and he captured *the* arm and *the* head's crown.

33:21 *et vidit principatum suum quod in parte sua doctor esset repositus qui fuit cum principibus populi et fecit iustitias Domini et iudicium suum cum Israhel*

"And he saw his prominence that, in

his part, *a* teacher was restored, who was with *the* people's leaders, and worked *the* Lord's fairnesses and His judgments with Israel.

33:22 *Dan quoque ait Dan catulus leonis fluet largiter de Basan*

To Dan likewise he said, "Dan *is a* young lion. He will flow in abundance from Bashan."

33:23 *et Nepthalim dixit Nepthalim abundantia perfruetur et plenus erit benedictione Domini mare et meridiem possidebit*

And he said to Napthali, "Napthali will enjoy abundance, and will be full of *the* Lord's blessing. He will possess *the* sea and *the* south."

33:24 *Aser quoque ait benedictus in filiis Aser sit placens fratribus suis tinguat in oleo pedem suum*

To Asher, as well, he said, "May Asher be blessed in children, pleasing his brothers. May he dip his foot in oil.

33:25 *ferrum et aes calciamentum eius sicut dies iuventutis tuae ita et senectus tua*

"His shoe *is* iron and bronze. As your youth's days, so your old age *will be*."

Moses' Final Blessing

33:26 *non est alius ut Deus rectissimi ascensor caeli auxiliator tuus magnificentia eius discurrunt nubes*

There is no other like *the* God of *the* most right. *The* One who ascends *the* sky *is* your helper. Clouds move around by His magnificence.

33:27 *habitaculum eius sursum et subter brachia sempiterna eiciet a facie tua inimicum dicetque conterere*

His dwelling is above and, underneath, everlasting arms. He will throw out *the* enemy before your face, and say, "Be crushed!"

33:28 *habitabit Israhel confidenter et solus oculus Iacob in terra frumenti et vini caelique caligabunt rore*

Israel will live confidently, and Jacob's eye alone, in *a* land of grain and wine. And skies will be clouded with dew.

33:29 *beatus tu Israhel quis similis tui popule qui salvaris in Domino scutum auxilii tui et gladius gloriae tuae negabunt te inimici tui et tu eorum colla calcabis*

You *are* blessed, Israel. Who is like you, *O* people, who is secure in *the* Lord, your help's shield and your glory's sword? Your enemies will deny you, and you will trample their necks.

Moses Dies on Mount Pisgah
Deuteronomy 34:1 *ascendit ergo Moses de campestribus Moab super montem Nebo in verticem Phasga contra Hiericho ostenditque ei Dominus omnem terram Galaad usque Dan*

Then Moses climbed up from Moab's plains over Mount Nebo, to Pisgah's peak, across from Jericho. And the Lord showed him all Galaad's land, even to Dan,

34:2 *et universum Nepthalim terramque Ephraim et Manasse et omnem terram usque ad mare Novissimum*

and all Napthali, Ephraim and Manasseh's land, and all *the* land, even to *the* Last sea,

34:3 *et australem partem et latitudinem campi Hiericho civitatis Palmarum usque Segor*

and *the* south part, and *the* broadness of Jericho's field, *the* city of Palms, even to Segor.

34:4 *dixitque Dominus ad eum haec est terra pro qua iuravi Abraham Isaac et Iacob dicens semini tuo dabo eam vidisti eam oculis tuis et non transibis ad illam*

And *the* Lord said to him, "This is *the* land for which I swore to Abraham, Isaac, and Jacob, saying, 'I will give it to your seed.' You have seen it with your eyes, and you will not cross into it."

34:5 *mortuusque est ibi Moses servus Domini in terra Moab iubente Domino*

And Moses, *the* Lord's slave, died there in Moab's land, at *the* Lord's command.

34:6 *et sepelivit eum in valle terrae Moab contra Phogor et non cognovit homo sepulchrum eius usque in praesentem diem*

And He buried him there, in *a* valley of Moab's land, across from Phogor. And man has not known his grave, even to *the* present day.

34:7 *Moses centum et viginti annorum erat quando mortuus est non caligavit oculus eius nec dentes illius moti sunt*

Moses was one hundred twenty years old when he died. His eye was not clouded over, nor were his teeth moved.

34:8 *fleveruntque eum filii Israhel in campestribus Moab triginta diebus et conpleti sunt dies planctus lugentium Mosen*

And Israel's children wept for him thirty days in Moab's plains. And *the* days of wailing and grieving were completed for Moses.

34:9 *Iosue vero filius Nun repletus est spiritu sapientiae quia Moses posuit super eum manus suas et oboedierunt ei filii Israhel feceruntque sicut praecepit Dominus Mosi*

Truly, Joshua, Nun's son, was filled with spirit and wisdom, because Moses had placed his hands on him. And Israel's children obeyed him, and they did as *the* Lord commanded Moses.

34:10 *et non surrexit propheta ultra in Israhel sicut Moses quem nosset Dominus facie ad faciem*

And another prophet like Moses has not risen up in Israel, whom *the* Lord knew face to face,

34:11 *in omnibus signis atque portentis quae misit per eum ut faceret in terra Aegypti Pharaoni et omnibus servis eius universaeque terrae illius*

in all *the* signs and wonders which He sent in through him, that He could do in Egypt's land, to Pharaoh and to all his slaves and to all his land,

34:12 *et cunctam manum robustam magnaque mirabilia quae fecit Moses coram universo Israhel*

and all *the* mighty hand and great miracles which Moses did before all Israel.

Volumes in the Latin Testament Project
from Searchlight Press
(All volumes available in print and e-book formats)

The Way of Wisdom:
Job, Proverbs, Ecclesiastes, Song
of Solomon
Latin-English Edition (2008)
English Edition (2008)

The Audacity of Prayer:
A Fresh Translation of the Book
of Psalms
Latin-English Edition (2009)
English Edition (2009)

The Latin Torah:
Genesis, Exodus, Leviticus,
Numbers, Deuteronomy
Latin-English Edition (2010)
English Edition with Commentary
(2011)

The Latin Nevi'im I
Joshua, Judges, 1 &2 Samuel,
1 & 2 Kings
(2012)

Mark:
A Latin-English, Verse-by-Verse
Translation
(2010)

Pastoral and General Epistles
from the New Testament:
A Latin-English, Verse-by-Verse
Translation
(2010)

Romans:
A Latin-English, Verse by Verse
Thranslation
(2011)

Searchlight Press
Who are you looking for?
Publishers of thoughtful Christian books since 1994.
5634 Ledgestone Drive
Dallas, Texas 75214
888.896.6081
info@Searchlight-Press.com
www.Searchlight-Press.com
www.JohnCunyus.com

www.ingramcontent.com/pod-product-compliance
Lightning Source LLC
Chambersburg PA
CBHW071916160426
42812CB00098B/1270